# Introduction to R
# and Statistics in Psychology

Visit the *Introduction to Research Methods and Statistics in Psychology* Companion Website at **www.pearsoned.co.uk/ mcqueen** to find valuable **student** learning material including:

- Multiple choice questions to help test your learning
- Links to relevant sites on the web
- Data Sets for all examples used in the book
- Quick Guides to give students a succinct procedural summary on one page
- Crosswords to help with familiarisation of key terms and to encourage independent thinking
- Flashcards to test your understanding of key terms
- Beginner's Toolkit that outlines crucial points for the nervous beginner

# Introduction to Research Methods and Statistics in Psychology

**Ronald A. McQueen**
**Christina Knussen**

PEARSON
Prentice
Hall

Harlow, England • London • New York • Boston • San Francisco • Toronto • Sydney • Singapore • Hong Kong
Tokyo • Seoul • Taipei • New Delhi • Cape Town • Madrid • Mexico City • Amsterdam • Munich • Paris • Milan

**Pearson Education Limited**
Edinburgh Gate
Harlow
Essex CM20 2JE
England

and Associated Companies throughout the world

*Visit us on the World Wide Web at:*
www.pearsoned.co.uk

First published 2006

10 0646750 X

ISBN-13: 978–0–13–124940–0
ISBN-10: 0–13–124940–1

**British Library Cataloguing-in-Publication Data**
A catalogue record for this book is available from the British Library

**Library of Congress Cataloging-in-Publication Data**
McQueen, R. A.
  Introduction to research methods and statistics in psychology / Ronald A. McQueen,
 Christina Knussen.
    p. cm.
  Includes bibliographical references and index.
  ISBN 0–13–124940–1
    1. Psychology—Research—Methodology—Textbooks. 2. Psychometrics—Textbooks.
  I. Knussen, Christina. II. Title.

BF76.5. M385 2006
150′.72—dc22                                          20050552349

10 9 8 7 6 5 4 3
11

Typeset in 10/12 pt Times by 72
Printed and bound by Ashford Colour Press, Gosport, Hants.

# Contents

**Preface**   xi

**Guided tour**   xiv

**Authors' Acknowledgements**   xvi

**Publisher's Acknowledgements**   xvii


**Part 1**   Introduction                                                    1

**Chapter 1**   Introducing research                                         3

1.1   Psychology, a definition                                               3
1.2   Psychology, its aims                                                   3
1.3   Psychology, its scope                                                  4
1.4   Research and scientific method                                        4
1.5   Beginning a research project                                         18
1.6   Reviewing the literature                                             21
1.7   Evaluating research                                                  25
1.8   Structuring a research project                                       27
        Review                                                             27
        Suggested further reading                                         27


**Part 2**   Planning a research project – the design                       29

**Chapter 2**   The nature of research design                              31

2.1    The purpose of a design                                             31
2.2    Problems with designs                                               32
2.3    The principles and language of design                               33
2.4    The world of variables                                              34
2.5    Dependent variables (DVs)                                           34
2.6    Independent variables (IVs)                                         35
2.7    Extraneous variables                                                39
2.8    Controls                                                            41
2.9    A medical model – the randomised controlled design                  42
2.10   The double-blind control                                            42
2.11   Variables and levels of measurement                                 44
2.12   Levels of measurement                                               44
2.13   Nominal (category) scales                                           46
2.14   Ordinal scales                                                      48
2.15   Ratio and interval scales                                           50
2.16   Changing the level of measurement                                   52
        Review                                                             54
        Suggested further reading                                         54

**Chapter 3**   Experimental research designs                                    55

  3.1   Introduction to experimental research                                    55
  3.2   Experimental design                                                       56
  3.3   Between-groups designs (independent groups designs)                       57
  3.4   Within-subjects designs (repeated measures designs)                       60
  3.5   Non-equivalent group (quasi-experimental) designs                         65
  3.6   Factorial designs                                                         66
  3.7   Randomised controlled designs revisited                                   68
  3.8   Mixed designs                                                             68
  3.9   Some reservations on factorial designs                                    70
        Review                                                                    71
        Suggested further reading                                                 71

**Chapter 4**   Correlational and regression designs                             72

  4.1   Correlational designs                                                     72
  4.2   The nature of correlation                                                 73
  4.3   The correlation coefficient                                               77
  4.4   Coefficient of determination                                             77
  4.5   Assumption of linearity                                                   77
  4.6   Misleading correlations                                                   79
  4.7   Partial correlation                                                       81
  4.8   Multiple correlation and regression                                       83
        Review                                                                    85
        Suggested further reading                                                 85


**Part 3**   Carrying out research – methods and procedures                      87

**Chapter 5**   The essentials of carrying out research – the participants       89

  5.1   The role of procedure                                                     89
  5.2   The stuff of research – whom will you use?                                 90
  5.3   Samples and populations                                                   91
  5.4   Sampling techniques                                                       92
  5.5   Non-probability sampling                                                  94
  5.6   Ensuring co-operation                                                    100
  5.7   Number of participants                                                   101
  5.8   Secondary research                                                       113
  5.9   Advantages of secondary research                                         113
  5.10  Disadvantages of secondary research                                      114
        Review                                                                   116
        Suggested further reading                                               116

**Chapter 6**   Collecting data                                                 117

  6.1   Carrying out ethical research                                            117
  6.2   Using questionnaires in research                                         124
  6.3   Special techniques for information gathering                             132
  6.4   What you need to know about psychological tests                          136
        Review                                                                   149
        Suggested further reading                                               149

**Part 4**  Tables, figures and descriptive statistics  151

**Chapter 7**  Describing data – tables, graphs
and descriptive statistics  153

7.1  Using numbers to represent the psychological world  153
7.2  Making sense of numbers  154
7.3  Tables and categorical variables  154
7.4  Figures and categorical variables  156
7.5  Tables and continuous variables  160
7.6  The stemplot  163
7.7  Figures and continuous variables  165
7.8  Continuous variables and the boxplot  167
7.9  Statistics  172
7.10  Dispersion  175
7.11  The normal distribution  178
7.12  Practical implications  182
7.13  The standard normal distribution  183
        Review  189

**Chapter 8**  Descriptive analysis and SPSS  190

8.1  Computer analysis and SPSS  190
8.2  Creating files in SPSS  191
8.3  Setting up data in SPSS  203
8.4  SPSS and descriptive statistics  206
8.5  Graphs and crosstabulated data  221
8.6  Screening data  224
        Review  227
        Suggested further reading  227

**Part 5**  Drawing inferences and testing hypotheses  229

**Chapter 9**  Introducing inferential statistics and tests
of differences  231

9.1  Inferential statistics  231
9.2  Tests of differences – between-groups comparisons,
        repeated measures and ANOVA  247
        Review  287
        Suggested further reading  287

**Chapter 10**  Tests of association  288

10.1  The chi-square ($\chi^2$) test of association  288
10.2  Correlation  295
10.3  Simple regression  299
10.4  The coefficient of determination  302
10.5  Correlation and simple regression in SPSS  303
        Review  309
        Suggested further reading  309

**Chapter 11**   Advanced analysis: Two-way ANOVA, partial correlation
and multiple regression                                            310

  11.1   Two-way ANOVA                                     310
  11.2   Locating an effect in ANOVA                       313
  11.3   Partial correlation                               319
  11.4   Multiple regression                               324
       Review                       328
       Suggested further reading    328

**Part 6**   Carrying out qualitative research                      329

**Chapter 12**   Introducing qualitative research                   331

  12.1   The differences between qualitative and quantitative research   331
  12.2   An example of a qualitative study                 332
  12.3   Qualitative or quantitative?                      335
  12.4   Representing the experiences of participants      335
  12.5   Previous research                                 335
  12.6   Availability of participants                      336
  12.7   Time factors                                      336
  12.8   Your supervisor                                   337
  12.9   Mixing methods                                    337
  12.10  Some approaches to qualitative research           338
  12.11  Qualitative approaches that involve the analysis of text   342
  12.12  Planning a qualitative study                      344
  12.13  Other points to consider                          349
  12.14  Collecting data                                   352
  12.15  Dealing with qualitative data                     357
  12.16  The quality of the research                       360
  12.17  Points to consider when writing up                361
       Review                       361
       Suggested further reading    362

**Part 7**   Writing up research                                    363

**Chapter 13**   Writing up research                                365

  13.1   The purpose of a report                           365
  13.2   Writing guidelines                                365
  13.3   The structure of a psychology report              367
  13.4   Tables and figures                                383
  13.5   Discussion                                        386
  13.6   References                                        387
  13.7   Appendices                                        390
  13.8   Presentation and style                            390
  13.9   Writing up qualitative research                   391
  13.10  Guidelines on writing up qualitative research     391
  13.11  Giving a presentation of your study               393

13.12   Practicalities: Giving a presentation                                    394
13.13   Assessment                                                              397
        Review                                                                  399
        Suggested further reading                                               399

**Appendix A**   Area under the normal curve                                     401
**Appendix B**   Critical values of $U$ and $U'$ for a one-tailed test at $\alpha = 0.025$
                 or a two-tailed test at $\alpha = 0.05$                          404
**Appendix C**   Critical values of $t$                                          405
**Appendix D**   Critical values of $T$                                          406
**Appendix E**   Table of $\chi^2$                                               407
**Glossary**                                                                    409
**References and reading list**                                                 421
**Index**                                                                       425

# Preface

For many students of psychology the prospect of planning and carrying out a research project is a daunting one, a prospect made worse for some since research, and all that goes with it – analysis, written reports, presentations – is now a universal requirement for undergraduate degrees.

Part of the problem is a conceptual one. Many people at the start of their student experience are simply unsure as to the nature and scope of psychological research. For those who do appreciate its role, however, there is often little relief, due to the fact that somewhere along the line statistics will rear its ugly head, and of all the concerns expressed by students, dealing with analytical procedures seems to be the most common. Nor is opting for a qualitatively based approach an 'easy way out', as many believe, since qualitative research places just as many demands on the researcher as its quantitative counterpart, only of a different kind. It is hardly surprising then that this particular topic and student angst seem to go so well together.

While no one would make the claim that understanding research and the analytical procedures that serve it is easy, there is no reason why it should be either intimidating or inaccessible. Regrettably, though, this is often the case since a great deal of what is currently written about the methods of psychological research – and much of this is of an extremely high quality – is more suitable for teachers, academics and researchers, people who usually have considerable experience of and a keen interest in the material. Too often this same material can be intimidating for the student who lacks experience in research, is new to analytical procedures or for whom the topic of methodology is a requirement rather than an interest.

With these points in mind, and with the intention of offering a practical guide to designing, carrying through and, indeed, surviving a research project, this textbook has been written. It is a book for students new to psychology, based on many years of teaching research methods, and incorporating the experience of having supervised innumerable projects at introductory, honours and postgraduate level. It has been written with an understanding of, and sensitivity to, the concerns and misgivings of undergraduates everywhere, and in the hope that the study of research methods, and all that goes with it, will become not only an accessible activity but a rewarding one also.

## The aims of this book

The purpose of writing this book is to provide a practical guide to the planning, implementation and presentation of research. While the scope and manner of presentation of the material makes it accessible to any student of psychology, irrespective of degree level, the text is directed primarily at undergraduate students embarking, perhaps for the first time, on the sometimes treacherous course of designing and carrying out a major piece of research.

Structurally, the book follows the accepted procedure for the conduct of any study – while recognising the unique nature of qualitative research – from the initial selection of a topic to the preparation of a final report. For the novice, this structure will in itself serve as a guide, leading from the conceptual processes involved in the development of ideas through all the intermediate stages of design, methodology and analysis, and offering real practical help whenever possible. For the more advanced student, each chapter can be regarded as a free-standing unit, offering in-depth treatment of a single topic, itself broken down into smaller, relatively independent sections. For example, for the student already involved in the design of a questionnaire, there is a section on important ethical considerations; for students at an earlier stage, there are sections covering decisions on whether or not to use closed- or open-ended items. For those at the very beginnings of a study there is help on the distinction between qualitative and quantitative approaches; for those at the planning stage of their study there is guidance on independent-group and repeated measures design; and for students at the end of the data-gathering stage, a detailed introduction to analytical techniques is offered, along with guidance on the use of SPSS. As a conclusion, the final chapter is concerned with presentation issues, both written and oral, with a section on procedures for referencing, which should come as a boon not just to student researchers, but to their supervisors also.

Fundamental to the entire book, however, is a sympathetic understanding of the student's approach to research methods. Many years of dealing with dismayed (and sometimes sobbing) undergraduates have gone into the design of this text, leading to a highly structured organisation of the material, and the adoption of a presentation style which we hope will be both engaging and informative.

## Features

The book is divided into a number of parts, presented in the conventional sequence of activities that comprise a research project, such that students lacking a background in research methods can progress from the most basic of decisions to the competent handling of data.

Each part, and the chapters within it, deals with a specific topic and, although reference is occasionally made to other parts of the book, each can be viewed as a stand-alone unit. In addition, most chapters feature helpful boxes which offer 'how to' guides, practical advice and checklists in every aspect of research methods. We have also – in response to requests from our own students – included an extensive glossary at the end of the book; key terms are identified in **bold** type within the text and we hope that this will be a useful feature.

In order to illustrate points we have made extensive use of examples, some unique to particular issues, and some serving as a running theme which we hope will provide a sense of continuity. These recurring themes include examples from experimental and social perspectives, in addition to a more lighthearted set of illustrations involving hedgehogs, which we hope will not offend.

In Parts 4 and 5, in which we introduce the statistical package, SPSS, we have adopted the convention of identifying commands in the text with a first-letter underscore. A sequence of command clicks then will appear as, Analyse, Correlate, Bivariate. . . The headings of the various windows and views which open as a result of the commands, we have identified with a first letter bold. Screen views and elements within screen views which you might see then will be referred to in the texts as, Test variable Grouping variable, and so on.

In line with current trends we have provided a companion website. However, rather than offering more of the same, we have tried to develop a site which is both informative and entertaining. Presented here are a variety of review and self-test features, in addition to an extensive range of FAQs (frequently asked questions) with detailed answers. There are crossword puzzles and data sets, there are downloadable guides to statistical analysis and much more.

We hope you enjoy the book.

*Ronald A. McQueen and Christina Knussen*

# Guided tour

**Key issues** at the start of each chapter introduce the key topics that are covered and summarise what is to be learned.

**A closer look at. . . boxes** focus on a particular topic to provide a more detailed explanation and provoke further discussion.

**Key terms** are highlighted in bold where they are first introduced, and definitions can be found in the glossary at the end of the book.

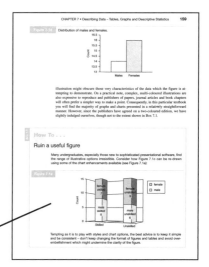

**How to. . . boxes** provide helpful hints and tips for carrying out the key stages and procedures of research.

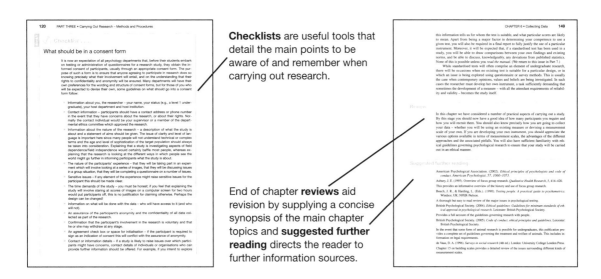

**Checklists** are useful tools that detail the main points to be aware of and remember when carrying out research.

End of chapter **reviews** aid revision by supplying a concise synopsis of the main chapter topics and **suggested further reading** directs the reader to further information sources.

The **Companion Website** at www.pearsoned.co.uk/mcqueen includes useful resources such as multiple choice questions, weblinks, data sets, quick guides, crosswords, flashcards and a beginner's toolkit for students.

# Authors' Acknowledgements

It almost goes without saying that a textbook of this nature cannot be the work of just two individuals – contributions by way of suggestions, guidance and advice have contributed in both small and large part to the finished work. We would like to thank the following:

Alan Tuohy for his expertise on statistical matters.

Paul Flowers for his guidance on qualitative techniques.

Marion Miller, our always helpful librarian.

David Bell and Cathie Wright for their assistance in so many ways.

Our academic reviewers whose comments, always candid, were invariably appropriate.

Morten and Emma, our editors, for their encouragement and occasional bullying.

Sarah, our desk editor, for putting the final book together.

Julie, for her work on the companion website.

Holly, the project manager, for being tolerant.

Needless to say, any gaffes which remain are ours and ours alone.

Finally, we wish to thank all our undergraduates, whose worries and concerns were responsible for our interest in writing this book in the first place.

# Publisher's Acknowledgements

We are grateful to the following for permission to reproduce copyright material:

We are grateful to SPSS for use of the screen images, copyright © SPSS Inc. SPSS is a registered trademark and the other product names are trademarks of SPSS Inc.; Screen image used in Box 1.7 is reproduced with permission from Google Inc.; Tables 6.3 and 6.4 adapted from the *Manual of the Eysenck Personality Scales* (Eysenck, H. J. and Eysenck, S. B. G., 1996), reproduced by permission of Hodder & Stoughton; Figure 6.6 from *Manual for the Eysenck Personality Questionnaire* (Eysenck, H. J. and Eysenck, S. B. G., 1975), copyright © 1991 H. J. Eysenck and S. B. G. Eysenck, reproduced by permission of Hodder & Stoughton; Table 6.5 adapted from the *Manual of the GHQ* (Goldberg and Williams, 1991), reprinted by permission of NFER-Nelson.

NHPA/Laurie Campbell (Part 1 opening image, p. 1); Corbis/Bettmann (Plate 1.1, p. 11); Corbis/Tim Davis (Part 2 opening image, p. 29); Mary Evans Picture Library (Plate 2.1, p. 43); AIP Emilio Segre Visual Archives, Physics Today Collection (Plate 2.2, p. 45); Getty/Hulton Archive (Plate 4.1, p. 73); Corbis/Hulton Deutsch Collection (Plate 4.2, p. 79); Getty/Bill Curtsinger (Part 3 opening image, p. 87); Empics/John Giles/PA (Plate 5.1, p. 95); Science Photo Library/Will and Deni McIntyre (Plate 6.1, p. 119); Getty/Daniel Bosler (Plate 6.2, p. 133); Alamy/Blickwinkel (Part 4 opening image, p. 151); Alamy/Genevieve Vallee (Part 5 opening image, p. 229); Corbis/David Michael Zimmerman (Plate 9.1, p. 232); Corbis/Kevin Fleming (Plate 9.2, p. 241); Photolibrary/ Picture Press (Plate 9.3, p. 246); Sir Ronald Fisher, copyright © Antony Barrington Brown, reproduced by permission of the Sir Ronald Fisher Memorial Committee (Plate 9.4, p. 263); Corbis/Helen King (Plate 9.5, p. 267); Alamy/Malie Rich-Griffith (Part 6 opening image, p. 329); Empics/Adam Davy (Plate 12.1, p. 333); Getty/Keith Brofsky (Plate 12.2, p. 339); Getty/Mike Powell (Plate 12.3, p. 353); Alamy (Plate 12.4, p. 356); Alamy (Part 7 opening image, p. 363).

In some instances we have been unable to trace the owners of copyright material, and we would appreciate any information that would enable us to do so.

# Introduction

## Part 1

**Introducing research**

Planning a research project—the design

Carrying out research—methods & procedure

Describing research findings— descriptives

Analysing research findings—inferential statistics

Carrying out qualitative research

Writing up and presenting the findings of research

NHPA/Laurie Campbell

Part 1 introduces the concept of psychological research, discusses why it is important and examines the various approaches which can be taken. Specific guidelines are offered on:

- how to commence a research project
- exploring the background to a topic
- conducting information searches
- making initial decisions on the type of study to be carried out

For beginning project students, this part represents the starting point of the research process and provides advice and suggestions on how to prepare to carry out a study; it is concerned with identifying research issues, proposing hypotheses and exploring relevant literature. Once a viable study has been decided upon, subsequent parts deal with the stages of designing and implementing your research, with concluding parts concerned with data analysis and writing up. The timeline strip on the previous page illustrates the sequential nature of the research process and indicates the relative position of each element. You will see that we are beginning, logically, at the beginning.

# 1 Introducing research

## 1.1 Psychology, a definition

Psychology is a relatively young discipline, not really arriving as a fully recognised sphere of scientific interest until the early 1900s. Of course the work of people like Freud, James and Adler had been well publicised before this, but their approach to the study of the mind had been largely introspective, and primarily philosophical in nature. Even the apparently more rigorous enquiries of people like Mesmer on hypnotism, or Galton on reaction times, were problematic, lacking the appropriate scientific methodology to allow them to test their theories successfully. However, with the establishment, in 1879, of a laboratory of psychological research in Leipzig by Wilhelm Wundt, we see, perhaps for the first time, a locus for this new discipline and by the turn of the twentieth century, as individuals from backgrounds ranging from medicine to engineering, or working in areas as diverse as industry and education, began to recognise a shared interest in human behaviour, the discipline of psychology was born.

Traditionally, the generally accepted definition of psychology is the scientific study of human behaviour, although nowadays this definition has to be quite loosely applied since psychologists are not just concerned with behaviour, but also with internal processes like thinking, judging and feeling. Nor, as was the case in Wundt's day, is all **research** laboratory-based – the developing interest in qualitative approaches has prompted a move away from experimentation in some areas, although the scientific element remains, in that most psychological research continues to be systematic and (up to a point) objective. To further complicate issues, there are some instances in which the participants in a **study** will be animal rather than human – occasionally there are practical or ethical reasons for using a non-human sample although the ultimate objective is usually to apply findings to human behaviour. And even here, this is a generalisation since there exists a respectable body of research of which the aim is an understanding of animal behaviour in its own right.

## 1.2 Psychology, its aims

The major aim of studying people is to increase our understanding about why we behave in the ways that we do. This is merely a reflection of other forms of scientific endeavour and is an expression of a general human curiosity about the world we live in. But there is more to psychology than mere understanding – like all other sciences, an evolution of understanding is part of the promotion of change, or intervention, for the attainment of some form of improvement in our environment. Fusion research for instance looks beyond an explanation of matter at atomic levels towards the possibility of a cheap energy source in the future; medical research has as its ultimate aim longevity and the elimination of disease. Similarly, psychology aims to apply an understanding of behaviour to an overall improvement in the human condition.

In this applied mode, psychology has met with mixed success. Certainly in the clinical sphere, huge advances have been made in the treatment of mental disorders, yet there are still many areas of mental functioning which remain poorly understood. Likewise, in the occupational setting, developments in testing have dramatically increased the likelihood that the right people will be hired for the right jobs, but there is still disagreement as to what makes an effective leader, or whether or not personality measures actually predict success. There is an additional problem here and it is an ethical one: as with all forms of investigation, it is possible to abuse the findings of psychological research, to use them, not for betterment, but for exploitation and manipulation. The commonly cited example is in the application of nuclear research to the weapons industry. But one might wonder whether it is any less exploitative for advertisers to use an understanding of human behaviour to persuade people to buy products which they do not need. This is an issue to which we will return later in Chapter 6, in the section on ethics.

## 1.3 Psychology, its scope

Since the early days when psychology was seen as a loose collection of interests, limited by the methods available to its researchers, the field has witnessed sustained growth – growth reflected in its popularity as an undergraduate topic and by the sheer scope of the subject. Psychologists today find themselves concerned with learning, cognition, social behaviour, developmental processes, work, consumerism, language, abnormality, emotion and many other spheres of knowledge. Yet this should not surprise us since any discipline purporting to be interested in people will inevitably find itself concerned with virtually every aspect of human endeavour. What links all these diverse threads of interest, however, is the way in which psychology approaches its subject; the unifying set of techniques, ethics and philosophy which comprise its methodology.

## 1.4 Research and scientific method

### 1.4.1 The nature of research

All scientists have their own particular view of the purpose of research, but essentially, research is carried out in order to firstly describe, then explain and ultimately predict, with each of these reflecting a progressively more sophisticated application. At its simplest level, research on any topic aims to describe a phenomenon or a process which has previously been inaccessible or only vaguely understood. For example, sleep, once an unmeasurable and unfathomable activity (sometimes regarded merely as the absence of wakefulness), can now be readily described as a complex altered state of consciousness involving several stages or cycles, each associated with differing levels of brain activity. More interestingly, it is now possible to attempt to explain what is actually going on during these processes, and why they occur – at least, up to a point. And finally, if these sleep processes have been accurately described, and if our explanations are indeed correct, we are now in a position to go for the big one – to make predictions. That is, we can now suggest what will happen if we deprive individuals of sleep for a specific length of time, or what the effects on behaviour would be if particular sleep cycles were interrupted. Each of these activities – describing, explaining and predicting – represents an essential function of research and together they constitute the goals of all researchers. But how are these goals achieved?

## 1.4.2 Scientific method

In order to understand a phenomenon, there are a number of things we can do. We can take an armchair, introspective approach and simply think about the world, applying our own past experience and self-knowledge. Much of what we believe to be true in life is based on this very approach – intuition, feelings or beliefs about the way things are contribute to how we perceive the world and, as a rough and ready rule-of-thumb guide to life, it's not a bad approach: the superstitious belief that walking under a ladder will give us bad luck will at least prevent the pot of paint falling on top of us – or even the painter; the fear of flying many of us experience will prevent us from becoming victims of an air disaster and our almost reflexive sense of danger in the presence of multi-legged creepy crawlies might prevent a fatal bite from the Australian funnel web spider. However, reliance on such a scheme for negotiating life is by no means foolproof and can, in some cases, lead to a complete misconception of 'the way things are'. The gambler who, on observing a run of ten reds on the roulette wheel, places his entire savings on black (because it *must* be black's turn) is likely to leave the casino minus his shirt because his intuitive view of the probability of events is flawed. Like many people, he has assumed that consecutive runs of the wheel are connected and that the laws of chance must eventually balance out. Similarly, the parent who, on observing two sunny weekends in a row, plans an outdoor children's party for the third, is inviting disaster. (The authors, showing a marked disregard for the British climate, can attest to this.)

Closer scrutiny of the flying example will also show the limitations of the intuitive approach since, in comparison to road travel, flying remains one of the safest modes of transport. And as for our poor arachnaphobic, unless he lives in Australia, that particular denizen is unlikely to be a problem, while most of the other species of wrigglers and scuttlers actually serve a useful function.

The point of all of the above is that the usual way we approach the world is flawed, subjective and judgemental (and, indeed, very human). It may get us by on a day-to-day basis, but it's not an approach designed to accurately describe, explain or predict. To be able to do this, we need a more rigorous, systematic and scientific approach to life – we need to adopt a **scientific method**, which is precisely what the first scientists felt.

Science really only takes off where intuition stops; many of our ideas about gambling, flying, spiders and the rest may well be true, but until they can be proved they remain at the level of heuristics, unsupported beliefs or even superstition. Science takes the next step and attempts to find this proof, using a methodology which has evolved over many years.

The starting point of scientific research is **theory**, and theory is simply a general set of beliefs about the way the universe, or a part of it, operates – nothing more or less than those very intuitions, rule-of-thumb heuristics and general beliefs discussed above. Theories can be vague, ill-defined and personal (I have this theory about why hedgehogs have spines . . . !) or they can be concise, well-structured and supported by a large body of evidence (as in behavioural learning theories). Either way, theories provide the descriptive and explanatory functions of research introduced at the beginning of this part. The major difference between theory and intuition, however, is that, while intuition is usually based on belief, feeling or even faith, theory is a much more systematic thing – any researcher attempting to develop a theory is constantly asking the questions: Does this describe . . . ? Does this theory explain . . . ? Consequently, a theory demands more thought and more enquiry than any heuristic – a theory will be based on observations, experience and the experiences of others; it will represent a balance of perceptions and information and it will be held up as presenting a better view of the world than possible alternatives. However, by far the most important aspect of a theory is that, if it provides an accurate description of the world, it will predict events which have not yet occurred.

### 1.4.3 Hypotheses

Psychological theories are always general views or propositions about people, representing the best descriptions and explanations we can come up with. We may have arrived at them through observing people, through thinking about our own behaviour or through discussions with others who share our interest in the human condition. However, such theories will never develop beyond the level of being just one of many possible explanations unless we can produce evidence to suggest that our theory is actually better than all the rest.

This is where the predictability issue comes in. If a particular theory represents an accurate description and explanation of events, it ought to predict what will occur or how people will behave in specific instances. Consider a theory of learning: if we believed that learning occurred simply by associating one event with another (a general theory) then we should be able to make a prediction, or a **hypothesis**, about what would happen in a particular learning situation. Assume we were able to find a dog noted for its uncontrollable drooling at the sight of food. If our theory of learning held true, then presenting some other stimulus (say, the sound of a bell) every time the animal was offered food would eventually lead to an association between the two events (food and the bell). Ultimately the dog would salivate to the sound of the bell only. If an experiment along these lines were tried, and the prediction borne out, then we would have evidence in support of our more general view of behaviour. The more our predictions come true and the more hypotheses we can accept, the stronger our theory becomes. If our hypotheses are rejected, or our predictions produce contradictory results, then our theory weakens.

One important point to note here is that, while it's all very well to propose hypotheses based on a general theory, unless the predictions which form a part of these hypotheses can be tested, the theory will never develop. The theory that humans evolved, not naturally from early mammals, but as a result of alien intervention and genetic engineering, is all very well, yet unless we can come up with a way to test this view, the theory will remain forever at the level of idle speculation. Theories concerning future developments are equally problematic – the proposition that some time in the future people will develop telepathic abilities is, by its very nature, incapable of generating a currently testable hypothesis. We will have to wait and see.

### 1.4.4 Experimentation

So far, the scientific process has been presented as a systematic development from general theories to more specific hypotheses. The next step is to consider how best to test these hypotheses. There are several options available to the researcher – surveys can be carried out, questionnaires compiled, observations made – the choice depending on a number of elements, such as the type of participants being used, the context in which the research is being carried out, ethical issues and practical problems. However, the approach most often associated with psychology is that of experimentation, and this will be our starting point.

The very term, **experiment**, implies control; an experimenter controls all aspects of the environment in which a study is carried out (as far as this is possible). She determines the nature of the participants taking part in her study; she decides on all tasks and activities which will form part of the experiment; and she controls the sequence in which events are experienced. But why would such a high level of control be required?

At the risk of sounding obvious, human behaviour is extremely complex. Any single human act can be linked to and influenced by a multitude of factors, all of which are tangled up in such a way that it is often impossible to identify cause-and-effect relationships. A researcher studying decision making would find the mix of possible influences daunting: motivation would obviously play a part, as we often choose things which will satisfy needs within us (a need to be loved, a need to be successful); learning too is important, since much of what we do is habitual in nature; and then there is perception, with different people seeing issues and problems in different ways. Gender will be an issue as well, since males and females will have been shaped by their upbringing to have different preferences, while personality factors may lead inward-looking introverts to rarely select the same options as the more outgoing extravert.

Just think of your own decision to study psychology as a subject – all of the above factors would have played some part in your decision, as would attitudes towards the course, aspirations, availability and what your friends did. Clearly, if asked why you chose to do this subject, once you started to really think about it you would be surprised by the number and variety of contributing factors. This is why the researcher, wishing to study such a complex process, may well choose to do so under laboratory conditions: here she can determine the type of decision to be made, control the environment in which the process occurs and restrict the many sources of variation among her participants. Only then does it become possible to isolate and manipulate specific factors and record their impact on the individual.

Occasionally some classes of behaviour are deemed too complex to be adequately studied even under the most rigorous of experimental conditions and in those instances, some researchers have resorted to using different and much less complex species. A great deal of what we now understand about learned behaviour has developed from studies on rats, pigeons and, in Pavlov's case, dogs – the rationale being that although the end product represents a universal phenomenon, in lesser species learning is easier to isolate and manipulate.

While experimentation is often seen as the backbone of any science, within a behavioural science like psychology, it is not without its critics. True, the method reduces the number of confounding, interrelated and sometimes downright nuisance factors which might interfere with an object of a study, yet in achieving this it is possible to argue that the essential nature of human behaviour has been lost. While there are undoubtedly some aspects of the individual which can best be studied under controlled laboratory conditions – functions of the brain, sensation and perception, reaction time, to mention but a few – much of what we do as part of our day-to-day lives is a product of many interacting, interfering and contradicting factors. A laboratory experiment may well be able to tease out pure, un-contaminated cause-and-effect relationships, but often at a cost: consider that most experimental participants are not "real" people but (with apologies to our readership) college or university undergraduates. This group is not typical of the population at large – students are bright, motivated, young and, generally speaking, happy to volunteer to participate in an endless cycle of mindless experiments dreamed up by their professors and peers. Add this bias to experimental tasks created for their simplicity and ease of measurement, and all in a clinical environment free from outside contaminants, and you have what can best be described as artificiality. In some cases experimentation can refine the context of behaviour to such a point where all relevance to real life has been lost and it becomes impossible, or at least pointless, to try and generalise from experimental findings to the real world. A big enough problem when dealing with humans, but what do you do when your participants are rats?

This issue is known, not surprisingly, as the **generalisation problem**, describing the sometimes problematic process of applying observations from one situation to another in which conditions might be quite different and for which the original findings might no longer be relevant. However, it also reflects a conflict between two methodological positions, or philosophies: that between a reductive analytic approach and a holistic perspective.

The classic, traditional method for studying just about anything can be described as a reductive analytic model (see Figure 1.1). This is a straightforward scientific approach whereby a given issue is reduced to its various components and the element of particular interest is then analysed. The examples of experimentation offered above reflected this philosophy. In the early days of medical investigation, if you wanted to know how the brain worked, you obtained a brain, sometimes by questionable means (discarding the rest of the body), and commenced an examination. This is largely why people still talk about the brain as "grey matter" – dead brains, lacking a continuous blood supply, are grey. They are also, of course, dead, making it difficult to apply findings to the fully functioning, living organ.

As an approach to investigation the reductive analytic method has merit. By removing a key component from its environment or context, you remove the possibility of contamination by other things. A good example here relates to early studies on leadership in which leadership situations – military, political and business – were reduced to their constituent components (which would include subordinates, type of task and other contextual factors), the leader isolated and then analysed in terms of their personality or behavioural styles.

The feeling here was that leaders were constantly interacting with other elements of a situation, and that variables like time constraints, task characteristics and type of subordinates would invariably reflect on how the leader behaved. It was argued that these other factors would fudge, obscure or contaminate the very leadership characteristics which were the focus of interest. As we have observed, however, these very "contaminating" factors are

---

**Figure 1.1**    A typical reductive analytic approach to research.

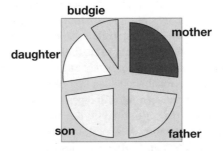

1. the situation (the family unit) is reduced to its component parts
2. the element of interest (the mother) is isolated
3. the isolated element is subjected to analysis

what provide the essence of this behaviour in real life, and the activity of attempting to reduce an essentially social process to its components serves only to dilute and obscure that
process. For this reason many early studies failed to properly describe and explain the actual interactions involved. In much the same way as motherhood can only be understood by
looking at how mothers behave within the family, so a true picture of leadership could not
emerge until leaders were viewed within the context of specific followers and particular
tasks; the removal of a mother from the family unit would provide little insight into how a
mother behaves, while at the same time destroying the integrity of the family itself.

This alternative, holistic view argued that any process which, in its normal functioning, interacts with other processes can only really be understood when viewed in its
context – the whole situation has to be considered, and not just its parts. Taking this particular view largely (though not completely) precludes the experimental approach. If we
wish to study behaviour in its natural context, using real people, doing real things, then we
have to adopt a different strategy, one in which the researcher does not become directly involved, does not manipulate and does not control. In this scenario the researcher becomes
an observer rather than an experimenter.

### 1.4.5    Observation

Observations can vary in nature from the kind of casual observations from which we notice, in an unplanned way, certain salient things about our environment, through the kind
of naturalistic or ethographic observations in which animals are studied in their natural
habitats, simply to see what they do, to a systematic form of observation in which the researcher has a pre-determined scheme relating to particular types of behaviours and structured methods for recording information.

This approach to the study of behaviour is truly holistic, in a way in which experimentation can never be. Participants observed in their 'natural habitat' tend to produce
more typical behaviours, a major implication of which is that findings of **observational
research** can usually be generalised quite validly to other, similar situations. Experimentation, as we pointed out, can produce findings which, because of the artificiality of the
experimental set-up (participants, task, context), can be difficult to generalise to real life.
Quite simply, the further our research setting is from real life, the greater the likelihood
that findings will be atypical.

However, before we go overboard in our praise of this method, it has to be recognised
that, just as with experimentation, the factors which make observation so valuable a research tool can also be regarded as its major drawbacks. Observing behaviour in natural
surroundings, without manipulation or attempts to control other factors, means that what
we see will be a product of many interactions. Consequently, identifying cause-and-effect
relationships will sometimes be impossible because several contributory causes will be
tangled up with one another. To further complicate the issue, it is not strictly true to claim
that an observation approach allows people to behave naturally; often, when we become
aware that we are being watched, our behaviour changes. Consider the common experience of passing a high street shop window and suddenly seeing yourself on a television
monitor: almost without thinking, the stomach is sucked in, the shoulders pressed back
and our normal slouching shamble replaced by a graceful stride. Or think of the student
whose performance on a statistical problem improves dramatically when the tutor peers
over her shoulder. Or her hapless neighbour, who falls to pieces in the same situation.
There are many examples of this phenomenon, known variously as a 'mere presence'
effect', a 'social facilitation/inhibition effect', an 'observer' or 'experimenter' effect and,

**A Closer Look At . . .**

# Observations

*I noticed a funny thing in the bank today . . .*

THE CASUAL OBSERVER

*During a trial of twenty interactions the number of eye contacts between tellers and customers increased by 40% when interactions were opposite-sexed, compared to an average of five contacts per minute for same-sexed individuals.*

THE SYSTEMATIC OBSERVER

in some situations, a Hawthorne effect (a term borrowed from an early series of industrial studies in which the impact of observers on work behaviour was noted). Whatever term is used to describe the effect, they all serve to demonstrate the same thing – the known presence of an observer invariably affects the behaviour of the observed in one way or another.

There is one final point to be made here, and it is an important one. Observation is, by its very nature, a human, judgemental activity in which we note when a behaviour occurs, and classify such behaviour, usually according to some kind of scheme. In planned psychological research we normally have a clearly defined set of behaviours in which we are interested, plus a logical plan for recording and coding what we see (see Box 1.1). However, because we are human, and since most of our everyday observations are coloured by a variety of factors – social, political, sexual, cognitive, motivational and so on – it is quite difficult to guarantee that what we apparently observe is actually what is happening. Consider the observation of a glance from one individual to another. If we are attempting to describe what has happened, how do we decide if the glance was casual, intimate, hostile, curious, friendly, aggressive, questioning, contemptuous or whatever; or even if the 'glance' itself actually took place? We rely on experience, we seek other cues – for example, was the glance accompanied by a smile? a frown? a raised eyebrow? We might even make a guess. In short, most forms of observation involve judgement of one kind or another and, as all psychology undergraduates quickly learn, human judgement in not something which can be wholly trusted.

It is important to point out, however, that many of the problems with observation methods can be dealt with – some through rigorous advance planning, and some through sophisticated statistical techniques which can effectively control for the influence of intervening factors, in an after-the-fact manner. Part 2, which deals with how studies are designed, will explore these matters more fully while Part 5 considers relevant statistical procedures.

## 1.4.6 Participant observation

One of the problems of being human (many would argue *the* problem) is that when it comes to observing anything – ourselves, other people, our society, other cultures – we do not do this as completely objective and honest recorders of what is actually there. We are not like that: we are not machines, we are not blank slates on which the reality of our surroundings is written in a passive manner. Rather we interact with our world, we are active in our judgement of what goes on around us and our perception of events is based on our

Plate 1.1    Anthropologist Margaret Mead, one of the best known ethnographers.
*Source*: Corbis/Bettmann

experience, our background and culture, and on who we are. In other words, we are sub-jective creatures, and our perceptions are therefore also subjective.

This tendency for people not to see the world as it is has been long understood and researchers in the field of visual imagery have used this understanding to illustrate such perceptual effects through various forms of visual illusion – an understanding shared by fairground magicians everywhere (see Figure 1.2). Nor are these effects restricted to the physical environment: the human tendency to perceive the world in anything but objective terms applies to the social world also, as the opposing sports fans in Box 1.2 illustrate.

It is because of this human characteristic (there is no point in calling it a failing since this is simply how we are) that the recurring question 'How do you know?' is so irritatingly

Figure 1.2    Necker cubes.

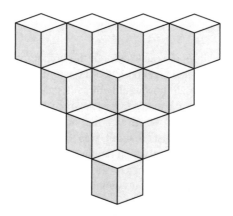

Box 1.2

**A Closer Look At . . .**

# Bias in judgement

*This was a triumph of skill over strength, of confidence over complacency in which the opposing team were outmatched, outplayed and outperformed. There is no doubt that the best team won.*

REVIEWER AND FAN OF THE WINNING TEAM

*This was an example of the worst excesses of football today, in which the winning team hacked its way to victory on the back of foul play and a blatantly partisan attitude from the referee. We were robbed!*

REVIEWER AND FAN OF THE LOSING TEAM

pointed. Whenever we report something, how do we know we are reporting what actually happened, as opposed to an interpretation of what occurred based on the fact that we are male as opposed to female; black as opposed to white; introverted as opposed to extraverted; wealthy as opposed to impoverished, and so on?

One way round this is to apply the rigours of science which we have introduced in the preceding sections. Awareness of our limitations has often led researchers along the route of experimentation and dispassionate observation in an attempt to control for our subjective tendencies, and a great deal of what is regarded as 'science' adheres to these processes. For some, however, even these rigorous approaches are not sufficient. It could be argued (and it often is) that no matter how carefully and objectively a researcher sets up an experimental study, it will be impossible for him to remain totally uninvolved or unaffected by the mix of social, cultural and personal influences which have made him what he is.

An alternative approach (and it is worth pointing out that this involves not just a procedural alternative, but also a philosophical one) is exemplified in the particular methodology of **participant observation**.

On the face of it this approach is the very antithesis of conventional scientific research in that it questions a number of the fundamental principles of scientific methodology:

- don't get involved
- begin research from the standpoint of theory
- be objective

In anthropological research the unique problems set by attempting to study cultures of which we had no experience and very little understanding precluded a dispassionate approach. After all, how could you understand something with which you had no experience by staying as far away from it as possible? Similarly, how could you develop theories about a society of which you had no understanding? The only solution, or at least so the early anthropologists thought, was to get involved.

Participant observation required that the researcher became involved with – indeed, became a part of – the society she was studying. Only by developing a history of experience within a particular society would it be possible to propose theories about its structure and functioning.

On the face of it, this approach runs counter to the principles of objective science, but in reality it was only a shrewd understanding of the issues surrounding the question: 'How do you know?' which forced the anthropologist to accept that allowing himself to be absorbed by the society he was studying was the only way in which it could be studied. Moreover, more than any other approach to research, participant observation can be regarded as truly holistic, a form of holism in which even the researcher has become a part of the whole.

Outside the anthropological setting, the approach has become more generally known as **ethnography**, a form of in-depth, holistic analysis of the structure and processes of culture. The approach came to wider prominence in the 1980s with the rise of what became known as feminist research, the aim of which was to investigate the changing role of women and their experiences in modern society. In particular, the approach underlined the point about bias in perceiving the world, whether such bias be determined by culture, experience or gender.

If all of this seems complicated, then it is. For most undergraduates, the rules and procedures for experimentation, or conventional observational research, are well within reach. For ethnographic research, however, the rules often seem vague, the procedures complex and the timescales lengthy. For this reason, few undergraduates could realistically attempt – nor would they be encouraged to attempt – an ethnographic study which required some form of participatory research, especially given the one- or two-semester timescale available for methodology projects. However, because the approach is now an accepted component in the repertoire of the modern-day researcher, and because there may well be instances in which undergraduate projects might benefit from an ethnographic perspective, further discussion is offered in Part 6. In addition, for those students especially interested in the area, the concluding section of this chapter offers some useful texts for further reading.

### 1.4.7 Field studies

It should be clear that the common methods of researching into human behaviour are not without their problems: an experiment usually has all the advantages of controlling for interfering factors at the expense of realism, whereas observation studies show the reverse – lots of realism, but limited controls. There is however another approach which, potentially, possesses the advantages of both, while minimising the disadvantages – field research.

A **field study** involves participants behaving in their natural surroundings, but with the researcher actively manipulating aspects of the environment and noting the outcome. This can be in a covert manner, in which confederates are used and unobtrusive observations taken, as in studies on pedestrians violating the red 'don't walk' signs at street crossings in response to the behaviour of a model, or it can resemble a conventional, controlled experiment in which a group of production workers operates under a new type of supervisory regime and their output compared with that of an identical group working under a standard management scheme. This kind of unobtrusive study offers the researcher an alternative, more holistic approach to research than is provided by conventional laboratory experimentation and which also goes some way towards dealing with the control difficulties which characterise observational methods. Field research, though, is not without its own set of drawbacks.

First, one of the guiding principles of psychological research is that participants involve themselves willingly, and on the basis of informed consent – that is, they are aware of what is being done and, given that awareness, have agreed to participate. Furthermore, it is an accepted standard now that participants have the right to withdraw from any research without prejudice and at their own volition. There is also an expectation that participants' rights on confidentiality and anonymity will be secured. However, in the kind of unobtrusive observation study which we have just described, participants are usually unaware that their environment has been manipulated, nor do they know that their responses are being recorded, or even videoed. Consequently they are not willing participants in the study, they have not had an opportunity to give informed consent and, arguably, their rights to anonymity and confidentiality have been violated. This is an important ethical issue, which will be more fully explored in Part 3.

Second, where the research is more overt in nature, involving for example manipulation within a hospital, school or factory, various forms of experimenter effect will come into play, possibly interfering with the aim of the study, much as we have already discussed in 1.4.5.

Lastly, any research involving changes or manipulations within an organisation runs the risk of interfering with and undermining normal organisational processes, practices and procedures. Consequently, unless a study can guarantee minimal disruption, or unless there is a strong rationale for the study, it is unlikely that such research would be permitted. Most organisations now support their own ethics committees, whose purpose is to safeguard the rights and wellbeing of their employees, patients and relevant individuals. Such committees nowadays are unlikely to approve research which is disruptive, unscientific or unethical.

### 1.4.8 Case studies

The implication in the methods discussed so far (experimentation and observation) is that large numbers of participants are involved in the research. This is based on the view that the more people for whom a prediction holds true, or across which observations are consistent, then the more likely we are to accept a hypothesis and provide evidence for a theory. However, there are certain situations in which it might not be possible to conduct research in the conventional way – we may have access to only a few participants, or the event we are interested in may be so unusual that there are only one or two participants to study. Consider trying to investigate coping behaviour of mothers with sextuplets, or the memory problems of people suffering accidental brain damage, and you'll get the idea. In situations like this, a **case study** approach is often the only option available to the researcher.

A case study is an intensive, detailed study of a single individual, group or event, using a variety of methods. Case study data are usually highly descriptive, and may take the form of interview notes, observations and video material; they can comprise introspections, narrative and psychometric measurements – in fact, anything at all which can offer an insight into an individual might be used. The approach rarely makes use of experimentation in the usual sense of the word, but may involve observation of behavioural change over a period of time as a result of a particular form of, say, drug treatment or therapy. Not surprisingly, given its application to studies on the efficacy of intervention, the case study approach has been closely associated with the clinical sphere, but it needn't be limited to this, since any instance of novelty or restricted participant numbers will lend itself to the technique. Studies of the experiences of astronauts, of people who have encountered near-death events or, indeed, of the mother with the large family would naturally advocate this type of in-depth approach.

The beginnings of an investigation or the exploration of a new area might also benefit from the extremely detailed analysis of a single participant – indeed, psychoanalysis was built on the personal introspections of the early theorists like Freud and the detailed case notes on individual patients. As a way of initially exploring issues, of gathering rich, descriptive data and providing the first steps in hypotheses generation, the case study approach is ideal.

As with all previous methods of research, however, the case study is not without its own problems. All the disadvantages of observer bias discussed earlier will come to bear on the single participant case – an observer may well attend selectively to the information presented to him, may overvalue some events at the expense of others and may even be guilty of a form of motivated perception, if the aim of the study is to promote a favoured belief or theory. The participant herself, if relying on memory or introspection to provide accounts of experiences and emotions, may fall victim to the many factors which influence our recall for past events. Not to mention the tendency, present in us all, to modify our view of the world and our role in it to play down anything which might show us in a poor light, or to modify our behaviour in terms of what we believe to be the researcher's expectations – a particular problem with the case study approach since the intensive nature of the relation-ship between those involved allows the participant to study the researcher even as she herself is being studied.

There is a final problem here, already encountered during our brief discussion on ex-perimentation: the generalisation problem. There are many reasons why it is sometimes difficult to expand findings from a study involving a sample to the population as a whole. We have already encountered some of these, and they include problems like the artificiality of an experimental situation, or the inability to control for interfering factors in an observa-tion study. In the case study, though, there is the added problem that there are often very few participants, and sometimes only one, and it would be difficult to make an argument for generalising observations from a single individual to society as a whole. However, this will not always be an issue, especially when the purpose of a study is not to find out some-thing about people in general, but about the target individual or group in particular. And where a broader perspective is the aim, a case study would be used only to provide a first, tentative hypothesis about human behaviour, which would be the starting point of a larger piece of research. For a fuller review of these issues, Part 6 offers an introduction to the qualitative techniques which form a large part of the case study approach.

### 1.4.9 Surveys

A method of data collection which is most often associated with marketing, political and social science research, but which has also found its place within psychological methodol-ogy (and is a special favourite among the undergraduate population), is the **survey**. Either as a kind of structured interview or in its more common printed, self-report format, sur-veys at their most basic level aim to generate primarily descriptive information. From the massive government census which attempts to describe the state of the nation in 10-yearly snapshots, through the ubiquitous market research interviews occurring on every street corner, to the frenetic political polling which takes place in the lead-up to every election, surveys provide huge quantities of descriptive information.

For the psychologist, however, concerned with hypotheses and theory, the quality of information generated by this simple survey is often too limited (proportion of the popula-tion who intend to vote Conservative at the next election; what percentage of income is spent on leisure pursuits; how many households own a microwave, etc.), although there are statistical techniques which allow certain inferences to be made with such data. The main contribution of the survey tradition to psychological research is not so much in the type of data it generates, but in the rigours of its approach to data gathering. Sampling techniques, methods for dealing with bias in our participants, ways of ensuring that a sample accurately reflects the population as a whole all owe much of their development to the simple survey, and provide an important foundation for developments in the next, and last, methodology to be discussed – questionnaire research.

### 1.4.10   Questionnaire-based research

We have previously stated that the survey is a frequently used method of data collection in psychological research – a great deal of data, especially at undergraduate level, is generated through the use of questionnaires. However, these are not the simple, descriptive devices of basic survey research, but sophisticated test instruments which can contain items on attitudes, perceptions, thoughts, feelings and behaviour. Furthermore, when combined with other, established instruments, such as personality measures, stress instruments, measures of self-esteem or any of a large number of **psychometric tests** which have been developed over the years – many of which are in themselves forms of questionnaire – we have at our disposal an extremely powerful technique for not just describing, but also explaining and predicting. A well-constructed questionnaire-based study can demonstrate relationships, explore differences and test hypotheses; in some respects it acts as an amalgam of observational and experimental approaches, with responses to questions serving as observations across a wide range of participants. Moreover, if the right kind of information is sought, real cause-and-effect relationships can be examined, allowing for similar kinds of controls to be exercised as those used in classical experimentation – always remembering of course that what is being measured is not what people actually do, but what they *say* they do.

An added advantage of the questionnaire, however, is that, as with most survey instruments, it is a potentially quick, cheap and straightforward method of obtaining information – large numbers of questionnaires can be administered simultaneously and, if items are correctly constructed, data can be readily collated using various kinds of scoring keys devised by the researcher. Moreover, since they require little in the way of facilities (laboratory space, computers, instrumentation, technical support), they are among the most readily implemented of research designs. There is, however, a danger in assuming that because questionnaire-based studies appear easy, cheap and straightforward to implement, they are in some way better than other approaches; some researchers would even go as far as to claim that, because of the nature of this method, it is almost impossible to obtain useful information of any sort (remember, these kinds of questionnaires go further than the basic

Box 1.3

### A Closer Look At . . .

## A sampling problem

*Unbelievably, 95% of our sample, representing the population at large, strongly agreed with the statement that the police in this country should be given increased powers of arrest, detention and personal exemption from prosecution. And more money.*

QUESTIONNAIRES ADMINISTERED TO A SAMPLE OF 200 INDIVIDUALS,
OUTSIDE THE OFFICES OF NEW SCOTLAND YARD, LONDON

survey in that they invite people to make judgements, state views and recall events, among other things, encouraging the possibility of bias in all its forms). Other potential problems can arise as a result of the process of handing out questionnaires – as with simple surveys, unless the sample filling in our forms truly represents the group or population we are interested in, any results will be seriously flawed and unrepresentative (see Box 1.3).

And finally, returning to the earlier comment about the apparent simplicity of the questionnaire, it is useful to remember that, in this kind of research, you get what you ask for – no more, no less. The skill of asking the right questions and in the right way is an exacting one, and will be discussed in greater detail in Chapter 6.

## 1.4.11   Secondary research

Research in which the individual or group responsible for the design of a study actively participates in its implementation is known as primary research, and information gleaned in this way is termed **primary data**. However, there are many instances in which the data required to answer a research question will have been already collected by others. Whenever we use data of this kind our research is termed secondary research and the data, **secondary data**.

Most research relies to some extent on secondary data – whenever we review the findings of previous research as part of a literature review, or consult government statistics, or even read a chapter in a textbook, we are using information which we ourselves played no part in gathering. However, it is possible, and indeed quite acceptable, to rely on secondary data as *the* data for a study. An investigator exploring changing trends in national earnings might find that the information she needs is already available in government census statistics, obviating the need to carry out a lengthy study of her own. Similarly, research into health and education issues can be well served by using General Household statistics (data collected at regular intervals and made available to researchers through the Office of National Statistics). In cases like this the researcher is able to explore and analyse existing data to meet the requirements of her own research. Not surprisingly perhaps, using secondary data for one's research has distinct advantages:

- Secondary data can be obtained quickly – the entire process of developing questionnaires or test instruments and carrying out lengthy research procedures is unnecessary.
- Secondary data can be obtained cheaply – though not always freely, since many organisations charge for access to their information, dispensing with the need to actively collect data which will in itself have clear funding implications for the research.
- The scope of secondary data will often exceed what the individual might achieve on his or her own – consider the national census; how many researchers could even dream of surveying every individual of voting age in the entire country?

Clearly, secondary data are of great potential value to the behavioural researcher. However (isn't there always a however?), there are a number of disadvantages to secondary data which must also be understood:

- Secondary data have usually been collected originally to meet a particular research purpose. Consequently, the way in which measures have been taken, or the range of response, might not meet the needs of the current research.
- Secondary data are often available only as summary data – it is not always clear what the original categories and responses might have been before the original researchers recoded variables, deleted certain data or summarised information.

- Secondary data are not always current. Most major government surveys, for instance, are carried out only every few years – research based on the most recent national census could be as much as nine years out of date.

Despite these drawbacks, secondary data research remains popular in many fields. Within psychology one of the relatively recent applications of secondary data is in the procedure of **meta-analysis**. This approach attempts to combine the findings of several studies on the same issue to provide a broader overview of a topic than is normally possible from a single, narrowly defined study. In much the same way that consulting a large body of literature provides a general picture of an area, meta-analysis, by aggregating the results of many independent studies, effectively performs a 'super study' of a particular issue, even though the data on which this is based were generated by other researchers. And finally, making use of secondary data is a favourite ploy of tutors and supervisors who will often use previous research and its findings as a training ground for their own students.

## 1.5 Beginning a research project

### 1.5.1 Choosing a research area

This is where it starts. As an undergraduate student of psychology or another of the behavioural sciences, you are now preparing to design and implement a study – either on your own or as part of a group – and the first question to be dealt with is: where do I begin?

The starting point is normally the selection of a **research area** – should the study be on the general topic of sensation? Should it be on developmental issues? occupational? forensic? How do you choose?

The simple answer is probably to begin with a general area which is of interest – one particular module in your course of study may appeal to you more than others and you might decide to conduct a study in this field, or there might be a contemporary issue which suggests a study to you. At the time of writing, current media topics are bullying in schools, attitudes towards the police and the problems of binge drinking. Any one of these issues would represent an interesting and fruitful research area, and scanning the newspapers remains a consistent source of research topics for the student of human behaviour, providing the student's natural desire to tackle the great issues of life can be tempered by practical considerations. Personal observation is another potential source of research – you may have noted something about the way human interactions change inside a lift, or how people sometimes appear happier on sunny days than rainy ones. Or perhaps a particular textbook has stimulated an interest in an issue (even reading this passage might have drawn you to the idea of looking at bullying in schools), or a recent article in a psychological or scientific journal might point to a new area of research (see Box 1.4). Even your poor, overworked tutors can be a useful source of mental stimulation – most university lecturers have their own pet research fields, and all of us are suckers for even a modest display of interest from students. It is only too easy to wheedle research ideas from academics who will be more than pleased to talk about what concerns them.

There is a special situation which, for some, offers a potential short-cut to research ideas, and it involves access to special participant groups. Many students, for matters of conscience, or for financial reasons, find themselves involved with participant groups

Box 1.4

How To . . .

# Come up with ideas for a research project

Choosing an issue to investigate is always a problem for undergraduates. As a first step any of the following can be useful sources of interesting research issues.

- Reading newspapers and watching news reports can identify a range of problems, aspirations and issues which are of current social concern.

- Pursuing an area of personal academic interest will usually lead to an issue which can form the basis of a study.

- Recognising staff interests will often point to interesting areas of possible research, in addition to identifying an ideal supervisor for a particular topic.

- Access to a particular group or organisation can sometimes be the starting point in identifying a research issue, either in terms of what the organisation does (for instance, working with a health-centred group might raise a number of health-related issues to explore) or in terms of structural, organisational issues (such as how leadership is exercised within the group, or motivation maintained or stress dealt with among the individual members).

- Reading current journal articles will be a guide to the issues other researchers are interested in, in addition to providing up-to-date references on related material. The bulletin of the British Psychological Society (BPS), *The Psychologist*, for example, is a good guide to not only current interests but also forthcoming attractions, offering a useful insight to future research trends.

outside the normal student population – some work part time in offices, some do weekends for burger chains, while others offer up their spare time to help out in nursery groups or as volunteer carers. In such instances, access to particular groups might in itself offer a source of rich ideas – in addition to solving the perennial problem of finding participants. Where such opportunities are available, they should be considered as extremely useful sources of inspiration, providing the ethical implications of doing so are understood; the step from convenience to exploitation is a short one.

Most students will readily settle on an area of interest from any one, or a combination, of the sources outlined above, but for those who still have difficulty choosing a topic, the simplest solution is to try a few of the approaches mentioned and generate a list of general topics. The next stage is to take each topic in turn and decide whether or not there is a specific aspect of this issue which is of interest – this becomes the **research question**.

## 1.5.2   Formulating the research question

The research question acts as a kind of anchor for a study – it identifies the area in which the research is being carried out, it precisely defines the aim of the research and, very often, it also indicates any sub-issues which might be involved in the study. In many instances it will also dictate the nature of the study, be it experimental, observational or whatever.

For these reasons, considerable thought should go into formulating the research question; get it right and it acts as a continual reminder of what a particular study is all about and provides a guide through all the subsequent stages of design, implementation and data analysis. Get it wrong and you will flounder. A common problem with undergraduate projects arises when students approach the data analysis part of a study with no clear idea of what kind of analysis they should be doing, and why. Some of this can be attributed to a generalised fear of statistics within the student population, but much of it will also be due to having lost sight of the research question, or having a question which is too vague and fails to provide sufficient direction.

Generally speaking, the research question provides a statement of the overall aims of a piece of research and indicates, in broad terms, what you are trying to do. This is different from the previous exercise of selecting a topic area in which to carry out your research, a distinction which, unfortunately, is a perennial source of annoyance to undergraduates everywhere. Choosing a topic is, as it appears, merely the selection of which field you wish to work in: clinical, educational, social, or whatever. Constructing a research question, however, requires that you select a quite specific issue from within this topic area. For instance, you might be interested in the general, medical issue of the factors influencing elevated blood pressure (hypertension). This interest might subsequently resolve into the research question of, 'What factors contribute to variation in blood pressure in a hypertensive patient group?', thus providing a starting point for the subsequent study, and a reminder of what it was all about. Such a research question identifies the area in which you will be working and also provides the important statement of what you are trying to do. However, the research question at this stage is still a relatively general thing. It requires refinement or qualification, so the next stage in the process is to turn our rather general question into something more specific – what precisely is it about hypertension which we wish to investigate?

### 1.5.3   Proposing a testable hypothesis

The research question gives us our starting point, but before we can begin our study, we need to hone in on something more specific – we need to refine our research question (see Box 1.5). Developing our medical example from the previous section, we now need to qualify the issue of what factors contribute to variation in blood pressure. To assist this

 **A Closer Look At . . .**

# Issues, questions and hypotheses

In refining our approach to a research issue we typically progress from the general to the specific:

■ I'm interested in the general area of social competence.
  (The research issue)

■ Are there gender differences in social competence?
  (The research question)

■ Mean social skills scores for pre-school females will be significantly higher than scores for pre-school males.
  (The hypothesis)

refinement, we would typically review previous research in the area, coming up with a number of more specific questions, such as: is personality related to elevated blood pressure, or self image, or exercise? And are there other factors involved – do women exhibit lower levels of hypertension than men? Does the frequency of exercise relate to blood pressure levels? Does the kind of exercise (for example, aerobic or anaerobic) have an impact? All these are logical extensions of the original question, the difference being that they now offer something specific which can be tested – they offer the basis for hypotheses.

### 1.5.4    Deciding on a type of study

We have already indicated that there are a number of ways to research an issue – we can design a laboratory experiment, we can conduct surveys, we can set up an observation study, and so on. The choice of which approach to take will involve a number of factors: do we want to study behaviour as it occurs in its natural habitat, without any kind of external interference or manipulation? Or do we want to control certain factors and study behaviour in a more rigid environment? In most cases, the research area and the research question will point to a particular type of study; in others, practical or ethical issues will play a part. For an undergraduate study, a particular department might not have the technical staff or equipment to support certain projects, where others might be rich in audio-visual suites and observation chambers. For some studies ample numbers of participants might be available, making a questionnaire-based **project** attractive, while for others, access to participants may be so limited as to necessitate a case study or other qualitative approach. Whichever approach is chosen, however, they all require the same adherence to the principles governing psychological research – the study should be systematic, professionally conducted and with due respect for the rights of the individual.

## 1.6    Reviewing the literature

A fundamental part of any study is a thorough knowledge of the area in which the research is to be carried out and a familiarity with other research on the same topic. Without this information we would never know that our brilliant, ingenious project had actually been published two years previously, or that the paper on which we are basing our own work had been subsequently refuted by the original authors. Moreover, the essential, reasoned justification for our work would be impossible unless we were able to provide a balanced review of previous research in the area. And to be able to do this we must read, and read widely.

In some cases this might involve tracking down back copies of newspapers – some research is based on contemporary issues, with relevant material available through library sources, either as hard copy (i.e., originals), on microfilm or, where facilities permit, on a computerised system. Unfortunately, many students – and even highly qualified researchers – often ignore the rich reservoir of material available through the popular media. After all, television and newspapers provide an expression of society's concerns and obsessions and anyone hoping to explore a contemporary social issue, like attitudes towards AIDS, the police or the provision of care in the community, could do worse than to review a few back copies of their local and national newspaper.

Textbooks, providing they are recent publications, also provide a useful source of background information, although it is in the nature of textbooks that the material covered is, of necessity, general. However, they can offer useful reviews of topics of interest, in addition to providing sources of more specific reading in their reference sections – including details of key articles on which much contemporary research will have been based. It is worth remembering, though, that textbooks provide secondary data: they present, summarise and often interpret original or primary work, and it is not always the case that such interpretations fully reflect the intentions of original authors.

For many students of psychology, however, research journals will provide their main source of background and reference material, and in a burgeoning science like psychology, the sheer number and variety of journals is both intimidating and satisfying. Journals are regular publications (sometimes monthly, quarterly or annually) closely attached to particular scientific domains and comprising a collection of articles, reports and research papers reflecting current work in particular fields. The studies described and the reports presented offer information on current research which is about as up to date as it is possible to get. Moreover, before any material is accepted for inclusion in a journal, it is subjected to a process of peer review, in which other researchers and academics have the opportunity to (usually anonymously) comment, evaluate and offer suggestions for improvement. Consequently, for anyone wishing to explore a particular issue in any detail, journals will represent a key source of primary information. Typical contents of a journal issue might be an editorial, commenting on any particular trends or themes represented in the particular issue, a number of research reports on a variety of topics within the discipline and possibly a book review or two.

For established researchers, keeping track of relevant research in their own area is usually quite straightforward – by and large they will subscribe to a relatively small range of journals, reflecting personal interest and providing a locus for their own publications. For undergraduates, however, perhaps embarking on their first major study, the wealth of sources and information available to them can be quite overwhelming. A cursory glance through any library catalogue of academic publications will turn up some 200 journals recounting psychological research, presenting a hopeless task for the un-initiated. Fortunately, information management (librarianship, for the novice) has evolved to the point that even the greenest of undergraduates can negotiate the wealth of information available to them to find what they want. Most psychologically relevant material is regularly catalogued and entered into what are termed Psychological Abstracts – as the name suggests, this is a listing of the abstracts, or summaries of various pieces of research, and they provide a brief but concise review of what a study was about and what the findings were. *Psychological Abstracts* is produced by the PsycINFO® department of the American Psychological Association (APA). It is a monthly printed index of journal articles, books and book chapters. Issues are organised by topic and contain author, subject and book title indexes. Annual author and subject indexes are also published to make searching easier.

Currently electronic searching is becoming the method of choice among undergraduates, and Box 1.6 illustrates a variety of useful websites. Typically, entering a few key terms will generate a full listing of relevant studies or abstracts (depending on the nature of the site), although care should be exercised in the selection of search terms – an unwary user who simply requests a search for any journal article with the word 'attitudes' in the title would spend weeks sifting through the mountain of returns. Selecting 'attitudes' and 'police', on the other hand, would generate a relatively small and much more specific selection of articles. More generally, Internet services provided by various search engines will usually provide plenty of references on most subjects of psychological interest. Of

A Closer Look At . . .

# Useful Internet resources

Most of the following are available on the Internet, but some may be accessible only through your campus library and might require a password (that is, some need to be paid for by your university). Check with your own library staff if in doubt.

Websites: simply type in the site name and follow your instincts.

- American Psychological Association
- British Psychological Society
- BUBL psychology sources (Buros Centre for Testing) – for locating psychology tests produced or published after 1989
- Classics in the history of psychology – full-text documents
- Cogprints – cognitive science electronic print archive
- Internet psychologist – a teach-yourself tutorial
- LTSN Psychology – learning and teaching support network for higher education
- Mental help net
- Psych web
- PsycPORT
- SOSIG – Psychology gateway

Electronic journal articles:

- Google scholar – an ideal starting point for keyword, or name searches of particular relevance for the academic. Also acts as an index of citations.
- The Psychologist – most departments subscribe to this; now full-text versions of back copies (to about 1997) are available online via the BPS website.
- PsycINFO – a major abstracting service for the behavioural sciences, usually provided under licence on campus. It covers books, book chapters, articles from 1,300 journals, conference proceedings, theses, government reports and papers. All aspects of psychology are covered as well as aspects of education, medicine, sociology, law and management. This is an extremely comprehensive resource and one of the most useful for the undergraduate.
- ASSIA – Applied social science index and abstracts (may be restricted to some university campuses) – indexes and abstracts the articles from 650 key English-language journals from 1987 onwards. Comprehensive coverage of social science topics including health, education, social work, gender, psychology, sociology, politics and race relations.
- Medline – a major bio-medical index which is useful for researchers interested in health-related issues.
- Journal Citation Reports – a useful site for evaluating journals: shows which journals are most often cited and which have the greatest impact on their field.
- Proquest newspapers – searches the main UK papers all at once and gives access to archives from about 1995 onwards (depending on newspaper).
- Social Science Citation Index – indexes 1,700 major social science journals from 1981, covering all social science disciplines. This is a useful site for tracking individual studies which have been cited in other research.

Box 1.7

A Closer Look At . . .

# A typical web-search result

**Scholar**

[BOOK] Mental representations: a dual coding approach
A Paivio - 1990 - Oxford
Cited by 467 - Web Search - Library Search

[CITATION] Imagery and verbal processes
A Paivio - New York: Holt, Rinehart & Winston, 1971
Cited by 420 - Web Search - Library Search

[CITATION] Concreteness, imagery, and meaningfulness: values for 925 nouns
A Paivio, JC Yuille, SA Madigan - Journal of Experimental Psychology Monograph Supplement, 1968
Concreteness, imagery, and meaningfulness : values for 925 nouns. By: Allan Paivio;
John C Yuille; Stephen A Madigan. Type: English : Book : Non-fiction. ...
Cited by 221 - Web Search - ncbi.nlm.nih.gov - Library Search

[CITATION] Dual coding theory: Retrospect and current status
A Paivio - Canadian Journal of Psychology, 1991
Cited by 109 - Web Search

[CITATION] Dual coding theory and education
JM Clark, A Paivio - Educational Psychology Review, 1991
Cited by 102 - Web Search

[CITATION] Working with emotions in psychotherapy
LS Greenberg, SC Paivio - Guilford, New York, 1997
Working with emotions in psychotherapy • By: Leslie S Greenberg ; Sandra
C Paivio • Publisher: New York : Guilford Press, ©1997. ...
Cited by 85 - Web Search - ncbi.nlm.nih.gov - Library Search

[CITATION] Mental Representations
A Paivio, A Paivio - A dual coding approach. New York, 1986
Cited by 53 - Web Search

[CITATION] Mental imagery in associative learning and memory
A Paivio - Psychological Review, 1969
Cited by 53 - Web Search

The output of a web search can be considerable and the above image is only a small part of the amount of information available on the Internet. The keyword for this particular search was 'Paivio', a central figure in the field of imagery, and typical output includes books and articles by the named individual, in addition to a listing of material in which the author has been cited. More refined searches can be carried out using additional keywords, ranging from the author's first name or initial, in case there are several Paivios out there, all of whom have been included in the search findings, to particular aspects of the individual's work which would limit the amount of material found.

particular use here is the Google.Scholar engine, a recent (at the time of publication) Internet search tool dedicated to academic and research literature. See Box 1.7 for a typical keyword search. The keyword was 'Paivio', a major figure in the field of information processing.

In the event that our study is based on one specific piece of published research – perhaps the aim is to develop an idea, or explore a novel aspect of previous work – then our starting point would be the Science, or the Social Sciences Citation Index. This particular index focuses on individual studies, and identifies any subsequent research which has cited the original. This is a useful method for following particular trends in a research area, but of a more specific type than that illustrated in Box 1.7.

For those keen to review research in progress, but not necessarily published, the Internet now offers direct links to individuals in university departments all over the country; information pages are appearing every day, outlining interests, publications and ongoing work. It is conceivable that, within a relatively short time, surfing the net will provide the most direct route to current psychological research.

## 1.7 Evaluating research

Much of the foregoing has emphasised the need to read widely around a topic before embarking on the design of a specific study. However, simply consuming journals and textbooks in an effort to amass information is, in itself, not enough – when we read and consider the work of others, we need to do so critically, adopting a questioning and sometimes downright suspicious perspective. The importance of this stance is obvious when one considers that, for the purposes of research, we are not merely trying to find out more about an issue, we are also looking for flaws in a theory, limitations in the way a study has been carried out, or possible sources of development. After all, it could well be that the very limitations of an early study provide us with the impetus for our own work, yet we would never have identified those limitations had our approach not been critical.

Asking questions while reviewing the work of others is a skill most undergraduates are expected to acquire as they progress through a degree course – the trick is in knowing what questions to ask. In the field of psychological research, this process is possibly more straightforward than in other areas, due to the manner in which research is carried out. Earlier, we emphasised the logical, systematic and scientific nature of psychology, and because the study of human behaviour now tends to follow an established structure, our questioning can follow similar systematic guidelines.

The first object of doubt in consideration of any study will be the literature review and background information cited in support of the research. We would want to know if the review seemed broad enough to provide thorough and balanced coverage of an issue:

- Are there any aspects of the research issue which, in your view, seem to have been overlooked, or not fully considered?
- Does the review provide a sound basis for the research question being explored?
- Do hypotheses follow logically from what has gone before?

If, at any time while reading a rationale for research, we find ourselves saying, 'Yes, but what about . . . ?' this could indicate a weakness or limitation.

If a review is broad in coverage, the research issue clearly stated and rationally justified, and the hypotheses logical extensions of what has gone before, the next area of concern is the design of the study. When we read this section, we are evaluating the plan drawn up by the researcher to examine the hypotheses. What we should be asking ourselves is:

- Does this seem like a good way of exploring the issue?
- Will all the considerations raised as being relevant to the research question be covered with this particular approach?

- Does it seem practical to research an issue in this way?
- Are there any ethical problems with this approach?
- Is there a better way to do this?

Once again, if we find ourselves saying, 'Yes, but what about . . . ?' then there may be some problem with the design.

If a researcher's plan for a study seems acceptable, the next thing we want to know is how well the plan was executed. Some studies, for instance, require many participants; yet obtaining volunteers in large numbers is not always possible. Our judgement here would have to be whether or not failure to obtain sufficient participants, or participants of the right type, detracts from the study in any way. Generally speaking, close scrutiny of the research procedure might highlight difficulties experienced by the researcher, or deviations from the original design which might lead us to question whether or not the research issue has actually been addressed.

When it comes to considering the results of a research study, many undergraduates find themselves bemused, if not intimidated, at the information presented to them. In part, this is due to the relative statistical inexperience common among early students and, while this is a facility which will develop as the individual matures, there are always some research designs which rely on complex analytical procedures inaccessible to most students. There is also the possibility that a researcher, due to his own statistical limitations or (and this is thankfully rare) a desire to deliberately mislead, may present results which are ambiguous or incomplete. Either way, it is sometimes difficult for the student to make a judgement on the validity of research findings from consideration of the results. However, there are some guidelines which can be applied:

- Are the results clearly presented – do tables and figures offer a clear indication of what happened?
- Is it made clear that the hypotheses have been supported or refuted?
- Do the results appear to address the issues raised during the literature review?
- Do the analyses seem appropriate?
- Do the data suggest some other form of analysis which has been overlooked?

Posing these questions will at least go some way towards evaluating the quality of research, yet this section of a published study will always be problematic since rarely will actual data be available to the reader. In most cases, if the reader wishes to look at actual scores or measurements, or even the precise calculations and computer outputs on which analyses are based, she must contact the researcher in question with a special request to look more closely at the data. Most undergraduates, reviewing literature for their own research, will be unlikely to gain access to primary data in this way.

The discussion section of a published study is often the most interesting, for it is here that the authors can explore their results in greater detail, consider the way in which they conducted themselves and, generally speaking, review the whole issue on which the study was based. The kind of questioning we should be considering here might take the following form:

- Have the authors effectively considered and explained the results, making it clear what the outcome of the study was?
- Did any unexpected findings emerge and were the authors able to explain these in light of the research question originally posed?
- Were the authors able to relate the findings to the research question?

- If the study failed to support the hypotheses, are the authors' explanations convincing?
- Have the authors recognised and discussed any limitations in their work?
- If the authors have speculated about their research findings, does this speculation seem justified?
- Does the study overall add anything to our understanding of the original issue?

All of the above examples represent typical questions which the student might ask of a piece of psychological research – the list is inexhaustive, and not all of these issues will be relevant to every study. The point, though, is that we should get into the habit of approaching published material from a critical point of view, an approach which will not only offer us an improved understanding of other people's work, but which might make us more professional in our own. After all, anything which we ourselves might someday publish will be viewed from precisely this critical perspective.

## 1.8  Structuring a research project

By now, if you have read the preceding sections you will have a good idea of how a research project is carried out. This final section presents an outline of the main steps.

- Selection of a field in which to carry out your study
- Carrying out a literature review on the topic
- Statement of a research question (what you are trying to do)
- Providing a rationale for the research question
- Refining your rationale into a number of specific and testable hypotheses
- Designing and planning an appropriate way of testing your hypotheses
- Implementing your plan and gathering data (carrying out the study)
- Analysing your data and presenting the results of the study
- Discussing your data, re-appraising the research question in light of your findings and considering the entire rationale, conduct and theoretical basis for your study

## Review

Part 1 has attempted to provide an overview of psychological research, explaining the reasons for conducting research, and providing a general guide to the many different approaches which can be taken to the study of human behaviour. The parts which follow will take you through the next set of stages in designing and carrying out a project, which include a number of practical guidelines to help make your own research more professional and, hopefully, personally satisfying.

## Suggested further reading

The following texts offer more details and alternative viewpoints on many of the issues raised in Part 1. The title of each article is self-explanatory and all are recommended. Where we suggest a textbook we identify relevant chapters.

Horn, R. (1996). Negotiating research access to organisations. *The Psychologist: Bulletin of the British Psychological Society*, *9*(12), 551–554.

Morgan, M. (1998). Qualitative research . . . science or pseudo-science? *The Psychologist: Bulletin of the British Psychological Society*, *11*(10), 31–32.

A useful review of the debate over quantitative and qualitative research.

Robson, C. (1993). *Real World Research – a resource for social scientists and practitioner-researchers*. Oxford: Blackwell.

A good general text emphasising non-laboratory research. Chapters 5 and 6 offer particularly useful coverage of small-scale surveys and case studies.

Salmon, P. (2003). How do we recognise good research? *The Psychologist: Bulletin of the British Psychological Society*, *16*(1), 24–27.

An up-to-date review of the continuing debate over qualitative and quantitative research.

Shaughnessy, J. J., & Zechmeister, E. B. (1994). *Research methods in psychology* (3rd ed.). New York: McGraw-Hill.

Chapter 9 provides a brief but useful discussion on meta-analysis.

Stevenson, C., & Cooper, N. (1977). Qualitative and quantitative research. *The Psychologist: Bulletin of the British Psychological Society*, *10*(4), 159–160.

Valentine, E. (1998). Out of the margins. *The Psychologist: Bulletin of the British Psychological Society*, *11*(4), 167–168.

A useful review of the debate over the history and philosophy of psychology.

# Planning a research project – the design

## Part 2

Introducing research

Planning a research project—the design

Carrying out research—methods & procedure

Describing research findings— descriptives

Analysing research findings—inferential statistics

Carrying out qualitative research

Writing up and presenting the findings of research

Corbis/Tim Davis

This part examines the different ways in which a study can be planned, or designed, identifying key research approaches and considering methods for dealing with the many pitfalls which lie in wait for the novice researcher. It covers the essential characteristics of good **research design**, explains the terminology and offers examples of the various design options with discussion on the advantages and disadvantages of each. As with other sections in this book, the companion website offers a structured, FAQ-based guide to the chapters which follow, reflecting typical concerns among undergraduates. In addition, a series of multiple-choice self-test questions are presented for review and assessment purposes. For students who have already identified a research issue to investigate, and who have gone as far as proposing hypotheses to test, Part 2 introduces the next stage in the research process – how to plan a systematic, scientific study which will effectively explore the research issue under investigation or test the specific hypotheses proposed. This part comprises three chapters, each dealing with a major set of design-related issues:

### Chapter 2

- considers the role of design in the overall research process
- introduces the different types of variables which comprise an essential component of any research, and the types of scale on which they can be measured
- discusses the practical implications of alternative levels of measurement for the design of undergraduate research projects

### Chapter 3

- introduces classical experimental design
- explains the distinctions between repeated measures and between-groups designs and provides guidance on the relative merits of each
- distinguishes between true and quasi-experimental approaches
- discusses more complex mixed and factorial designs and offers practical advice for the benefit of undergraduate researchers

### Chapter 4

- considers correlation and regression-based designs, with discussion on their differences from experimental procedures
- outlines the assumptions underlying correlation
- introduces complex partial correlation and multiple regression designs

# 2 The nature of research design

Chapter 2 introduces the principles of research design, explaining the terminology, showing how the design element fits into the overall research procedure and highlighting the mistakes which are often made by students new to the topic. The different types of variables which feature in all research are considered in detail, and we compare the different scales on which they can be measured, offering advice on when each type of scale is appropriate. The main topics covered are as follows:

- independent variables
- dependent variables
- extraneous variables
- controls
- the language of design
- inappropriate designs
- different levels of measurement

## 2.1 The purpose of a design

There is a typical sequence of activities to be found in psychological research which to some extent defines the field and also expresses its basis in the scientific tradition. (Note, though, our later discussion in Part 6 on the qualitative method, which has its own tradition and its own processes.) This normally begins with the posing of a question, the research question, followed by an evaluation of existing research – a **literature review** – and the proposition of a research rationale and a statement of aims and hypotheses. These represent the initial, preparatory stages of a research project and reflect the general coverage of Part 1. However, up to this point all we would have is a proposal for what would comprise a fruitful or interesting piece of research, without any kind of strategy for actually carrying it out. We therefore require a plan for setting up a study which will, in the first instance, test the stated hypotheses, and in the second, address the broader issues raised by the research question. This plan is the research design, and in a scientific report, the section which describes how a study was carried out is itself termed the design section.

At a general level, the design is a plan of campaign, a sketch of how to carry out a study. Knowing the research question which forms the basis for our study and having offered a number of specific predictions (hypotheses) about what we expect to find, we are merely trying to come up with an appropriate strategy for testing these predictions and examining the issue. What we are saying to ourselves is, 'I know what I want to find out; what's the best way of doing it?' Specifically, we want a practical plan which is ethical,

Box 2.1

## A Closer Look At . . .

# Consequences of poor design

> '. . . no useful findings can be reported due to participants' complete inability to follow even the simplest of experimental instructions.'

> '. . . the survey was abandoned following receipt of only two postal questionnaires from a possible sample of 100.'

> '. . . the favourable response of the sample to proposed increased national funding of psychological research had to be disregarded on discovery that, inadvertently, all respondents were delegates at the annual BPS conference.'

scientifically rigorous and, above all, foolproof. The last thing we need is to have carried out some brilliant piece of research, only to have some interested but irritating observer (usually our supervisor) point out that we forgot some obvious factor which negates our findings. Aside from being extremely annoying, we will also have wasted time – our own and our participants' – in what has become a pointless enterprise. To avoid this, a design must be comprehensive and well-thought-out. Like all human endeavours, from decorating our bedrooms to investigating problem-solving in a cognitive experiment, the quality of the finished piece of work is a function of the preparation. Box 2.1 suggests some consequences of a lack of foresight.

## 2.2  Problems with designs

Many undergraduates have real problems with the design part of a research project. Some of these are due to conceptual difficulties with the terminology of design – dependent and independent variables for instance are often confused in some project reports, while the precise nature of a within-subjects design is clearly a complete mystery for others. Another problem often presents itself with the writing up of this section of a report, and it is a temporal one: typically a student project will follow the sequence of a research idea, hypotheses, some thoughts on how to carry out the study, the study itself, analysis and final write-up. Often it is only at writing up that any real thought is given to the formal design characteristics of the study, which seems paradoxical since, if the study was carried out, it must have been to some kind of plan. Unfortunately such plans are often vague, ill-defined things which are refined and changed as the study progresses and it wouldn't be the first time a tutor is asked, as late as the write-up stage, something like, 'Do we say our participants were randomly assigned to groups?', or, to return to a previous point, 'Which of these is our dependent variable?' To make matters worse, since this write-up stage occurs at the end of the study, many students seem unable to resist providing a summary of procedural matters (what they actually did) in place of a design (what they planned, originally, to do). Hardly surprising then that, with so much scope for errors and confusion, the design part of a report is often the least satisfactory. The next part of this chapter will

Box 2.2

**How To . . .**

# Express a design, and not

*A design . . .*

A between-groups post-test experimental design was employed, with a treatment group providing a measure on the dependent variable of task performance under the condition of performance feedback, and a control group providing a measure on the dependent variable under the condition of no feedback.

*Not a design . . .*

Twenty participants were assigned to an experimental group and 20 to a control group. There was a mix of males and females in both groups and the age range was 21–25. The experimenter read out the following instructions, 'This is an experiment on problem-solving. You will be given a sheet containing a number of simple arithmetic questions and you should try to answer as many as you can in the next five minutes. Begin now.' And so on.

The first example contains all the elements we would expect in a formal design section. The particular type of research design is identified (experimental as opposed to correlational) along with its major characteristics (between-groups; post-test). The dependent variable is specified (measure of performance on an experimental task) as is the independent (performance feedback, comprising two conditions – presence or absence).

The second example contains primarily procedural information and is inappropriate for this part of a report, yet unfortunately reflects the content of many an undergraduate write-up.

address all of these issues while a review of the examples in Box 2.2 will illustrate the difference between a design and procedural matters.

Recall that the whole point of a design is to plan a study which will effectively explore an issue, answer a question or test a hypothesis (unless the research is qualitative, in which case the aims might be quite different: see Part 6). To do this successfully we need to be able to identify a number of things – we need to know what we are going to measure, whom we are going to measure, and we need to know what can go wrong. Most importantly we need to know these things before we start our study – or at least, try and anticipate them. A vague and badly worked out set of football game tactics will end in a shambles and inevitable defeat. A sound game plan, on the other hand, with everyone knowing exactly what they are supposed to be doing, stands a much better chance of succeeding. Things can still go wrong of course – our team may not be on form, playing conditions might not be to our liking, there may be unexpected injury and the other team might just be superior. Research plans are much the same, and **Murphy's Law** is pervasive, warning us that if something can go wrong then it probably will; even the best thought-out designs can end in disaster, but at least this will be less often than in the case of no design at all.

The next section begins our consideration of the key components of a good research plan, and introduces the sometimes complex language of design.

## 2.4 The world of variables

We have already intimated that our universe comprises an almost infinite number of variables, which are just things that can vary or change. This is true of the psychological universe as well as the physical, and our particular interest is here, in such phenomena as intelligence, personality, reaction time, abilities, wellbeing, stress, information processing and so on. The list is rather extensive. We know that all of these phenomena can be characterised by particular structures, based on their composition and expressed in the methods we employ to measure them (some variables are measured in terms of categories, some are measured on a scale, and so on). This in part reflects the inherent nature of our environment – most physical events have absolute zero as a starting point (volume, sound, light) as do many human characteristics (age, various behavioural and performance measures) and so can be measured on what is known as a **ratio scale**. Gender, on the other hand, is a category variable and is measured on what is termed a **nominal scale**. However, it is important to be aware that such classifications are often a matter of convenience, reflecting more a preference or orientation in the observer than anything intrinsic to the variable itself. A researcher may prefer to view age in terms of the three categories of *Young, Middle-aged* and *Elderly*, as opposed to the actual age of individuals in years and months. The essential nature of the variable has not changed, only the way the researcher has chosen to perceive it (see 2.12).

The point of this discussion is that when we talk about different kinds of variables the distinctions are often imposed, by us, the observers and researchers. It is we who choose how to perceive them, it is we who decide on which kinds of scale they should be measured, and it is we who decide on the kind of relationships among variables we wish to explore. This is particularly relevant with regard to independent and dependent variables, the stuff of experimental psychology, in which we attempt to identify cause-and-effect relationships. What must be understood is that there are no naturally occurring independent or dependent variables – there are only variables. It is up to us, with our perceptions and research aims, to classify them.

## 2.5 Dependent variables (DVs)

The starting point in research design is to identify what we want to measure. A statement of the obvious perhaps, but it wouldn't be the first time that an unfocussed undergraduate student has asked, in embarrassed tones, what it is she is supposed to be looking at, usually when the study is completed and she is confronted by reams of statistical output. Moreover, if the study is exploratory, the identification of issues may well be the aim of the research rather than the starting point. Having said this, a common way to deal with uncertainty over what is to be measured is to return to the research question posed at the outset. For example, the issue of whether or not females are more prone to addiction than males implies that we should be measuring alcohol intake, drug use, or some other form of overindulgence (chocolate, sex, shopping). If we believe that some psychology tuition methods are superior to others, the implication is that we should be measuring some aspect of academic performance, something which follows on from, is determined by, or which is *dependent upon* different tuition methods, and so on. Looking at our hypotheses will tell us even more explicitly what the study is trying to achieve (and if it doesn't, then our hypotheses are probably flawed). In the addiction example, for instance, a hypothesis might be that addictive behaviour in young adolescents will vary according to gender. This allows us to be more specific about what we are measuring – some aspect of addictive behaviour, as measured by an appropriate instrument, using young male and female adolescents as participants. These aspects of behaviour which we are trying to measure are the **dependent variables**; they represent the outcome of the study and they provide the quantitative data which allow us to answer the research question. They are termed *dependent* because they are believed to be caused by (dependent upon) other factors – some possibly naturally occurring and some the result of the researcher's manipulation. In the case of the gender-linked addiction example, the proposition is that addictive behaviour is dependent upon (caused by) the gender of the individual; in the tuition example, we are trying to demonstrate that pass grades are dependent upon particular tuition methods. Remember, when in doubt always return to the research issue and hypotheses – what questions are you asking and what are you predicting. It is a relatively short step towards identifying what outcomes could be measured in answer to these questions, and it is this step which identifies the dependent variables. (In fact, occasionally the dependent variable is also termed the outcome variable, though more commonly in correlation research, an approach which will be considered in subsequent sections.)

Sometimes, the outcome of a study can be measured in more than one way, allowing for the possibility of two or more dependent variables. Consider the example of a study in which performance on some experimental task is to be the dependent variable (dependent on some factor such as training, experience, attention or some other eventuality). In such cases a straightforward and readily available measure is usually taken as an indication of performance, such as the time, in seconds, taken to carry out the task. However, other measures will also be possible – the number of errors made during performance of the task, for instance. One might expect that one measure would serve to reinforce the other, which would in itself be a useful finding: the more experienced a participant is, the shorter is the time to complete the task, and the fewer errors made. An alternative outcome, however, might be that while the time taken to perform a task would remain constant, irrespective of experience, the number of errors produced would decline. An experienced cyclist might take the same time to cycle from point A to point B as would a novice, but he would run over fewer migrating hedgehogs (make fewer errors). Had this study been carried out using only the dependent variable of time, the relationship between experience and performance would not have been demonstrated. Using more than one dependent variable, however, demonstrates that a relationship does exist, which otherwise might have been overlooked. Box 2.3 illustrates the point.

## 2.6 Independent variables (IVs)

The previous section identified the dependent variable as one of the essential components in quantitative study, that aspect of the psychological world which changes, and whose change can be measured as a consequence of the influence of some other factor. That

Box 2.3

## A Closer Look At . . .

# Research with more than one dependent variable

Perceptual accuracy tests often require job applicants to compare columns of letters and numbers. Scores can be taken in terms of time to complete the task and number of inconsistencies overlooked (errors). In the example below the task would be to identify differences between each comparison line and its corresponding standard line.

| Standard | Comparison |
|---|---|
| 123aabbcedeff | 123aabbccdeff |
| ssaaddfghh456 | ssaaddfghh456 |
| 789gghjjunndf | 788gghjjumndf |

Figures 2.1 and 2.2 demonstrate a paradoxical effect in which an independent factor can give rise to very different outcomes. If we were to measure performance on a perceptual

**Figure 2.1**    Time (minutes) to complete a perceptual task, by experience (in months).

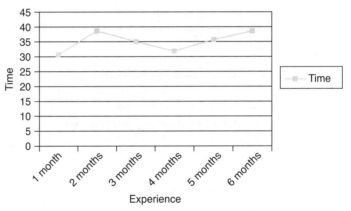

**Figure 2.2**    Number of errors made in a perceptual task, by experience (in months).

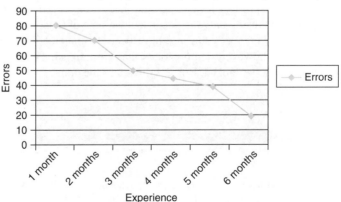

accuracy task we may well find that experience has little effect on the speed with which the task is completed. However, were we to take a different measure of performance, such as the number of errors made, we might observe a change with experience.

Often when there is more than one way to measure some treatment effect, the choice of which to adopt is obvious. In the perceptual accuracy example above, since the aim was to assess accuracy, the better choice would be errors, as opposed to speed. In other cases, appropriate options are less obvious and the researcher must rely on judgement, experience and whatever guidance might be present in the relevant literature. On a final note, it will be observed that both these variables (speed and errors) are what are termed interval/ratio scaled variables.

other factor, the aspect of the environment which is (assumed to be) responsible for changes in a dependent variable, is termed the **independent variable**.

It is called independent because variations on this variable are not dependent upon, or influenced by, any other factor in the study. Manipulation of this variable is under the control of the researcher – it is she who assigns participants to groups and who selects how comparisons are to be made. Consequently, this variable can be regarded as relatively independent of any other factor (except of course the judgement of the researcher who makes the initial decision on which variables to include in a study).

The relationship between these two kinds of variable is assumed to be a cause-and-effect one, with changes in an independent variable producing some kind of corresponding change in the dependent one. In fact, the general aim of most research is to demonstrate that such a relationship is present. Is word recall influenced by the encoding system used to memorise stimuli? That is, are variations in experimental participants' ability to recall a list of words (dependent variable) determined by differences in the mnemonic system adopted (independent variable)? Do reaction time scores decline as the measured amounts of alcohol ingested by participants increase? That is, are changes in reaction times (dependent variable) caused by changes in alcohol consumption (independent variable)? Are scholastic grades (dependent variable) a function of the gender of the individual (independent variable)? These are all examples of attempts to point to relationships between the two different kinds of variable, a process which underlies much psychological research.

We have already seen that a study need not involve just one dependent variable, and the same is true of independent variables. Certainly, a common design for a research project – especially at undergraduate level – attempts to relate one independent variable to one dependent one. This is the classic experimental design and makes for simplicity, both in the conduct of a study and at the analysis stage, where statistical procedures for this design are relatively straightforward. However, as we are continually reminded by experience, people are complex and it is rare that any event in our world would be influenced by only one factor. The notion of multi-causality implies that for any event, there will be many influences at work.

The implication for research is that a number of independent variables are likely to be present in the determination of some dependent, or outcome variable, and it is here that an important decision must be made by the researcher: do we concentrate on a single factor which we believe is the key causal variable, and in so doing somehow eliminate or minimise the impact of all the other factors? Or do we attempt to include all the important variables and examine their combined effects on the dependent variable?

The solution to this dilemma is never easy and provides one of the trickiest challenges for the researcher, not to mention its impact on the overall quality of the research itself. Get it wrong and opt for the single independent variable design and you risk ignoring or obscuring key causal factors. Alternatively, combining several independent variables might serve only to dilute the effects of a single, key factor.

Ultimately these risks have to be borne by the individual, but they can be minimised: knowing the research area in detail and building on a thorough literature review of the particular issues being explored in a study will allow a pretty good guess as to the likely relationships between independent and dependent variables. After all, the process whereby hypotheses are proposed would have required the researcher to make a number of judgements about cause and effect from an early stage, helping to at least reduce the chances of choosing the wrong option.

Returning to our earlier example in which we examined performance on some experimental task, let us assume that the literature implied that, not only would experience be a factor, but that there might be a gender difference also. It would of course be possible to carry out two separate studies, one in which performance was measured as a function of the participants' experience, and a second in which males and females were compared.

Box 2.4

## A Closer Look At . . .

# Interacting independent variables

In a study on a performance task, male and female participants are differentiated by three levels of skill. Performance is measured by error rate and the results are described in Figure 2.3.

Inspection of the graph demonstrates that for male participants error rates remain relatively constant, irrespective of skill level. For female participants, however, while error rates remain similar to those of males for inexperienced and novice skill levels, error rates decline noticeably at the experienced level. This is the nature of the interaction: neither gender nor skill level alone determines variation in error rates. Both variables act in combination.

**Figure 2.3**     Error rates on an experimental task as a function of both gender and skill level.

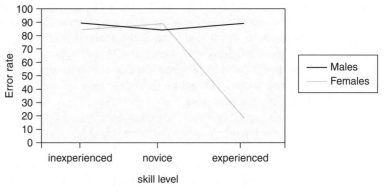

This though would be clumsy, time consuming and organisationally demanding. More important, by treating both factors separately we are ignoring the possibility that they might act in combination to influence performance, and we risk overlooking any possible interaction between the two. Box 2.4 illustrates the point, demonstrating that the independent variables do not act on the dependent variable on their own, but in combination. Specifically, in this example, the participant's gender is not the sole determinant of performance on the task; it depends also on his or her experience level.

There is one final point worth mentioning before we leave our consideration of variables – most independent variables can also be dependent variables, depending on the research context. Consider a study trying to demonstrate that stress proneness (as measured by some form of questionnaire) might be caused, or at least influenced by, geographical area, with the driving, competitive urban dweller suffering more continual pressure than his more laid-back, rural counterpart. Here, stress proneness is the dependent variable. In another study, however, a researcher might be interested in the relationship between stress proneness and alcohol abuse, testing the assumption that a high susceptibility to stress will be linked to maladaptive coping strategies. In this instance, stress proneness has adopted the role of an independent variable.

In short, as we have already argued, there is a case for suggesting that there are no independent or dependent variables in the universe, only variables. It is how we perceive and use them that makes the difference.

## 2.7    Extraneous variables

While it is the aim of most studies to demonstrate a relationship between an independent and a dependent variable, there will be instances in which this anticipated relationship will fail to materialise. One obvious reason for this is that there *is* no relationship between the variables and that our study was based on an inappropriate premise. (Consider an investigation trying to equate the hours of exercise taken by individuals in a week to their performance in an examination. We would be very surprised to find any relationship between the two variables.) Another possible explanation, however, is that there is a relationship between the variables under investigation, but a relationship which has been obscured, or interfered with, by some other, unanticipated factor – an **extraneous variable**.

Extraneous variables are so called because they lie outside the planned structure of a study – either ignored, on the assumption that their influence on some dependent variable will be minimal, or unanticipated by the researcher and acting as nuisance factors which interfere with the planned scope of a study. They are, in effect, all the other independent variables which comprise the multi-causal nature of human activity and their effects have to be anticipated as far as possible.

The previous section raised the problem in terms of what can be done with all these variables through the use of more than one independent factor; if the researcher believes that change in some outcome is determined by a combination of, or interaction between, two independent variables, then these variables become a part of the research design itself. However, if the aim of a study is to concentrate on the influence of one key variable on its own – even though it is recognised that other factors will be at work – then all other possible causal factors are seen, not as contributory elements, but as irritants whose effects have to be minimized, or controlled. By treating these factors, not as independent variables in their own right, but as extraneous elements in a study which have to be somehow eliminated, the impact of the key independent variable (or variables) can be examined.

The issue ultimately resolves into a matter of perspective. In any given situation a large number of variables will always be present; whether or not we choose to treat them as independent or extraneous variables, however, depends on how we view the outcomes we are ultimately interested in. If we believe a particular dependent variable changes as a function of several factors, and we want to explore the relative importance of these factors, either in combination or by way of interactions, then we are treating our causal factors as independent variables. If, on the other hand, we want to determine the precise influence of only one factor on a dependent variable, then all the other influencing factors have to be treated as extraneous variables. To adapt the concluding statement to the section on independent variables, there are no independent, dependent or extraneous

Box 2.5

**A Closer Look At . . .**

# A distinction between independent or extraneous variables?

It has been argued that our ability to recall information is a function of how we approach the learning task, in terms of how motivated we are (Baddeley, 1993). To test this an equivalent-groups experiment is designed in which an incidental group is presented with a task involving a list of common nouns, and an intentional group is presented with the same task, plus an instruction to memorise the words. A confounding element of this design is the suggestion, from the literature, that the nature of the stimulus words will in itself influence recall. Specifically, some words – abstract words – are encoded semantically whereas concrete words are encoded using both semantics and a system of imagery, and the argument is that these different coding systems will affect the ease with which words can be recalled (Paivio, 1971).

If the researcher accepted that both the motivational and the encoding factors were possible determinants of recall, but was interested primarily in the motivation element, then the coding factor would be treated as an extraneous variable, to be controlled for:

| Independent | Extraneous | Dependent |
| --- | --- | --- |
| motivation | coding system | word recall |
| (incidental vs intentional) | | |

If, however, the researcher, knowing that both motivation and coding system were important determinants of recall, wished to determine the combined effects of both variables on recall, then both would be treated as independent factors:

| Independent | Extraneous | Dependent |
| --- | --- | --- |
| motivation | none | word recall |
| (incidental vs intentional) | | |
| coding system | | |
| (concrete vs abstract) | | |

As we have already argued, the psychological universe comprises many variables; it is up to the researcher, and the nature of the research question, whether they will be viewed as independent or extraneous variables.

variables in the universe, only variables. It is what we do with them that makes the difference. How extraneous variables are dealt with is considered in the next section. In the meantime, Box 2.5 looks more closely at the 'independent-or-extraneous' issue.

## 2.8   Controls

The procedure whereby the influence of extraneous variables on some dependent measure is minimised or removed is termed a **control**. In a study which attempts to relate some personality measure (independent variable) to an index of stress (dependent variable), in which the likely influence of gender has to be minimised, then we say that the gender effects are controlled for.

There are a number of ways in which extraneous variables can be dealt with. Since typical sources of such influences are the characteristics of the participants themselves (age, gender, education, personality, etc.), one way to deal with extraneous variables is to control how individuals are assigned to groups. In the above example, relating personality types to stress, if we felt that females were inherently more stress prone than males anyway, this gender-linked effect could well obscure the personality factor we are interested in. A simple control is to ensure that the gender composition of one group (high extravert personality, for example) matched the gender composition of the other (low extravert personality). More simply, we ensure there is the same number of males as females in each group. This would serve to minimise the influence of this particular extraneous variable, or at least ensure that its effects were similar in both groups. It is important to be aware, though, that such deliberate manipulation of participant characteristics is only appropriate when we are pretty certain that a particular conflicting factor is present. Otherwise, by far the preferred method for dealing with individual differences among participants is to have them randomly assigned to groups, a procedure which is an important component in experimentation, and which is discussed in some detail later.

This process of **matching** participant characteristics can be extended to most extraneous factors – participants can be matched on the basis of age, education, personality, shoe size and, in fact, on almost any variable which might be regarded as extraneous to a research design. Unfortunately, the process of matching tends to prove costly in terms of sample size – if the only factor we wanted to match participants for was, for instance, gender, then there is little problem: there are lots of men and women around. However, if we re-consider the previous stress prone example – if it were shown that, in addition to gender, age might be considered an extraneous variable, and health, and occupation, and social class – if we tried to find even just two groups of participants, both matched on all of these factors, it is extremely unlikely that we would have more than a handful of participants to compare in the different personality conditions. This then is the problem with using matching procedures to control for extraneous variables: if we attempt to take into account the multitude of ways in which people differ, we find that there will be very few who actually share the same nature, background and psychological composition, certainly too few for any kind of practical study. In reality, however, most researchers accept the impossibility of eliminating all sources of variability, opting for what they believe will be the main nuisance factors for their particular study, or relying on a randomisation procedure to minimise confounding effects. Taking this approach of course allows for the possibility of key influencing factors being over-represented; but then, psychological research can never be perfect and it would not be the first time that an otherwise sound study has been undermined by the influence of an unexpected extraneous variable.

## 2.9   A medical model – the randomised controlled design

Randomisation procedures are regarded as a 'gold standard' for research in other areas, in particular the medical field. Typically medical research is concerned with the impact of novel treatments, interventions or new drug regimes on patient health and the standard design would involve a treatment group and a non-treatment, or control group. The key to the success of this approach, however, lies in the way in which patients are assigned to each group: in order that the real effects of an intervention can be maximised (by controlling for variations within the participant groups) a randomisation procedure is used, ensuring that, as far as is possible, both groups are equivalent prior to the intervention or treatment. If this can be demonstrated, then any change in health or wellbeing following treatment can reasonably be attributed to the treatment and not to some other factor involving patient characteristics. In fact, all of this is merely an application of the basic experimental procedure which forms the foundation of classical psychological research – the rules are the same, but the language differs. In the medical model this type of design is termed a **randomised controlled trial (RCT)**, although since medical research is often referred to as clinical research, the *RCT* abbreviation will sometimes stand for *randomised clinical trial*. A more detailed description of this model can be viewed in Altman and Dore (1990), while a more general overview can be found in Jadad (1998).

## 2.10   The double-blind control

There is a particular kind of control which is worth mentioning, not because it is special or different in some way from other kinds of procedure – after all, there are only variables and it is up to us what we do with them – but because the procedure puts the role of the researcher herself into perspective. From much of the foregoing discussion on variables, it would be easy to get the impression that most of the problems with extraneous effects are to be found in the participants used for a study; their biases, personal characteristics and limitations seem to be continually interfering with the research process and it is the lot of the overworked but brilliant researcher to deal effectively with all these problems. This view, however, is somewhat demeaning of our participants, and presents ourselves in a positive light which is more in the mind of the researcher than in reality. Of course, we as researchers are just as flawed, possessing the same quirks and foibles as our participants – we are all people after all – and because of this, the possibility exists that limitations within a study may be due to factors in ourselves. Moreover, since any given study is likely to concern a hypothesis of our own devising, we are likely to have a keen (if not vested) interest in its outcome. A famous example of a failure to recognise the role of the researcher in inadvertently manipulating outcomes is found in the salutary tale of Clever Hans.

In 1890 the Russian aristocrat Wilhelm von Osten claimed ownership of a mathematically aware stallion, which could tap out solutions with a hoof. This horse could perform (apparently) basic arithmetic calculations, on instruction from its owner. At this particular time, when interest in evolution and matters psychological was high, stories of this 'intelligent' animal aroused interest within the scientific community across the length and breadth of Europe. Von Osten claimed that he had trained his prize stallion to perform various simple calculations on demand and over the next several years the traditional lecture circuit featured Clever Hans as often as the most learned professors in their various fields

Plate 2.1   Clever Hans: The horse who could not count, although his owner could.
*Source*: Mary Evans Picture Library

of science. In 1904, however, the experimentalist Oskar Pfungst was able to show that the cleverness was not the horse's but the owner's. In a convincing demonstration, Pfungst proved that Hans was only able to perform in the presence of its owner. Placing von Osten out of view rendered the horse – mysteriously – incapable of even the simplest of arithmetic calculations, let alone simultaneous equations. The explanation was simple: Hans, the horse, could not of course do sums. But what it could do was respond to the various non-verbal cues given off by its owner. Pfungst was able to show that the horse would paw the ground in response to subtle changes in posture from von Osten. When his owner was not visible, the horse could not perform. The horse couldn't count, but what it could do was respond to the expectations of its owner.

In recognition of this type of problem and to control for what we might term a researcher effect, the double-blind control has evolved, a technique which achieved a certain amount of fame in the explosion in drug trials during the 1960s, but which has its place in any situation in which some factor within the experimenter might unwittingly influence an outcome, as in the Clever Hans example.

Visualise a study in which a new 'smart' drug is to be tested on humans. The drug is believed to improve learning and problem-solving ability and volunteers have been selected to participate in an appropriate drug trial. If only one group of participants were used, and they knew they were taking an intellect-enhancing substance, the expectation associated with this knowledge could in itself produce an improved performance on some task, hence masking a possible real drug effect.

The normal method of dealing with this is to use a second group, the members of which receive a placebo (i.e., a neutral substance), and with none of the participants knowing who has been given the real drug. Participants are blind to the experimental manipulation in a **single-blind design**. However, the fact that the researcher knows which is the real drug group might lead him to signal the fact (through non-verbal cues), or to allow his expectations to influence the recording of results. To control for this effect, the researcher himself also must be blind to the experimental manipulation; hence the term **double-blind control**, with neither participant nor researcher being aware of the manipulation. In practical terms the allocation of participants to groups is usually carried out by some third party, not directly involved in the study, some procedures for which are described in the next part.

## 2.11  Variables and levels of measurement

In previous sections on independent and dependent variables, we stated that the starting point for designing many studies is to identify *what* it is we are trying to measure. The logical next step in this process is to decide *how* we are going to measure it.

A variable is the most general of all terms to describe absolutely anything in the universe which can change (or vary). The level of rainfall in Scotland is a variable; age is a variable; different reference groups to which we might belong are variables, as are scores on attitudinal and personality questionnaires. More significantly, anything which can vary can also be subjected to analysis, whether qualitative or quantitative, an important point when it comes to assessing the outcome of a study.

In psychological research the aim is usually to examine the ways in which variables are related to one another, with a particular (although not exclusive) interest in causal relationships. For instance, we might want to show that practice in a certain activity leads to an improvement in the performance of some experimental task, that belonging to one group as opposed to another determines success in solving a memory problem, that measures of psychological wellbeing vary depending on which day of the week it is. All of these are variables – they are aspects of our world which can vary, or change, and they comprise one of the main tools of the researcher; being able to demonstrate that one variable changes due to the influence of some other factor is, by and large, the whole point of the research process.

The observant reader might have noticed something odd in the above explanation, concerning the nature of the variables used as examples. Undoubtedly factors like group membership, days of the week and performance are all variables – they can change. But each of these factors is clearly different from the others in some significant way: the time taken to perform a task, or the number of errors made, is somehow different from whether or not it is a Monday or a Tuesday. And both of these, in turn, are different from the type of variable which identifies whether or not participants belonged to an experimental group as opposed to a control group. They are all certainly variables, but each is a different kind of variable. Understanding these differences is a relatively straightforward matter and requires merely that we look more closely at the composition of a variable, considering its components, the relationship among these components and the ways in which a variable can be measured. The next three sections demonstrate this process.

## 2.12  Levels of measurement

Most aspects of our universe can be measured in more than one way, with the choice of particular method a function both of the nature of what is being measured and of the researcher's judgement and preference. Measuring a participant's age, for instance, can be a precise thing, in which age is expressed in years, months and weeks, reflecting the true character of this particular variable. Alternatively, age can be expressed in terms of a particular

Plate 2.2    S. S. Stevens, the American experimental psychologist.
*Source*: AIP Emilio Segre Visual Archives, Physics Today Collection

category into which it falls (16 to 25; 26 to 35, etc.) or merely as an order of relative magnitude (old, middle-aged, young). Each of these measurement systems varies descriptively, in terms of precision, and also in terms of what can be done with the information. The existence of different measurement systems, though, can be problematic, and a common source of anxiety among undergraduates is how best to measure the various components of a study. However, historically, this problem has not been confined to undergraduate students.

In 1941 the American experimental psychologist S. S. Stevens presented a classification of measurement scales before the International Congress for the Unity of Science, a classification which emerged from a number of years of intensive research within the scientific community in general, and in the field of psychophysical measurement in particular. This was followed up in 1946 with the publication in the journal *Science* of an article titled 'On the Theory of Scales of Measurement', which has since become the accepted standard classification system for the measurement of quantitative variables. Debate over the most effective systems for measuring aspects of signal detection (sound, loudness, pitch, etc.) had ultimately led Stevens to propose four different measurement scales, varying in level of precision. The scales were *nominal, ordinal, interval* and *ratio* and they represent the classifications which are now in common usage throughout psychology and other sciences. This classification in contemporary psychology is arguably incomplete, ranging as it does from the purely quantitative to the 'almost' qualitative, and this can be explained by the fact that Stevens and his colleagues were embedded in the empirical tradition with its emphasis on numerical measurement. As is explained below, nominal scales merely apply a numerical notation to information which differs qualitatively: a control group and an experimental group are often identified by the values 0 and 1 respectively, yet these numbers are merely descriptive labels – they have none of the usual characteristics of numerical values. However, in recent times psychological research has been making increasing use of a qualitative approach, one in which the very process of measurement is seen as inappropriate. Research of this nature would be unable to find a place anywhere within Stevens's notation yet, since a qualitative orientation represents a fruitful and increasingly popular approach to psychological research, allowance must be made for it in any classification system. It is perhaps fitting then to merely make the point that there are a number of quantitative measures available to us and there are a number of qualitative measures which can be taken. And the two sets of measures differ, as Table 2.1 in Box 2.6 illustrates.

It is clearly inappropriate to include qualitative data on any 'dimension of measurement', since in qualitative research descriptions of the environment are not numerical in

Box 2.6

A Closer Look At . . .

# A modern perspective on measurement

Table 2.1     Different methods of measurement.

| What is measured | Type of scale | Measurement perspective |
|---|---|---|
| A variable measured on a scale with a zero origin | ratio | quantitative |
| A variable in which the intervals between adjacent scale values are equal | interval | quantitative |
| A variable whose elements are identified in terms of being greater than or less than other elements | ordinal | quantitative |
| A variable whose elements are identified as belonging to a different class or category from others | nominal | quantitative |
| An element of the environment which is expressed in terms of a descriptive narrative, often as a transcription | not applicable | qualitative |

nature; rather, data take the form of verbal or written descriptions of events, perceptions, thoughts and feelings. Certainly such descriptions might be coded in various ways into categories, placing the information at the nominal end of Stevens's system, and in some studies this is precisely what happens. However, there exist sets of procedures which are uniquely qualitative and many would argue that attempting to quantify information of this nature subverts the distinctive character of qualitative research. The rest of this chapter will concentrate on the quantitative **levels of the measurement scale** which have become central to psychological research, while qualitative research is considered in detail in Part 6.

## 2.13  Nominal (category) scales

Much of what occurs in our universe can be explained in terms of the group or category to which particular events belong, and this represents one of the simplest ways in which things can vary. The traditional experimental independent variable is a category variable, insofar as the components, or elements, which make up the variable are categories. In its simplest form there are normally two categories (the presence of an effect, or treatment, and the absence of an effect), with participants being assigned randomly to one or other of the conditions, or groups, but we can readily identify other category variables which contain many components – a more complex experimental variable might comprise 3 elements (the absence of a treatment and two levels of an experimental treatment); astrological sign comprises 12 categories; whereas the Myers-Briggs (Myers & McCaulley, 1985) typology of personality allows for 16 types. Questionnaire responses often employ nominal scales, as in the YES/NO response to a question, or the choices A, B or C to a multiple-choice item.

In the traditional experiment the independent variable is nominally scaled with, usually, two conditions – a control and an experimental. When naturally occurring groups comprise an independent variable, there may be several conditions, or categories, as with astrological sign.

An important consideration here concerns the relationships among the various components of category variables, relationships which are purely qualitative as opposed to quantitative. This means that being in one particular category simply makes you different (in a qualitative sense) from people in other categories; there is no implication of such differences being quantifiable in any way and the categories exist in name only, with the names simply supplying descriptive characteristics of each category. Hence the frequently used term *nominal variable*. If we consider the variable of gender, the terms *male* and *female* describe the characteristics of participants in each category, but make no suggestion of any intermediate, quantifiable steps between the two. They are merely different. Moreover, to suggest that the male category is in some way better that the female category would be totally inappropriate (not to mention a danger to the health of one of the authors) for this kind of variable.

In terms of research, nominal variables are used most frequently as grouping variables, allowing participants to be observed, compared or measured on the basis of their belonging to one group or another. A quasi-experimental approach comparing males with females on some measurable aspect of attitude or behaviour is a common design element, while other studies might involve such variables as personality type, ethnic group, regional location or even the random assignment to experimental groups A, B or C.

Another common setting for nominal variables is in survey and market research, in which the information being sought from participants is in terms of which particular response category they would choose for a given variable. A market researcher, for example, might be interested in people's preferences for breakfast cereal, or a political researcher might be trying to measure attitudes towards a referendum issue (possibly using a questionnaire item such as, 'Are you in favour of membership in the European economic community?'). Here, the nominal variable of food preference might have four categories – corn flakes, bran, muesli and kippers – while the attitudinal issue of support for a political

**Figure 2.4** Frequency of response (Yes/No) to the questionnaire item, 'Are you in favour of membership in the European economic community?'

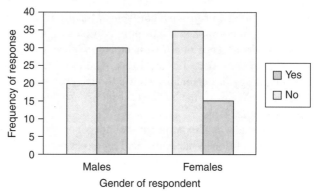

issue might only have two – Yes and No. Figure 2.4 offers an example of how responses might be expressed.

Using the language of research design, all such variables are category or nominal variables, although the more accurate terminology would be nominally scaled category variables, since the components which comprise them are measured on a nominal scale.

## 2.14 Ordinal scales

The grouping of events into categories (treatment group, responses on a survey item, etc.) is expressed merely in terms of qualitative differences among them. It is, however, possible in the categorisation of variable components to imply a quantitative relationship. Hence, participants in Group A might differ from participants in Group B, not just by being different, but in terms of the direction these differences take. If, instead of subdividing a variable into nominal categories (Group A, B, C) we use the categories of 'best', 'next best' and 'worst', we have altered the way the variable is measured from a nominal scale to an **ordinal scale**, in that the components can be presented in some kind of numerical order. It can still be classed as a category variable, but now there is a quantitative element in the relationship among the components. It is important to be aware, however, that the relationships among the elements of an ordinal variable can only take the form *greater than* or *less than*. There is no implication of how much greater or less and, while being able to place categories in some sort of order is a useful development in the measurability of our universe, it only goes a little way towards numerical sophistication.

There are, however, a number of statistical procedures available for the analysis of outcome data which are in an ordinal format and, consequently, some quantitative researchers prefer to work more with ordinal than with nominal variables. The use of ordinal categories, however, is not simply a matter of individual preference – sound practical or statistical reasons will always determine the nature of the variables to be used in a study.

In a race between a sports car, a hare, and a hedgehog, the sports car came first, the hare second, and the hedgehog third. This is an example of how events are measured on an ordinal scale. This type of measurement will not show by how much the sports car outpaced the hare, or how far behind the hare the hedgehog came; only the order in which they came.

Typically, ordinally scaled variables are found in cases where participants are assigned to categories or groups on the basis of some kind of ranking or order effect (high income; moderate income; low income, or a researcher's estimate of most extravert; moderately extravert; introvert); or on the basis of the way in which responses and behaviour are themselves ranked. Asking participants to rank breakfast cereals in order of preference, as opposed to merely selecting their favourite one (as in the previous nominal example), will produce ordinally scaled data (see Figure 2.5). Similarly, when a study requires participants to respond to a questionnaire item which offers a range of options, these options can often take the form of ordered categories. A typical item on research surveys might take the form:

How likely are you to finish reading to the end of this chapter?

☐ highly likely   ☐ likely   ☐ unlikely   ☐ highly unlikely

In this instance the response categories are not only different from one another, but they provide a specific order of response. An individual choosing one of the categories is

**Figure 2.5**   Responses to an item on breakfast preference.

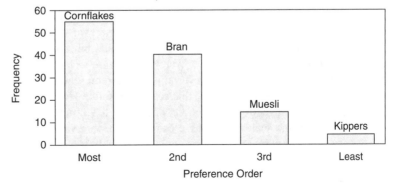

placing himself on an imaginary probability continuum, and can therefore be described as more likely than some or less likely than others to produce the stated activity. What cannot be ascertained, of course, is just how much more likely one category is than another. It is the classic grade school problem most of us have experienced at some time – if all we know is that Carol was first in arithmetic and Jonathan second, we actually have very little information on the relationship between the two pupils, other than the order in which they performed on the test. Lacking would be any information on the magnitude of this relationship, which would considerably enrich our understanding of what actually occurred. Consider how much more useful it would be to know that Carol's mark was 85, and Jonathan's 84, or even that Carol scored 85 and Jonathan only 40. In both examples we have a far greater understanding of the relationship between the two pupils than if all we knew was that one scored higher than the other. This is the problem with all ordinal variables.

## 2.15 Ratio and interval scales

This final type of variable incorporates the most sophisticated form of scale, and is often the most preferred by numerically oriented researchers, and certainly statisticians, due to the type and amount of information provided. Here, the components of the variable are not discrete categories, nor are they categories which are ordered according to some ranking system. In fact, the elements which comprise this type of variable are not really categories at all, but rather a range of values which differ from one another in a systematic way. By way of example, if performance on some experimental task were to be measured under conditions of varying temperature, then both variables in this study would be interval scaled. Temperature is represented by a range of values, but more importantly, the difference (interval) between one temperature and another is the same as the difference between any other two temperatures. (That is, the interval between 14° and 15° represents the same change as the difference between 26° and 27°.) Note that temperature here is expressed on the scale developed by the Swedish astronomer, Celsius (1701–1744), on which the freezing point of water is established as 0°C, the significance of which will become clear on our discussion of ratio scales.

Likewise, if performance on the task can be measured by speed of response, or number of errors, these variables comprise a range of values, each of which differs by the same amount from the next. The difference between interval and ratio measures concerns the existence of a true zero point – the point which represents the total absence of a phenomenon (illumination, noise, force). **Interval scales** may well have an arbitrary zero point, as does the Celsius temperature scale, but this is not the same as a true zero, or starting point for the scale. Were temperature to be measured on the scale proposed by Kelvin (1824–1907), however, this would represent a ratio scale, since the starting point or lowest possible limit of this scale is absolute zero (roughly −273°C). Similarly, variables like age, or response rate, or income have true zero points which reflect the beginning of the scale; all of these examples are interval, but these latter cases are also ratio (although in real terms a zero point may rarely be employed). Figure 2.6 in Box 2.7 illustrates the measurement of an interval-scaled variable. Note how this is depicted, graphically, in a different manner from the previous nominal and ordinal examples.

## A Closer Look At . . .

# The measurement of ratio- and interval-scaled variables

Both errors and temperature are continuous variables. Errors are measured on a ratio scale (with a true zero point) and temperature (°C) is measured on an interval scale. Box 2.8 further distinguishes between ratio and interval scales.

**Figure 2.6**    Errors on a cognitive task as a function of temperature.

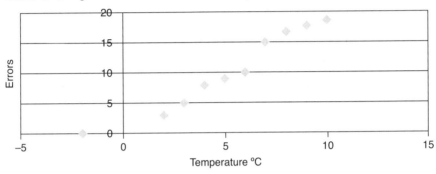

## Practicalities . . .

# What you really need to know about ratio and interval scales

The distinction between interval and ratio scales is one of which much is made in the statistical world, and many tutors believe that their students should be aware that different measurement systems are required for the different types of variable. Commendable as this is, many students privately ask themselves, what difference does this make, really? In practical terms, the truth is, very little. Aside from the desirability of understanding the measurement world as best we can, in much psychological research it doesn't really matter whether a variable is interval or ratio scaled, other than that it allows us to attach a label to different types of scale. In Stevens's time, when the objects of interest were essentially physical phenomena, such as sonic pitch, tone, level of illumination and so on, it was genuinely useful to have different ways of measuring scaled variables. Today, it is often sufficient to recognise that a variable is measured on a continuous scale and it makes little difference if the scaling is interval or ratio.

The advantage which the interval- (and ratio-) scaled variable has over other forms of measurement lies in its susceptibility to statistical analysis. Most quantitative research relies on statistical procedures to support hypotheses, validate theories and answer research questions, and while both nominal and ordinal variables have their own procedures, many researchers feel that only when data are available in at least interval format can useful analysis begin. (Note, this is not a position with which the authors necessarily agree but we nonetheless recognise the levels of sophistication possible with interval-scaled variables.) The calculation of averages, measures of spread and other valuable statistics are possible only with interval-scaled variables, allowing an impressive range of analytical techniques to be used. This issue is explored in greater detail in Chapter 6, under the section on questionnaire design.

The point of the preceding discussion has been to introduce the measurement foundations of psychological research and, while we hope it has been both informative and interesting, students may well be wondering what the implications are for their own undergraduate studies. In practical terms, the way in which a particular variable can be measured is often self-evident and beyond the control of the researcher. This is especially true when an independent variable comprises naturally occurring and mutually exclusive groups – gender is a good example, social class another, and personality as expressed in various Type theories a third. Likewise, many dependent variables will automatically lend themselves to a particular level of measurement, as in different response categories to a questionnaire item, or when the measurement of some outcome is in terms of either the presence or absence of a particular behaviour. In cases like this the details of the research design are almost entirely dependent on the nature of the variables comprising the study (i.e., the type and number of groups we are comparing and the nature of the measurements we take). Similarly, the type of statistical analysis most appropriate for the data is also largely predetermined by the nature of the variables – statistical procedures based on calculations of average, for instance, would be impossible for nominally scaled dependent variables (e.g., yes/no responses to a questionnaire item).

Complications occur for the undergraduate when any or all of the variables being explored in a study are measured on interval/ratio scales, for the composition of the variables no longer determines either the particular research design or the most appropriate mode of analysis – an element of choice now exists. A characteristic of the different measurement scales is that a more powerful scale can always be transformed, or recoded into a weaker or simpler scale, although the reverse is not true. A study relating age to decision time on some cognitive task, for example, might measure both the independent variable (age) and the dependent variable (decision time) on interval/ratio scales. However, it would be perfectly reasonable to change the way age is measured, moving from a ratio scale of years and months to an ordinal scale of old, middle-aged and young.

Changing the level of measurement is not difficult, as the following example shows:

Age: 18,19,20,23,24,25 . . . 26,27,40,41,42,43,44,50,51,52,55,59 . . . . . . 60,61,62,63,

Age:      Young      |                    Middle-aged                    |                    Old

There are a number of cautions to be mentioned concerning this process. The first involves the decision on how many categories are needed. In the present example, why select three categories as opposed to two (younger/older)? Alternatively, why not have many age groups (15–19; 20–24; 25–29; 30–34, etc.)? There are three factors which will help you decide.

- The extent to which there are likely or logical distinctions within the range of values making up the variable. In the exploration of certain attitudes, for instance, we might expect participants over 30 to hold certain views, while those under 30 might hold different views. If we believe there are no further divisions within the overall age range then we opt for a two-category variable. However, should we feel that teenagers will represent a different attitude group, as would those of pensionable age, then we expand the number of categories in our variable to include these additional groups, and so on.

- Conventional or traditional divisions within the range of values. In some areas of research various typical categorisations have evolved. In political research, for example, particular income groups have been identified as exhibiting particular voting behaviours and these groupings are now regularly polled at the onset of each election. In research involving personality measures, a common distinction is between extraverts and introverts, achieved by transforming a single, continuous extraversion scale into two categories on the basis of a cut-off point.

- The number of participants who may be represented by each category. A researcher might have required four age categories but finds the number of participants in one group too few to allow for any meaningful comparisons. In such cases categories are usually expanded to absorb stray participants who are not sufficiently plentiful to form a grouping of their own.

Ultimately the decision on how to re-structure a variable – or indeed, whether to do this at all – must be an informed judgement, and rarely based on just a single factor; there will need to be a logic for reducing a continuous variable to categories, and the number of categories will follow this logic. Previous research will also be helpful and it would be reasonable to adopt a similar strategy to the treatment of variables as other researchers in a particular area have done. The costs of recoding variables must also be understood. Changing from a continuous to a category form of measurement will usually change the type of statistical analysis appropriate to the data, often with an alteration to the power of that analysis, in terms of its likelihood of detecting the presence of an experimental effect.

It should be clear from the above discussion that changing the way a variable is measured is not something to be undertaken lightly, so much so that we return to the issue in Part 4, when we consider the practicalities of recoding variables. Different types of statistical analysis relevant to different measurement systems are considered in Part 5.

Box 2.9 compares variable types in relation to research hypotheses.

A Closer Look At . . .

# Different types of variables

The following are examples of different research hypotheses. Independent and dependent variables are identified in each case, as are the variable types, in terms of their levels of measurement.

*Mean recall rates on a word memory task will differ between an experimental group trained in a mnemonic scheme and a control group learning by rote.*

| Independent variable | Dependent variable |
| --- | --- |
| Experimental condition | Scores on a recall task |
| Nominally scaled variable | |
| Categories: 2 | |
| Experimental group; control group | Interval-/ratio-scaled variable |

*Male and female psychology students will make different choices on a behavioural questionnaire comprising dichotomous-response items.*

| Independent variable | Dependent variable |
| --- | --- |
| Gender | Responses to questionnaire items |
| Nominally scaled variable | Nominally scaled variable |
| Categories: 2 | Categories: 2 |
| Males; females | Yes; no |

*Ranking in a statistics test will depend on the personality type of the individual student.*

| Independent variable | Dependent variable |
| --- | --- |
| Personality type | Test ranking |
| Nominally scaled variable | Ordinally scaled variable |
| Categories: 2 | Categories: $n$ |
| Type A; type B | 1st, 2nd, 3rd, 4th . . . $n$th |

*The number of road accidents on a given stretch of road will be related to variations in temperature.*

| Independent variable | Dependent variable |
| --- | --- |
| Temperature | Traffic accidents |
| Interval-scaled variable | Ratio-scaled variable |
| Temperature, °C | Number of recorded accidents |

## Review

Chapter 2 has introduced what can be regarded as the building blocks of research, the variables which provide the basis for both manipulation and for measurement in research. The different types of variables have been described and advice on how they can be measured offered, along with some practical guidelines for the undergraduate. The next chapter in Part 2 takes our view of the variable universe to the next stage in which one of the central research designs in psychology is introduced – experimental design.

## Suggested further reading

Dyer, C. (1995). *Beginning research in psychology: A practical guide to research methods and statistics*. Oxford: Blackwell.

This is a good general textbook on research and contains a straightforward overview of different designs.

Lofland, J., & Lofland, L. H. (1995). *Analysing social settings: A guide to qualitative observation and analysis* (3rd ed.). Belmont, CA: Wadsworth.

Addresses the quantitative – qualitative debate within psychology and provides an insight into the conduct of qualitative research. This is a useful introduction for students contemplating a qualitative study.

# 3 Experimental research designs

## Key Issues

Chapter 3 introduces what is often regarded as the cornerstone of psychological research, experimental design. The essential elements of true experimentation are discussed in detail, and comparisons are made with quasi and non-experimental designs. In particular we contrast the classic between-groups and repeated measures approaches, outlining the advantages and disadvantages of each. We also offer advice on the sometimes tricky procedures of counterbalancing. We end the chapter with an introduction to more complex designs involving many factors.

- experimentation
- between-groups designs
- within-subjects designs
- repetition effects and how to deal with them
- quasi-experimental design
- factorial designs
- randomised control designs
- mixed designs

## 3.1 Introduction to experimental research

In Part 1 the purpose of research was discussed in terms of describing, explaining and predicting something about the psychological world we live in. The methods available to us for doing this are many and varied and we discuss these in some detail in Part 3. However, whether or not the approach is survey, questionnaire-based, observation or interview, most of the methods used in our research will share a number of important elements and adhere to a common language of design. The exception here is qualitative research which, as we have previously stated, possesses certain unique characteristics requiring different treatment, and these issues are discussed in Part 6. However, for much of the work carried out by undergraduates – whether survey, observation or whatever – the general approach will be quantitative and usually experimental in nature.

By experimental we refer not so much to the rigid, laboratory-based work of the cognitive psychologist, but to the more general set of procedures (this does not of course exclude laboratory research) whereby individuals are manipulated into different groups, groups are compared on some factor and relationships among variables are explored. In most cases, as far as design elements and technical language are concerned, it does not matter whether we are using surveys, interviews or, indeed, experiments; the components of our research are the same: there will be independent variables and dependent variables, there will be causes and there will be effects, there will be predictors and there will be outcomes, there will be extraneous variables and there will be controls. In this respect it could be argued that most psychological research is, at the very least, quasi-experimental in nature, in that it follows a common set of rules. These rules, and the language associated with them, form the basis of this chapter.

## 3.2 Experimental design

In most (though not all) instances, the research process aims to explore whether or not a relationship exists between or among variables. Does changing the presentation rate of stimulus words affect the accuracy of recall, for instance; do the different genders express different attitudes in response to a persuasive communication; does performance on a problem-solving task vary with a measure of self-perceived ability? Specifically, the aim in all these examples is to demonstrate that the relationship between the independent and dependent variable is causal. To achieve this we adopt an experimental design.

We have already remarked that experimental design does not just mean laboratory research but rather refers to any type of study which incorporates a number of key characteristics. Chief among these are the measures taken to control for the possible effects of extraneous variables, factors which might obscure or interfere with the relationship between an independent and a dependent variable. The most important of these is the way in which participants are assigned to different groups, or experimental conditions.

The purpose of an experiment is to demonstrate that a particular experimental manipulation or intervention results in a predicted outcome. For example, we might set up a study to demonstrate that exposing participants to a list of subliminally embedded food objects in an otherwise innocuous visual presentation will result in high scores on a hunger index. However, this on its own is not enough to prove a causal link between the independent and the dependent variable, since there could be many explanations for high scores in this scenario. In order to argue a causal case with any conviction we are required to demonstrate that, not only does the presence of the experimental treatment (the embedded subliminal images) result in high scores on the response measure, but that its absence fails to produce the predicted behaviour. Only then can we claim to have demonstrated a cause-and-effect relationship. The basic experimental design therefore usually involves a comparison between two groups on some **outcome** measure – an experimental group in which a treatment or intervention is present, and a control group in which the treatment is absent. The expectation is that (if a cause-and-effect relationship really exists) an effect will be observed in the treatment condition and be absent in the non-treatment condition.

The presence or absence of an effect, while an essential requirement of experimental design, is only meaningful providing we can demonstrate that the effect was due to variation in the independent variable, and not some other extraneous factor. The obvious culprit in the scenario we are describing is the fact that we have two different groups in our study. Who is to say that a difference in some measure between the two groups is determined by the independent variable, as opposed to the fact that the groups possess different characteristics? We have different people in each group, after all, and participant differences remain one of the key confounding factors in any study. The solution is to strive for equivalence between the groups, and the procedures whereby this can be attained are discussed in the next section.

As we have seen, the most basic kind of research design involves two groups being compared on some outcome measure, with any observed differences between the groups evaluated for statistical significance (hence, a **between-groups design**). Typically, in the case of a conventional experiment, one group is exposed to some kind of experimental procedure (a treatment), and the second group is not, so as to serve as a comparison with the treatment group. This comparison group is then termed the **control group**, and the group receiving the treatment is termed the **experimental group**. The assumption is that, if both groups were equivalent prior to the experiment, yet demonstrated differences after the experiment, then the change must have been due to the experimental treatment.

There are three methods for ensuring equivalence in the between-groups design: matching, expanding the design and randomisation. Matching we discussed in Chapter 2, and while there are certain circumstances in which this will be an appropriate solution to the problem of different groups, it will be recalled that obtaining a perfect match between two groups of participants is almost impossible and places considerable demands on a participant pool (meaning that in order to eliminate or omit non-matches, numbers in the groups may become very small). In fact, the matching of participant characteristics across groups is rarely done and in the event that a particular variable is identified as a potential extraneous factor, the preference in these circumstances is often to expand the design to incorporate this factor as an additional independent variable. An example of this approach has been illustrated previously (see Box 2.4) and is further discussed in the section on factorial design.

The third technique for establishing equivalence, randomisation, is by far the most common in an experimental design, and usually the most preferred. The assumption is that, if we start with a population which is homogeneous (in which everyone is more or less the same as everyone else, in the most general terms) and randomly draw from it two samples, then on any measure we care to take we would expect both groups to be roughly similar. A requirement for this is that at the point of drawing from the population, each individual could be placed into either group, with an equal probability, and that this placement is random. What this does is create two groups which are clearly not identical (how could they be, with different members in each?) but which are probabilistically equivalent. It is this notion of probability which is important here, since if any individual could just as easily be in one group as in the other, then it follows that both groups must be (more or less) the same, or equivalent. Consequently it is assumed that if both groups were compared on some measure prior to any form of treatment or intervention, they would exhibit similar scores; if differences are evident after manipulation, we can reasonably assume that they are the result of the manipulation. It would of course be possible to actually take a measure from both groups as a **pre-test**, to assure ourselves of their initial similarity, and sometimes a design will require this, but it is not always necessary, since the randomisation process is seen as sufficient to ensure equivalence. Consequently, most designs of this type are termed **post-test**, since the only measure taken is after the experimental manipulation or treatment has occurred.

In design terminology this particular scenario is known as a **post-test randomised between-groups experimental design**. It forms the basis of much psychological research and because of the extent to which extraneous variables can be controlled – including unpredictable ones – any proposition of a causal relationship between independent and dependent variables is said to possess **internal validity**. Moreover, an experiment which conforms to this design, in which assignment to groups is randomised, is known as a **true experiment**.

There remains a final point to be made on the subject of between-groups designs. So far we have been considering the two-group case, and all our discussions and examples have involved this particular scenario. The reasons for this have hopefully been made clear – the two-group design, in which measures taken from a treatment group are compared with those from a control group, is regarded as the classic experimental position; adopting a control versus treatment approach which incorporates appropriate measures for dealing with extraneous variables provides us with the most economical method for demonstrating cause-and-effect relationships. Moreover, as will be noted in Parts 4 and 5, a number of statistical techniques have been developed specifically for this particular type of design, and a considerable proportion of psychological research conforms to this approach.

The astute reader, however, will have deduced that not all research settings will fit comfortably into this two-group structure – in a study exploring the relationship between learning style and word recall we may well compare a mnemonic group to a rote learning group, but there are many different mnemonic styles and our interest might be in exploring possible differences among them, as well as comparing them against a control condition. The procedure here is quite straightforward and merely requires that we expand the number of groups in our study to include all the conditions. Hence, for this example, we might have a control group learning words by rote, an experimental group learning words in terms of what they rhyme with, a second experimental group learning words in terms of their meaning and a third learning by association. As with the two-group case, a number of statistical techniques exist to analyse data from many-group designs, all of which are fully covered in the later parts on statistical procedure. The following sections consider variations on the experimental theme and the examples in Box 3.1 provide illustrations of the different research designs.

Box 3.1

**A Closer Look At . . .**

# Different experimental designs

### Research setting

Participants are drawn from a population and randomly assigned to a control group and an experimental group. The experimental group is trained in a word-association mnemonic prior to the presentation of a list of common nouns. The control group is presented with the word list without training. Subsequent recall of the presentation words is compared between the groups.

### Research design

Post-test randomised between-groups experimental design with two conditions, A (mnemonic) and B (rote) of a single independent variable (learning strategy).

### Research setting

Participants are drawn from a population and randomly assigned to a control group and two experimental groups. The experimental groups are trained in either a word-association or a rhyming mnemonic prior to the presentation of a list of common nouns. The control group is presented with the word list without training. Subsequent recall of the presentation words is compared among the groups.

*Research design*

Post-test randomised between-groups experimental design with three conditions, A (mnemonic 1), B (mnemonic 2) and C (control) of a single independent variable (learning strategy).

*Research setting*

In a study on dual processing theory (Paivio, 1971), a research sample is presented with a list of common nouns comprising equal numbers of concrete and abstract stimuli. Subsequent recall of concrete and abstract words is examined in terms of the prediction that different encoding systems will be used to process the different classes of stimuli.

*Research design*

Within-subjects design with two repeated measures, A (concrete) and B (abstract) on a single independent variable (type of stimulus).

*Research setting*

In a study on the 'availability heuristic' (Tversky & Kahneman, 1974), a sample drawn at random from an undergraduate population completes a 'fear of crime' questionnaire. The participants are subsequently presented with information on local crime statistics before responding again to the questionnaire. Responses are compared for the before- and after-presentation conditions.

*Research design*

A pre-test, post-test within-subjects design with two conditions, A (control; pre-presentation test), B (treatment, post-presentation test) on a single independent variable (presentation).

*Research setting*

In a study investigating the role of experience on error rate on a co-ordination motor task, a sample of novice cyclists is drawn from the cycling community. Error rates on a standard route are noted at novice level, after six months' cycling experience, and after one year, and the rates compared.

*Research design*

A post-test within-subjects design with three conditions, A (novice), B (six months) and C (one year) on a single independent variable (experience). (Note, there is no provision for a control group in this type of design, so a pre-test condition is unnecessary.)

*Research setting*

In an experiment exploring the effect of music on problem solving, a sample drawn at random from a population completes a number of problem-solving trials in silence and while listening to preferred music. To control for possible **order effects**, half of the participants complete the task in the silence condition first, while the other half experience the music condition first.

*Research design*

A partially counterbalanced, pre-test–post-test within-subjects design with two conditions, A (absence) and B (presence) on a single independent variable of music.

Box 3.2

## Practicalities . . .

# Achieving equivalence

The between-groups experimental design with two conditions is the classic technique for demonstrating the existence of a cause-and-effect relationship; typically one group of participants is exposed to some experimental treatment while a second group is not, and comparisons are made between the two. The key element of this approach is the equivalence of the groups, achieved through a process of random assignment. In practical terms this can create problems for you, the researcher – selecting a large sample from a population, then tossing a coin to decide which group each individual should be assigned to will probably result in unbalanced groups. (In 20 tosses of a coin, for instance, it would not be impossible to obtain 15 heads and 5 tails.) More useful, and practical, would be to use one of the many computer packages to generate random numbers. In Table 3.1, participants identified by case numbers 1 to 12 were allocated to groups 0 or 1 by drawing a random sample of exactly 6 from the total number of cases. This was achieved in SPSS in the Data menu, under the Select Cases command. Similar functions are available in Minitab and other packages.

Table 3.1   Participants randomly assigned to two groups, through a random sampling procedure in SPSS.

| Case | Group |
| --- | --- |
| 1.00 | 1 |
| 2.00 | 0 |
| 3.00 | 0 |
| 4.00 | 1 |
| 5.00 | 0 |
| 6.00 | 0 |
| 7.00 | 1 |
| 8.00 | 1 |
| 9.00 | 1 |
| 10.00 | 1 |
| 11.00 | 0 |
| 12.00 | 0 |

## 3.4 Within-subjects designs (repeated measures designs)

The major alternative to the between-groups design is the **within-subjects design**. Here, each participant experiences each condition of an independent variable, with measurements of some outcome taken on each occasion. As in the between-groups situation, comparisons are still made between the conditions, the difference being that now the same participants appear in each group or level. Consequently, all the requirements for an experimental design are met – there is a condition in which a treatment or intervention is present, and there is a condition in which it is absent (repeated measures are taken from the group, both before and after some treatment is applied); the 'groups' are equivalent (in that the same people are in each condition) minimising the possible confounding effects of extraneous variables. In a memory study, for example, a group of participants might be required to recall lists of common nouns under different conditions of interference; during the interval between initial learning of one particular list and recall, participants might experience a passive activity, such as watching television (the control condition). In a repetition, the same participants learn a different set of common nouns with a more active, problem-solving activity taking place between initial learning and recall (the experimental condition). Participants would then be compared on their recall under each of the conditions. Comparisons are not being made between different sets of participants, but within the same participants across different conditions.

The major advantage in using a within-subjects design, and one of the reasons many researchers opt for the approach whenever possible, is that it almost entirely eliminates the problem of individual variability which represents the main drawback of between-groups designs. Recall that, when different participants comprise the different categories of an independent variable, any observed differences on a corresponding dependent variable, while possibly due to the experimental factor under investigation, could be equally due to different people being in each group. Even if variation in an outcome measure is not directly caused by variation among participants, such individual differences will often interfere with or possibly dilute a true relationship between independent and dependent variables.

A further advantage of the within-subjects approach is that participant numbers are much reduced – even the most basic of between-groups studies requires a minimum of two groups, whereas a similar study using the within-subjects procedure needs only one. The same individuals are used for each condition, making the approach especially useful in situations where there are only a few available participants. In undergraduate research, where competition for a limited participant pool is often fierce, a willingness to accept smaller sample sizes might be a distinct advantage, although this must be balanced against the fact that participants may well be exposed to a more lengthy procedure involving repeated measures.

In addition to the arguments for using **repeated measures designs**, there are some instances in which no other method is feasible. **Longitudinal** research, for instance, in which a number of variables expected to change over time are measured, really could not be attempted in any other way. The alternative **cross-sectional** approach which uses different groups of participants of different ages, all measured at a single point in time, while more immediate will most likely exhibit huge variability due, not simply to individual differences, but also to the widely different age groups used. Comparing a group of 20-year-olds with a group of 60-year-olds goes beyond mere age differences, incorporating considerable changes in culture, society and experience which will have a huge impact on almost any measurable variable. A longitudinal approach, using repeated measures, can follow the changes and developments taking place within the same group over a number of years – today's 17-year-old participant is the 7-year-old we observed 10 years ago.

Other situations in which the within-subjects design is to be preferred are those in which the relationships between an independent and a dependent variable are believed to be real, consistent but very slight and possibly difficult to demonstrate. Under such circumstances a between-groups design with all its attendant sources of participant variability would probably completely obscure such effects. The only way of demonstrating a causal link between an independent and a dependent variable when an effect size is small is by eliminating extraneous factors as far as is possible. The within-subjects design is a good solution here.

By and large, many between-groups studies can be redesigned to take advantage of the within-subjects approach, reducing the need for large participant pools and controlling for a good deal of undesirable variability. A major exception is when the independent variable providing the basis for comparison in a study is of the participant profile variety (typical of most quasi-experimental research; see the section which follows). These are characteristics like age, gender, class and personality type – key descriptive aspects of an individual which place them into some mutually exclusive category. Consequently, when independent variables take this form the only possible design is between-groups. Within-subjects designs are really only possible when the independent variables involve either treatment or temporal differences.

Despite the generally positive regard many researchers have for the within-subjects approach to research, the procedure is not without its own problems. The main drawback is the simple fact that *it is* the same people who experience all the conditions within a variable, allowing for the very real possibility that experience of one treatment will influence measurements on another. The most obvious **repetition effect** is a practice phenomenon – in studies involving performance, if the same participants are used in a before and after design (i.e., participants are tested in the no-treatment condition, and then re-tested after some intervention), it is likely that an improvement in task performance is partially due to the participants simply getting better at the task. If it is the case that exposure to repeated treatments, irrespective of order, results in a generalised practice effect, there is little the researcher can do, other than resort to a between-groups design, swapping the practice problem for the individual differences problem. As ever, the choice as to which design will be the most appropriate comes down to a matter of judgement on the part of the researcher, and a decision as to which effect will prove the more serious.

The type of repetition effect most difficult to deal with is that which is unpredictable – experience of one treatment might improve performance in another condition, as in a practice effect, but not in a third; or prior experiences might inhibit performance at a later stage. Furthermore, the order in which treatments are experienced might produce differing effects. The solution to this problem is to manipulate the order in which participants experience conditions, such that while one individual might be presented with treatments in the order A, B, C, another would undergo the treatments in the order B, A, C and so on. This process, known as **counterbalancing**, serves to reduce the influence of any one particular repetition effect by restricting the number of participants to whom it would apply.

There are various ways in which counterbalancing can be performed. The most complete and effective method is termed, not surprisingly, complete counterbalancing. Here, every possible order of treatments is presented to participants repetitively until everyone has experienced all combinations. While this is the most effective method for dealing with a mixture of known and unknown repetition effects – the effect of any one order is balanced against every other order – there is an obvious drawback. The more conditions there are in an independent variable, the more combinations of different orders are possible and, as the number of conditions increase, so the counterbalancing procedure becomes rapidly impractical, not to mention exhausting for your participants. Box 3.3 illustrates the problem. Realistically, this version of complete counterbalancing is only practical for up to four conditions, after which the procedure begins to place considerable demands on participants. More useful, certainly in an undergraduate context, would be a counterbalancing procedure in which the number of combination treatments is reduced, while at the same time trying to ensure that repetition effects are minimised. Unlike the previous procedure, each participant encounters each treatment only once, but in a different order from the next participant, and so on. An obvious advantage of this approach is that, in a study involving a number of conditions, there is a good chance that the researcher will still be alive at the end of it (death by old age or following a revolt by participants is minimised). The disadvantage is that any interaction effects between individual participants and order of treatment presentation cannot be controlled for. This is a serious problem which should not be overlooked if we are taking the trouble to counterbalance in the first place. There are ways round this of course, but the procedures are potentially complex and there are several models for producing an effective counterbalancing design. Procedures also exist for partial counterbalancing in which only some of all possible orders are tested. Such procedures, though, go beyond the introductory nature of this book and moreover, few undergraduates will have either the time or resources to operate at this level of complexity with possibly the majority of supervisors steering their protégés towards something more economical. However, in the event that your own work *is* more complex than a basic two-treatment, or even three-condition repeated measures design, we recommend the Shaughnessy and Zechmeister (1994) text, which offers an acceptable discussion on advanced counterbalancing techniques. Alternatively, the Christensen (2004) text provides a number of counterbalancing illustrations which should cover most of the designs likely to be considered by undergraduate researchers. Finally, in Box 3.3 we offer some practical guidance on counterbalancing which you may find useful.

By way of a concluding comment, it will have become apparent that the basic two-condition within-subjects design can be readily developed to incorporate many conditions, in much the same way that the basic between-groups experiment can be expanded

Box 3.3

How To . . .

# Balance repetition effects in a within-subjects design

In a within-subjects study, when participants experience a series of conditions, with measurements being taken on each repetition, the order in which they encounter each condition can influence the outcome measure. This is not a mere practice effect, but a more complicated experimental or order effect. To control for this we can vary the order in which participants experience each condition; if we allow for all possible ways in which the order of presentation can vary, this will balance out the effects of any particular permutation. However, this procedure can generate its own set of problems:

Consider two studies investigating the recall of lists of common nouns under different conditions of learning. In the first study, two conditions are present: a control condition in which participants attempt to memorise a word list by rote, and an experimental condition in which they are required to make use of a mnemonic technique, such as considering each word on the list in terms of what it rhymes with. The following design is implemented:

*A completely counterbalanced within-subjects design with two conditions, A (control) and B (rhyme), on an independent variable (learning style).*

Participants in this experiment experience repetitions of the experimental treatments as shown:

| All participants | Order 1 | A, B |
| --- | --- | --- |
| All participants | Order 2 | B, A |

In a more complex study, a second mnemonic approach is added, one in which partici-pants are required to consider the meaning of each word. The design becomes:

*A completely counterbalanced within-subjects design with three conditions, A (control), B (rhyme) and C (meaning) on an independent variable (learning style).*

| All participants | Order 1 | A, B, C |
|---|---|---|
| All participants | Order 2 | B, A, C |
| All participants | Order 3 | C, A, B |
| All participants | Order 4 | C, B, A |
| All participants | Order 5 | A, C, B |
| All participants | Order 6 | B, C, A |

Clearly things are getting out of hand – even with only three conditions, which is far from excessive, we require 6 different presentation orders to counterbalance all possible order effects. Just one more learning condition (another mnemonic system) and our experiment would require 24 separate presentations to allow for all the different permutations. With five conditions our experiment becomes so cumbersome as to be almost impractical. (Five conditions would generate 120 different permutations to allow for all possible order combinations.) In addition to this problem the demands on participant time, patience and co-operation will quickly become intolerable. The only solution, when faced with this kind of prospect, is to adopt one of the methods of incomplete counterbalancing. In the mem-ory example above, for instance, it would be permissible still to cover all possible order combinations, but with each individual experiencing only some, but not all permutations:

| Participants 1–5 | Order 1 | A, B, C |
|---|---|---|
| Participants 6–10 | Order 2 | B, A, C |
| Participants 11–15 | Order 3 | C, A, B |
| Etc. | | |

This particular solution, and variants of it, will reduce the demands on the individual, but often at the cost of requiring a larger sample so that enough participants are experiencing each of the permutations. Alternatively, if neither complete nor incomplete counterbalanc-ing is seen as acceptable in a particular study, it would be necessary to consider adopting a partial counterbalanced design in which only a selection of all possible orders is adopted. Alternatively, changing to a between-groups design is a possibility although this will give rise to its own set of problems, as outlined in the section on between-groups approaches.

to a many-groups situation. Certainly a large number of studies will conform to the stan-dard *treatment present/treatment absent* situation (or before/after, as it is commonly called in within-subjects research), but there will be many cases in which we wish to compare several measures, or conditions of an independent variable. By way of example, a medical study may aim to explore the effects of exercise on resting blood pressure among a sample of hypertensive patients. There are various ways in which this could be done – a between-groups design would make use of two different groups of patients, one taking exercise and one not. However, if we feel that there will be several other factors which contribute to high blood pressure and that a between-groups design will allow for too many uncontrolled extraneous variables, we could opt for a within-subjects design. A basic structure might be a before-and-after design in which measures are taken from a single sample before and then after commencement of an exercise regime. In the event though that there is evidence of a long-term or cumulative effect of exercise, we would want to take measurements a number of times during the course of an exercise regime – say, after a month, then at three-month intervals over the space of a year. As might be anticipated, statistical techniques exist for such expanded repeated measures designs and if you feel sufficiently brave, a look at Part 5 and our treatment of the repeated measures ANOVA provides an example.

## 3.5   Non-equivalent-groups (quasi-experiments)

In a **quasi-experiment** the same general principles of experimental design apply, in that the aim is to demonstrate a relationship, hopefully causal, between an independent and dependent variable. In this instance, however, rather than adopting a randomising procedure to assign individuals into one group or another, the researcher makes use of groups which already exist. For instance, a study might be concerned with differences between males and females on some opinion measure, in the lifestyles of different occupational groups, or in the coping strategies of one type of personality as opposed to another. In a variant of the quasi-experiment, groups being compared need not always be of the nominal categorical type – a variable measured on an interval or ratio scale can readily be used to create the different conditions of an independent variable by use of a cut-off score. This is a common technique in undergraduate research and is often found in studies comparing different personality types on some dependent measure. Here, a score on an extraversion scale (for example, as measured on Eysenck's EPQ[1]) might be compared to the mean or median value of a group of participants, with participants with scores above the mean assigned to an extravert group, and those with scores below the mean assigned to an introvert group. There are many such examples in which **cut-off assignment** can be used as a means of generating comparison groups and as an approach it is recognised as a useful design for demonstrating causal relationships, though not as good as the fully randomised experimental design.

In the language of research design, the different groups which are being compared represent the different categories of an independent variable. They could be the male and female components of a gender variable; or they could be an experienced versus inexperienced category of a skill variable in the cycling example we have been using (based on some cut-off value). Other frequently used terms for the components of an independent variable are **conditions** (the gender variable comprises two conditions – male and female) and **levels** (in one of our cycling examples there are two levels of skill – experienced and inexperienced, while in others we have added the third level of novice). In psychological research which adopts the quasi-experimental stance, the assumption is that the different groups to which people belong are sufficient to account for differences in a range of dependent measures. In true experimentation, on the other hand, the underlying assumption is that the two (or more) groups should be essentially similar (equivalent) at the outset, in

[1] Eysenck's Personality Questionnaire (Eysenck & Eysenck, 1975).

terms of some dependent variable we are interested in observing or measuring, but that this will change following the researcher's manipulations.

Another difference between the two approaches is that while true experimentation usually takes place in the laboratory, quasi-experimentation tends to be more 'real world' in context. As such it is the kind of design often favoured by social psychologists and it is used exclusively in survey research, since the opportunity to randomly assign participants to different conditions is limited in the real world. However, the key issue here is the demonstration of causality. It will be recalled that the main strength of the true experiment lies in the confidence with which we can argue a causal relationship between an independent and a dependent variable. This is due primarily to the fact that the randomisation procedure ensures equality (almost) between comparison groups at the outset of a study. In quasi-experimental research, though, the use of pre-existing or naturally occurring groups requires that our groups are different in significant ways at the outset. (If we devise a study to compare males and females on some measure we do so in the belief that the fact of their gender makes them different.) The problem is that if such groups are **non-equivalent** in one way, there is reason to assume they might be non-equivalent in others, differences that can act as extraneous variables on some outcome measure. This means that attempts to argue causality when comparing naturally occurring (and therefore non-equivalent) groups are more problematic.

A final note on terminology is that the term *quasi-experiment* is found most often in the broad area of social science research, which incorporates, among others, the fields of sociology, social policy, economics and politics. In psychological research the preference is usually for the more informative term, *non-equivalent-groups design*. *Quasi* means nearly or similar to, whereas *non-equivalence* explains the particular way in which a study is nearly (or not quite) an experiment.

## 3.6 Factorial designs

There are many variants on the basic experimental model, one of the most frequently employed being the factorial design. Recall that the simple experimental design – involving equivalent or non-equivalent groups – is attempting to examine a relationship between an independent variable and a dependent variable. Recall also that one of the confounding factors in any design is the effect of other variables present in a study. In previous discussions we have chosen to regard such additional variables as extraneous factors whose effects have to be controlled for. An alternative position would be to regard all such variables as potentially influential and we expand our study to include them as independent variables in their own right; hence the term **factorial research**, research which investigates the effects of several variables, or factors, on some outcome measure.

When we adopt a multi-factor approach to psychological research we design studies which have two or more independent variables, each of which can have two or more conditions. Not only are we looking for differences between the conditions of each individual factor, but we are also interested in possible interactions among the factors themselves. This type of study is termed a *factorial design*, and is carried out as follows.

Let's return for a moment to our hypothetical study of hedgehog-fearing cyclists. In this example it has been argued (not unreasonably) that performance on the task would be largely a function of level of skill – with performance measured in the number of errors made, or poor hedgehogs run over. Previously, while it was accepted that other factors might also have an impact on performance, these additional elements were treated largely as nuisance variables to be eliminated or controlled. However, should we decide that these other factors are important in their own right, and that, far from having their effects minimised, they should themselves be regarded as causal factors, then we have moved to a many-independent variable study. In a variant of our hedgehog example, assume that we have identified two main factors likely to cause variability in performance – skill level (novice or expert) and terrain (easy or difficult). A study set up on this basis would be termed a 2 × 2 (two by two) factorial design – there are two factors or independent variables in the study, both of which comprise two levels. Had we identified three levels of skill and two levels of terrain, this would give us a 3 × 2 factorial design. Moreover, if we proposed the existence of a third independent variable, such as gender (male or female), then we would have a 3 × 2 × 2 design.

If all of this sounds unnecessarily complicated, it is because factorial designs don't consider just the isolated or **main effects** of variables. If this were all we were interested in there would be nothing to prevent us carrying out a series of isolated studies in which each variable was considered on its own: we would perform one study in which performance is measured for skilled and novice cyclists, and a second study in which performance is measured for easy and difficult terrains. What we would miss with this approach is the possibility of an **interaction** – for example, that skill level on its own might not dictate performance, but that its impact depends on the type of terrain. Box 3.4 illustrates how the two factors might interact.

## A Closer Look At . . .

## A factorial design with interactions

From inspection of the graph in Figure 3.1, the results of our study on cycling show that while skill level is a key determinant of performance, its effects depend on the second factor, terrain. When the ground is easy, experienced and novice riders produce similar numbers of errors. It is only with difficult terrain that the effects of skill level can be observed – skill level and terrain are interacting factors.

**Figure 3.1**    Errors on a performance task by terrain and skill level.

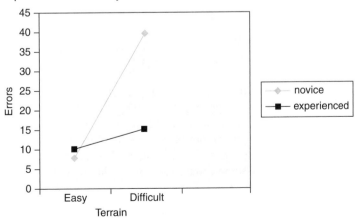

The great advantage of this type of study is that, not only can we observe the main effect of each independent variable on its own, but also, because every possible combination of conditions is considered, any interaction effects can be seen as well. This opportunity to explore interactions is of immense importance since, as we have observed, events in our social world are often the outcome of a large number of interacting factors – and to fully appreciate such events we must have access to these interactions.

An important consideration with factorial designs is the issue of causality. In the previous discussion on experimental design the point was made that only the equivalent-groups design permitted a strong causal argument: the random assignment of participants to groups offered the greatest control over the effects of extraneous variables and it is the preferred model for the researcher. It was noted, though, that some studies will make use of pre-existing or naturally occurring groups, requiring a modification to the basic experimental design to one which is quasi-experimental, or based on non-equivalent groups. The approach is valid and sometimes it is the only design which fits a particular context, although the drawback is the relative weakness of the causal argument. Because group membership has not been manipulated by a process of random assignment, there is a greater likelihood of confounding factors. Factorial designs which make use of non-equivalent groups suffer from the same limitations and the interpretation of both main and interaction effects must be made with caution.

## 3.7 Randomised controlled designs revisited

We have previously remarked that research in the medical field has adopted the classical experimental paradigm as its preferred model. Known as the randomised controlled trial (RCT), the approach relies on the assumption of equivalence when a control group and a treatment group are compared on some clinical measure, or in terms of response to an intervention. However, the basic two-group comparison study represents only one variety of the RCT, and it will be the case that some medical research will attempt to explore the effects of more than one factor on some outcome measure. For example, different patient groups might be compared on the efficacy of two different pain-relief drugs, each of which can be administered in different strengths, in what is obviously a factorial design. We mention this to make the point that there are certain fundamentals in research and that what we might term sound practice will be present in many disciplines, although terminology will vary. The RCT in the field of medicine is a case in point.

## 3.8 Mixed designs

Inevitably, in the design of a study involving more than one independent variable – a factorial design – factors might not always fall into just one class and we will have a mixture of equivalent group factors and non-equivalent group factors. Alternatively, the investigation of a topic might not be possible with a between-groups design on its own and there may be a requirement for an element of repeated measures as well. When a particular design involves some combination of the different design elements it is known as a **mixed design**, and there are several types.

- A common mixed design is one which combines equivalent and non-equivalent groups. Members of a group of skilled cyclists and a group of novice cyclists might be randomly

Table 3.2     The number of errors made by skilled and novice cyclists over two different types of terrain.

|  | Skilled | Novice | Totals |
|---|---|---|---|
| Easy | 5 | 10 | 15 |
| Difficult | 5 | 50 | 55 |
| Totals | 10 | 60 | |

assigned to one of two terrains, varying in degree of difficulty; male and female under-graduates might be randomly assigned to either a control or an experimental group in a memory study, and so on. However, the same reservations about causality mentioned previously will also apply here: individuals who differ by virtue of their gender or skill level are likely to differ in other ways as well, and caution is required when arguing causality. This will apply to both main effects and interaction effects.

In the example shown in Table 3.2, if we observe a difference in total errors between the easy and difficult terrains, we can be confident that differences in terrain determined differences in errors, since the assignment to each condition was random (making the groups probabilistically equivalent). However, the same cannot be said of total error differences in the skilled and novice conditions, since these groups existed already and are therefore not equivalent. Differences here may well be due to any number of unknown factors and observed differences must be interpreted cautiously. The same is true of any observed differences among the interacting cells, or sub-groups, when any of them involve some element of non-equivalence.

A second type of mixed factorial design is one in which both between-groups and within-subjects elements are present. A medical researcher investigating the long-term effects of a hypertension-reducing drug, suspected to have different effects depending on the sex of the patient, might follow a group of male and a group of female patients on the medication at three-monthly intervals over the course of a year. The between-groups factor is the sex of the patient, with two levels (male and female), while the within-subjects factor is expressed by the repeated measurements taken at four different times. Table 3.3 demonstrates the structure of this example. We have not shown totals.

Finally, the most complex of the mixed designs would involve a combination of all these elements – equal and unequal groups, between-groups and repeated measures. Extending our medical example, if there were two new drugs, the male and female patients might be assigned randomly to one or other of the two medications, and again measures taken at three-month intervals. Table 3.4 illustrates this.

It should be apparent from the above discussion that factorial designs allow a high level of sophistication in research, with the opportunity to combine different types of variable in ways which enable studies to be carried out on almost any topic. And this is only a part of what is possible. There is, for instance, no (theoretical) limit on the number of

Table 3.3     Measures of diastolic blood pressure (dbp) of male and female patients taken at three-month intervals.

| Dbp | Time 1 | Time 2 | Time 3 | Time 4 |
|---|---|---|---|---|
| Male | 100 | 98 | 90 | 85 |
| Female | 100 | 102 | 95 | 95 |

Table 3.4  Measures of diastolic blood pressure (dbp) of male and female patients on two different hypertension-reducing drugs, taken at three-month intervals.

|  | Time 1 | | Time 2 | | Time 3 | | Time 4 | |
|--------|--------|--------|--------|--------|--------|--------|--------|--------|
|  | Drug A | Drug B | Drug A | Drug B | Drug A | Drug B | Drug A | Drug B |
| Male | 100 | 100 | 98 | 98 | 90 | 95 | 85 | 96 |
| Female | 100 | 100 | 102 | 95 | 95 | 85 | 95 | 80 |

independent variables which can be included in this design, or the number of repetitions over which measurements can be taken. It is also possible to design factorial studies in which other factors can be treated as extraneous variables and controlled for, although consideration of such complex designs go beyond the introductory scope of this book.

## 3.9  Some reservations on factorial designs

Factorial designs allow for more complex studies than is possible with the basic experiment in which two or more groups are compared on a single independent variable. However, being able to measure simultaneously the effects of several factors on some dependent variable (as opposed to carrying out several studies, each of which looks at the relationship between a single independent variable and a dependent variable) is not the only advantage of the factorial approach. The key here is that interactions among variables can be explored and this is a huge development in research terms. It has to be said that the analysis of such interactions is complex and 10 to 15 years ago would not have been possible in the average undergraduate programme – students would certainly have been advised against such designs and directed towards something less statistically demanding. Nowadays, though, there are many computer packages available which make the required analyses accessible to undergraduates and there is no reason why such designs should not be attempted. Some words of caution are required, though, concerning factorial designs: just because it is now possible to carry out quite complex studies (complex in terms of the number of independent variables considered) it is not always desirable to do so. There are many experimental studies in which the basic two-group, single independent variable design is the most appropriate. The point is that merely because we can carry out complicated research does not mean we should. The complexity of our design must always be a matter of judgement, judgement based on the number of factors we believe will influence a dependent variable, and whether or not we wish to view all of these factors as potentially causal, or extraneous.

A final note here is a practical one: factorial designs, whatever their merit, are heavy on sample sizes. If we were to take a minimum sample size of 30 as being sufficient for most comparison purposes, then in a typical two-group design we would need 60 participants in our study (30 in each condition). Were we to consider a factorial design with two independent variables, each with two groups, or conditions, then to maintain our minimal 30 participants per group we would require 120 participants. (Imagine trying to persuade 120 people to participate in your study.) Quite simply, the more variables we wish to include in our study, the more participants we will require, and for most undergraduates this will be a major problem. Factorial designs may be desirable in some circumstances, but they are costly in numbers. We conclude with a statistical point: the more interacting factors we include in our design, the more difficult it becomes to tease out particular effects. In spite of the accessibility of sophisticated statistical analyses, it remains the case that when we are obliged to perform large numbers of comparisons, as is required in factorial studies, the likelihood of demonstrating real effects becomes reduced. This point is further discussed in Part 5.

## Review

In this chapter the essential characteristics of the experiment have been introduced, with emphasis on causality. You should now be able to distinguish between true and quasi-experimentation, appreciate the differences between repeated measures and between-groups designs, and recognise how the basic experiment can be expanded into factorial and mixed designs. In the next chapter, our interest in causality is replaced with an emphasis on the demonstration of association, as a different type of research design is considered – that of correlation and regression.

## Suggested further reading

Christensen, L. B. (2004). *Experimental methodology* (9th ed.). Boston: Allyn & Bacon.

An excellent guide to experimental design with accessible arguments on the advantages and disadvantages of the various procedures. Describes a number of counterbalancing models.

Shaughnessy, J. J., & Zechmeister, E. B. (1994). *Research methods in psychology* (3rd ed.). New York: McGraw-Hill.

Of special interest for those proposing complex repeated measures designs. This contains a useful section on counterbalancing procedures which is both informative and of practical value.

# Correlational and regression designs

Chapter 4 introduces correlational designs and distinguishes these from the experimental designs considered in the preceding chapter. The nature of correlation is explored, the use of scatterplots to express correlated relationships is illustrated and the features of the correlation coefficient are demonstrated. More complex correlational designs are introduced with our discussion on partial correlation and regression. Guidelines are offered on when correlations are appropriate and the issues involved in setting up this type of design are discussed. Key points include:

- the features of correlation designs
- the correlation coefficient
- the coefficient of determination
- different types of correlation illustrated
- linear and non-linear relationships
- partial correlation
- multiple correlation and regression

## 4.1 Correlational designs

In our discussions on experimental design we stated that the aim of this particular research approach was to demonstrate that a causal relationship exists between an independent and a dependent variable. Moreover, a key characteristic here was that, while the dependent variable can be measured on any of the scales as proposed by Stevens, the independent variable tended to be measured on an ordinal or nominal scale – hence the typical experimental scenario in which a control and an experimental group are compared on some measure. This is not the case with correlations.

Firstly, correlational designs explore only whether different variables are associated with one another – they are not able to demonstrate whether such associations are causal as opposed to coincidental. Therefore they cannot be classed as experimental designs. A second point is that correlations are symmetrical. This means that observed associations can be in either direction. Consider the example in which anxiety and stress proneness are related (as indeed they are in real life). Conceivably people high in anxiety will also tend to be prone to stress, but it is equally possible that the more prone to stress we are the more anxious we become. It is often not possible to determine the direction of a relationship and consequently the use of the terms *independent* and *dependent variable* is inappropriate, especially given our reservations about the causal argument. Having said this, there are many researchers who persist with the terminology of experimental design in correlation studies, especially when the nature of a relationship is intuitively apparent. Unlike the anxiety and stress proneness example, there are many instances in which causality might be implied – study time and exam performance, for instance, might suggest that study time, as an independent variable, determines (causes) variation in exam performance, a dependent variable. The fact remains that no matter how obvious an association might seem, correlational relationships cannot be considered causal. The preference, then, in correlational designs is to talk not of independent and dependent variables but of predictors and **criterion variables** (sometimes called outcome measures). This allows us to argue that while one variable might predict another, it does not necessarily cause it. (Barometer readings may well predict changes in weather conditions, but in no way do they cause them.)

## 4.2 The nature of correlation

In its typical form correlation is a **bivariate** method – it is concerned with an association between two variables, although many research projects may involve a number of bivariate correlations carried out at the same time. An unusual element of this approach is that the term *correlation* describes not only a research design but also a set of statistical procedures, those used to determine and express the nature of the relationship between two variables, as first developed by Francis Galton in 1888 during his research into heredity, and subsequently by Karl Pearson (1894). Specifically correlations can vary in terms of *strength* and *direction*, as the next example shows.

Following growing speculation about a possible relationship between incidents of road rage and variations in temperature, a researcher notes the frequency of reported traffic incidents under this category over a given time interval, and records the temperature at each observation. The data obtained are shown in Table 4.1.

Table 4.1 illustrates the key characteristic of a correlation study – each observation comprises two measures, a pair of events which are believed to be associated. Note that,

Plate 4.1    The theorist Francis Galton.
*Source*: Getty/Hulton Archive

Table 4.1    Temperature values (°C) and their associated road rage rates.

| Observation | Temperature (°C) | No. of rage incidents |
|:-----------:|:----------------:|:---------------------:|
| 1 | 11 | 1 |
| 2 | 11 | 3 |
| 3 | 13 | 4 |
| 4 | 15 | 4 |
| 5 | 18 | 6 |
| 6 | 19 | 8 |
| 7 | 22 | 11 |
| 8 | 25 | 15 |
| 9 | 31 | 13 |
| 10 | 34 | 20 |

on the first observation, when the temperature is 11°C, one incident of road rage occurred. On the second observation, temperature was again 11°C, but this time three incidents occurred. When the temperature reached 13°C, there were four incidents, and so on.

When this information is plotted on a graph Figure 4.1 is generated. Known as a **scatterplot**, each plot indicates both a measure on the predictor variable, and its associated criterion value. Given that we have stated that correlations are symmetrical and that it is not always clear in which direction the predictor-criterion relationship goes, it normally makes little difference on which axis a particular variable is plotted. However, when we do suspect a particular type of relationship, the convention is to plot the predictor variable (a possible independent variable) on the horizontal, or *x*-axis, with the criterion (or dependent variable) on the vertical, or *y*-axis.

Table 4.1, containing the temperature/rage data, has already suggested that a relationship might exist between the two variables, a relationship depicted visually in the graph. As temperature increases, so apparently does the incidence of road rage.

Figure 4.1    Association between temperature (°C) and incidents of road rage.

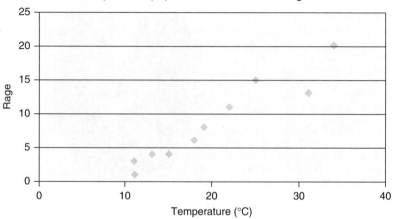

In the above example, the relationship between the two variables is of a particular kind – as one variable changes, the other variable changes in the same direction (as temperature increases, the number of reported road rage incidents also increases). In such cases we state that a **positive correlation** exists between the two variables. Moreover, in this example, because for each unit increase in temperature there is an almost proportional increase in rage rates, we can make a judgement that there is a *strong* correlation between the variables (something to be confirmed, or otherwise, by the appropriate statistic). A similar illustration appears in Box 4.1, in which a hypothetical relationship between the amount of time students spend studying and exam marks is shown. Amazingly, there appears to be a strong positive correlation between these two variables, which might come as something of a surprise to many readers.

Frequently we come across relationships which clearly demonstrate strong correlations between variables, but in which the direction of the relationship is different from that previously considered. In other words, as one variable changes in one direction, the corresponding variable changes in the other – a **negative correlation**. Box 4.1 offers the example of relating exam performance to the number of hours spent in social behaviour – going to the pub, clubbing, watching movies, spending time with friends and so on. Almost as surprising as the previous finding, it would seem that the more time our hypothetical students spend socialising, the poorer is their exam performance, with those whose entire spare time is spent down at the pub doing worst.

## A Closer Look At . . .

# Correlation

The scatterplot shown in Figure 4.2 demonstrates a strong positive correlation between the two variables: as one variable (study time) increases, so the other (exam performance) also increases. Moreover, as one variable changes the other changes by an (almost)

**Figure 4.2** Association between study time (hours per week) and exam performance.

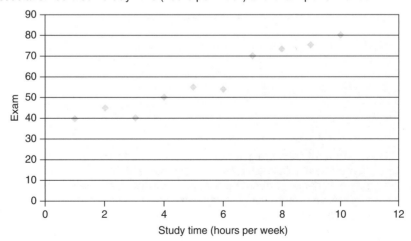

proportional amount. (Note: If the change were perfectly proportional, the plots would form into a straight line.)

Figure 4.3    Association between social time (hours per week) and exam performance.

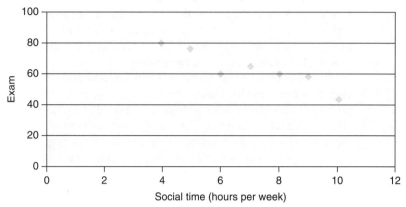

In Figure 4.3 there is still a strong relationship between the variables, since as one changes, the other changes by a similar amount. In this instance, however, as social-isation time increases, exam performance decreases, indicating that the correlation is a negative one.

Figure 4.4    Association between exercise (hours per week) and exam performance.

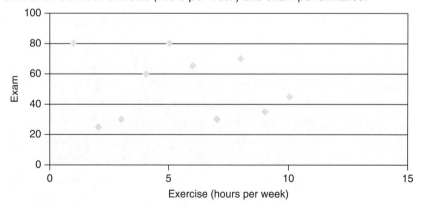

In the final correlation example, the scatterplot in Figure 4.4 shows a weak, if not non-existent, relationship between the two variables. In fact, with such a clearly unrelated pair of variables, without resorting to statistics (which would be pointless in this case) it is impossible even to suggest whether such a relationship is positive or negative. The find-ing here would be that varying amounts of physical exercise seem to have no bearing on examination performance.

## 4.3   The correlation coefficient

The nature and strength of a relationship between variables is indicated by the **correlation coefficient**, a statistic denoted by the letter $r$, and expressed as a value which ranges from +1, through 0, to −1. The sign (+ or −) indicates whether or not an association is positive or negative, as in the examples shown in Box 4.1. The value of the coefficient is a measure of the strength of the relationship, such that as this value approaches 1, change in one variable is matched by a similar change in the other. Correlation coefficients with a value of 1 almost never occur, expressing as they do a perfect relationship and probably a function of two associated variables which are actually measures of the same thing. Correlations approaching zero indicate that there is little or no association between variables, as would be the case in the third example in Box 4.1 (shown in Figure 4.4), comparing exam performance with the hours spent in exercise. The coefficient is sensitive to extreme scores and can be understated if associations are not linear, as discussed in the next section. Part 5 presents a more detailed review of the correlation statistic.

## 4.4   Coefficient of determination

We have used the terms *predictor* and *criterion* to identify the two variables associated in a bivariate correlation design. However, the correlation coefficient tells us only about the strength and the nature of a relationship. In the example in which anxiety and stress proneness are correlated, we may well observe a correlation coefficient ($r$) of 0.60 (an arbitrarily chosen value), which would tell us firstly that the relationship is a positive one (as measures on one variable change, measures on the other change in the same way). The second thing we know is that this is quite a strong relationship – even with a relatively small sample size, a correlation coefficient of 0.60 can be considered quite meaningful. In predictive terms, though, we can say little more than that if anxiety scores are high, stress proneness scores will also tend to be high. Squaring the correlation coefficient produces another statistic known as the **coefficient of determination**, and denotes the amount of variation in one variable which is explained, determined or predicted by the other. Hence in this current example, with an $r$ of 0.60, the corresponding $R^2$ value would be 0.36; the terminology now falls into place and we can say that anxiety predicts 36% of the variation in stress proneness. Of course, since correlations are symmetrical, it is also true that stress proneness predicts 36% of variation in anxiety scores. We will return to the coefficient of determination and its applications in our consideration of regression.

## 4.5   Assumption of linearity

Correlation is a widely used and powerful research approach, but, as with all attempts to study the psychological world, it is not without its own set of problems. One of the difficulties encountered when looking at things which are related is the fact that such relationships are not necessarily consistent, or linear. Consider the case of exam preparation and the common undergraduate problem of motivation. Most students would agree that without a certain level of motivation, studying is an extremely difficult, if not low-priority, activity. Not until examinations or assignments begin to loom, and pressure starts to mount, do many students find within themselves the ability to sit down with notes and textbook. We might then hypothesise that there will be a relationship of sorts between motivation level and examination performance, since the more motivated students will study more and therefore be better prepared. However, as most of us know from experience, this relationship between motivation and performance is not necessarily linear – it is by no means the case that increasing motivation levels will produce a consistent improvement in assessment performance. In the case of the poor student who has left her studying to within one week of a final examination (hard to believe, we know), while she may be highly motivated to study, the associated high level of stress (not to mention panic) might in fact interfere with her ability to concentrate. Motivated or not, the last-minute studier might ultimately do worse than the moderately motivated student who has been working for much longer. Figure 4.5 in Box 4.2 illustrates the point.

There are many instances in which the curvilinear relationship can catch out the unwary researcher, especially when a study involves some developmental or age-related process. However, this would be a problem only if purely statistical evidence of a relationship were

Box 4.2

## A Closer Look At . . .

## Non-linear associations

Motivation, as measured by a psychological arousal questionnaire, demonstrates a strong relationship with examination performance. However, this relationship is not linear, but curvilinear, adopting what is termed an inverted-U shape (roughly). Up to a certain point, increasing levels of psychological arousal relate positively to exam performance. Beyond this point, the direction of the relationship changes and increasing arousal becomes associated with a decline in performance. Calculation of the correlation between these two variables would underestimate the relationship and therefore a different approach – that of regression analysis – is required in such circumstances.

**Figure 4.5** Association between arousal level and exam performance.

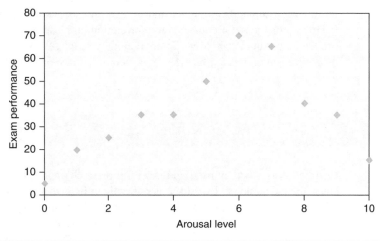

sought. Relying on a numerical value as a measure of correlation (the correlation coefficient) would lead us to assume there was an extremely weak relationship between the two variables – the strong positive effect would be effectively cancelled out by the negative. A glance at the pictorial presentation of the relationship though would immediately show that these two variables are in fact closely linked; a salutary lesson indeed to the unwary researcher.

## 4.6 Misleading correlations

We have already made the point that one of the most important issues concerning this type of design involves the notion of causality. Normally, when a dependent variable is linked with some independent factor, the implication is that change in the outcome measure is in some way caused by, or at least influenced by, the independent variable. This, by and large, is the point of experimental research and a great deal of Part 2 has been devoted to considering the many factors which can undermine attempts to demonstrate such a relationship. With correlational research, the already questionable cause-and-effect relationship is further complicated by the fact that, just because two events occur in juxtaposition, it doesn't mean that one has caused the other. Box 4.3 provides a simple but effective example of this phenomenon.

# A Closer Look At . . .

# The strange relationship between shoe size and intelligence

Plate 4.2    Shoes in the entryway of a preschool.
*Source:* Corbis/Hulton Deutsch Collection

There are many things in our universe which are related. Our mistake is often to assume that such associations are meaningful in some way, when in fact they might be related merely because they happen to be in the same universe, or because both are related to some third variable, as the following example illustrates.

Figure 4.6     Association between age (years) and shoe size.

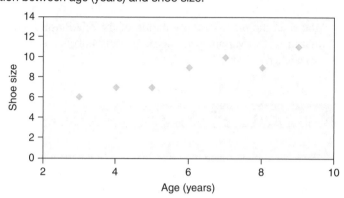

In Figure 4.6 we observe that as young children age, their shoe size increases. Not surprising since, in our early years, the maturation process includes physical growth.

Figure 4.7     Association between age (years) and a measure of general mental ability (GMA).

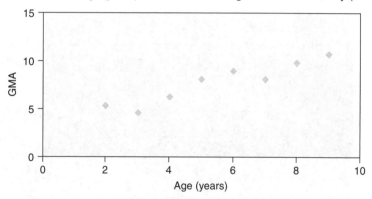

As with the previous example, in Figure 4.7 there is a relationship between certain aspects of intellectual functioning and age (five-year-olds perform better on some intellectual tasks than four-year-olds, four-year-olds do better than three-year-olds, and so on). Once again, intellectual development is a part of the age-related maturational process.

**Figure 4.8**    Association between shoe size and a measure of GMA (general mental ability).

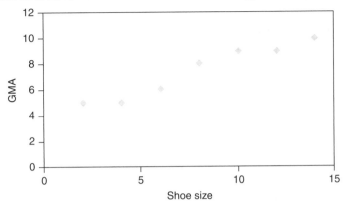

This final example in Figure 4.8 demonstrates the ground-breaking discovery that, the bigger your feet, the brighter you are likely to be. The authors firmly believe, however, that this apparent relationship is purely accidental, or spurious. The two events are related only because they are both surface expressions of a deeper, more fundamental process – the profound and all-encompassing developmental process which occurs with age.

## 4.7 Partial correlation

We have already remarked in our consideration of experimental design that for any effect there will probably be more than one cause. Responses to this are twofold: either the design is modified to concentrate on a single predictor while controlling for all others, or the design is broadened to include all relevant factors as independent variables. In this respect, correlation is the same. It is worth repeating that for any observed event there will rarely be just one causal factor or predictor. To the extent that our interest is in one particular association it is likely that in many cases a relationship between a predictor and a criterion variable will be obscured by the presence of other variables.

Consider our example of anxiety and stress proneness. If our interest was in the extent to which anxiety scores predicted stress proneness but we knew that neuroticism also related to both variables, we might decide that our association could be properly explored only by eliminating the neuroticism effect. This is achieved by a procedure called **partial correlation** in which the effects of one or more variables are removed from an association. The steps in this procedure and guidance on interpreting partial statistics are given in Part 5. Meanwhile, Box 4.4 provides an example.

A Closer Look At . . .

## A partial correlation

Imagine that the diagram represents the relationship between two variables, anxiety and stress proneness. The shaded area expresses how much the variables overlap, or to put it another way, how much of one variable is explained or predicted by the other. In our anxiety and stress proneness example, a correlation coefficient of 0.60 produced an $R^2$ of 0.36. The area of overlap in the diagram then would account for 36% of the variation in stress proneness (or anxiety, since all such relationships are symmetrical). Consider now the presence of a third variable, neuroticism, which correlates with both anxiety and stress proneness (not an unreasonable proposition). Using the same type of diagram (a Venn diagram, named after John Venn, an English mathematician, 1834–1923), we could express the influence of this additional variable as follows:

Now that the third variable of neuroticism has been added it can be seen that some of the original association between anxiety and stress proneness can be attributed to neuroticism (the darker area). Removing the effect of neuroticism, known as partialling out, will show the real relationship between anxiety and stress proneness.

The last diagram expresses the partial correlation between anxiety and stress proneness, with the effect of neuroticism removed.

Note: The statistical procedures for carrying out partial correlations are outlined in Part 5.

The procedures for controlling for, or incorporating, the effects of other variables in correlational studies are much the same as in the group-comparison approach. We can attempt to keep other potential influences constant, or we can decide that the influence of other factors is important and therefore incorporate them into our design.

The first option is not always available in correlation research, since we are often dealing with naturally occurring events over which we can exert no or little control (this is why correlation studies are often regarded as non-experimental). However, there are some things we can do. In our temperature example, for instance, if we had taken temperature readings from different countries across the world, along with corresponding local road rage reports, we might have found that the variation in these traffic incidents was largely based on cultural factors, or other variables of a national or geographic origin. The logical solution would be to restrict our observations to one particular location. Then, if we still generated the same relationship between temperature and rage, we could be more certain that the key factor was indeed temperature change, and not the geographic region in which the observations were made. Of course if, having removed the effects of geographic region, we no longer observe our relationship, then we have made a major error in judgement.

In situations where, rather than trying to eliminate the effects of one or more additional independent variables, we wish to include them in our design, then the second of our options can be applied. In this instance, instead of the usual bivariate (two-variable) approach, we adopt what is known as a multi-correlational design. In its implementation this is a straightforward procedure, involving the simultaneous gathering of data on all the variables which are believed to be interrelated. Determining the combined effects of several variables on some outcome is more complex, requiring sophisticated statistical analysis and familiarity with the procedures of **multiple correlation** and regression analysis. Complex as these techniques are, a number of statistical computer packages exist which deal with the process in a manner accessible to undergraduates. However, at this stage it is enough merely to illustrate the procedure – later sections of the book will look more closely at analytical techniques.

Returning to the example of our stress-prone friends, we had previously been interested in the association with anxiety to the exclusion of all other factors. In order to explore just this one relationship a partial correlation procedure was appropriate. However, should we change the nature of our research aim such that we are interested in just how many factors predict stress proneness, and what the relative importance of each predictor is, we treat all our identified variables as predictors in a procedure known as multiple regression.

If we have identified a number of possible predictors of stress proneness – anxiety, which we have already considered, but also a personality variable like neuroticism and another like locus of control, and possibly even the age of the individual – a multiple regression procedure will provide us with, firstly, a multiple correlation in which all our predictors in combination are correlated with the criterion variable. Squaring this value, as we have done before with a correlation coefficient, provides us with the **squared multiple correlation** (often abbreviated to SMC) which would tell us what proportion of variation in stress-proneness scores can be predicted by a combination of anxiety, neuroticism, locus of control and age. Finally, the procedure allows us to identify the relative importance of each predictor and indeed, whether any of our variables are not predictors at all. In many respects then, multiple correlation and regression perform a similar function to

Box 4.5

**A Closer Look At . . .**

# Multiple correlation and regression

The Venn diagram shows one possible outcome of a study investigating the combined effects of four predictor variables on an outcome measure (stress proneness). Each predictor on its own will account for some of the variation in stress proneness, but in combination it appears that a considerable proportion of variation in the criterion can be explained.

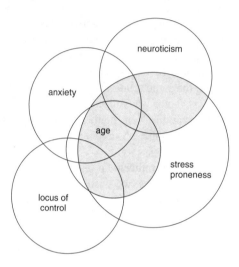

Moreover, the relative importance of each factor can be seen, in terms of how much variance is predicted. Regression analysis expresses statistically what the above diagram illustrates visually, and the calculations for this example are shown in Part 5. See Box 4.6.

Box 4.6

**Practicalities . . .**

# And correlations

When both variables in our study are continuous – that is, measured on an interval or ratio scale – the preference is for a correlational design. You may feel that one of these variables is clearly an independent one, yet it would be more appropriate to use the terms **predictor** and **outcome variables**. Moreover, the approach will not allow you to argue that a causal relationship exists between the pair of variables, since correlation fails to permit this. What you can do, however, is correlate a pair of variables while controlling for the possible interfering effects of some third variable, or indeed of several variables. Alternatively, it is possible to investigate the combined effects of several variables on some outcome measure.

Finally, although we have made the point that correlation is appropriate for interval-scaled variables, there exist procedures for including category variables in a correlation. While we don't cover such procedures in the later sections on statistical analysis it is worth noting that a correlational design need not be limited to continuous variables alone.

factorial experiments and in the same way they provide an opportunity to design quite sophisticated and complex studies. Box 4.5 offers an illustration, and statistical procedures for carrying out and interpreting regression analysis are discussed in Part 5.

## Review

In this chapter correlation and regression have been introduced, with particular emphasis on how they differ from the experimental approach. The assumptions underlying correlations have been considered and the issue of causality has been re-visited.

This completes Part 2 in which we have explored the basic elements of research design, beginning with a consideration of the types of variables encountered in a study and outlining the various ways in which variables can be related. The classical designs have been discussed in terms of comparing different groups of participants, or using the same participants repeatedly, along with the relative merits and disadvantages of each approach, and an introduction has been made to more sophisticated designs. A correlation approach has been discussed and regression introduced.

By the end of Part 2 you should be able to plan a study, identify independent and dependent elements and devise ways of dealing with extraneous factors. It should also be clear how a particular study fits in to the traditional between-groups, within-subjects, or correlational designs.

## Suggested further reading

Christensen, L. B. (2004). *Experimental methodology* (9th ed.). Boston: Allyn & Bacon.

An excellent guide to experimental design with accessible arguments on the advantages and disadvantages of the various procedures.

Dyer, C. (1995). *Beginning research in psychology: A practical guide to research methods and statistics*. Oxford: Blackwell.

Contains a good overview of different research designs.

Howitt, D., & Cramer, D. (2000). *An introduction to statistics in psychology* (2nd ed.). Harlow, Essex: Pearson/Prentice Hall.

Although a statistics textbook, the introductory sections on correlations and factorial experiments are clearly expressed.

Lofland, J., & Lofland, L. H. (1995). *Analysing social settings: A guide to qualitative observation and analysis* (3rd ed.). Belmont, CA: Wadsworth.

Addresses the quantitative–qualitative debate within psychology and provides an insight into the conduct of qualitative research.

Shaughnessy, J. J., & Zechmeister, E. B. (1994). *Research methods in psychology* (3rd ed.). New York: McGraw-Hill.

Of special interest for those using complex repeated measures designs. This contains a useful section on counterbalancing procedures which is both informative and of practical value.

# Carrying out research – methods and procedures

## Part 3

Introducing
research

Planning a research
project—the design

Carrying out
research—methods
& procedures

Describing research
findings—
descriptives

Analysing research
findings—inferential
statistics

Carrying out
qualitative research

Writing up and
presenting the
findings of research

Getty/Bill Curtsinger

Let us assume you have now designed the perfect study, you've identified the key variables, considered everything that could go wrong and built failsafes into your plan. The next step is to put your plan into practice. This part deals with procedural details of implementing a design. Chapter 5 is concerned with sampling issues and considers the various ways in which we can obtain participants for our research, while Chapter 6 deals with issues involved in questionnaire design and the use of standardised tests in research.

# 5 The essentials of carrying out research – the participants

## Key Issues

Chapter 5 is the first of two procedural chapters and is concerned with the 'who' of research. Here we discuss the type of individual who might be an appropriate participant in your research, we consider what would be a suitable number of participants in different situations and we consider how the participants can be recruited. The emphasis then is on the relationship between samples and populations, on different sampling procedures and on the many factors which determine sample size. We offer general guidelines on all of these issues, in addition to providing specific realistic advice on the practicalities of obtaining research participants. This chapter discusses:

- the role of procedure in the research process
- participant characteristics
- sampling techniques
- sample size
- power
- secondary research
- practical issues in sampling

## 5.1 The role of procedure

In Parts 1 and 2 we looked at what might be regarded as the intellectual, or thinking, components of a study – carrying out a literature review, identifying research issues, designing the study and so on. Now it is time to get out there and put your design into practice, known technically as the procedural part of a study. For some this can be a daunting moment, being the point at which all their ideas now must be put into action with all the attendant possibilities for disaster. Others find the actual implementing of a study the most satisfying part of the whole exercise – an opportunity to see their plans come together, and the point at which real data or insights begin to emerge. Either way, the process is not without its own set of pitfalls, and what follows is an attempt to identify the common procedural approaches, the likely problems which might occur in their implementation and conduct, and ways of dealing with them.

One of the many concerns of undergraduates during this stage of their research relates to participants: what kind of participants should they get? How do they get them? How many do they need?

The first question ought to be a straightforward one to answer since in many respects the whole research issue in general, and the research question in particular (see Part 1), will probably have identified a number of important population characteristics, especially if the study is along quasi-experimental lines in which the independent variables are themselves participant or profile variables as they are sometimes termed. If, for example, a study is exploring gender effects on some index of social activity, it is clear that our participants would have to comprise a mix of males and females. If we are concerned with attitudinal differences among university students taking different degrees, then our participants would of course be students, differentiated by course of study, and so on.

The design element of a research project (Part 2) will have further refined our participant characteristics, since the purpose of a design is to develop a plan which will answer the research question while at the same time preventing extraneous or confounding factors from interfering with the study. Since many such interfering factors are themselves participant variables, dealing with them is often enough to narrow down our requirements for participants even further. By way of illustration, our gender and social activity example had logically required that our participant pool include both males and females. However, in the design of an appropriate study, we may have concluded that, if genetic factors contribute to social activity in females but not in males, such differences will become diluted over time, as boys acquire the skills which girls are potentially born with. Therefore our participants are not just males and females, but males and females young enough for the

Box 5.1

## How To . . .

# Choose participants

In most studies the nature of the research topic will in itself identify the type of individuals who should participate.

| Research topic | Possible participants |
| --- | --- |
| A study investigating gender differences in social behaviour. | Males and females of varying ages |
| A study investigating gender differences in social behaviour, controlling for the effects of acquired factors. | Male and female children of pre-school age |
| A study investigating gender differences in social behaviour during the performance of a psychomotor task. | Male and female cyclists of varying ages |
| A study investigating revenge behaviour of small insectivores of the family Erinaceidae on perambulating socially aware hominids. | Hedgehogs of varying ages |

effects of genetic factors to be still visible. In short, we may decide that our participants should be of pre-school age.

In our student example above, if our review of previous attitudinal research intimates that the predicted differences might require time to evolve, or crystallise, then not only are we looking for students following different career paths, but students in their later or final years of study. Box 5.1 discusses possible participants for various research topics.

In most instances the nature of the participants required for a particular study can be readily identified by the nature of the research topic itself.

## 5.3    Samples and populations

The key to grasping the significance of the 'whom do I study?' problem lies in an understanding of the relationship between **samples** and **populations**, and an appreciation of how the phenomenon we are studying varies within the population. By population, we mean the entire set or sub-set of entities which comprise the group we are interested in. This could be the population at large, representing humanity in general, or it could be pre-school children or particular social groups; it could be the student population of your own university or college, or it could even be – for a neuro-psychologist studying brain functions – other species. Whenever we carry out a piece of research a typical aim is to demonstrate that what we discover in the course of our observations, experiment or survey is relevant to the wider population. Of course, the ideal way to ensure this relevance would be to test everyone in that population; this way we could say with certainty that 'this is what people do,' or 'university undergraduates behave in this way in this situation'. Unfortunately, testing an entire population (currently standing at some 7,000 million people) is just a bit impractical, with even sub-sets of this group being so large as to be out of reach. So research, even the most impressively funded, tends to concentrate on a smaller version of a population – a sample. The hope is, of course, that what we learn about the sample will be true of the wider population, and the trick is to ensure that the individuals who comprise our sample are really representative of the population we wish to explore, an issue briefly considered in Part 1. However, irrespective of the size and scope of the population, the aim in studying a sample will always be representativeness: if our population contains both males and females, our sample must have a similar distribution; if there are varying ages in the population, our sample must reflect such age differences also. And if the proportion of males to females in the general population is uneven, then our sample too should ideally reflect this imbalance.

It is worth noting, however, that the cause of representativeness can be over-championed. Case studies are concerned not with the population as a whole, but with the specific object of the case itself – be it an individual, a family group, a school or a hospital. In effect, the membership of the case *is* the population. There are other instances in which slavish adherence to the principles of representativeness can generate unnecessary complications in a study when the object of investigation is not susceptible to particular sources of variation. In many areas of cognitive psychology (e.g., testing visual acuity or responses to audio signals, or memory) and in some medical research, it might be safe to assume that some measures will not vary as a result of, say, gender and personality, or regional location and culture. In instances like this, while it might not be true to say that just any participants would do, it is likely that the much-put-upon undergraduate would be an acceptable research participant here. What a researcher learns about vision and hearing, for instance, from a student sample is likely to be true of the population at large, up to a point – for even these relatively universal functions will vary with age and so generalisations from an undergraduate sample would have to be made with caution. Likewise, medical research on the effects of a new stress-reducing drug might not depend on the individual's profile characteristics (gender, age, class and so on), since the emphasis is on purely physiological factors. When studying more complex, interacting social variables, however (opinions, motivation, stress, psychological wellbeing, economic disadvantage, voting intentions), when measures are likely to vary among individuals and groups of individuals, the issue of representativeness becomes central.

When research involves dependent variables which are known (or assumed) to co-vary with other factors (general health, for instance, will vary depending on our age, gender, class, etc.), the need for participants in a sample to truly reflect the salient characteristics of the population becomes an important requirement. Otherwise we would find ourselves in the position of claiming that a finding is true of the particular group studied, but not necessarily of anyone else, a problem known variously as **sampling bias**, **situational bias** and **situation specificity**, all reflecting the possibility that particular groups might be over-represented in a study. While all researchers should be aware of this issue, the problem of sampling is particularly keen when research is based on the survey method. How often have opinion samples, market research surveys and political polls been discounted or proved wrong because the sample studied failed to accurately reflect the population at large? The voting polls taken prior to the 1992 general elections in the UK were way off the mark in predicting a Labour landslide largely as a result of sampling problems, in addition to a gross underestimation of the 'last minute' factor in voting behaviour. In survey research, the choice of sample is often *the* issue. So how do we ensure that a survey adequately taps the true range of population characteristics? The next section may provide some answers.

## 5.4    Sampling techniques

There are numerous methods for obtaining participants for a study, and they differ in terms of cost, effort and the extent to which they will generate samples which are a fair representation of the general population. This latter denotes the most important distinction and refers to the extent to which we can learn something about a population from what we discover in the sample.

### 5.4.1    Random sampling (probability sampling)

Most undergraduates, especially in their early years as novice researchers, persist in claiming that random samples were drawn from a population to provide participants for their research. In almost every case this will be a false claim since student projects tend to be based on some non-probability sampling procedure, as outlined in subsequent sections. In honest **random sampling**, as the term suggests, a number of individuals are picked from the population totally at random and in the absence of any selection criteria whatsoever, except – and this is a major exception – that every single member of the population has an equal probability of being selected for the sample (which is why the procedure is also known as **probability sampling**). The advantage of this approach is seen in its fairness and objectivity, since everyone in the population has the same chance of being selected. In an ideal world, this would be the survey researcher's preferred method of sampling because any group drawn in this way would be truly representative of its population. The only problem is in ensuring that the process of drawing participants is truly random – that a crofter on the Isle of Skye has as much chance of becoming a participant as a stockbroker in London. In order to achieve this we would require an accurate **sampling frame**, which is a comprehensive list of every member of the population. Drawing from this frame would then be carried out using modern computer software or the older, but just as effective, tables of random numbers. (Large, national surveys might use census information for a sampling frame, or sometimes the voting register is used.) In reality, as we have previously intimated, many so-called random samples have more in common with what is sometimes known as **area sampling**, a process of restricting the available population to particular areas, clusterings or locations. The undergraduate who randomly samples from his own neighbourhood, rather than travelling the country in his search for participants, is guilty of this, running the risk that the particular section, or sub-set, of the population from which he is drawing his sample is in some way unusual; a pre-election opinion poll taken in the west of Scotland, for instance, would generate very different findings from a similar poll in the English home counties. Having said this, however, for practical reasons most undergraduate studies must rely on a highly restricted population for participants, using, for example, schools in the area or business premises in the neighbourhood. Provided the dangers of using a local population are understood – people in one location being more similar than if people from different locations were considered, or even certain rare characteristics being over-represented – the approach is acceptable, not to mention pragmatic. Most student projects are carried out for illustrative, training or assessment purposes and it is unlikely that any undergraduate would have a sufficiently accurate sampling frame of any population to apply a random sampling procedure – let alone the time, money or resources – and in reality most research of this nature will fall into one or other of the categories in the next section on non-probability sampling. This type of work is designed to introduce appropriate principles and procedures and supervisors will always make allowance for the often suspect sampling approaches taken by students (everyone in my class; my mum and her friends; all the unemployed men on my street; and so on). Having said this, the random approach is of course the preferred method for drawing participants from a population, especially in funded research, in that it allows us to gather data from a population even when we know little about the characteristics of that population. However, to prevent us from over-sampling from a particularly rare group, or underestimating common features in a population, sampling has to be extensive with large numbers of participants drawn. The magnitude of this task makes the approach viable only for major research, marketing or government organisations, with the unfortunate undergraduate restricted, as we have already intimated, to more local or convenient populations, with all the attendant problems.

### 5.4.2 Stratified sampling

One of the advantages of random sampling mentioned above was that we didn't need to know all that much about a population in order to draw a fair, representative sample from it. However, in many cases we do actually know a great deal about populations – how they are structured, the different sub-groupings or strata which comprise them and the relative proportions of people who fall into the various categories. We know, for example, that people can be classified by social status, by earning bracket, by educational qualification and so on. Researchers have been able to use this knowledge to modify their sampling procedures such that much smaller samples can be drawn, in which the sample represents a smaller (but arguably more typical) version of the population as a whole. The procedure, particularly useful to those involved in survey design, is termed, not surprisingly, **stratified sampling**, in which a population is divided into a number of pre-determined sub-groups on the basis of existing groupings or strata, or according to some pre-determined design characteristic.

In normal random sampling, ensuring that particular groups are not over- or under-represented by chance requires that large numbers of people must be drawn (e.g., a random sample could easily comprise a greater proportion of middle-class individuals than exists in the general population). However, knowing how the population is structured (stratified), and knowing the relative membership of each stratum, we can draw a series of random samples based on a separate sampling frame for each sub-group, and drawing the same proportion from each group as exists within the population as a whole. This is a useful development of simple random sampling in that it ensures that important (i.e., important to the research issue) sub-groups within the population are fairly represented. It also, as we have indicated, means that smaller samples can be drawn, with all the attendant implications for cost.

## 5.5    Non-probability sampling

The other major approach to sampling, which incorporates a variety of procedures, is **non-probability sampling**. As the name suggests, this approach does not afford every individual in a given population the same likelihood of being selected. It is important to realise therefore that with this second approach, sampling will not be as representative of the wider population as probability sampling, and consequently our freedom to genereralise from sample findings ought to be more limited. Simply because not everyone has the same chance of being selected there is an increased likelihood of sampling bias whereby, for all sorts of reasons, certain groups may become over-represented. On the other hand, it is precisely this bias which, in some situations, makes non-probability procedures appealing.

### 5.5.1    Quota sampling

On the face of it, **quota sampling** looks a lot like stratified sampling – a population is stratified according to particular categories relevant to the research, a number to be selected from each stratum is decided, reflecting the relative proportion of each group to the whole population, and field workers are sent into the streets to fulfil their quotas. Typically, an interviewer might be charged with obtaining a number of respondents within a particular age group, of a given sex, or with a certain occupational status. Where this differs from stratified sampling, however, is that the selection of individuals in any quota group is left to the field worker. Quota sampling is undoubtedly cheaper and speedier than random sampling and, like its stratified counterpart, it ensures that particular groups are represented. However, because the approach is not truly random it is risky trying to generalise too much from quota-determined findings. Consider a field worker charged with surveying attitudes to some issue of 100 people in the 18–25 years age category. Because they are left to their own devices in how they choose respondents, there is a strong possibility of sampling bias affecting selections. The researcher might decide to base her selections on the users of a university library – a typical undergraduate ploy – where, in the space of a single afternoon, the entire quota of 100 might be filled. Much easier, surely, than trying to stop people in the street – except that all 100 respondents would in this instance reflect one particular and unique social grouping. How typical, you might ask, are university students of the wider 18–25 years age group? Or even (excuse the cynicism here), how typical of the student population would be a sample drawn from a university library? By and large, quota sampling remains a popular method for exploring certain social and political issues, although largely for its cheapness and (sometimes) the illusion of control it offers the researcher. It is useful certainly for providing a quick overview of issues but its limitations and the potential for sampling bias must always be kept in mind.

### 5.5.2 Purposive sampling

Occasionally, particular population sub-groups may have demonstrated an uncanny facility for predicting larger population trends. For instance, it is now recognised in political circles that certain constituencies – for whatever reason – often provide typical patterns of voting intention; sometimes predictions on the proportions of Labour or Conservative voters turning out can be quite accurate based on observations of such benchmark constituencies. Therefore, rather than randomly sampling from the entire voting population, election researchers will find it convenient to target those particular regions which have been identified as useful indicators, in what is termed **purposive sampling**. Similarly, market researchers attempting to gauge responses to new products will tend to target particular groups as being the most typical consumers in certain areas – this could be a specific age group, people within a particular income band or those living within a particular

Plate 5.1   During elections, some constituencies are closely observed due to a history of predicting national voting trends.
*Source*: Empics/John Giles/PA

geographic area. Without doubt, purposive sampling runs counter to all the sage advice about randomness and the need for representativeness, yet in certain areas it does appear to work and for those organisations favouring the approach, its cheapness, speed and practicality outweigh any disadvantages of a non-probability approach.

### 5.5.3    Snowball sampling

When an area of psychological enquiry concerns a particular sub-group with which the researcher has very little contact, **snowball sampling** presents a method of accessing a larger sample than might otherwise have been possible. In research into criminal cultures or drug networks, a researcher may have contact with only one or two members. Such contacts, however, might be in a position to recommend others from their group or, alternatively, they might act as unpaid assistants and agree to distribute questionnaires among their own acquaintances, with these in turn contacting yet others. This is a useful technique for gaining access to groups which would normally be out of reach of the researcher, either as a means of exploring unknown social networks or as a method of obtaining participants. If the aim of the research is to identify the structure and networks of unusual cultures this is a practical first step since it will offer insight into who knows whom, which sub-groups might exist and the relationships among them. As merely a source of participants, on the other hand, the dangers of the approach should be pretty clear in light of our previous discussion – using untrained confederates to not only select others for inclusion in the sample, but also to administer questionnaires (and give instructions, advice and suggestions, etc.) is an open invitation for sampling bias. It is worth pointing out that the example above, involving criminal or drug cultures, is unlikely to form the basis of undergraduate research (it would not be approved by most departmental ethics committees) and it is used here purely for the purposes of illustration. Having said this, however, snowball sampling involving different issues remains a popular choice for many undergraduate projects: it would not be the first time a student researcher had sent off a friend or parent to persuade work colleagues to fill in questionnaires exploring job satisfaction, motivation and other issues of interest to the organisational psychologist. Unfortunately, it would also not be the first time that the student researcher failed to fully appreciate the limitations of the approach.

### 5.5.4    Accidental sampling

**Accidental sampling** or, as it is sometimes known, **convenience sampling** makes no attempts at representativeness at all. Everyone – and anyone – that the researcher happens to encounter in a certain place, or between certain times, becomes a member of the sample. Now this is fine so long as representativeness is not an issue, and the approach can be used at the developmental stage of a survey, for instance, when particular items or modes of questioning are being tried out. To be frank, it is probably also acceptable for many undergraduate projects in which the aim is more to develop research skills than further psychological understanding, just so long as the considerable potential for bias is understood. As we have previously mentioned, one of the most irritating things for a supervisor to read in a student project is how a "random sample" was drawn from students in the library, or the canteen, or the pub. Box 5.2 summarises this consideration of sampling.

A Closer Look At . . .

# Sampling procedures

### Probability sampling

#### 1. Simple random sampling

*Each member of a population has an equal chance of being drawn. Sampling is truly random and based on a comprehensive sampling frame.*

#### 2. Stratified sampling

*A population is sub-divided by known strata and participants are sampled randomly from within each stratum.*

### Non-probability sampling

#### 1. Quota sampling

*A population is sub-divided by known strata but participants are not drawn randomly within each stratum.*

#### 2. Purposive sampling

*A particular sector of a population is deliberately targeted. Sampling is not random; rather, specific individuals are selected because they possess certain characteristics of typicality or predictive power.*

#### 3. Snowball sampling

*Population members act as agents of the researcher by sampling from colleagues, friends or associates. Useful when a population is largely inaccessible to the researcher.*

#### 4. Accidental sampling

*Sampling follows no predetermined plan and is a matter of convenience only.*

### 5.5.5    Samples – how to get them

It's all very well knowing whom you want to take part in your study; getting them is another matter altogether. In the case of an observation study in some kind of natural setting there is really no problem, since everyone in the situation is potentially a participant. Studying people unobtrusively in a bank would automatically incorporate all customers, tellers and bank staff into your sample, although there are certain constraints on this kind of study which must be understood before it can be implemented. The section on ethics in Chapter 12 is of particular relevance here.

The real problem in obtaining participants is that, with the notable exception of naturalistic observation research, everyone in a study must be participating willingly. Commendable as this notion is, it does give rise to problems of its own – given the previous discussion on representativeness, how typical can our sample be of the general population if entire sub-groups (those engaging in criminal activity, or heavily stressed individuals) refuse to participate in our study, especially if these characteristics are known to be sources of variation within our dependent variable, or they are of particular interest to us? Having said this, however, all the various codes of practice governing the behaviour of psychological researchers are in agreement on this point: individuals should not participate in any research without their consent, against their will or without their knowledge. So how are you going to get people flocking to take part in what you might well regard as cutting-edge research but which, from the individual's perspective, is as stimulating as watching hedgehogs hibernating?

For the majority of undergraduate projects, participants are usually drawn from other undergraduates (recall our discussion in the previous section on convenience sampling), with the keen first-year student taking the brunt of the offensive. Indeed, some colleges and universities make it clear that there is an expectation for students – psychology undergraduates in particular – to participate in departmental research, whether carried out by fellow students or academic staff. The argument is that a student of psychology is likely to learn as much about the processes of research by participating in it as by carrying it out, providing a detailed debriefing forms part of the experience. However, reasonable as this argument might be, it is nevertheless at odds with the general principle that participants in research should be willing volunteers. Moreover, making such expectations explicit detracts from the fact that most students of the discipline are genuinely interested in what other people are up to, and will quite happily volunteer, if only in the knowledge that someday they too will be looking for participants.

As a population, undergraduates are often suitable as a basis for research – when projects are designed for demonstration purposes or when dependent variables are pretty universal within the population at large (not affected by age, social class, region, etc.), rigorous sampling procedures are unnecessary. Research in the cognitive field is a good example.

Occasionally, though, undergraduates will prove inappropriate as research participants. In situations where an understanding of certain social/psychological phenomena would interfere with the course of a study, you clearly don't want psychology or social science students. After all, how valid would a study be on decision making if your participants have detailed knowledge of the influence of bias and heuristics on individual judgement? There is also the more widespread problem that, as a group, the student population is not typical of the population at large. Students tend to be well educated, bright and highly motivated; if they are also volunteers, then you have an unusual group indeed. Consequently, any findings which emerge from a student-based group might not generalise well to the population at large, simply because of their atypicality. In some respects this can be regarded as an extreme case of a **local sampling effect**. On the other hand, sometimes the student population represents the only practical group. An experiment requiring repeated measures with the same participants over a period of time is unlikely to be popular, let alone possible, with members of the general public; fellow students may represent the only available group for this type of research, providing the longitudinal element is relatively short term. As ever, though, the decision on which participants to use rests with the researcher and must be made based on a judgement balancing the relative importance of design needs, practicality and convenience, and by weighing the extent to which our dependent variables are likely to co-vary with other factors not present within the student sample.

### 5.5.6    Special groups

When a research project is of the quasi-experimental variety – that is, when the design revolves not just around any particular manipulation on the part of the researcher, but on the selection of particular types of participants – access to special groups might be sought. In the past it has not been unusual for undergraduate researchers to explore vocational aspirations among third form school pupils in deprived as opposed to wealthy communities, or to study achievement motivation among managerial staff in various organisations. Some enterprising individuals might even have obtained access to local maternity units in order to evaluate perceived pain levels among mums-to-be. However, while such creative work has been possible in the past, it is becoming increasingly difficult for researchers of any stature – let alone undergraduates working on final projects – to work with certain, special groups. Part of the problem relates to a growing sensitivity towards outsiders, particularly within educational and health institutions; recent developments concerning changes in status and accountability have made many individuals at managerial level in these organisations extremely cautious about, if not suspicious of, any research which might reflect badly on policy, practices and procedures. Indeed, it is now a common requirement that any proposal for research in a health or educational sphere, no matter what the source, be considered by an appropriate committee and assessed on the grounds of ethics, potential disruptiveness and public relations. At the time of writing a new set of regulations has just been published governing research involving any element within the National Health Service (NHS), covering both practitioners and patients. While these regulations are unlikely to be an issue for most undergraduate projects it is important to be aware of their existence in the event that a health-related study is contemplated. In any event, since such evaluation committees tend to meet at irregular intervals, the time constraints on most student projects make the use of such groups impractical.

---

Box 5.3

## Practicalities . . .

# Of sampling

In most instances, participants in your research will be drawn from the local undergraduate population to which you yourself belong. This is especially true in the early academic years when research projects will be designed and implemented primarily for demonstration and illustration purposes. It will always be important, however, to consider the extent to which what is being measured or observed varies within the general population, and to be prepared to comment on the generalisability – or otherwise – of any findings. In later years, when you will be encouraged to extend your participant pool to include family, friends, workmates or special groups to which you might have access, the same reservations apply: such samples will usually be biased in some way. This is not necessarily a problem at this level of research however, provided these limitations are clearly spelled out in the research write-up, and provided you make it clear that sampling was convenience, local, snowball or whatever. One thing is certain: it is unlikely to be of the probability or random type and any pretence that it is will only irritate your supervisors.

Occasionally an individual might, by dint of personal background, experience or contacts, have access to groups which might otherwise be inaccessible. Some students work part time in offices, some act as helpers in nurseries or school libraries, and some even offer their spare time for voluntary work among people with social problems. In such cases it is often possible to carry out a practical study within a special participant group, not as a result of some back-door enterprise, but simply because approval is more likely to be granted to a personal request from someone known, than if a proposal arrived cold, through the post from some anonymous source. It wouldn't be the first time that a tutor, trying to guide a supervisee towards a practical research topic, asks if the student has access to some particular or unusual group. More than a few studies have evolved not from some burning research issue, but simply because of the availability of a particular section of the population. Box 5.3 offers additional comments on participant sampling.

## 5.6 Ensuring co-operation

In some ways research with undergraduates is the easiest to organise, especially when the design is experimental in nature – the population is relatively captive and most of your peers will co-operate with whatever strange research scenario you have devised. When your study involves members of the wider population, however, as would be the likely case in survey-based research, problems can arise. Approaching people in the street can be a soul-destroying experience. Just recall the deftness with which all of us manage to avoid the desperate-looking market researcher in the high street and you will recognise the difficulties. Most of us don't like being diverted from our goals and everyone striding down a busy street is going somewhere – to the shops, to meet friends, to the office after an over-extended lunch, to catch a lecture; much better to approach people whose goals have been attained, or even thwarted. Waiting rooms, queues, libraries will all likely provoke more co-operation than trying to stand in the way of some poor woman, laden down with shopping and children who just knows she's going to miss the last bus home. At least in a face-to-face situation, once you have caught someone's attention, the chances are he or she will be reasonably happy to answer your questions or fill in your questionnaire. This is by no means true in the much more anonymous case of postal questionnaires.

Many surveys use the device of postal questionnaires because they are cheap – no more than the price of a stamp – and huge sections of the population can be reached quickly. Unfortunately, the approach is also prone to generating the poorest response rate of all data-gathering techniques, with one or two notable exceptions. The problem is that few people see any reason to respond to a "cold" questionnaire; in the face-to-face scenario, there are all kinds of subtle pressures and rewards present which make it likely that someone will take the time to answer your questions, no matter how banal: you provide a distraction to a boring wait at the bus stop, they like your face or they are touched by your expressions of relief and deep joy to find someone who isn't running away from them. Either way, despite its own set of problems, the direct approach will usually produce a co-operative response due to factors which are simply not present in the more distant postal approach.

Receiving a questionnaire through the post lacks the warmth and human contact of the direct, one-to-one approach. Add this to the requirement of not just filling in the questionnaire, but also posting it back – a chore, even if a stamped addressed envelope is provided – and we should be surprised that anyone takes the bother to respond at all. Most

Box 5.4

How To . . .

# Encourage questionnaire responses

While it is true that undergraduate researchers will be unable to coerce, offer incentives to, or make unjustified promises to respondents, there is much that they can do to encourage people to complete and return questionnaires.

- Making contact with an individual who is in a position to encourage returns can be helpful. This could be a group leader or a club secretary who may be in more direct contact with the respondent group. This can be easier than it sounds since often you will have made an initial contact with such a person to seek permission or to set up your study in the first place.

- A polite reminder sent to respondents or contact individuals after about two weeks will often stimulate a response.

- Avoiding traditionally busy or holiday periods should ensure a higher response rate than if you post out questionnaires at Christmas, or during school holiday periods.

- Ensuring that forms are attractive, clear, error-free and easy to fill out is more likely to encourage co-operation than an untidy, over-long and complicated instrument.

Note: it is likely that, once issues of anonymity and confidentiality have been resolved, electronic mailing will become a common method for administering and collecting questionnaires. The new technology approach may well raise a completely new set of issues, but it seems reasonable to suggest that, at the very least, all of the points listed above will still apply when the e-mail replaces the postage stamp.

people would probably prefer to expend the energy in steaming the stamp off the envelope than to answer questions on a form. The exceptions are when there is a legal obligation, as in the case of the national census – there is a threat of fine or imprisonment for non-compliance – or when there is a positive reward on offer, as when we fill in forms to obtain credit, or it is implied that answering questions and returning on time will make us eligible to win 10 million pounds, or when it is clearly in the interests of respondents to comply. Unsurprisingly, none of these methods is generally available to undergraduates – they lack any authority to coerce respondents, they are usually too close to financial embarrassment to offer rewards and it is in the nature of undergraduate-level research that it will not improve the condition of any group or individual. To suggest otherwise would constitute a serious breach of ethical guidelines. What then can the undergraduate do to encourage respondents to return their questionnaires? Box 5.4 offers some suggestions.

## 5.7 Number of participants

Along with 'whom should I choose?' the question 'how many should I get?' ranks as one of the most common asked of tutors. Unfortunately most students are constantly surprised at how such an apparently simple question can stimulate such a variety of complex and sometimes unhelpful responses. 'It depends' is probably the most common response, along with the equally enigmatic 'how many can you get?' Clearly this is not a simple issue and the mere fact that students invariably have concerns about participant numbers indicates an intuitive appreciation that this is an important issue.

In essence, sample size relates to how useful, or powerful or reliable a study is. An attitude survey using only five respondents will tell us virtually nothing about a larger population; an experiment exploring gender differences in spatial ability, comparing only two males and two females, will demonstrate little beyond the skills of the particular individuals involved. Clearly in both examples numbers will be too few either to accommodate the variability in attitudes which would exist in the population, or to overcome possible large individual differences which might obscure a more general gender effect. But what would be an appropriate number? At what point can we reasonably claim that attitudinal measures within our sample probably reflect attitudes in the wider population? How large do our comparison groups need to be before we can claim that an observed difference represents a true gender effect, and not some other extraneous influence? Is a sample size of 20 adequate? or 50? or 100? Should minimum group sizes be 5, or 10, or 20?

This issue is an important one in research, and recent years have seen an expansion of interest in ways of determining appropriate participant numbers. Calculations can be complex, involving several elements, and most introductory texts tend to avoid doing more than airing the question of sample size. Increasingly, though, journal editors are requesting such calculations from their contributors and therefore it would seem appropriate for even the novice researcher to have an understanding of the issues. The next two sections take a closer look at sample size from two different perspectives, while the statistical underpinnings are introduced in Part 4.

### 5.7.1 Sample size in estimating population characteristics

When a research project takes the form of a survey, the aim is to determine something about a population by means of studying a small sample drawn from that population. In order that our study possesses any validity, the sample must be typical, or representative of the overall population. It is this notion of representativeness which is of central importance to all surveys, and which in large part is related to sample size.

### Variability

Any social/psychological issue will be characterised by variability – be it opinions, actions, beliefs, rituals and behaviours. This is expected due to the complexity of modern society and the people who inhabit it: an opinion on any issue, for instance, will vary depending on age, gender, occupation, personality, income, ethnic background, political affiliation, geographic location, level of industrialisation, other attitudes and so on. There is an extensive list of factors which will influence any number of attitudinal issues, and those mentioned so far represent only the tip of the iceberg. The point is that if we are hoping to draw a representative sample from a population in which there is considerable variability, then our sample has to be pretty big to take this level of variation into account. The opposite of course is also true – if what we are interested in is subject to few influences and there is consequently very little variability in the population, then samples can be smaller. To recall an earlier example, if we were studying cloned hedgehogs, where every member of the population was identical and there was therefore no variability

Box 5.5

## A Closer Look At . . .

# Sample size

In an ideal world sample sizes (*n*) can be precisely calculated, providing that certain things are known by the researcher:

1. the extent to which what we are interested in varies within the population (a measurement known as the standard deviation, *SD* or $\sigma$)

2. the margin of error we are prepared to tolerate when generalising from our sample to the population (*E*)

3. the level of confidence we require in our estimates of the population (*z*)

This is worked out using the following formula, based on what is known as the standard error statistic. (If the terms in this formula are unfamiliar, Part 4 provides a comprehensive introduction to statistics.)

$$n = \left(\frac{z \times \sigma}{E}\right)^2 \qquad\qquad (5.1)$$

(*Source:* Adapted from Sarantakos, 1998, p. 159.)

Imagine the following scenario: the faculty librarian wishes to know how much time, on average, psychology students spend in the library (reading, researching, in study groups, etc.). She is prepared to accept a margin of error (*E*) of 1 hour either way and wants to be 95% confident that her estimate will be accurate. (Requests for funding, space allocation and forward planning might well depend on such estimates.) Assuming we know (don't ask) that library time varies within the whole student population with a standard deviation of 4 hours, all of this translates into the following:

$z = 1.96$; *SD* or $\sigma = 4$; $E = 1$

(*Note:* you will be wondering where on earth we picked this number for *z* from. In statistical terms confidence can be expressed either as a percentage [95%] or as a transformed *z*-score [$z = 1.96$]. This is similar to the process of converting actual marks in a certificate exam to grades of 1, 2, 3, etc. A look at Part 4 and our discussion on the normal distribution should make this clearer.)

The formula then becomes:

$$n = \left(\frac{1.96 \times 4}{1}\right)^2 = 7.84^2 = 61.5$$

In other words, given our requirements and the information available, we need 62 students in our sample. (The convention is to round up in such cases.)

whatsoever, then a sample of one would suffice. If our identical hedgehogs had been brought up in differing environments, however, we would need more in order to allow for this and, as the possible sources of variability increased, so too would our need for bigger and bigger samples. Consider Box 5.5; the example here shows a formula-based method for estimating sample size in which variance – the extent to which some aspect of the population varies – is a key element. In our example, what we are interested in (library time) varies on average by only about 4 hours within the student population. However, if we had found that there was more variation in the amount of time students spent in the library, producing a standard deviation (a measure of variability) of 6 hours, then our sample size would have to be larger. In fact, the formula would require 138 participants for our study. (You might want to try this relatively simple calculation for yourselves, by substituting the value 6 for the existing value of 4 in the formula in Box 5.5.)

Variability is clearly an important element in determining sample size but there are other factors to be considered. These are shown in the example in Box 5.5, and discussed in more detail below.

## Margin of error

Whenever a sample is used to estimate some aspect of a population (in a fear of bullying study we might measure the fears of a sample of primary school children on a rating scale and estimate average concerns within the larger school population, for instance), there will always be some difference between the two measures – that of the sample and that of the actual population parameter. This causes error in our population estimates. This margin of error, sometimes known as **sampling error**, is susceptible to sample size such that the larger our sample, the smaller our margin of error (the difference between the sample and population characteristics). The reason for this should be becoming clear now in light of our previous discussions on samples – when something varies within the population (there are short people and there are tall people, for example) a small sample might easily over-represent some elements to the detriment of others.

'*I have worrying news – the human race is growing taller!*'

'*Ah, no – there are only seven people in your sample, and as it happens they are all members of the basketball team.*'

'*Ah, right!*'

With larger samples, extremes will be evened out, sampling bias reduced and the character of the sample will assume a closer and closer approximation to the population. Return again to our example in Box 5.5. We had originally stated that we were prepared to accept a margin of error of 1 hour in our study on student activity. Supposing we wanted to be more precise and required that our sample predictions came much closer to the character of the whole population: supposing we wanted to reduce our margin of error to 0.5 of an hour. Substituting this new value in our formula would require a dramatic increase in sample size to 245. This in fact represents a general rule of sampling in surveys – whenever we wish to reduce our margin of error by half, we need to quadruple our sample size, a daunting requirement for any researcher.

## Level of confidence

An important element of all behavioural research concerns the confidence we have in our research findings. Historically the convention has been to express this in terms of percentages, as in '*we are 90% confident that this finding is true; that this difference is real*', and so on. Another way of looking at this is we are confident that in 90 cases out of 100 this prediction would be supported, or this difference would be observed. Of course, the converse would be to admit that 10% of the time our findings would not be supported, and indeed many researchers report their findings in this manner – as in an effect being observed as significant (real, meaningful) at the 10% level (sometimes expressed as the 0.10 significance level). Over the years psychologists, along with other social and medical researchers, have come to accept that a 95% confidence level is sufficiently rigorous for most applications. Certainly, they could be wrong in their claims 5% of the time, but by and large this is seen as an acceptable risk. Occasionally, though, when there is risk to life in making a mistake or serious money could be lost by, for instance, implementing potentially damaging policies on the basis of research findings, a researcher wants to reduce the possibility of being wrong. In this instance a confidence level of 99% may be adopted, reducing the possibility of making an inappropriate judgement (a Type I error) to 1%. But there is a price to be paid. Consider again the example in Box 5.5. Here the confidence level has been set at the usual 95%. Note that this is expressed as the value 1.96, which might seem a little confusing but merely represents the transformation of values from a percentage scale to a different scale (known as a scale of $z$-scores). The process is fully discussed in Part 4 and if this current section has lost you it might be worth having a look ahead to our consideration of distributions, $z$-scores and statistical significance. Otherwise, read on.

A 95% confidence level, when transformed into a $z$-score, gives a value of 1.96, and this is the value found in our formula. Increasing our confidence level to 99% would result in a corresponding $z$-score of 2.58 (you might confirm this by consulting Appendix A) which, when substituted into the formula, would generate a value for $n$ of 107. In other words, if the same study were carried out but the researcher wanted to be extra certain of not making a mistake, he would need a sample size of 107. Finally, if we were to put all of these things together, a measure of variation of 6 hours in library time, a margin of error of only 0.5 hour and a confidence level of 99%, we would need a sample size of:

$$n = \left( \frac{2.58 \times 6}{0.5} \right)^2 = 30.96^2 = 959$$

Clearly the estimation of sample size for any study is a complicated thing – there are a number of elements which have to be considered and as each one varies there is a direct, knock-on effect on sample size. However, the deeper thinkers among our readers may be feeling a little uncomfortable about the previous discussion. How, you might well ask, are we able to include a measure of population variation in our formula when surely the whole point of studying samples is to estimate such population characteristics? Well, it is possible to approximate a measure of population variation by looking at the sample (if what we are interested in varies dramatically within our sample it's a safe bet this will be true of the population also), but by then we have already carried out our study and the question of sample size becomes spurious. So how do researchers get round this?

One solution is to carry out a small-scale, pilot study in which the sample variation can be used as a basis for estimating the variation in the population. We can then apply our formula prior to the full-scale study. This of course takes time and money and besides, to obtain a reasonable estimate from the sample it would have to be of a reasonable size, bringing into question the need to repeat the exercise at all. In reality, much funded re-search tends to adopt rule-of-thumb guides to sampling and many of the major survey organisations accept a sample of 1,000 as being acceptable. It is a manageable number (for a large research group) and ought to be representative; any more than this has a min-imal impact on margin of error.

For undergraduates it should be apparent that some of these guidelines on sampling will be inappropriate – no student will be able to gain access to 1,000 possible respond-ents and the formula for estimating sample size contains too many unknowns. Which is why, returning to the introduction to this section, when a student asks a supervisor 'how many should I get?' the response is most likely to be, 'how many can you get?' By and large most undergraduate research is carried out using limited samples – we have already intimated that this inappropriateness will be partly due to unrepresentativeness. Now we can add to this the issue of small sample sizes. Practical constraints and the nature of this kind of research make it unlikely that the average student project will have anything like a suitable sample size but then, arguably, given the function of this work at undergraduate level, does it really matter?

Most undergraduate research is carried out for the purposes of demonstration, illustration and the gaining of experience and it is accepted that samples will be neither rep-resentative nor sufficiently large. What is important, however, is that students understand this, that they are aware that findings must be expressed with reservations and that whatever is noted about the sample is unlikely to be true of the population as a whole (see Box 5.6).

Box 5.6

## A Closer Look At . . .

## Limitations of research

No piece of research is ever perfect and the researchers will always have some doubts about the accuracy or relevance of their findings. They may not always say so and many a government department or political party has fudged statistics to suit their own ends. In undergraduate research, however, one of the important functions of reporting findings is to demonstrate that you understand the limitations of your work. Whether or not a study has unearthed anything remarkable or even noteworthy is largely irrelevant. What is im-portant, and what you will be assessed on, is the extent to which you displayed initiative, you were objective and systematic, your approach was ethical and that you were aware of the problems and limitations of the research.

Although the findings of this survey indicated extreme attitudes in the area of new police powers of arrest, the process whereby respondents were drawn raises con-cerns about how far these results can be generalised: undoubtedly a local sampling effect was present and analysis of the characteristics of participants in-dicated that four important ethnic groups were not represented. Nor were there any females. Furthermore, given that the sample size was limited to ten, it is clear that findings are likely to be relevant only to this group and not typical of the popu-lation as a whole. The range of attitudes expressed within the sample suggests that the issue generates many viewpoints within the population and that to reliably estimate attitudes here would require a truly random sample of 1,000 participants.

When the purpose of a study is to test specific hypotheses, as in an experimental design, most of the previous discussion on sample sizes applies. Thus, if we aimed to compare two groups on some measure (an occupational psychology major might compare a group of unskilled workers with a managerial group on some measure of psychological health, with a view to exploring a hypothesis about the relationship between occupational status and wellbeing), we would wish to ensure that both samples were truly representative of their populations, both in terms of number and type. Consequently, all the sampling issues which we have already considered above – variability, level of confidence, etc. – are relevant here. We would want to demonstrate that when we support or reject a hypothesis (e.g., that there is no significant difference on a measure of psychological wellbeing between a sample of unskilled workers and a sample of managerial workers), this finding is true of the population as a whole, and not merely of the particular groups we sampled in our study. In practice, however, few researchers – and certainly not undergraduates – will draw the large numbers of individuals for their study required by conventional sampling guidelines. Instead, they consider the amount of variability in the population, the type of analytical test which will be used to determine whether or not an effect is present (some tests are better than others) and they defend this in terms of **power**. There are calculations available to determine precisely how powerful a research procedure is – similar in many ways to our earlier calculations for estimating sample size in survey research – and power can be explained simply as the extent to which a procedure or a specific test will correctly identify a significant difference (or effect) where one really exists. This is expressed as a probability value, and is a measure of reliability: the likelihood that our findings are true, and that they can be replicated. It is not our intention to say much more on the topic at this stage – power calculations can be difficult and currently beyond the scope of what might be expected at an undergraduate level. For a practical look at these issues, Box 5.7 offers an illustration.

Box 5.7

A Closer Look At . . .

# Power, and how some tests are better than others

Some statistical tests are more powerful than others in that, with the same data, one test would demonstrate, for instance, the presence of a significant difference between two measures while another would not. Consider the slightly spurious example (though of personal interest to the authors and those keen on fishing everywhere) of two groups fishing for trout on the same stretch of a waterway, but using different lures. The Morpeth to Newcastle Tyne waterway team are fishing with multi-coloured lures, while the Forth and Clyde canal team are using monochromatic bait. Each member is timed on how long it takes to land the first trout and the average times of each group are compared. Our question is this: if there is a difference between the average catch times (there nearly always is), is this due to a real effect of the different lures, or is this just a chance effect?

For the sake of this example, let's assume the team using the multi-coloured lure took on average 3.4 minutes before landing a catch, whereas the monochrome group took 4.3 minutes. The result of one type of test, the Mann-Whitney $U$-test, indicates that this difference is not sufficiently large to be explained as anything other than a chance event. The result of a more powerful test, such as the Student's $t$-test, indicates that this difference between the average times, based on the number of participants in each group, is too great to be explained away as a purely chance thing, and that the type of lure made a real (statistically significant) difference. Table 5.1 gives the numbers:

Table 5.1   Comparison of the Mann-Whitney $U$-test and the Student's $t$-test on the same data.

| Test | Statistic | Probability ($p$) | Decision |
|------|-----------|-------------------|----------|
| Mann-Whitney test | $U = 25$; $n1 = n2 = 10$ | 0.063 | not significant |
| $t$-test | $t(18) = 2.28$ | 0.028 | significant |

Clearly then, demonstrating that an effect or an event is present or not is far from being an exact science. As we have been at pains to mention elsewhere, it depends.

An important consideration here is the nature of the data. In the present example, the data are normally distributed, making the $t$-test the more appropriate test. In a situation like this the Mann-Whitney $U$-test is considered to be only about 95% as powerful as its counterpart. However, were the data to deviate too far from normality (see Part 4, where the normal distribution is discussed at length), the $t$-test becomes less powerful, in that the probability of detecting a real difference when such a difference exists declines. Increasingly, when data are **skewed**, the Mann-Whitney $U$-test becomes more appropriate, and more powerful.

Note: as with all our statistical examples, the data set on which the above analyses are based can be viewed on our companion website as *MKt&U.dat*.

It is sufficient for us to make the point that if a study uses only 10 participants in each comparison group we would be less likely to demonstrate the existence of an effect (a difference between the groups, for instance) than if each of our samples comprised 20 or even 30 participants. Similarly, as we have suggested in Box 5.7, research using one particular kind of test, such as the $t$-test, will be more likely to detect an effect where one exists, than if another kind of test were used on the same data, such as the Mann-Whitney $U$-test. Put simply, a study which uses a larger sample will be more powerful than one based on small numbers; a study which uses one kind of statistical test can be more powerful than one which uses a different form of analysis or, to be more accurate, a study which uses the most appropriate test for the characteristics of the data will be the most effective.

Again, in practice, research which aims to test hypotheses can be carried out with relatively small sample sizes – as a general rule it would be nice to maintain 20 to 30 participants per group, but in fact most statistical tests will allow analyses to be carried out using smaller numbers, and group sizes of 10 or so are not uncommon. However, as sample sizes decline, the chances of correctly demonstrating an effect are reduced. See Part 5 for illustrations of some of the common forms of analysis and Box 5.8 for an illustration of the above discussion.

Box 5.8

A Closer Look At . . .

# Power and sample size

Consider a study in the field of organisational psychology, in which we examine differences in psychological health between skilled and managerial workers. We may have postulated that managerial workers earn more, have a better lifestyle and have more interesting work than the skilled workforce. Consequently, on a self-rating scale on which individuals are asked to rate their perceived level of wellbeing over the previous 12 months, we might hypothesise that average scores of psychological health will be significantly higher for the managerial group than the skilled group. (By significant we mean that the difference is sufficiently large, or consistent, so as not to be explained away as a purely chance effect. See Part 4 for the relevant discussion on probability and statistical significance.)

If we worked with two extremely small samples – say, 10 managers and 10 skilled workers – and observed average health ratings of 5.0 and 4.2 respectively, we might feel that with such small numbers of participants this difference is not meaningful, and could well be explained away by all manner of things. And in fact, if we applied one of the standard difference tests used in these circumstances, this impression would be confirmed.

Table 5.2 provides much of the relevant information on our study – it shows the average health measures being compared; it shows the $t$-value (a transformed measure of the magnitude of this difference) and it indicates the probability of obtaining this difference. (We have omitted measures of variation in the interests of clarity in this example.) By convention, unless a significance value is 0.05 or less, then we accept that there is no *real* effect and that any observed difference can be explained by chance, or some form of error.

In the present example, the difference between 5.0 and 4.2 is not significant. Consider now what happens when a larger sample – say, 20 – is drawn from each population of managers and skilled workers. The observed difference in wellbeing scores may stay the same, but when this difference holds true across a larger number of individuals, the outcome of our study is very different indeed (see Table 5.3).

A final point remains to be made concerning the relationship between significance and power. If in this current example we had obtained only 5 participants in each group,

Table 5.2    Comparison between mean wellbeing scores of managers and skilled workers, showing $t$-value and exact probability ($N = 20$).

| Group | n | Mean (average) score | t-value | Probability (p) |
|---|---|---|---|---|
| Managers | 10 | 5.0 | | |
| Skilled | 10 | 4.2 | 1.37 | 0.207 |

Table 5.3    Comparison between mean wellbeing scores of managers and skilled workers, showing $t$-value and exact probability ($N = 40$).

| Group | n | Mean (average) score | t-value | Probability (p) |
|---|---|---|---|---|
| Managers | 20 | 5.0 | | |
| Skilled | 20 | 4.2 | 2.31 | 0.027 |

$\rightarrow$

yet comparisons of wellbeing yielded a statistically significant difference, we would not be convinced that this finding was particularly reliable – with such small numbers, many factors could have contributed to this finding, such as individual differences and error. We would argue that, significant or not, this was not an especially powerful test because the sample size was so small. We return to this issue in the section on Type I and Type II errors in Part 4.

### 5.7.3    Sample size and variability

As the roughest rule of thumb we have suggested that, in an experimental study in which different groups are compared on some measure, a minimum sample (group) size should be 10. We chose this lower limit purely on the pragmatic grounds that the interpretation of many statistical tests becomes impossible when sample sizes are lower. Imposing a limit like this, however, can be of use to the undergraduate trying to determine participant numbers since with each new variable, or condition within a variable, numbers will have to increase. Consider the following example:

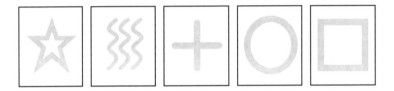

In a study on parapsychology it is believed that the correct identification of a sequence of hidden Zener cards will be determined by personality type. In a quasi-experimental design, the dependent variable is the score (number of correct identifications) on the Zener task while the independent variable is personality type, as defined by an appropriate test. In this instance there are two conditions in the independent variable – introverted and extraverted, as determined by a cut-off score on the Eysenck Personality Questionnaire (Eysenck & Eysenck, 1975).

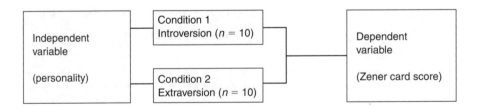

In this example, with only two conditions, if we stick to our informal rule of 10 participants per condition, we would need a total participant pool of 20 for our study, just about sufficient for a conventional difference test. Suppose though that our exploration of the literature had raised the unusual suggestion that astrological sign might be linked to the ability to read hidden Zener cards: our study would change accordingly.

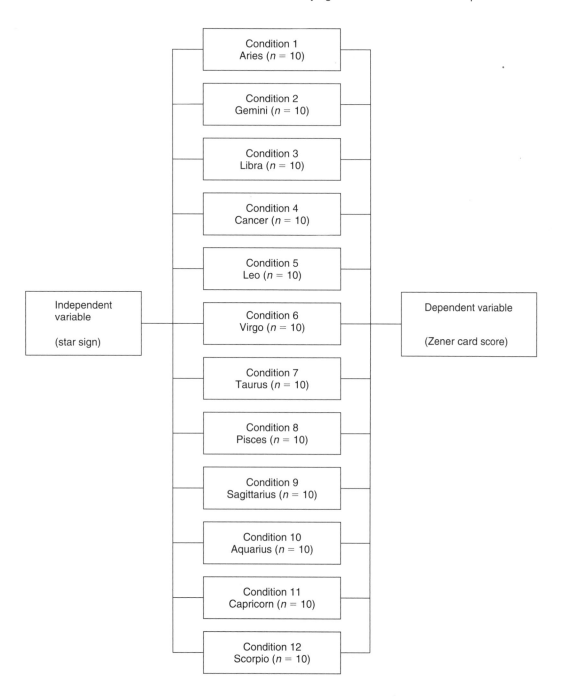

In this scenario, following our 10-participants-per-condition guideline, we would require 120 (10 × 12) participants. And if we should decide that both these variables (personality and astrological sign) interact in terms of determining a Zener card score, then our participant pool expands to an unwieldly 240, as the truncated example below indicates.

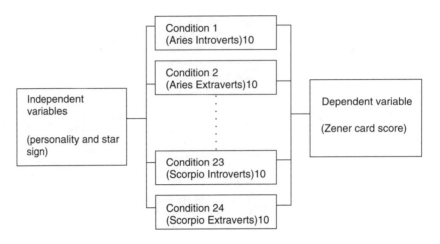

This particular quasi-experiment is in danger of spiralling out of the novice researcher's control, and should we decide that gender may also be an important variable here we approach participant numbers which will be unavailable to the average undergraduate (480). Clearly our novice would have been ill-advised to get into this pickle in the first place, but it is a common fault among psychology undergraduates, especially in their early years, to be too ambitious – to design too many variables into a study, or to attempt to measure the effects of too many conditions. The solution most favoured among the student body is simply to reduce group sizes and our hapless researcher might well consider that 5 participants per group would be adequate, or 4, or even 3. The problem here should be obvious: reducing group size increases the effects of individual differences within groups, and these individual differences eventually obscure any real influence of the independent variables. With small numbers, any differences between conditions are likely to be due to specific individual characteristics and little else. In terms of analysis, small group sizes are problematic and any apparent statistical effects are likely to be completely spurious.

The solution to this problem, and the one most likely to be offered by tutors and supervisors, is to firstly limit the number of independent variables in a study. While it is true that most events will have many causes, it is always possible to identify and isolate a finite number of key factors to study. Inspection of the literature on a given issue will usually offer guidance and most tutors will often advise as to what would be manageable.

A second guideline is to keep down the number of conditions within a variable. It is often possible to categorise conditions into more manageable numbers – astrological signs, for instance, can be grouped into the four elemental categories of air signs, earth signs, fire signs and water signs. Alternatively, in the presence of a large number of conditions, we might select just two to compare. If people vary according to star sign, any two signs ought to do.

It remains to say that, while most undergraduate studies will not be particularly powerful (in that sampling procedures will be convenient rather than conforming to the requirements of probability research, and sample sizes will be small), it is still expected in any report that these issues be raised; the students should make it clear that the limitations of their particular study are well understood. It is also worth mentioning that by the time the junior researcher embarks upon funded research there will be an expectation of a clear statement of how powerful (or not) this research is. After all, if someone is paying you good money he or she has a right to know how useful (accurate, relevant, valid, powerful) your findings are likely to be. For more discussion of number of participants, review Box 5.9.

Box 5.9

Practicalities . . .

# How many participants?

It remains for us now to stick our necks out – if your research is to be survey based, how many participants should you aim for in your sample? A minimum of 30 is needed, but preferably more. Less than this and, even in the context of an undergraduate study, you might as well not bother, unless the intention is to conduct a case study, in which case the sample size is determined by the characteristics of the case itself. In hypothesis testing, where experimental conditions will be compared, group sizes ought to be about 10. This number should be tempered by the number of conditions you have, by the variability of whatever it is you are measuring and the size of the difference you might expect. As we stated earlier, whenever a tutor is asked how many participants should be sought, the answer is usually 'it depends'.

## 5.8 Secondary research

It is a common, if not self-evident, expectation among researchers that they will be involved in all stages of their research – from the initial identification of issues, through the design and implementation of a study, to the analysis of data and reporting of findings. While not common in psychology, in the broader social sciences there often exists the opportunity to base one's research on work which has been carried out by others, quite legitimately, incurring a huge saving in time, effort and money – **secondary research**. Several agencies, primarily but not exclusively governmental, conduct regular surveys designed to review the nature of society and chart the changing state of the nation. The National Census is one example, providing 10-yearly snapshots of the UK going back to 1851. The General Household Survey (GHS) is another, an annual survey carried out by the Social Survey Division of the Office for National Statistics, and providing information on some 10,000 households across the country. Typical information found in the GHS concerns income, housing, economic activity, education and health. A survey like this is a huge resource and often provides a basis for preparatory work in primary research. Secondary data also serve as a major teaching platform and many readers of this book will be currently working with experimental or survey databases (created by other people, or even made up by a tutor) as part of their undergraduate training to develop their own analytical skills. However, the use of secondary sources is not without its problems, for while there are some clear advantages to working in this way, there are disadvantages also.

## 5.9 Advantages of secondary research

Access to official secondary information often incurs some cost, in terms of fees to the relevant research or publishing body. However such fees rarely come anywhere near the costs of carrying out the primary research. Where time is important, it is obviously quicker to consult information which already exists than to design, carry out and analyse a primary study of your own, providing of course the secondary information meets your needs.

From a teaching or training point of view, secondary data provide an opportunity to practise important research and analytical procedures on a large body of information normally out of reach for the undergraduate – as we have previously intimated, primary undergraduate research often involves very small samples; what luxury to work with a sample of some 10,000 individuals!

Secondary data can provide a useful basis for the initial exploration of a population. When samples are large, as they usually are in big social surveys, they often offer an insight into the character of a group which will be studied later, as part of a primary research project (e.g., we can discover important things about the distribution of age, occupation and marital status of a population, or we can determine the political, religious and ethnic structures of a population).

Although primarily descriptive in nature, secondary information will often lead to the identification of social issues which might be more intensively investigated in subsequent primary research (e.g., if one of the large-scale social surveys indicated that people in the north made more demands on health and welfare services than did those in the south, this could initiate further research into health, education or economic issues for the different regions).

## 5.10 Disadvantages of secondary research

Because the studies which provide secondary information were designed and carried out by someone else, it follows then that they were intended to meet that someone else's own particular needs. This is probably the biggest drawback of using secondary information, since the original research might not have asked the questions *you* would have liked to ask, or might not have sampled from all the groups you would have liked to look at. Having said this, many of the major social surveys are sufficiently broad to be applicable to a wide variety of studies but it will always be the case that the needs of a particular researcher will never be fully met by secondary information.

Although most secondary information is usually accompanied by explanatory notes (a **codebook**, detailing what questions were asked and how responses were encoded), it will not always be clear how decisions were made when assigning categories or summarising data. The example below, in which participants are asked to classify themselves on an index of perceived psychological wellbeing, might well reach the secondary researcher as shown:

WELL: Psychological wellbeing

MISSING VALUES:     −9

VALUE LABELS: WELL

1 = LOW

2 = MEDIUM

3 = HIGH

Here, all the researcher knows is that psychological wellbeing was classified into three categories, and unless categorisation was based on some generally accepted and understood system, he has no way of knowing whether wellness covers chronic conditions of anxiety and depression, or whether the categories relate only to popularized ideas of psychological/emotional health. Nor will it be clear whether scores were based on self-rating or on some other type of measure, such as a diagnostician's evaluation or an objective test (see Box 5.10 for a fuller example of codebook information).

Finally, a rather obvious problem with secondary data is that by the time they reach the new researcher they are (often) no longer current. The time factor involved in collecting and analysing primary data means that some survey data are out of date by as much as a year before the secondary analyst gets hold of them. For undergraduates the problem is even worse since poor, under-funded departments will often only acquire older (and cheaper) survey data sets for their students. It would not be unusual for students to be working with material which is as much as 10 years out of date – hardly likely to offer a contemporary picture of "living in the UK".

 **A Closer Look At . . .**

# Codebook information

When the information from an original study becomes available to later researchers, it is known as secondary data. These later researchers are therefore presented with what is in effect a *fait accompli* – the primary study has been carried out, data gathered, variables re-coded and so on. There is almost no opportunity for a later researcher to modify any of the information from the original study, other than by further summarising or re-coding. However, so that use can be made of these secondary data, codebooks are usually provided which comprise information on all the measurements taken, the questions asked and the types of responses generated by questionnaires. The following is an example of what is found in a typical codebook.

List of variables

| Name | Position | Label |
|------|----------|-------|
| HEDGE1 | 1 | SPECIES OF HEDGEHOG, EITHER EUROPEAN OR LONG-EARED |
| HEDGE2 | 2 | ENVIRONMENT IN WHICH HEDGEHOGS ARE OBSERVED |
| PROB1 | 3 | MAZE-RUNNING SPEED OF HEDGEHOGS ON MAZE 1 |
| PROB2 | 4 | MAZE-RUNNING SPEED OF HEDGEHOGS ON MAZE 2 |
| PERS | 5 | PERSONALITY OF HEDGEHOG SAMPLE |
| WELL | 6 | PSYCHOLOGICAL WELLBEING OF HEDGEHOG SAMPLE |

| | | |
|------|------|------|
| HEDGE1 | | SPECIES OF HEDGEHOG, EITHER EUROPEAN OR LONG-EARED |
| MISSING VALUES | | −1 |
| VALUE LABEL | −2 | NA |
| | 1 | EUROPEAN HEDGEHOG |
| | 5 | LONG-EARED HEDGEHOG |
| | 7 | BROOM, MISTAKEN FOR HEDGEHOG |

Codebook information of this type is generally useful and sometimes essential in explaining the contents of databases which are likely to contain abbreviations and coding understood only by the primary researcher. For instance, without this explanation, who would ever have guessed that HEDGE1 provided profile information on the sample, such that cases identified by the number 1 referred to European hedgehogs, while 2 referred to the long-eared variety. However, codebook explanations are not always clear – we do not know, for instance, why there is a gap between 1 and 5 in the categories of hedgehog. Does this mean that there are other varieties which (for reasons not explained anywhere) did not feature in this particular study? Or is it the case that in order to minimise mistakes in entering large amounts of data the researcher chose to select numerical values which were not only quantitatively quite different from one another, but also widely spaced on conventional number keyboards? (This latter explanation is often, though not always, the reason for the apparently odd choice of numbers used to assign categories.) And then, what do brooms have to do with hedgehogs?

(*Note*: codebook information is often supplied as a hard copy accompaniment to a data file. It is also usually available as part of the file itself and can be reviewed or printed off to suit the researcher.)

## Review

Chapter 5 has introduced a key issue in research, that of sampling. Different procedures for obtaining participants have been discussed, the vexed question of sample size has been addressed and practical advice has been offered on procedural matters. The chapter which follows advances the research process to the data-gathering stage.

## Suggested further reading

Bryman, A. (2001). *Social research methods*. Oxford: Oxford University Press.

This is a useful general text covering most aspects of social research methods. Chapter 4 in particular offers extensive coverage of sampling issues.

de Vaus, D. A. (1996). *Surveys in social research* (4th ed.). London: University College London Press.

This text is devoted entirely to the design and implementation of survey-based research. The presentation is highly detailed but covers everything the undergraduate might ever need to know about sampling, sample size and questionnaire design.

Sarantakos, S. (1998). *Social research* (2nd ed.). London: Macmillan Press.

Good general coverage is offered on sampling procedures. Various formulae are offered for the calculation of sample size.

# 6  Collecting data

Key Issues

Chapter 6 is the second of our procedural chapters and is concerned with how to gather information – the data which will allow us to answer a research question, explore an issue or test a hypothesis. The first part of the chapter deals with ethical matters and considers the type of participant you can reasonably expect to take part in your research; issues concern vulnerable groups, deception, research involving animals and the key features of informed consent. Since it is an expectation that all undergraduate research conforms to appropriate ethical standards, we offer specific advice on how participants should be treated at all stages of the research process. We also provide a typical consent form which can be used as a template for your own research.

The second part of the chapter deals with questionnaires, a data-gathering instrument which features prominently in much undergraduate research. We consider the different ways in which questionnaires can be designed, we discuss different response scales, along with their advantages and disadvantages, and we provide advice on the various stages involved in their development.

The concluding part of this chapter deals with standardised tests; many of you will consider using existing tests of personality, attitude, ability or some other measure as part of your study. In this event there is much that needs to be understood about psychological tests and we offer detailed discussion on the evolution of tests, their characteristics and how they should be administered and interpreted. Key points include:

- carrying out of ethical research
- informed consent
- questionnaire design
- response scales – closed-ended, open-ended, rating scales, Likert scales, semantic differential
- the use of standardised tests
- test norms
- test reliability
- test validity

## 6.1  Carrying out ethical research

It is important to be aware that, before you can inflict a study on an unsuspecting public, you are bound by certain constraints on your behaviour – especially those concerning your willing participants. Aside from the implicit moral obligation of any psychological researcher to prevent distress among those individuals who give up their time to help out, there exist a number of guidelines which should always be considered in the design and implementation of any study. Developed over many years of research, and based on broadly accepted moral, behavioural and ethical values, these guidelines have been produced by the various overseeing bodies and are available in full in their many publications, relating both to human and (where appropriate) animal participants.

A summary of the main points of these guidelines is offered below and students should note that, while they are only guidelines, most supervisors would decline to supervise an undergraduate project if they are not adhered to. Moreover, as we appear to be evolving into an increasingly sensitive, not to say litigious society, academic institutions are themselves becoming more cautious about the nature of research carried out in their name. In any event, ignoring these points should be considered only in exceptional circumstances, and with the strongest possible justification since, by and large, they reflect powerful human values and not simply professional ones.

### 6.1.1    Sampling

Where participants are to be drawn from specific populations (workers in an organisation, patients in a hospital, pupils in primary schools), you should be aware of any possible disruption to normal institutional functioning which your study may cause. It is therefore important that approval and authorisation be sought from appropriate individuals or bodies before your work commences. Indeed, some institutions (e.g., hospital boards) require research proposals to pass their own form of ethics committee before approval is given. Furthermore, any reporting on the findings of a study must include details of all procedures used to obtain participants, to ensure the consent of participants and to seek the approval of relevant bodies.

### 6.1.2    Apparatus

*Apparatus* refers to any instrument, device or questionnaire which is used to aid the collection of data. In the case of standard equipment, such as a tachistoscope (a device for back-projecting images onto an enclosed screen for pre-determined durations), it is important that all operations are fully understood and the regulations governing use are fully adhered to. In the case of standard questionnaires and psychometric tests, the instructions for administration and scoring must be followed. Further, no such instrument should be used without a thorough awareness of norms, limitations, applications, reliability and validity studies, such that in no way can participants be disadvantaged by your lack of familiarity with the manual. (This issue is covered in detail later in this chapter.)

In the case of non-standard equipment, details of any unusual features should be included, insofar as they have a bearing on the design of the study; otherwise it is enough to state that, for instance, in a maze-running experiment, 'a maze was constructed comprising an equal number of left and right hand turns'. In the case of non-standard questionnaires, a full copy, with rationale for each element, must also be included as part of the report. Undergraduates often fail to do this, to their cost, since it is often the case that findings will be interpreted in terms of the procedures used to develop and score items. The reason for so much detail is not simply replicability, although this is often important, but also to ensure that ethical standards are maintained. If a researcher is unable to provide such depth of information or, worse, is unwilling to do so, then the research is clearly suspect.

Plate 6.1    Various mazes can be constructed for laboratory rats to explore, differing in complexity.
*Source*: Science Photo Library/Will & Deni McIntyre

### 6.1.3    Procedural issues

Participation in any psychological study is normally voluntary and you must ensure that participants are aware of this, and that they are able to withdraw *at any time* during a study, without prejudice (i.e., without any fear of sanction and with an assurance of no negative consequences of withdrawal), a right which extends even beyond the data-collection stage. At no time must you coerce or use deceit (which is not in itself a part of the study) to obtain co-operation. In the event that some type of deception forms part of the experimental manipulation, you must ensure that participants are fully debriefed (i.e., told exactly what has happened and why).

If a situation is encountered in which participants are not able to provide **informed consent** themselves, steps must be taken to protect the individual: if people with neural damage, young children, or individuals exhibiting other forms of cognitive disorder are to be approached as participants, consent must be obtained from those who have their interests at heart. These could be relatives, parents, carers or medical staff. And even then, unless there is sound reason for pursuing a particular research interest, such individuals should not be used in a study. Increasingly, academic departments are now requiring participants to sign a consent form, stating that they fully understand the purpose of the study in which they are participating and that they are aware of their rights, both legally and morally. Box 6.1 offers an example of a typical consent form which might reasonably be used as a template for much undergraduate research.

If the data collected in a study are to be kept confidential (as they must be), you must take steps to ensure that not only is this so, but that it is seen to be so, especially by your participants – people who have willingly agreed to participate in your research in the belief that they will be treated fairly and with respect. This is especially true if the data might be considered private and personal to participants. Again, reported research is now expected to include details of how the confidentiality of responses has been ensured.

Box 6.1

# What should be in a consent form

It is now an expectation of all psychology departments that, before their students embark on testing or administration of questionnaires for a research study, they obtain the informed consent of participants, usually through an appropriate consent form. The purpose of such a form is to ensure that anyone agreeing to participate in research does so knowing precisely what their involvement will entail, and on the understanding that their rights to confidentiality and anonymity will be ensured. Many departments will have their own preferences for the wording and structure of consent forms, but for those of you who will be expected to devise their own, some guidelines on what should go into a consent form follow:

- Information about you, the researcher – your name, your status (e.g., a level 1 undergraduate), your host department and host institution.

- Contact information – participants should have a contact address or phone number in the event that they have concerns about the research, or about their rights. Normally the contact individual would be your supervisor or a member of the departmental ethics committee which approved the research.

- Information about the nature of the research – a description of what the study is about and a statement of aims should be given. The issue of clarity and level of language is important here since many people will not understand technical or complex terms and the age and level of sophistication of the target population should always be taken into consideration. Explaining that a study is investigating aspects of field dependence/field independence would certainly baffle most people, whereas explaining that the research is looking at the different ways in which people see the world might go further in informing participants what the study is about.

- The nature of the participants' experience – that they will be taking part in an experiment which will involve looking at a series of images, that they will be discussing issues in a group situation, that they will be completing a questionnaire on a number of issues.

- Sensitive issues – if any element of the experience might raise sensitive issues for the participant this should be made clear.

- The time demands of the study – you must be honest; if you feel that explaining the study will involve staring at scores of images on a computer screen for two hours would put participants off, this is no justification for claiming otherwise. Perhaps the design can be changed!

- Information on what will be done with the data – who will have access to it (and who will not).

- An assurance of the participant's anonymity and the confidentiality of all data collected as part of the research.

- Confirmation that the participant's involvement in the research is voluntary and that he or she may withdraw at any stage.

- An agreement check box or space for initialisation – if the participant is required to sign as an indication of consent this will conflict with the assurance of anonymity.

- Contact or information details – if a study is likely to raise issues over which participants might have concerns, contact details of individuals or organisations who can provide further information should be offered. For example, if you intend to explore people's understanding of phobias, you would be expected to include information or helpline numbers for the National Phobics Society, or a local health education centre.

**A sample consent form:**

Thank you for agreeing to take part in this study.

My name is (*name*) and I am (*status; department; university or college*).

This study is investigating (*nature and aims of study*).

It will involve (*nature of participant's experience; the time demands of the study; sensitive issues*).

Please note that your participation in this study is entirely anonymous and voluntary, and that you may withdraw at any point. All the information gathered during the course of this study will remain confidential and will be seen only by (*state who will have access*).

If you have any concerns about this study or would like more information, please contact (*contact person and contact number*).

If, having read and understood all of the above, you agree to participate in this study, please place a tick in the box below.

☐

**Optional:**

If you have any concerns about issues raised during this study, please contact any of the information lines below:

(*contact details*)

As a general rule, participants should never be placed under undue stress. However, should induced stress form a part of a study, advance preparations must be made in terms of controlling such stress, and for preventing or dealing with possible catastrophic consequences (both physiological and emotional). Generally speaking no undergraduate would be permitted to conduct a study along these lines nor, unless in exceptional circumstances, would an experienced researcher. The days of Milgram, in which participants were placed under great personal stress in the false belief that they were inflicting pain on others, have gone! (Note: references for both the British Psychological Society [BPS] and American Psychological Association [APA] sets of ethical guidelines are provided at the end of this book. These should be consulted prior to the commencement of any undergraduate study.)

### 6.1.4 General

All of the above are merely guidelines to enable you to conduct yourself and your research in an ethical, humane and fair manner. They should not be regarded as constraints, rather as a series of reminders that when you carry out a piece of research you are dealing, not with abstract sources of data, but with real people who have rights of privacy, sympathy, and expectations of fairness of treatment to which all of us are entitled.

While most departments, and certainly most supervisors, are keen to encourage initiative and creativity among their students, it is likely that ethical considerations will increasingly be an overriding factor in determining the type of research which is granted approval. Vulnerable groups of any kind (children, hospital inmates, prison inmates) are unlikely to feature among 'approved' populations for study. Topics which may prove stressful, disturbing or anxiety provoking to participants will not generally be approved. The use of standardised tests which might force vulnerable participants to confront difficult issues would not be allowed. In addition, students are now required to present to all potential participants a consent form in which their rights (both moral and legal) are clearly defined (see Box 6.1). There will inevitably be exceptions to these general guidelines – some undergraduates will have legitimate access to special groups (perhaps through working in some counselling capacity with a socially vulnerable group), some may be allowed to participate in ongoing departmental research and there may be other circumstances in which a normally prohibited topic may be approved. By and large, though, there will be real restrictions on what an undergraduate will be allowed to tackle. The point to be remembered is that, in most instances, undergraduate research is for demonstration and assessment purposes, and for the gaining of experience. Consequently, deviating from any of the guidelines governing ethical research will rarely be justified at this level. Box 6.2 offers a review of ethical guidelines.

Box 6.2

## A Closer Look At . . .

# Ethical guidelines

All psychological research today must adhere to a set of ethical guidelines designed to protect the rights and preserve the dignity of participants, while at the same time ensuring the safety of the researcher. In its most recent publication, the BPS working party on ethical practices has produced a set of minimum guidelines (BPS, 2004) which it believes should represent best practice in psychological research. In addition, every psychology department today has in place its own recommendations governing research at all levels, from undergraduate to postgraduate. Below we offer a checklist of questions you should ask of your own research. Answers to these questions will determine whether a study will be conducted in an ethical manner, with due concern for the welfare of participants.

### A. Matters of openness and the rights of the individual

1. Will participants be informed that their involvement in a study is entirely voluntary?
2. Will it be explained that participants are free to withdraw from the study at any time, both during its conduct and after its completion, without prejudice?
3. Will it be made clear to participants that their contribution to any part of the study will be totally confidential and that it will be impossible for any individuals to be identified by any party not directly involved in the research?
4. In the event that individual contributions will not be anonymous (perhaps the identity of participants must be retained in order to match different scales) how can participants be assured of confidentiality beyond the requirements of the research design?
5. Will it be made clear what participation in the research will be like? In particular will participants be informed about time demands, about the nature of any activities required of them or about the type of questions they might be asked as part of the study? This is especially important in cases where test or interview items are designed to explore personal or sensitive issues.

6. If a study is questionnaire based, will it be made clear that participants need not answer questions they do not want to answer?

7. Will participants be invited to complete a consent form in which all the points mentioned above are fully explained?

The point of the above guidelines is to ensure that involvement in any study is based on the principle of informed consent; that is, with the full knowledge of what the study is about, with an understanding of what the experience will be like, and with an awareness of the steps taken to protect rights and dignity.

## B. Matters concerning special and vulnerable groups

8. In the event that participants are unable to give informed consent (the sample may include very young children, or individuals who have difficulty in understanding or communicating), what steps have been taken to ensure the informed consent of those responsible for their welfare? (These might be the parents or teachers of children, or the carers of other disadvantaged groups.)

9. If a study will involve members of a school, an element of the health service, a community organisation or a commercial business, what steps have been taken to obtain authorised approval to carry out the particular research?

10. If a sample to be used in research might be described as vulnerable – insofar as participants might respond negatively to questioning or to items on a measurement scale what steps have been taken to deal with potentially catastrophic situations? (Confronting a group of phobic individuals with probing questions about their fears could produce a range of negative reactions from feelings of discomfort to uncontrollable panic attacks.)

Research involving special or vulnerable groups raises a variety of important issues for the researcher. Whenever children are involved in research our society is increasingly concerned about protecting their wellbeing and currently, aside from the need to obtain permission from parents and teachers and school officials, the researcher will require to be vetted by an appropriate criminal records authority – the Criminal Records Bureau (CRB) in England and Wales, and the Scottish Criminal Records Office (SCRO) in Scotland. Most departments now have in place procedures for interacting with the appropriate authority. Moreover, depending on the nature of the research, some studies will require approval by the ethics committee of the relevant education authority.

Research in the health service carries with it additional problems in that now all studies must be scrutinised by an appropriate ethics committee, arranged through the newly formed (at the time of going to press) Central Office for Research Ethics (COREC). Moreover, research within any type of organisation risks disruption of care, productivity and social structures and the researcher will be required to take steps to minimise such disruption.

With vulnerable groups especial care is required to protect participants from all forms of harm. If there is a danger of individuals becoming distressed during the course of a study, safeguards must be set in place to provide counselling or therapy and the contact numbers of appropriate helplines should be made available as an additional support for the research participants.

## C. Deception

11. Is there an intention to mislead participants about the purpose, or about any part of the study?

12. If deception features in a study, will participants be fully debriefed on completion of their involvement? Will they be informed that they have a right to withdraw from the study following debriefing?

The use of deception in research is a controversial one, in which the need to research a particular issue must be balanced against all the points made previously about informed consent and the rights of the individual. Within the context of undergraduate research, though, the issue will almost never arise since, with research at this level, a need to know will never be sufficient to outweigh the need for openness.

### D. Research with animals

Non-human research is unlikely to feature at all at undergraduate level and for this reason we merely note that (rightly) a number of rigorous and legally binding safeguards are in place governing the care and welfare of all animals used in research. The BPS offers advice for anyone planning research of this type.

## 6.2 Using questionnaires in research

### 6.2.1 Questionnaire design – how to get information

By this stage in our research, we have hopefully decided on the issue we are going to explore, we know whom we are going to use and we have decided on the key components of our hypotheses. We also know what kind of information we want from our participants, the precise data needed to test our hypotheses and to ultimately explore the research issue in question. So how are we going to get this information?

Some research designs will use standardised instruments to generate information (health questionnaires, stress measures, personality tests, etc.); others will rely on an outcome measure of a laboratory experiment (reaction times, frequency of correct responses to stimuli, or changes in decision times). Many designs, though, will require custom-made procedures to gather information, as researchers devise questionnaires to assess attitudes to numerous issues, to obtain information on what people do in various social situations, to measure opinion on a wide range of social and political issues or to explore the distribution of different categories of person in the population. Gathering information of this sort might appear, on the face of it, straightforward – they are all simple question-and-answer scenarios, whether they involve interviews or questionnaires. The reality is somewhat more complicated in that the development of a 'good' questionnaire is not just a skill but almost an art in itself. The following sections attempt to make the process a little easier, explaining the pitfalls and offering solutions.

Probably the simplest rule of information gathering is 'if you want to know something, ask', and, by and large, this is the most useful rule to follow when designing a questionnaire or interview schedule. Just ask your participants to tell you what you want to know. Most people are honest, disingenuous and, once they have agreed to participate in a study, usually willing and co-operative. Unfortunately, a common perception of psychology is one of a somewhat sneaky profession, relying on methods of deception and misdirection for its information. Even among students of the discipline, there is a view that participants have to be tricked in some way into giving honest, objective responses and, unfortunately, such a view will only continue to encourage the sense of suspicion and mistrust directed at elements of the profession by outsiders. Such a lamentable state of affairs has its origins in the type of research allowed before guidelines were established by the psychological societies and various educational and medical associations which govern the activities of their members. Contemporary researchers now frown on the needless use of deceptive techniques (see the earlier section on ethics). In most instances – with certain qualifiers – the direct approach is best: if you want to know something, ask. The qualifiers are important, though.

The general rule of *ask and ye shall be answered* holds true most of the time. But sometimes the nature of response can be influenced by who does the asking and how the asking is done. Consider the following question:

Have you ever, at any time in your life, committed a crime?

This is an apparently simple question, if asked by a social researcher guaranteeing absolute confidentiality. Imagine the nature of response if the same question were asked by a serving police officer conducting research into criminal behaviour among undergraduates. So the *who* of a question is important and what every researcher must ask him or herself is: 'will the fact that *I* am asking a particular question affect the response?'

The other major qualifier is the *how* of a question. The example above (Have you ever, at any time in your life, committed a crime?) can only generate either a Yes or No response. Modifying the question to . . .

What crimes, no matter how small or insignificant, have you ever committed in your life?

. . . is likely to produce a very different class of response. Aside from the fact that this could be described as a leading question (it assumes people do commit crime) the asker has no control over the type and quantity of response. Anything from a 'How dare you . . .' to a two-page list of guilt-ridden confession is possible. And so, the *how* of a question is an important consideration. The following section describes the most common ways of asking questions and the kinds of responses each produces.

## 6.2.2 Types of scale

There are two broad types of question available to the researcher: one in which the researcher controls the nature of the response and one in which the participant is free to respond in any way. Both have their uses and their disadvantages, and the decision as to which method to apply is one the researcher must make in terms of the context of the research and the quality of the information required.

### Closed-ended questions

**Closed-ended questions** occur where the possible range of responses is pre-determined by the tester. (The opportunity for free response is closed to the person answering.) There are many forms of this type of item, the simplest of which allows for answers on a dichotomous scale.

| Response | *n* | % |
|---|---|---|
| Yes | 120 | 60 |
| No | 80 | 40 |

Table 6.1     Responses of 200 psychology students to an attitude question item: 'Do you like the book?'

### Dichotomous-category scaled items

**Dichotomous scales** are used for questions offering only two answer choices.

> Do you like the book?
>
> Yes          No

The data questions like this produce are in the grand tradition of survey techniques. Participants respond by selecting one or another of the nominally scaled categories and sample data can be presented simply, by referring to the numbers, proportions or percentages of participants who selected each category. Table 6.1 and Figure 6.1 demonstrate the economy and elegance of this approach.

Table 6.1 and Figure 6.1 both display an at-a-glance summary of the data, and the Yes/No distinction represents one of the simplest – and most common – item formats available to researchers. However, care must be taken not to confuse simplicity with impoverishment. True, the Yes/No response options provide only limited information; but when other variables are introduced, the basic dichotomous distinction suddenly becomes quite sophisticated.

Consider the above example when we wish to further analyse the Yes/No choice in terms of the student's gender, or age group, or study options; suddenly we have more than straightforward descriptive data – we can begin to make comparisons and to make inferences. We have now moved, and quite painlessly at that, to a point where the number-devouring statistician begins to take an interest (see Figure 6.2).

The dichotomous example is only one of a variety of closed-response formats. There is no reason why we should stick to just two possible responses when, with most questions we might want to ask, there are invariably several types of response possible.

### Multiple-category scaled items

**Multiple category scales** are used for questions offering three or more choices for the respondent.

Figure 6.1     Responses of 200 psychology students to an attitude question: 'Do you like the book?'

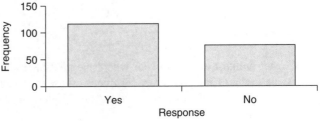

Figure 6.2

Responses of males (*m*) and females (*f*) to a questionnaire item: 'Do you like the book?'

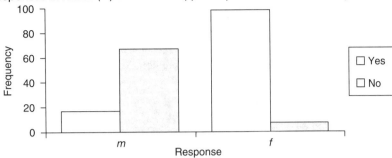

During the current semester, which of the following modules have you enjoyed most?

a. developmental psychology ☐

b. personality and individual differences ☐

c. organisational behaviour ☐

d. research methods ☐

Just as with the previous example, the response categories are independent of one another: that is, there is no relationship of magnitude or order between any one category and another, only of difference – the essence indeed of all nominal scales. Similarly, the display of this type of data is equally straightforward, as Figure 6.3 demonstrates:

Figure 6.3

Frequency of response (*f*) to the question: 'During the current semester which of the following modules have you enjoyed most?'

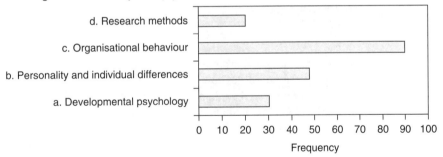

### Rating scales

**Rating scales** are scales which rate some attribute from negative to positive, low to high, weak to strong.

Moving along the continuum of sophistication, but still retaining control of how participants can respond, are scaled items. Instead of requiring participants to choose from a number of response categories which differ in type from one another (as in the dichotomous and multiple examples above), we focus on just one category and require participants to indicate their strength of feeling on the issue. In the 'do you like this book' example, participants could give only the following responses: Yes (they do) or No (they don't).

Interesting as such responses are, they nonetheless obscure the range of feeling within each category; that is, one Yes respondent might be transcendentally ecstatic about the textbook, whereas another might merely be expressing a 'yeah, it's OK' attitude. This kind of internal distinction is lost in fixed-category items, but is accessible in rating scales in which, at its most basic level, nominally scaled responses are transformed into ordinally scaled ones. Consider the re-structuring of the previous Yes/No item.

I am enjoying this book:

not at all                                                                                    tremendously

| 1 | 2 | 3 | 4 | 5 |

Not only does this provide a more detailed picture of how strength of feeling varies across an issue, it also moves the relevant information away from the descriptive and towards the more traditionally quantitative. What this means is that, while in the previous examples participants differed in the type of response they made, now participants differ in terms of, at the very least, the order and even magnitude of response. It also moves the analysis of data towards a format with which many quantitative researchers feel more comfortable: we now have measures of central tendency (average) and variability to play with. In other words, we have **parametric data**.

However, the presentation of more sophisticated data like this should be no less straightforward than for the earlier examples, provided we are familiar with the concepts of sample statistics. Table 6.2 and Figures 6.4 and 6.5 demonstrate this:

Table 6.2     Mean and standard deviation of response to an attitude question.

|  | (mean) | (standard deviation) |
|---|---|---|
| I am enjoying the course: | 3.75 | 0.64 |

The mean provides a measure of central tendency (average) of the responses on the issue and the SD (standard deviation), a measure of how much, on average, scores varied around this value. Part 4 explains these concepts in greater detail. See Figure 6.4.

In Figure 6.4 the median, or middle value, indicated by the dark bar in the middle of the rectangle (some statistical packages represent this as an asterisk *), is approximately 3.7; the interquartile range (the range of scores from the lower quarter to the upper quarter of the distribution of scores) as indicated by the upper and lower limits of the enclosed rectangle, is approximately 3.2 to 4.2; and the overall range of responses, shown by the

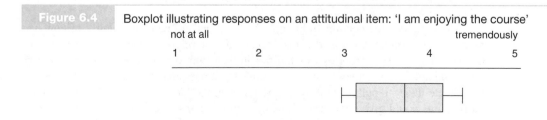

Figure 6.4     Boxplot illustrating responses on an attitudinal item: 'I am enjoying the course'

upper and lower 'whiskers', is approximately 3.0 to 4.4. This particular method of descriptive illustration is termed a boxplot and is further explained in Part 4.

As with our categorical examples, we can of course make our analysis more sophisticated with the inclusion of additional independent profile or participant variables. For instance, we can compare the different genders on the same scale, or different seminar groups, or whatever. The example shown in Figure 6.5 demonstrates this:

**Figure 6.5**   Responses of male and female participants to an attitudinal item: 'I am enjoying the course'

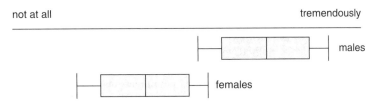

A special variant of scaled items comes to us from Likert (1932). In this approach, participants are asked to provide their level of agreement with a statement. Usually (though not always) corresponding numerical values are absent and appended only later when the researcher converts response categories to their quantitative equivalents. For example, in the following illustration, participants choose one of the agree/disagree categories. The choice made will ultimately place their attitude on some kind of (assumed) linear scale and means that standard deviations and all kinds of comparisons can be produced in the time-honoured manner of parametric statistics, even though by rights this is actually an ordinal scale, with the numbers referring to categories rather than points on a continuum. Many researchers, especially undergraduate ones, choose to ignore this, however, and continue to treat these types of data as if they were interval and hence susceptible to parametric analysis. There is debate on the issue and arguments range from the purists who would gladly have their students shot for treating category data as if they were continuous, to the pragmatists who take the line that 'well, if it's going to show something, why not?' Definitely a case for checking with your supervisor. The de Vaus reference in our suggested further reading section also provides useful background material on different types of scale. (Note: if these statistical terms are foreign to you, the next part of this book introduces basic statistical concepts.)

**Likert scale**

The **Likert scale** is a response scale where the respondent indicates the amount of agreement/disagreement with an issue. It is usual to construct Likert scales with an odd number of response categories (typically five), allowing for a neutral central category.

Psychologists are nice people.

| strongly agree | agree | neutral | disagree | strongly disagree |
|---|---|---|---|---|
| (+2) | (+1) | (0) | (−1) | (−2) |
| 5 | 4 | 3 | 2 | 1 |

Normally, with this type of item, respondents are presented with only the worded response options (*strongly agree, agree*, etc.). The numerical scales are shown to indicate how the researcher might transform actual responses to numerical scale values. Two such transformations are shown here, one in which the middle value is given as a zero on a positive-to-negative scale, and the other in which this value is shown as 3, on a 1-to-5 scale. If the researcher is going to pretend that the scale represents a numerical continuum of values (as in an interval scale) the variant with a zero point is probably the most useful, certainly the most intuitive, since the zero point on the scale represents an absence of opinion or view. Adopting a similar line with the 1-to-5 scale will lead to problems of interpretation, since values of 3 on a series of items might be intuitively interpreted as reflecting a stronger attitude than values of 2 or 1, when in fact scores of 3 represent an absence of opinion or attitude strength. Far better to treat the numbers as categories on an ordinal scale and avoid confusion altogether.

This method whereby actual scale values are obscured can have its advantages. A problem with asking participants to choose a numerical value indicating a particular view or attitude is that sometimes people are unclear as to how their feelings can convert to a number; or they may be reluctant to select extreme values, or they may be unsure of how one scale value differs from the next. Replacing numbers with choice categories (as in the Likert scale) will sometimes alleviate this problem, in addition to making items more user-friendly. A development of this approach in which participants are indirectly placed on some scaled position is the semantic differential, shown below:

### Semantic differential

With **semantic differential** the respondent rates an issue on a number of bipolar categories. The choice of pole can indicate intensity of feeling on the issue.

Research projects are: (choose one of each pair of response options)

| | |
|---|---|
| good | bad |
| easy | difficult |
| useful | worthless |
| challenging | problematic |
| interesting | boring |

In its simplest form, items at one pole can be given a positive value, and items at the other pole a negative value. A simple arithmetic count of both positive and negative choices can produce an overall score which will be indicative of the general attitude towards an issue.

### Visual analogue scales

Expressing attitudes or feelings is often difficult since such things don't always translate easily into a number. The semantic differential described above is one way of dealing with this. Another method is the **visual analogue scale**. Typically this is a horizontal line, 100 millimetres in length and anchored at each end by one extreme of an issue. Such scales can be used to measure like or dislike for something, and for measuring constructs such as fear and anxiety. They have also been used extensively in pain research.

Please indicate with a cross on the line how much pain you are in at the moment.

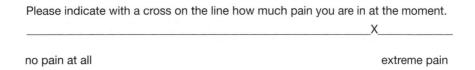

no pain at all                                                                    extreme pain

Since such scales are of a standard length (100 mm), an ordinary ruler can be used following administration to convert a response to a numerical value on a 10-point (10-centimetre) scale, as shown:

| 1 | 2 | 3 | 4 | 5 | 6 | 7 | 8 | 9 | 10 |
|---|---|---|---|---|---|---|---|---|----|

## Open-ended questions

With **open-ended questions** the individual is free to offer any response. The researcher relinquishes control of how the respondent can behave. In fact, open questions are not really questions at all. Rather, they are scenarios or situations created artificially in which respondents are encouraged to air their views or feelings. In this respect they have much in common with what are termed **projective techniques**, as used in a clinical setting, or for the measurement of personality variables. Given free choice, we all tend to project some part of ourselves onto a situation, and this is the principle behind the open-ended question. What we say or write in response to an unrestricted item is an expression of our feelings, values and attitudes.

### Unstructured items

**Unstructured items** are questionnaire items which allow the subject to answer in an unlimited fashion.

What do you think of the book so far? _____

Note that in items of this type the researcher does in fact have some control over how much of a response an individual can make, although the content will still remain unpredictable. Leaving the item as it stands invites a very brief response, possibly only a single word. Allowing several blank lines, or even a page, might encourage a much fuller response.

### Word association

Using **word association**, the individual is asked to respond with the first thing that comes to mind on presentation of the cue word.

What do you think of when you hear the following?

research project          exam          statistics

### Sentence completion

In **sentence completion**, the participant is offered an incomplete sentence and asked to continue in his or her own words.

> I chose to study psychology because _____.

Note that the comment about controlling the length of response (as encountered in the 'What do you think of the book so far?' example earlier) is relevant here.

The great advantage in not restricting responses is that the full variety of human thoughts and feelings is available to the researcher. The disadvantage is that it is available in a totally unstructured and uncontrolled form. Responses to any of the above can range from a few words to hours of introspective rambling. Accordingly, the approach lies more at the qualitative end of the research dimension (in terms of the type of information generated), but for quantitative researchers the data produced by open-ended questioning are more problematic: given the wide range of possible responses, considerable judgement is required and each participant's response must be inspected for common themes or threads of thought which offer an insight into the unique nature of the individual.

As a general principle, unless the components of an issue and the range of possible responses to a question are well understood, a study would normally be piloted using some form of open-ended enquiry. This would identify the type and range of responses likely, any sources of ambiguity, possible response bias among the respondents, overlap among items and so on. Only then would the more direct, closed-type items be used. The rule in closed-type items is simple: you will get only the information you ask for, so you had better have a good idea of what you are likely to get!

## 6.3 Special techniques for information gathering

### 6.3.1 Focus groups

The previous section on questionnaire design ended with the sage advice that if you don't ask the questions, you won't get the answers. But how do you know which questions to ask? Or to what extent a particular issue is important or relevant to your sample group?

It would seem then that, even before we consider our very first questionnaire item, we should know in advance what we are looking for. In many cases, this will have been established following an appropriate literature review: issues would have been identified at this stage and hypotheses developed. However, there are certain situations in which a research issue, or its key components (and hence a workable hypothesis), cannot readily be identified in this way; many elements of attitudinal and behavioural research are simply not accessible via the standard route and have to be explored in a more direct manner. One particular method of doing this, originating and widely used in the marketing sphere, is the focus group.

One of the key functions of the marketing process is to find out how people are likely to respond to new products, publicity campaigns and marketing information. If this is done well, we, the consumers, respond positively when a product is released on the market

Plate 6.2    A focus group.
*Source*: Getty/Daniel Bosler

and (so the manufacturers hope) go out and buy it. Poorly done, the result is a marketing disaster and possible bankruptcy. The attempt by Ford to launch America's first small, economical automobile in a culture of gas-guzzling monsters was an abysmal failure, and even today comedians make jokes about their parents being the first in the street to buy an Edsel. Similarly, the attempt by British Leyland in the 1970s to persuade us that an Austin Allegro with a square steering wheel was a must, ended in fiasco. (Oddly enough, the square-wheeled Allegro is now something of a collector's item.)

These examples represent classic marketing disasters – public opinion was seriously misjudged and important informational cues missed. By and large, however, marketing strategists tend to get it right (or right enough) by relying on a variety of techniques to gauge opinion, evaluate campaigns and judge consumer response. One of the mainstays of the approach is the focus group.

Much as the term suggests, focus groups are essentially discussion groups comprising either randomly or carefully selected panels of individuals brought together to discuss, or focus on, specific issues. Discussion can be free-flowing or controlled, but it is always under the guidance of a moderator, or facilitator, whose role is to maintain the focus of the group's attention on the issue, and to further probe or develop important themes. As an exploratory instrument, focus groups are superb sources of information, allowing a skilled researcher excellent insight into the values, beliefs, fears and aspirations which comprise most attitudes. Not surprisingly then, the approach has become an important tool in recent years in social, and especially political, research. Opinion, though, is divided as to both the value of the focus group and the procedures involved. In some quarters, the focused approach is seen as a preparatory procedure only, a way of refining ideas, getting to grips with the scope of a particular issue or developing a theory sufficiently to generate hypotheses (as intimated in our discussion of open-ended questions). For others, the focus group is an end in itself, with the information generated providing the essential and necessary data for a study, as discussed in Part 6. And certainly, given the vast amount of potential information generated in this format – hours of audio tape, pages of transcriptions and so on – its appeal as a qualitative research tool is obvious. However, it is in the first context that focus groups are probably of most use to undergraduate researchers, providing as it can a way of coming closer to an issue, of developing a greater understanding of the components of attitudes and of identifying key or relevant issues which will ultimately form the basis of a questionnaire.

With its increasing application within the behavioural sciences, several guidelines have evolved covering the use of focus groups and related procedural issues: how to sample, optimal group sizes, the composition of groups (whether or not members should be strangers or people known to each other) and so forth. There are views on the roles of moderators, on how to collect information and how it should be analysed. For the majority of undergraduate studies, though, a focus group *approach* is probably of more value than adopting a full procedure. In most cases a student is merely interested in identifying or refining important issues so that questionnaire instruments can be designed which will ask the right questions and provide sufficient coverage of an issue to deal appropriately with a given research topic. Such a scaled-down version will still require planning – participants have to be recruited to participate; individual characteristics have to be identified if these are going to be important variables in a study; topics for discussion have to be prepared, along with procedures for guiding or focusing discussion, dealing with awkward individuals and recording data. Equally important, especially if the research is dealing with a sensitive topic, is the thought which must be given to protecting vulnerable members of the group and on dealing with upset or catastrophe. Generally speaking, untrained undergraduates would be discouraged from using a focus approach to explore highly emotive or disturbing issues without a great deal of supervision and forward planning. Indeed, most research ethics committees would reject an undergraduate proposal to explore feelings and attitudes towards sensitive issues when participants of the focus group were themselves the victims of, for example, abuse or assault. Approval of this type of study might be granted only if supervisors were present at each focus session and experience of intervention could be guaranteed.

By and large, many undergraduates tend to use this procedure badly, calling brief, informal discussion meetings with relatively few individuals, failing to adequately control discussion and failing to record data in any systematic way. Often this process is seen merely as a precursor to the more important business of interview schedule or questionnaire design; students forget that they will ultimately have to justify every issue covered, and every item contained in any instrument. This can be done only if the issues have been properly explored and understood in advance. In Part 6, the use of focus groups in qualitative research is discussed in more detail.

### 6.3.2    Pilot research

Most of us feel that by the time we reach the stage of implementing our research design, we have worked out everything to the last detail: we have completed our literature review and therefore know how other practitioners have fared in their research; we have identified all potential sources of bias; and we have used an appropriate procedure to focus on the key issues and develop a foolproof questionnaire. However, complacency at this stage is to admit to a poor regard for the vagaries of human nature – misunderstanding instructions, misperceiving the researcher's intent, refusal to co-operate and so on are all events which can ruin the best conceived study. The solution of course is to pilot your method: try it out on a small sample of the population you will eventually be working with. This is the only way to refine the elements of a design, to identify questionnaire items which are misleading, confusing or offensive. Such pilot work need not be extensive – indeed in designs where participant pools are limited, pilot studies must be constrained – but they can be thorough: a survey or questionnaire administered to a small sub-set of our sample, in addition to some kind of focused interview, can be useful in identifying limitations and areas of improvement. Mistakes at this stage can be easily remedied; identifying flaws only after a major study has been implemented is hugely wasteful, not to mention demoralising.

### 6.3.3 Using standardised instruments in research

Many studies will make use of standard scales, existing questionnaires or psychometric tests as part of their data-gathering procedure, either as devices for assigning individuals to different conditions, or as a key source of data, as in an outcome measure. For example, an existing stress inventory could be used to assign people to the categories of either stressed or unstressed in a study of job burnout in modern organisations, categories which will comprise the various elements of an independent variable. Alternatively, standard instruments could provide us with our dependent measure, as in a wellbeing questionnaire measuring the impact of unemployment in particular regions, or an established job satisfaction instrument assessing responses to supervisors differing on androgeny scores in an academic context. By and large, using existing scales as part of a study can make life a little easier for the researcher: normally, before a test can be released on to the market, it must demonstrate that it is fit for its purpose; a great deal of preparatory work has invariably gone into the design and construction of any psychometric instrument. This provides the researcher with a useful measurement or classification tool without the need for the lengthy process required in developing a new instrument from scratch. However, using an existing test correctly requires familiarity with the general principles underlying measurement and scaling, in addition to an understanding of the essential characteristics of the particular test or questionnaire itself. Such a level of competence can be attained only through many years of experience with measurement scales; furthermore, the major publishers and distributors of tests have for some years provided training courses in various aspects of assessment while, more recently, the BPS has introduced an accreditation scheme whereby potential test users are obliged to undertake specific training before they are regarded as qualified to use particular tests. This is an important consideration, since failure to understand how a test has developed, or what specific responses mean, or a failure to prevent bias in administering or scoring, can lead to misinterpretation of scores and misleading – or even damaging – information being fed back to the testee. Equally dangerous is the potential for exploitation when tests are used by unqualified or unscrupulous people and it is largely for these reasons that the BPS introduced its scheme.

The observant reader might have realised by now that most undergraduates are unlikely to have either the experience or training to include existing scales as part of their research repertoire with any personal competence. The assumption is that it is the competence of the supervisor and the department to which they belong which allows the use of such instruments, not the students, although in all cases the users will be expected to familiarise themselves thoroughly with whichever test they will be using.

## 6.4 What you need to know about psychological tests

While it would be nice to test every aspect of some issue under investigation, such that we could explore a group or culture's entire history, or measure every aspect of an individual's life as it relates to the issue we are interested in, this is clearly impractical. (Any such test would be not only unwieldy, but would probably take a lifetime to administer.) What established instruments actually do is study a small but carefully chosen sample of some topic, issue or behaviour, in the hope that we can generalise from the specific to the global, in much the same way that a survey, while its main interest is the entire population, can only ever explore a small section of that population. Hence, a vocabulary test cannot address every word in a person's repertoire; rather it deals with a sample of what the individual knows.

To be of any use in predicting or describing what people do in general, this sample of items must be **representative** of the overall area, both in terms of type and number of items. An arithmetic test using only five items, for instance, or only items on multiplication, would be a poor test of arithmetic skill. A good test, on the other hand, would have to include items on addition, subtraction, multiplication and division. Furthermore, we might be unhappy if such a test omitted items involving fraction or decimal calculations and we might also expect some measure of computational abilities such as dealing with square root, power or factorial calculations. The underlying point here is that it would be impossible to develop a good, representative test of any aspect of human endeavour unless the composition of that behaviour had been fully considered in advance – in our arithmetic example we could develop a sound test only if we had a thorough understanding of the scope and composition of arithmetic skill to begin with.

While we expect test designers to demonstrate a sound knowledge of their particular area, it is equally important that we, as ultimate users of tests, also understand a good deal about the issues we are exploring. How else could we judge whether or not a test was a good one for our purposes, or, given a number of similar tests, how would we know which was the most appropriate?

### 6.4.1 Standardisation

Even the best measurement scale in the world will be wasted unless we can ensure that scores reflect the subject we are interested in, as opposed to some other factor. Notorious 'other factors' which can affect apparent performance on a test are instructions given to participants, their level of anxiety about the test, motivational factors, methods of collecting data and scoring procedures – nothing less, in fact, than the extraneous variables discussed in Chapter 2. Unless every individual who completes a test does so under identical, standardised conditions, any observed effects might simply reflect **procedural variations** rather than actual differences in behaviour. Box 6.3 illustrates the point.

Fortunately, test constructors are well aware of this issue and are able to employ several procedures to reduce the effects of administration variability. The Eysenck Personality Questionnaire, or EPQ (Eysenck & Eysenck, 1975), a favourite among psychology undergraduate researchers, is a good example (see Figure 6.6). It's a pre-printed test with restricted response categories and instructions clearly printed on every copy. Even scoring has been taken out of the hands (or judgement) of the administrator, being achieved via

# The standardisation problem

Instructions given to a group of university students prior to the administration of a standard intelligence test:

### Instruction A

The test you are about to complete is one of the most advanced tests of intellectual functioning yet devised. Your scores on this test will be considered by a team of experts and their decision will partially determine whether or not you are allowed to enter the honours stream next session. It is therefore important that you do well.

### Instruction B

I'm afraid today's video presentation is cancelled due to the technician's inability to remove the cling film wrapping from the tape. For want of something better to do, we've found this intelligence test – it's not an especially good test but it might be a bit of fun and it will give you something to do.

Each set of instructions is in its own way inappropriate (and also unethical) in that each actively cues respondents to approach the test in a particular way. It would be unsurprising to obtain two completely different sets of scores not measuring intelligence, but more likely motivation or – especially among those receiving Instruction A – test anxiety.

standard scoring stencils. Finally, interpretation of individual profiles can be guided by reference to printed norms, a procedure with which all test users must become familiar.

### 6.4.2   Norms

Contrary to popular belief, there is no pre-determined pass or fail level in most tests. It would be nonsense to talk of passing a stress or personality test, for instance, although the notion might seem less bizarre if we are dealing with something like arithmetic for which some form of pass levels can realistically be set. (Most students will be aware that the various exams they sit, which test their knowledge of or competence in particular subjects, have clearly defined pass and fail levels.) In fact, outside of such measures of achievement, in the majority of tests, individual scores are compared against other scores which have previously been collated by the test designer. This comparison function is obtained by first administering the test to a large, representative sample of those with whom the test will subsequently be used (the **standardisation sample**). This provides us with a **norm**, which is simply a measure, or series of measures, indicating how people typically (or normally) perform on this test.

Norms can take various forms, although usually they comprise a measure of average performance (being the arithmetic average, or mean of the scores of all the participants in the standardisation sample), and a measure of the extent to which scores tend to vary above and below this average (given as a standard deviation; see Part 4). The point of

**Figure 6.6** An extract from the Eysenck Personality Questionnaire, showing the scoring template, superimposed. (Copyright © 1991 H. J. Eysenck and S. B. G. Eysenck. Reproduced by permission of Hodder & Stoughton.)

ADULT EPQ-R

| | Age | Sex M / F | P | E | N |
|---|---|---|---|---|---|
| | | | L | A | C |

INSTRUCTIONS: Please answer each question by putting a circle around the 'YES' or 'NO' following the question. There are no right or wrong answers, and no trick questions. Work quickly and do not think too long about the exact meaning of the questions.

■ PLEASE REMEMBER TO ANSWER EACH QUESTION

PAGE 1

ADULT EPQ-R: Scoring Template 1

| | | | |
|---|---|---|---|
| 1 | Do you have many different hobbies? | YES (E) | NO |
| 2 | Do you stop to think things over before doing anything? | YES | NO (P) |
| 3 | Does your mood often go up and down? | YES (N) | NO |
| 4 | Have you ever taken the praise for something you knew someone else had really done? | YES | NO |
| 5 | Do you take much notice of what people think? | YES | NO (P) |
| 6 | Are you a talkative person? | YES (E) | NO |
| 7 | Would being in debt worry you? | YES | NO (P) |
| 8 | Do you ever feel 'just miserable' for no reason? | YES (N) | NO |
| 9 | Do you give money to charities? | YES | NO (P) |
| 10 | Were you ever greedy by helping yourself to more than your share of anything? | YES | NO |
| 11 | Are you rather lively? | YES (E) | NO |
| 12 | Would it upset you a lot to see a child or an animal suffer? | YES | NO (P) |
| 13 | Do you often worry about things you should not have done or said? | YES (N) | NO |
| 14 | Do you dislike people who don't know how to behave themselves? | YES | NO (P) |
| 15 | If you say you will do something, do you always keep your promise no matter how inconvenient it might be? | YES | NO |
| 16 | Can you usually let yourself go and enjoy yourself at a lively party? | YES (E) | NO |
| 17 | Are you an irritable person? | YES (N) | NO |
| 18 | Should people always respect the law? | YES | NO (P) |
| 19 | Have you ever blamed someone for doing something you knew was really your fault? | YES | NO |
| 20 | Do you enjoy meeting new people? | YES (E) | NO |
| 21 | Are good manners very important? | YES | NO (P) |
| 22 | Are your feelings easily hurt? | YES (N) | NO |
| 23 | Are *all* your habits good and desirable ones? | YES | NO |
| 24 | Do you tend to keep in the background on social occasions? | YES | NO (E) |
| 25 | Would you take drugs which may have strange or dangerous effects? | YES (P) | NO |
| 26 | Do you often feel 'fed-up'? | YES (N) | NO |

PLEASE TURN OVER

these measures is that, provided the people who tried out the test during these initial stages are representative of the broader population, what is true for the sample should be true for everyone. This is a crucial point: for statistical purposes a standardisation sample of 600 or so participants would be fine, providing what we are measuring is pretty stable in the population. If, however, a test is being designed to measure some trait which is known (or suspected) to be influenced by many factors (it can vary with age, sex, social class, occupation, etc.), then the sample would need to be much larger to allow the different sources of variability to be reasonably well represented. In the development of the Eysenck Personality Inventory, or EPI (Eysenck & Eysenck, 1964), the forerunner of the EPQ, the test developers used a standardisation sample of more than 5,000 participants. With a sample this large, they were able to explore scores on the extraversion and neuroticism scales by age, sex and some 47 different occupational groups, a diversification which would not have been possible with smaller numbers of participants. The point of this protracted discussion on norms and samples is that, if a test is to be used as part of a student project (or indeed for any research purpose), it is important to be aware of how relevant the norms are to the group being studied. A standardisation sample which is small, or which does not allow for sources of variation, might be of limited value in describing the larger population.

Returning to the EPI, the large standardisation sample allows us not only to state that the average extraversion score for all males in the sample was 13.19 and for females, 12.60, but also that the average for male students was 13.80 with female students 13.49. Similar information is available for many other occupational sub-groups and for different age groups. See Box 6.4 which shows an extract from age norms taken from the later EPQ-R (Eysenck & Eysenck, 1991).

Providing an average measure of performance on a test is a common method of presenting norms, but there are others. More typical, and more informative in some ways, are norms which are expressed as **percentiles** – a measure of the percentage of the standardisation sample which scored at or below a particular level. Hence, if a test manual informs us that a score of 35 on an abstract reasoning test is at the 50th percentile, then we know that 50% of the standardisation sample scored 35 or less; if we are told that a score of 59 lies at the 95th percentile, then we know that 95% of the standardisation sample scored 59 or less, and so on (see Figure 6.8).

### 6.4.3  Test reliability

Every measuring instrument, if it is to be of any use, must demonstrate a number of important qualities. The first of these is that it must be sensitive to the character of whichever variable – be it some physical property or a social phenomenon – it is measuring, and accurately detect any changes which might occur. Equally important, it must not indicate change where no change has taken place. This may sound strange, but consider an everyday measuring instrument, such as a ruler. If we measure the height of a table on a Monday and obtain a measure of 1 metre, but on Tuesday obtain a height of 1.3 metres, there are two things which can have occurred. The first is that the table (for some bizarre reason) has changed its dimensions in the course of a day and is now 0.3 metre taller than it was on Monday, a change which has been accurately detected by our ruler. Alternatively, the table has not changed; rather it is the ruler which has changed – possibly some temperature-sensitive metal was used in its manufacture and the thing actually shrank overnight. Before the advent of plastic-coated materials, traditional fabric tape measures

Box 6.4

A Closer Look At . . .

# Test norms

In the development of most psychological tests, one of the tasks of the designer is to determine typical score profiles for the population for whom the test is intended. Conventionally this takes the form of a measure of average (usually the arithmetic mean) and a measure of how much, on average, people tend to vary about this mean (given as a standard deviation). There are other methods for indicating typicality – we can determine what percentage of respondents are likely to score at, or below, particular levels of a test, in which case our typical scores take the form of percentiles, or percentile ranks. (We might find that 80% of respondents tend to score on or below a given score on some test, which would make this score the 80th percentile. People performing at a higher level might score on the 90th percentile, and so on. See Part 4.) All such attempts to demonstrate typicality are part of the process of establishing norms: they are measures of how people normally respond to a particular test. Some tests are offered with only the most general of norms (e.g., we will be given typical scores for broad groups only, such as those for males and females). Other tests which have received more thorough development might have gender norms subdivided by age category. And some might even provide norms by gender, age, occupational category and so on. Table 6.3, extracted from the EPQ-R, shows extraversion and neuroticism scores for two different age groups.

The interpretation of normative data like these requires some basic statistical understanding, and Chapter 7 (Part 4) provides a good introduction to the various descriptive measures presented in Table 6.3. Figure 6.7 illustrates the distribution of extraversion scores for males in the 16–20 years age group, using the normative data. The mean is shown as the score obtaining the highest frequency, and the variation around this mean is given as standard deviation units. Specifically, we see that the average extraversion score for this sample

Table 6.3 Age norms (mean and SD) for extraversion and neuroticism. Adapted from the *Manual of the Eysenck Personality Scales (EPS Adult)* (Eysenck & Eysenck, 1996, Table 2).

**Males**

| Age (years) | Extraversion | | | Neuroticism | |
| --- | --- | --- | --- | --- | --- |
| | *n* | Mean | SD | Mean | SD |
| 16–20 | 108 | 15.97 | 5.26 | 11.12 | 5.68 |
| 41–50 | 55 | 11.91 | 5.09 | 11.22 | 5.95 |

**Females**

| Age (years) | Extraversion | | | Neuroticism | |
| --- | --- | --- | --- | --- | --- |
| | *n* | Mean | SD | Mean | SD |
| 16–20 | 161 | 15.47 | 4.99 | 14.03 | 4.85 |
| 41–50 | 50 | 12.36 | 4.95 | 10.94 | 5.92 |

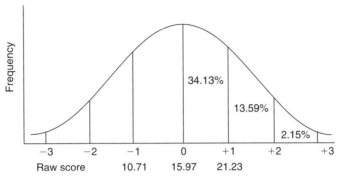

**Figure 6.7** Mean and standard deviations of extraversion scores for males in the 16–20 age group.

is 15.97, with respondents varying, on average, 5.26 points above and below this score. Another way of expressing this, given the characteristics of a normal distribution, is that 68.26% of this sample scored somewhere between 10.71 and 21.23 on this particular test.

Note that the mean score given in Table 6.3 for extraversion relates only to one particular age group for male respondents on this particular version of the EPQ scale. Average extraversion scores for other age groups differ from this, and there are clear gender differences as well. Moreover, different versions of these scales show quite marked differences in mean scores. In the EPQ-R Short Scale, for instance, the male mean for the 16–20 age group is 8.16, based as it is on a smaller number of items. The point is that there is a danger – commonly found among undergraduates – of latching onto numerical values as if they are absolute measures of particular constructs. It would not be the first time that a student has tried to interpret an individual score on a personality test in the belief that average performance could be expressed as a given value (such as 15.97), while forgetting or being unaware that norms will vary for particular age groups, for males and females and for whichever form of a test has been used.

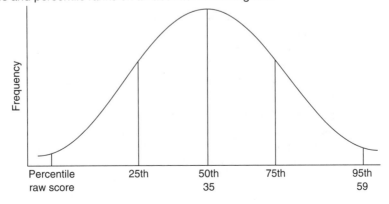

**Figure 6.8** Scores and percentile ranks on an abstract reasoning test.

were notoriously unreliable in wet conditions and it was the wise surveyor who refused to work in the rain. The point of this example is that, with a standardised test, we always try to ensure that the first case is the typical one: when a change is signalled it must be the aspect of the psychological environment which is changing and not the instrument itself. In other words, a test must demonstrate consistency, or **reliability**. There are a number of ways in which this might be done:

## Test-retest reliability

The simplest and most direct method for demonstrating that a test is behaving consistently is to measure the same thing twice – **test-retest reliability**. The same test is administered to the same participants and the two scores compared, using a form of correlation procedure. Obvious problems here are practice effects, which could actually produce a poor comparison between two presentations of the same test simply because our testees were getting better at the task. This could lead us to wrongly assume the instrument is not reliable when in fact the opposite is the case – the test has been sensitive to the change in behaviour. Alternatively, if participants recall their original responses and attempt to reproduce them, an artificially high correspondence between the two measures might occur, demonstrating more the reliability of participants' memories than the stability of the test. Only tests not affected by repetition can be assessed in this way, or alternatively, a sufficient time interval between pairs of testings can dilute the effects of both practice and memory. Of course, leaving a lengthy time interval between testings allows for the intervention of other variables which might affect performance on the task, which merely serves to indicate that demonstrating test reliability will never be completely straightforward.

## Alternate form reliability

When there is a danger of straightforward repetition producing a misleading reliability measure – as in the memory issue – two different forms of the test can be given to the same participants and the scores correlated, referred to as **alternate form reliability**. Care should be taken to ensure that the two forms of the test are truly equivalent and of course practice can still influence performance.

There is a method for assessing reliability without the need for two repetitions of the same or parallel forms of the same test – **split-half reliability**. In this variant, a test is administered once only, the items split in half and the two halves correlated. Sometimes a straight split is made, with the first half of a test compared with the second half, while at others times the split is in terms of odd-numbered items versus even-numbered ones. However, this method is not so much a measure of temporal reliability (consistency over time) as of internal consistency (where all the items themselves are measuring in the same direction), and should not be regarded as an alternative to either of the previous approaches; this provides a check of how reliable the individual items are. If a good comparison is achieved, the items are deemed to be consistent and the test largely reliable (insofar as all the items are measuring the same construct). There are of course a number of problems in attempting to demonstrate reliability, with practice and memory effects having already been discussed. Equally important are procedural and administration factors – any variations across successive repetitions of a test will adversely affect reliability measures. Nor is the split-half approach without its problems, because the strength of the comparison may vary according to

Box 6.5

A Closer Look At . . .

# Reliability

It is an important characteristic of all psychological tests that, whichever aspect of the individual they measure, they do so consistently. This means that test scores must be closely linked to what is being measured: if an aspect of behaviour remains constant in real life, the test should reflect this stability. If the aspect of behaviour changes, test scores must also change. This is known as reliability and all well-developed tests ought to be able to demonstrate this. Moreover, measures of test reliability and explanation of how these measures have been obtained must be readily available to the test user. The test manual which accompanies most tests will normally offer such information, and the extract from the EPQ-R manual, shown in Table 6.4, is a good example.

The extract in Table 6.4 is typical of the information found in a good test manual, in support of the reliability of a scale or scales. Other information which one would expect to find in a manual would be the type of reliability demonstrated (test-retest or alternate form), the size of the sample used to investigate test reliability, the precise nature of the reliability coefficient and a full citation of the authors of the research. In the current example, in addition to the tabulated information of which Table 6.4 is an extract, we are informed elsewhere in the manual that the reliabilities shown are test-retest reliabilities, with one month between administrations; that the sample comprised 109 males and 120 females; and that the reliability coefficients are given as alpha coefficients (Eysenck & Eysenck, 1996, pp. 14–15). The many studies investigating the reliability of the scales are also cited in full with brief descriptions of the findings in each case.

**Table 6.4**  Test-retest reliability coefficients for males and females on the extraversion (*E*) and neuroticism (*N*) scales of the EPQ-R. Adapted from the *Manual of the Eysenck Personality Scales (EPS Adult)* (Eysenck and Eysenck, 1996, p. 19, Table 5).

|  | *E* | *N* |
| --- | --- | --- |
| Males | 0.83 | 0.76 |
| Females | 0.89 | 0.81 |

how the split is made. There are statistical ways of dealing with reliability problems, and the actual correlation between two testings is not based on the conventional calculation most undergraduates are familiar with, but rather on a development which attempts to counterbalance the deficiencies of the reliability procedure in general. The manuals which accompany most tests ought to provide details of the procedures used to establish reliability, together with the associated **reliability coefficients**. See Box 6.5.

## Test validity

The next crucial quality that a test should possess is **test validity**. This is simply an expression of the extent to which a test is actually measuring what it is supposed to be measuring, although the methods available to demonstrate this quality are often far from simple. In terms of test characteristics validity is possibly even more important than reliability. After all, reliability only tells us that, whatever the test is measuring, it is doing so consistently. It doesn't necessarily inform us about what the test is actually measuring, or how good a job it is doing of measuring it. If a test is demonstrably valid, though, we know it is doing what it claims to do. Unfortunately, in the historical development of testing some of the early forms of intelligence test, for instance, were subsequently shown to be invalid when it was observed that they could not be completed successfully without a conventional Western educational background – they had more to do with scholastic aptitude than with what people regard as pure intelligence (whatever that might be). This is an aspect of validity, and this example also offers an idea of the scope of the problem. Given that many tests attempt to measure the traits which *underlie* behaviour (creativity, personality, intelligence, etc.), the problem of validity becomes a difficult one. Having said this, a number of methods are available which go some way towards demonstrating the fitness of particular tests, and the different types of validity are discussed in the following sections.

### Content validity

If a test is to demonstrate **content validity** then the content of the test must accurately and adequately reflect the content of the phenomenon under investigation. In the case of an opinion or attitude measure for example, the content of the test should be based on a thorough understanding of the attitude, related views, associated measures and likely values expressed; knowledge tests should be a fair representation of the topics which comprise the information base. Your exam at the end of a typical methods module, for instance, should be a good expression of the course of study, reflecting topic diversity, issues raised and recommended readings given. If it does not meet the terms of these criteria students have every right to complain about the lack of content validity present in their exam (the content of the test failed to reflect the content of the course). However, many such tests can become overloaded with items which lend themselves to objective testing. While it is easy enough to explore an individual's familiarity with information aspects of an issue, how do you measure something like critical appraisal? And, as previously mentioned, early intelligence tests primarily comprised items on academic skill rather than abstract reasoning, creativity and the like. Achievement tests in particular will invariably be examined in terms of their content validity.

### Face validity

**Face validity** is often confused with the previous test feature since, as with content validity, the concern is with the appearance of a test. However, face validity is not a true indication of validity, being concerned only with what a test appears to measure, and having little to do with what is actually being measured. Nevertheless, this represents a useful feature of any test because there will be a relationship between how people view a test and their willingness to participate; if we see an instrument as childish, irrelevant or even insulting, we will certainly not give it our full attention. Box 6.6 illustrates this issue.

In some cases, especially in the area of opinion studies, it is not always possible to ensure face validity: in a situation where a participant may not respond honestly if the true purpose of the test is known, we may be tempted to disguise part of the test content. This of course must be done with extreme caution and only with considerable justification. It should be understood that this approach actively deceives participants and adherence to ethical guidelines (as published by the various research governing bodies such as the BPS and APA) must be ensured. See Box 6.7 for an illustration of the problem, and also the section on questionnaire design in which this issue is further explored.

How To . . .

# Ensure face validity

> Orange ice lollies cost 50p each, raspberry lollies 35p and lemon ones 40p. If a schoolboy has £1.60 to spend in his tuck shop, and he wants to buy each of his three friends a different flavour, which flavour of ice lolly can he then buy for himself?

The above problem would be a good (valid) item in a test of general arithmetic reasoning. However, if the item appeared in a test designed for trainee electrical engineers, the response would more likely be derisory laughter than the correct answer (which is raspberry lollies, for the computationally challenged). For this particular group the item would not have face validity and some re-wording would be in order:

> Assume 1-millimetre copper cable costs £35 per 100 metre drum, 1.5 mm cable £40 per drum and 2.5 mm cable £50 per drum. If a project buyer needs electrical cable of each size and has £160 to spend, of which diameter cable can he buy 200 metres and stay within his budget?

This is the same item as the previous one except, for this group, it now has face validity. (By the way, the correct answer is 1-millimetre cable, in case you haven't got the idea yet.)

### Criterion related validity

When a test is developed to diagnose something about an individual's present circumstances, or to predict something about a person's future, validation can sometimes be achieved by comparing test scores to some other indicator (or criterion) of what the test is trying to measure. An occupational selection test, for example, can be checked against later job performance (which is actually how such tests are validated); a neuroticism test can be checked against medical records, or friends' ratings of behaviour; a scholastic achievement test can be checked against assignment ratings; and so on. Within this general procedure of relating test scores to some other criterion, there is a particular condition concerning the temporal relationship between the test and its criterion measure (i.e., when we actually obtain this validating information). This relationship is determined by the nature of the test itself – whether or not it is measuring something about an individual's current circumstances, or whether it is predicting something about the future.

### Concurrent validity

The criterion against which scores are to be checked is obtained at the same time for **concurrent validity**. This is the type of proof which is necessary when a test is assessing some aspect of a current condition (as in a diagnostic test).

### Predictive validity

In a test which predicts something (as with aptitude tests), a follow-up study is carried out to test the strength of the prediction, called **predictive validity**. Most selection tests, as used by industrial or occupational psychologists, will be obliged to demonstrate criterion

## A Closer Look At . . .

# Concealing the true nature of research

Armed with a limited budget and charged with identifying the 20% of pensioners most in need of additional subsistence payments, you devise a questionnaire to determine differing levels of deprivation.

*Please indicate on the scale below how adequate your pension is in meeting your individual needs.*

| 1 | 2 | 3 | 4 | 5 |
|---|---|---|---|---|
| totally inadequate | inadequate | acceptable | adequate | more than adequate |

(Note: the wording used for the response categories would be chosen to reflect the type of question and the nature of the respondent.)

If other items on the questionnaire are like this, approximately 99% of our sample will fall into our most needy category – simply because it is obvious what the questionnaire is about, and what the consequences of particular responses will be. And human nature being what it is . . .

Modifying the appearance of items, however, might provide a subtler if more indirect route to the information you are looking for – for example, if items appear to be measuring more general behaviour than obvious levels of deprivation:

*Please indicate how often you eat a hot meal in the course of a week?*

| 1 | 2 | 3 | 4 | 5 |
|---|---|---|---|---|
| never | rarely | sometimes | often | every day |

Or

*Approximately how much do you spend on fuel in the course of a week?*

Or

*On average, how many times do you go shopping during the week?*

Items like this allow us to infer certain things about respondents, indirectly, and it could be argued that for some types of information this form of indirect questioning is the only way of ensuring an honest or unbiased response. However, an approach of this type is potentially deceptive insofar as the purpose behind items is obscured, and runs counter to the spirit of openness which forms the basis of current ethical principles. One might adopt the line that the ultimate aim of this particular study is to improve the lot of as many individuals as possible, and moral rectitude will overcome any niggling doubts about deception. However, suppose the same type of study were used in order to reduce benefits to individuals deemed well enough off not to need so much financial support. Therein lies a dilemma for the researcher – is the need for information so great that the means by which we obtain it are always justified?

related predictive validity, since everything from an interview to a job sample test is predicting something about job candidates. If a selection test is described as having predictive validity, then during its design phase it might have been administered to job candidates as part of a general selection and recruitment process. Subsequent assessment of individuals actually hired by the company would be compared with the predictions made on the original test, and if a good match is obtained, the test is declared valid. Only then would it be developed for future use in the selection process.

A problem here is criterion contamination, in which the independent measure can become contaminated by knowledge of the test results and therefore ceases to be truly independent.

*"He looks sick, what do you think?"*

*"Yeah, now that you mention it . . . "*

This is a tricky problem to overcome in many cases since it is common for the individual responsible for an original assessment to be the same person involved in subsequent evaluations. The only way round this is to ensure that independent assessments are truly independent – follow-up measures should ideally be taken by individuals who have no detailed knowledge of previous evaluations.

### Construct validity

**Construct validity** indicates the extent to which a test measures some theoretical construct or concept, such as intelligence, creativity or personality. Not surprisingly this is the most diffi-cult type of validity to demonstrate, since the concepts being measured – as the name sug-gests – are really theoretical entities whose existence is inferred by observation of related ac-tivities. Consequently, validation of such concepts is also indirect: measurements of activities which are believed to be related to, expressions of, or caused by, some underlying factor.

Age differentiation is one such indirect method of validation. If a trait is expected to vary with age, scores on the test should reflect this variability. For instance, if the under-standing of certain concepts (e.g., prejudice) is part of a developmental process, we should be able to observe this by comparing older children with younger ones. If people become more conservative as they get older, measures of attitudes towards many issues should differ between a middle-aged sample and a young sample.

Correlation with other tests is another commonly used validation method whereby a new test should compare well with existing tests of the same trait. (The Binet test of intelligence – one of the earliest examples of this type of test – and the later Wechsler Adult Intelligence Scale were often used to validate new tests of intelligence.) Of course, any new test must have genuine advantages over what already exists. It might be easier to administer, more comprehensive, applicable to a broader sample; otherwise there is little point in developing something new.

Administration to extreme groups offers another method of validation, such that if two groups are known to differ markedly on a trait, the test should reflect this difference (a per-sonality test, for instance, might clearly distinguish between previously identified extreme extraverts and extreme introverts). This is a particularly crude measure, however, since it will demonstrate only that a test is capable of identifying broad differences and not how well it measures fine distinctions (for instance, between mild and indeterminate introverts).

In fact, in the case of construct validity, a number of independent measures would be used to provide a comparison function, and most manuals for specific tests will offer ex-tensive detail on how precisely the test was validated. See Box 6.8 for an example.

Box 6.8

## A Closer Look At . . .

# Test validity

An issue which is central to all psychological tests is the extent to which we can be confident that the test is measuring what it is supposed to be measuring. This is termed validity and there are many forms, as outlined in the main text of this chapter. Demonstrating validity, however, is a complex task, linked to the nature of the construct being measured – sometimes validity can be shown by correlating scores on a new test with scores on some existing or similar measure. A new arithmetical reasoning test in which the scope and depth of the concept is well understood can be matched to one of many existing instruments, or to scholastic assessments. With less-well-defined concepts, such as personality, intelligence or psychological wellbeing, it is more difficult: sometimes test assessments must be compared against interview evaluations, or longitudinal studies are required to determine the veracity of predictions made on the basis of a test, and sometimes research is required in several countries to demonstrate the cross-cultural validity of a measure.

In the manual of the General Health Questionnaire, or GHQ (Goldberg & Williams, 1988), a test designed to detect psychiatric disorders in community and non-psychiatric settings, a wide and comprehensive range of validation methods is described. In its development, the GHQ has been administered along with other measures of psychological health, such as the Profile of Mood States, or POMS (Worsley, Walters, & Wood, 1977), it has been matched to evaluations based on clinical interviews, and it has been used to predict GP consultations.

Table 6.5 is typical of the information available in the manual for the GHQ.

The GHQ is an extensively researched instrument which has been used in many situations and many cultures. For every application the manual provides details of validation research, with full citations and a commentary to aid the user in determining the efficacy of the instrument for current applications. Every student intending to use an instrument like the GHQ must become familiar with the relevant manual to determine the relevance of the instrument to particular groups in particular contexts.

**Table 6.5**    Correlation coefficients between scores on the GHQ-60 and a standard Clinical Interview Schedule (CIS) from three validation studies.

**GHQ-60**

| Investigators | Year | Research interview | Correlation coefficient |
| --- | --- | --- | --- |
| Goldberg and Blackwell | 1970 | CIS | 0.80 |
| Goldberg | 1972 | CIS | 0.77 |
| Munoz et al. | 1978 | CIS | 0.81 |

Adapted from the *Manual of the GHQ* (Goldberg & Williams, 1991, p. 44).

All of the foregoing discussion represents essential reading for anyone contemplating using a standard testing instrument as part of their study. For anyone who aims to make use of an existing test it is important to understand how it was devised, how reliable it is and what steps were taken to prove its validity. Familiarity with test norms is vital, since this information tells us for whom the test is suitable, and what particular scores are likely to mean. Apart from being a major factor in determining your competence to use a given test, you will also be required in a final report to fully justify the use of a particular instrument. Moreover, it will be expected that, if a standardised test has been used in a study, you will be able to draw comparisons between your own findings and existing norms, and be able to discuss, knowledgeably, any deviations from published statistics. None of this is possible unless you *read the manual*. (We return to this issue in Part 7.)

While standardised tests will often comprise an element of undergraduate research, there will be occasions when no existing test is suitable for a particular design, or in which an issue is being explored using questionnaire or survey methods. This is usually the case when contemporary opinions, values and beliefs are being investigated. In such cases the researcher must develop her own instrument, a task sufficiently demanding that sometimes the development of a measure – with all the attendant requirements of reliability and validity – becomes the study itself.

## Review

In this chapter we have considered a number of practical aspects of carrying out a study. By this stage you should now have a good idea of how many participants you require and how you will recruit them. You should also know precisely how you are going to collect your data – whether you will be using an existing measure or devising a measurement scale of your own. If you are developing your own instrument, you should appreciate the various options available in terms of measurement scales, the advantages of the different approaches and the associated pitfalls. You will also have sufficient familiarity with ethical guidelines governing psychological research to ensure that your study will be carried out in an ethical manner.

## Suggested further reading

American Psychological Association. (2002). *Ethical principles of psychologists and code of conduct. American Psychologist, 57,* 1060–1073.

Asbury, J. E. (1995). Overview of focus group research. *Qualitative Health Research, 5,* 414–420.

This provides an informative overview of the history and use of focus group research.

Beech, J. R., & Harding, L. (Eds.). (1990). *Testing people: A practical guide to psychometrics.* Windsor, UK: NFER-Nelson.

A thorough but easy to read review of the major issues in psychological testing.

British Psychological Society. (2004). *Ethical guidelines: Guidelines for minimum standards of ethical approval in psychological research.* Leicester: British Psychological Society.

Provides a full account of the guidelines governing research with people.

British Psychological Society. (2005). *Code of conduct, ethical principles and guidelines.* Leicester: British Psychological Society.

In the event that some form of animal research is possible for undergraduates, this publication provides a complete set of guidelines governing the treatment and welfare of animals. This includes information on legal requirements.

de Vaus, D. A. (1996). *Surveys in social research* (4th ed.). London: University College London Press.

Chapter 15 on building scales provides a detailed review of the issues surrounding different kinds of measurement scales.

# Tables, figures and descriptive statistics

## Part 4

Introducing
research

Planning a research
project—the design

Carrying out
research—methods
& procedures

Describing research
findings—
descriptives

Analysing research
findings—inferential
statistics

Carrying out
qualitative research

Writing up and
presenting the
findings of research

Alamy/Blickwinkel

Part 4 deals with the data generated in quantitative research – what we do with the numbers produced by an observation study, survey or experiment; how we present them; and the most appropriate form of analysis. In particular, it focuses on how we can use numerical information to make sense of the psychological world.

Chapter 7 deals with basic concepts in describing data – using tables, graphs and introducing descriptive statistics – while Chapter 8 is concerned with the practical issues of setting up data files and working with modern statistical software. In particular, the SPSS statistical package will be used to illustrate procedures and outputs, a package which is becoming one of the most frequently encountered quantitative tools in academic and government departments. (*SPSS* is an abbreviation of *Statistical Package for the Social Sciences*, although the acronym is sometimes expressed as *Superior Performance Statistical Software*.) By the end of this part you will be able to:

- understand the principles behind tabular and graphical presentation of data
- prepare tables and figures according to appropriate conventions
- describe your data using appropriate statistics for central tendency and dispersion
- create a file for your data in SPSS
- generate a variety of basic, descriptive statistics in SPSS
- produce graphs in SPSS appropriate to your data
- be able to interpret the sometimes complex output typical of computer software

As with all sections of this book, the aim is to introduce essential concepts; those interested in more advanced ideas and techniques should pursue some of the articles cited in the *Suggested further reading* sections at the end of most chapters.

# 7

# Describing data – tables, graphs and descriptive statistics

## Key Issues

Chapter 7 provides an in-depth treatment of the quantitative methods we use to describe our world. We show how tables are constructed and present the rules for their use in reports and publications. Different types of graphs are compared and we offer illustrations on their use and construction. The chapter concludes with extensive consideration of descriptive statistics; we demonstrate the computation of measures to indicate average, spread and deviations from the normal, based on the premise that this will represent your first introduction to quantitative techniques. Our examples and explanations therefore make no assumptions about prior knowledge, and the presentation of ideas and procedures is designed to be accessible and user-friendly. More specifically, this chapter covers the following topics:

- description of the psychological world
- tables, figures and categorical data
- tables, figures and continuous data
- measures of central tendency
- measures of dispersion
- the normal distribution
- skewness and kurtosis

## 7.1 Using numbers to represent the psychological world

So, the study is complete and you have now amassed a great deal of information, and if your research was quantitative in nature, this information will take the form of numbers. The proportion of Yes or No responses to an opinion questionnaire, measures of attitude on rating scales, scores on some kind of performance measure in an experiment – these are all typical. In addition, you will also probably have key information on your participants: profile information such as gender, age category, personality type and so on. These too will probably be in the form of numbers, and here is an important point: the central philosophy of a quantitative approach is that everything in the universe can be represented numerically. This allows widely diverse elements to be compared using a common classification and measurement system. Hence, the strength of an opinion on a social issue might be expressed as a value between 1 and 7; membership of a particular occupational class as one of five numerical categories (1 = professional; 2 = managerial, etc.) with even a person's gender expressed simply as 1 for males and 2 for females. (Ouch! We can hear the complaints already, so make that 0 = male and 1 = female, if you prefer.) Using numerical values in this way is termed **coding**, and some of the principles of and practical issues involved in the procedure have been discussed in Part 3 of this book, in the section on questionnaire design. Further discussion on coding procedures is available in the next chapter of Part 4.

Once the notion of numbers being symbols which represent other things is understood, the next stage in the quantitative process is to make use of the significant characteristics of numbers – they can be added, subtracted, multiplied and divided. In other words, they can be manipulated.

## 7.2 Making sense of numbers

Choosing to represent the world numerically is only the beginning of the quantitative process. After all, taking a series of measurements on a sample of participants – be it height, age, membership of particular groups or scores on some attitudinal variable – will only provide you with a list of numbers. And if this is a long list the numbers quickly become unintelligible. Yet the quantitative approach is intended to make sense of the world, so techniques have evolved to deal with this.

Irrespective of what we intend to do with our data, be it to describe (the purpose of this chapter) or to draw inferences, compare groups or explore relationships (the themes considered in Part 5), there are usually three things we *can* do with our data: we can organise our numbers into tables, we can generate figures, or pictures, from the data, and we can calculate descriptive statistics. This is especially true of the procedures outlined in the following sections, in which techniques are considered for describing, summarising and illustrating the psychological world with quantitative data – **descriptive techniques**. The point of this is to impose order on what is often a disorganised set of data, to group similar types of data into classes or categories, to demonstrate relationships or differences, or simply to present data in a manner which is clear to the viewer. Box 7.5 provides an illustration of the three methods of describing data.

The first set of examples which follow concern nominal or ordinal data. It will be recalled from our discussion on levels of measurement in Part 2, that data can be either continuous (interval and ratio) or discrete (nominal or ordinal), comprising qualitatively different categories. In the case of discrete or categorical data, our options for describing are restricted, primarily, to two methods – tables and figures. Many descriptive statistics (apart from percentages and frequency counts) are unsuitable for these data and a certain amount of common sense is required to present your data to the reader.

## 7.3 Tables and categorical variables

At their most basic, tables allow us to organise numerical information in a way that imposes some order on our data, serving the important descriptive functions of summarising and simplifying.

In the illustrations which follow we have adopted, in large part, the guidelines supplied by the APA and BPS. While these are conventions as opposed to strict rules which must be followed slavishly, it is nevertheless sensible practice to adhere to such guidelines where possible. Whenever we have deviated from the recommendations this is usually to allow us to illustrate particular points, or in cases where recommendations for journal articles are inappropriate for the format of a textbook. We do signal such deviations. There follows a summary of APA (2001) guidelines for the presentation of tables.

- Every table should be identified by a title which should be brief, but informative, clearly stating what the data contained within the table illustrate. The title should appear either above or beneath the table and placement should be consistent within a single document (that is, always one or the other).

- All tables should be numbered sequentially. The APA advises against the use of suffixes (Table 4a, Table 4b, etc.), preferring a unique numerical identifier for each illustration (Table 4, Table 5). In this textbook, however, containing as it does many tables and figures, we have deliberately opted for suffixes as a means of organising our illustrations. This is not necessary in a research paper which would contain a small number of tables and the preference of the APA can be more readily adopted.

- In structuring tables, separators should be confined to horizontal lines. APA and BPS journal editors seem to dislike vertical lines. This is partly to impose consistency in the way tabular information is presented, and partly because horizontal lines are more straightforward to set up for printing purposes.

- Tables should be independently intelligible – it should be clear from the title and headings what the table is about without the need to refer to the text.

(Note: further discussion on the placing and formatting of tables occurs in Part 7.)

Imagine a research scenario in which we are interested in the performance of skilled versus unskilled individuals on some co-ordination task (readers are alerted to the imminent return of hedgehog-based examples). As part of our study we may feel it relevant to report on, or describe, the key characteristics of our sample, and what better way to do this than in a table?

Tables 7.1a and 7.1b are good examples of simple tables which reduce, summarise and describe information in a way which is both easy to follow and meaningful.

In the examples below tables have been used to organise information in a way which both summarises and describes, a particularly appropriate technique for nominally scaled data (information characterised by the class or category to which it belongs, as in male or

**Table 7.1a**    The distribution of males and females in a sample.

| Gender | Value | Frequency | % |
|--------|-------|-----------|-----|
| Male | 1 | 14 | 46.7 |
| Female | 2 | 16 | 53.3 |
| Total | | 30 | 100.0 |

**Table 7.1b**    Distribution of skilled and unskilled cyclists in a sample.

| Skill level | Value | Frequency | % |
|-------------|-------|-----------|-----|
| Skilled | 1 | 15 | 50.0 |
| Unskilled | 2 | 15 | 50.0 |
| Total | | 30 | 100.0 |

Table 7.1c Crosstabulation of participants' gender by cycling skill level.

| Gender | Cycling skill level | | Total |
| --- | --- | --- | --- |
| | Skilled | Unskilled | |
| Male | 8 | 6 | 14 |
| Female | 7 | 9 | 16 |
| Total | 15 | 15 | 30 |

female). Tables 7.1a and 7.1b are known as **frequency tables** (the frequencies with which participants fall into each category are reported; percentages are also shown, which is a common feature of such tables). Table 7.1c is slightly more sophisticated, being a **contingency table**. Contingency tables are combination tables whose contents are the result of a **crosstabulation**, a procedure whereby frequencies are reported across two different nominal or ordinal variables – in this case we are presented with information about individuals who were both male and skilled and so on, the outcome of a simple counting procedure. (For the sake of completeness, the placing of any one individual in the table is contingent upon both gender and skill level.)

While most studies require that the researchers report on any relevant characteristics of their participants, this is especially true of survey-based research, in which the description of the disposition of a sample is often an important aim of the study – how many voters claimed they would support Conservative at the next election, as opposed to Labour; how many respondents voted yes on the issue of a single European currency; of these, how many were male, middle class and living in rural communities, and so on. In research which is quasi-experimental, the nature of the participants is also of importance, since particular profile characteristics (such as gender or personality type) will often comprise the conditions of an independent variable. It is worth pointing out that one would not normally go to the trouble of creating tables for the simple information shown in Tables 7.1a, 7.1b and 7.1c, all of which might be better expressed in the text. We do so here purely for illustration purposes. Note also that we have adopted a convention of using letter suffixes in our titles. This is a convenience allowing us to group tables together and is not, as we have previously indicated, the preference of the APA or BPS.

## 7.4 Figures and categorical variables

While no one would deny the importance of tabular illustrations, it must be said that some of us are uncomfortable with this approach. Aside from the fact that many of us seem to have an inherent fear of numbers, causing us to shy away from even the most informative of table, presenting information pictorially often has more immediate impact. It should be pointed out, though, that most researchers (and editors) prefer summary and descriptive data as tables because of their precision, and a review of most current journals will readily confirm this preference. Graphs tend to come into their own at the data-screening stage of analysis, when they can often point to problems with our data (such as the presence of extreme scores, or distributions which deviate from the normal) which might be more difficult to identify from a table. Graphs can be colourful, striking even; moreover, apart from appealing to an apparent liking for visualisation, they can often emphasise effects which

**Figure 7.1a**    Distribution of males and females.

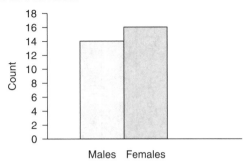

**Figure 7.1b**    Distribution of skilled and unskilled cyclists.

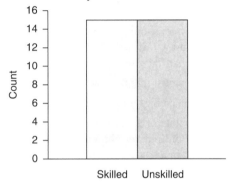

could easily be overlooked in complex and information-rich tables. Figures 7.1a and 7.1b reproduce the information displayed in the preceding tables.

Figures 7.1a and 7.1b are termed bar charts, or bar graphs, since the number of cases in each category is expressed by a vertical bar, or column. Conventionally, categories are shown on the horizontal, or *x*-axis, with the frequency, or count, shown on the vertical, or *y*-axis. The number of observations – male/female or skilled/unskilled – can be read against the vertical scale. As with tables, we would not normally generate figures simply to indicate frequencies in such a simple example, nor would we duplicate information which is already present in a table. The use of figures is most appropriate when data are more complex and trends may not be obvious from a table. Inspection of the figures in section 7.7 will illustrate this point.

Finally, charts can also be of the combination variety, in which measures on more than one variable can be shown, as in Figure 7.1c, a 'stacked' bar chart which replicates the crosstabulated data in Table 7.1c.

The generation of such charts is relatively straightforward – they can be hand-drawn, or computer generated, which is fast becoming the norm as the availability of cheap PCs increases; most current word-processing and spreadsheet packages will allow a graph-creation facility and good presentation-standard charts are now readily available. However, there are certain guidelines which should be followed to ensure that diagrams can be easily understood and that they are true expressions of the data they represent.

- All graphs must be titled as figures, and each figure should have its unique identification number. Titles should be placed either above or below the figure itself, and placement should be consistent for all figures in a document.

**Figure 7.1c** Distribution of sample by gender and skill level.

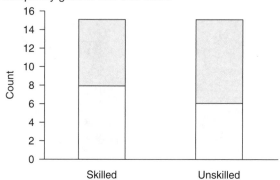

- Figure numbers should be sequential and linked to any tabulated data from which they have been drawn, if appropriate (Figure 7.1c is based on the data in Table 7.1c). As with tables, suffixes are discouraged (although we use them in this textbook).
- Figure titles must indicate clearly what the chart shows.
- Each axis on a chart must be clearly labelled.
- The horizontal (or *x*) axis in a chart usually shows the categories which comprise a nominal or ordinal variable, or shows the independent variable (either categorical or continuous) in a study.
- The vertical (or *y*) axis usually shows the count or frequency with which observations occurred, or shows the dependent variable in a study. (In correlation research, the variable known as the *predictor* is shown on the *x*-axis, and the variable known as the *criterion* is shown on the *y*-axis. Part 5 explains these terms in greater detail.)
- By convention, the vertical axis should be three-quarters the length of the horizontal axis; this is especially important when two charts showing the same scales are to be compared. Note, though, that modern computer software often defaults to settings in which both axes will be the same length. In practice this is not a problem providing consistency is maintained.
- The scale on the *y*-axis (and the *x*-axis when two continuous-scaled variables are plotted) should have zero (0) as its origin. Following this convention allows for the direct comparison of different charts drawn from a single data set. Failure to do so makes such comparisons problematic; this will also affect the proportional difference between, for instance, the bars on a bar chart in much the same way that manipulating the length of the axis will. Figure 7.1d offers an illustration, in which Figure 7.1a has been re-drawn, creating the impression that there were many more females in the sample than males, when in fact the difference in numbers is small (16 females to 14 males). Unfortunately most graph-drawing packages tend to emphasise the overall proportions of the chart to the detriment of the scales on the axes and it is the wise undergraduate who inspects the origins on figures before they attempt to interpret what they see.

(Note: further discussion on the use of figures can be found in the Part 7 of this book.)

Generally speaking, in the preparation of graphs, most researchers tend to shun over-embellishment, partly as a matter of taste, and partly because too many features in an

**Figure 7.1d** Distribution of males and females.

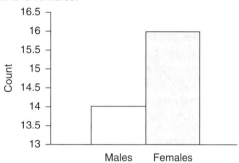

illustration might obscure those very characteristics of the data which the figure is attempting to demonstrate. On a practical note, complex, multi-coloured illustrations are also expensive to reproduce and publishers of papers, journal articles and book chapters will often prefer a simpler way to make a point. Consequently, in this particular textbook you will find the majority of graphs and charts presented in a relatively straightforward manner. However, since the publishers have agreed on a two-coloured edition, we have slightly indulged ourselves, though not to the extent shown in Box 7.1.

Box 7.1

## How To . . .

# Ruin a useful figure

Many undergraduates, especially those new to sophisticated presentational software, find the range of illustrative options irresistible. Consider how Figure 7.1c can be re-drawn using some of the chart enhancements available (see Figure 7.1e):

**Figure 7.1e**

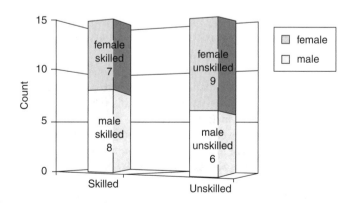

Tempting as it is to play with styles and chart options, the best advice is to keep it simple and be consistent – don't keep changing the format of figures and tables and avoid over-embellishment which might undermine the clarity of the figure.

## 7.5    Tables and continuous variables

When measures are taken on a continuous variable – scores on an ability or personality scale; physical measurements such as height or shoe size; or performance scores, like the number of words correctly recalled in a cognitive experiment, or the number of hedgehogs stunned in a cycle race – the mere noting of such scores as they occur is not especially helpful. Consider the unorganised array of scores in Table 7.2a, based on a hypothetical study in which the intellectual ability of a sample of participants is recorded:

Table 7.2a    Unordered array of ability scores on a sample of 110 participants.

| | | | | | | | | | |
|---|---|---|---|---|---|---|---|---|---|
| 154 | 131 | 122 | 100 | 113 | 119 | 121 | 128 | 112 | 93 |
| 133 | 119 | 115 | 117 | 110 | 104 | 125 | 85 | 120 | 135 |
| 116 | 103 | 103 | 121 | 109 | 147 | 103 | 113 | 107 | 98 |
| 128 | 93 | 90 | 105 | 118 | 134 | 89 | 143 | 108 | 143 |
| 85 | 108 | 108 | 136 | 115 | 117 | 110 | 80 | 111 | 127 |
| 100 | 100 | 114 | 123 | 126 | 119 | 122 | 102 | 100 | 106 |
| 105 | 111 | 127 | 108 | 106 | 91 | 123 | 132 | 97 | 110 |
| 150 | 130 | 87 | 89 | 108 | 137 | 124 | 96 | 111 | 101 |
| 118 | 104 | 127 | 94 | 115 | 101 | 125 | 129 | 131 | 110 |
| 97 | 135 | 108 | 139 | 133 | 107 | 115 | 83 | 109 | 116 |
| 110 | 113 | 112 | 82 | 114 | 112 | 113 | 142 | 145 | 123 |

Surprisingly perhaps, the presentation of data, even in this raw form, constitutes a table. Although we have previously stated that the purpose of a table is to display, organise and summarise data, the presentation of raw scores in the format of Table 7.2a is still sufficient to enjoy the status of a table – true, there is no attempt to summarise, and raw data by their nature are unorganised. But it does display the data, and that is sufficient. However, data in this format are not particularly useful since inspection of a table of raw, unorganised data is unlikely to tell us much about the sample from which it was collected. In particular, as researchers, we are interested in such things as central tendency (average scores) and dispersion (the extent to which scores vary), and the first step towards these goals is to organise the data.

The conventional method for organising large arrays of raw data is to reduce the amount of information to the point where we can begin to determine trends (averages and variation). The simplest way to do this is to create a frequency distribution based on the original data, as in Table 7.2b.

What we have done here is reduce the 110 original scores into score categories, while retaining a count of the number of individual scores falling into each one. Hence, we find that 3 of the raw scores fit into the 80–84 category, while 5 of the original scores fit into the 85–99 category and so on, while ensuring that each category is the same size, or interval (i.e., 5 scores in width). This is why such continuous data are termed *interval* data. (See Box 7.2 for an illustration of the procedure for generating frequency distribution tables.)

Although there are no hard and fast rules for determining the number of intervals to have in a frequency distribution, or the size of the interval itself, a general guideline would

Table 7.2b    Frequency distribution of ability scores.

| Class interval (*i*) | Frequency (*f*) |
| --- | --- |
| 80–84 | 3 |
| 85–89 | 5 |
| 90–94 | 5 |
| 95–99 | 4 |
| 100–104 | 12 |
| 105–109 | 14 |
| 110–114 | 17 |
| 115–119 | 13 |
| 120–124 | 9 |
| 125–129 | 9 |
| 130–134 | 7 |
| 135–139 | 5 |
| 140–144 | 3 |
| 145–149 | 2 |
| 150–154 | 2 |

BOX 7.2

## How To . . .

# Generate a frequency distribution from raw data

The following raw data comprise numbers of stunned hedgehogs (errors) for a sample of 30 cyclists.

Table 7.3a    Unordered array of hedgehog (error) scores.

| | | | | |
| --- | --- | --- | --- | --- |
| 19 | 32 | 28 | 30 | 16 |
| 7 | 41 | 21 | 23 | 22 |
| 35 | 15 | 16 | 26 | 26 |
| 8 | 11 | 15 | 14 | 14 |
| 13 | 13 | 16 | 16 | 13 |
| 16 | 21 | 20 | 16 | 11 |

To convert Table 7.3a into something more useful, the following steps are required.

(i)   Choose sufficient intervals to allow several observations in each category. In this instance, with only 30 observations, 6 intervals might be recommended.

(ii)  Take the difference between the lowest and highest value and add 1 (here, this equals 35).

(iii) Divide this figure by the chosen number of intervals to determine the interval width – adjust the interval size up or down to ensure the interval width is an odd number, so that the middle value is always a whole number. In this example an interval width of 5 will accommodate all the values.

(iv) Set the range of the first interval to accept the lowest score in our array, plus any others which fit this first range. (In this case, the first interval might be 5–9 and we find that two of the raw scores will fit.)

(v) Show the frequency with which scores fall into each interval.

Inspection of Table 7.3b informs us of a number of things. Firstly there is a bunching of observations around the 10 to 24 range, with a tailing off of cases above and below. Secondly we note that the range of observations is approximately 5 to 44. We say approximately since we don't know if anyone actually scored 5 (or 44), or whether the relevant scores merely occupy these categories. More correctly we would use the mid-points of intervals, and our compromise range would become 7 to 42 (hence our earlier suggestion that when class intervals are determined, they comprise an uneven value range, allowing for the mid-point to be a whole number). And finally, we can note that the most frequent set of observations occurs in the 15–19 interval. Since this is the modal range, and therefore the score of 17 becomes the modal value, we can judge that the arithmetic average of this distribution of scores will be close to this. (The actual arithmetic average is 19 for this array of scores which, for a rule-of-thumb guide, is acceptably close to our estimate.) Note that there are certain cautions concerning the use of a modal value to estimate average, to do with the way in which the other scores are spread around this value. This is discussed in detail in the later section on statistics.

Table 7.3b    Frequency distribution of hedge-hog (error) scores, based on the raw data in Table 7.3a.

| Interval ($i$) | Frequency ($f$) |
|---|---|
| 5–9 | 2 |
| 10–14 | 7 |
| 15–19 | 9 |
| 20–24 | 5 |
| 25–29 | 3 |
| 30–34 | 2 |
| 35–39 | 1 |
| 40–44 | 1 |

be to choose something between 5 and 20 intervals. Fewer than 5 and we find that most of our observations are crammed into too few categories to give a picture of either average or spread, while much more than 20 and we risk having categories with too few, or even no observations at all. This of course is linked to the overall number of original scores, and the range of scores, from lowest to highest. If we are measuring extraversion with a small sample, on a scale where the lowest score is 5 and the highest 25, we might opt for intervals of width 3, allowing for 7 intervals altogether. With our ability example, on the other hand, with a large sample and a range of scores from 80 to 154, we can have many more intervals, knowing that there will be several observations in each. Moreover, an interval width of 5 scores will provide for 15 intervals, which is within our guidelines.

The frequency distribution in Table 7.2b fulfils all the functions we expect in a good table – it displays the data in an organised format, it summarises and it allows us to describe important characteristics of the sample. In particular, we can now make a judgement about typicality, in that most of the participants scored in the range of 100 to 119, with the most frequent scores occurring in the 110–114 interval. This is known as the **mode**, or modal interval, and is often a good approximation of the actual average. (In fact, the arithmetic average for this array of scores is 114, making the mode not a bad approximation.) Equally useful, we can determine that the overall range of scores is roughly between 80 and 154. Neither of these judgements is possible from the table of original, raw data.

Now it is true that in achieving this frequency table we have lost important information – we no longer know the precise scores obtained by each individual, only that, for instance, three participants scored somewhere within the range of 80–84 and so on. Despite this loss, the opportunity to make informed judgements about a sample from a summary table is often seen as outweighing all other factors. In addition, a number of illustrative graphs can be generated from such summary data, which forms the basis of the next section.

## 7.6 The Stemplot

The **stemplot**, or stem-and-leaf plot as it is often called, is a bit of an oddity since it is neither a table nor a graph, although it seems to possess elements of both. Given to us by Tukey (1972), it is perhaps best thought of as a table which looks like a graph and which can be interpreted in a similar manner. Although generally a useful way of describing data, the stemplot would not normally appear in a formal report, being primarily a screening tool allowing us to inspect data for deviations from normality.

Consider the data shown in Table 7.3a, concerning the fates of unfortunate hedgehogs during a cycle race. Converting these data into a stemplot would produce Table 7.4a.

To the left of the divide in a stemplot table is the stem, or basic structure of an array of scores, shown as units (0), 10s (1), 20s (2) and so on, to accommodate the full range of the raw data. To the right of the divide are the leaves, the actual values associated with the respective stems. Thus, from the table we note that there were two values in the units stem, being 7 and 8. There were three values in the 30s stem, being 30, 32, 35 and so on. The useful point about this type of table is that it also provides a picture of the distribution of scores. As we shall see in the next section on graphs, a chart representing the data in the stem-table would look very much like the table itself. Box 7.3 provides a guide to producing stemplots.

The example in Table 7.4a has used the major divisions of units, 10s, 20s and so on as the stems for the stemplot, which is the usual method for generating this particular figure,

| Table 7.4a | Stemplot of hedgehog (error) scores, based on the data in Table 7.3a. |
|---|---|
| 0 ┊ 78 | |
| 1 ┊ 1133344556666669 | |
| 2 ┊ 01123668 | |
| 3 ┊ 025 | |
| 4 ┊ 1 | |

but other subdivisions are possible, particularly when there are a large number of observations within each stem range. In these cases it is possible to reduce the range of each stem such that, instead of the stem for 10s ranging from 10 to 19, we have two stems, the first from 10 to 14 and the second from 15 to 19. Given the example in Table 7.4a, this would become Table 7.4b:

Table 7.4b    Modified stemplot of hedgehog (error) scores, based on the data in Table 7.4a.

| 0 | |
|---|---|
| 0 | 78 |
| 1 | 1133344 |
| 1 | 556666669 |
| 2 | 01123 |
| 2 | 668 |
| 3 | 02 |
| 3 | 5 |
| 4 | 1 |
| 4 | |

## How To . . .

# Generate a stem plot

Plotting a stemplot is a convenient method of both tabulating and showing a picture of an array of data. It is especially useful for data which spread across a wide range of values (e.g., 0 to 100), but less so for narrow ranges (e.g., 5 to 20). Production of stemplots is straightforward and we can illustrate this using the raw ability data in Table 7.2a.

(i)   Order the data from the lowest value to the highest, as in Table 7.5a. This really does make it easier.

Table 7.5a    Ordered array of 110 scores, based on the ability data in Table 7.2a.

| | | | | | | | | | |
|---|---|---|---|---|---|---|---|---|---|
| 80 | 93 | 101 | 107 | 110 | 113 | 117 | 122 | 128 | 135 |
| 82 | 94 | 102 | 107 | 110 | 113 | 117 | 123 | 128 | 136 |
| 83 | 96 | 103 | 108 | 110 | 113 | 118 | 123 | 129 | 137 |
| 85 | 97 | 103 | 108 | 110 | 114 | 118 | 123 | 130 | 139 |
| 85 | 97 | 103 | 108 | 111 | 114 | 119 | 124 | 131 | 142 |
| 87 | 98 | 104 | 108 | 111 | 115 | 119 | 125 | 131 | 143 |
| 89 | 100 | 104 | 108 | 111 | 115 | 119 | 125 | 132 | 143 |
| 89 | 100 | 105 | 108 | 112 | 115 | 120 | 126 | 133 | 145 |
| 90 | 100 | 105 | 109 | 112 | 115 | 121 | 127 | 133 | 147 |
| 91 | 100 | 106 | 109 | 112 | 116 | 121 | 127 | 134 | 150 |
| 93 | 101 | 106 | 110 | 113 | 116 | 122 | 127 | 135 | 154 |

(ii)   Identify and note the stems. In this example the first set of values begin in the 80s, and end in the 150s. The stems therefore range from 8 to 15.

(iii)  Identify and note the unit values for each stem. For the 8 stem (i.e., values in the 80s) we find the values 80, 82, 83, 85 and so on. These are expressed as 0, 2, 3 and 5. Table 7.5b shows the completed table.

Table 7.5b    Stem plot of 110 ability scores.

| | | |
|---|---|---|
| 8 | ⦙ | 0 2 3 5 5 7 9 9 |
| 9 | ⦙ | 0 1 3 3 4 6 7 7 8 |
| 10 | ⦙ | 0 0 0 0 1 1 2 3 3 3 4 4 5 5 6 6 7 7 8 8 8 8 8 8 9 9 |
| 11 | ⦙ | 0 0 0 0 0 1 1 1 2 2 2 3 3 3 3 4 4 5 5 5 5 6 6 7 7 8 8 9 9 9 |
| 12 | ⦙ | 0 1 1 2 2 3 3 3 4 5 5 6 7 7 7 8 8 9 |
| 13 | ⦙ | 0 1 1 2 3 3 4 5 5 6 7 9 |
| 14 | ⦙ | 2 3 3 5 7 |
| 15 | ⦙ | 0 4 |

A number of things are immediately apparent from a stemplot table. Firstly we can determine the absolute range of the data, in this case from 80 to 154. Secondly we can determine the modal range, merely by noting the stem value in which the greatest number of scores fall – the stem of 11, which means all values from 110 upwards, but not as high as 120. (Recall that the actual arithmetic average for this array of data is 114.) And finally, inspection of the shape of the table tells us how far scores vary around the most frequent range.

A point to note here is that not all statistical software will generate stemplots and so these must be often done manually, using either a standard spreadsheet or a table function in a word-processing package. This is rarely a problem once the principle of stemplots has been grasped.

(Note: the particular statistical package we have used to illustrate descriptive statistics in Chapter 8 – SPSS – is one which does offer stemplots as part of its Explore facility.)

## 7.7    Figures and continuous variables

We have made the point that graphs can offer an alternative, and sometimes more immediate, representation of a data set than a table and there follows a review of the ways in which continuous data can be presented in this way.

Generally speaking, a chart aims to offer a picture of the data collected in a study such that, merely by inspection (i.e., looking at it) we can make certain inferences, in particular about central tendency (average), dispersion (the extent to which scores vary about the average) and whether our data differ from what we might expect. Consider the data in Table 7.2b, in which ability scores have been organised into class intervals. Were we to

**Figure 7.2a** Bar chart showing the distribution of ability scores of 110 research participants.

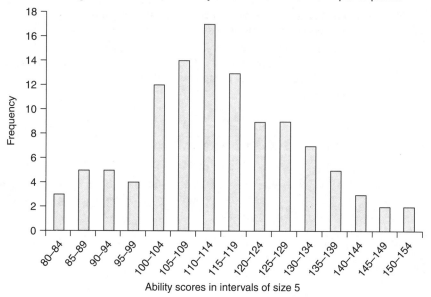

Ability scores in intervals of size 5

create a bar chart, similar to those appearing in 7.1.4, with a bar for each interval, we would produce a figure like Figure 7.2a.

However, since the categories which comprise this particular data set are actually intervals of a continuous variable, they are more appropriately shown as a histogram, in which the various 'bars' adjoin, to indicate that each interval blends into the next, as in Figure 7.2b.

Figure 7.2b is termed a histogram and is one of the standard ways of representing continuous data. Note that, rather than showing the class intervals on the *x*-axis (80–84) we have instead given the mid-points of each interval (82, 87, etc.) which is an alternative method of labelling the category axis. An advantage of doing this – apart from making the axis label less cluttered – is that if we were to join all these mid-points with a single line,

**Figure 7.2b** Histogram showing the distribution of 110 ability scores.

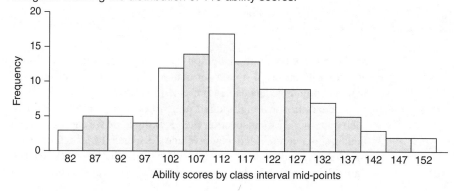

Ability scores by class interval mid-points

**Figure 7.3a**    Frequency polygon of ability scores of 110 participants.

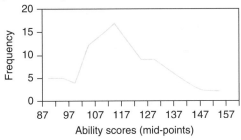

**Figure 7.3b**    Frequency polygon of ability scores of 110 male and 110 female participants.

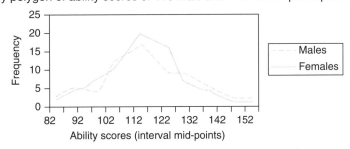

dispensing with the bars which form the histogram, we produce a line graph termed a frequency polygon, as in Figure 7.3a.

An advantage of this type of graph is that, because the figure itself is a much simplified version of the histogram on which it is based, and therefore less complex, we can display data from more than one source in the same chart. Imagine that the ability scores which comprise our current example are drawn from a population of male psychology undergraduates. If we were to draw similar data from a female population, we could compare both samples on a single graph, as in Figure 7.3b.

The value of presenting data in graphical format is the immediacy of the illustration. In the histograms and frequency polygons shown in this section, key characteristics of the data are readily seen. Central tendency is obvious merely by inspection of where the graphs peak, variation is also apparent by noting the starting point and end point of the graphs and any peculiarities of the data are also easy to spot. For instance, in our ability data for males, there is a dip in cases around the 102 score point, which is not evident in the female sample. Other important characteristics of a data set can also be noted in graphical format, which are often not visible if we only consult a table of data (see our discussion of kurtosis and skewness in section 7.11).

## 7.8    Continuous variables and the boxplot

An alternative method for expressing a continuous-scaled variable is to use a boxplot. Figure 7.4 is typical, based on our ability score example.

**Figure 7.4**    Boxplot of ability scores of 110 participants.

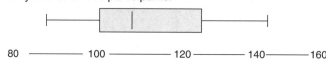

Figure 7.4, based on the raw ability data shown in Table 7.2a, is known as a **boxplot** and is another common illustrative chart, utilising the measures of median, IQR and overall range. Many people new to this mode of presentation find boxplots unintelligible, yet once their principle is understood, they quickly become a useful tool for the researcher, especially for screening data, although they are rarely used in formal reports.

The median is a measure of central tendency which indicates the middle value in a distribution of scores, and given by a bar or an asterisk running through the rectangle in the centre of the graph. The upper and lower quartiles are shown by the upper and lower limits of the rectangle itself, which contains the middle 50% of all the data, while the overall range of values is shown by the horizontal lines resembling the plunger on a syringe. (These lines are actually termed the 'whiskers' of the plot. In fact, this type of graph used to be known as a box-and-whiskers plot.)

Inspection of this chart would suggest that the average ability score is about 110, the interquartile range (the range in which the middle half of the scores fall) about 20 (100 to 120, approximately) and the overall range of scores going from 85 to 150. (The actual values were median = 115; IQR = 19; range = 74 – not too bad an estimate from a graph.) Procedures for creating a boxplot are given in Box 7.4.

---

Box 7.4

## How To . . .

## Generate a boxplot

The procedure for creating a boxplot from an array of data is extremely straightforward, requiring merely that we arrange our data in an array from lowest to highest and begin subdividing it, first into two halves, and then into quarters, by position. Consider a group of cyclists covering a standard cycle run, and a note being taken of the number of errors made by each one.

6   7   7   8   6   7   8   9   5   5   7   6   2   3   4   4   5   4   3   4

(i) Our first step is to re-arrange these raw data into an ordered array of scores, from lowest to highest:

2   3   3   4   4   4   4   5   5   5   6   6   6   7   7   7   7   8   8   9

(ii) The next step is to identify the middle value, by counting from each end. If the distribution comprises an uneven number of scores this will be a single value. Otherwise we merely take the average of the two scores on either side of our mid-point, as in this case.

2   3   3   4   4   4   4   5   5   5   |   6   6   6   7   7   7   7   8   8   9

(iii)  The median is given as the middle value of a distribution, the value which divides an array of scores into two equal halves. In this instance there is no single value which represents the mid-point, so we would take the two points on either side (5 and 6) and take the average. Thus the median for this array is 5.5.

(iv)  Take each half of the distribution, as located on either side of the median, and identify the quarter positions, in the same way the median was identified in the previous step. Again, if the quarter points, termed quartiles, do not fall on a single value, take the average of the scores on either side.

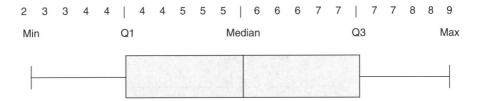

We have now identified the lower quartile (Q1) as 4, the median as 5.5 and the upper quartile (Q3) as 7. We also note that the minimum value is 2 and the maximum 9.

(v)  Replace the data in the ordered array with an idealised boxplot, ensuring the features of the graph mirror the information on the array itself. (The boxplot is termed *idealised* since the plot will match the symmetrical segments of the data set, as opposed to the actual scale on which the scores are measured.)

(vi)  The final step is to fit our ideal plot onto the interval scale on which the original measurements are based (see Figure 7.5).

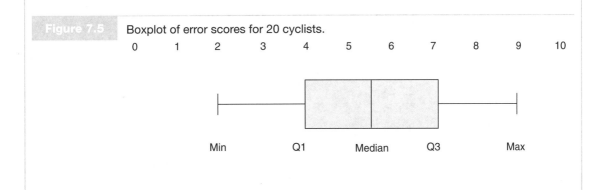

**Figure 7.5**    Boxplot of error scores for 20 cyclists.

The astute reader may have noticed that, while this section is ostensibly concerned with the use of graphs to describe data, a number of our illustrations have wandered into statistical territory. This should not be a problem though, and is explained by the fact that all of the ways of expressing the important characteristics of data (tables, graphs and statistics) are really just different perspectives of the same thing. Not surprisingly then there will be considerable overlap among the different methods, and this is especially true in consideration of the next section on the normal distribution. In the meantime, Box 7.5 illustrates the three methods of expressing data we have chosen to adopt. Box 7.6 compares different types of figures.

## A Closer Look At . . .

# Ways of describing data

Consider a recurring example concerning a group of novice cyclists negotiating a standard route. During a single trial a note is taken of the number of hedgehogs run over, taken as a measure of performance, an error rate for each cyclist. If there are 30 cyclists and the raw data are collected, our first view of events might be as an unorganised array of error scores. Note that Tables 7.6a and 7.6b are identical to Tables 7.3a and 7.3b.

Table 7.6a   Unordered array of error scores.

| | | | | |
|---|---|---|---|---|
| 19 | 32 | 28 | 30 | 16 |
| 7 | 41 | 21 | 23 | 22 |
| 35 | 15 | 16 | 26 | 26 |
| 8 | 11 | 15 | 14 | 14 |
| 13 | 13 | 16 | 16 | 13 |
| 16 | 21 | 20 | 16 | 11 |

On its own such an array is of limited use – we gain no impression of central tendency (average), or of the way in which error rates might vary among the riders merely from inspection of the data. There are three things we can do to make sense of what has occurred in this small-scale observation study.

1. A summary table:

Table 7.6b   Frequency distribution of error scores, based on the raw data in Tables 7.6a.

| Interval (*i*) | Frequency (*f*) |
|---|---|
| 5–9 | 2 |
| 10–14 | 7 |
| 15–19 | 9 |
| 20–24 | 5 |
| 25–29 | 3 |
| 30–34 | 2 |
| 35–39 | 1 |
| 40–44 | 1 |

The table is one way of organizing, describing and summarizing data. We can determine, for instance, the most common error rate among our participants and suggest that on average the cyclists are leaving tyre marks on between 15 and 19 unfortunate hedgehogs. We can also note that the fewest casualties are likely to be 5, with the most careless of our cyclists seeing off 44.

2. A figure:

**Figure 7.6**    Histogram of hedgehog scores, based on the data in Table 7.6a.

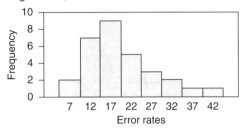

Describing our data in a figure such as Figure 7.6 offers an immediate, visual impression of what occurred in our study. Clearly there is a bunching of cases in the 15–19 error group, with a large number of observations immediately below and a more gradual tailing off beyond. The minimum and maximum values are evident (although not given precisely) and the image allows us to form an impression of the extent to which rates vary around a central value. While it is possible to make precise judgements from a table, many people prefer the visual impact of a figure. Moreover, as the size of a data set increases, the interpretation of tables becomes difficult, while the immediacy of a figure tends to remain. Having said this, the fact remains that most researchers, and most journal editors, still prefer the accuracy afforded by tables with graphs being used primarily for initial screening or general illustration purposes.

3. Statistics:

| | |
|---|---|
| Mean errors | 19.14 |
| Standard deviation | 8.05 |
| Skewness | 0.98 |

Using statistics to represent our data is the third method we can adopt. Here, numerical values are used to describe some of the important characteristics of a variable – a measure of central tendency (mean), a measure of dispersion (standard deviation) and a measure of the symmetry of the range of scores (skewness). There are other measures we could report which provide a fuller picture of the data. These and the statistical examples already discussed are considered in detail in section 7.9.

Box 7.6

## A Closer Look At . . .

# Comparing different types of figures

The function of a graph is to display data in a visual format. The three examples below, based on the stunned hedgehog data in Table 7.6b, present three different views of the same information. Note that the stems in the stemplot have been modified to reflect the

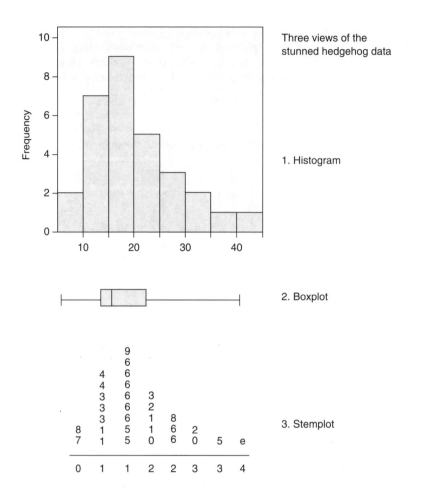

Three views of the
stunned hedgehog data

1. Histogram

2. Boxplot

3. Stemplot

intervals which were used to create the histogram. Note also that the stem of 4 is
characterised by the letter *e*, indicating that the highest score in this distribution can be
considered an 'extreme' score, and not typical of the rest of the distribution. The notion of
extreme scores is considered in more detail in the next chapter.

## 7.9 Statistics

The third method for making sense of our universe is quite different from the previous
two: tables and graphs both tend to provide a broad view of the data, with illustration and
description being their primary function. Statistics, on the other hand, can express and
summarise substantial amounts of data with a single value. This is what a **statistic** is – a
numerical value which represents a body of data according to certain established conventions, plus (usually) an associated symbol which identifies the particular aspect of our
data being expressed. Moreover, a statistic is often merely the first step in a more complex
analysis – in the way that a measure of average can often be used as the basis for comparison with other measures of average. The discussion which follows illustrates the point,

while Box 7.9 later in this chapter presents common statistical symbols and their associated meanings.

## 7.9.1 Central tendency

When trying to describe or illustrate the typical characteristics of a variable, we often opt for some measure of **central tendency** (statistical jargon for average) which best represents our information. Consequently we describe the heights of a group of undergraduates in terms of an arithmetic average and, because we are used to using this kind of statistic in our everyday lives, we readily understand that average is only a part of the story; while most people will cluster around some central measure, we nonetheless accept that some people will gain higher scores than this, and some lower. Observing that the average height of a group of undergraduates is 5′ 9″ recognises the fact that there will be some students who measure 5′ 10″, or even 6′. Similarly, there will be some people who measure 5′ 8″ or 5′ 7″, but by and large, most of the people will measure round about the 5′ 9″ mark. This is what average is all about, the almost universal tendency for anything we care to observe to cluster around some central or typical measure. (Some readers may be uncomfortable with our use of old-style imperial measures, preferring metres and centimetres. It is, however, an age thing and we like feet and inches.)

The term 'average' is usually taken to represent the arithmetic average, in which all the scores or values in a set of observations are summed and then divided by the number in the set. Statistically, this is known as the arithmetic **mean** (symbolised by $\bar{x}$) and it is the most precise of all the different measures of centrality based, as it is, on actual scores. However, there are situations in which the mean, irrespective of its accuracy, may not fulfil the function of indicating typicality. This can occur when a distribution contains one or more extreme scores, or outliers, as in the following examples.

We measure the attention span (in minutes) of male and female undergraduates during an introductory psychology lecture.

(i) the attention span scores of male undergraduates

    5,6,7,7,8,8,8,9,9,10,11,12,                mean = 8.3

(ii) the attention span scores of female undergraduates

    5,6,7,7,8,8,8,9,10,11,120                 mean = 18

In example (i) the arithmetic mean works out as 8.3, which, by inspecting the distribution of spans, is fairly typical of the way scores are clustered in this group. In example (ii), however, the mean is 18, which clearly is typical of none of the members of this particular group. (If you are wondering how such an extreme score as 120 could find its way into a group whose real average is closer to 8, admittedly this is unusual. Perhaps a passing alien of unusual curiosity joined the class to see what we humans were up to, or perhaps we made a mistake in measuring our students. Either way, the calculated mean is going to be misleading.)

To deal with such problems, which are really quite common (not the part about the alien), an alternative measure of central tendency is available to us which is not so sensitive to extreme values. This is the **median**, which is simply the middle value in a range of scores (arranged in order from lowest to highest that is, rather than simply presented in the order in which data were gathered). In example (i), the median would be 8. In case (ii) the median is also 8, a much more representative value than the arithmetic average, and a statistic not in the least influenced by the extreme score of 120.

This tendency for the middle value in any range of scores to provide a good measure of average is a universal phenomenon, allowable by the fact that the measurement of every human characteristic will always produce a clustering of observations which will typify the majority. Height, shoe size, intelligence, attention span, whatever – there is invariably a measure, or range of measures, which is most typical of that particular trait. Hence, the middle value will always fall within this common or most typical cluster, which is why the median is usually a good measure of average.

Box 7.7

## A Closer Look At . . .

# The mean, median and mode

If students are drawn at random from the undergraduate population and their shoe size measured, the following arrays of scores might be produced.

1. 2,2,2,3,3,4,5,5,5,5,5,6,6,7,7,8,9

Each of the three measures of average is suitable here, with the mean, median and mode giving a score of 5.

2. 5,5,6,7,7,7,8,8,9,9,10,10,10,10,11,11,12,13,14

Here, the mean is 8.95, the median is 9 and the mode – in fact, there are two modes, making this measure of average inappropriate here. Both the mean and median are the most useful measures of central tendency in this instance. If you are wondering why there appear to be two groupings of 'typical' sizes, this could be attributed to the fact that this particular sample comprises a mixture of males and females, and that their shoe sizes are sufficiently different to give two distinct clusters.

3. 5,5,6,7,7,7,8,8,9,9,10,11,25,37

In this final example, the occurrence of two extreme scores at the top end of the range (probably recording errors) will artificially pull the calculated arithmetic average towards this extreme. Hence, the mean here would be 11. The median, however, immune as it is to the effects of such extreme scores, would be the much more reasonable 8, with the mode not far away, with 7.

(Note 1: in the event that a median fails to land on an actual middle value, as will be the case with all even-numbered arrays, the procedure is to take the average of the two adjacent scores. Thus, a median falling between the values of 5 and 6 would become 5.5.)

(Note 2: a useful hint for embryonic statisticians is to compare the mean and median values in a distribution. If the distribution is normal, as in comprising a typical clustering around some middle score with cases tailing off evenly at either side, the median and the mean will be close to one another. However, when extreme scores are present, or the distribution is not symmetrical, the calculation of the mean will be influenced and noticeable differences will be observed in comparison to the median.)

There exists a third measure of central tendency, which is really a rule-of-thumb indicator, termed the mode. The mode, or modal value, is the most frequently occurring score in a series of observations and as such, often provides the simplest and speediest estimate of average. Providing the trait or characteristic being measured is of the kind where most people are scoring around some typical level, the mode will give a similar value to the other two measures. In both of the above examples, the mode is 8. Box 7.7 illustrates all three measures of central tendency.

## 7.10 Dispersion

In describing the characteristics of a variable it should now be clear that relying solely on measures of central tendency provides only part of the picture. Much of the discussion in the previous section involved problems associated with how widely, or unevenly, scores varied around some central measure, called **dispersion**. This aspect of any variable or distribution is of considerable interest to researchers.

Much in the same way that even the layperson has an intuitive grasp of the concept of average, so too do most of us have a working understanding of dispersion, even if we lack the statistical skills to generate appropriate measures.

Think back to school days and class exams: if you scored 46 in an arithmetic test and stated that the class average was only 45, you would be more likely to impress parents and friends by pointing out that the top mark was 47. Alternatively, if you scored 50 to the same mean of 45, you might just keep quiet about the fact that the total range of marks was from 0 to 100!

What we have been applying here is the simplest measure of dispersion, the **range**, which is a statement of the lowest score to the highest. In the example below, showing an ordered array of the error rate of 16 cyclists, the range is 8, with a minimum of 2 and a maximum of 10.

2,3,3,4,5,5,6,6,6,6,7,7,8,8,9,10

However, as we have already discovered with central tendency, trying to reduce a large amount of information to a typical, representative value is not without its problems – in particular, the misleading effects caused by extreme scores. In much the same way, a simple range, or a statement of minimum and maximum values, can be equally inappropriate when extreme scores are present. The example below illustrates the point: the minimum and maximum values are given as 5 and 37 respectively, with a corresponding range of 32. This implies a broad spread of scores, yet we know that the majority of participants in this group had shoe sizes in the 5–11 range.

5,5,6,7,7,7,8,8,9,9,10,11,25,37

Fortunately, just as with measures of average, there exist alternative ways to represent spread which are not susceptible to extremes.

One such measure is related to the median and is known as the **interquartile range**, or IQR. Just as any array of scores can be divided in two by the median or middle value, so can it be further subdivided: if we take the lower half of a distribution and divide this in turn by half, we obtain two quarters. Similarly, if we take the upper half and further divide this, we also obtain two quarters. These two further subdivisions are known as the lower quartile and the upper quartile (or Q1 and Q3). See below.

| | | | | | | | | | | | | | | | | | | | | |
|---|---|---|---|---|---|---|---|---|---|---|---|---|---|---|---|---|---|---|---|---|
| 5 | 5 | 6 | 7 | 7 | \| | 7 | 7 | 8 | 8 | 9 | \| | 9 | 10 | 10 | 10 | 10 | \| | 11 | 11 | 12 | 13 | 14 |

Q1      Median      Q3

7      9      10.5

All we need do is subtract the value at the first quartile from the value at the third (Q3 − Q1), and we have the interquartile range, which is a measure of spread in which the top and bottom quarters have been removed, thus eliminating any extreme values. In the above example the IQR would be from 7 to 10.5, which comes to 3.5.

There exists a third measure of spread which, like the mean, is based on the actual scores or values found in a distribution. Termed the **standard deviation**, which we discussed earlier in the text, this provides an indication of how much, on average, scores deviate from the mean. Specifically, if we were to learn that the mean score on an abstract reasoning test for a sample of undergraduates was 100, with a standard deviation of 5, we would know that most of our sample deviated by 5 points above and below this average value. In fact, based on an understanding of distributions, we could state that 68% of our sample scored between 95 and 105. The process whereby we are able to make this statement is fully explained in the later section on the normal distribution, while the procedure for calculating the standard deviation is outlined in Box 7.8.

Box 7.8

## How To . . .

## Calculate the standard deviation

Consider an example in which the shoe sizes of a group of undergraduates are measured, as shown:

2,2,2,3,3,4,5,5,5,5,5,6,6,7,7,8,9

The calculated mean (obtained by adding up the individual sizes and dividing by the number of observations) is 4.9. They have small feet! To find out how much each score varies or deviates from this value, we perform a simple subtraction:

| Mean ($\bar{x}$) | Score ($x$) | Score − mean ($x - \bar{x}$) |
|---|---|---|
| 4.9 | 5 | 0.1 |
| 4.9 | 6 | 1.1 |
| 4.9 | 7 | 2.1 |
| . | . | . |
| . | . | . |
| . | . | . |

In approximately half the cases, taking each score from the mean will produce a positive value, as above. Because, however, about half of the scores in a distribution will be greater than the mean, the results of some of these calculations will be negative values, as below:

| Mean ($\bar{x}$) | Score ($x$) | Score – mean ($x - \bar{x}$) |
|---|---|---|
| . | . | . |
| . | . | . |
| . | . | . |
| 4.9 | 2 | −2.9 |
| 4.9 | 2 | −2.9 |
| 4.9 | 2 | −2.9 |
| 4.9 | 3 | −1.9 |

In many statistical calculations, negative values are problematic and statisticians have developed ways of dealing with them. In the calculation of the standard deviation, they are eliminated by squaring the result of each subtraction:

| Mean ($\bar{x}$) | Score ($x$) | Score – mean ($x - \bar{x}$) | (Score – mean) squared ($x - \bar{x}$)$^2$ |
|---|---|---|---|
| . | . | . | . |
| . | . | . | . |
| 4.9 | 5 | −0.1 | 0.01 |
| 4.9 | 6 | −1.1 | 1.21 |
| 4.9 | 7 | −2.1 | 4.41 |
| . | . | . | . |
| . | . | . | . |

The total deviations can now be obtained by adding up all these squared values but what we really want is an average of these, obtained simply by dividing by the number of observations. However, just when we thought we had the answer, we mustn't forget that we are currently dealing with squared scores and not the original values, and this must be rectified. Taking the square root will finally provide the statistic known as the standard deviation (SD), the formula for which is shown below:

$$sd = \sqrt{\frac{\sum (x - \bar{x})^2}{n}}$$  (7.1)

In summary, the standard deviation is obtained by:

(i)   subtracting the mean from each score
(ii)  squaring this value
(iii) summing these values and taking an average
(iv)  taking the square root

Box 7.9

## A Closer Look At . . .

# Common statistical symbols and their meaning

| | |
|---|---|
| $x$ | a score, or the column heading for a variable in univariate analysis. Where more than one variable is present, the notations become $x_1, x_2 \ldots x_n$. |
| $y$ | a score, or the column heading for the second variable in bivariate analysis. Also the variable heading for the dependent variable in two-group comparisons. |
| $\Sigma$ | the sum of . . . (whatever follows). |
| $\Sigma x$ | the sum of the scores. If the scores were 1,2,3,4,5, then $\Sigma x = 15$. |
| $x^2$ | the square of the score, or scores. If the scores were 1,2,3,4,5 they would become 1,4,9,16,25. |
| $\Sigma x^2$ | the sum of the squared scores. From the previous example, $\Sigma x^2 = 55$. |
| $(\Sigma x)^2$ | the sum of the scores, which is then squared. In this case we would add the scores 1,2,3,4,5 (= 15), then square this value = 225. |
| $\sqrt{}$ | the square root. For example, $\sqrt{225} = 15$. |
| $!$ | factorial. For example, $!5 = 5 \times 4 \times 3 \times 2 \times 1 = 120$. |
| $\bar{x}$ | a sample mean obtained by: $\Sigma x / n$. For example, $15/5 = 3$. |
| $sd$ or $s$ | a sample standard deviation, used as an estimate of the population standard deviation. Obtained by: |

$$sd = \sqrt{\frac{\Sigma(x - \bar{x})^2}{n}}$$

| | |
|---|---|
| $\mu$ | a population mean. |
| $\sigma$ | a population standard deviation. |
| $n$ | the number of observations in a sample or a sub-sample. |
| $N$ | the number of observations in a population, or in a total sample. |
| $s^2$ | sample variance. |

Because it is based on actual values the standard deviation is a very accurate and powerful statistic. For the same reason, however, it is also susceptible to extreme values and if a distribution becomes too skewed in one direction, the standard deviation ceases to be of value in representing that distribution.

The terms in this formula are standard statistical notations. Box 7.9 provides full details of relevant terms.

## 7.11  The normal distribution

A major characteristic of our world is the tendency for certain patterns to repeat themselves. One such pattern, observed whenever we measure an event, attitude, response or behaviour, is the tendency for most people to congregate around some middle value, with

Box 7.10

## A Closer Look At . . .

# Skewness

When a distribution contains more than the usual proportion of observations near one of the two ends of the measurement scale, it is said to be skewed (Pearson, 1894) (see Figure 7.7b). In this example, there are a disproportionate number of observations close to the higher end of the distribution. This is known (counter-intuitively, perhaps) as a negative, or left skew, referring to the direction of the elongated tail, rather than the position of the bunching of scores. This tendency for some distributions to deviate from the expected shape can be represented statistically, and calculated using the expression for the alpha 3 measure of skewness, given at (7.2), as:

$$\alpha_3 = \frac{\sum (x - \bar{x})^3}{n \times sd^3} \tag{7.2}$$

The calculations involved in this formula are somewhat complex and these days are better left to the many computer programmes available to us. The next chapter covers this more than adequately. For the moment it is sufficient to note that for normal distributions the skewness value will be zero, with deviations above and below indicating increasing levels of skew.

It is worth mentioning that a simple rule-of-thumb method for estimating skewness is to compare the mean with the median, reminding yourself of the tendency for the mean to be affected by extreme scores in a way in which the median is not. Skewness is indicated when discrepancies begin to appear between the two measures of central tendency.

fewer and fewer people falling into more extreme categories. This always happens if the group we are observing reflects the 'normal population' – normal in that there is the expected variation among individuals in the group we are measuring. Putting it another way, this is the pattern we normally see whenever we observe any human or psychological phenomenon. When we fail to observe this typical outcome we talk of a distribution being characterised by skewness (see Box 7.10).

We have already witnessed this effect to some extent with our previous example on stunned hedgehogs (Box 7.6), in which there is a bunching of scores towards the lower end of the distribution, making for a slightly skewed, or asymmetrical, appearance. But the notion holds true for most other factors, such as age of participants in a sample, measures of stress, personality or indeed any aspect of our lives in which there is scope for variation.

Early studies of general intelligence, for instance, show that most of us will cluster around some average measure, usually given the arbitrary value of 100 (based on Terman and Merrill's (1960) development of the original Binet mental age and chronological age relationship). As with height, there will be some people who will score in higher ranges (e.g., 105–110), but there will be fewer of these. At more extreme ranges (e.g., 110–120) there will be fewer still. This typical pattern is illustrated in Figure 7.7a, a

Figure 7.7a     Histogram showing the distribution of scores about a mean of 100, based on hypothetical mental ability data.

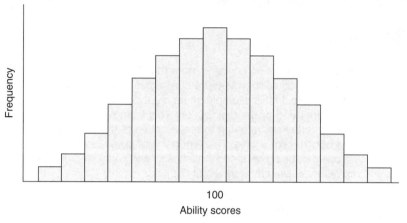

Figure 7.7b     Negatively skewed distribution of mental ability scores.

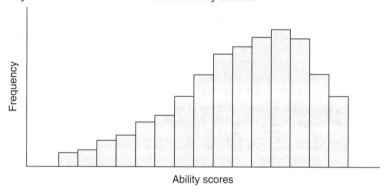

histogram in which the heights of each bar represent the number of observations giving particular scores. (Note: the uses of and methods for producing histograms are outlined in section 7.7.)

This pattern, of course, will only occur providing the group being measured is normal. (Recall that this use of the expression 'normal' is a statistical one, referring to a typical, or expected pattern.) If, by some chance, the observations on intelligence were made on an unusually bright group (who mentioned our students?) there would be more than the usual (or normal) proportion of intellectually superior people in our sample. Therefore the distribution of scores would reflect this skew, as illustrated in Box 7.10.

There is another issue concerning the shape of a distribution which should be noted at this stage, and this is termed **kurtosis**. Like skew, kurtosis describes a deviation from the normal distribution; unlike skew it does not imply a loss of symmetry. Rather, kurtosis is a measure of what can be termed the 'peakedness' of a distribution and relates to the extent to which measures or scores are spread evenly across the intervals on a measurement scale, as opposed to clustering unusually towards some median value. Figure 7.8a illustrates a distribution characterised by positive kurtosis, in that it shows considerably more peakedness and heavier tails than would be found in a normal distribution. It is almost as if a distribution has been squashed in at the sides and forced upwards to relieve the pressure.

**Figure 7.8a**   Leptokurtic distribution.

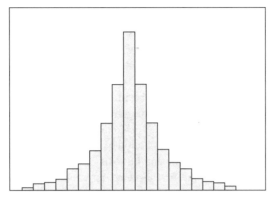

If respondents to an attitudinal item attempt to manipulate their responses by avoiding either extreme of a scale, there will be an unusual clustering of scores around this central value, producing the type of distribution shown in Figure 7.8a. This is sometimes termed a distribution characterised by high kurtosis, positive kurtosis, or by its definitional name, a **leptokurtic** distribution.

If, however, in the same example respondents failed to cluster to any great extent around some central value, but rather spread themselves more evenly across a range of response categories, a **platykurtic** distribution is likely, as in Figure 7.8b.

In this example, rather than being squeezed from the sides, it is as if a normal distribution has been squeezed from the top, producing a distribution with a flatter peak and lighter tails. This particular shape is known variously as a platykurtic distribution, a distribution with low kurtosis, or a distribution with negative kurtosis, for which the formula, termed the alpha 4 expression, is given at (7.3) as:

$$\alpha_4 = \frac{\sum (x - \bar{x})^4}{sd^4} \tag{7.3}$$

Note that today, undergraduates will almost never be expected to calculate this, or similar formulae (such as that for skewness), since these are given as part of most computerised analyses. We offer them merely for completeness and to serve as an indication of the procedures and the measures used in their calculation.

**Figure 7.8b**   Platykurtic distribution.

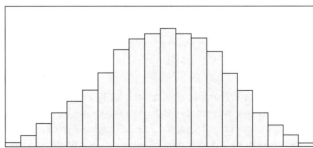

Given that kurtosis is a measure of peakedness, every distribution will, by definition, possess some measure of kurtosis, unless it takes the form of a flat line. Consequently, the value for a normal distribution is always 3. However, most statistical packages have adopted the convention of expressing this as a zero, allowing for the practice of leptokurtic distributions being expressed by a positive value, with platykurtic distributions showing negative values. The point is that kurtosis, as applied in modern statistical software, is an expression of the extent to which a distribution's peakedness varies from normal. In this respect kurtosis can be interpreted in the same way as skew, insofar as we can imagine zero skew representing the normal distribution, with positive and negative values indicating higher and lower peakedness respectively. Nevertheless, this remains an artificial transformation and a reflection of the programmer's need for consistency.

So why are skew and kurtosis of interest beyond providing a picture of the shape of a distribution? In the first instance, any notable skew or kurtosis might indicate a problem in sampling procedures, in that a sample drawn for an experiment or observation study could be biased in some way (see Part 3), such bias expressed as a deviation from the normal distribution. A second explanation might be that the measure being used (an attitudinal scale for instance) might encourage respondents to behave in a particular way, as in always opting for extreme responses, or by clustering around some middle value. This could easily lead to skewed distributions, or to distributions exhibiting high kurtosis. At this level both skew and kurtosis are actually quite useful, since they point to potential problems in the way a sample is drawn, or in the way a questionnaire has been designed. However, in terms of statistical analysis, when distributions demonstrate either of these characteristics, certain restrictions become apparent with conventional statistical tests. Quite simply, most of the statistics which are used to describe the characteristics of different variables, and most of the tests which are used to explore possible differences between different groups, are all based on the assumption of normality – that the variables described will conform to the characteristics of the normal distribution. When skew or kurtosis are present the conventional methods of describing data become inappropriate: we have already discussed the limitations of the mean when data are skewed (see section 7.9). Similarly, some statistical tests suffer in accuracy and power when data deviate from the normal – tests of means, for instance, seem especially vulnerable when data are skewed, while variance tests are adversely affected by kurtosis. This seems to be a particular problem in our own field since it is not uncommon for psychological variables to deviate from normality (Micceri, 1989). On the other hand, many of the tests used in psychological research are robust in that, up to a point, they can be applied even in the presence of non-normal distributions. The arguments here are quite complex and statisticians continue to argue the virtues and failings of different analytical techniques. Suffice it to say that a deviation from normality in any study should be noted, either as an indication of flaws in sampling or data gathering, or as potential limitations of whichever statistical analysis we use to test our hypotheses. Ways of dealing with such problems are considered in the next chapter.

## 7.12 Practical implications

The novice researcher will undoubtedly be growing worried about our warnings over skew and kurtosis, and what these mean for their own research. In fact, deviations from normality are quite common features of undergraduate work, based as it is on small samples – studies relying on 30 or fewer participants will always be susceptible to skew due to error and sampling bias, effects which progressively disappear as samples become larger. Kurtosis is more of a problem since, even with large samples, a badly designed questionnaire or measurement scale might still encourage undue peakedness. The point is that, for various reasons, data in undergraduate research are likely to be non-normal. Mostly this presents no difficulties since conventional parametric tests are able to deal with such deviations without losing much of their efficiency. In the event that either skew or kurtosis is considered to be significant there are strategies available. One is to resort to non-parametric analysis, which does not depend on measures of central tendency and dispersion reflecting normality. The other requires modifying the data in some way so that they acquire the character of a normal distribution. The procedures for this are given in the next chapter.

Finally, one might wonder how we tell when skew or kurtosis become a problem. The decision is based on a statistic known as the standard error and a general rule-of-thumb is that, if the obtained statistic (for either skew or kurtosis) exceeds twice the standard error, then the distribution deviates significantly from normality and steps must be taken to correct for this. A simple formula for calculating the standard error of skew is given by Tabachnick and Fidell (2001), as:

$$S_S = \sqrt{\frac{6}{n}} \tag{7.4}$$

where $S_s$ is the term for standard error and $n$ is the sample size.

Given an obtained value for skew – either from the formula at (3) or, more likely, as part of a statistical output – we judge the extent by which this deviates from zero by:

$$z = \frac{S - 0}{S_s} \tag{7.5}$$

where $S$ is the obtained value of skew.

A similar procedure – again from Tabachnick and Fidell (2001) – is available for kurtosis. Given an obtained value from the formula at (7.2) the standard error of kurtosis is:

$$S_k = \sqrt{\frac{24}{n}} \tag{7.6}$$

with the corresponding $z$-value given by:

$$z = \frac{k - 0}{S_k} \tag{7.7}$$

where $k$ is the obtained value for kurtosis.

By convention, if the calculated $z$-value for skew or kurtosis equals or exceeds 1.96 then we say these values deviate significantly from zero. Alternatively we can resort to the standard error multiple mentioned previously, although this is less precise. (Note: $z$-scores are discussed in detail in Box 7.11.)

## 7.13 The standard normal distribution

In most instances the kind of skewness and kurtosis illustrated in the previous examples will not occur if the group we are observing is typical, or normal, or the sample an honest reflection of the population at large (bearing in mind that psychological variables do seem

| Figure 7.8c | Characteristic shape of a normal distribution. |

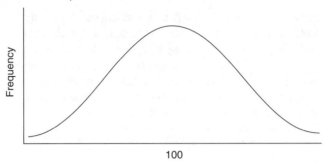

to be prone to problems of non-normality). You might recall the discussion in Part 3 in which sampling issues were considered: in particular, the problem of inadvertently over-representing particular groups was noted, a problem which could easily give rise to a skewed distribution. If sampling is carried out properly, and if what we are measuring conforms to the typical human pattern, the type of distribution we obtain is called a **normal distribution**. Statisticians usually prefer to display such trends, not in the form of histograms, but in the form of a bell-shaped or inverted U curve, as in Figure 7.8c.

All normal distributions share this typical shape, and they also share similar characteristics:

1. The shape of the distribution is always symmetrical.

2. The highest point of the distribution represents the mean. (And because this distribution is so symmetrical, this point will also represent the median and the mode.)

3. Furthermore, due to this symmetry, each half of the distribution will account for 50% of the scores, or cases (see Figure 7.8d).

4. Dividing the normal distribution into equal halves is only the beginning of the descriptive potential for this particular shape: for example, we can identify the particular score below which only 25% of the sample falls (Figure 7.8e). Likewise, we can identify a similar score at the other end of the distribution, above which 25% of the sample falls. This is a procedure we have already considered in the section on dispersion, when the concept of quartiles was introduced (see section 7.10).

| Figure 7.8d | Symmetry of a normal distribution. |

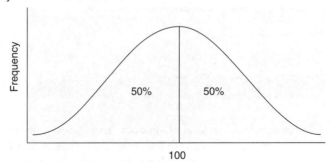

Figure 7.8e     Further sub-divisions of the normal distribution.

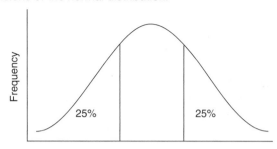

In case no one's noticed, it's worth pointing out that we have actually progressed from looking at concrete examples involving a sample, some kind of measure of average and a range of scores, to what is in effect a theoretical model of just about any human characteristic one might think of. Just as the mean is a useful statistic which typifies or symbolises a range of scores, so too the **standard normal distribution** (as it is termed when it serves as a model, rather than a representation of some concrete measure) offers a general picture of the way most aspects of human behaviour manifest themselves – a lot of people clustering around some middle value, with the number of cases declining the further removed they are from this point, in either direction.

The significance of this evolution from the real to the theoretical is that if most actual human characteristics conform to an approximation of this normal shape, then whatever can be deduced from the standard normal distribution (i.e., the theoretical model) will hold true for real life. Consequently, because all normal distributions share the same symmetry, it is possible to identify standard distances from the mean, and to know what proportions of scores fall on either side of these points. For this, we use the formula for the standard deviation (SD), already encountered at Box 7.9:

$$sd = \sqrt{\frac{\sum(x - \bar{x})^2}{n}}$$     (7.1)

This formula allows us to divide our distribution into three equal proportions on either side of the mean: 1, 2 and 3 standard deviations above the mean, and −1, −2 and −3 below the mean, as in Figure 7.8f.

In case we are in danger of losing anyone at this point, it is worth recalling that in this perfectly balanced distribution, a line down the centre will divide the distribution into two

Figure 7.8f     Proportions of the area under the normal distribution.

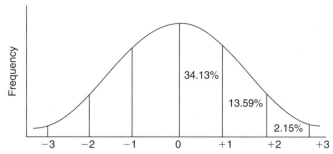

equal halves. Similarly, a distribution based on some real psychological element, be it a measure of cognitive ability, scores on a personality inventory or responses on an attitudinal questionnaire, so long as it conforms pretty well to the now typical shape, will also be divided in two by some measure of centrality – in other words, the mean. By way of illustration, if a study demonstrates that scores on a particular cognitive ability test are normally distributed, with a mean of 100, we know therefore (because of our increasing understanding of the characteristics of this kind of shape) that 50% of the participants measured have scored close to or below this value, while the other 50% scored close to or above 100 per trial.

Developing from here we can now return to the notion of the standard deviation, recognising that what this particular statistic does is divide a distribution (providing it approximates the characteristic shape of the normal curve) into six segments, or intervals, based on the absolute range of scores. And because all normal distributions are symmetrical, we can expect to find that about 34% of the scores are between the mean and 1 SD above. Another 34% are between the mean and 1 SD below. Since the number of cases decline the further away we travel from the mean, the interval between the first and second SDs will comprise 13.59% of all observations, with the third and last interval containing the remaining 2.15%.

For example, if we discovered that our sample of ability scores had a mean of 100 and an SD of 5, we would know that the dividing points above the mean are 105, 110, 115. Similarly, the dividing points below the mean are 95, 90, 85.

Actual [raw] ability scores

| 85 | 90 | 95 | 100 | 105 | 110 | 115 |
| I | I | I | I | I | I | I |

| −3 | −2 | −1 | 0 | +1 | +2 | +3 |

Equivalent standard deviation values

In this sample, therefore, about 68% of the ability scores fall between 95 and 105 (see Figure 7.8g).

Thus for any normal curve, if we divide the distribution into three equal parts above and below the mean, we know that the proportion of scores falling between the particular values will always be: 34.13%, 13.59% and 2.15%. While these proportions remain constant, the actual values which represent the different standard deviation positions will obviously change.

**Figure 7.8g** Proportion of scores falling between standard deviation values (shown as %).

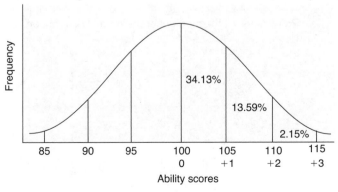

Figure 7.8h Normal distribution of ability scores ranging from 70 to 130.

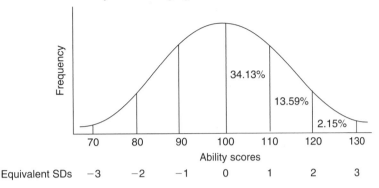

For example, Figure 7.8g is based on a hypothetical distribution of ability scores ranging from 85 to 115 overall. If we conducted a similar study with a different sample, we might find that, although our mean was again 100, the range of ability scores might be broader, as in 70 to 130. With individuals spread out across this more extensive ability range, then our standard deviation value would be different: for example, 10. Figure 7.8h illustrates this point.

Therefore, while the shape of our new distribution would be the same as in the original example, and while the proportion of scores falling between any given standard deviation points would be the same, the actual raw scores reflecting these standard units would be different.

To calculate where any individual score falls in a distribution, we need to transform it into the same kind of measure as standard deviation scores – reminding ourselves that the standard deviation allows us to divide up a distribution in terms of percentages. Known as a *z*-score, this tells us how many SDs a score of, say, 103 is above the mean, or how many SDs a score of, say, 94 is below the mean. The significance of this information is demonstrated in Box 7.11.

A Closer Look At . . .

## z-scores

To understand the relationship between a single score and a distribution of scores of which it is a part, the score must be transformed into a form which can be interpreted in terms of our standard normal distribution. Once this transformation has taken place, we can now view our score in terms of percentage differences above or below the mean.

Transforming a score into a *z*, or standardised, score can be achieved via the formula shown below:

$$z = \frac{x - \bar{x}}{\sigma} \qquad (7.8)$$

With a mean of 100 and an SD of 10, a raw score of 103 converts to a *z*-score of +0.3, and a raw score of 94 has a *z*-score of −0.6. With a mean of 100 and an SD of 5 (as in Figure 7.8g), a raw score of 103 has a *z*-score of +0.6, and a raw score of 94 has a *z*-score of −1.2 and so on. However, aside from offering a visualisation of how far a particular score deviates from its mean, more precise information can be offered. Recalling that normal distributions can be subdivided into standard deviation units, each with its own known percentage of observations, it ought to be possible to interpret any individual score also in terms of percentages. This is precisely what can be done with z-scores.

Consulting the statistical tables which invariably form an appendix to any modern statistics textbook will identify the tables of proportions of area under the normal curve. Such tables state the proportion, or percentage of cases which, for a given mean and standard deviation, will fall between a z-score and its mean, or which will fall beyond z. Appendix A at the back of this book is the relevant table for this example.

By way of illustration, if our score of 103 above generated a z-score of +0.6, the appropriate statistical tables indicate that 22.57% of all the scores which made up that particular distribution fall between this score and the mean. Alternatively, the same tables will indicate that 27.43% of all scores fell above this score (see Figure 7.8i).

To summarise this section we re-state that all behavioural elements possess the same approximate characteristics – most observations will congregate around some central value, with decreasing numbers falling above and below. Presenting these common characteristics graphically invariably produces an approximation to the normal distribution, a theoretical distribution which nonetheless allows us to predict the proportion or percentage of observations which will fall between any two points, irrespective of the actual scores which comprise the real distribution, as the example in Box 7.12 demonstrates.

**Figure 7.8i**    Position of an individual score on the standard normal distribution.

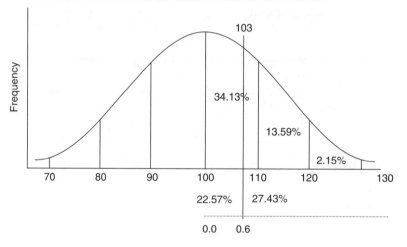

Box 7.12

**A Closer Look At . . .**

# The standard normal distribution

A study among the readership of this book identified a mean reading time (average time anyone can stand to read this text before nodding off or suddenly remembering an urgent engagement elsewhere, like cleaning the bathroom) of 7 minutes, with an SD of 2 minutes.

We therefore know that approximately 68% of our readers can manage between 5 and 9 minutes at any time (see Figure 7.8j).

**Figure 7.8j**    Distribution of reading times.

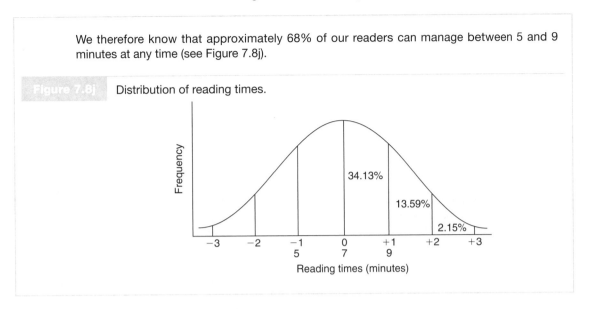

## Review

In this chapter, we presented the first steps you can take to understand and describe your raw data, using tables, figures and descriptive statistics. In the next chapter, we show how to generate these descriptive statistics in SPSS.

# 8 Descriptive analysis and SPSS

## Key Issues

In Chapter 8 we introduce the SPSS computer package, representing one of the most common analytical programmes currently available to the undergraduate population. We show how to create files in SPSS, how to enter data and how to cover all the procedures for formatting, coding and transformation. The screening of data for errors and anomalies is demonstrated, using worked examples, screenshots and step-by-step guides. The chapter concludes with detailed consideration of the procedures for generating tables, figures and descriptive statistics, along with practical hints on using SPSS and interpreting complex statistical output. This chapter focuses on:

- creating files in SPSS
- entering and coding data
- generating tables and figures in SPSS
- using descriptive statistics
- making sense of SPSS output
- dealing with errors, anomalies and extreme scores

## 8.1 Computer analysis and SPSS

In the last decade advances in statistical computing have been extremely rapid, with numerous systems proliferating in an attempt to capture a section of a huge market. Initially available only as mainframe facilities in large academic departments, such systems became progressively accessible to owners of small portable machines until today, anyone with a half-decent PC or Macintosh computer now has at his or her disposal the type of analytical power once available only to major universities.

Software, too, has undergone a revolution with the once cumbersome command-driven packages giving way to more user-friendly, menu-driven approaches. This method of manipulating files and carrying out complex operations has proven extremely successful and now, with the advent of Windows software for PC owners, advanced statistical software is within reach of us all.[1]

There are many different varieties of statistical software, and university and college departments – as well as individuals within those departments – all have their own preferences. However, increasingly, one particular system has been developing – at least in Europe – as the academic industry standard, the system known as **SPSS** (Statistical Package for the Social Sciences). It is this particular system which will form the basis for the following

[1]Windows is either a registered trademark or trademark of Microsoft Corporation in the United States and/or other countries.

illustrations. It should be noted, however, that other programmes such as Minitab and Statistica share similar features, both in the setup procedures for various analyses and in statistical output, such that familiarity with any one system usually transfers quite well to the rest.

## 8.2  Creating files in SPSS

Let us assume that the superb piece of research which you so painstakingly designed has been completed and now you find yourself staring at a small mountain of data – numbers, ratings, piles of completed questionnaires, complicated checklists or reams of dialogue. The chances are that for many, the thoughts which accompany such a mass of information go along the lines of "what am I going to do with all these numbers?" The answer couldn't be simpler (aside from the fact that you should have thought about this earlier, but we won't be unkind to the novice researcher) – these numbers are going to be sorted, simplified and summarised; they will be reduced to descriptive statistics which will impose meaning on the factor or behaviour they represent and they will be used to draw inferences and test hypotheses. They will also form the basis for a variety of graphs and charts which will illustrate, highlight and describe. Some of these procedures and the different types of tabular, graphical and statistical methods for describing and summarising have been discussed in detail in the previous chapter. It is now appropriate to consider how we might take advantage of modern computer software to do all this work for us. But before any of this is possible, we must create a space to store our information – we must create an SPSS data file.

Those new to computer statistical software might be daunted by the scale of a package like SPSS, but it is relatively simple to use, as the following sections will demonstrate.

### 8.2.1  The basics of working with SPSS: Setting up variables and data entry

The first contact with SPSS takes the form of a blank spreadsheet, a kind of template which opens automatically when the programme is activated (by clicking or double-clicking on the SPSS icon similar to Figure 8.1). At this stage the spreadsheet comprises merely a grid of empty cells, devoid of data and not even titled, but forming the basis of a file in which all the information from a study can be stored. However, the SPSS spreadsheet is more than simply a bin for information; it offers the capacity to manipulate data and perform complex analyses via the symbols and menu options which form a part of it. Figure 8.2 illustrates the major elements of a typical blank spreadsheet: there are a number of empty cells (many thousands of these in fact, although only a screen's worth will be visible at any one time without scrolling).

This particular image is based on version 12 of SPSS, currently (at the time of going to press) the most up-to-date of the releases. Moreover, the layout is similar to earlier versions (back to version 6) and is relevant to both Macintosh and PC equipment.

The title of the particular spreadsheet or data set is always shown, although initially this appears as a file called 'Untitled'. Not until you actually enter some data into the spreadsheet and save your work are you given the opportunity to give your data set, and

**Figure 8.1**

**Figure 8.2**

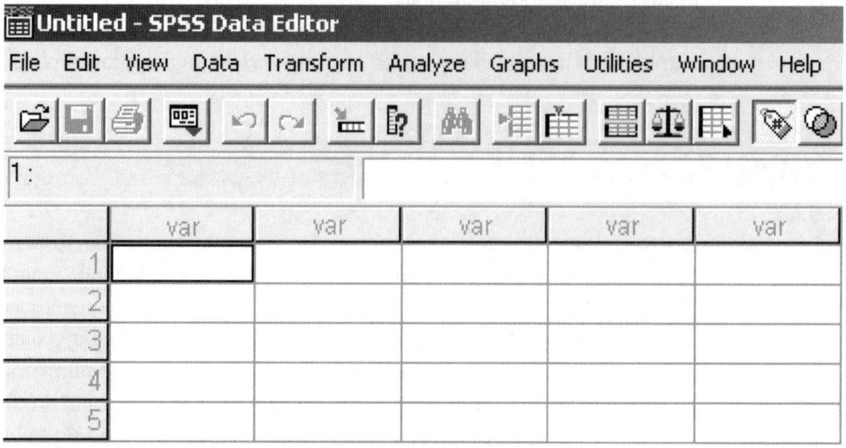

![SPSS Data Editor window showing Untitled file with menu bar (File, Edit, View, Data, Transform, Analyze, Graphs, Utilities, Window, Help), toolbar, and empty spreadsheet grid with columns labeled var and rows numbered 1 to 5.]

your file, an appropriate name – a function which becomes available when you first try to save your data in the File menu with the Save as . . . command. (Note: after a file has been named, updating the information contained in it requires only the Save command. If you were to use the Save as . . . again you are effectively creating a new file and will be asked if you wish to replace the previous one. This can be quite confusing at first.)

Beneath the title area is a ribbon of buttons, a series of small symbols or icons which, when selected (by a single left-button mouse click), perform various functions – for example, one switches the view from the data spreadsheet (containing all the numbers and values generated in your research, and termed **data view**) to a **variable view** (offering details of each variable in your file, along with explanatory information); one changes the way the data appear, and one initiates printing (Figure 8.3):

**Figure 8.3**

Not all of these buttons will be available until the spreadsheet contains data, and in fact when the first untitled file is opened several of the symbols will be 'greyed out', indicating that they are currently de-activated. In the sample empty spreadsheet in Figure 8.2, for instance, the printer icon is unavailable, and will not become active (as above) until there is something to print.

The final part of this window (a window is whatever is currently on the screen) is the menu bar running along the top. Opening any of these menu items (by clicking and holding the mouse button depressed, or simply clicking in the PC versions) will display the various functions available under each heading. Generally speaking the main categories of operation are File Handling (opening new files, saving, etc.), Editing (copying, pasting and moving information about) and statistical functions. Box 8.1 offers an example of the menu items at work.

### 8.2.2 Coding data

Once a study is completed you will have available large amounts of data. Some of these will be what are termed **profile** or **participant data**, which comprise descriptive information on the individuals who participated in the study. Often these also comprise the

A Closer Look At . . .

# Menus in SPSS

All operations and functions within SPSS are accessed in the same way – using the mouse and selecting any of the menu items with a single button click will explore all the operations available under each heading (see Figure 8.4).

Opening the File menu at the top of the data spreadsheet will allow access to the type of functions shown. Selecting a particular function is achieved by dragging the arrowhead over each option until the desired one is selected. Releasing the mouse button at this point automatically selects this option and SPSS will perform the desired activity. All the other menu items work in the same way although, as with the assortment of toolbar symbols beneath the menu, not all operations will be available at any particular time. It is also worth noting that many operations can be carried out using a combination of keystrokes (e.g., Ctrl + S to save a file, or Command + S for Macintosh users). These are always shown on the menu if they are available and experienced users often prefer to work this way because of speed. In Figure 8.4 the File menu has been opened and the Open sub-command selected. From here we can choose a variety of different types of files to be opened.

**Figure 8.4**

independent variables in an experimental study, or the predictor in a correlation design. For example, you will probably have numbered your participants to enable you to identify cases while at the same time ensuring the anonymity of the actual participants. You are likely to know, for instance, if they were male or female, how old they were, whether married or single, extraverts or introverts, working or unemployed, users of private or NHS health facilities and whether they cycled or not (or whatever was relevant to the particular study). If the study took the form of a true experiment, you will also have information on which experimental condition participants were assigned to (e.g., control or experimental). Finally, you are likely to have a number of outcome measures – responses to questions on a survey, scores on a number of questionnaire items or performance measures on some experimental task.

Not all of this information will necessarily be, initially, numerical: the participant-profile details are likely to be simply categories into which individuals can be placed (male or female, control or experimental). Likewise, response or outcome data will often be in a non-numerical format – nominal categories chosen by respondents (yes/no/don't know). Similarly, scaled responses on questionnaires are often in the format "strongly agree/agree/uncertain/disagree/strongly disagree" (see Part 3). However, if the intention is to carry out some form of quantitative analysis on your data, all of the relevant information must be transformed into a numerical format. Box 8.2 demonstrates the procedure.

Box 8.2

A Closer Look At . . .

## Viewing data

When we create a data file to hold all the information on our research there is more than one way in which we can display it. The most basic level of display is known in SPSS as the data view, which shows (not surprisingly) the actual numerical data we have gathered. Figure 8.5 is an extract from the MK data set on cyclists and hedgehogs which presents the findings of a hypothetical performance study (*MKGdists.dat*).

To remind ourselves what all these numbers mean we can choose what SPSS terms the variable view, a separate part of the display in which we can enter descriptions and explanatory information about our variables. See Figure 8.6.

**Figure 8.5**

|    | case | experien | gender | ea_good |
|----|------|----------|--------|---------|
| 1  | 1    | 1        | 1.00   | 2       |
| 2  | 2    | 1        | 2.00   | 3       |
| 3  | 3    | 1        | 1.00   | 4       |
| 4  | 4    | 1        | 2.00   | 3       |
| 5  | 5    | 1        | 1.00   | 4       |
| 6  | 6    | 1        | 2.00   | 5       |
| 7  | 7    | 1        | 1.00   | 4       |
| 8  | 8    | 1        | 2.00   | 3       |
| 9  | 9    | 1        | 1.00   | 3       |
| 10 | 10   | 1        | 2.00   | 5       |
| 11 | 11   | 2        | 1.00   | 1       |
| 12 | 12   | 2        | 2.00   | 1       |
| 13 | 13   | 2        | 1.00   | 0       |

| 32 |

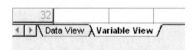

◄ ► \ Data View ⋋ Variable View ╱

**Figure 8.6**

|    | Name     | Type    | Width | Decimals | Label                      | Values        |
|----|----------|---------|-------|----------|----------------------------|---------------|
| 1  | case     | Numeric | 8     | 0        |                            | None          |
| 2  | experien | Numeric | 8     | 0        | level of cycling experience | {1, novice}... |
| 3  | gender   | Numeric | 8     | 2        |                            | {1.00, male}... |
| 4  | ea_good  | Numeric | 8     | 0        | easy terrain;good conditions | None        |
| 5  | ea_bad   | Numeric | 8     | 0        | easy terrain;bad conditions | None         |
| 6  | mod_good | Numeric | 8     | 0        | mod terrain;good conditions | None         |
| 7  | mod_bad  | Numeric | 8     | 0        | mod terrain;bad conditions | None          |
| 8  | chal_goo | Numeric | 8     | 0        | challenging t;good conditions | None       |
| 9  | chal_bad | Numeric | 8     | 0        | challenging t;bad conditions | None         |

In this view we can type in relevant information, such as that the variable 'experien' is a numeric variable, the numerical value used to identify cycling experience, that it has no decimal places and that the variable itself stands for 'level of cycling experience'. There are more options for customising your variables, as explained in later sections, but for the moment it is useful to appreciate that when presented with a data set (especially when encountering secondary data for the first time) we can readily discover what all the variables are and all the numbers mean by choosing the variable view. In a final refinement, we can combine some of the variable information with the basic data. When in data view, selecting the label symbol (so called because it controls how a variable element is labelled – it even looks like a shipping or airline luggage label) switches the numerical codes to the categories they represent (Figure 8.7).

**Figure 8.7**

This process of changing category information into numbers is known as **coding**, and is relatively straightforward (Figure 8.8). A participant who happens to be male can be represented in the 'gender' variable by the value 1; females can be represented by the value 2, and so on. Moreover, statistical software is at its most contented when dealing with numbers so the procedure has many merits; in fact, the only problem is when the researcher loses track of what all the numbers mean, which is not uncommon, although SPSS allows a record to be kept of such explanatory information in variable view, as illustrated in Box 8.2. Alternatively, a full record of all the variables and numerical codes used in a data set can be obtained as a codebook, using one of a number of special commands, as demonstrated in Chapter 5 in the section on secondary research. The actual logic and the processes behind coding are shown in Box 8.3.

**Figure 8.8**

| | case | experien | gender | ea_good |
|---|---|---|---|---|
| 1 | 1 | novice | male | 2 |
| 2 | 2 | novice | female | 3 |
| 3 | 3 | novice | male | 4 |
| 4 | 4 | novice | female | 3 |
| 5 | 5 | novice | male | 4 |
| 6 | 6 | novice | female | 5 |
| 7 | 7 | novice | male | 4 |
| 8 | 8 | novice | female | 3 |
| 9 | 9 | novice | male | 3 |
| 10 | 10 | novice | female | 5 |
| 11 | 11 | skilled | male | 1 |

Box 8.3

How To . . .

# Code data

When collecting data during the course of a study it is sometimes not possible and occasionally undesirable to record information numerically. Participant profile information is invariably presented in terms of specific categories (male/female; married/single), while some response variables are often more comfortably expressed qualitatively. Many participants for instance are happier when allowed to respond to descriptive categories rather than numerical scales. Compare the examples below.

How satisfied are you with your course of study so far?
completely dissatisfied ☐   dissatisfied ☐   neutral ☐   satisfied ☐   completely satisfied ☐

Please rate on the scale below your level of satisfaction with the course so far. Selecting 1 indicates complete dissatisfaction; selecting 5 indicates complete satisfaction.

| 1 | 2 | 3 | 4 | 5 |
|---|---|---|---|---|
| ☐ | ☐ | ☐ | ☐ | ☐ |

While qualitative categories might be preferable for some participants, if the ultimate aim of a study is quantitative analysis, such descriptive categories must be recoded – which simply means replacing category information with an appropriate numerical value.

| Subject No | | | 14 |
| gender | M ☐ | F ☒ | 2 |
| marital status | single ☒ | married ☐ | 1 |
| condition | control ☐ | experimental ☒ | 2 |

How do you feel about the book so far?

| brilliant | good | limited | awful | |
|---|---|---|---|---|
| ☒ | ☐ | ☐ | ☐ | 4 |

In the above example, all of the items offer descriptive, qualitative responses to participants. However, in order to analyse the data in terms of, for example, the percentage of males and females responding to a particular attitudinal category, or even to determine the number of single versus married participants who participated in the control and experimental conditions, it is necessary to convert this information into a format which is more accessible to conventional statistical software. Hence, male participants are coded with the value 1, and females, 2. (One of the contributors to this text wishes to point out that the convention of using 1 = male and 2 = female should not convey any sense of order or magnitude; the numbers merely differentiate between the classes on a nominal scale.)

Likewise, other profile information can be coded numerically – 'married' can be represented by the (arbitrary) value 2, with 'single' coded as 1, or the other way around; it doesn't really matter, providing it makes sense and we are consistent. Responses on outcome measures are coded in the same way, with the proviso that when response alternatives indicate degree, as in 'greater than' or 'less than', the numerical codes must reflect this. Consequently, coding of an item along the lines of 'to what extent do you agree with . . . ?' would generate an ordinal scale (1 2 3 4 5) in place of the categories 'strongly agree', 'agree' and so on. Many researchers take the additional step of regarding ordinally scaled categories as representative of points on a continuous scale. This allows for a number of operations to be carried out, such as calculating a mean response across a number of related categories, as in the example below:

Item: What do you feel about the book so far?

| brilliant | good | limited | awful | |
|-----------|------|---------|-------|---|
| ☒ | ☐ | ☐ | ☐ | 4 |

Item: How good do you feel the statistical explanations have been?

| brilliant | good | limited | awful | |
|-----------|------|---------|-------|---|
| ☐ | ☒ | ☐ | ☐ | 3 |

Item: How effective do you feel the graphical illustrations are in this text?

| brilliant | good | limited | awful | |
|-----------|------|---------|-------|---|
| ☐ | ☐ | ☒ | ☐ | 2 |

If we represent the descriptive terms of 'awful' to 'good' by the numbers 1 to 4 (with the higher values reflecting a more positive attitude) then an average value of 3 would represent the above responses. Overall, the attitude towards the textbook is positive. Note that adopting this approach to what are essentially ordinal data breaks certain rules about levels of measurement (see Part 2). By rights, responses such as those above are categorical responses arranged on an ordinal scale. Hence we understand that selecting the response of 'brilliant' is better than 'good', which in turn is better than 'limited', but this is not the same as measuring responses as 4, 3, or 2. Category responses of this type are not scalar and the intervals or gaps between each response category are indeterminate. It should therefore be inappropriate to apply parametric analyses to this type of data. However, as we have explained elsewhere, many people do so.

### 8.2.3   Coding and recoding continuous data

The examples above have all assumed that participant characteristics will conform to nominal or ordinal scaling (i.e., male-female; young, middle-aged, elderly) but there will be many instances in which profile data will be measured on an interval or ratio scale. For instance, it may be that our study aims to examine the possible relationship between personality and stress-proneness, in which case the personality variable can be considered an element of profile data. So, instead of a category, our personality descriptor will consist of a continuous measure on, for example, the EPQ (Eysenck & Eysenck, 1975). This approach is typical of a correlation design in which all elements of a study are continuous variables. It is, however, possible to recode continuous data, converting it to category format, something which might be desirable to bring a particular variable into line with other independent factors, when these variables are themselves categorical. Box 8.4 offers an example in which an age measure is recoded into a categorical variable.

Box 8.4

## How To . . .

# Recode continuous variables

A typical set of profile data might contain – aside from a participant's case number, which is merely an identifier and does not feature as a variable in a study – the participant's gender, the experimental condition in which he or she participated and his or her age. These data may well have been recorded as two category variables (gender and condition) and one continuous variable, as shown in Figure 8.9:

**Figure 8.9**

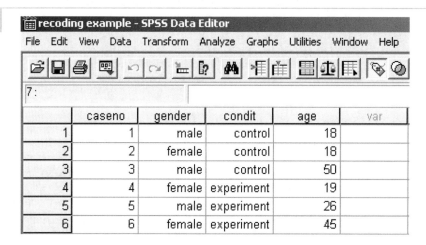

If, for the purposes of a particular study, it was felt that age would be better expressed as a category variable, the continuous range of ages can be recoded into a nominal or ordinal scale. The first step here is to decide on an appropriate cut-off, or cut-offs, for the continuous variable based on the logic of the study, or on the literature. Detailed consideration of this process can be found in Part 2. For the moment, if we adopt three age ranges of less than 25, 26 to 45, and 46 and above as our new age categories of young, middle and older, the recoding procedure is carried out as follows:

Step 1.   With the data editor window open, select Transform from the menu, Recode and then Into Different Variables (Figure 8.10).
   Had we opted for Into Same Variables, our new variable would have replaced the existing age values and we would have lost this information permanently.

Step 2.   The recode window opens. All the variables in our data set will be shown in the left-hand Variables window. We select the variable we wish to recode (click on the variable 'age'), then click the arrow key (Figure 8.11), which sends 'age' to the Numeric Variable → window.

Figure 8.10

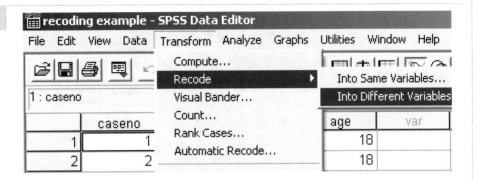

Step 3.  Move the cursor to the blank space under **N**ame in the **O**utput Variable box. Type in the name of the new variable. In this example we choose 'agegroup' as our new variable name.

Figure 8.11

Step 4.  Before we can change our original 'age' variable to the new 'agegroup' one, we must explain how our old values are going to be recoded into the new values. Click on the **O**ld and **N**ew **V**alues button (Figure 8.12).

Figure 8.12

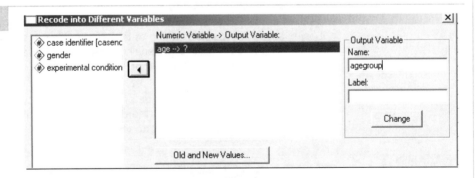

Step 5.  The next window to open is the **O**ld and New Values window. We note that in the **O**ld Value sector (Figure 8.13) we can recode either a variable comprising discrete values (e.g., the categories 1, 2, 3) into something else, or we can recode a variable which comprises a range of scores. In the current example the variable we are recoding is a continuous variable, made up of a range of scores and the procedure is relatively straightforward requiring only that we identify particular ranges in the **O**ld Value sector, and state the new categorical value it is to be replaced by in the **N**ew Value sector. We offer the procedure for recoding the age range 26 to 45 by way of illustration.

**Figure 8.13**

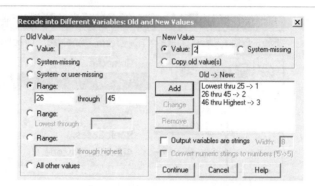

1. Select (click the appropriate button) the range category we wish to operate. For our first category, 25 and under, we would choose the **R**ange, Lowest thru, and enter the value 25 in the blank box (i.e., lowest value in the age range through, and including, 25. This means we don't actually need to know what the lowest value is). For the third category of 46 and older, we would choose the **R**ange, through Highest, and enter the value 46 in the blank box. For the second category of 26 to 45, we choose the open **R**ange option and enter the values 26 and 45 in the blank boxes.

2. Since the 26 to 45 range will represent the second of our three age categories, we move the cursor to the blank **V**alue box in the **N**ew Value sector. Type the value 2. (We are using the values of 1, 2 and 3 to identify the new age ranges, although we could use any old numbers.)

3. Click **A**dd, which adds this transformation to the SPSS file. The transformation itself will be shown in the **O**ld → New window, allowing us to check our recoding. Note that a common error among novice researchers is to forget to add the last transformation and move straight to the **C**ontinue button, which ends the transformation procedure. This leads to one of the transformations not being saved and causes no end of trouble with later analyses. Trust us on this point – it happens often and usually remains undiscovered until a supervisor remarks, 'there's something wrong with this data'.

4. Click **C**ontinue, which returns us to the original Recode window. Click **C**hange, which completes the change of the original 'age' variable to the new 'agegroup' variable. Inspection of the data window will show that the new 'agegroup' variable has been added to the file (Figure 8.14).

**Figure 8.14**

| caseno | gender | condit | age | agegroup |
|---|---|---|---|---|
| 1 | male | control | 18 | young |
| 2 | female | control | 18 | young |
| 3 | male | control | 50 | older |
| 4 | female | experiment | 19 | young |
| 5 | male | experiment | 26 | middle |
| 6 | female | experiment | 45 | middle |

When working with large data sets it is easy to lose track of all the changes, recodes and transformations which might have been made. This can cause real difficulties later if we encounter errors, or if we wish to subsequently change, for instance, some of the categories comprising our variables. It is important then to keep a record of how data are recorded and what changes were made. This can be done manually, by keeping a simple diary of events, or the Syntax window available in SPSS can be employed. It will be noted that the various windows available for most SPSS functions contain a Paste button. Selecting this after each procedure has been set up pastes a record of what we have done into a special Syntax window, which can be viewed at any time. The example below contains a record (in words) of how we recoded the continuous age variable into a category variable comprising three age groups.

RECODE

age

(Lowest thru 24 = 1) (25 thru 45 = 2) (46 thru Highest = 3) INTO agegroup.

EXECUTE.

### 8.2.4   Entering data and naming variables

Each variant of statistical software has its own set of preferences concerning data handling, but all share certain conventions, the most fundamental of which relates to how data are entered. The typical format is that all cases are identified by a participant or case number, in a single column. Traditionally this is the first column of data entered into any data set, although with the current version of SPSS this is no longer strictly necessary, since all the rows in its spreadsheet are numbered and actually identified by the system as case numbers. However, we have found it a useful discipline to begin all data entry by identifying, numerically, each individual who participated in a study. This sets the scene as it were and makes it easier to deal logically with subsequent data entry and to correct errors. It also makes it easier to track individuals at the later analysis stage, especially where extreme scores occur on some measure.

Many undergraduates experience difficulty with this initial stage, and understandably so since the common method of presenting data in journal articles and textbooks distinguishes among participants in terms of group or category, as Table 8.1a illustrates:

Table 8.1a    Number of hedgehog-defined errors for two groups of cyclists.

| Novice cyclists | Skilled cyclists |
| --- | --- |
| 25 | 7 |
| 13 | 8 |
| 27 | 10 |
| 22 | 5 |
| 30 | 7 |
| 23 | 4 |

When dealing with data in this format the intuitive way to enter it into a statistical spreadsheet is to mimic the two-column table. While this is fine for publication or illustration purposes, it is not the way most statistical software works, as the next section demonstrates.

Table 8.1b    Recall scores of participants in an experimental and a control condition in a memory study.

| Participant | Condition | Recall score |
|---|---|---|
| 1 | control | 25 |
| 2 | control | 22 |
| 3 | experimental | 15 |
| 4 | experimental | 12 |
| 5 | control | 19 |
| 6 | experimental | 18 |
| 7 | experimental | 14 |
| 8 | control | 21 |
| - | - | - |
| $n$ | - | - |

## 8.2.5    Data entry – between-groups designs

The trick in error-free data entry is to begin, as mentioned earlier, with a single column listing of every participant or observation which comprised a particular study. Each successive column contains information relevant to its associated case, whether it be participant or grouping characteristics, or outcome measures on some experimental task. Table 8.1b illustrates the point, presenting data for an experimental study. One group of undergraduates participated in a memory experiment in which learning was carried out under a condition of intrusive background noise. Subsequent word recall was measured and compared to that of participants in a control group who did not experience the intrusive noise. (Note: this particular design conforms to that of a true experiment, as opposed to a quasi-experiment, and if you've no idea why, a review of Part 2 will be useful.)

All between-groups data are organised in this way, with a separate column devoted to each variable. In Table 8.1b, participant 1 was in the control condition and returned a recall score of 25. Participant number 3 was in the group which took part in the experimental condition and returned a recall score of 15, and so on. The approach can of course be extended to allow for any number of variables, as is the case with traditional behavioural research – generally speaking most studies, even at undergraduate level, will generate considerable quantities of information, such that for each individual participant or case there can be several associated measures.

## 8.2.6    Data entry – within-group designs

When entering data for a within-subjects design, the general principle of one participant (or case) column followed by separate columns for each variable still holds. For example, if in the word recall experiment outlined in Table 8.1b we decided that differences between the control and experimental groups were being confounded by the effects of individual differences (i.e., the participants were just different and differences in word recall had nothing to do with the presence or absence of noise), we might opt instead for a within-subjects design in which the same participants participated in both conditions, as in Table 8.1c.

Table 8.1c    Word recall under two conditions of background noise.

| Participant | Recall under control condition (no noise) | Recall under experimental condition (noise) |
|---|---|---|
| 1 | 25 | 15 |
| 2 | 22 | 18 |
| 3 | 19 | 12 |
| 4 | 20 | 17 |
| - | - | - |
| n | - | - |

Here again, there is a single column devoted to identifying the individual or case number, with successive columns providing information relevant to each case. By way of example, participant 1 correctly recalled 25 words in the no-noise condition, but only 15 in the noise condition.

## 8.3    Setting up data in SPSS

The first step in setting up a data file in SPSS is to recognise that all computer-based analytical systems appear initially dim, unhelpful and occasionally intransigent. Of course, software producers and distributors like to emphasise user-friendliness and the sophisticated help functions which come with their products, yet the truth is that all such systems are designed not to be nice or awkward, but to obey. Few systems will make suggestions, none will make allowances and all of this makes life difficult for the novice. However, providing we appreciate that no statistical package will do any more than we tell it to do, then we are on the way to developing an effective working relationship.

Translated into actions this means that we must always explain what we are doing and what we expect in response. The majority of errors can usually be traced back to a failure to adequately or fully 'explain' what is required. The next few illustrations demonstrate the main steps in setting up a data file in SPSS.

### 8.3.1    Naming and defining variables

For any analytical system to be able to work with a set of data – generate tables, draw graphs and make comparisons – it needs to be able to identify the variables which comprise the data set. This is the first task in data entry and it is initiated by left-clicking, or double-clicking (using the mouse button) on the column heading cell found at the top of the first empty column of data cells, or by selecting the variable view window at the bottom of the data window, as we have previously intimated. See Box 8.5 for a full illustration of these procedures.

Box 8.5

## How To . . .

## Define variables in SPSS

Figure 8.15

| | Name | Type | Width | Decimals | Label | Values | Missing | Columns | Align | Measure |
|---|---|---|---|---|---|---|---|---|---|---|
| 1 | VAR00001 | Numeric | 8 | 2 | | None | None | 8 | Right | Scale |

Selecting the variable view in SPSS activates an (initially) empty spreadsheet in which we can type in details of the variables in our research, as in Figure 8.15. This example shows the default settings for all data (i.e., the way SPSS describes variables until we do something to change this description). Intimidating at the outset, the variable window quickly becomes a straightforward tool for the novice, once all its parts are explained, as follows.

The settings in Figure 8.15 refer to the first variable in our analysis (1) and SPSS has assigned it the **N**ame VAR00001. Our first action would be to replace this with a variable name of our own choosing (case, gender, group, family, score or whatever) with the advice that our name is kept relatively short – this keeps the column widths manageable. In fact, most previous versions of SPSS would not allow variable names longer than eight characters. The **T**ype of variable is currently shown as Numeric, which will suit most of the variables you are likely to use, although you could have other types, such as string (this would be people's names, or towns, or countries) or date. These other options become available by clicking at the top of the **T**ype column. The width of our numeric variable is set at eight characters in the **W**idth column and whatever number we type in SPSS will automatically round it to two decimal places (2 **D**ecimals).

The next setting is an important one: since our variable name will often comprise an abbreviation or some personal code we often wish to attach a more useful descriptive label. For example, our variable name might be simply 'errors', and we expand on this in the label column by typing in 'number of stunned hedgehogs'. If a variable measures responses to questionnaire items, our variable names might be merely 'Q1', 'Q2', etc., and our label the actual questions.

Sometimes a variable will be of the category type, with the variable name being a collective for a number of groups or categories. For instance, the variable 'gender' will be made up of two groups (male and female); the variable 'class' might have five, and so on. Recall, though, that SPSS does not actually work with alphabetic information (words), although it will display them. Thus, categories such as male and female have to be represented by numerical values (e.g., 1 and 2), and the next settings column, **V**alues, allows us to tell SPSS which numerical values stand for which categories. You can then decide whether categories will be displayed as numerical values, or by their descriptive labels by checking (or un-checking) the **V**alue labels item in the <u>V</u>iew menu. You can even toggle between the two types of display by clicking the label symbol we introduced earlier, at Figure 8.7.

The **M**issing column is another important one in SPSS; from time to time and for various reasons, some of our data for some of our participants will be missing. Sometimes survey respondents will refuse to answer a particular item on a questionnaire (they might object to the intrusive nature of an item, or question its relevance), some items will be omitted by accident and some will so obviously have been misunderstood that a response to a particular item might have to be ignored (as when a participant selects two options from a response scale). Similarly, the researcher can make mistakes in recording or transcribing responses – all expressions of a natural human fallibility which result in the occasional finding that some of our data are missing.

Most undergraduate researchers, not familiar with the peculiarities of computer software, or the significance of missing pieces of data, might take the line 'so what?' So there is a piece of missing information, so participant number 24 forgot to complete item 19, so I'm not sure if the response to this particular item is a '3' or a '5'. Just type in a zero or leave the cell blank and go on to the next one.

Neither of these options is recommended: a blank space, while it will be picked up by SPSS as a missing value in a list of values, might actually be caused by the person entering the data inadvertently mis-keying, and SPSS will not discriminate between a genuine missing value and incompetence on the part of the operator – they all look the same, as it were. Using a zero is not a good idea either, since zero is itself a value, or can represent a category within a coded variable. However, it is important to let SPSS know if any values have been omitted – even a simple calculation like the arithmetic average will be undermined by miscounting the number of cases or values. Moreover, it is sometimes useful for the researcher to be able to identify cases or participants who did not respond to particular items in the event that they represent an interesting sub-group of the population.

The convention for dealing with missing values is to enter an extreme or bizarre value which could not form part of a conventional set of values within a specific variable, and which is clearly distinguishable from legitimate values. Hence, if a response to a given item is of the nominal Yes/No variety (typically coded 1 and 2 respectively) then no response at all could be expressed as the value 9, or 99 or whatever. Providing SPSS is informed that whenever it encounters 99 it is to treat this as a missing value, then calculations won't be affected and any such cases can be readily spotted. Moreover, if at some stage we wished to take a closer look at all of our respondents who failed to respond to a particular item on a questionnaire, we need only request a listing of all those scoring 99 on a particular variable. The missing values can therefore be used as identifiers in their own right.

**C**olumns is a throwback to the early days of computing when data were stored on punchcards. Each punchcard was divided up into 80 columns and every piece of information on a case allocated a certain number of these columns. Our own variable has been allocated a space of 8 columns (characters).

**A**lign is self-explanatory, in that our data can be centred, left or right aligned in the column.

**M**easure is the final setting and allows us to describe the kind of scale on which our variable is measured, be it nominal, ordinal or interval.

The example in Figure 8.16 is taken from the MK *recoding example* data set, showing how four of the variables have been set up.

**Figure 8.16**

| | Name | Type | Width | Decimals | Label | Values | Missing | Columns | Align | Measure |
|---|---|---|---|---|---|---|---|---|---|---|
| 1 | caseno | Numeric | 8 | 0 | case identifier | None | None | 8 | Right | Scale |
| 2 | gender | Numeric | 8 | 0 | | {1, male}... | 9 | 8 | Right | Nominal |
| 3 | condit | Numeric | 8 | 0 | experimental condition | {1, control}.. | 9 | 8 | Right | Nominal |
| 4 | age | Numeric | 8 | 0 | | None | 999 | 8 | Right | Scale ▼ |

In this instance our third variable is 'condit'; it is a numerically defined variable and the full descriptive label describes it as an 'experimental condition'. In its composition, the variable comprises two conditions, each represented by its own numerical value. For example, the control condition is represented by the value 1, with the code for the experimental condition currently hidden, although becoming available with a single click of the mouse button in the **V**alues cell. Any missing cases are identified by the value 9, and the variable was measured on a nominal scale.

## 8.4  SPSS and descriptive statistics

In Chapter 7, a large number of tables, graphs and statistics were used to illustrate various points about measures of central tendency, dispersion and the general presentation of quantitative information. The sections which now follow deal with the procedures for generating this type of descriptive information in SPSS, based around a hypothetical example of a study in which male and female students were asked to provide measures of their attitudes towards various issues. These could have been anything from the siting of contraceptive machines in the university toilets to liking for small, spine-covered hog-like mammals. The actual measures themselves are not important, serving only to provide a platform for the illustrations which follow. And in fact, this is an important point: most procedures for describing and analysing data don't distinguish among different possible research contexts, such that once we become familiar with a particular set of analytical tools we can apply them to answer many research questions. We have opted for the one about our favourite small, spine-covered mammals and Box 8.6 demonstrates the procedures for describing data.

Box 8.6

## How To . . .

# Generate descriptive statistics in SPSS

Descriptive statistics in SPSS are easily obtained through the <u>A</u>nalyze menu at the top of the data spreadsheet. (In earlier versions of SPSS this was shown as a Statistics item on the menu.) When selected, a number of statistical operations are offered (Figure 8.17). Based on the *MKhedgehogs2* data set.

Figure 8.17

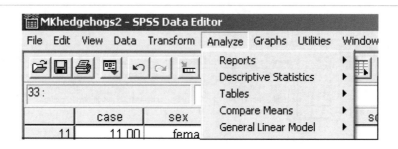

Figure 8.18

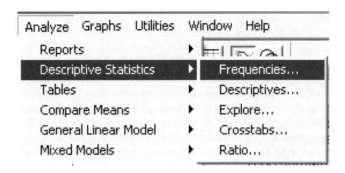

Generally speaking the options available within these menus remain constant irrespective of which version of SPSS is used, but there are some differences: we have already mentioned that this Analyze menu was previously known as a Statistics menu, and the General Linear Model was previously found as ANOVA. The important thing is not to be intimidated by such variations – simply try them and see what they offer.

The next step in our analysis is to choose what we want from the available options: in this instance, we will select Descriptive statistics (Figure 8.18).

The basic descriptive options are shown in Figure 8.18, and selecting any one of them will open a further window which allows us to select which variable we intend to describe. Selecting Frequencies, for instance, would produce the window shown in Figure 8.19:

Figure 8.19

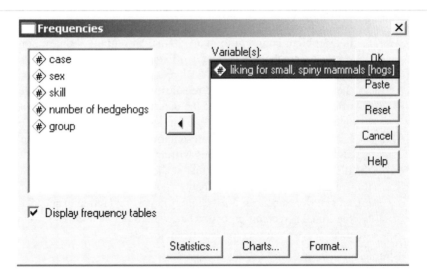

Selecting variables for any kind of analysis in SPSS follows the same general sequence – all the variables in a data set are displayed in a scrolling box on the left part of the window, where one or more can be selected using conventional mouse clicks. In Figure 8.19, a number of variables from our hypothetical spiny mammal study are

**Figure 8.20**

shown – the participant case, or identification number, the individual's gender and attitude score, along with other variables which will form part of subsequent illustrations. An arrow button (Figure 8.20) transfers the selection to a variables window on the right from where, depending on the particular analysis being carried out, a number of additional options can be selected. A final OK will produce an appropriate output which will either be tabular, graphical or both – selecting the Statistics or Charts buttons gives us a number of options to expand or restrict output, while ignoring them effectively leaves the decision to SPSS and you will get the default presentation.

As we have previously explained, tables represent one of the standard methods of describing numerical data and most types of modern software – word processing, database and spreadsheet packages – offer excellent facilities for the production of high-quality tables. For most purposes the table facilities within SPSS are adequate, as Table 8.2, based on our hedgehog study, illustrates.

The Frequencies command is suited to the analysis of a single variable which comprises category data (although it can be used as a screening device for continuous variables, by selecting the condensed format which is one of the available options). Category examples include the number of males and females in a sample (as in Table 8.2), the number of participants in a control or experimental condition, or the frequency with which respondents to a questionnaire item opted for a Yes as opposed to a No response on some issue. However, in the event that tables are not as informative as they might be – and this is a problem common to many statistical outputs – the option of seeing the same data presented graphically is usually offered, as in Figure 8.21.

The bar chart in Figure 8.21 presents the same information as in Table 8.2, showing the distribution of males and females who participated in our study. As with most charts it offers a visual illustration of the data which is often more immediate and easier to grasp than tabulated information. It often does this, of course, at the expense of precision yet it is the preferred method of presentation in many fields: newspaper articles in particular and various trade publications writing for a diverse readership will opt for this approach. It should be noted, though, that academics tend to prefer tables for their very precision. We discussed this issue in Chapter 7, making the point that figures of this nature would almost never appear in a psychology report or journal article. Their main use is as part of the initial screening process when we are perhaps looking for a general overview of our data, or we are trying to identify anomalies.

Table 8.2     Output 8.1 – Distribution of males and females in an attitudinal study.

|       |        | Frequency | Percent | Valid percent | Cumulative percent |
|-------|--------|-----------|---------|---------------|--------------------|
| Valid | male   | 19        | 55.9    | 55.9          | 55.9               |
|       | female | 15        | 44.1    | 44.1          | 100.0              |
|       | Total  | 34        | 100.0   | 100.0         |                    |

Figure 8.21 Distribution of male and female participants in an attitudinal study.

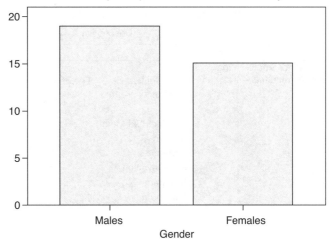

Table 8.3   Output 8.2 – Descriptive statistics for an attitudinal variable.

Descriptive Statistics

| | N | Minimum | Maximum | Mean | Std. Deviation |
|---|---|---|---|---|---|
| Liking for small, spiny mammals | 34 | 13.00 | 28.00 | 19.3529 | 3.93032 |
| Valid *N* (listwise) | 34 | | | | |

When the data are continuous, or interval scaled, the <u>D</u>escriptives command is appropriate, offering relevant parametric statistics on central tendency and dispersion. As with most SPSS operations numerous options are available, allowing the user to determine how much information will be displayed. In our current example, asking for descriptive statistics of the 'hogs' variable (measures of liking for small, spiny mammals), the <u>D</u>escriptives command produces Table 8.3 at Output 8.2. Considerably more information, however, is available via the <u>E</u>xplore command which provides not only an extensive statistical breakdown of a given variable, but also a number of graphical views. Moreover, unlike the <u>D</u>escriptives command, <u>E</u>xplore allows us to inspect a variable by different categories – here we can break down our attitude measure by the gender of the individual. Consequently there are really two outputs, one for males and one for females. Box 8.7 offers the entire output generated on the hedgehog data.

Box 8.7

# A Closer Look At . . .

## Full descriptive output in SPSS

The <u>E</u>xplore command in SPSS offers the most comprehensive analysis of continuous data – detailed tables providing information on average, spread and skewness; stem-and-leaf tables (stemplots); and a variety of pictorial representations. In Output 8.3 in Table 8.4

Table 8.4    Output 8.3—Full descriptive statistics on an attitudinal variable, by gender.

Descriptives

| | Gender | | | Statistic | Std. Error |
|---|---|---|---|---|---|
| liking for small, spiny mammals | male | Mean | | 17.9474 | 0.93806 |
| | | 95% Confidence Interval for Mean | Lower Bound | 15.9766 | |
| | | | Upper Bound | 19.9182 | |
| | | 5% Trimmed Mean | | 17.6637 | |
| | | Median | | 17.0000 | |
| | | Variance | | 16.719 | |
| | | Std. Deviation | | 4.08892 | |
| | | Minimum | | 13.00 | |
| | | Maximum | | 28.00 | |
| | | Range | | 15.00 | |
| | | Interquartile Range | | 4.00 | |
| | | Skewness | | 0.996 | 0.524 |
| | | Kurtosis | | 0.601 | 1.014 |
| | female | Mean | | 21.1333 | 0.76760 |
| | | 95% Confidence Interval for Mean | Lower Bound | 19.4870 | |
| | | | Upper Bound | 22.7797 | |
| | | 5% Trimmed Mean | | 21.0926 | |
| | | Median | | 21.0000 | |
| | | Variance | | 8.838 | |
| | | Std. Deviation | | 2.97289 | |
| | | Minimum | | 17.00 | |
| | | Maximum | | 26.00 | |
| | | Range | | 9.00 | |
| | | Interquartile Range | | 4.00 | |
| | | Skewness | | 0.321 | 0.580 |
| | | Kurtosis | | -0.837 | 1.121 |

the hedgehog data have been examined by the nominal variable of 'sex'. (We are interested in whether or not liking for spiny mammals depends on whether you are male or female.)

A table produced by the Explore command is undoubtedly comprehensive – there are several measures of central tendency (mean, trimmed mean, median), of dispersion (range, interquartile range, variance, standard deviation), of normality (skewness, kurtosis) and a number of crude descriptive measures (minimum, maximum). The choice is impressive: how much more would anyone ever want to know about a measure? The choice is also – especially to an undergraduate new to statistics – intimidating. So, in order to minimise the threat-value of such information overload, we will attempt to explain the contents of Table 8.4 in some detail.

## Measures of central tendency

The first few elements of Table 8.4 offer several measures of central tendency, as follows:

(i)   Mean: the arithmetic average, given here as 17.9474 (for males).
(ii)  Five percent trimmed mean: the arithmetic mean of the data after the top and bottom 5% of values have been removed, or 'trimmed' (17.6637). This feature eliminates the effects of extreme scores and outliers which would influence the calculation of the

conventional mean. When sample sizes are small, however, the loss of any data might be unacceptable. In this instance both the trimmed and actual mean values are similar, indicating that the presence of any extreme scores has not adversely affected the calculation of the mean.

(iii)  Median: the middle value in the ordered array of values. Comparing the median with the mean provides a good indication of how skewed a distribution might be. When skew is present the median might be a more appropriate measure of average. Here, both the mean and median values are similar indicating that the shape of the distribution of male scores is essentially normal. However, the mean does show a slightly higher value than the median (17.9474, as opposed to the median value of 17.000), indicating a slight positive skew, since means are drawn towards the elongated tails of a skewed distribution.

(iv)  Standard error: this is short for the standard error of the mean, and it provides a measure of the extent to which the sample mean in question is likely to be close to the mean of the population from which it has been drawn. In general terms, the smaller this value is, the less error there is; moreover, the standard error is partly a function of the sample size, so the larger the sample the less error there will be. In terms of describing the characteristics of a variable this is not particularly important and can usually be ignored, but if we are interested in the extent to which a sample is a fair reflection of a population (as we would be if our research were survey based), the standard error becomes an essential piece of statistical information. The '95% confidence interval' in Table 8.4 is based on the standard error, and concerned with estimating population characteristics (the lower and upper bounds in Table 8.4). The values given here indicate the range within which we are 95% confident that the population mean will fall, which works out as 2 standard errors above and 2 standard errors below the mean (approximately). The obsessive among you might wish to consult the descriptive statistics table and demonstrate this for yourselves. A review of Part 3, in which we discuss the estimation of sample sizes, might also be of interest, as will sections of Part 5, in which we look more closely at the role of the standard error in estimating population characteristics.

## Measures of dispersion

The next several elements of the Table 8.4 offer several measures of variation, or dispersion, as follows:

(i)  Variance: described as the average of the squared deviations from the mean, this is a measure of how much, on average, squared scores varied about the mean score. The variance is an essential element in many statistical calculations, but at a purely descriptive level its use is limited since the value of this statistic is based on the *squared* deviations from the mean. Consequently, for most observers the variance provides little insight into the extent to which individual scores varied about the mean (although if this turned out to be a really big number, then we might assume a lot of variation). Here the variance is given as 16.719, with the calculation based on the formula:

$$\text{variance} = \frac{\Sigma (x - \bar{x})^2}{n} \tag{8.1}$$

Details of the calculation of variance are given in Chapter 7.

(ii)  Standard deviation: this measure provides the square root of the variance, which means that the average of individual variations about the mean is returned to the scale on which original scores were measured. Consequently, the standard deviation provides a more intuitively useful indication of variation than the variance and is a good descriptive statistic. In this example the standard deviation is given as 4.08892 which, for the statisticians among our readership, is the square root of the variance (16.719).

$$sd = \sqrt{\frac{\Sigma(x - \bar{x})^2}{n}}$$

(7.1)

(iii)  Minimum, maximum and range are self-explanatory, being the lowest score in the distribution, the highest score and the difference between the two. Providing a distribution is normal in shape and there are no outliers, all three measures are good indications of variation. The presence of even a single extreme score though will lead to an over-estimation of variation.

(iv)  Interquartile range (IQR): if our distribution were ordered from lowest to highest value and the quartiles identified, this is a measure of the range between the first and third quartiles (i.e., the middle 50% of scores). The advantage of this measure is that it does not incorporate any extreme scores which would exaggerate the crude range (lowest to highest score). Chapter 7 discusses quartiles and their derivation in detail. It should be pointed out, however, that the IQR is not intuitively meaningful and many of us will struggle with trying to make sense of a middle range of scores and what this might mean for an entire distribution, especially in the absence of a boxplot.

### Measures of normality

The last two elements of Table 8.4 provide measures of the extent to which our distribution varies from a normal distribution. In particular they are measures of the shape and symmetry of our data, important features when we progress to inferential statistics, since data which are asymmetrical might require some form of transformation prior to analysis, or the employment of a non-parametric test.

(i)  Skewness: a measure of the extent to which scores are concentrated near one end of a distribution, giving rise to an elongated tail towards the other end. With highly skewed distributions, both the mean and the standard deviation are poor measures of central tendency and spread respectively, which is why parametric analyses (based as they are on both of these measures) become problematic. Examples of skewed distributions can be inspected in Chapter 7, where there is discussion on the implications of asymmetric distributions. As a guide, normal distributions have a skew value of zero. We can consider a distribution to be *significantly* skewed when the skew statistic (shown in Table 8.4 as 0.996 for males) is greater than two standard errors of skew. In this instance, while there is evidence of positive skew, this is not significant.

(ii)  Kurtosis: a measure of the 'peakedness' or 'flatness' of a distribution. As with skew there are implications for statistical analysis when kurtosis becomes significant, and again, these issues have been discussed in Chapter 7. As a guide, SPSS would describe a normal distribution as having zero kurtosis (although this is a transformed score since normal distributions actually possess a kurtosis of 3). Consequently a positive kurtosis value denotes a distribution with a sharper than normal peak, with negative kurtosis denoting a flatter than normal peak. Kurtosis becomes significant when the statistic (here given as 0.601 for males) is greater than two standard errors of kurtosis, although as sample sizes increase, even significant kurtosis becomes unimportant. In the current example there is evidence of slight positive kurtosis, but not significantly so.

The next part of the typical Explore output takes the form of graphical presentation of the data. Figures 8.22a and 8.22b contain two histograms, one each for the groups of

**Figure 8.22a**   Distribution of male responses on an attitudinal item.

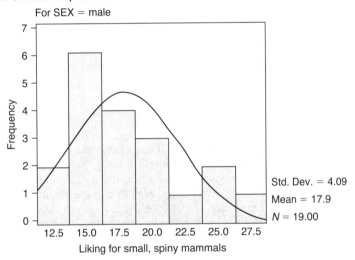

**Figure 8.22b**   Distribution of female responses on an attitudinal item.

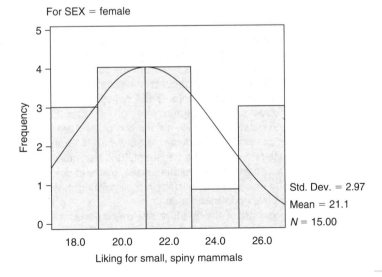

| Figure 8.23 | Boxplot showing distribution of responses on an attitudinal item by gender. |

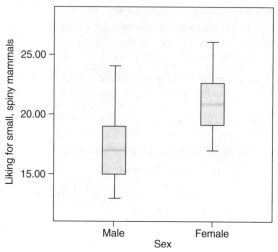

male and female participants. If our study had investigated an issue in terms of three groups (e.g., young, middle-aged, elderly), there would have been three histograms offered. In our examples we asked for the additional (and satisfyingly useful) option of having a smoothed distribution curve fitted to the histogram, which allows us, at a glance, to obtain an impression of skewness, if present – a skewed distribution would differ quite markedly from the superimposed normal curve. It should be noted though that with the small samples typical of undergraduate research, distributions will rarely appear normal. This is not a problem since with larger numbers, elements of asymmetry are often smoothed out. From the graph alone, at Figures 8.22a and 8.22b, we would estimate the male and female means as approximately 17 and 21 respectively (a pretty good estimate when compared to the actual values which are shown beside each chart). Both distributions also exhibit slight positive skewness, although this could well be a feature of the small sample sizes.

In the final illustration offered by this particular package a single chart directly comparing the distributions of both groups is offered, in the form of boxplots. Figure 8.23 is extremely useful in that, at a glance, we can estimate averages (median values) for each group, in addition to the measures of interquartile range, minimum and maximum and crude range. The differences between the groups are clear and more immediately appreciated than were we to consult Table 8.4 only. For more information on boxplots and how they are constructed, see Chapter 7.

It is worth noting that, while the various graphs are available as part of the descriptive output, they can also be produced via a separate Graphs menu in the menu strip at the top of the data and variable spreadsheet. This particular menu offers a wide range of chart types, plus facilities for manipulating sizes, text and colour. It means that a whole range of graphs can be generated from data in their own right, without the need to go through one of the Descriptives command menus.

Finally, as part of the Explore set-up options, we can request stem-and-leaf diagrams. We have encountered these in Chapter 7, and we have made the point about the unusual nature of these illustrations. Stem-and-leaf diagrams, or stemplots as they are sometimes known, possess elements of both tables and charts – tables in that all of the actual data which comprise a variable are present, and charts in that the arrangement of the tabulated data creates a picture of what the distribution looks like. With our hedgehog data, Explore will provide two diagrams, one for each of the break-down conditions (male and female). Note in Table 8.5 that the emboldenment is that of the authors to highlight the key elements of the table.

The final option in the Descriptive Statistics sub-menu is the Crosstabs command. Concerned with nominal or ordinally scaled data, Crosstabs provides frequency counts of pairs of related variables – a crosstabulation is performed in which a count is made of the number of events which occur across two categories. For instance, in our hedgehog study we can determine how many of the males were also skilled cyclists; how many of the females were also unskilled cyclists, and so on (see Figure 8.24).

**Table 8.5**    Stem-and-leaf diagram for an attitudinal variable by gender.

Liking for small, spiny mammals Stem-and-Leaf Plot for sex = male

| Frequency | | Stem & Leaf | |
|---|---|---|---|
| **4.00** | | **1** | **. 3344** |
| **11.00** | | **1** | **. 55667788999** |
| **3.00** | | **2** | **. 244** |
| 1.00 | Extremes | (> = 28) | |

Stem width:        10.00
Each leaf:         1 case(s)

Liking for small, spiny mammals Stem-and-Leaf Plot for sex = female

| Frequency | | Stem & Leaf | |
|---|---|---|---|
| **5.00** | | **1** | **. 77899** |
| **7.00** | | **1** | **. 0012223** |
| **3.00** | | **2** | **. 566** |

Stem width:        10.00
Each leaf:         1 case(s)

**Figure 8.24**

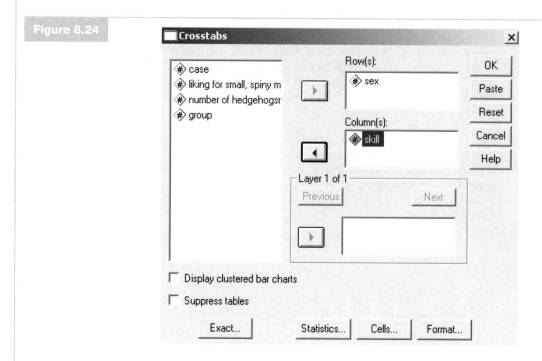

The example in Output 8.4 in Table 8.6 presents the typical tabular output, in this instance for the two category variables in the hedgehog data set – cycling skill level and gender. (All will be revealed presently.)

Table 8.6    Output 8.4—Crosstabulation of skill level by gender

Sex Skill Crosstabulation

|  |  |  | Skill |  | Total |
|---|---|---|---|---|---|
|  |  |  | Novice | Experienced |  |
| Sex | Male | Count | 10 | 9 | 19 |
|  |  | % within sex | 52.6 % | 47.4% | 100.0% |
|  | Female | Count | 7 | 8 | 15 |
|  |  | % within sex | 46.7 % | 53.3% | 100.0% |
| Total |  | Count | 17 | 17 | 34 |
|  |  | % within sex | 50.0 % | 50.0% | 100.0% |

The type of table shown in Table 8.6 is termed a 2 × 2 contingency table, there being two variables in the analysis, each comprising two categories. Occasionally the more informative notation of 2R × 2C is used, making it clear how the data are laid out – with two categories in the Row variable, and two in the Column. In its basic format each cell displays only the number of observations or cases applicable to its particular categories, such that in this illustration we can see that, in the novice group, there were 10 males and 7 females. More useful for descriptive purposes is the translation of cell counts into percentages, thus reducing the sometimes misleading effects of uneven participant numbers represented in each category. In the setting up of this example, an option (see Figure 8.25) allowed the specification of what actually appears in the various cells: percentages were selected for the row variable and the cells now provide the additional information that, for the female cyclist condition, 52.6% of the cases were novices and 46.7% were experienced cyclists. It will be noted that the Crosstabs: Cell Display window (obtained by clicking the <u>C</u>ells button in the **C**rosstabs set-up window) offers many more options. However, since these relate to drawing inferences and go beyond the mere description of data they will not be discussed at this point. We return to crosstabulation in Part 5.

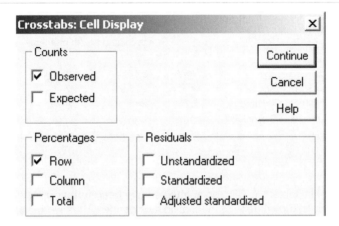

The 2 × 2 case is the simplest of the crosstabulation relationships possible for, as we are aware, variables can be subdivided into many components. We could measure preference for beer or lager among different astrological signs for instance, and this would give us a 2 × 12 contingency table; we could obtain an impression of preference in reading material by equating the personality type of participants with the type of newspaper most frequently read. If there are two major personality types (e.g., extraverts and introverts) and two types of paper (tabloid or broadsheet), we would be back to the 2 × 2 contingency table, and so on. Box 8.8 offers a more complex application of crosstabulation in addition to providing a word of caution in the use of this procedure.

## A Closer Look At . . .

# Crosstabulation

In a health study investigating aspects of psychological wellbeing, a sample of 500 participants is drawn from three regions – Scotland, the Midlands and South England. (See the *MK crosstabs* data set in our companion website.) Psychological wellbeing is assessed by questionnaire response to an item on the number of general practitioner (GP) visits in the previous year for stress-related problems (none; once; up to three; more than three). Respondents' gender is noted, allowing a breakdown of the basic two-variable relationship by a third, control variable, as is shown in Tables 8.7, 8.8, and 8.9.

In Table 8.7, wellbeing is presented simply in terms of geographical region. It can be seen, for instance, that the highest number of GP visits is recorded for the Midlands, with 38.7% of the Midlands sample recording up to three GP visits in the previous year, and almost the same percentage recording more than three visits. Participants from South England, on the other hand, recorded the fewest visits. Note that because it is easy to become overwhelmed with information in the conventional crosstabs output, we have restricted the cell contents to row percentages only. Cell contents are readily controlled in the Crosstabs: Cell Display window.

**Table 8.7**     Output 8.5 – GP visits for stress-related health problems by major UK region.

| % within major UK region | | Stress-related health problems | | | | |
|---|---|---|---|---|---|---|
| | | None | Once | Up to three | More than three | Total |
| Major UK region | Scotland | 22.4% | 26.9% | 27.4% | 23.4% | 100.0% |
| | Midlands | 4.7% | 17.3% | 38.7% | 39.3% | 100.0% |
| | S. England | 26.7% | 30.0% | 29.3% | 14.0% | 100.0% |
| Total | | 18.4% | 25.0% | 31.3% | 25.3% | 100.0% |

In Table 8.8, GP appointments have been further broken down by a control variable, as it is known: that of the individual's gender. Thus we have a measure of psychological wellbeing by geographic region for males, and psychological wellbeing by region for females.

This is quite a sophisticated development and allows us to explore our data in more detail – we could for instance determine whether or not women's psychological health reflects the general trend, or is there perhaps something unusual about this group?

**Table 8.8**     Output 8.6 – GP visits for stress-related health problems by major UK region.

| Sex | % major UK region | | Stress-related health problems | | | | |
|---|---|---|---|---|---|---|---|
| | | | None | Once | Up to three | More than three | Total |
| Male | Major UK region | Scotland | 19.8% | 27.0% | 28.8% | 24.3% | 100.0% |
| | | Midlands | 1.2% | 2.4% | 38.6% | 57.8% | 100.0% |
| | | S. England | 32.1% | 24.4% | 26.9% | 16.7% | 100.0% |
| | Total | | 17.6% | 18.8% | 31.3% | 32.4% | 100.0% |
| Female | Major UK region | Scotland | 25.8% | 25.8% | 25.8% | 22.5% | 100.0% |
| | | Midlands | 9.0% | 35.8% | 38.8% | 16.4% | 100.0% |
| | | S. England | 20.8% | 36.1% | 31.9% | 11.1% | 100.0% |
| | Total | | 19.3% | 32.0% | 31.6% | 17.1% | 100.0% |

We could continue this process of further sub-dividing our data and it might be of interest to explore wellbeing not only by region and gender, but also by occupational category. However, if we do continue with this process we begin to encounter problems.

While initially a sample size of 500 might have seemed adequate, when this is sub-divided by six occupational classes, three regions and two genders, a random distribution would leave us with only about 13 cases per category. If numbers were further diluted across three age groups, for instance, the likely numbers falling into any cell are further reduced with some combinations (e.g., male, professional, middle-aged, from South England) only sparsely distributed among all the possible cells. This problem is intensified when we rely on percentage values alone in cells: 4% of a sample of size 50 is only two people.

A related problem, which will be considered at greater length in Part 5, concerns the use of crosstabulations to analyse the distribution of observations. In a search for patterns among responses, or in an attempt to judge whether actual observations deviate substantially from our expectations, certain statistical techniques can be applied to crosstabulated data. However, to be effective these techniques impose certain conditions on the data, one of which concerns minimum numbers of cellular observations, or rather, minimum numbers of what we would expect in particular cells – when this becomes small, the data are no longer susceptible to statistical analysis.

An obvious solution to the problem of numbers is to increase the sample size. However, often this is not possible, especially in undergraduate research, so an alternative solution would be to reduce the number of sub-divisions. In the example in Table 8.8, ignoring the regional differences would make more cases available for each cell since we would be looking at GP visits by gender only (and more expected values, which is important from the point of view of further analysis). Opting for only two or three categories of GP visit – such as *none*, *once* and *more than one* – would considerably increase the pool of participants available for each cell and might produce the added gain of achieving the requirements for statistical analysis. Of course, the disadvantage of taking this approach is that important distinctions among participants can be lost and it is up to the individual how important this is in terms of the overall research issue.

A final point brings us back to the essential purpose of descriptive statistics – that they are intended to summarise, describe and illustrate. Unfortunately, contingency tables, while they do meet these requirements, sometimes fail to do so immediately and with clarity. They provide too much information for the at-a-glance effect and often require close inspection for any patterns to emerge. Consider again Tables 8.7 and 8.8: there is no question that they contain relevant data, and in a precise format, but gaining an overall impression of how individuals are distributed across the various cells will not be immediate. This is even more of a problem when we expand on the information offered in each cell. So far we have restricted our output to percentage information only, but we could easily include in each cell the actual number of observations on which percentage calculations were based; we might also include the number of expected observations for each cell, producing the much more intimidating (though complete) output as shown in the detail below in Table 8.9.

Table 8.9    Output 8.7 – GP visits for stress-related health problems in two regions.

|  |  | None | One | Up to three | More than three |
|---|---|---|---|---|---|
| Scotland | Count | 22 | 30 | 32 | 27 |
|  | Expected count | 19.6 | 20.8 | 34.7 | 35.9 |
|  | % within major UK region | 19.8% | 27.0% | 28.8% | 24.3% |
| Midlands | Count | 1 | 2 | 32 | 48 |
|  | Expected count | 14.6 | 15.6 | 25.9 | 26.9 |
|  | % within major UK region | 1.2% | 2.4% | 38.6% | 57.8% |

On the other hand, consider Figure 8.26, a combination bar chart showing similar information. Here we can see the overall level of GP visits broken down by gender.

Number of GP visits by gender

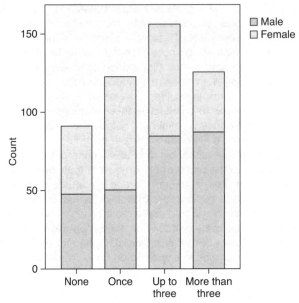

It looks like the male participants in our study aren't doing too well. Box 8.9 explains the process of crosstabulation in more detail.

Box 8.9

**Practicalities . . .**

## Using crosstabulations

Crosstabulation is the typical procedure for describing and demonstrating associations between nominal or ordinal variables. As such it is a particularly useful procedure for dealing with survey data in which both profile information and response data are categorical. Such data include responses to questionnaire items which are measured on a Likert-type scale (strongly agree, agree, etc.) which, despite the common interpretation of such scales, actually comprise ordinal categories. The word of caution here is to be alert to the relationship between sample size and the number of categories comprising each variable to be crosstabulated. The general rule is that if the expected number of cases for any cell in the contingency table drops below five, subsequent analysis becomes difficult. Exploring an association between 10 males and 10 females, and a Yes/No response to an opinion item is probably fine, whereas exploring an association between the same 20 individuals and a five-category Likert scale would most likely spread participants too thinly across the categories to be of any use either as an illustration or for the purposes of analysis. A solution is to collapse the number of categories which comprise a variable, allowing the opportunity for more cases to fall in any given cell: for example, items on a 5-point Likert scale could be compressed into three categories. Alternatively, a profile age variable comprising six age groups can be reduced to two. Always remember that whenever we manipulate variables in this way we lose information.

| strongly agree | agree | undecided | disagree | strongly disagree |
|---|---|---|---|---|
| agree | | undecided | | disagree |

| age: <15 | 16–20 | 21–30 | 31–40 | 41–50 | 51–60 |
|---|---|---|---|---|---|
| 30 years and younger | | | 31 years and older | | |

## 8.5  Graphs and crosstabulated data

As a final refinement, we could break down our distribution of GP visits by gender, for each of the geographic regions, in much the same way as we obtained separate contingency tables. The procedure, though, is slightly more complex than merely selecting options.

Our intent here is to generate a graph, similar to that in Figure 8.26, but for each of the regions, Scotland, the Midlands and South England. This is achieved by selecting, initially, only those cases (participants, observations) in the Scottish sample, generating a combination chart, then repeating the exercise for the remaining samples. The procedure for selecting cases and drawing stacked graphs is as follows:

Step 1.  Open the Data menu option and choose Select Cases (Figure 8.27).

Figure 8.27

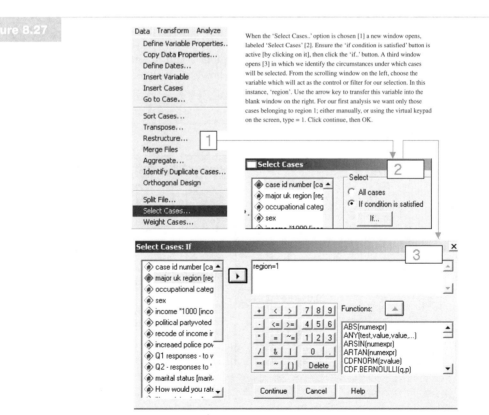

When the 'Select Cases..' option is chosen [1] a new window opens, labeled 'Select Cases' [2]. Ensure the 'if condition is satisfied' button is active [by clicking on it], then click the 'if..' button. A third window opens [3] in which we identify the circumstances under which cases will be selected. From the scrolling window on the left, choose the variable which will act as the control or filter for our selection. In this instance, 'region'. Use the arrow key to transfer this variable into the blank window on the right. For our first analysis we want only those cases belonging to region 1; either manually, or using the virtual keypad on the screen, type = 1. Click continue, then OK.

Step 2.    Now that only those cases in 'region' 1 are available for analysis, the first graph can be drawn. Open the Graphs menu and select Bar (Figure 8.28).

**Figure 8.28**

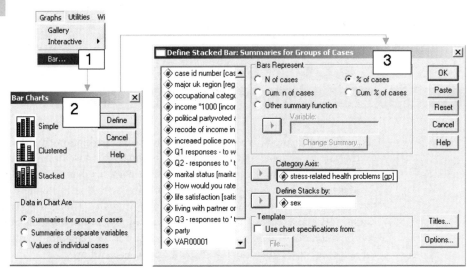

In 'Graphs' choose Bar . . . [1]. In the 'Bar charts window [2] select the 'stacked' option, ensure the 'Summaries for groups of cases' is active [by clicking on the button next to it], then select 'Define'. The next window [3] allows us to determine how our chart is going to look, and what variables will be used. From the variables window on the left, select the GP variable and transfer it to the 'Category Axis' box. Transfer the SEX variable into the 'Define stacks by:' box.

We can choose our bars to represent many things [number of cases, cumulative number, and so on] but since we wish to compare three regions which may comprise different number of cases, we choose the % of cases option. Click OK.

Step 3.    Repeat this procedure for 'region' 2 and 3. Graphs can be customised and re-sized. Figures 8.29a to 8.29c show the results:

**Figure 8.29a**    GP visits in Scotland.

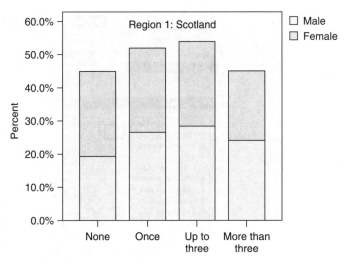

| Figure 8.29b | Percent GP visits in the Midlands. |

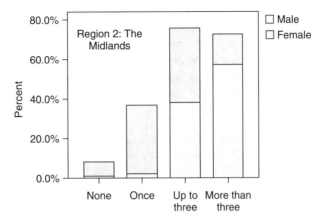

| Figure 8.29c | Percent GP visits in South England. |

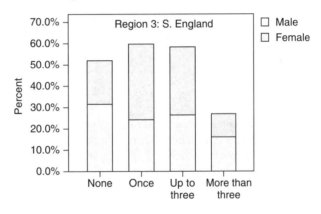

Read more about selecting cases in Box 8.10.

## Box 8.10

## Practicalities . . .

# Selecting cases

The ability to select particular cases for analysis is a useful one and we might envisage a situation in which we wish to select the male participants in a study for more detailed analysis, or participants in a control condition. However, following any Select Cases procedure it is good practice to return to the Data menu, choose the Select Cases option, and then click All cases in the Select sector, which restores the full data set. Otherwise all subsequent analyses will be carried out on the reduced sample. This is a common problem among undergraduates using SPSS and often not discovered until later stages of analysis.

## 8.6    Screening data

When data are collected following a study it is always our hope that, as a result of proper sampling procedures, reliable and valid measurements and diligent recording, such data will be complete and normally distributed. Unfortunately the reality is often different: in undergraduate research sampling is usually far from random. Measurement instruments can also cause problems when, for instance, scales are too narrow to discriminate adequately among individuals, or response categories are ambiguous. Nor can recording procedures be totally relied upon and mis-coding of data is not just confined to undergraduate work. The outcome can be distributions which are skewed, full of missing values and featuring outliers and extreme scores. In many cases, especially in introductory courses, such problems will likely be tolerated by tutors in the interests of offering research experience, or when other aspects of the research process are emphasised. However, it should be noted that, apart from being untidy and reflecting possible problems in research design and procedure, data which deviate too far from the normal or which exhibit some of the other problems mentioned above cannot be effectively described using many of the common descriptive measures. The mean, for instance, is of limited value in providing a measure of central tendency for a highly skewed distribution; the presence of extreme scores makes a nonsense of minimum and maximum values. Moreover, when data are flawed, subsequent inferential analyses can be problematic. It is therefore important that we understand how problems with data occur, and how we can deal with them.

### 8.6.1    Missing values

We have already discussed missing values but it is worth re-stating the point that it is useful to identify instances where data are missing. It may be that there is a particular item on a questionnaire which respondents are avoiding, or whose wording is ambiguous, and we may wish to identify cases where this has occurred. Alternatively there may be particular individuals who have omitted certain responses and it might be useful to identify these also. The procedure for dealing with missing values is relatively straightforward and requires inspection of records, questionnaires or other form of data collection, or such gaps in data can be picked up at the data entry stage. Once missing values have been identified, recall that they must be coded in an appropriate way so that they can be, firstly, readily identified in the data set and, secondly, excluded from analysis when, for instance, a test is performed in SPSS. Procedures for coding missing values have been described elsewhere and you are reminded to review Box 8.5.

### 8.6.2    Outliers and extreme scores

Encountering outliers or extreme scores in a data set can be both problematic and illuminating. Consider the following (hypothetical) attention spans (in minutes) for a sample of 13 undergraduates during an introductory psychology lecture:

2 3 3 4 5 5 5 6 7 7 8 9 50

If we were to express these data in terms of a simple range we would state that attention span ranged between 2 and 50 minutes. If this were all the information we had, and given

Boxplot of attention span, showing ranges for outliers and extreme scores.

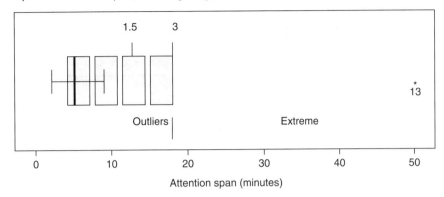

our tendency to assume an even or normal distribution of values between two end points in an ordered array, we might mistakenly imagine that average span would be found at around 25 minutes. The reality is that average attention span is more like 5 minutes (this is what a median would tell us). The actual calculated mean for these data is 8.8 which, while not 25, is still untypical since extreme scores tend to pull arithmetic averages towards them. So how do such unusual scores arise? Usually as a result of error – misreading data and mis-keying data are the most common sources of extreme values. On the other hand, extreme scores can also alert us to something interesting going on in our study: it may be that in the attention span example there was indeed a student who managed to stay awake for 50 minutes and it would be in our interests to find out more about this person (and to learn how we could get more students like this).

We have used the terms *outlier* and *extreme* here merely to indicate values which don't seem to fit the rest of a data set. In SPSS, however, they have particular meaning, as shown in Figure 8.30.

In a boxplot SPSS determines that any value which falls between 1.5 and 3 IQRs (interquartile ranges) above or below the third or first quartile is classed as an outlier. (Recall that in the boxplot, the box itself represents the IQR.) Extreme scores are any which lie beyond 3 IQRs, as shown in Figure 8.30.

### 8.6.3 Non-normal distributions

When distributions are severely skewed subsequent inferential analyses become problematic. A way of dealing with this is to normalize the data through one of a variety of transformations. There are no set rules for this; rather, a procedure should be adopted which is the most successful in creating a more normal-like distribution. A common approach for moderately skewed data is to compute a new variable based on the square roots of the original (skewed) data. This is achieved as follows:

Step 1.   In the Transform menu select Compute.

Step 2.   In the Compute Variable window, type in the name of the new variable you are about to create. In the present example a variable in the *MKhedgehog* errors data set has been chosen for transformation. The variable 'errors' exhibits signs

Figure 8.31

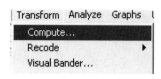
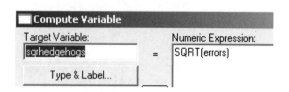

of skewness and we intend normalizing the variable by taking the square root of each value. Hence, the new variable has been named 'sqrhedgehogs'.

Step 3. In the **N**umeric Expression box, enter the procedure which will perform the transformation. This can be attempted manually, for simple mathematical transformations, or a selection is made from a list of common expressions in the **C**ompute **V**ariable window (Figure 8.31).

Step 4. With the transformation complete a new variable will be created in the data set. This should be inspected to determine whether the transformation has reduced the skew, either by examining descriptive statistics, or by generating appropriate graphs. Figures 8.32a and 8.32b demonstrate the hedgehog error variable for both the original data and for the transformed values.

It can be observed that in the original form, the hedgehog data are slightly skewed. Following transformation, the data appear more normal.

It must be pointed out that in most cases, slight to moderate skew will rarely influence subsequent analysis and can be largely ignored. Where transformations are to be considered, however, there are a number of strategies which can be adopted – the square root approach is only one. This is quite a complex area and a number of useful texts are available which explore the issues in some detail. These are provided among our listing of recommended reading.

Figure 8.32a    Histogram of original data.

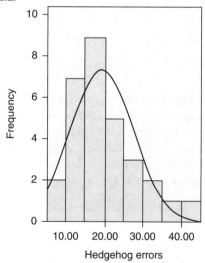

**Figure 8.32b**    Histogram of normalized data.

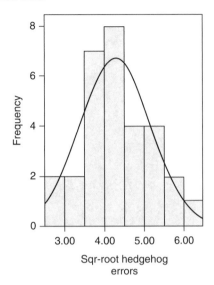

Sqr-root hedgehog
errors

## Review

This concludes the section on describing data. The aim, as in all sections of this book, has been to introduce general principles and provide examples of those principles in operation. Moreover, Chapter 8 has attempted to provide an introduction to one of the commonest statistical packages available to students. Students should now be able to create a data file in SPSS, enter data correctly, format the data and perform elementary descriptive analyses.

## Suggested further reading

Howitt, D., & Cramer, D. (2003). *A guide to computing statistics with SPSS 11 for Windows*. Harlow, Essex: Pearson/Prentice Hall.

A useful and detailed guide to the statistical procedures available in SPSS. Contains many worked examples.

Kinnear, P. R., & Gray, C. D. (2000). *SPSS for Windows made simple: Release 10*. Hove, East Sussex: Psychology Press Ltd.

This is very much a 'how to do it' text, comprising relatively easy to follow guidance on all aspects of SPSS.

Langdridge, D. (2004). *Introduction to research methods and data analysis in psychology*. Harlow, Essex: Pearson/Prentice Hall.

Provides good general coverage of descriptive statistics and also introduces SPSS.

# Drawing inferences
# and testing hypotheses

## Part 5

Introducing
research

Planning a research
project—the design

Carrying out
research—methods
& procedure

Describing research
findings—
descriptives

**Analysing research
findings—inferential
statistics**

Carrying out
qualitative research

Writing up and
presenting the
findings of research

Part 5 goes beyond the description of data, which formed the basis of Part 4, and considers how these data can be used to make decisions. Did one group perform better than another? Do these observed differences signify a genuine, as opposed to a chance difference? Do these results support my hypothesis? Was the theory correct? The major statistical tests, both parametric and non-parametric, will be introduced and the procedures for making statistical decisions explained. The emphasis in the following chapters is on selecting the most appropriate form of analysis and the interpretation of statistical output. Once again, output and analyses have utilized SPSS.

Chapter 9 reviews the principles of inferential statistics and introduces difference testing, through consideration of the following:

- probability
- the role of statistical significance in testing hypotheses
- the role of power and effect size in making statistical decisions
- the distinction between parametric and non-parametric tests
- single sample tests, comparing a sample with a population
- between-groups tests, comparing two conditions
- between-groups tests, comparing three and more conditions
- within-subjects tests, comparing two conditions
- within-subjects tests, comparing three and more conditions

Chapter 10 introduces the principles behind, and procedures for performing, tests of association, through consideration of the following:

- the chi-square test of association
- correlation
- simple regression

Chapter 11 introduces complex modes of analyses which, while relevant to the more advanced student, are still well within the grasp of most undergraduates. The chapter focuses on:

- partial correlation
- multiple regression
- two-way analysis of variance

# Introducing inferential statistics and tests of differences

## Key Issues

Chapter 9 is essential reading for those of you who are ready to analyse the data collected in your study in order to test a hypothesis or answer a research question. Here we introduce the principles of inferential statistics, explaining the role of probability in making informed decisions and evaluating different types of tests in terms of their power, applicability to different research designs and their suitability for different types of data – parametric and non-parametric. In all cases we offer step-by-step procedures for calculation, worked examples in SPSS and explanations of statistical output. The emphasis in this chapter is on difference testing and includes discussions of:

- hypothesis testing and probability
- one- and two-tailed tests
- sample and population comparisons
- parametric and non-parametric data
- between-groups comparisons
- within-subjects comparisons
- ANOVA

## 9.1  Inferential statistics

Descriptive statistics are in themselves important means to understanding the characteristics of data. However, the parameters usually taken to describe variables – specifically, measures of spread and central tendency – can be further, although not exclusively, used to draw inferences. (See section 9.1.7 on parametric and non-parametric data.) Comparing the means of two samples can be the first step in demonstrating that a genuine difference exists between two groups, or that a particular experimental treatment has a real effect on some outcome. This is what **inferential statistics** is all about – making deductions and drawing conclusions. In the first chapter of this book the purpose of research was defined as describing, explaining and predicting aspects of the world in which we live. Describing and, to some extent, explaining have been considered in the previous chapter on describing data. Understanding the psychological world and the people who inhabit it, however, requires a more detailed appreciation of the information we gather and a sophisticated ability to manipulate it which goes beyond the purely descriptive. And if we ever hope to be able to predict behaviour, we need to demonstrate that events which we observe or effects we encounter during the course of an observation study or experiment are not mere chance occurrences. Not surprisingly then, inferential statistics rely heavily on the concept of **probability**.

### 9.1.1   Probability explained

Whenever a researcher attempts to make a point, support a hypothesis or test a theory, she is trying to show that a particular set of observations is not merely a chance occurrence. This is not an easy task, due to the richness and variety of the countless elements which comprise human experience. No two people are ever alike – even identical twins, as we know, cannot share the same physical space and are therefore subjected to differing experiences and influences throughout their lives. Consequently, selecting any two people at random and looking for differences in measurable characteristics will produce a breath-taking lack of commonality. But this is normal. Each of us inherits a unique genetic pattern, whose contribution to individual singularity is further enhanced by particular parental interactions and selective exposure to peer influences, attitudes, values, education, opportunities and cultural forces. The wonder of this is that there remains sufficient common ground within humanity for any level of predictability whatsoever.

The point we are trying to make here is that whenever we look at any two individuals or groups we should *expect* there to be differences between them, and this is the researcher's problem. If we devise a study to demonstrate that a new form of learning strategy is more effective than traditional methods, how do we know that any differences between a sample using the new techniques and a sample using the traditional strategies is nothing more than a reflection of the very human tendency for variation? How do we know that the new approach had a *real* effect?

The answer lies in probability. Every event in the world, every occurrence, happens with its own particular level of likelihood or probability: the chances of someone having a puncture while driving home from work is pretty unlikely in these days of modern tyre technology, but it can happen (and often does, usually at the busiest junctions). Having two punctures is even less likely (less probable), while experiencing three flat tyres is unusual in the extreme. If our hapless driver discovered four flats – and the spare – he could quite reasonably assume that something was going on.

Plate 9.1   Understanding probability can help predict the likelihood of any given number coming up with each roll of the dice.
*Source*: Corbis/David Michael Zimmerman

Making decisions about the outcome of research operates in a similar manner. Comparing two groups of participants on any measurable characteristic – be it height, shoe size, verbal ability or personality – will always produce differences. In fact, given what we have just said about human variability, we would *expect* differences. Moreover, we would be prepared to accept that such differences might reasonably range from the marginal to the moderate. Comparing the average heights of two groups of undergraduates, for example, could easily produce the heights of 1.9 metres and 1.8 metres respectively, showing a very slight difference between the two. We could, however, discover mean heights of 1.9 and 1.6 metres, and still not be too surprised. After all, while this difference of 0.3 metres is less likely than our previous finding, it is still possible, given this known tendency for variation in all things human. Mean heights of 1.9 and 1.4 might start us wondering, though, while 1.9 and 1.0 would make us extremely suspicious – just like the driver with all the punctures. This is how statistical decisions are made: when an event occurs which is so unlikely that, even within the bounds of human variability it is remarkable, then we can claim that a discovery has been made or an effect demonstrated. Three simultaneous punctures might be possible, but four is a conspiracy. A difference in heights between 1.9 and 1.6 metres might be unusual, but that between 1.9 and 1.0 metre might suggest that our samples have not been drawn from the same population.

The question now to be addressed is "how unusual is unusual?" Certainly we all have an intuitive idea of what is unusual but possible as opposed to what is downright impossible, but this is a subjective thing, based on feelings and, occasionally, misperceptions about the laws of chance. The example in Box 9.1 is a good illustration.

Box 9.1

## A Closer Look At . . .

# Events and possibilities

Certainty — Every day it will rain somewhere

Every day it will rain somewhere in the UK

Hedgehogs will eventually develop intelligence equal to that of humans

Some day pigs will fly

Impossibility — There will come a time when all students understand the difference between Type I and Type II errors

The rule, which has become the accepted norm for making statistical decisions, is that if an event occurs (a difference between groups, the outcome of a manipulation) when the chances of it occurring naturally are less than 5 times in 100, then this event is deemed too unusual to be plausible, or within the acceptable range of variability. The event is then given the status of being **statistically significant**.

This cut-off – known as the 5% or .05 significance level – is deliberately far removed from high-probability events (it will rain somewhere on any given November day in Britain, for instance) to ensure as far as possible that when we decide an effect is present, a change has occurred or whatever, that we are not merely seeing an unusual but not completely out of the ordinary event. The astute reader will have noticed the essential flaw in this approach: even an event so unlikely that we might expect to see it, naturally, only 5% of the time, is still possible in an infinitely variable universe. Because of this, we can be led to false conclusions in our research, as the next section demonstrates.

### 9.1.2  Scope for errors

Every event in the universe exists on an imaginary continuum running from certainty to impossibility, with the full range of probabilities in between (see Box 9.1). The convention is to view events as 'different' only when the probability that they will occur is as unlikely as .05 or less. However, the danger here is that such events, though rare, could still occur by chance alone. In fact, according to the rules of probability, events of this rarity could actually occur by chance 5% of the time. Or to put it another way, if we use this level of probability to identify events as significantly different from what we might normally expect, we will be wrong approximately 5% of the time. In research terminology this is known as a **Type I error** – the possibility that an apparently significant finding can actually be explained in terms of unusual but nonetheless valid variations and individual differences. This is expressed formally as the probability of rejecting the null hypothesis when the null hypothesis is true. Alternatively, a **Type II error** can occur when we wrongly accept that an unusual event is merely an extension of chance occurrences when in fact we have a significant finding. Expressed formally, a Type II error is the probability of not rejecting the null hypothesis when it is false. More simply, whatever we decide in research, there is always some chance that we will be wrong. Figure 9.1 illustrates the location of the .05 significance level in a range of probabilities.

One solution to this problem, of course, would be to push our cut-off point further along the continuum of probability, not accepting a finding unless it is even less likely than the 5 times in 100 level. And indeed, some researchers eager to avoid Type I errors do just that, refusing to accept a finding as being significant unless the probability of its occurrence is 1 in 100 or less (known as the 1% or .01 significance level). Unfortunately, while a finding significant at this extreme level might seem more robust, it will also be more difficult to demonstrate due to the need for a really clear-cut effect, or a huge sample. Even then there are problems in interpreting significance, as section 9.1.4 will show.

### 9.1.3  One- and two-tailed tests

An added complication to the problem of significance concerns whether or not our hypothesis and our test is **one-tailed** or **two-tailed**. This is a question which often causes difficulties in comprehension for those new to statistical analysis, but it needn't, once the principle is understood.

**Figure 9.1**     Illustration of the location of the .05 significance level in a hypothetical range of probabilities.

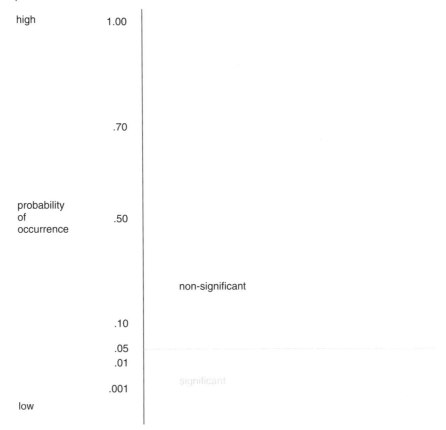

Suppose we were concerned with an industrial process of some kind, say the brewing of a particular variety of ale. To ensure that a new batch measures up to what we normally expect from this brew, we take a number of bottles off the production line and subject them to analysis – looking at flavour, strength, colour and so on. We might even invite a few friends round to assist in the assessment process.

While modern production methods are now well controlled and the chances of a particular sample deviating from the norm are slim, this was not always the case. In the past it would have been quite likely in this kind of study to find samples deviating markedly from the expected norm. The point of this particular study would be to determine whether variation is within an acceptable range, or whether the sample characteristics are so far removed from what would normally be expected of this brew that the batch would be destroyed.

From the way this hypothetical example has been expressed, it should be clear that when we are comparing our sample to the expected characteristics of the population as a whole, we are prepared for differences to be in either direction – that is, that the new batch will be different from our expectations; it might be stronger or weaker, it might be fuller flavoured, or insipid. Figure 9.2 illustrates this.

Figure 9.2 can be taken to represent the known characteristics of the particular brew we are interested in. There will be a mean for this population and variation about this

Figure 9.2   Samples and populations. Any sample drawn from a population is likely to differ in some way from the typical characteristics of that population.

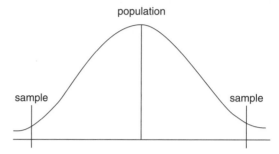

mean. When we compare our sample statistics to these population parameters, we could find that our sample is placed somewhere beyond the mean (stronger, fuller flavoured, etc.). But equally, we could find our sample falling below the mean (weaker, less flavourful, etc.). Since the ends of this kind of distribution are known as 'tails', our sample could lie at either tail, and therefore any test which allows for this either-or case is termed a *two-tailed test*.

This allowance for observations to fall at either tail of a distribution requires further explanation in probability terms. So far we have argued that an event will be deemed statistically significant if it occurs with a probability of .05 (5%) or less. However, if we try to test this in a two-tailed manner, we would be wrong to examine the 5% cut-off point at each tail, since what we would be doing is checking for the occurrence of an event which appears only 5% of the time in one direction and 5% of the time in the other direction. In reality we end up using a 10% significance level!

To ensure then that we evaluate an event in terms of only the .05 level, this measure of extremeness must be spread between the two ends of a distribution, meaning that, in practical terms, the actual cut-off point of a two-tailed test is 2.5% in either direction. See Box 9.2 for a fuller explanation.

Box 9.2

 A Closer Look At . . .

# One- and two-tailed tests

A quality control chemist with statistical leanings suspects that a current batch of dark ale will not be typical of the usual brew, due to a problem during the production process. Making a number of selections at random from the current production line, our closet statistician has colleagues rate the ale on an index of taste. His expectation, and hence his hypothesis, is that the sample drawn from this current batch will be different from the known characteristics of this particular beer. However, he does not know in what way the sample will differ so he proposes an hypothesis which covers all eventualities – specifically, the sample could differ from the known characteristics of all previous batches (the population), but it could differ in either direction (i.e., stronger than or weaker than). This is a two-tailed hypothesis (see Figure 9.3).

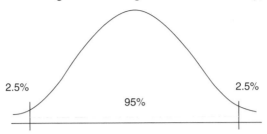

Figure 9.3    Normal distribution showing the critical regions for a two-tailed hypothesis.

If our embryonic statistician selects the usual .05 cut-off for his test then he is proposing that the sample batch cannot be considered unusual unless it differs from the expected range of flavour in a way which would only ever happen 5% of the time. Another way of looking at this is that 95% of the time variations from the population average will be within an acceptable range. If, however, the new batch falls outside that 95% limit, then it must be considered statistically different from the expected norm. Figure 9.3 shows the range in which the sample must fall to be considered different – also apparent is the way in which the remaining 5% of rare differences have to be divided between the two extremes of the distribution. In practical terms what this means is that to be considered significant within a two-tailed context, a particular event must be further out along the rarity continuum than we might have expected; it is almost *as if* we are using a 2.5% cut-off level rather than the 5% one, although in probability terms this is not the case.

All of the above is relevant only if the researcher is unsure of the way in which his sample might differ from the population. If, on the other hand, he was pretty sure that the new batch would not be so flavourful as the normal brew, then in his comparison with the population he would be looking only at the lower end of the distribution, or at one tail. Consequently, his hypothesis changes from 'the mean taste rating of the sample will differ from that of the population', to 'the mean taste rating of the sample will be less than that of the population' (Figure 9.4).

Clearly, while he is still working within his 5% boundary, all of our researcher's scope for unusualness is at the same end of the continuum. Comparing this distribution in Figure 9.4 with that in Figure 9.3, it should be clear that basing a judgement on only one tail of a distribution is more likely to produce a result than if he had to consider both ends – but only if he gets the direction right. This is the problem with one- versus two-tailed tests: it is more difficult to find evidence in support of a two-tailed prediction, but a two-tailed test will nonetheless pick up a significant finding no matter at which end of the continuum it

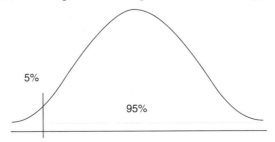

Figure 9.4    Normal distribution showing the critical region for a one-tailed hypothesis.

**Table 9.1** Statistical output comparing sample statistics with a population parameter.

| | No. of cases | Mean | SD | SE of mean |
|---|---|---|---|---|
| Sample | 30 | 153.27 | 8.92 | 1.64 |
| Population | | 156 | | |

| Mean difference | 95% confidence interval | | t-value | df | Two-tailed significance |
|---|---|---|---|---|---|
| | lower | upper | | | |
| −2.73 | −6.062 | .595 | −1.68 | 29 | .10 |

falls. One-tailed tests, on the other hand, are effective only if the researcher has chosen the right direction to explore.

Returning to our beer-tasting study, on averaging judgements across 30 observations, a mean measure of 153.267 is obtained (totally meaningless, but representing flavour for the purpose of this example).

In the past, and using similar measures, this particular ale has produced a score of 156 on the same flavour index. Clearly the two averages are different, but what our researcher must now decide is whether the sample is too different from the population to be considered *really* different (a statistically significant difference).

An appropriate test here is the one-sample *t*-test, in which a sample statistic (sample mean) is compared with a known population parameter (population mean) and a formula applied to ascertain the likelihood that the sample comes from this population. Alternatively, the standard error, introduced in Part 4 and further discussed in later sections of this chapter, can be utilised to determine the extent to which the sample deviates from the population. (The formula for the calculation of the one-sample *t*-test is given in section 9.2.1, as is the SPSS procedure.) The relevant statistics are shown in Table 9.1.

Inspection of Table 9.1 demonstrates that, given everything else we know about the sample (its size, the spread of scores around the mean) the observed difference of 153.27 from the population mean of 156 would occur with a probability of .10 (or 10% of the time). Large as this difference is, it is not large enough to be statistically significant – that is, it does not fall at or beyond the conventional cut-off level, as Figure 9.5a demonstrates.

However, had our researcher been convinced that the new batch of ale would score lower on the index of flavour, then he could have applied a one-tailed test, whereby he could concentrate his attention at one end of the continuum. In this instance, the observed difference suddenly achieves statistical significance, as in Figure 9.5b.

**Figure 9.5a** Two-tailed comparison between a sample and a population.

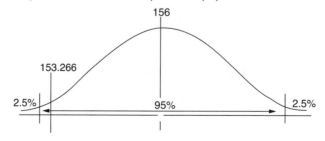

One-tailed comparison between a sample and a population.

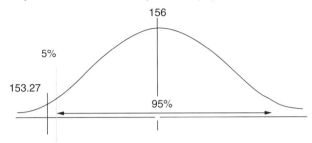

By way of a final demonstration, returning to the statistical output, we observe that the two-tailed probability of obtaining this difference at either end of a distribution is .10. Converting this to a one-tailed probability is achieved by halving the two-tailed value. Thus the probability of obtaining this observed difference, below the population mean, is .05.

(Note: this example is based, somewhat loosely, on the life of William Gosset, employee of a well-known Irish brewing family and occasional statistician, known more familiarly as Student, originator of the *t*-test in its various forms.)

Hopefully by now the notion of events being evaluated in terms of their probability of occurrence is understood, but if there is still some puzzlement over this, Box 9.3 should illustrate the point.

### 9.1.4   Effect size and power

Much of the previous discussion might have created an impression that statistical significance in research is the benchmark for any study, and while to some extent this is true, the role of significance in determining an outcome is slightly more complex. Almost 20 years ago Jacob Cohen (1988) argued that significance should be interpreted in terms of a combination of effect size and sample size. If an experiment, for instance, demonstrated a tiny and indeed meaningless difference between a control group and an experimental group on some measure, yet this for a huge sample (e.g., 2,000 participants), then this tiny difference would probably be significant. This is the classic Type I error. More important in research, however, is the opposite scenario in which a Type II error is made. Recall that this occurs when the researcher mistakenly accepts the **null hypothesis** as being true when in fact it is false. A difference between a control and an experimental group may be moderate, or even large, but if the sample sizes are too small a statistical test may fail to find significance. This will certainly not happen if the size of an effect is small.

This seems such an obvious issue it is surprising that it has taken the research establishment until very recently to recognize it. Only now, in the past few years, are journal editors requiring submissions to include a statement on effect size and power, with **power** being a measure based on the probability of rejecting the null hypothesis when it is

Box 9.3

## A Closer Look At . . .

# Probability

Imagine you and a close friend are constantly disagreeing about what to do at weekends – where to go, who to go with and so on. To resolve these differences a coin is usually tossed – your friend's 'lucky' coin, and invariably the fall is in her favour. She doesn't call it her lucky coin for nothing! However, you are now becoming suspicious that there might be something more sinister behind your friend's luck since you can no longer remember any occasion when you got to do what you wanted. In short, you suspect your friend is using a bent coin; you suspect your friend of cheating.

Stealing into her room one night you retrieve the questionable coin and prepare to carry out an experiment: you will toss this coin 100 times and observe the outcome. Your recollection is that in resolving differences your friend always calls Heads, and nearly always wins: therefore your expectation is that in this experiment there will be an unusually high number of Heads. The problem is this: what constitutes unusual?

If this coin were fair, then at each toss there would be two possible outcomes, Heads or Tails, with each equally likely. In 100 tosses then, you might expect 50 Heads and 50 Tails. Of course, due to variations in a variety of factors (wind speed, hand used to flip coin, height of flip) you would accept some deviation from the expected distribution. For instance, 55 Heads and 45 Tails might pass without remark, as might 60 Heads and 40 Tails. But what about 70 Heads and 30 Tails? Would this be unusual enough to convince you that your friend is a cheat? Would you risk a friendship of many years standing on a 70–30 distribution? Perhaps not – this is unusual but not impossible. But what about 90 Heads and 10 Tails? Surely this event is rare enough to prove our suspicions?

This is how statistical decisions are made: we do not live in a perfect universe and so will always accept that actual events will vary somewhat from our expectations. However, when an event occurs which is so unusual that we might expect to witness it by chance only 5% of the time, we argue that such an event is no longer within the accepted range of variability. This event, whether it be the extent to which a sample mean differs from a population parameter, or the extent to which observed choices on a questionnaire differ from what is expected, can be regarded as statistically significant. As with our surreptitious coin tosser there comes a point beyond which we will no longer accept events as being attributable to chance alone. In statistical terms this is known as the point of statistical significance. (In fact, in this particular example, a split of 60–40 would be rare enough in statistical terms to state that the coin was biased, although in defence of our friendship we would probably still make allowances for our friend and choose a much more remote event as our cut-off point.)

false. Power calculations are complex and will not be covered here, especially since they are unlikely to feature in undergraduate research. However, it is important to realise that restricting our interpretation of findings to significance levels might not be sufficient. There may be many instances in which a test provides a significance value greater than .05 (and therefore not statistically significant) when in reality the null hypothesis is false, simply because the sample size is not sufficient to demonstrate a particular effect size.

9.1.5   Comparing samples and populations – an overview

Much psychological research, particularly survey-based research (unless you happen to be a government, or at least a university), is based on samples since it is generally impractical to observe, interview or test every member of a population – a point we have made repeatedly. However, it is usually our ultimate intention to generalise our sample findings to the wider population: we want to argue that what is true for the few will be true for the many. All of these issues have been extensively explored in Part 3 and anyone unclear about sampling issues might wish to review the sections on sampling.

In order that we *can* generalise from the few to the many it should be clear that this is possible only if we can demonstrate that our sample actually belongs to the population we are ultimately interested in. In a zoological study aiming to learn something about social hierarchies within the common hedgehog population, we would be in serious trouble if the sample we studied comprised a rare European species. (Well, they do look much the same to the uninitiated.)

By the same token, if our study centred on number recall within a particular age group (say the 18-to-25-year band), we might well wonder how useful a sample with a mean age of 16 would be. The problem is that no matter how rigorous our sampling procedures the characteristics of a sample will always differ to some extent from the population from which it was drawn. But how different must our sample be from the population before we have to say that the sample was not drawn from that population?

While the relationship between samples and populations is a central one in psychological research, this is not an exclusive context – in most areas of human endeavour the same concerns are present.

Plate 9.2   Modern production processes minimise variability in ways not always possible when studying human behaviour.
*Source*: Corbis/Kevin Fleming

Consider industrial processes which today are highly organised, usually automated and incorporating sufficient checks and balances to ensure a consistent quality of product. However, given the potential for variability which exists in our universe, there is always some chance that a current process (and therefore product) will differ slightly from previous standards – and sometimes not so slightly. Consider the unfortunate owner of what has become known as a 'Monday morning car', a vehicle which in all respects looks like every other of the same model, yet in which nothing works. This is a readily understood factor of modern industrial life and most manufacturing processes contain a quality control element. For instance, a steel foundry will compare a current smelt with the quality of previous output; a pharmaceutical company will check the purity of medicines against previous standards; and a brewer will test a current batch of ale against earlier brews (see Box 9.2 for an illustration).

Because, as we have already stated, samples are rarely a perfect match of the population from which they are drawn, industrial processes tend to make similar allowances to the psychological researcher. Hence, a Ford Focus can still be called a Ford Focus providing it conforms to, or falls within, a specified range of variability on certain characteristics set by the manufacturer. A current batch of malt whisky can still be called malt whisky as long as it matches – within particular tolerances – certain malt characteristics and so on. As with behavioural research, though, the question is how far can our sample deviate from the known population characteristics before we have to reject the batch? There would come a point at which the flavour, strength or colouring of our whisky would be too different from the norm to be accorded the brand label. Thus our question has expensive connotations, when a rejected product might run into hundreds of motor vehicles, or many thousands of litres of sub-standard malt whisky. So how do we make this judgement?

## 9.1.6 Comparing samples and populations – the standard error of the mean

The following attempts to explain some of the theoretical background to the procedures which allow us to compare samples with populations and, in particular, to answer the question, 'does this sample come from that population?' In psychological research (although not exclusively so, as the previous section on industrial quality control illustrates) this is an important question. In some instances it represents the starting point for quantitative research: an educational psychologist studying scholastic achievement among children from low-income families, known to average 200 points across a bank of standard scholastic tests, may find herself interviewing members of a sample whose children are averaging 175 points across the same range of tests. The researcher would want to know whether this sample actually comes from the wider population of families whose children score 200, or whether this sample in fact represents a completely different – and much more disadvantaged – group. Specifically, is this difference between 200 and 175 an acceptable variation from the population average, or is the difference too great? This is important, since if the 175-point scores represent acceptable variation within the general population, then the researcher could happily use this sample for her research. However, if it were demonstrated that children producing 175-point scores do indeed represent a quite different group from the population norm, then any findings from this sample could not be generalised to the wider population. It would be pointless using this particular group in the hope of learning something about the population.

In other instances, rather than representing a starting point for further research, the extent to which a sample differs from a population is the central issue in the research. Consider another educational question, slightly closer to home, in which a head of department wants to know if this year's psychology students (the sample) really are performing more poorly than those of all previous years (the population). The number of passes achieved for Psych1 may be fewer than in the past, but is this difference marginal and part of acceptable variation in performance, or are this year's students really different? This type of question may be part of the normal monitoring process typical of all colleges and universities, in which case the aim is largely descriptive, or it might reflect a more investigative, inferential stance in which the head of department is concerned that a change in teaching strategies, a decline in staff morale (due to a woefully poor salary structure) or a revision of recruitment standards has affected student performance. In either event the question remains the same: 'does this sample belong to that population?' The answer lies in an understanding of a statistic known as the standard error of the mean, or sometimes simply the **standard error**.

The standard error reflects the extent to which an element within a population varies. Specifically, if a population characteristic varies widely, any sample drawn from that population could itself deviate markedly from the population average yet still be regarded as reasonably coming from the population. If, on the other hand, variation within the population is only slight, then a sample which differs markedly probably doesn't belong to the population. It should be no surprise then to note that the formula for calculating the standard error is based partly on the population standard deviation:

$$SE = \frac{\sigma}{\sqrt{n}} \qquad\qquad (9.1)$$

Where *SE* is the abbreviation for *standard error of the mean*
σ is the population *standard deviation*
*n* is the *sample size*

The standard error informs us how far a sample can deviate from a population before we can claim it was drawn from a different population. The full procedure for determining the standard error is outlined in Box 9.4, but for the moment it is sufficient to state that once we have calculated the standard error we are in a position to say that if our sample mean is greater than two standard errors beyond the known population mean (either greater than or less than), then this sample does not come from that population. More accurately, we are 95% confident that the sample does not belong to the population. Yet remember our previous discussion on Type I errors; we could be wrong, and in fact, 5% of the time we would be.

Returning to our hypothetical study on low-achieving families (population mean = 200 points; sample mean = 175 points), suppose the standard error calculation produced a value of 20. According to what we have said above, providing our sample mean falls between two standard errors on either side of the population mean, the sample was drawn from the population. In this instance, the range within which we are confident that samples might reasonably fall (given what we know about variation within the population) would be 160 to 240.

Population mean = 200
Standard error = 20
2 × standard error = 40
95% confidence interval = 160 to 240

Box 9.4

**A Closer Look At . . .**

# The standard error of the mean, and how to calculate it

The following is a step-by-step guide for calculating the standard error of the mean, and includes an explanation of how this particular statistic is used to compare samples with populations.

Consider a hypothetical situation in which we draw a large number (hundreds) of samples from a particular population. For each of these samples we calculate a mean score on some relevant variable. If we create a distribution of all these sample means, the following will be observed (Figure 9.6a):

- The distribution of these sample means is normal in shape.
- The calculated mean of the sample means (MSM) = the population mean.
- The standard deviation of these sample means is called the standard error of the mean (SE).
- The standard error is calculated thus: $SE = \sigma/\sqrt{n}$. See equation (9.1).
- Ninety-five percent of all the sample means fall between two SEs of the MSM.
- Most importantly, because the MSM and the population mean are the same, 95% of all sample means fall between two SEs of the population mean.

Example: A tutor learns that this year's psychology students have scored an average of 58 in their term examination. Since the mean exam mark for previous years is 55 (with a standard deviation of 5) the tutor wants to know whether this year's students are really just like those of all the previous years and the difference between the marks is merely part of chance variation, or are these students really different from those in previous years? If there are 20 students in this year, the calculation of SE would progress as follows:

$$SE = \sigma/\sqrt{n};$$
$$= 5/4.47;$$
$$= 1.118$$

Figure 9.6a
Distribution of sample means showing two standard errors above and below the MSM.

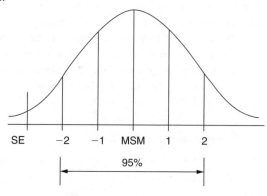

If we now use this information to interpret the distribution of means, we find the following (Figure 9.6b):

Figure 9.6b    Distribution of sample means: MSM = 55 and SE = 1.118.

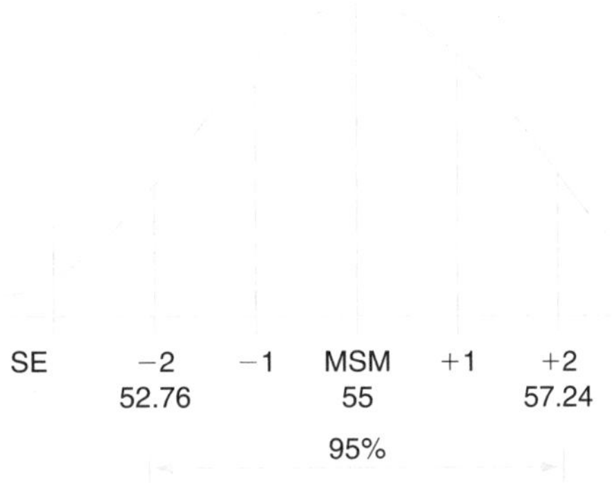

| SE | −2 | −1 | MSM | +1 | +2 |
|---|---|---|---|---|---|
|  | 52.76 |  | 55 |  | 57.24 |

95%

According to our calculations, 95% of all sample means are likely to lie between 52.76 and 57.24. Since our current year mean of 58 lies outside this range, we assume it does not come from the population whose mean is 59. This year's students are really different.

Thus, our sample with a mean of 175 could well have been drawn from the population with a mean of 200. Our researcher then can justifiably use this sample for her study, knowing that it represents the wider population which is her ultimate interest.

For the sake of completeness, this range of acceptability derived from the standard error is termed the **confidence interval**, and expresses the range of population values within which we are 95% confident that sample means will fall. Box 9.4 illustrates the calculation of the standard error and its application.

### 9.1.7   Parametric and non-parametric data

There are many different types of data, meaning that, depending on the kind of information you have gathered during a study, your data can look different and tell you different things about participants. For instance, some of your data might be in the form of a simple numerical code to identify the sex of participants (1 denoting male participants and 2 denoting females) with values only indicating different from, as opposed to better than; some might be in the form of a response on a Likert scale of agreement to certain attitudinal items (strongly agree, agree, disagree, strongly disagree), such that values indicate some kind of greater than/less than ordering. Yet other data might appear as a score on a continuous scale, such as response time (in milliseconds) to a visual stimulus, or score on an objective personality inventory. These different types of data, which reflect the various ways in which we can measure things, have been discussed in Part 2. This discussion is reviewed here.

Data in which participants or events are identified by the category to which they belong, with membership of a particular category serving a purely descriptive function (as in being male as opposed to female, or being a member of an experimental group as opposed to a control group), are termed *nominal data*. Any numerical values associated with categories are for identification purposes only and possess no quantitative meaning. Nor is there any numerical relationship among them.

Data in which participants or events are identified by the position in which they appear in some ordered array running from best to worst (or tallest to smallest, least to greatest) are termed *ordinal data*. Numerical values associated with particular positions indicate the order in which observations appear (1st, 2nd, 3rd, etc.); relationships among numerical values indicate only greater than/less than. There is no allowance for how much greater than/less than with these kinds of data. Both nominal and ordinal data are often termed merely category data, with supplemental information on whether the categories are nominally or ordinally scaled.

Data in which participants or events are measured on some kind of continuous scale, ranging from zero to *n*, are termed *ratio data* (age, income, extraversion scores). Where measurement scales lack zero as a starting point (as in temperature, which can have negative values, or one's financial standing at the bank), such data are termed *interval data*. Both types of data are often treated similarly and are described collectively as continuous or continuous-scaled data. With this latter type of data (continuous) it is possible – and the convention – to both express and summarise variables in terms of their key, defining characteristics, or parameters. These defining parameters are given usually as a measure of central tendency (mean) and a measure of dispersion (variance, or standard deviation). Consider how we are used to talking about average response time, mean temperature and so on and you have the idea – all such variables are composed of parametric data. On the other hand, a variable like sex cannot be expressed in terms of some key, summarising characteristic (there's no such thing as an average sex, for instance). Likewise astrological signs cannot be expressed in terms of parameters, and this is the rule: interval and ratio data are parametric since they can be expressed in terms of defining parameters. Ordinal and nominal data are **non-parametric** since they cannot be thus expressed.

Plate 9.3   These hedgehogs can be timed in a running race, or merely ranked as first, second or third past the post.
*Source*: Photolibrary/Picture Press

The extension of this distinction concerns the methods available to us for analysis. In the simplest of terms, parametric data can be analysed using parametric statistics, a type of analytical approach which relies on measures of central tendency and dispersion for their computation. Non-parametric data, on the other hand, possessing as they do no such defining measures, must be analysed using non-parametric statistics – a brand of computational procedure which relies instead on ranks (e.g., 1st, 2nd, 3rd, etc.) and other types of qualitative relationship. An illustration follows.

Envisage a study in which an animal behaviourist is investigating the maze-running abilities of small mammals. Two groups of hedgehogs are released into a complex assault course and a record is taken of the sequence in which they pass the finishing line. If a parametric approach were to be taken to analysis, the time taken for each runner would be noted, a mean time calculated for each group and the difference between the means examined in terms of probability.

A non-parametric approach would be different – rather than time taken, group membership of the runners would be noted as they pass the line. The logic is that if there is no difference between the two species of hedgehog, there would be no clear pattern to the runners: both early arrivals and late-comers would comprise a mix of both groups. However, if the early runners comprise a bunching of one particular group (e.g., the 1st, 2nd, 3rd, 4th and 5th places all go to the common species) with a concentration of the other group arriving near the end, this is evidence of a difference between the groups. The significance of this difference would still be determined via probability, but in this case what is being compared is the pattern of ranks, rather than actual values.

## 9.2  Tests of differences – between-groups comparison

### 9.2.1  One-sample *t*-test

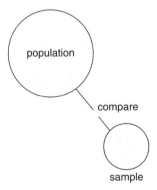

This test belongs to a suite of tests known as goodness of fit tests and is used to determine whether a sample derives from a population with known characteristics, or in predicting population parameters from a sample. The technique is based on the work of William Gossett who in 1908 developed the principle as a quality control measure in the brewing industry, the obvious application here being to determine the extent to which a current brew (the sample) deviates from the typical characteristics of a brand of ale (the population). However, the procedure is applicable to any research situation in which we wish to compare the characteristics of a sample to a population. We have noted previously (9.1.6)

that the standard error is a common method of comparing samples with populations. But this approach requires that the population standard deviation is known, and the assumption is that sample size will be greater than 30. When neither condition is met the one-sample $t$-test is a good alternative. Inspection of the formula at (9.2) demonstrates the role of the standard error in the computation of $t$.

$$t = \frac{\bar{x} - \mu}{s/\sqrt{n}}$$
(9.2)

Where $\bar{x}$ is the sample mean
$\mu$ is the population mean
$s$ is the sample standard deviation
$n$ is the sample size

Consider the example from Box 9.4, in which a tutor observes that marks in this year's psychology class (average 58) appear higher than in the past (average 55). Previously we tested the hypothesis that the current class came from the same population as those of previous years (i.e., that the difference in grades was a chance occurrence) by calculating the standard error and determining the 95% confidence interval, yet the same hypothesis can be tested using the one-sample $t$-test. This would be especially appropriate if we did not know the standard deviation of the previous marks, or if (as in the present case) the sample size were smaller than 30.

*Example:*
Given:
population mean $= 55$
sample mean $= 58$
sample standard deviation $= 3$
sample size $= 20$

Then, applying the formula at (9.2)

$$t = \frac{58 - 55}{3/\sqrt{20}}$$

$t = 4.5$

Traditionally we would consult a $t$-distribution for the sample size given, usually shown in standard statistical tables, to determine whether our sample with a mean of 58 is likely to have come from a population with a mean of 55. Inspection of the table of critical values of $t$ in Appendix B indicates that, for a sample size of 20 (and hence, degrees of freedom of 19), our obtained $t$ of 4.5 is greater than the table value (2.093) at the .05 level for a two-tailed test. In the modern world of computer analysis, contemporary statistical packages now do this work for us, as the following example, based on the *MK* marks SPSS database, demonstrates:

Step 1.    From the data editor menu, select <u>A</u>nalyze, then <u>C</u>ompare Means, then <u>O</u>ne-Sample T Test (Figure 9.7).

Step 2.    From the One-Sample T Test window, select the variable 'marks' from the variables window on the left and transfer this to the **T**est Variable(s) box on the right. In the Test Value box, enter the value against which the 'marks' data are to be compared. In this case the test value is the population mean of 55. Select OK (Figure 9.8).

Step 3.    Inspect the output. Note the $t$-value (4.5) and compare the given significance value (.000) with the conventional cut-off value of .05.

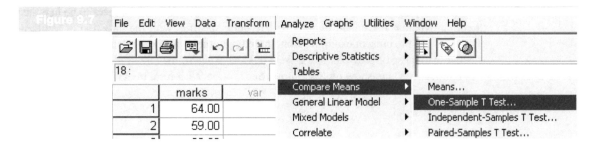

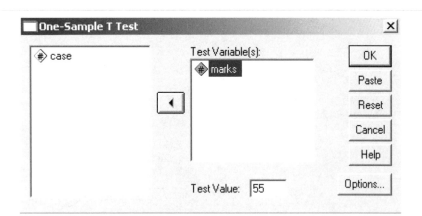

In the psychology class example we conclude that the sample whose mean was 58 did not come from the population whose mean was 55. This would be expressed formally as,

$$t(19) = 4.51, \quad p < .001$$

The tutor can be pleased – this year's group is significantly different from those of previous years.

Note that when a probability value is given as .000 in statistical output (as in Table 9.2), this is expressed as .001 (or as <.001). It should be further noted that the significance value is two-tailed, which is the default for SPSS. Recall from our discussion on one- and

Table 9.2    Output 9.1 – One-sample test.

| | | | Test Value = 55 | | | |
|---|---|---|---|---|---|---|
| | | | | | 95% Confidence Interval of the Difference | |
| | *t* | *df* | Sig. (two-tailed) | Mean Difference | Lower | Upper |
| marks | 4.512 | 19 | .000 | 3.000 | 1.61 | 4.39 |

two-tailed hypotheses in Part 4 that the two-tailed case allows for differences to be in either direction, whereas one-tailed hypotheses are quite specific, with the direction of a difference given. In the present example, a one-tailed hypothesis would be that the current group is better than those of previous years. We would have determined the truth of this by halving the significance value shown in the output. See section 9.1.3 for a review of this topic.

### 9.2.2 Independent-samples *t*-test

An **independent-samples *t*-test** is a test which compares the means of two different groups measured on some outcome variable. It is also known as the Student's independent

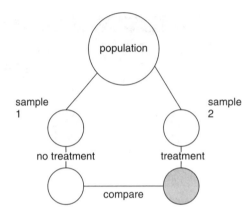

*t*-test (after Student, the pseudonym adopted by William Gossett), the unrelated *t*-test and the unpaired *t*-test.

When two groups comprising different participants are compared on some measure (this could be an attitudinal measure, a behavioural measure, or a score on an experimental task) a between-groups test is appropriate. Such tests determine whether an observed difference between the groups is so great that it cannot be explained in terms of chance variation. As we have previously intimated (in section 9.1.1) differences are deemed to be 'too great' when their likelihood of occurrence falls to 5% (we might expect to notice such a difference only 5 times in every 100 observations), although there are some occasions when we would require a difference to have a probability of occurrence of 1% or less before we feel chance alone cannot explain them. These cut-offs are termed the .05 and the .01 significance levels respectively.

When only two groups are compared as in the classic experimental paradigm (control group vs. experimental group) and the data meet parametric requirements (the data are interval and normally distributed), the independent-samples *t*-test is appropriate. The test is also suitable for quasi-experimental designs in which two existing groups are compared on some measure (e.g., males and females).

$$t = \frac{\bar{x}_1 - \bar{x}_2}{\sqrt{\left[\frac{\left(\sum x_1^2 - \frac{(\sum x_1)^2}{n_1}\right) + \left(\sum x_2^2 - \frac{(\sum x_2)^2}{n_2}\right)}{(n_1 - 1) + (n_2 - 1)}\right]\left(\frac{1}{n_1} + \frac{1}{n_2}\right)}} \qquad (9.3)$$

To perform this test, means and standard deviations are calculated for both groups. The observed difference between the means is interpreted in terms of their respective standard deviations and sample sizes, as shown in the formula at (9.3) and expressed as a *t*-value. This value is a transformed measure of the extent to which the groups differ, such that the greater the difference in means, the greater the *t*-value. The logic is that an observed difference is evaluated against the probability of obtaining such a difference by chance alone, and if this probability falls below .05, we claim a significant difference exists. Consider the following example:

A sample of 24 male undergraduates is drawn from the student population and divided at random into two groups. Group 1 attends a presentation from a male 'nutritionist' extolling the gastronomic virtues of a newly branded flavour of crisp, namely, hedgehog flavour. Meanwhile, Group 2 is attending an identical presentation though in this instance from an attractive female 'nutritionist'. Both presentations conclude with the information that this particular delicacy would be available that day in the campus shop (the result of an unfortunate earlier experiment involving cyclists). As part of a marketing exercise, the participants in both groups are asked to rate how likely they would be to sample the new crisps, on a 7-point scale running from Never to Highly likely.

This particular scenario is typical of the persuasive communication field in which the covert purpose of the study is to investigate the impact of the source of a communication, rather than the communication itself. Specifically an experiment of this sort would be exploring the hypothesis that male participants would respond differently to a message originating from an attractive female source, than to the same message from a male source. The data from this study are shown in Table 9.3, along with the computational steps for calculating *t*. The data are based on the *MK attitude* data set.

Table 9.3    Attitude scores for two groups of male students, differentiated by communication source. Scores are likelihood ratings of trying a novel product, measured on a 1–7 scale.

| Communication source | |
|---|---|
| **Male** | **Female** |
| 2 | 4 |
| 1 | 5 |
| 2 | 5 |
| 3 | 6 |
| 2 | 5 |
| 5 | 6 |
| 2 | 5 |
| 4 | 4 |
| 1 | 7 |
| 2 | 4 |
| 2 | 7 |
| 5 | 7 |

Substituting the derived values in Table 9.3 into the formula in (9.3),

$$\bar{x}_1 = 2.58$$

$$\bar{x}_2 = 5.42$$

$$\sum x_1^2 = 101$$

$$\sum x_2^2 = 367$$

$$\left(\sum x_1\right)^2 = 961$$

$$\left(\sum x_2\right)^2 = 4225$$

$$n_1 = 12$$

$$n_2 = 12$$

$$t = \frac{2.58 - 5.42}{\sqrt{\left[\dfrac{\left(101 - \dfrac{961}{12}\right) + \left(367 - \dfrac{4225}{12}\right)}{22}\right]\left(\dfrac{1}{12} + \dfrac{1}{12}\right)}}$$

$$t = 5.4$$

The independent $t$-test (unpaired $t$-test, independent-samples $t$-test or unrelated $t$-test) compares the means of two samples and produces a value – the statistic, $t$ – which is a measure of the difference between these two means. The resulting $t$-value can then be matched against the relevant statistical tables – see Appendix B – and a decision made whether or not the observed difference is statistically significant. For 22 $df$, a probability level of .05 and a two-tailed test, the table value is given as 2.074. Our obtained value of $t$ is greater than the table value, therefore we reject the null hypothesis.

Statistical analysis of the present data in SPSS follows, based on the data set *MKattitude2* comprising two variables, 'attitude' and 'source'.

**Step 1.** From the menu, select Analyze, then Compare Means, then Independent-Samples T Test (Figure 9.9).

**Step 2.** In the test editor window, transfer the dependent variable from the **Variables** window into the **T**est Variable(s) box. In the present study, 'attitude' is the dependent variable. Had our study involved several attitudinal variables we

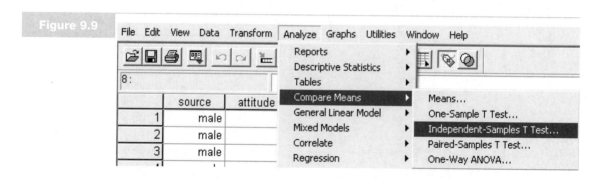

Figure 9.9

Figure 9.10

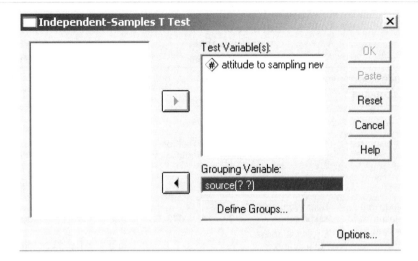

could have transferred them all to the test window and performed a series of *t*-tests in succession. (Note that SPSS is unhelpful in labelling this the **Test Variable(s)** window since it does not use this term consistently for other types of analysis. Consider this as the location for the variable which is to be tested in the analysis.)

Step 3. Transfer the independent variable – 'source' – into the **Grouping Variable** box. (Again this is not too helpful. Consider this as the variable composed of the groups or conditions to be compared.) You will notice that when the independent variable is placed in the **Grouping Variable** box, a suffix has been added, showing two question marks (??). SPSS is requesting the numerical values used to differentiate the groups (Figure 9.10).

Step 4. Click the **D**efine Groups button. In the Define Groups window, enter the numerical values used for each group, and click **C**ontinue. In the data set for this example the Male source was represented by the value 1, with the Female source identified by the value 2 (Figure 9.11).

Step 5. Inspect the output (Table 9.4).

Recall that our male students were exposed to information concerning a (mythical) new snack food product, one group from an attractive female source and one from a

Figure 9.11

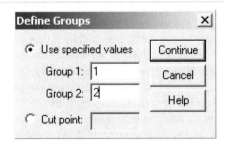

**Table 9.4**    Output 9.2 – Group statistics.

| | Source of communication, male or female | N | Mean | Std. Deviation | Std. Error Mean |
|---|---|---|---|---|---|
| Attitude to sampling new product | Male | 12 | 2.58 | 1.379 | .398 |
| | Female | 12 | 5.42 | 1.165 | .336 |

Independent Samples Test

| | | Levene's Test for Equality of Variances | | t-test for Equality of Means | | | | |
|---|---|---|---|---|---|---|---|---|
| | | F | Sig. | t | df | Sig. (2-tailed) | Mean Difference | Std. Error Difference |
| Attitude to sampling new product | Equal variances assumed | .221 | .643 | −5.438 | 22 | .000 | −2.833 | .521 |
| | Equal variances not assumed | | | −5.438 | 21.400 | .000 | −2.833 | .521 |

non-attractive male source. Following the communication they completed an attitudinal measure to rate how likely they would be to try the new food.

The $t$-test output in Table 9.4 contains a great deal of information, which might appear initially intimidating. However, if we consider the output in stages, it should become manageable.

There are two elements to the output shown for the $t$-test, the first containing simple descriptive statistics on the dependent variable, as a function of the independent variable. The most important information here relates to the mean measures on the attitude scale for each group – those with the male source producing a mean of 2.58, and those with the female source producing a mean of 5.42. Clearly these means are different, but it is the function of the $t$-test to determine whether or not this difference is sufficiently large to be statistically significant.

One detail remains, however, before the test finding can be interpreted, and it has to do with variance (the extent to which individual observations in a sample vary around the mean). The $t$-test, while designed to test for differences between the means of two samples, nevertheless assumes that the distributions within each sample, and hence the average variation about the means, are similar. If this is not the case – and this in itself can be an interesting finding – a modification to the $t$-test formula is necessary. The decision is made with relative ease, by comparing the variance within one sample with the variance within the other. The simplest method for this comparison is via an $F$-test, in which the variance of one group is simply divided by the variance of the other – if they are similar, they will effectively cancel one another out. A more powerful form of this type of comparison test is the Levene's test for the Equality of Variances, as shown in Table 9.4, which provides the probability that the two variances are equal. We can see that in our example, a probability of .643 is shown, an indication that the distributions comprising each sample are similar. Indeed, even by inspecting the standard deviations of both samples we would have come to the same conclusion – they are quite similar. Had the probability value dropped below .05, though, we would have had to accept that the variances were unequal and inspect that section of the output under the heading: Equal variances not assumed.

The final part of the table relates to the $t$-test itself. Selecting the 'Equal variances assumed' option (based on the result of the Levene test), we note the $t$-value of −5.438 (which is a transformed measure of the difference between the sample means) and the associated significance value of .000. What this is telling us is that the likelihood of obtaining such a difference between two sample means by chance alone is so remote that the probability value falls off the end of the scale as it were – certainly well below our conventional .05 cut-off and less even than the more remote .01. (It is worth reminding ourselves that when the probability of an observed difference between means is so remote, computer software often prints the value .000. This does not mean that the probability of this particular occurrence is zero, nor does it mean that the observed difference was not significant, both common errors among undergraduates. To avoid error, this should be written as .001.) In other words, the source of the communication made a statistically significant difference to participants' responses to the attitude item. This is expressed formally as,

$$t(22) = -5.44, \quad p < .001 \text{ (two-tailed)}$$

When working with $t$-tests there are two points to be appreciated. The first is that the value of $t$ reflects the magnitude of the actual difference between the two sample means being compared. The bigger this difference, the bigger will be the $t$-value and the more likely that this difference will be significant. The second point concerns the fact that $t$-values can be both positive and negative, a possible source of anxiety for some students. In practice, the sign is unimportant, merely reflecting the difference between the sample means being compared. If the larger mean is subtracted from the smaller, the difference will of course be a negative value. It is the magnitude of the $t$-value which is important, not its sign.

Box 9.5 details how to perform an independent-samples $t$-test in SPSS.

### 9.2.3 The Mann-Whitney U-test

The **Mann-Whitney $U$-test** is an independent-groups, between-groups non-parametric test for comparing two groups or conditions. When two groups comprising different participants are compared on some measure (this could be an attitudinal measure, a behavioural

---

Box 9.5

How To . . .

## Perform an independent-samples $t$-test in SPSS

Step 1.  From the command menu strip select Analyze, then Compare Means, then Independent-Samples T Test.

Step 2.  In the test editor window, select from the variable list the dependent variable in your analysis and transfer it to the **T**est Variable(s) box.

Step 3.  In the test editor window, select from the variable list the independent variable in your analysis and transfer it to the **G**rouping Variable box.

Step 4.  Click the Define Groups button.

Step 5.  In the Define Groups window enter the two numerical values you assigned to Group 1 and Group 2.

Step 6.  Click Continue in the Define Groups window.

Step 7.  Click OK in the test editor window.

Step 8.  Consult the Levene table and decide whether the $t$ statistics from the 'equal variances assumed' or 'equal variances not assumed' ranges should be used.

Step 9.  Interpret the output in terms of the $t$-value and the significance value for a two-tailed test. Adjust the significance value accordingly if a one-tailed test is used.

measure, or a score on an experimental task) a between-groups test is appropriate. Such tests determine whether an observed difference between the groups is so great that it cannot be explained in terms of chance variation. As we have previously intimated, differences are deemed to be 'too great' when their likelihood of occurrence falls to 5% (we might expect to notice such a difference only 5 times in every 100 observations), although there are some occasions when we would require a difference to have a probability of occurrence of 1% or less before we feel chance alone cannot explain them. These cut-offs are termed the .05 and the .01 significance levels respectively.

When only two groups are compared as in the classic experimental paradigm (control group vs. experimental group) and the data do not meet parametric requirements (the data are ordinal, or interval but not normally distributed), the Mann-Whitney $U$-test is appropriate. The test is also relevant in quasi-experimental research when existing, or natural, groups are compared on some nominal or ordinal measure.

To perform this test, data from the two groups are treated as if they comprise a single distribution. This single array of measures is then ranked from lowest to highest and the original identity of the groups is restored. The logic is that if there is no real difference between the groups, the ranks will be fairly evenly distributed – each group having similar proportions of low and high ranks. If the groups really are different, we might find that all the low ranks are occurring in only one of the groups, with high ranks occurring in the other group. Applying the relevant formula allows us to determine whether or not our observed difference is sufficiently large to be statistically significant, as the following example shows:

Twenty volunteers, randomly assigned to a control condition and an experimental condition, are presented with a list of common nouns. Participants in the experimental group are required to perform a distracting task during presentation while in the control condition there is an absence of distraction. On a subsequent recognition task the number of correctly recognised words is noted for each participant. The issue is whether the presence or absence of a distraction task made a difference to the number of words recognised (see Table 9.5).

Step 1. The scores of individuals in each group are treated as if they belong to a single array.

Step 2. The combined scores are ranked from lowest to highest.

Step 3. The identity of the groups is restored and the ranks assigned to each group are summed.

It will be noted that there is a higher proportion of high ranks in Group 1. To determine the significance of the observed difference between the groups, the statistic $U$ is calculated, from the following formula:

$$U = (n_1 \times n_2) + \frac{n_1(n_1 + 1)}{2} - \sum R_1 \qquad (9.4)$$

Substituting our values,

$$U = (10 \times 10) + \frac{10(10 + 1)}{2} - 139$$

$$U = 16.00$$

Table 9.5    Word recognition scores and ranked scores for two independent groups.

| Case | Group | Rscore | Rrscore | |
|------|-------|--------|---------|---|
| 1 | 1 | 12 | 19.5 | |
| 2 | 1 | 13 | 17.5 | |
| 3 | 1 | 12 | 19.5 | |
| 4 | 1 | 15 | 20.0 | |
| 5 | 1 | 13 | 17.5 | |
| 6 | 1 | 14 | 19.0 | Sum of ranks in Group 1 = 139 |
| 7 | 1 | 9 | 8.5 | |
| 8 | 1 | 7 | 4.0 | |
| 9 | 1 | 11 | 13.0 | |
| 10 | 1 | 9 | 8.5 | |
| 11 | 2 | 10 | 11.0 | |
| 12 | 2 | 11 | 13.0 | |
| 13 | 2 | 6 | 2.0 | |
| 14 | 2 | 7 | 4.0 | |
| 15 | 2 | 5 | 1.0 | Sum of ranks in Group 2 = 71 |
| 16 | 2 | 9 | 8.5 | |
| 17 | 2 | 11 | 13.0 | |
| 18 | 2 | 9 | 8.5 | |
| 19 | 2 | 8 | 6.0 | |
| 20 | 2 | 7 | 4.0 | |

Key: Case = participant number (1–20); Group = condition (1 = control; 2 = experimental); Rscore = recognition score (words correctly recognised); Rrscore = the rank of each score.

Traditionally we would consult statistical tables to determine the significance of this calculated $U$-value. Inspection of Appendix B indicates that the table value for $U$ with $n_1 = 10$ and $n_2 = 10$ is 23. Since our obtained $U$ is less than the table value, following the decision rule given, we reject the null hypothesis. The steps for analysing the recognition data in SPSS are outlined below.

Step 1. Enter data with Variable 1 = case (participant number); Variable 2 = group (control or experimental); Variable 3 = recognition score (rscore) (Table 9.6).

Step 2. From the command menu strip select Analyze, highlight Nonparametric Tests, then select 2 Independent Samples (Figure 9.12).

Table 9.6

| case | group | rscore |
|------|-------|--------|
| 1 | control | 12 |
| 2 | control | 13 |
| 3 | control | 12 |
| 4 | control | 15 |
| 5 | control | 13 |

**Figure 9.12**

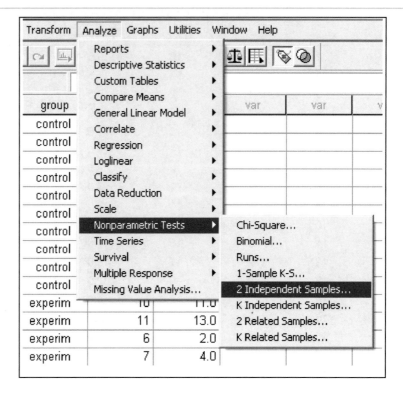

This operation produces the test editor window shown in Figure 9.13. This window has a number of features which should be noted:

1. There are several possible tests we could apply to our data. The Mann-Whitney is the default test, as shown by the checked box, and so this part of the editor window should be left alone.

2. The left-hand side of the editor window shows a box in which all the variables in our data set are listed.

3. The right-hand side of the window shows two boxes which we use to set up the particular analysis we want. The **T**est Variable List box will contain the dependent variable in our analysis (the variable we are testing, in this instance, 'word recognition score').

**Step 3.**  Select the variable 'word recognition score' in the variables box, and then click the arrow button in the middle of the test editor window to send this variable into the **T**est Variable List box.

**Step 4.**  Identify the independent variable in our data set (the grouping variable) and in a similar manner, transfer this variable into the blank **G**rouping Variable box.

If the above steps are carried out successfully, the test editor window will now resemble Figure 9.14.

Note that the variable 'group', now in the **G**rouping Variable box, is highlighted in Figure 9.14, and followed by two question marks (??). SPSS needs to be told which particular numerical values were used to identify or define the different groups.

Figure 9.13

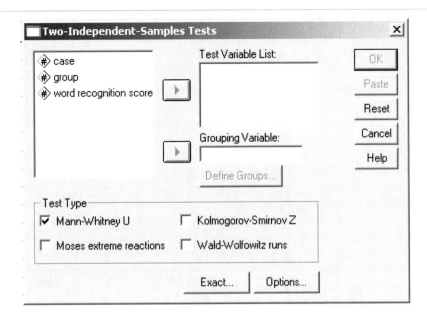

Step 5. Click the Define Groups button to advance to yet another window (Figure 9.15) in which we can complete our test set-up, as follows:

SPSS recognises that there are two groups in this analysis and requires us to type in the numerical code we used to identify the first group, and the code which identifies the second group. In this instance it so happens that we used the values 1 (control) and 2 (experimental), but we could readily have used the values 0 and 1.

Figure 9.14

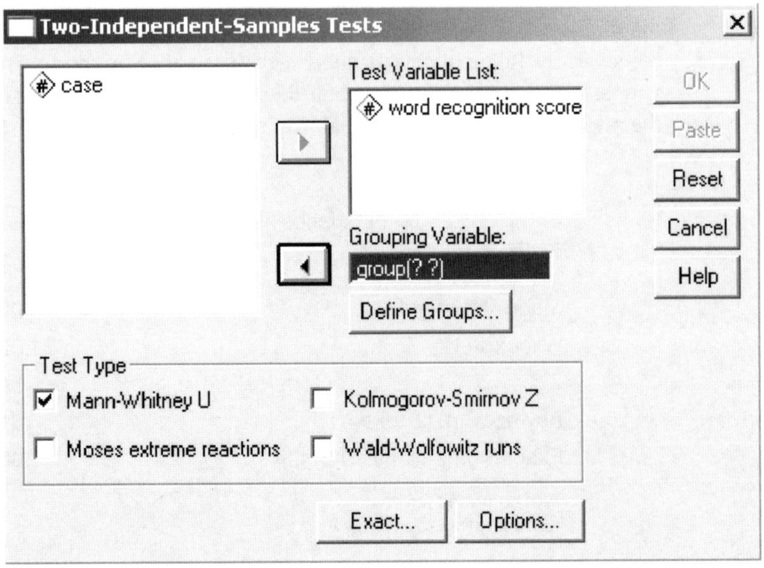

**Two-Independent-Samples Tests**

case

Test Variable List:
word recognition score

OK
Paste
Reset
Cancel
Help

Grouping Variable:
group(? ?)

Define Groups...

Test Type
☑ Mann-Whitney U          ☐ Kolmogorov-Smirnov Z
☐ Moses extreme reactions  ☐ Wald-Wolfowitz runs

Exact...     Options...

Figure 9.15

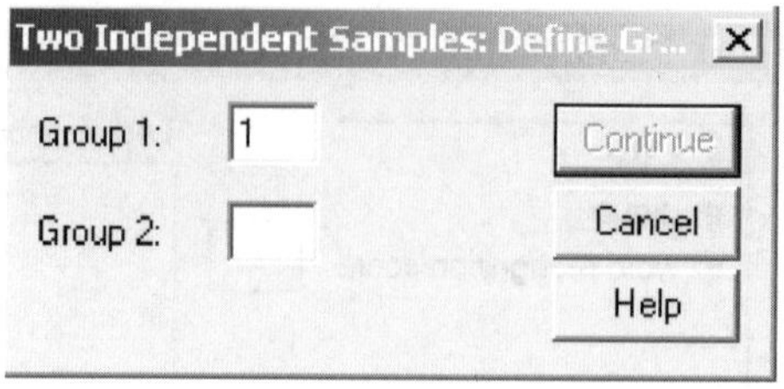

**Two Independent Samples: Define Gr...** ☒

Group 1: | 1

Group 2: |

Continue

Cancel

Help

To complete the set-up select <u>C</u>ontinue, which returns us to the previous test editor window, and then click OK. The output of the analysis is then shown (see Table 9.7):

Table 9.7 Output 9.3 – Ranks.

|  | GROUP | *N* | Mean Rank | Sum of Ranks |
|---|---|---|---|---|
| Word recognition score | Control | 10 | 13.90 | 139.00 |
|  | Experimental | 10 | 7.10 | 71.00 |
|  | Total | 20 |  |  |

SPSS output is invariably comprehensive and sometimes overwhelming. Of the output from the Mann-Whitney *U*-analysis, the only sections which are relevant are shown in Table 9.8. Table 9.7, a table of ranks, gives the sum of the ranks for each group, which fortunately matches the values from our manual calculation. In Table 9.8 we note the calculated *U*-value is 16. Again this matches our manual calculation. Finally, the probability of obtaining the observed difference between the two groups is given as .010. We conclude that the difference in word recognition scores between the control and experimental group is significant at the .01 level.

Note that this output also provides a *z*-score; as sample size increases beyond 20, the distribution for *U* approaches normal and therefore the probability for *z* (Asymp. Sig.) becomes as useful as that associated with *U* (Exact Sig.) and can be interpreted in the same way as all *z*-scores. Indeed, when there are too many tied ranks in the calculation for *U*, the *z*-value and associated probability becomes more powerful.

Table 9.8 Test statistics[b] for 'group' variable.

|  | Word recognition score |
|---|---|
| Mann-Whitney *U* | 16.000 |
| Wilcoxon *W* | 71.000 |
| *Z* | −2.590 |
| Asymp. Sig. (2-tailed) | .010 |
| Exact Sig. [2*(1-tailed Sig.)] | .009[a] |

[a]Not corrected for ties.
[b]Grouping Variable: GROUP.

Box 9.6

How To . . .

## Compute a Mann-Whitney *U*-test in SPSS

Step 1.  From the command menu strip select Analyze, highlight Nonparametric Tests, then select 2 Independent Samples.

Step 2.  In the test editor window, select from the variable list the dependent variable in your analysis and transfer it to the **T**est Variable List box.

Step 3.  In the test editor window, select from the variable list the independent variable in your analysis and transfer it to the **G**rouping Variable box.

Step 4.  Click on the Define Groups button.

Step 5.  In the Define Groups window enter the two numerical values you assigned to Group 1 and Group 2.

Step 6.  Click **C**ontinue in the Define Groups window.

Step 7.  Click OK in the test editor window.

Step 8.  Interpret the output in terms of the *U*-value, the significance value (Exact Sig.) and the z-score, with its corresponding significance value (Asymp. Sig.).

Note also that this particular output also provides a value for Wilcoxon *W*. This is based on a different non-parametric test, the Wilcoxon Rank Sum Test which does the same thing as the Mann-Whitney *U*, although computations are even simpler – the statistic *W* is merely the sum of the ranks in the smaller sample. This is of little consequence to the undergraduate researcher since the decision to reject or accept a null hypothesis is the same. We merely mention it because SPSS provides the information. The formal expression of the *U*-test becomes,

$$U (n_1 = n_2 = 10) = 16.00, \quad p < .01$$

Box 9.6 gives step-by-step instructions for computing a Mann-Whitney *U*-test in SPSS.

By way of a final comment, tutors are often asked whether non-parametric tests are as "good" as parametric. By good we assume our students mean whether we would make the same decision to accept or reject a null hypothesis using the different tests. In the case of the Mann-Whitney *U*-test, probably yes, since the test is almost as powerful as the independent *t*-test. However, it must be said that any test basing its calculations on actual scores or measures must be more powerful than a similar test using only ranks.

### 9.2.4  One-way analysis of variance

The **one-way analysis of variance (ANOVA)** is a between-groups, independent-samples parametric test comparing three or more groups or conditions.

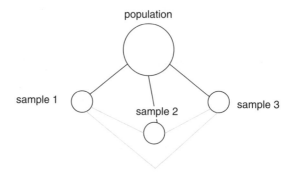

In ANOVA many groups drawn from a single population can be compared.

In Part 2 it was explained that while the two-category independent variable was typical of research designs (control group vs. experimental group; male vs. female) there were many instances in which a causal factor would comprise a number of components. Comparing the general health of the five different occupational classes is one example previously cited; measuring performance on a task under four different experimental conditions would be another. In fact there are many situations in which an independent variable will not fit conveniently into the two-group scenario, and this has particular implications when it comes to analysing the data from such a study. In section 9.2.2 of this chapter the *t*-test was offered as a powerful group comparison test. However, its application is limited to the two-group. For more complex comparisons of the kind described, what is needed is analysis of variance.

Developed by Sir Ronald Fisher as an instrument for agricultural research, ANOVA, as it is more commonly termed, is an extremely sophisticated analytical tool. As such it is ideally suited to the multi-category case. However, the procedure is also complex and requires a little explanation.

### 9.2.5    Analysis of variance explained

In the previous section, it was shown that real-life investigations don't always fall neatly into the two-group comparison design. The social class example, for instance, contained 5 groups while the independent variable in the astrological sign case comprised 12 categories. These are all merely extensions of the two-category situation however – they still involve only one independent variable (class, star sign, experimental condition or whatever) and differ only in the number of elements into which the independent variable can be sub-divided.

In ANOVA terminology, the independent variable is usually called a factor, and the various sub-divisions, levels. The above examples would be analysed by what are called single-factor or one-way ANOVAs (one independent variable). Furthermore, if different participants are used for each condition or level, they would be termed unrelated or between-groups ANOVAs; had a repeated measures design been used, they would be related or within-group ANOVAs. (In case anyone's forgotten the difference between repeated measures and between-groups designs, a review of Part 2 is recommended.)

Plate 9.4    Sir Ronald Fisher.
*Source*: Copyright © by Antony Barrington Brown, reproduced by permission of the Sir Ronald Fisher Memorial Committee.

The next question most newcomers to statistics ask is, apart from the opportunity to learn new jargon, what advantage does ANOVA have over *t*-tests? Why not just carry out a series of *t*-tests on all the various pairs of conditions? Well, actually, you can, but the following example shows why you shouldn't:

If we devised a study to determine whether personality scores varied depending on the star sign people were born under, a *t*-test approach would require that we compare the following groups:

| | |
|---|---|
| Aries vs. Gemini | Aries vs. Cancer |
| Aries vs. Leo | Aries vs. Virgo |
| Aries vs. Sagittarius | Aries vs. Capricorn |
| Aries vs. Aquarius | Aries vs. Pisces |
| Aries vs. Taurus | Aries vs. Gemini |
| Aries vs. Libra | Gemini vs. Leo |
| Gemini vs. Virgo | Gemini vs. Cancer |

Etc.

For one thing, ANOVA explores all these relationships in a single step, rather than in the multiple repetitions which would be required by the *t*-test. For another, in a situation in which lots of *t*-tests are carried out, chance alone would throw up the occasional apparently significant finding and lead to a misplaced interpretation of the data. Finally, the single-factor ANOVA is merely the beginning of what this sophisticated technique can do.

Unfortunately there is a cost: ANOVA will tell us only that a difference exists *somewhere* among the various comparisons being made, not necessarily where. However, since there are ways round this, it is a small price to pay.

So why analysis of *variance*?

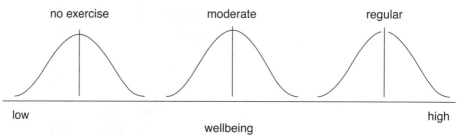

**Figure 9.16**   Distribution of responses on a wellbeing questionnaire for groups taking no exercise, occasional exercise and regular exercise.

We already know that when data are collected from some sample on an outcome measure, the mean provides the most common descriptive statistic. However, we also know that scores vary around this mean, a variance which is due to two things: (1) individual differences among participants; and (2) error (mistakes in measurement, misclassification of participants, random occurrences, etc.). This variance within a sample and around the sample mean is known as the within-group variance and is one of the key ANOVA measures.

Consider an example in which we hypothesise that the general psychological wellbeing of a number of participants will be determined by the amount of physical exercise they take (based on the healthy body–healthy mind notion). If three groups are compared, one taking no exercise, one taking occasional exercise and one taking regular exercise, we might observe the distributions as shown in Figure 9.16.

Here we can see that each of the groups is represented by a mean score somewhere along our wellbeing continuum. We also observe that, within each group, there is variation about the respective means – there is within-group variance for each sample. Moreover, because the sample distributions are different, there will also be variance between the participants in one group and participants in another group. This is known as between-groups variance, another important ANOVA measure, and attributable to three things:

1. Individual differences
2. Error
3. A real difference, or treatment effect

Such between-groups variance can be considerable, as in the above example (where the samples are clearly scoring at different levels on the outcome measure), or negligible, as in the example in Figure 9.17.

What ANOVA aims to do is determine whether or not the observed differences among these distributions are significant, or mere chance occurrences, given the effects individual differences and errors have on measurement. More specifically, if participants were in different groups, would the differences between them be greater than if they were in the same group? The significance of these differences is tested using Fisher's $F$-statistic:

$$\frac{\text{between-groups variance}}{\text{within-group variance}}$$

**Figure 9.17**  Alternative distribution of responses on a wellbeing questionnaire.

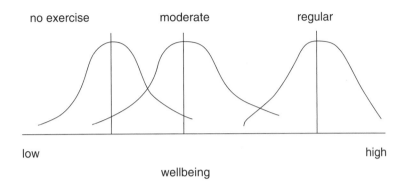

The logic of this is that when we compare individuals – whether in the same group or in different groups – much of the variation between them is due to the same things: individual differences and error. Applying the $F$-ratio procedure then we have:

$$\frac{\text{individual differences; error; treatment effect}}{\text{individual differences; error}}$$

Once the common sources of variance are eliminated from both the numerator and the denominator, anything left over must be attributable to the treatment effect. If this is small (expressed as a small $F$-value) then assigning participants to one group or another has little impact on the variability among participants. If this is large, however (expressed as a large $F$-value), then this signifies that belonging to one group as opposed to another makes a real difference, and one which cannot be attributable to either individual differences or error (since these common elements have now cancelled one another out).

There is a third measure of variance used in ANOVA, and this is termed the total variance. This is obtained by treating individual participants as if they belong to one, single distribution as opposed to their own particular group. A grand mean can be calculated for all participants, irrespective of sample, and the measure of variance for the combined participants provides the total variance. See Box 9.7 for a worked example of the one-way ANOVA.

In the language of ANOVA, variance is given as the average of the sum of squares, or $SS$ (the sum of the squared deviations from the mean), such that the within-group variance is known as $MSwithin$, between-groups variance as $MSbetween$ and the total variance as $Total SS$. Box 9.7 illustrates the derivation of these terms.

Consider the following example:

In a medical study post-operative recovery time for two groups of patients is recorded. The groups differ in the amount of exercise taken prior to surgery, with one group taking no exercise and one group taking moderate exercise. The null hypothesis is

*(text continues on p. 268)*

Box 9.7

A Closer Look At . . .

# The language of ANOVA

The measurement of any variable generally produces a conventional type of distribution (see Figure 9.18):

**Figure 9.18**

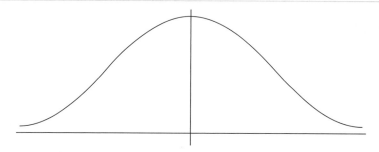

This typical arrangement of scores is usually expressed in terms of a measure of central tendency, such as the mean, but it is clear that this is an artificial measure since all the scores which comprise this distribution vary to a greater or lesser degree from this middle value. Moreover, while many forms of analysis rely heavily on the mean, analysis of variance, as the term suggests, is more concerned with how scores vary or deviate from the mean. This is calculated as follows:

1. Once the mean has been established, each individual score in a distribution is compared with this central value:

| Mean | Score | Difference (score – mean) |
|------|-------|---------------------------|
| 50 | 25 | −25 |
| 50 | 60 | +10 |
| 50 | 48 | −2 |
| 50 | 55 | +5 |
| . | . | . |
| . | . | . |
| . | . | . |

2. In order to eliminate negative values from our calculations, each score is squared:

| Mean | Score | Difference (score – mean) | Difference$^2$ |
|------|-------|---------------------------|----------------|
| 50 | 25 | −25 | 625 |
| 50 | 60 | +10 | 100 |
| 50 | 48 | −2 | 4 |
| 50 | 55 | +5 | 25 |
| . | . | . | . |
| . | . | . | . |
| . | . | . | . |

3. Adding up all these values gives us a measure of the total variation (squared) within a distribution. Another way of expressing this is that we now have a sum of the squares (sum of the squared deviations) or, as ANOVA terminology prefers it, *SS*.

To compute the *F*-statistic, which tells us whether or not a manipulation or treatment has had an effect, we need to generate a number of different measures of variation. We need to know the amount of variation within each group – *SSwithin*; we need to know the variation between the groups – *SSbetween*; and we also need to know the total variation for the combined groups – *TotalSS*.

However, just when we think we have got the hang of ANOVA, there is one additional step required before calculation of Fisher's *F*-statistic can be carried out. Specifically, ANOVA is concerned not with the total variation for each of the within and the between conditions; rather it is based on measures of *average* variation (for which the statistical term is variance). Hence, the within variance used in calculations is based on within/df (the within-group variation divided by the appropriate degrees of freedom for each sample); the between-groups measure is based on between/df (between-groups variation divided by the number of groups – 1); the total variances measure is based on total/$n - 1$.

This may appear complex, but all this does is to provide a measure of average variation for each component. At the end of this exercise we would be left with:

Mean squares within (*Mean SS within* or *MSwithin*)

Mean squares between (*Mean SS between* or *MSbetween*)

The one-way ANOVA output presented in this chapter demonstrates the application of the analysis of variance terminology.

Plate 9.5   Different levels of exercise might affect our health in important ways.
*Source*: Corbis/Helen King

that prior exercise makes no difference to post operative recovery time. For ease of illustration this example is restricted to two groups but is readily expanded to three or more groups (e.g., no exercise, moderate exercise, intensive exercise). The steps in the calculation are shown (see Tables 9.9a and 9.9b).

Calculation of a one-way ANOVA

Step 1. Calculate the grand mean and total sum of squares (*Total SS*).

Step 2. Calculate the within-group sum of squares (*SSwithin*).

Step 3. Calculate the between-groups sum of squares (*SSbetween*).

Step 4. Calculate degrees of freedom.

Step 5. Calculate mean sum of squares for within and between.

Step 6. Calculate *F*-value (mean SS between/mean SS within).

Step 7. Interpret the *F*-value.

Step 1.

Table 9.9a

| Case | Exercise | Recovery time (x) | (x-mean) | (x-mean)$^2$ |
|------|----------|-------------------|----------|--------------|
| 1 | 1 | 4 | −0.89 | 0.79 |
| 2 | 1 | 3 | −1.89 | 3.57 |
| 3 | 1 | 3 | −1.89 | 3.57 |
| 4 | 1 | 4 | −0.89 | 0.79 |
| 5 | 1 | 5 | 0.11 | 0.01 |
| 6 | 1 | 3 | −1.89 | 3.57 |
| 7 | 1 | 4 | −0.89 | 0.79 |
| 8 | 1 | 3 | −1.89 | 3.57 |
| 9 | 1 | 3 | −1.89 | 3.57 |
| 10 | 2 | 5 | 0.11 | 0.01 |
| 11 | 2 | 6 | 1.11 | 1.23 |
| 12 | 2 | 6 | 1.11 | 1.23 |
| 13 | 2 | 7 | 2.11 | 4.46 |
| 14 | 2 | 8 | 3.11 | 9.68 |
| 15 | 2 | 7 | 2.11 | 4.46 |
| 16 | 2 | 6 | 1.11 | 1.23 |
| 17 | 2 | 6 | 1.11 | 1.23 |
| 18 | 2 | 5 | 0.11 | 0.01 |
| Grand mean = 4.889 | | | | *Total SS* = 43.78 |

**Key:**
Case: patient number
Exercise: exercise regime prior to surgery
1 = no exercise; 2 = moderate exercise
Grand mean = 4.89
*Total SS* = 43.78

Step 2.

Table 9.9b

| No exercise | | | Moderate exercise | | |
|---|---|---|---|---|---|
| Recovery time (x) | (x-mean) | (x-mean)² | Recovery time (x) | (x-mean) | (x-mean)² |
| 4 | 0.44 | 0.19 | 5 | −1.22 | 1.49 |
| 3 | −0.56 | 0.31 | 6 | −0.22 | 0.05 |
| 3 | −0.56 | 0.31 | 6 | −0.22 | 0.05 |
| 4 | 0.44 | 0.19 | 7 | 0.78 | 0.61 |
| 5 | 1.44 | 2.07 | 8 | 1.78 | 3.17 |
| 3 | −0.56 | 0.31 | 7 | 0.78 | 0.61 |
| 4 | 0.44 | 0.19 | 6 | −0.22 | 0.05 |
| 3 | −0.56 | 0.31 | 6 | −0.22 | 0.05 |
| 3 | −0.56 | 0.31 | 5 | −1.22 | 1.49 |
| Mean = 3.56 | | WithinSS = 4.22 | Mean = 6.22 | WithinSS = 7.56 |

**Key:** WithinSS = (4.22 + 7.56) = 11.78

Step 3.  Between-groups SS = *Total SS – WithinSS* = (43.78 − 11.78) = 32

Step 4.  Between-groups *df* = 1 (No. of groups − 1)
Within-group *df* = 16 (*n* group 1 – 1 + *n* group 2 − 1)

Total *df* = 17 (*n* − 1)

Step 5.  Mean SS Between = 32 (32/1); Mean SS Within = .736 (11.78/16)

Step 6.  *F* = 43.47 (32/.736)

Recall that differences between groups in an ANOVA design are interpreted in terms of how much of the variation between groups can be explained by variation within groups. This is the *F*-ratio:

$$F = \frac{\text{Between-groups variance}}{\text{Within-group variance}} = \frac{MeanSSbetween}{MeanSSwithin} \tag{9.5}$$

In the present example this is given as:

$$F = \frac{32}{.736} = 43.47$$

The traditional convention would be to consult appropriate tables to determine whether the amount of residual or unexplained variance, as given by the *F*-ratio, is too great to be explained as chance variation. Contemporary researchers though rely on statistical packages. The procedure for performing the present analysis in SPSS is given below:

Step 1.  From the menu strip select <u>A</u>nalyze, <u>C</u>ompare Means and <u>O</u>ne-Way ANOVA (Figure 9.19).

Step 2.  With the ANOVA set-up window displayed, select the dependent variable in the analysis – 'recovery' – from the variables window on the left and transfer it into the **D**ependent List box. (We could enter a series, or list of dependent variables which would be analyzed sequentially.) Select the independent

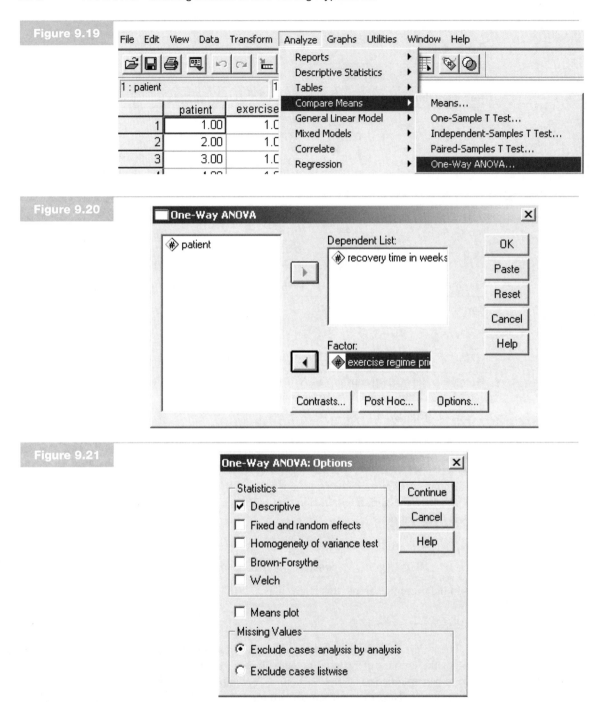

**Figure 9.19**

**Figure 9.20**

**Figure 9.21**

variable – 'exercise' – and transfer it to the **F**actor box. Recall that in ANOVA, an independent variable is called a factor (Figure 9.20).

**Step 3.** Select the required options. There are three possible additional procedures we can choose from. **C**ontrasts and **P**ost Hoc we will deal with later. For the moment, selecting **O**ptions takes us to yet another window in which we would choose **D**escriptive (Figure 9.21).

This is an important option to request in SPSS, since, on its own, the ANOVA calculation ends with an *F*-ratio and an associated probability value. This would tell us whether a significant difference existed among the levels of a factor, but not the nature of this difference. Opting for **D**escriptive as we have shown will provide a table of means for the factor levels which we can use to interpret the ANOVA table.

Step 4. Inspect Output 9.4 (see Tables 9.10 and 9.11).

Table 9.10    Output 9.4.

Descriptives

recovery time in weeks following surgery

|  | N | Mean | Std. Deviation | Std. Error |
|---|---|---|---|---|
| no exercise | 9 | 3.5556 | .72648 | .24216 |
| moderate exercise | 9 | 6.2222 | .97183 | .32394 |
| Total | 18 | 4.8889 | 1.60473 | .37824 |

Table 9.11

ANOVA

recovery time in weeks following surgery

|  | Sum of Squares | df | Mean Square | F | Sig. |
|---|---|---|---|---|---|
| between groups | 32.000 | 1 | 32.000 | 43.472 | .000 |
| within groups | 11.778 | 16 | .736 |  |  |
| Total | 43.778 | 17 |  |  |  |

The significance value given by SPSS is .000 (actually .001), well below the conventional .05 cut-off. We reject the null hypothesis and inspect the means in the descriptives table. We conclude that exercise prior to surgery significantly affects recovery time. Expressed formally, this is given as,

$$F(1,16) = 43.47, \quad p < .001 \text{ (two-tailed)}$$

The above example demonstrates the simplicity of the ANOVA approach and hopefully the manual calculation which precedes it has explained the rather elegant logic behind the procedure. Unfortunately there is a snag with ANOVA – a significant *F*-ratio informs us only that a difference, or an effect, is present among the factor levels. It does not tell us where. In the two sample case above this was not an issue, since inspection of means clearly showed how the levels differed, much as in the case of the *t*-test. However, when a factor has three or more levels (which is the more appropriate design for ANOVA) a significant *F*-ratio will not tell us whether this is due to a significant difference between levels 1 and 2, levels 1 and 3, levels 2 and 3 and so on – or indeed, whether all levels differ significantly from one another. To determine where within the levels of a factor a significant difference lies, we need to carry out an additional procedure. We need to perform a **post hoc test**.

### 9.2.6   Post hoc testing in ANOVA

In recent years a variety of tests have been developed to identify the precise nature of an effect in an ANOVA design, after the analysis of variance itself has been performed. Known as post hoc tests they bear certain similarities to the *t*-test insofar as they compare pairs of factor levels and assign a probability value to each difference. We have previously stated, though, that multiple paired comparisons using *t*-tests are inappropriate since the risk of Type I errors is high (viewing observed differences as being significant when they are in fact chance occurrences). Post hoc tests make allowance for this and are more conservative than conventional *t*-tests. The following example replicates the exercise-recovery time study, this time using three groups, no exercise, moderate exercise, intensive exercise. Performing a one-way ANOVA on the *MKrecovery1* data set as before, following the steps in section 9.2.5 will produce the output shown in Tables 9.12 and 9.13:

Table 9.12     Output 9.5.

Descriptives

recovery time in weeks following surgery

|  | N | Mean | Std. Deviation | Std. Error |
|---|---|---|---|---|
| no exercise | 9 | 3.5556 | .72648 | .24216 |
| moderate exercise | 9 | 6.2222 | .97183 | .32394 |
| intensive exercise | 9 | 5.7778 | 1.20185 | .40062 |
| Total | 27 | 5.1852 | 1.52005 | .29253 |

Table 9.13

ANOVA

recovery time in weeks following surgery

|  | Sum of Squares | df | Mean Square | F | Sig. |
|---|---|---|---|---|---|
| Between Groups | 36.741 | 2 | 18.370 | 18.895 | .000 |
| Within Groups | 23.333 | 24 | .972 |  |  |
| Total | 60.074 | 26 |  |  |  |

Note that the ANOVA output informs us that a significant effect is present among the three levels of exercise. Table 9.12 shows the mean recovery times and we might speculate about whether the significant ANOVA probability is due to the difference between no and moderate exercise, between no and intensive exercise or between moderate and intensive. This would remain speculative though, until we carry out an appropriate post hoc test, using the following procedure:

Step 1.   In the ANOVA set-up window, select the Post Hoc option. This opens the PostHoc Multiple Comparisons window. From here select Tukey. There are several possible tests available and all differ slightly from one another, but the Tukey Honestly Significant Difference (HSD) test is suitable for most applications, especially at undergraduate level (see Figure 9.22).

Step 2.   Click Continue and inspect Output 9.6 (see Table 9.14).

Figure 9.22

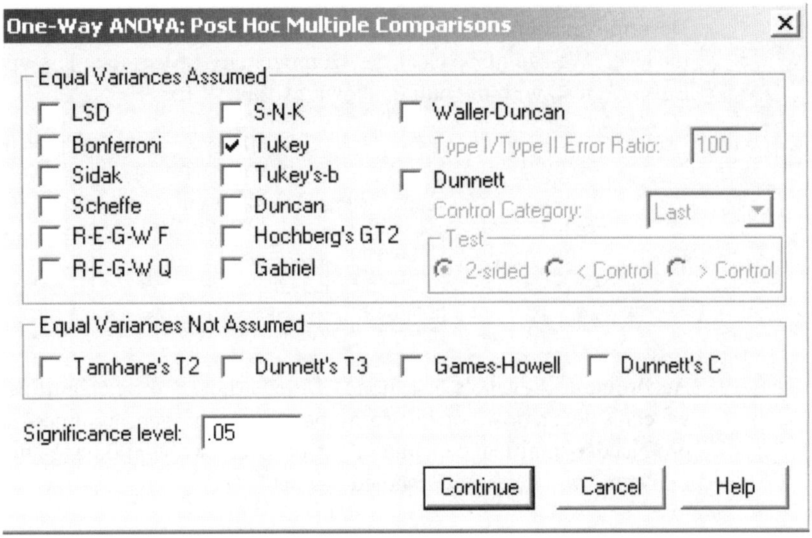

One-Way ANOVA: Post Hoc Multiple Comparisons dialog box.

Table 9.14    Output 9.6.

Multiple Comparisons

Dependent Variable: recovery time in weeks following surgery

Tukey HSD

| (I) exercise regime prior to surgery | (J) exercise regime prior to surgery | Mean Difference (I-J) | Std. Error | Sig. | 95% Confidence Interval | |
|---|---|---|---|---|---|---|
| | | | | | Lower Bound | Upper Bound |
| no exercise | moderate exercise | −2.66667* | .46481 | .000 | −3.8274 | −1.5059 |
| | intensive exercise | −2.22222* | .46481 | .000 | −3.3830 | −1.0615 |
| moderate exercise | no exercise | 2.66667* | .46481 | .000 | 1.5059 | 3.8274 |
| | intensive exercise | .44444 | .46481 | .611 | −.7163 | 1.6052 |
| intensive exercise | no exercise | 2.22222* | .46481 | .000 | 1.0615 | 3.3830 |
| | moderate exercise | −.44444 | .46481 | .611 | −1.6052 | .7163 |

*The mean difference is significant at the .05 level.

Interpretation of the Tukey output is straightforward – each condition, or level, is compared with all other levels of the factor and a significance value assigned to the difference. So, we note that when no exercise is compared with both moderate and intensive, the differences are significant (shown as .000 and .000 respectively). When moderate exercise is compared with the other two levels, the difference between this and no exercise is confirmed (.000) but the difference with intensive exercise is not significant (.611).

The full story now behind our study is that it makes a significant difference to postoperative recovery time to take exercise. However, it makes no difference whether exercise is moderate or intensive.

There remains a final point to be made concerning the interpretation of ANOVA output. Recall that with the $t$-test we had to make allowance for occasions when the variances of the groups being compared were not equal. The same allowance has to be made in ANOVA. Referring to the Post hoc Multiple Comparisons window in Table 9.14, there are two types of post hoc tests available – one assuming equal (or similar) variances between the factor levels and one not. Equality of variance is determined via the ANOVA options set-up window, as shown at Step 3 in 9.2.9. This window was used previously to select **D**escriptive, so that the ANOVA output would also show descriptive statistics for each factor level. We can also select the **H**omogeneity of variance test option which will perform Levene's test, with the output shown in Table 9.15:

Table 9.15    Output 9.7 – Test of Homogeneity of Variances.

recovery time in weeks following surgery

| Levene Statistic | df1 | df2 | Sig. |
|---|---|---|---|
| .642 | 2 | 24 | .535 |

According to Levene's test, none of the variances differ significantly from any other and we can select a post hoc test from the 'equal variances assumed' sector. Had Levene's test produced a significance value of .05 or lower, we would have chosen a post hoc test from the 'equal variances not assumed' sector.

Box 9.8

## How To . . .

# Perform a one-way analysis of variance

Step 1.   From the menu, select **A**nalyze, **C**ompare Means, then **O**ne-Way ANOVA.

Step 2.   In the test editor window, select from the variables window on the left of the window, the dependent variable in the analysis (or variables, if several ANOVAs are to be done) and transfer to the **D**ependent List box.

Step 3.   In the test editor window select from the variables list the independent variable in the analysis and transfer this into the **F**actor box.

Step 4.   Click the **O**ptions button and in the Options window check the **D**escriptive box and the **H**omogeneity of variance test box. Click **C**ontinue to return to the test editor window.

Step 5.   Click the **P**ost Hoc button and in the Post Hoc Multiple Comparisons window check the **T**ukey box. Click **C**ontinue to return to the test editor window.

Step 6.   Click OK to perform the ANOVA.

Step 7.   Inspect the ANOVA output, noting the following:

a.   If the probability associated with Levene's statistic is .05 or lower, repeat Step 5 but select a test from the **E**qual Variances Not Assumed sector.

b.   Check the degrees of freedom for both the between-groups and total variances. They should confirm that all factor levels were included in the analysis.

Step 8.   Inspect the post hoc multiple group comparisons output and determine which comparison(s) produced a significant difference. Note that SPSS indicates significant comparisons with an asterisk (*), although the significance values themselves are usually sufficient.

(Note: Step 8 is not required if the probability associated with the ANOVA fails to reach significance.)

On a practical note, when inspecting the output from an ANOVA, special attention should be paid to the degrees of freedom ($df$). If an analysis comprised three groups, the particular degrees of freedom would be $(k - 1) = 2$, as in the present example. Similarly, if a sample comprised 27 participants, the relevant degrees of freedom would be $(n - 1)$ for the total sample $= 26$, and $(n - 1)$ for each of the groups in the analysis. The within-groups $df$ for three groups each comprising 9 participants would be 24 $[(9 - 1) + (9 - 1) + (9 - 1)]$. In ANOVA, inspection of the between-groups $df$ in particular is to be strongly recommended: it would not be the first time that, in the setting up of the data for analysis, one of the groups to be compared is omitted. The only clue that this has occurred would be in the degrees of freedom, which in the between-groups case would be one less than it ought to be. Inspection of the Within and Total $df$ would also provide a clue but we would need to know the total sample and group size. Unfortunately this is often overlooked in our eagerness to get to the $F$-statistic. A quick guide to ANOVA can be reviewed in Box 9.8.

It is worth noting at this point that, as with our previous statistical tests, there exist non-parametric equivalents to the one-way ANOVA – the Kruskal-Wallis test is a good example, being a straightforward expansion of the Mann-Whitney test to include three or more conditions when data are ordinal (i.e., ranked). For anyone wishing to pursue their interest in non-parametric tests any of the standard statistical texts cited at the end of the book will serve as a useful source.

### 9.2.7 Within-group comparisons – paired $t$-test

In a **within-group parametric comparison test** two repeated measures are taken on a single group. It is also known as a dependent $t$-test, related-samples $t$-test and correlated $t$-test.

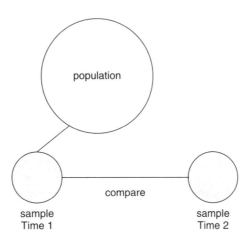

In Part 2 a particular type of design was outlined which had some advantages over the conventional two-group comparison. Rather than use different individuals in each category (e.g., one set of participants in a control group and another set in an experimental), the same people can be used in both conditions. The advantages of this approach are that fewer participants are needed in a study, and the complicating effects of individual differences are minimised. This also makes the paired $t$-test a more powerful type of test

Table 9.16     Word recall under two conditions.

| Case | Rote condition | Association condition | $d$ | $d^2$ |
|------|----------------|------------------------|-----|--------|
| 1 | 10 | 11 | 1 | 1 |
| 2 | 15 | 11 | −4 | 16 |
| 3 | 11 | 10 | −1 | 1 |
| 4 | 12 | 12 | 0 | 0 |
| 5 | 14 | 14 | 0 | 0 |
| 6 | 12 | 15 | 3 | 9 |
| 7 | 13 | 16 | 3 | 9 |
| 8 | 15 | 18 | 3 | 9 |
| 9 | 16 | 12 | −4 | 16 |
| 10 | 14 | 14 | 0 | 0 |

$\Sigma d = 1$

$(\Sigma d)^2 = 1$ where $d$ is the difference between the scores of the two conditions

$\Sigma d^2 = 61$

$n = 10$

than its independent-groups equivalents (see 9.1.3) since the probability of making a Type II error is reduced. A worked example follows:

Consider an experiment in which two forms of learning strategy were investigated. A group of 10 volunteers attempted to memorise a list of 20 common nouns using a rote learning procedure. A subsequent test measured the number of words correctly recalled by each participant. At a later date the same participants took part in a second memory experiment, this time using a system of word association explained to them by the experimenter. Again, after an interval, recall of the word stimuli was measured. The relevant analytical information is shown in Table 9.16, comprising the recall scores for each condition with relevant calculation steps. Differences between the conditions, squared differences and computational elements are shown.

The computation of the paired $t$-test provides a $t$-value which expresses the magnitude of the difference between the two repeated measures. The formula is shown at (9.6).

$$t = \frac{\sum d / n}{\sqrt{\dfrac{\sum d^2 - \left[\dfrac{(\sum d)^2}{n}\right]}{n(n-1)}}} \tag{9.6}$$

Substituting the values from Table 9.16, we have:

$$t = \frac{1/10}{\sqrt{\dfrac{61 - \left(\dfrac{1^2}{10}\right)}{10(10-1)}}}$$

$$= .12$$

Inspection of Appendix C identifies a table value of 2.262 for a .05 level of significance for a two-tailed test. Since the obtained $t$ is less than the table value, we accept the null hypothesis.

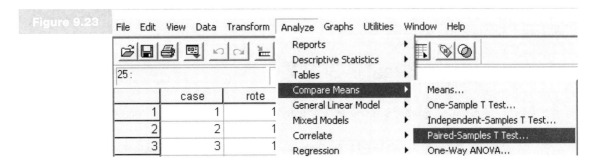

Figure 9.23

To perform the same test in SPSS, the following steps should be followed:

Step 1.  From the menu select Analyze, Compare Means and then Paired-Samples T Test (Figure 9.23).

Step 2.  In the test editor window, select the pair of variables to be compared from the variables window and transfer them to the **P**aired Variables box. Click OK (Figure 9.24).

Step 3.  Inspect the output (Table 9.17).

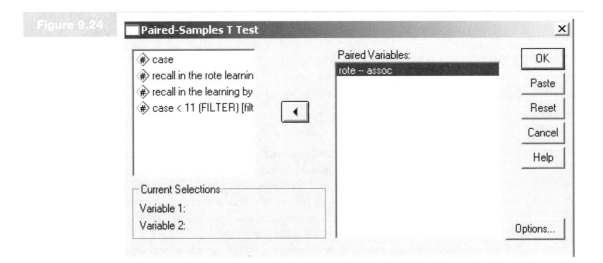

Figure 9.24

Note that the variable, case < 11, indicates that we used a sub-set of the data for this example.

Table 9.17    Output 9.8 – Paired samples test.

| | Paired Differences | | | | | | | |
| | | | | 95% Confidence Interval of the Difference | | | | |
| | Mean | Std. Deviation | Std. Error Mean | Lower | Upper | t | df | Sig. (2-tailed) |
|---|---|---|---|---|---|---|---|---|
| Pair 1  recall in the rote learning condition − recall in the learning by association condition | −.100 | 2.601 | .823 | −1.961 | 1.761 | −.122 | 9 | .906 |

Box 9.9

**How To . . .**

## Perform a paired *t*-test in SPSS

Step 1.  From the menu select <u>A</u>nalyze, <u>C</u>ompare Means and then <u>P</u>aired-Samples T Test.

Step 2.  In the test editor window select the two variables to be compared and transfer to the **P**aired Variables box.

Step 3.  Inspect the output.

The first part of the paired *t*-test output is concerned with the differences between the two measures. Inspection of the *t*-value shows that this is small (reflecting a small difference between the measures), confirmed by the probability value of .906: therefore $p > .05$, and we accept the null hypothesis. This is expressed formally as,

$$t(9) = -0.12, \quad p > .05$$

A quick guide to performing the paired *t*-test is given in Box 9.9.

### 9.2.8  Wilcoxon signed rank test

The **Wilcoxon signed rank test** is a within-group non-parametric comparison test in which two repeated measures are taken on a single group. When a single group of participants is measured on two separate occasions (this could be an attitudinal measure before and after exposure to a persuasive communication, a score on an experimental task under two different conditions or some behavioural measure before and after some treatment or intervention) a within-participants test is appropriate.

When only two measures are taken on a single sample of participants, and the data do not meet parametric requirements (the data are ordinal, or interval but not normally distributed) the Wilcoxon test is appropriate.

To perform this test, scores or measures taken from each individual are compared; the difference between each pair of scores is taken and the values of the differences are ranked from lowest to highest without consideration of whether the observed differences are positive or negative. Once ranked, the sign of the original differences is attached to the ranks. The positive ranks are summed and the negative ranks are summed, and the statistic, *T*, is taken as the sum of the smaller of the two sums. The following example illustrates the procedure.

Ten hypertensive patients participate in a clinical trial of a new blood-pressure controlling drug. A measure of diastolic blood pressure is taken prior to the first administration of the new drug and a second measure is taken after a one-month regime on the medication. The issue is whether the new drug made a difference to the health of the sample.

Table 9.18    Diastolic blood pressure before and after an intervention.

| Case | Bp_pre | Bp_post | Diff | Rdiff | |
|------|--------|---------|------|-------|---|
| 1 | 95 | 96 | −1.00 | 2.000 (−) | |
| 2 | 90 | 85 | 9.00 | 9.000 | |
| 3 | 89 | 90 | −1.00 | 2.000 (−) | Sum of +ve ranks = 49 |
| 4 | 100 | 89 | 11.00 | 8.000 | |
| 5 | 135 | 100 | 39.00 | 10.000 | |
| 6 | 88 | 89 | −1.00 | 2.000 (−) | Sum of −ve ranks = 6 |
| 7 | 90 | 80 | 10.00 | 7.000 | |
| 8 | 93 | 91 | 2.00 | 4.000 | |
| 9 | 101 | 89 | 12.00 | 9.000 | |
| 10 | 92 | 85 | 7.00 | 6.000 | |

**Key**: Case = participant number (1–10); Bp_pre = blood pressure prior to intervention; Bp_post = blood pressure post-intervention; Diff = difference between pre- and post-measures; Rdiff = rank of the differences. (Note: the sign of the differences is ignored for the purpose of ranking, then subsequently restored to the ranks for the purpose of summation.)

The logic is that if there is no real difference between the two sets of measures there should be roughly the same distribution of positive and negative ranks (see Table 9.18). Where a real difference is present, this would be reflected in an imbalance in the distribution of positive and negative ranks. To determine whether this imbalance represents a significant difference between the two measures, appropriate tables would be consulted in terms of the calculated $T$, which in this example equals 6 (the smaller of the two summed ranks). Although such calculations are not onerous, the modern approach is to utilise a statistical package; the steps for analysing these data in SPSS are outlined below.

Step 1.  Enter data with Variable 1 = case (participant number); Variable 2 = the first measure taken on the sample (bp_pre); Variable 3 = the second measure (bp_post) (Table 9.19).

Table 9.19

| case | bp_pre | bp_post |
|------|--------|---------|
| 1 | 95 | 96 |
| 2 | 90 | 85 |
| 3 | 89 | 90 |
| 4 | 100 | 89 |
| 5 | 135 | 100 |
| 6 | 88 | 89 |
| 7 | 90 | 80 |
| 8 | 93 | 91 |
| 9 | 101 | 89 |
| 10 | 92 | 85 |

Figure 9.25

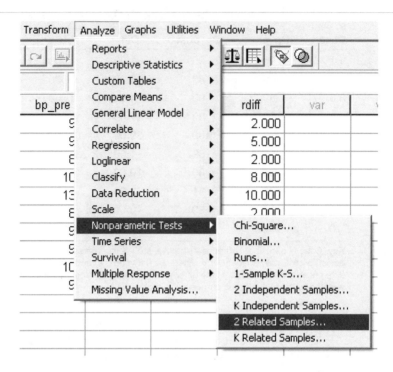

**Step 2.** From the command menu strip, select <u>A</u>nalyze, <u>N</u>onparametric Tests, then <u>2</u> Related Samples (Figure 9.25).

This operation opens the test editor window as shown in Figure 9.26.
There are several features of this window which should be noted:

1. There are a number of possible tests we could apply to our data. The Wilcoxon is the default test, as shown by the checked box, and so this part of the test editor should be left alone.

Figure 9.26

2. The left-hand side of the editor window shows a box containing all the variables in our data set.

3. The right-hand side shows a blank box or window, into which we will transfer the variables which comprise our two measures. This is achieved by selecting the bp_before and the bp_after variables, then clicking the arrow button. The test editor window changes as indicated in Figure 9.27:

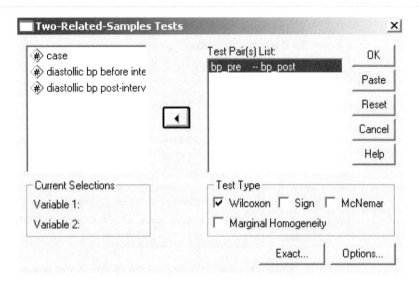

Clicking OK takes us to the output of the analysis, as follows:

Table 9.20   Output 9.9 – Wilcoxon Signed Rank Test.

|  |  | N | Mean Rank | Sum of Ranks |
|---|---|---|---|---|
| Diastolic bp Post-intervention − diastolic bp before intervention | Negative Ranks | 7[a] | 7.00 | 49.00 |
|  | Positive Ranks | 3[b] | 2.00 | 6.00 |
|  | Ties | 0[c] |  |  |
|  | Total | 10 |  |  |

[a]Diastolic bp post-intervention < diastolic bp before intervention.
[b]Diastolic bp post-intervention > diastolic bp before intervention.
[c]Diastolic bp before intervention = diastolic bp post-intervention.

Table 9.21   Test Statistics[b].

|  | Diastolic bp post-intervention − diastolic bp before intervention |
|---|---|
| Z | −2.197[a] |
| Asymp. Sig. (2-tailed) | .028 |

[a]Based on positive ranks.
[b]Wilcoxon signed rank test.

## How To . . .

# Perform the Wilcoxon signed rank test in SPSS

Step 1. From the command menu strip, select <u>A</u>nalyze, <u>N</u>onparametric Tests, then <u>2</u> Related Samples.

Step 2. In the test editor window, transfer the two variables representing the measures taken on the sample, into the **T**est Pair(s) List box.

Step 3. Click the OK button.

Step 4. Interpret the output, in terms of the z-score given and the associated probability value.

The output for the Wilcoxon test comprises two tables. Table 9.20 shows the sums of the positive and negative ranks (you will note they are the same as in our manual calculation). Table 9.21 presents us with a z-score and an associated probability. This is the probability of obtaining the observed differences between our two measures, given as .028. We conclude that the difference in diastolic blood pressure levels before and after an intervention is significant at the .05 level. This is expressed formally as,

$$z(n = 10) = -2.2, \quad p < .05 \text{ (two-tailed)}$$

Box 9.10 explains in detail how to perform the Wilcoxon signed rank test in SPSS.

### 9.2.9 One-way ANOVA, related

Three or more repeated measures are taken on an interval-scaled variable with the same participants used under each experimental condition.

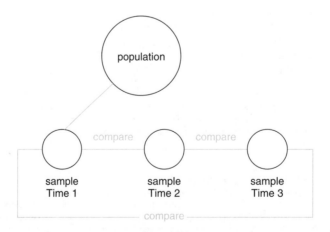

During our previous discussion on different research designs it was proposed that the two-sample comparison study represented a typical experimental paradigm. Consequently particular statistical tests are available for these very scenarios – the independent t-test and its non-parametric equivalents. Similarly, when a design is of the within-subjects variety (a single sample is tested on more than one occasion) the paired *t*-test is available for the typical two repeated measures case. However, as with between-groups designs, repeated measures on a single sample need not be restricted to only two repetitions. There are many research scenarios in which a whole series of measures might be taken on a sample, with a view to identifying significant differences among any of the measures. And, as with the between-groups approach, it is ANOVA which provides the extension of the two condition case.

Note that there is a non-parametric equivalent to the repeated measures ANOVA – the Friedman test, which expands the principles of the Wilcoxon test to the three or more samples case. We will not be covering the Friedman test here but refer you to one of the general statistics texts cited at the end of this book. There follows an example of the computation of the one-way related ANOVA in SPSS.

Consider our group of enthusiastic cyclists and their impact on the hedgehog population. If we were to take the number of hedgehogs run over on a standard circuit as an indicator of cycling skill, measures taken at different times during their training would reflect their progress from novice to experienced. We note the number of errors made at Time 1 (hedgehogs run over at the start of the training period), the number of errors made at Time 2 (six weeks into training) and the number of errors made at Time 3 (the end of the training period). We use a one-way related ANOVA to test whether a significant difference in error rates is present within our time factor. The independent variable is the within-subjects *time* factor, of which there are three levels. The dependent variable is the error rate.

Step 1. From the menu, select <u>A</u>nalyze, <u>G</u>eneral Linear Model, then <u>R</u>epeated Measures (Figure 9.28).

Step 2. In the Define Factor(s) window, provide a name for the independent variable (the within-subject factor) in the experiment. This is currently shown as factor 1 and should be overwritten with the chosen variable name. In the present example we type *time* in this space. Enter the number of levels which comprise the 'time' factor, in this case, 3. Click <u>A</u>dd to update the settings for the analysis. The Define Factor(s) window now appears as shown in Figure 9.29.

Step 3. Click <u>D</u>efine. The standard test editor window opens. From the variables list on the left, select, in order, the 1st, 2nd and 3rd measures which comprise the levels of the independent variable. Transfer these to the **Within-Subjects** Variables box on the right (Figure 9.30), which changes to show the selections (Figure 9.31).

Step 4. Click OK and inspect the output (see Tables 9.22 and 9.23).

**Figure 9.28**

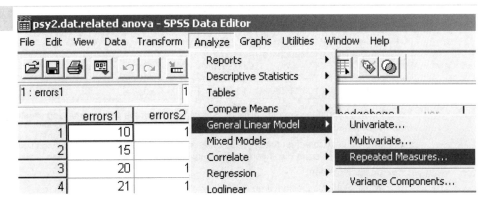

Figure 9.29

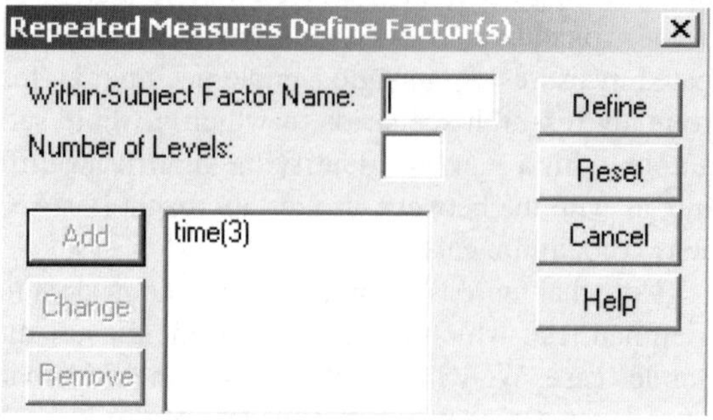

**Repeated Measures Define Factor(s)**    ☒

Within-Subject Factor Name: [＿＿＿＿]

Number of Levels: [＿＿＿]

| Add | time(3) |
| Change | |
| Remove | |

Define
Reset
Cancel
Help

Figure 9.30

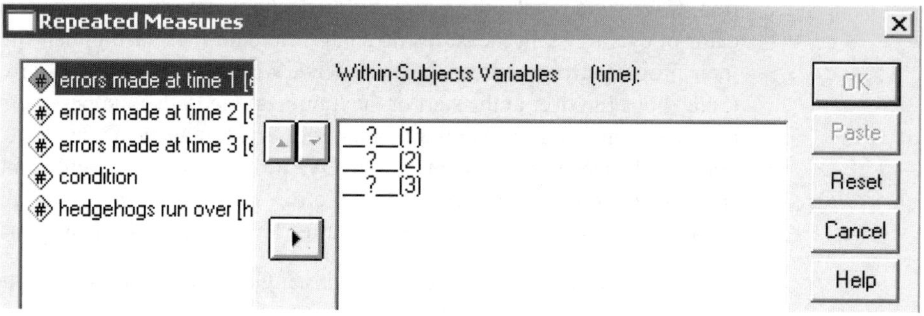

**Repeated Measures**    ☒

# errors made at time 1 [
# errors made at time 2 [
# errors made at time 3 [
# condition
# hedgehogs run over [h

Within-Subjects Variables   (time):

__?__(1)
__?__(2)
__?__(3)

OK
Paste
Reset
Cancel
Help

Figure 9.31

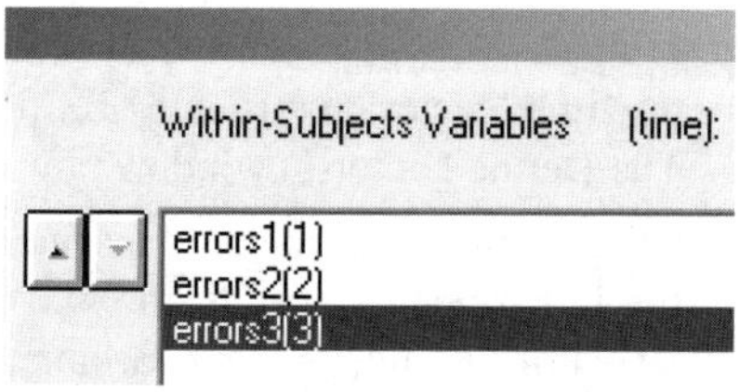

Within-Subjects Variables   (time):

errors1(1)
errors2(2)
errors3(3)

Table 9.22    Output 9.10 – Mauchly's Test of Sphericity.

Measure: MEASURE_1

| Within Subjects Effect | Mauchly's W | Approx. Chi-Square | df | Sig. | Epsilon[a] | | |
|---|---|---|---|---|---|---|---|
| | | | | | Greenhouse-Geisser | Huynh-Feldt | Lower-bound |
| time | .920 | 1.082 | 2 | .582 | .926 | 1.000 | .500 |

Tests the null hypothesis that the error covariance matrix of the orthonormalized transformed dependent variables is proportional to an identity matrix.

   a. May be used to adjust the degrees of freedom for the averaged tests of significance. Corrected tests are displayed in the Tests of Within-Subjects Effects table.

   b. Design: Intercept

      Within Subjects Design: time

Table 9.23    Tests of Within-Subjects Effects.

Measure: MEASURE_1

| Source | | Type III Sum of Squares | df | Mean Square | F | Sig. |
|---|---|---|---|---|---|---|
| time | Sphericity Assumed | 121.111 | 2 | 60.556 | 5.328 | .011 |
| | Greenhouse-Geisser | 121.111 | 1.852 | 65.393 | 5.328 | .013 |
| | Huynh-Feldt | 121.111 | 2.000 | 60.556 | 5.328 | .011 |
| | Lower-bound | 121.111 | 1.000 | 121.111 | 5.328 | .037 |
| Error(time) | Sphericity Assumed | 318.222 | 28 | 11.365 | | |
| | Greenhouse-Geisser | 318.222 | 25.929 | 12.273 | | |
| | Huynh-Feldt | 318.222 | 28.000 | 11.365 | | |
| | Lower-bound | 318.222 | 14.000 | 22.730 | | |

Note that output from a repeated measures ANOVA is both considerable and complex, and from an undergraduate viewpoint, possibly one of the more intimidating SPSS functions. We have not shown the full output here, only that which is relevant to the present example.

Tables 9.22 and 9.23 have similarities with the unrelated ANOVA output we are now familiar with – we have values for sum of squares, *df*, mean square, *F* and a significance value. Note, however, that for our within-subjects factor of 'time' we have shown several versions of this output, one labelled **Sphericity** assumed, and a number of alternatives, in particular the **Greenhouse-Geisser**. One of the requirements of data in the repeated measures context is sphericity. This can be considered as similar to the requirement of homogeneity of variance in the between-groups case, which we have previously discussed (see independent *t*-test; one-way unrelated ANOVA), except that sphericity refers to covariance – the correlations among scores at different levels of the within-subjects factor. If all of this is becoming a bit too intimidating, it is enough to be aware that if we are unable to assume sphericity in our data then there is an increased chance of making a Type I error (wrongly rejecting a null hypothesis). In the above example we find that if sphericity is assumed, the *F*-value of 9.328 has a corresponding probability of .011, which is significant at the .05 level. If sphericity is not assumed there exist a number of modifications to the *F*-test which lead to a more conservative decision being made (one which reduces the likelihood of making a Type I error). One such is the Greenhouse-Geisser test which we have shown in Table 9.23. The significance value here is .013 which differs only marginally from the sphericity assumed *p*-value, and would not cause us to change our decision – that a significant difference exists among our measures of error.

How do we know which *F*-test is the most appropriate for our data? Along with the ANOVA output, SPSS also offers the **Mauchly test of sphericity**.

The significance value shown is the probability that the data are spherical. This is given as .582, well above our .05 cut-off, and so in our within-subjects effects table we can opt for the *sphericity assumed* F-*value* and associated probability.

Shrewd readers will recall that this is not the end of our analysis, for ANOVA tells us only if an effect is present within our data, not where it is. So far all we know is that when we compare our three measures of error within our cycling group, the probability that they are the same is .011 (i.e., they are *not* the same). But how do they differ? Does the measure at Time 1 differ significantly from Time 2? Does Time 1 differ from Time 3? Does Time 2 differ from Time 3? In the two-sample design there is no problem, we merely examine the mean scores in each sample and inspection alone tells us which group scored higher. But when we are comparing three measures it is not so simple. During the ANOVA set-up, had we chosen the Descriptive option we would have been given Table 9.24 as part of the general output:

Table 9.24    Output 9.11.

Descriptive Statistics

| | Mean | Std. Deviation | N |
|---|---|---|---|
| errors made at time 1 | 15.13 | 3.159 | 15 |
| errors made at time 2 | 13.47 | 3.739 | 15 |
| errors made at time 3 | 11.13 | 3.583 | 15 |

In this case Table 9.24 is not particularly helpful – we can see that there are differences, but we don't know whether this merely reflects chance variation. The solution is the same as in the unrelated ANOVA case: we carry out some form of post hoc paired comparison test, in which every possible pair of measures is tested for a significant difference (see section 9.2.6). In the within-subjects context this is slightly more complex than our previous experience with post hoc tests. The recommended approach is to perform a series of paired $t$-tests which encompasses all possible pairs, while applying what is termed the **Bonferroni** correction for repeated paired comparisons. Normally a post hoc test makes its own adjustments for multiple comparisons but the Bonferroni procedure requires the researcher to make the appropriate computation (strictly speaking the Bonferroni is not a post hoc test, rather it was designed for planned contrasts between pairs of measures. It can though be used in the post hoc setting). The logic is as follows:

In ANOVA we assign a probability value (typically) of .05 to the entire analysis. If we subsequently sub-divide our analysis into a number of components, this assigned probability of .05 must be shared out among the components. (This is a bit like sharing our significance value between both tails of a distribution in a two-tailed test.) Therefore, if our subsequent testing requires three paired $t$-tests, then our cut-off for significance becomes .016 (.05/3). This is what is meant by being conservative. The procedure for performing a paired $t$-test is given in section 9.2.7 and output for the present example is shown in Table 9.25:

Table 9.25   Output 9.12.

| | Paired Differences | | | | | | | | |
|---|---|---|---|---|---|---|---|---|---|
| | | | | 95% Confidence Interval of the Difference | | | | | Sig. |
| | Mean | Std. Deviation | Std. Error Mean | Lower | Upper | t | df | (2-tailed) |
| Pair 1  errors made at time 1– errors made at time 2 | 1.667 | 4.287 | 1.107 | –.708 | 4.041 | 1.506 | 14 | .154 |
| Pair 2  errors made at time 1– errors made at time 3 | 4.000 | 5.385 | 1.390 | 1.018 | 6.982 | 2.877 | 14 | .012 |
| Pair 3  errors made at time 2– errors made at time 3 | 2.333 | 4.562 | 1.178 | –.193 | 4.860 | 1.981 | 14 | .068 |

Inspection of the output indicates that, with the Bonferroni correction for multiple paired comparisons, only the second comparison achieved significance (Time 1 and Time 3).

This all seems terribly complicated but it is really only tedious and perhaps a little clumsy. The sequence of operations given in Box 9.11 will hopefully simplify the procedures for the related ANOVA.

How To . . .

# Perform a one-way ANOVA – a quick guide

Step 1. From the menu select Analyze, General Linear Model, then Repeated Measures.

Step 2. Name the Within-subjects factor and state the number of levels. Click Add.

Step 3. Click Define.

Step 4. Select the variables which comprise the levels of the within-subjects factor.

Step 5. In the Options window, select Descriptive. Click OK.

Step 6. Inspect the output for the Mauchly test of sphericity against the .05 level.

Step 7. Inspect the ANOVA table and note the significance value. If the probability associated with the Mauchly test >.05, use the Sphericity Assumed output. If the probability associated with the Mauchly test <.05, use the Greenhouse-Geisser alternative.

Step 8. If the probability associated with the $F$-test in ANOVA < .05, perform sufficient paired $t$-tests to test all possible pairs.

Step 9. Apply the Bonferroni correction to adjust the alpha level in line with the number of paired comparison tests being carried out. (Divide .05 by the number of comparisons to be made.)

## Review

Chapter 9 has introduced the key statistical concept of probability and shown how the interpretation of all statistical analyses is based on this. The second part of the chapter considered the common statistical methods for testing hypotheses in experimental designs. You should now be able to identify appropriate tests of differences for between-groups and within-subjects designs, perform the necessary steps in SPSS and correctly interpret statistical output.

## Suggested further reading

Howitt, D., & Cramer, D. (2000). *An introduction to statistics in psychology* (2nd ed.). Harlow, Essex: Pearson/Prentice Hall.

This text provides a good review of the standard statistical tests and offers examples of their use in the literature, along with a sensible set of recommendations on when particular tests are appropriate.

Kinnear, P. R., & Gray, C. D. (2000). *SPSS for Windows made simple: Release 10*. Hove, East Sussex: Psychology Press Ltd.

A comprehensive manual of SPSS procedures, providing step-by-step guidelines for most statistical tests with explanations of output. A straightforward and easy to follow text, though it does not consider the background to the various research designs.

# 10 Tests of association

## Key Issues

The emphasis in Chapter 10 is on tests of association. Two major procedures are considered – the first relevant to research in which associated variables are category in nature, and the second in which the associated variables are continuous. We provide worked examples of the procedures, SPSS guides and detailed interpretation of statistical output. Chapter 10 focuses on these topics specifically:

- crosstabulation
- the chi-square test
- correlation
- simple regression

## 10.1 The chi-square ($\chi^2$) test of association

Many survey- and questionnaire-based studies are of the category-category design. That is, the independent or causal variable comprises a number of categories, but the dependent or outcome measure is also composed of categories; as when the choice of response to an item (Yes/No) is related to the gender of the respondent (male/female). (Note: while both these examples refer to nominally scaled variables, the following discussion relates equally well to cases in which either or both variables are ordinally scaled.)

In this type of design the most appropriate form of analysis is by a combination of crosstabulation and chi-square ($\chi^2$). **Chi-square** assesses the association between two variables when both are measured on a nominal or ordinal scale. The chi-square (pronounced ky-square, as in *kyak*) test of association, to give it its full title, compares actual observations with what would be expected were chance alone responsible for the distribution of events. As the difference between observations and expectations increases, this is reflected in the magnitude of the statistic. In the example above, if there was no difference between male and female respondents in the choice of response to a particular item, we would expect a random, and more or less equal distribution of male and female responses in each of the yes/no categories. If this is not the case, if we find there are, say, more female responses in a particular category than we would expect, then there is evidence for an association between response and gender.

A problem with this particular statistic is that it merely informs us that there is an effect of some kind within the associated variables, but not where. This is why a crosstabulation is useful, since inspection of the cells which comprise a contingency table can often identify the source of an effect. The example below provides an illustration.

A number of individuals classified as either Type A or Type B personality types respond to an item from a stress-proneness questionnaire. The particular item asks the question:

How often do you feel unsatisfied with the course your life is taking?

never ☐                    occasionally ☐                    all the time ☐

A sample output is shown in Table 10.1:

**Table 10.1**    Crosstabulation of two personality types and three response categories.

| Personality type | Response category | | | |
| --- | --- | --- | --- | --- |
| | **Never** | **Occasionally** | **All the time** | **Total** |
| Type A | 7 | 24 | 44 | 75 |
| Type B | 43 | 17 | 15 | 75 |
| Total | 50 | 41 | 59 | 150 |

Table 10.1 illustrates the pattern of responses for the two personality types. We note, for instance, that among Type As, 7 respondents said they never felt unsatisfied, 24 occasionally and 44 felt unsatisfied all the time. We also note there is a different pattern for the Type Bs. What we can't say at the moment is what the expected pattern of responses would be if there were no association between these variables (i.e., if it made little difference to how participants responded if they were either Type A or B). Determining the expected frequency of response for any cell is given by the formula at (10.1):

$$E = \frac{Row\ Total \times Column\ Total}{n} \tag{10.1}$$

Where $E$ = Expected frequency
and $n$ = number of participants

To determine the expected frequency of response in the first cell (Type A responding 'never'), we merely substitute into the formula:

$$E = \frac{75 \times 50}{150}$$

$$= 25$$

If we were to repeat this exercise for all cells we would have a picture of how the overall pattern of observed responses differed from what we might have expected, as in Table 10.2.

At a descriptive level it is clear that actual responses have differed from what we might have expected were there no relationship between these two variables. To determine

Table 10.2  Crosstabulation of two personality types and three response categories with expected frequencies shown in parentheses.

| Personality type | Response category | | | Total |
| --- | --- | --- | --- | --- |
| | Never | Occasionally | All the time | |
| Type A | 7 (25) | 24 (20.5) | 44 (29.5) | 75 |
| Type B | 43 (25) | 17 (20.5) | 15 (29.5) | 75 |
| Total | 50 | 41 | 59 | 150 |

this difference between what we observed ($O$) and what we might have expected ($E$) we apply the chi-square test, using the formula at (10.2).

$$\chi^2 = \sum \frac{(O - E)^2}{E_i} \qquad (10.2)$$

Where $O$ = Observed frequency
$E$ = Expected frequency
$E_i$ = Expected frequency for a given cell

Substituting in the formula gives us:

$$\frac{(7 - 25)^2}{25} + \frac{(24 - 20.5)^2}{20.5} + \frac{(44 - 29.5)^2}{29.5} + \frac{(43 - 25)^2}{25} + \frac{(17 - 20.5)^2}{20.5}$$
$$+ \frac{(15 - 29.5)^2}{29.5} = 41.4$$

To interpret this value for chi-square we would either consult appropriate statistical tables, or inspect the output from an analysis in SPSS. The procedure for calculating chi-square is shown, based on the *MKpsy2* data set.

Step 1. From the menu, select <u>A</u>nalyze, <u>D</u>escriptive statistics, then <u>C</u>rosstabs (see Figure 10.1).

Step 2. In the test editor window, select from the variable list on the left which variable will be the row variable in our crosstabulation and which will be the column variable. (Note that it doesn't actually matter which is which, although if one variable has many categories, selecting this as the column variable is probably better since SPSS will split tables containing too many row categories.) Transfer these to the appropriate boxes on the right of this window (Figure 10.2).

Step 3. Click on the <u>S</u>tatistics button and select <u>C</u>hi-square from the options provided. Click <u>C</u>ontinue Figure 10.3).

Figure 10.1

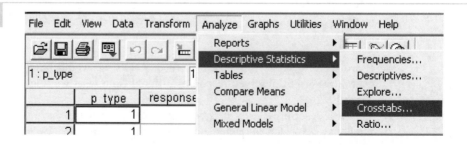

Step 4. Return to the test editor window and click the <u>C</u>ells button to open the Cell Display window. The settings in this window determine how much information will be displayed in the contingency table output. Select **O**bserved, **E**xpected, **R**ow and Unstandardized. Click <u>C</u>ontinue, then OK (Figure 10.4).

Step 5. Inspect the output.

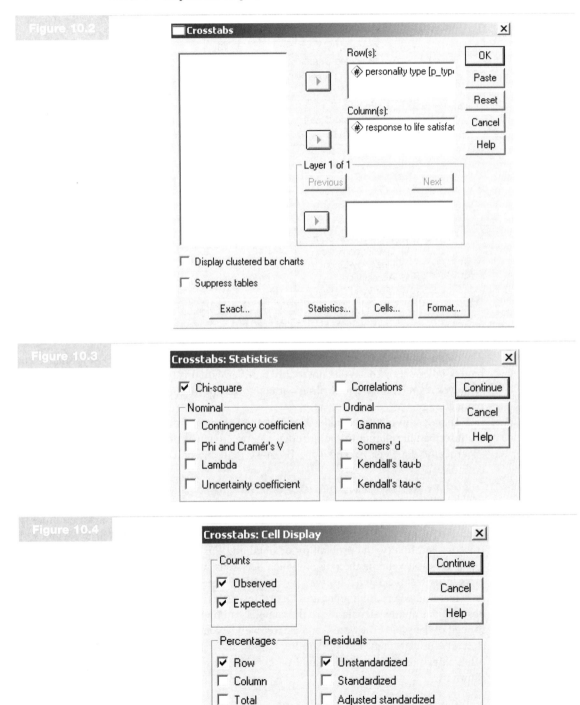

**Figure 10.2**

**Figure 10.3**

**Figure 10.4**

Table 10.3    Output 10.1.

personality type * response to life satisfaction Q Crosstabulation

| | | | response to life satisfaction Q | | | |
| | | | never | occasionally | all the time | Total |
|---|---|---|---|---|---|---|
| personality type | type A | Count | 7 | 24 | 44 | 75 |
| | | Expected Count | 25.0 | 20.5 | 29.5 | 75.0 |
| | | % within personality type | 9.3% | 32.0% | 58.7% | 100.0% |
| | | Residual | −18.0 | 3.5 | 14.5 | |
| | type B | Count | 43 | 17 | 15 | 75 |
| | | Expected Count | 25.0 | 20.5 | 29.5 | 75.0 |
| | | % within personality type | 57.3% | 22.7% | 20.0% | 100.0% |
| | | Residual | 18.0 | −3.5 | −14.5 | |
| Total | | Count | 50 | 41 | 59 | 150 |
| | | Expected Count | 50.0 | 41.0 | 59.0 | 150.0 |
| | | % within personality type | 33.3% | 27.3% | 39.3% | 100.0% |

Table 10.4

Chi-Square Tests

| | Value | df | Asymp. Sig. (2-sided) |
|---|---|---|---|
| Pearson Chi-Square | 41.369[a] | 2 | .000 |
| Likelihood Ratio | 44.912 | 2 | .000 |
| Linear-by-Linear Association | 38.695 | 1 | .000 |
| N of Valid Cases | 150 | | |

[a] 0 cells (.0%) have expected count less than 5. The minimum expected count is 20.50.

The output in Tables 10.3 and 10.4 is typical of modern statistical output – informative but hugely intimidating to anyone not totally familiar with this type of computerised analysis. However, there is a trick to dealing with any mass of information, and that is to take it a piece at a time.

There are in fact three tables here, but the first part of the output which interests us is the information relating to the difference between actual observations and expectations; specifically, did Type As and Type Bs make random choices among the three response categories?

Under the heading *Chi-square* in Table 10.4 is the name of the particular statistic which will be used to make our decision. Most software offers several calculations of the chi-square statistic, but we will rely on the Pearson, which is the one most commonly used. The next value is the chi-squared statistic itself (41.369), followed by degrees of freedom and finally, the probability of obtaining this particular distribution of observations. This last value is the one on which decisions will be made, since it represents the probability that the actual observations match our expectations, assuming chance were the only factor in determining our participants' responses. In this instance the probability that observations and expectations are the same is so remote that the value actually drops off the end of the scale as it were – and clearly well beyond the conventional .05 cut-off level. (Recall that extremely low probability values, indicating hugely significant effects, are often shown as .000, which should be expressed as .001.) Expressed formally, this is shown as,

$$\chi^2(2, N = 150) = 41.37, \quad p < .001$$

In our example chi-square tells us that the two personality types are not choosing randomly among the response alternatives. However, it does not tell us in what way actual choices are deviating from expectations: for this, inspection of the contingency table (Table 10.3) is necessary, which is why chi-square is rarely used on its own; the addition of a crosstabulation is needed to further explore the relationship between the two variables.

It is easy to appreciate how the contingency table (Table 10.3) can appear scary to the novice. There is a lot of information on offer but again, provided it is considered a piece at a time, it becomes manageable.

At the top and to the left of the cells in Table 10.3 the numbers simply refer to the numerical values assigned to each category. To the right and at the bottom are the sums of all the observations in each row or column, along with the corresponding percentage of the whole which they represent. It is inside the cells, though, that the most useful information is to be found.

Each cell contains four values, as follows:

> Count (the number of observations falling inside a particular cell)
> Expected count (the number of observations we would expect)
> Row percentage (% of each personality type responding in each category)
> Residual (observed values – expected values in each cell)

Taking the first cell in Table 10.3, the count is 7, representing the number of Type A individuals who chose the 'Never' response. Converted to a percentage of the entire group of Type As this is given as 9.3%. The expected value, however, if choice were a random event, is 25, producing a residual of $-18$. In other words, there are 18 fewer observations in this cell than would be expected. (The calculation of expected values is explained in the formula at equation 10.1.)

Normally statistical software presents only the count of observations in each cell, and additional information must be selected from the options when setting up the crosstabulation command. Of particular value is the residuals option, permitting the speedy identification of particular cells in which actual observations vary dramatically from expected values – particularly useful if we have to scan a very large table. In our example, the category 'Never' shows the greatest discrepancies, for both measures of personality.

Note: if at Step 3 we had also selected the option **Lambda**, we would have obtained additional information about the relationship between our two variables, under the heading **PRE (proportional reduction in error)**, which is yet another table available through the general crosstabulation menus. If this option is chosen, a measure of association will be offered, Lambda, which indicates how much our independent variable (personality type) actually predicts the dependent (response).

In our example shown in Table 10.5 the Lambda is given as 0.308 when 'satisfaction' is taken as the dependent variable in the analysis. This tells us that there is a 30% reduction in error in predicting the satisfaction response by knowing the personality type of the individual. (This is why Lambda is termed a Proportional Reduction in Error statistic.) If the two independent and dependent variables had been completely unrelated, the corresponding Lambda would have been 0.0, or thereabouts. (Note that the Lambda table allows for either factor to be taken as the dependent variable, in addition to a 'symmetric' value, which is a compromise between the two; in the context of this example though 'satisfaction' is deemed to be the appropriate outcome measure.)

This concludes our consideration of the category-category type of relationship, although this represents an introduction only and the crosstabulation procedure can be used for more sophisticated applications than we have offered here. For instance, our example

Table 10.5    Output 10.2.

Directional Measures

| | | | Value | Asymp. Std. Error | Approx. T | Approx. Sig. |
|---|---|---|---|---|---|---|
| Nominal by Nominal | Lambda | Symmetric | .386 | .066 | 4.957 | .000 |
| | | personality type Dependent | .480 | .068 | 5.598 | .000 |
| | | response to life satisfaction Q Dependent | .308 | .070 | 3.854 | .000 |
| | Goodman and Kruskal tau | personality type Dependent | .276 | .066 | | .000 |
| | | response to life satisfaction Q Dependent | .147 | .039 | | .000 |

has only considered two variables in its analysis – participants' personality type and response to a life satisfaction questionnaire item. We might have further analysed the link between these variables by a third, control variable, such as the gender. Hence we would have obtained outputs examining the personality-satisfaction relationship for males and the personality-satisfaction relationship for females. Finally it should be noted that the variables used in our example reflect the simplest of category types – in which one variable comprises two, and the other three categories. The crosstabulation procedure is equally relevant when our variables comprise many categories. We may, for instance, have explored people's life satisfaction by their astrological sign, in which case our independent variable would comprise twelve categories. Similarly, instead of 'never', 'occasionally' and 'all the time' variables, responses could have been reduced to the simpler Yes/No categories. There really is no limit in how sophisticated the nominal-nominal design can be. A quick guide to chi-square can be found in Box 10.1.

How To . . .

## Perform a chi-square analysis in SPSS

Step 1.  From the menu, select Analyze, Descriptive Statistics, then Crosstabs.

Step 2.  Enter the two variables to be evaluated, one into the **R**ow(s) box and one into the **C**olumn(s) box. If a control variable is to be included, select this third variable and transfer to the **L**ayer 1 of 1 box.

Step 3.  Click **S**tatistics and select **C**hi-square. If further information on the relationship between the variables is required, select also **L**ambda. Click **C**ontinue.

Step 4.  Click **C**ells and select the information required for each cell. At the very least **C**ount should be selected. Further selections might be **E**xpected, **r**esiduals and one of the **p**ercentages.

Step 5.  Inspect the output and note the **P**earson's chi-square. Note also the **l**ambda statistic.

## 10.2 Correlation

As we considered in Part 2, many studies will involve exploring the relationship between two interval-scaled variables. Relating working hours to stress levels is an example of such an approach, since both measures can vary along their own continua. Matching measures of extraversion to attention span is another and equating trait anxiety to different measures of blood pressure is a third. All these examples are similar in that they represent pairs of linked observations of continuous data, in the procedure termed correlation.

**Correlation** refers to the relationship between two continuous variables (co-relationships). Specifically, the variation in one variable is said to be associated with the other in some way, and the following example shows this.

Imagine that in our continuing interest in the phenomenon of road rage we have observed that, on a particular stretch of urban motorway, as traffic density rises the reported incidence of road rage also rises. That is, we have two variables which appear to be related, as in Table 10.6a.

Merely by inspection we suspect that there is a relationship between the two variables: as $x$ (traffic density) increases, $y$ (incidence of road rage) also tends to increase. By convention, this type of relationship is presented graphically, and usually in the form of a scatterplot, where each plot on the graph represents a pair of values – in the example below every plot represents a density value and its corresponding road rage value (see Figure 10.5).

In our previous discussion of descriptive statistics (see Part 4) we explained that there are three ways in which variables can be effectively described – by tables, by graphs and by statistics, and this is precisely the case with the data from correlational studies. The twin rows of data for traffic density and road rage shown in Table 10.6b represent the conventional tabular presentation of correlated variables, and it is important to realise that each pair of values actually represents a single observation, in which two measures were taken at the same time.

Inspection of the tabulated data suggests that some kind of relationship is present for as scores on one variable (traffic density) increase, so do scores on the other (incidence of

Table 10.6a    Variations in road rage with traffic density (vehicles per 300 metres).

| $x$ density | 10 | 12 | 15 | 15 | 20 | 25 | 26 | 28 | 29 | 30 |
|-------------|----|----|----|----|----|----|----|----|----|----|
| $y$ road rage | 5 | 4 | 5 | 6 | 6 | 10 | 20 | 19 | 25 | 26 |

Figure 10.5    Scatterplot showing the relationship between traffic density and road rage.

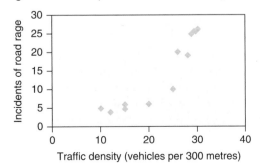

Table 10.6b    Details from Table 10.6a.

| Observation | Traffic density | Mean number of rage incidents |
| --- | --- | --- |
| 1 | 10 | 5 |
| 2 | 12 | 4 |

road rage). As we have observed, however, trends are not always immediately apparent through tables, especially with large amounts of data, and it sometimes requires the simplified but more immediately illustrative effect of a chart or figure to identify a pattern. Hence the scatterplot in Figure 10.5 demonstrates the general nature of the relationship – that as one variable increases, so does the other. Moreover, this pattern of change reflects a close link between the two variables since, for a given increase in density, there is a proportional – as opposed to a random or unpredictable – increase in reported rage.

In the language of correlation, the above example demonstrates a strong positive correlation: strong because as one variable changes, the other changes by a similar amount, and positive since as one variable changes the other changes in the same direction (i.e., as one increases, the other variable also increases). Box 10.2 reviews a number of examples previously introduced in Part 2, and demonstrates the different types of correlated relationships.

**Box 10.2**

A Closer Look At . . .

## Correlational relationships

Figure 10.6 illustrates a strong positive correlation between two variables.

Given the language of correlation introduced so far (i.e., strong, positive) it can be rightly assumed that correlations can also be weak, and negative. Generally speaking we would expect that those who indulge in regular weekly study time will perform better in

**Figure 10.6**    Scatterplot showing the relationship between study time and exam performance.

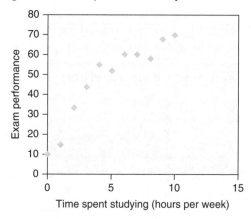

examinations than those of us whose idea of research is investigating how many pints of beer we can lift from a standard pub counter in a given evening. Compare Figure 10.6 with Figure 10.7:

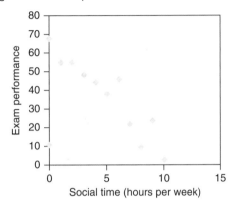

**Figure 10.7** Scatterplot showing the relationship between social time and exam performance.

In Figure 10.7 there is still a strong, but negative relationship between the two variables, insofar as when one variable changes the other changes by a similar amount. However, while one variable increases (social/pub time) the other one *decreases*. This will probably come as a great surprise to the majority of undergraduate students.

The final example, shown in Figure 10.8, illustrates a weak relationship.

Not surprisingly, taking varying amounts of exercise will have little or no effect on examination performance, indicated by the absence of any kind of pattern.

(Note: these examples have been exaggerated to illustrate particular points. With large databases it is not always possible to detect an obvious pattern from a scatterplot alone, although this is still usually more straightforward than trying to interpret a substantial table.)

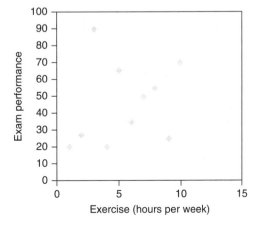

**Figure 10.8** Scatterplot showing the association between exercise and exam performance.

So far we have demonstrated two of the common methods for describing correlated data – tables and graphs. The third and final approach is that which attempts to represent and describe relationships through the use of symbols, and their related numerical values, in the form of statistics.

The convention for representing the relationship between two variables statistically employs the symbol $r$, which is an expression for the **coefficient of correlation**, from Pearson (1896). Its full title is the Pearson product–moment correlation, although today it is known more simply as Pearson's $r$, and in numerical terms it is expressed as a value ranging from $-1$ through 0 to $+1$, with the strength of a particular relationship indicated by how close the calculated value approaches $+/-1$. Weak relationships will of course be indicated by values closer to zero. The formula for calculating the statistic is given below, and the manual calculation for this example is shown. It is worth pointing out that, while the formula appears intimidating, the expressions which comprise it are actually quite straightforward. In any event, it is rare now for undergraduates to be expected to perform such calculations manually, the norm being – for better or worse – to rely on computer software.

$$r[\text{Pearson}] = \frac{\sum XY - \dfrac{\sum X \sum Y}{N}}{\sqrt{\left( \sum X^2 - \dfrac{(\sum X)^2}{N} \right)\left( \sum Y^2 - \dfrac{(\sum Y)^2}{N} \right)}} \tag{10.3}$$

where $X$ = the scores on one variable

$Y$ = the scores on the second variable

$N$ = the total number of cases

Substituting the values calculated in Table 10.7 into the formula, we have:

$$r[\text{Pearson}] = \frac{3240 - \dfrac{55 \times 524}{11}}{\sqrt{\left( 385 - \dfrac{3025}{11} \right)\left( 29032 - \dfrac{274576}{11} \right)}}$$

$$r = .93$$

Aside from providing a measure of the magnitude of a relationship, $r$ also describes the direction of a relationship. If the calculated value for $r$ is positive, this signifies that as one variable increases, so too does the other. The exercise and exam illustration in Box 10.2 (Figure 10.6) and at (10.3) is an example of a positive relationship. In fact, by inspecting the plots on the graph we can see that this is also a strong relationship, and the actual calculated value for $r$ in this instance is $+.93$. (Note that the data on which these illustrations are based are available on our companion website. See *MKexam_study* data.)

Negative values for $r$ indicate that, as one variable increases, the other decreases, as in the social time and exam illustration in Box 10.2 (Figure 10.7). Here, as the time spent on social indulgence increases, exam performance, as expected, decreases. The actual value in this hypothetical example is $-.90$.

The third and final chart in the sequence (Figure 10.8) demonstrates a poor relationship – as one variable increases (exercise) the other variable seems to vary independently. The actual value of $r$ here is $+.002$, an extremely weak relationship in which the sign ($+$ or $-$) is largely irrelevant. The computation of correlation in SPSS is considered later in this chapter, along with the way correlation should be reported.

**Table 10.7**    Raw data on study time and exam performance with summary statistics for the computation of Pearson's *r*.

| Study time | | Exam performance | | |
| x | x² | y | y² | xy |
|---|---|---|---|---|
| 0 | 0 | 10 | 100 | 0 |
| 1 | 1 | 15 | 225 | 15 |
| 2 | 4 | 33 | 1089 | 66 |
| 3 | 9 | 44 | 1936 | 132 |
| 4 | 16 | 55 | 3025 | 220 |
| 5 | 25 | 52 | 2704 | 260 |
| 6 | 36 | 60 | 3600 | 360 |
| 7 | 49 | 60 | 3600 | 420 |
| 8 | 64 | 58 | 3364 | 464 |
| 9 | 81 | 67 | 4489 | 603 |
| 10 | 100 | 70 | 4900 | 700 |

$\Sigma x = 55$

$(\Sigma x)^2 = 3025$

$\Sigma x^2 = 385$

$\Sigma y = 524$

$(\Sigma y)^2 = 274576$

$\Sigma y^2 = 29032$

$\Sigma xy = 3240$

$n = 11$

## 10.3  Simple regression

One of the problems with correlation is that with large numbers of observations (anything from 50 and above) even the normally effective scatterplot might fail to identify any obvious trend in terms of the association between variables. Certainly the correlation coefficient, if calculated, will tell us whether an association is positive or negative and we could inspect the magnitude of the calculated statistic as a guide to the strength of the relationship. Another difficulty is that, while we are always reluctant to suggest a causal link between two correlated variables, we often wish to make use of one variable as a predictor of the other. In general terms we can predict that (from Figure 10.6) the more we study the better we will do in exams, but what we cannot do is predict a specific exam mark from a given length of study. At least, not from the scatterplot, nor from the correlation coefficient. What we need is the **regression line**.

The regression line, sometimes known as the line of best fit, or the least squares line of regression, acts in much the same way as a mean for a single variable. Just like the mean, the regression line expresses the typical relationship between two variables, and just like the mean of a single variable, there is no requirement that any of the correlated observations actually fall on the regression line. The example in Figure 10.9 offers an illustration.

Figure 10.9 Association between study time and exam performance with three proposed best-fitting lines.

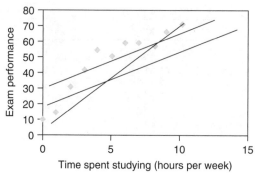

Figure 10.9, based on the data shown in Table 10.7, shows the association between study time and exam performance. If we were required, for example, to predict the exam performance for a study time of 5 hours though, we would not be able to do so, at least not with any precision. What is needed is a straight line which best expresses the relationship between study time and performance. We could try drawing such a line manually, by inspection, but as Figure 10.9 demonstrates, this is never easy and it is impossible to determine which of the three lines shown would best fit the data. How we do this is illustrated in Figure 10.10.

Needless to say, no one actually performs such a tedious procedure and conventionally the regression line is determined using the formula for a straight line, given as:

$$y = a + bx \text{ or } y = bx + a \tag{10.4}$$

in which $a$ is the y-intercept (the point where the line will intersect the y-axis, or, alternatively, the value for $y$ when $x = 0$) and $b$ is a measure of the slope of the line, or, alternatively, the amount of change in the $y$ variable for every unit change in $x$. Essentially what this formula gives us is a starting point for our regression line, plus a value for any other point along the line. Enough to extrapolate the full length of the line.

Figure 10.10 Illustration of a procedure for drawing the regression line. If we were to draw various lines which appear to fit the data plots, then measure the distance between each point and line, both above and below, square these values, then the line which best balances (minimises) the squared distances above and below, will be the best-fitting line.

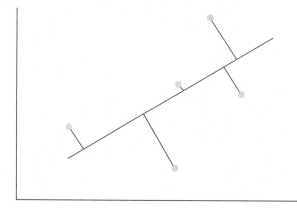

The formulae for determining $a$ and $b$ appear intimidating at first, but closer inspection reveals that most of the expressions are already available once the original correlation has been calculated.

$$b = \frac{\Sigma XY - \left(\frac{\Sigma X \Sigma Y}{N}\right)}{\Sigma X^2 - \frac{(\Sigma X)^2}{N}} \qquad (10.5)$$

The formula for $a$ is now easily calculated, using elements which are readily available:

$$a = \frac{\Sigma Y - b\Sigma X}{N} \qquad (10.6)$$

Using the data in Table 10.7, we substitute into the formulae at (10.5) and (10.6) as follows:

$$b = \frac{3240 - \frac{55 \times 524}{11}}{385 - \frac{3025}{11}} = 5.64$$

$$a = \frac{524 - 5.64(55)}{11} = 19.44$$

The formula $y = a + bx$ becomes $y = 19.44 + 5.64x$. This informs us that the point at which the regression line crossed the $y$-axis is 19.44, and the slope of the line is 5.64. This means that for every unit (hour) of study time, exam performance increases by 5.64 marks. Figure 10.11 illustrates this.

A more precise way of showing how this line is drawn manually is merely to calculate any other point on the line. Given that we already know the origin ($a$) a second point

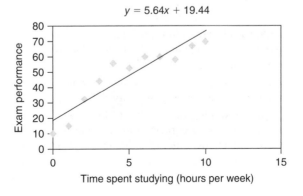

**Figure 10.11**  Scatterplot showing the association between study time and exam performance with the best-fitting line of regression and the regression equation shown.

$y = 5.64x + 19.44$

**Figure 10.12** Detail from Figure 10.11 showing the y-intercept (circled) and the predicted y-value for x = 10 (circled).

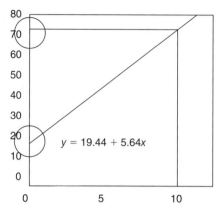

is sufficient to draw the full line. If we take a measure of 10 for $x$, then substituting into our regression formula we have,

$y = 19.44 + 5.64(10)$
$y = 19.44 + 56.4$
$y = 75.84$

Figure 10.12 illustrates the relationship between the calculated value and the plotted data. The intercept is circled and is a good match for the value given in the formula (19.44), and the predicted value for $y$, when $x$ is given as 10, is also a good match for the calculated value (75.84).

## 10.4 The coefficient of determination

The application of regression to predict a value for $y$ from a given value for $x$ is undoubtedly a useful development of the correlation coefficient. However, many undergraduates often assume that just because we *can* predict one value from another, such prediction is reliable and accurate, often forgetting that the original correlation on which the regression analysis is based might not be particularly strong. A useful method for interpreting the association between two variables, as expressed in the regression equation, is to calculate the **coefficient of determination**. This is the simplest of all procedures and requires only that we square the correlation value. Thus, a correlation given as $r = .5$, would become $r^2 = .25$. Interpretation is equally straightforward, with the $r^2$ value providing a measure of the proportion (or percentage) of one variable which can be predicted (or determined) by the other. In the case of our study time – exam example, the correlation of .93 becomes $r^2 = .86$, informing us that 86% of the variation in exam performance can be predicted by study time. Therefore, prediction of exam success based on the regression equation will be pretty good. On the other hand, had the correlation been .5, with a corresponding $r^2$ of .25, we would be less confident in being able to predict exam scores from study time alone, since apparently 75% of the variation in exam scores is determined by other factors.

The procedures for calculating correlations and the regression equation are shown below, based on the MK exam-study data. These data are also shown in Table 10.7.

Step 1.   From the menu, select <u>A</u>nalyze, <u>C</u>orrelate, then <u>B</u>ivariate (Figure 10.13).

Step 2.   In the Bivariate Correlations set-up window, select from the variable list on the left, the two variables to feature in the analysis, and transfer them to the **Variables** box on the right. Note that the Pearson correlation is already selected. Click OK (Figure 10.14).

Step 3.   Inspect the output (Table 10.8). Note the duplication: study time is correlated with exam and exam with study time. Note also that any variable correlated with itself gives a value of 1, which can be ignored. The correlation is given as $r = .927$, which matches our earlier manual calculation. A significance value is given for this correlation, and the sample size is also shown.

Figure 10.13

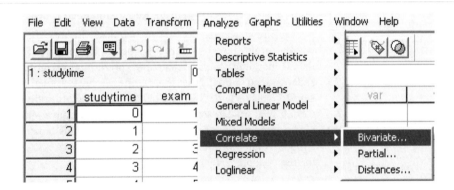

Figure 10.14

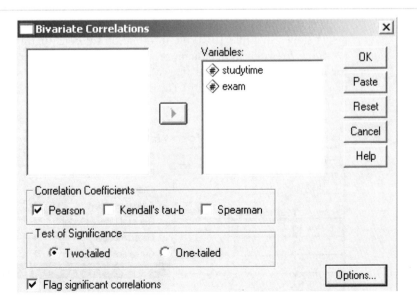

Table 10.8     Output 10.3.

Correlations

|  |  | studytime | exam |
|---|---|---|---|
| studytime | Pearson Correlation | 1 | .927** |
|  | Sig. (2-tailed) |  | .000 |
|  | N | 11 | 11 |
| exam | Pearson Correlation | .927** | 1 |
|  | Sig. (2-tailed) | .000 |  |
|  | N | 11 | 11 |

**Correlation is significant at the 0.01 level (2-tailed).

This is expressed formally as,

$$r = .93, \quad p < .001 \text{ (two-tailed)}, \quad n = 11$$

To perform a simple regression analysis on the same data, follow the steps below:

Step 1.    From the menu select Analyze, Regression, then Linear (see Figure 10.15).

Step 2.    In the Linear Regression set-up window (Figure 10.16), select the variable which might be considered to be a dependent variable and transfer to the Dependent box. Select the predictor variable and transfer to the Independent(s) box. Note that, while we have argued that correlations do not signify causality, SPSS nonetheless uses the terminology of cause-and-effect. Certainly it makes some sense to do it as we have shown. Note also that the set-up window appears somewhat daunting. This is because the procedure is a simpler version of the more complex multiple regression which is considered in the next chapter.

Step 3.    Click OK and inspect the output.

The regression output shown is a detail from the full SPSS output. In the model summary shown in Table 10.9 the relevant information is the value for $R$, which is the correlation value and given as .927. The value for $r^2$ (expressed as $R$ square) is .858. In the coefficients shown in Table 10.10 the information for constructing the regression equation ($y = a + bx$) is given in column $B$ of the Unstandardised Coefficients sector. The value for $a$ is the (Constant), and the value for $b$ is adjacent to study time. The equation becomes: $y = 19.455 + 5.636x$. The rest of the table can be ignored for the time being.

Figure 10.15

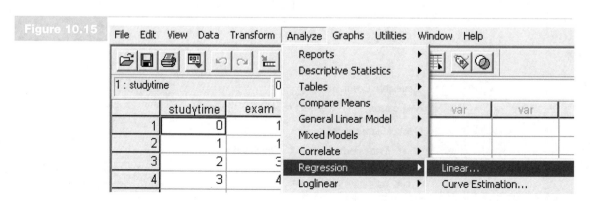

Figure 10.16

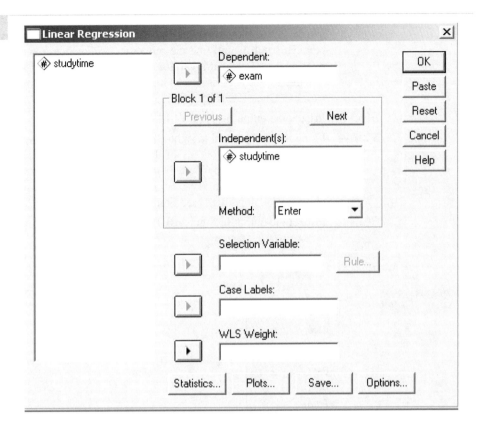

Table 10.9   Output 10.4.

Model Summary

| Model | R | R Square | Adjusted R Square | Std. Error of the Estimate |
|---|---|---|---|---|
| 1 | .927[a] | .858 | .843 | 1.315 |

[a] Predictors: (Constant). exam

Table 10.10

Coefficients[a]

| Model | | Unstandardized Coefficients | | Standardized Coefficients | t | Sig. |
|---|---|---|---|---|---|---|
| | | B | Std. Error | Beta | | |
| 1 | (Constant) | 19.455 | 4.513 | | 4.311 | .002 |
| | studytime | 5.636 | .763 | .927 | 7.389 | .000 |

[a] Dependent Variable: exam

Producing a scatterplot of the correlated variables and fitting the regression line is accomplished as follows:

Step 1.   From the menu, select <u>G</u>raphs and then <u>S</u>catter. The Scatterplot selection window opens. **S**imple is already selected; click **D**efine.

**Step 2.** In the <u>S</u>imple Scatterplot set-up window (Figure 10.17), select the variable which will be plotted on the *y*-axis (the vertical axis) and transfer to the **Y** Axis box. This will usually be the outcome, or dependent variable in a correlated relationship. Select the variable to be plotted on the *x*-axis (horizontal) and transfer to the **X** Axis box. This is usually the predictor, or the independent variable. Click OK (Figure 10.18).

**Step 3.** Inspect the output in Figure 10.19.

**Step 4.** Using the cursor, double right-click within the graph. This opens a graph editor window. Click once on any of the plot marks within the graph, open <u>C</u>hart in the menu, select <u>A</u>dd Chart Element, then select <u>F</u>it Line at Total. Closing the window returns to the SPSS output showing the original scatterplot with the regression line now fitted (see Figure 10.20).

**Step 5.** Inspect the output in Figure 10.21.

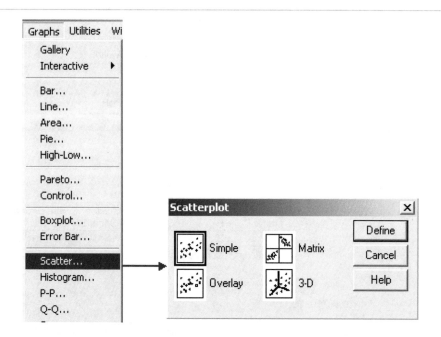

Figure 10.17

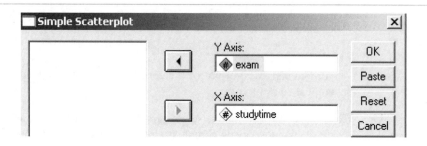

Figure 10.18

**Figure 10.19**    Output 10.4.

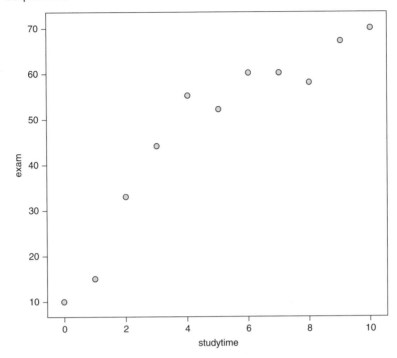

**Figure 10.20**

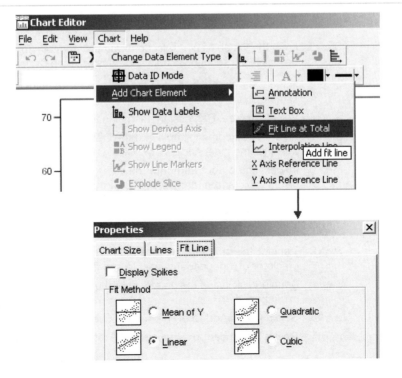

**Figure 10.21**    Output 10.5.

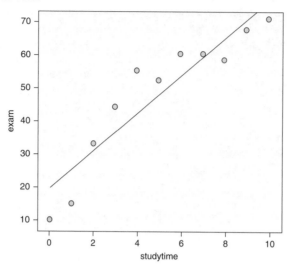

A quick guide to carrying out a correlation and simple regression is shown in Box 10.3.

Box 10.3

## How To . . .

# Perform correlation and simple regression in SPSS

Step 1.   Select <u>A</u>nalyze, <u>C</u>orrelate, then <u>B</u>ivariate.

Step 2.   From the **V**ariables box select one variable and transfer to the **I**ndependent(s) box. Select a second variable and transfer to the **D**ependents box. Click OK.

Step 3.   Inspect the output and note the value for *r*, the significance value and the sample size.

Step 4.   Select <u>A</u>nalyze, <u>R</u>egression, then <u>L</u>inear.

Step 5.   Enter the outcome variable into the **D**ependent box, and the predictor variable into the **I**ndependent box. Click OK.

Step 6.   Inspect the output and note the value for *r* and for $r^2$. Inspect the Coefficients table and under Column B of the Unstandardised Coefficients, note the value for *a* adjacent the (Constant) and the value for *b* adjacent the predictor variable.

Step 7.   Select <u>G</u>raph, <u>S</u>catterplot, <u>S</u>imple, and then <u>D</u>efine.

Step 8.   Transfer the outcome or dependent variable into the **Y** Axis box, and the predictor or independent variable into the **X** Axis box. Click OK.

Step 9.   Double-click inside the boundary of the scatterplot. Single-click on any plot marker.

Step 10.   Select <u>C</u>hart, <u>A</u>dd Chart Element, <u>F</u>it Line at Total.

Step 11.   Check the **Linear** box, then click the **F**it Line box. Close the window.

Chapter 10 has explored the types of analyses appropriate for research designs in which, rather than differences between groups or conditions, the aim is to examine relationships between variables. However, the procedures outlined here represent only the beginnings of what can be done with correlation and regression and while the coverage of Chapter 10 will be more than adequate for the majority of undergraduate research projects, for those of you interested in something more complicated and sophisticated, the next chapter introduces what we have referred to as advanced analyses.

## Suggested further reading

Howell, D. C. (1997). *Statistical methods for psychology* (4th ed.). Belmont, CA: Duxbury.

There are many textbooks currently available on statistics, but this one by Douglas Howell is probably one of the most accessible. The material is far from simple but the style is straightforward and clearly written with an understanding of the trepidation with which most undergraduates approach statistics. Aside from covering all the major tests, Howell also provides the mathematical background to the different procedures.

Kinnear, P. R., & Gray, C. D. (2000). *SPSS for Windows made simple: Release 10*. Hove, East Sussex: Psychology Press Ltd.

This text remains the essential manual for anyone struggling with SPSS – procedures for almost every test you will need to use are offered here, along with explanations of the often cumbersome output provided by SPSS.

# 11 Advanced analysis: Two-way ANOVA, partial correlation and multiple regression

## Key Issues

In Chapter 11 we consider the types of analyses appropriate for more complex research designs. Studies exploring the effects of several independent variables are considered, detailed SPSS procedures are outlined and the complex output from such analyses is explained. Given the demanding nature of these procedures we have provided a broad range of illustrations and a comprehensive series of screenshots. Topics include:

- two-way ANOVA
- locating effects in ANOVA
- partial correlations
- multiple regression

## 11.1 Two-way ANOVA

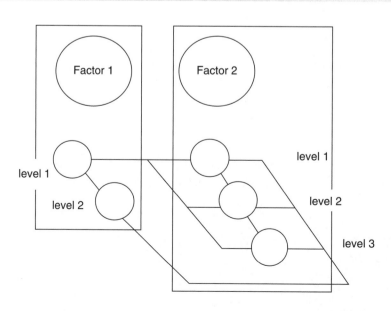

Just as it is common for independent variables to comprise more than two categories, so it is often the case that a study comprises more than one independent variable. In Part 2, considerable discussion was offered on this issue, with particular attention paid to the problem of whether the existence of several independent variables should be dealt with by controls, or by incorporating them into the design. In the event that we decide that more than one factor is having an effect on some outcome measure, and providing these factors are nominal in character, we are led once again towards analysis of variance.

In the case of more than one causal factor, successive one-way ANOVAs are as inappropriate as repeated *t*-tests would be to test a single factor containing more than two categories, and for the same reasons – sooner or later, successive tests will throw up an apparent significant finding which is really a naturally occurring though rare event (Type I error). Moreover, when two or more factors are impinging on a dependent variable, it will often be the case that they will not do so independently, having rather an interactive or **interaction effect**. Once again, the notion of interacting factors is discussed in Part 2 and ought to be reviewed if this idea is causing confusion.

If our design is of this more complex variety, the type of ANOVA required is termed a **two-way ANOVA** (or sometimes factorial or multi-factor ANOVA). A two-way ANOVA is a parametric test in which different levels of two or more factors are compared on some dependent measure. An example follows.

Assume that in a study previously outlined, in which psychological wellbeing is thought to be related to particular levels of exercise, we are subsequently led to suspect the presence of a second factor which might affect wellbeing – a personality variable encountered previously as the Type A/Type B distinction. Now the prediction might be that the competitive element in the Type A personality would interact with exercise to have an effect on wellbeing scores, in a way that Type B would not. Or stated more simply, the effects of exercise on wellbeing would vary according to personality type.

The ANOVA logic is the same as in the one-way case, with multiple conditions being compared in terms of variance and the procedure is as follows, based on the *MKp_ex_wellbeing* data.

Step 1. From the menu, select Analyze, General Linear Model, then Univariate (see Figure 11.1).

Step 2. In the Univariate set-up window, select from the variable window on the left the dependent variable in the analysis and transfer to the **Dependent Variable** box. Transfer the independent variables in the analysis into the **Fixed Factor(s)** box. Click OK (Figure 11.2).

Figure 11.1

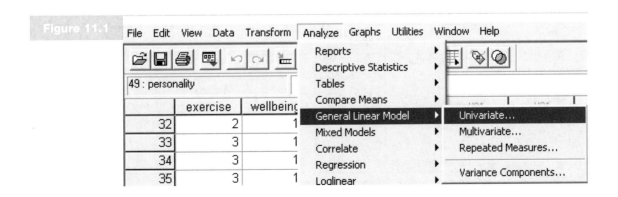

**Figure 11.2**

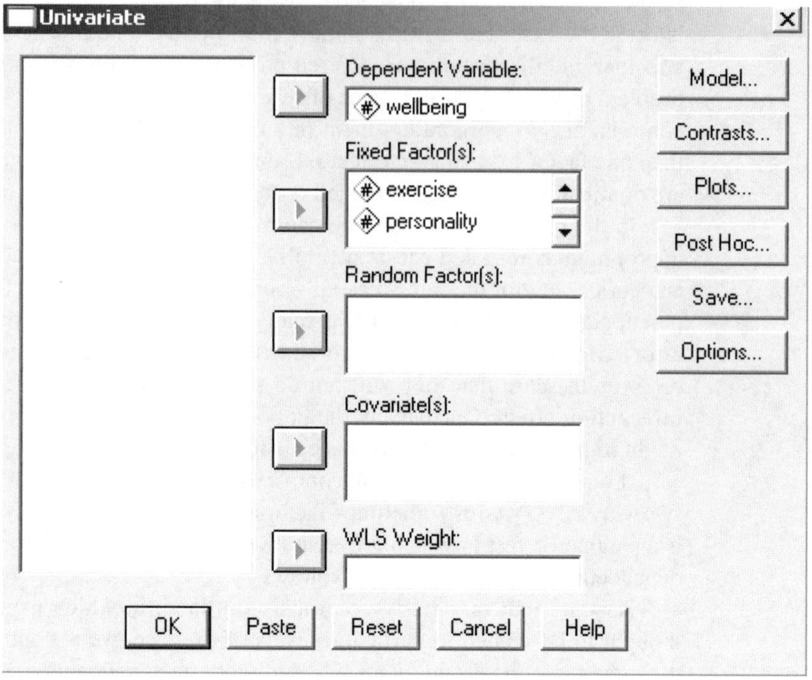

Step 3.  Inspect the output in Table 11.1.

The multifactor output is similar to that from the one-way analysis, except there is more of it, as one might expect. The key difference is that there are three elements to the more sophisticated output. The first deals with an overall effect in which all combinations of exercise level and personality type are considered. This is given as the **corrected model** and there are 6 ($2 \times 3$) possible combinations here, hence the degrees of freedom are shown as 5, and the significance level given is .008. This is expressed formally as,

$$F(5, 42) = 3.61, \quad p = .008$$

**Table 11.1**    Output 11.1.

Tests of Between-Subjects Effects

Dependent Variable: wellbeing

| Source | Type III Sum of Squares | df | Mean Square | F | Sig. |
|---|---|---|---|---|---|
| Corrected Model | 84.000[a] | 5 | 16.800 | 3.614 | .008 |
| Intercept | 14076.750 | 1 | 14076.750 | 3028.033 | .000 |
| exercise | 45.125 | 2 | 22.563 | 4.853 | .013 |
| personality | 2.083 | 1 | 2.083 | .448 | .507 |
| exercise* personality | 36.792 | 2 | 18.396 | 3.957 | .027 |
| Error | 195.250 | 42 | 4.649 | | |
| Total | 14356.000 | 48 | | | |
| Corrected Total | 279.250 | 47 | | | |

a. R Squared = .301 (Adjusted R Squared = .218)

Box 11.1

## How To . . .

# Compute a two-way ANOVA in SPSS

Step 1.  Select Analyze, General Linear Model, then Univariate.

Step 2.  From the variable list, transfer the dependent variable in the analysis to the **D**ependent Variable box.

Step 3.  Transfer the independent variables in the analysis to the **F**ixed Factor(s) box.

Step 4.  Inspect the output for an overall effect, shown in the **Corrected model**; for **Main effects**; for an **Interaction effect**.

Therefore, somewhere within our analysis there is a significant effect. The second element concerns **main effects**, which describe the impact of each factor, or independent variable, on its own. In this case, the table informs us that there is a significant main effect of the variable 'exercise' (significance value .013). This is expressed formally as,

$$F(2, 42) = 4.85, \quad p = .013$$

'Personality', however, has almost no impact whatsoever on wellbeing scores (significance value .507). As previously, we use the .05 level as our critical significance value. This is expressed formally as,

$$F(2, 42) = 0.45, \quad p = .507$$

The third major element in the multifactor output examines interactions. In this case, however, we can see that the effect of exercise on wellbeing is modified by the personality type of participants (significance value .027). We interpret this to mean that exercise is a key determinant of psychological wellbeing, but that its effects are modified by the personality type of the individual. At least, according to this particular study. This is expressed formally as,

$$F(2, 42) = 3.96, \quad p = .027$$

Box 11.1 explains how to compute a two-way ANOVA in SPSS.

## 11.2  Locating an effect in ANOVA

In Chapter 9, in which ANOVA was introduced, it was explained that this procedure will determine that a significant effect exists among a number of comparisons, but not where this effect is. What the present example indicates is that a significant difference in wellbeing measures was detected somewhere among the three different exercise categories and that exercise interacted with personality type in some way. What we really want to know, however, is which of these groups was significantly different from another. If there had been no interaction and only two groups in our exercise factor there would be no problem: as with the *t*-test, a significant finding is easily explained in terms of the

Table 11.2    Output 11.2 – Descriptive Statistics.

**Dependent Variable: wellbeing**

| Exercise | Personality | Mean | Std. Deviation | N |
|---|---|---|---|---|
| No exercise | Type A | 17.50 | 2.000 | 8 |
| | Type B | 19.38 | 1.188 | 8 |
| | Total | 18.44 | 1.861 | 16 |
| Moderate exercise | Type A | 16.50 | 2.330 | 8 |
| | Type B | 15.75 | 1.389 | 8 |
| | Total | 16.12 | 1.893 | 16 |
| Intensive exercise | Type A | 18.00 | 2.777 | 8 |
| | Type B | 15.63 | 2.722 | 8 |
| | Total | 16.81 | 2.926 | 16 |
| Total | Type A | 17.33 | 2.371 | 24 |
| | Type B | 16.92 | 2.535 | 24 |
| | Total | 17.13 | 2.438 | 48 |

difference between the two means, and inspection of descriptive statistics would be sufficient to determine the direction of the difference. However, in the case of three or more groups within a factor it is not so easy, and with two factors interacting it becomes quite problematic.

Consulting a table of means is not a particularly satisfactory way of trying to locate effects when there are multiple factors, or multiple levels within factors, although many undergraduates do precisely this in order to explain an ANOVA finding. Table 11.2 is produced by selecting Options at Step 2 of the procedure outlined in Box 11.1, then checking **D**escriptive for the Exercise × Personality interaction.

A table of means on its own is clearly not enough – just by looking at how the means of groups differ will not tell us if the significant difference was, say, between Type As taking no exercise and Type Bs taking intensive exercise, or whatever. An alternative to inspecting means is to generate a figure in which the pattern of effects might become more obvious. This still doesn't tell us where the significant difference is but a figure will often illustrate the nature of an interaction more clearly than will a table, and for this reason inspection of the graph for a two-way ANOVA is extremely useful.

Step 1.    From the menu, select **G**raphs, **L**ine, then **M**ultiple. Click **D**efine (Figure 11.3).

Step 2.    In the **D**efine Multiple Line window (Figure 11.4), click the **O**ther summary function button, select the dependent variable in the analysis from the variables window on the left and transfer it to the **V**ariable box.

Select one of the factor variables and transfer to the **C**ategory Axis box. Transfer the other factor variable to the **D**efine Lines by box. Click OK.

Step 3.    Inspect the output in Figure 11.5.

Inspection of the graph suggests there is some difference between the two personality types taking no or moderate exercise, but that the difference is considerable for those taking intensive exercise. The pattern is clearer and most undergraduates will be content to leave the analysis at this stage. However, we can take one more step, and it is a somewhat

Figure 11.3

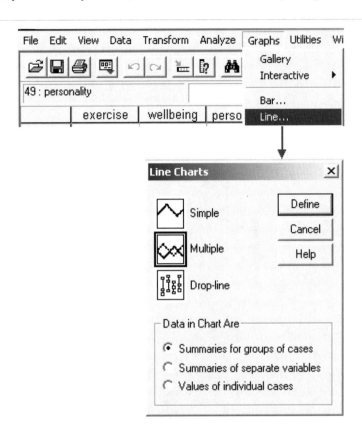

Figure 11.4

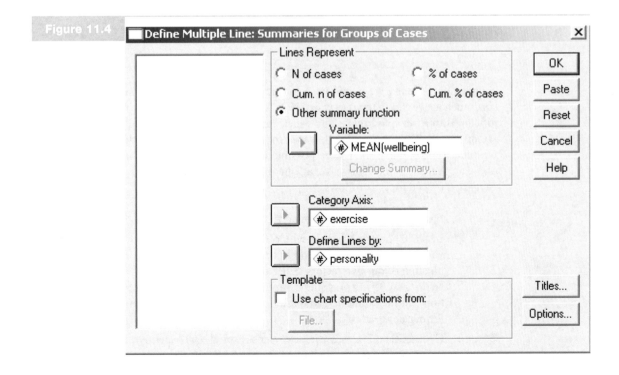

**Figure 11.5**     Output 11.3.

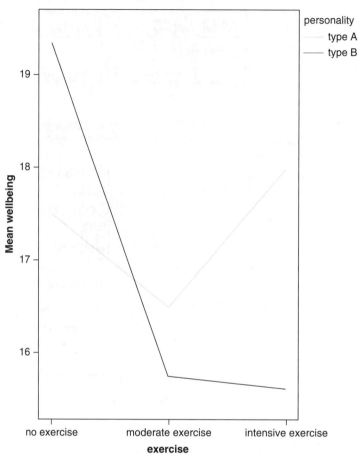

complex one. Ideally we would wish to carry out some form of multiple group comparison, much as we did in the one-way ANOVA example. A post hoc test would identify significant differences and make allowance for the increased likelihood of a Type I error. Unfortunately SPSS makes no allowance for multiple comparisons in the two-way case so we need to be creative. If it were possible to reorganise our data so that it looks like a one-way ANOVA, then we have at our disposal the full range of post hoc tests. A suggested procedure is as follows:

Step 1.    From the menu, select Transform, then Compute (Figure 11.6).

Step 2.    In the Compute Variable window (Figure 11.7), type in the name for a new variable which we are going to create. This variable will comprise every combination of our two factors. Since this example is for a $2 \times 3$ ANOVA, there will be six new levels of a single variable. We have called the new variable 'condition'. In the Numeric Expression box type '1'. This will be the first condition for our new variable.

Step 3.    Click If. The If Cases window opens. Here we will identify the particular combination from the original two factors which will comprise the first condition in

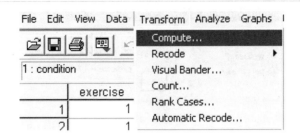

Figure 11.6

our new variable. Condition 1 will comprise those taking no exercise (1) who are also Type A (1). This can be typed directly or the virtual keypad can be used. Click Continue (Figure 11.8).

Step 4. Click OK when returned to the Compute Variable window. This returns the Data window, and shows the first condition in the new variable (Figure 11.9).

Step 5. Repeat Steps 1 through 4, this time changing the Numeric Expression to 2 (Step 2), and changing the combination of levels in the If cases window to exercise = 1 and personality = 2. At Step 4, you will be prompted to 'Replace existing variable' to which the response is 'Yes'. The data spreadsheet will now show two conditions for the new variable.

Step 6. Repeat until all six levels of the new variable have been established.

Step 7. In Variable View, use the Value Labels function to identify the different levels of the new factor. For instance, the value 1 might become 'noex/typeA', identifying those Type A individuals in the no exercise condition. Value 2 might become 'noex/typeB', and so on. While not an essential step for computational purposes it is important in that it allows you to interpret output tables; consider Table 11.4 where the descriptive labels make it clear where the significant differences occur.

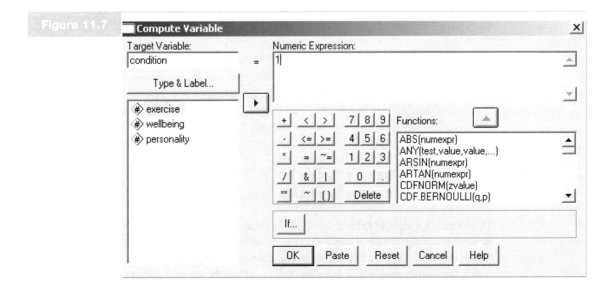

Figure 11.7

**Figure 11.8**

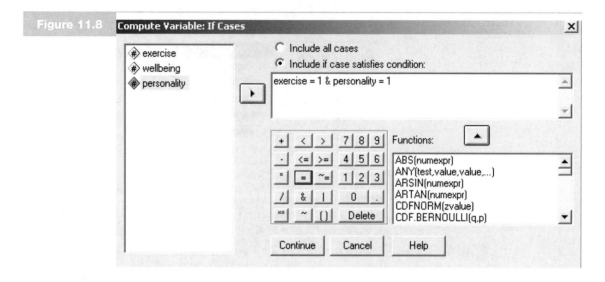

**Figure 11.9**

|    | exercise | wellbeing | personality | condition |
|----|----------|-----------|-------------|-----------|
| 1  | 1        | 15        | 1           | 1.00      |
| 2  | 1        | 16        | 1           | 1.00      |
| 3  | 1        | 20        | 1           | 1.00      |
| 4  | 1        | 19        | 1           | 1.00      |
| 5  | 1        | 16        | 1           | 1.00      |
| 6  | 1        | 18        | 1           | 1.00      |
| 7  | 1        | 20        | 1           | 1.00      |
| 8  | 1        | 16        | 1           | 1.00      |
| 9  | 1        | 18        | 2           | .         |
| 10 | 1        | 21        | 2           | .         |

Step 8. Perform a one-way ANOVA as in Chapter 9 and select the **Tukey HSD** test from the **Post** hoc option.

Step 9. Inspect the output: Table 11.3 is the standard ANOVA table, which confirms the findings in our earlier analysis. The probability value for the *F*-ratio is the same as the overall value computed for the two-way ANOVA (.008). This is an important check and indicates whether the complicated transformation outlined above has been successful. It also confirms that the principle of modifying the format of the data to fit a one-way model is a valid one.

Step 10. Inspect the paired comparison table.

This detail is a sample from a much more comprehensive tabular output. SPSS assists us in identifying significant comparisons with an asterisk (*). Thus we see that in our study which explored the relationship between exercise level, personality type and wellbeing, significant differences occur between the mean wellbeing score of participants in the no

Table 11.3    Output 11.4.

ANOVA

wellbeing

|  | Sum of Squares | df | Mean Square | F | Sig. |
|---|---|---|---|---|---|
| Between Groups | 84.000 | 5 | 16.800 | 3.614 | .008 |
| Within Groups | 195.250 | 42 | 4.649 |  |  |
| Total | 279.250 | 47 |  |  |  |

Table 11.4    Output 11.5 – Multiple comparisons.

Dependent Variable: wellbeing
Tukey HSD

| (I) condition | (J) condition | Mean Difference (I − J) | Std. Error | Sig. | 95% Confidence Interval | |
|---|---|---|---|---|---|---|
|  |  |  |  |  | Lower Bound | Upper Bound |
| noex/typeB | noex/typeA | 1.875 | 1.078 | .515 | −1.34 | 5.09 |
|  | modex/typeA | 2.875 | 1.078 | .104 | −.34 | 6.09 |
|  | modex/typeB | 3.625* | 1.078 | .019 | .41 | 6.84 |
|  | intex/typeA | 1.375 | 1.078 | .796 | −1.84 | 4.59 |
|  | intex/typeB | 3.750* | 1.078 | .014 | .53 | 6.97 |

*The mean difference is significant at the .05 level.

exercise/Type B condition and the mean wellbeing score of participants in the moderate exercise/Type B condition ($p = .019$) and between the mean wellbeing score of participants in the no exercise/Type B and the mean wellbeing score of participants in the intensive exercise/Type B condition ($p = .014$). No other significant differences were observed. It is worth noting that since post hoc tests are conservative, effects which we might anticipate from inspection of a figure, for instance, often disappear once allowance is made for repeated paired comparisons.

## 11.3 Partial correlation

Once we understand that any event in the psychological world (an outcome measure, or dependent variable) is unlikely to be determined by just one causal factor (independent variable, or predictor), we are closer to appreciating the real world than when our explorations were based on the single independent variable–single dependent variable scenario. Accepting this level of complexity in life requires an equally complex method of analysis. We have already encountered one such sophisticated approach in the two-way ANOVA, which has the potential for exploring the effects of many predictors on some outcome measure. ANOVA, as we now appreciate, is the preferred approach when our predictors are nominal or ordinal (category) in nature. When our predictors are interval (continuous), we are in the realm of correlation and regression.

There are two approaches we can adopt to the many-predictor/one outcome case, and the decision on which to choose is based largely on what the researcher is trying to do. For example, returning to our earlier road rage study, we may have ascertained from various sources (previous research, an exploratory study or issues raised during a focus group session with convicted offenders) that a number of things are likely to be linked, causally, to incidents of aggressive driver behaviour. These might be vehicle density, temperature, personality and driving experience. If the point of our study is to explore the combined effects of all these factors on road rage, or to determine the relative contributions of each on the outcome measure, then our approach is that of multiple regression. We have already observed that, in simple regression (see Chapter 10) we can state how much variation in an outcome measure is predicted by an independent variable. Multiple regression allows us to do the same, but with many (multiple) predictors. Similarly, we have noted that, in simple regression, the regression coefficient ($b$, in the regression formula, $y = a + bx$) provides a measure of how much a dependent variable changes for a given change in a predictor. The same is true for multiple predictors – with multiple regression we can identify the relative contribution of each factor, in addition to determining whether or not such contributions are statistically significant.

Supposing, however, that our research aim differs from the multiple predictor case. Imagine that a city planning department, charged with developing a new traffic system which, among other things, would minimise the incidence of dangerous road rage, identifies the same factors as likely contributors to this particular type of aggressive driving behaviour. Undoubtedly driver experience will play a part, as will personality. There is evidence that rage also varies with temperature, but these are all factors beyond the control of the planning unit. So what if research indicates that high-scoring extraverts feature most often in incidents of road rage – are the planners going to insist that drivers take an extraversion test before being allowed inside the city boundaries? Or will traffic barriers go up when temperatures rise above 20 degrees? Unlikely. However, it is within the ability of the planners to control traffic density, via speed limits, filter systems, CCTV and warning signs. To justify the expense, though, they need to know the precise contribution of the density factor – would it be the case that, once the effects of the other factors were removed, traffic density still remained a major influence of road rage? To test this, the planners have to examine the correlation between density and rage, with all the other factors removed. The procedure is termed **partial correlation**, a correlation between two variables from which the effects of a third have been statistically removed.

Conventional bivariate correlation explores a relationship between two variables, expressing this as a correlation coefficient ($r$). By way of illustration, we may note that the incidence of street muggings seems to rise every time there is an increase in sunspot activity. If this relationship is noted over a 10-month period and a correlation performed, we might demonstrate that $r = .895$. This is significant and, if squared, would allow us to argue that approximately 80% of variation in muggings can be explained by changes in sunspot activity. Impressive, one would think.

Supposing, however, that it is pointed out to us that the rate of muggings also varies with temperature ($r = .903$), and, moreover, that sunspot activity also varies with temperature ($r = .938$). This presents us with something of a problem – since all three variables are intercorrelated, it is possible that the apparent relationship between any two is exaggerated. More specifically, since temperature correlates with sunspot activity, and sunspot activity correlates with the rate of muggings, some of the variation in muggings presumably can be explained by temperature. The following diagram (Figure 11.10) might clarify this.

The illustration shows that the amount of variation in muggings explained solely by sunspot activity is in the region A. That explained by temperature is the region B. The variation

Figure 11.10

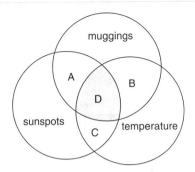

within region D is explained by a combination of sunspots and temperature. Therefore, the correlation between sunspot and muggings is exaggerated by the region D, part of which is attributable to temperature. Thus, if we were to remove the obscuring effect of temperature we would find that the true sunspot effect is less: A rather than the original A + D.

We can see in Output 11.6 in Table 11.5 the zero-order correlation between muggings, sunspots and temperature. It is termed zero-order since this is the basic correlation with nothing removed, or controlled for. (Note that this example is presented for illustrative purposes and we would suggest that, practically, such a small sample would not contribute to a credible analysis.) The computations for both zero-order and partial correlation are performed by following the steps as shown:

Step 1. From the menu select Analyze, Correlate, then Bivariate (Figure 11.11).

Step 2. Enter all the variables which are to be intercorrelated into the **Variables** box. Click OK (Figure 11.12).

Step 3. Inspect the output. Note that a significant correlation is present between each pair of variables (Table 11.5).

Step 4. From the menu, select Analyze, Correlate, then Partial (Figure 11.13).

Step 5. In the Partial Correlations window, enter the two variables whose relationship we wish to explore into the **Variables** box. Enter the variable we wish to remove from the relationship into the **Controlling for** box. Click OK (Figure 11.14).

Step 6. Inspect the output.

Table 11.5    Output 11.6.

Correlations

| | | average temperatures | mugging rates over 12 months | sunspot |
|---|---|---|---|---|
| average temperatures | Pearson Correlation | 1 | .903** | .938** |
| | Sig. (2-tailed) | | .000 | .000 |
| | N | 10 | 10 | 10 |
| mugging rates over 12 months | Pearson Correlation | .903** | 1 | .895** |
| | Sig. (2-tailed) | .000 | | .000 |
| | N | 10 | 10 | 10 |
| sunspot | Pearson Correlation | .938** | .895** | 1 |
| | Sig. (2-tailed) | .000 | .000 | |
| | N | 10 | 10 | 10 |

**Correlation is significant at the 0.01 level (2-tailed).

Figure 11.11

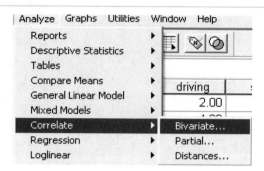

Figure 11.12

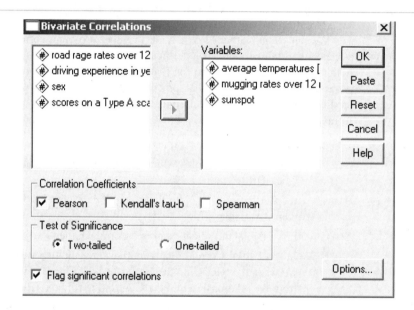

Figure 11.13

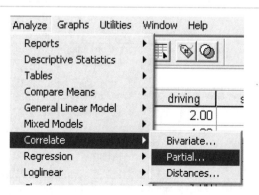

Figure 11.14

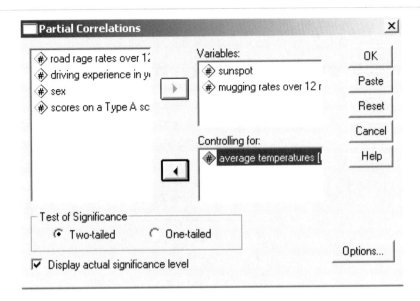

The remarkable observation which can now be made is that by removing the effects of temperature, the original strong correlation between sunspots and muggings is reduced. Table 11.6 shows there is a weaker relationship between these two factors and that what we were led to believe at the outset was largely the result of a third factor – temperature.

This has to be an upsetting revelation for most undergraduates: suddenly nothing is certain anymore. Relationships between variables are no longer straightforward and what was previously thought of as statistically rigorous findings now depend on the influence of other factors. However, we should try not to become too disturbed – after all, since the first chapter of this book we have been at pains to point out that nothing in the world is simple and that for any event there may be numerous causal and contributory factors. The trick has always been to identify what those other factors are and to make a judgement about which were important and which could be ignored. The success with which we can do this will often determine the ultimate value of our research.

As a final comment here, the thoughtful reader might just have guessed that partial correlation lends itself to mathematical solution, and this is true. Consider the present example – it is possible to remove the effects of temperature from the sunspot-mugging relationship using the following formula, from McGhee (1985).

Table 11.6     Output 11.7.

Correlations

| Control Variables | | | sunspot | mugging rates over 12 months |
|---|---|---|---|---|
| average temperatures | sunspot | Correlation | 1.000 | .323 |
| | | Significance (2-tailed) | . | .396 |
| | | df | 0 | 7 |
| | mugging rates over 12 months | Correlation | .323 | 1.000 |
| | | Significance (2-tailed) | .396 | . |
| | | df | 7 | 0 |

Box 11.2

# How To . . .

## Compute a partial correlation in SPSS

Step 1.   Select Analyze, Correlate, then Partial.

Step 2.   Transfer the variables to be correlated to the **V**ariables box.

Step 3.   Transfer the variable to be controlled for to the **C**ontrolling For box. Click OK.

Step 4.   Inspect the output and compare with the zero-order correlation.

(Note: zero-order correlations can be computed separately, or by selecting Options in the Partial Correlation window. From here **Z**ero order can be selected.)

$$r_{x_1y \cdot x_2} = \frac{r_{x_1y} - r_{x_1x_2} \times r_{yx_2}}{\sqrt{(1 - r_{x_1x_2}^2)(1 - r_{yx_2}^2)}} \qquad (11.1)$$

Where $x_1$ = predictor (sunspot)

$y$ = criterion (muggings)

$x_2$ = variable to be partialled (temperature)

$r_{x_1y \cdot x_2}$ = correlation between predictor and criterion with $x_2$ controlled for.

Substituting our calculated correlation values into the formula (11.1), we have:

$$r_{xy \cdot x_2} = \frac{.895 - (.938)(.903)}{\sqrt{(1 - .88)(1 - .82)}}$$

$$= .35$$

which is a pretty good approximation.

Box 11.2 lists how to compute a partial correlation in SPSS.

## 11.4  Multiple regression

**Multiple regression** involves assessing the combined effect of a number of predictors on a criterion variable. Without apology we decided that the last procedure in this part had to involve our favourite small, spiky mammals once more. Consequently, in a study investigating the number of hedgehogs squished by cyclists, three variables were considered as possible influencing factors. They were the 'age' of the riders, their 'extraversion' scores and their cycling 'experience.'

Each of these potential causal factors was selected on the basis of arguments that they would all in some way relate to the levels of coordination required to circumnavigate hordes of scuttling and leaping hedgehogs across a standard cycle route. To determine the combined effects of all three factors, multiple regression analysis is carried out, as follows:

Step 1.   From the menu select Analyze, Regression, then Linear (Figure 11.15).

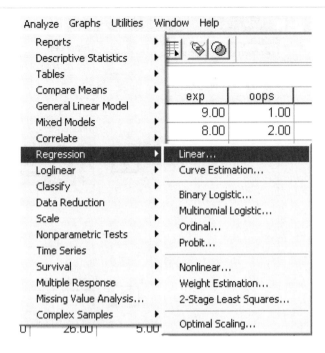

Figure 11.15

Step 2.    In the Linear Regression window (Figure 11.16), enter the criterion or outcome variable in the study into the **D**ependent box. Transfer all the predictor variables to the **I**ndependent(s) box. Click OK.

Step 3.    Inspect the output.

The output from a multiple regression analysis is both complex and considerable, and the table we provide represents only a part of what is available with this analysis.

Table 11.7 shows the regression model adopted, with all the variables identified. Table 11.8 is an ANOVA table which can be interpreted as indicating whether or not there is a real relationship between the variables. If there is no significant probability then the predictors do not significantly predict variation in the dependent variable. In the present example $p < .01$.

Table 11.9 is the Model Summary, which gives the $R^2$ (shown as $R$ Square) value. Standing at .566 the implication is that 57% of the variance in hedgehogs run over can be explained by a combination of the various causal factors. However, since these factors *are* acting in combination it is quite possible that the effects of one particular factor are being obscured or exaggerated by the effects of others – therefore it is possible that one or more of the independent variables is having a greater or lesser impact on the decline of the hedgehog population than at first appears.

Looking at the final Coefficients table (Table 11.10), we observe a number of columns of data. The first of these simply identifies the various variables in the analysis. The second column, headed 'B', refers to the value $b$ in our old friend $y = a + bx$, where $b$ is a measure of the slope of the regression line or, alternatively, the amount of change in the $y$ (outcome) variable for every unit change in the $x$ (independent) variable. Hence, for every increase on the extraversion scale of 1, there is a corresponding change to the number of hedgehogs stunned of 0.206, and so on. The full formula for this particular design then would be,

$$y = 5.697 - .0046x_1 + .206x_2 - .515x_3$$

Figure 11.16

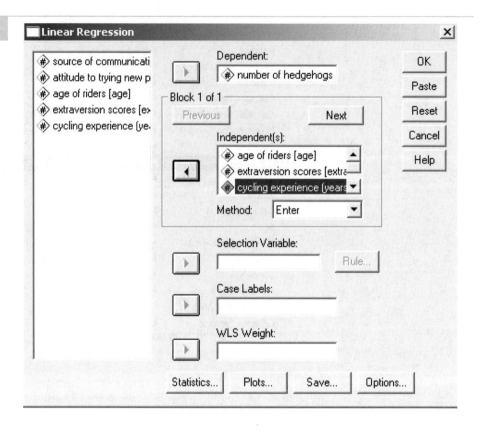

where $x_1$, $x_2$ and $x_3$ refer to the variables 'age', 'extraversion' and 'cycling experience' respectively.

The next important section here is found under the 'Beta' column heading (sometimes given as $\beta$), the values here being the standardised coefficients encountered in the

Table 11.7    Output 11.8—Variables Entered and Removed

| Model | Variables Entered[a] | Variables Removed[a] | Method |
|---|---|---|---|
| 1 | cycling experience (years), age of riders, extraversion scores[b] | – | Enter |

[a]Dependent variable: number of hedgehogs run over.
[b]All requested variables entered.

Table 11.8    ANOVA

| Model | | Sum of Squares | df | Mean Square | F | Sig. |
|---|---|---|---|---|---|---|
| 1 | Regression | 382.741 | 3 | 127.580 | 41.787 | .000[a] |
| | Residual | 293.099 | 96 | 3.053 | | |
| | Total | 675.840 | 99 | | | |

[a]Predictors: (Constant), cycling experience (years), age of riders, extraversion scores.
[b]Dependent variable: number of hedgehogs run over.

Table 11.9

Model Summary

| Model | R | R Square | Adjusted R Square | Std. Error of the Estimate |
|---|---|---|---|---|
| 1 | .753[a] | .566 | .553 | 1.74732 |

a. Predictors: (Constant), cycling experience (years), age of riders, extraversion scores

Table 11.10

Coefficients[a]

| Model | | Unstandardized Coefficients | | Standardized Coefficients | t | Sig. |
|---|---|---|---|---|---|---|
| | | B | Std. Error | Beta | | |
| 1 | (Constant) | 5.697 | 1.210 | | 4.710 | .000 |
| | age of riders | -.047 | .028 | -.117 | -1.647 | .103 |
| | extraversion scores | .206 | .050 | .314 | 4.123 | .000 |
| | cycling experience (years) | -.515 | .075 | -.515 | -6.876 | .000 |

a. Dependent Variable: number of hedgehogs run over

'B' column. This deals with the problem of different predictors being measured on different scales, and allows us to compare directly the effects of several independent variables with each other, much in the same way that comparisons in fractional calculations are effected by transforming several fractions to a common denominator. For completeness, values are standardised by multiplying the value of b for a given predictor by the ratio of the standard deviation of the independent variable to the standard deviation of the dependent variable, as in the formula:

$$Beta = b \frac{sx}{sy} \qquad (11.2)$$

If this is all a bit too much, however, a general rule of thumb is that the larger the beta ($\beta$) value, the more important is the variable in predicting or determining variation in the dependent variable. The sign too is important, with a positive value indicating that as the predictor increases so too does the criterion measure. A negative value indicates that as the predictor increases, the criterion decreases. In the present example, for an increase of one standard deviation in extraversion scores, the number of hedgehogs run over increases by .314 (as measured in standard deviations). Accordingly, it would appear that the variables responsible for the decline in the hedgehog population are cycling experience, extraversion scores and age, in that order. The final two columns describe $t$-values and their associated probabilities. These test the regression coefficients and can be interpreted as indicating whether a given independent variable significantly predicts variance in the dependent variable with all other variables controlled for. Therefore we can state here that of all the independent variables which could be included in an attempt to predict the number of hedgehogs run over, experience and extraversion of the rider were the only ones which made a significant difference. In other words, when it comes to accounting for the decline in the hedgehog population, experience and personality are the dominant factors.

Box 11.3 instructs how to compute a multiple regression in SPSS.

Box 11.3

## How To . . .

# Compute a multiple regression in SPSS

Step 1. Select Analyze, Regression, then Linear.

Step 2. Transfer the dependent variable in the analysis to the **D**ependent box.

Step 3. Transfer the predictor variables in the analysis to the **I**ndependent(s) box. Click OK.

Step 4. Inspect the output and note the following: the values in the **B**eta column indicate the relative importance of each variable as a predictor. The significance values associated with the $t$-scores identify predictors which significantly influence the outcome variable. The values in column **B** are used to generate the expanded regression equation, with **a** expressed by the Constant.

## Review

This concludes the statistical element of this book. In Chapters 9 and 10 we have offered an introduction to statistical procedures which ought to be sufficient for the majority of undergraduate projects. In the present chapter we have introduced more advanced procedures which should be enough for even the most ambitious of studies. While we have tried to cover statistical analyses in a reader-friendly manner, if you continue to experience difficulties with the various procedures we have outlined, our suggested reading section will be helpful.

## Suggested further reading

Field, A. (2000). *Discovering statistics using SPSS for Windows: Advanced techniques for beginners*. London: Sage.

A comprehensive and accessible book offering more detail on advanced statistics. Well worth a look.

Kinnear, P. R., & Gray, C. D. (2000). *SPSS for Windows made simple*. Hove, East Sussex: Psychology Press Ltd.

The standard 'how to' manual. Covers all the statistical procedures in SPSS and provides guidance on interpreting statistical output.

Langridge, D. (2004). *Introduction to research methods and data analysis in psychology*. Harlow, Essex: Pearson Education.

A slightly more advanced text, but offers good, readable coverage of advanced statistical analyses.

Tabachnik, B. G., & Fidell, L. S. (2001). *Using multivariate statistics* (4th ed.). Needham Heights, MA: Allyn & Bacon.

While not for the faint-hearted, this is *the* definitive text on advanced statistical analysis. If it's not in here it doesn't exist, but it's not an easy read. For the undergraduate this is the book to keep at the back of the mind: when everything else fails, Tabachnik and Fidell will cover it. And it is worth noting that every one of your tutors will probably have a copy hidden away on their bookshelf somewhere. Anyone into belly dancing will find this book a must!

# Carrying out qualitative research

## Part 6

Introducing
research

Planning a research
project—the design

Carrying out
research—methods
& procedure

Describing research
findings—
descriptives

Analysing research
findings—inferential
statistics

**Carrying out
qualitative research**

Writing up and
presenting the
findings of research

Alamy/Malie Rich-Griffith

In our experience, increasing numbers of students are interested in the idea of conducting qualitative research and, while some decide in the end to conduct a more traditional quantitative study, others continue and are successful in their endeavour. Our aim in this section is to give you an idea of what qualitative research entails, and to help you decide whether or not to conduct a qualitative study. We do not pretend here to present an authoritative treatise on the nature of qualitative research, but we can guide you to books and articles that provide more detail. The following topics are addressed in this section:

- The differences between qualitative and quantitative research.
- Qualitative or quantitative? Points to consider when making the decision.
- Forms of qualitative research.
- Planning your qualitative study.
- Other points to consider, including the ethics of the research.
- Collecting data.
- Analysing data.

# 12 Introducing qualitative research

Quantitative research reflects the philosophy that everything in the psychological world can be described according to some kind of numerical system – for example, a person's gender can be represented by the number 1 (for male) or 2 (for female); views on various kinds of attitudinal questionnaires can be expressed as numbers on a scale (e.g., 1 indicating total disagreement, and 7 representing total agreement); and many forms of behaviour can be similarly quantified. All of us have encountered rating scales and numerical measures at one time or another and this is where the term 'quantitative' comes from. The underlying belief is that only by reducing aspects of our universe to a common numerical system can precision be achieved; only then can we can carry out comparisons, project trends and identify differences among individuals, groups and experimental conditions. Furthermore, expressing phenomena in numerical terms opens the way to a range of statistical techniques that allow researchers to describe and draw inferences according to certain conventions with which most of us are familiar (see Part 4). In short, the quantitative approach is concerned with averages, variation, differences and relationships, and it represents one of the major research approaches within psychology, both historically and at the present time.

There is, however, an alternative approach. Qualitative research is sometimes defined only in opposition to quantitative research: that it does not involve statistics, for example, or that it does not rely on the objectivity that supports the quantitative approach. However, to presume a simple dichotomy does neither form of research justice. First of all, there are many different types of qualitative research, encompassing quite distinct approaches, methodologies and philosophies, and it is difficult to make generalisations that do justice to all types. Second, the demarcation lines between qualitative and quantitative methods are not as fixed as they might appear, in that, for example, the extent to which one can say that a quantitative approach is scientific or objective has been strongly debated (see Potter, 1998). Finally, although this is open to argument, quantitative and qualitative approaches need not be in direct opposition to one another; in our opinion, the two approaches can happily coexist, or even overlap, within the same study (see Bryman, 1988). However, there is a crucial experiential difference between the two forms of research: a qualitative study relies on the skills and abilities of the researcher in a way that is not normally acknowledged or expected in quantitative research. This is made clear in Parker's (1994, p. 2) definition of qualitative research as 'the interpretative study of a specified issue or problem in which the researcher is central to the sense that is made'. In other words, when

**331**

Box 12.1

## A Closer Look At . . .

# Qualitative, quantitative or just research?

Some researchers regard quantitative and qualitative orientations as quite distinct from one another:

←------------------------→          ←------------------------→
        quantitative                              qualitative

Others regard quantitative and qualitative orientations as different points on a general continuum of research approaches.

←--------------------------------------------------------------→
quantitative                                                  qualitative

you conduct a qualitative study, it is *your* understanding of the data, and of what happened during the study, that constitutes the analysis. Being 'central' in this way is hard work, and it can be very time consuming; qualitative research demands an extra level of involvement on the part of the researcher. Having said this, it can be both rewarding and exhilarating, particularly if the end result offers insight into an experience that was not previously well understood.

## 12.2  An example of a qualitative study

Imagine yourself as a social psychologist going to a darts match with the aim of exploring the behaviour of the fans. Taking a quantitative approach, you might begin with a theory about audience behaviours, and a set of hypotheses about what the fans will do under varying circumstances (when, for example, their player is winning, losing or the match is abandoned). A structured questionnaire might be given out before and after a match, the scores compiled, averages calculated and conclusions drawn from statistical analysis. Alternatively, you could act as an observer and complete detailed behavioural checklists, prepared in advance, to note the frequency of occurrence of different events. But supposing you don't begin with a theory, let alone any hypotheses – suppose you don't actually have any idea how fans behave at darts tournaments, and there is no literature to provide anything more than the vaguest of clues. In addition, you might feel that numerical data provide information on the measurable aspects of behaviour only, and very little information about the experience of life as a fan. In this case you might decide to observe what goes on around you at darts matches, taking notes, recording conversations and interviews or even videoing behaviour. Or you might feel that the detached approach isolates you too

Plate 12.1    How do we conduct research into areas with which we have no expertise?
*Source*: Empics/Adam Davy

much from what is actually happening and you decide that the best way to understand is to become one of the fans yourself – to travel with others to and from tournaments, to meet socially and to experience games yourself as part of the crowd. With this approach your data are quite different: they include detailed descriptive and narrative notes, diaries and transcriptions of interviews; there will be recordings of how people feel and what they think, as opposed to merely what they do. There will even be information on how you, as a researcher, feel about what's going on. This is qualitative information and Box 12.2 offers an illustration of the difference between quantitative and qualitative approaches to this study.

A Closer Look At . . .

# How qualitative and quantitative approaches differ

Often the same scenario, when looked at from different points of view, can be described in very different ways. The quantitative researcher, writing on the behaviour of darts supporters, might offer the following:

The mean number of hostile displays (as measured by the hostility scale) across 15 games was 21.65 ($SD = 5.35$) for the home supporters and 13.93 ($SD = 4.62$) for the visitors during the same period. An independent $t$-test was used to examine the hypothesis that home supporters would exhibit more hostile displays than would visitors. A significant difference was found on hostility scores between the two groups . . .

The qualitative researcher might produce something like this:

> The first of three major themes to emerge from the interviews with fans centred on the extent to which fans from opposing teams enjoyed the company of one another. For example, one of the interviewees from the first match made the following comment: 'You need to come when the guys from the Green Man are playing – their fans are great. We know the same songs, like, and we take it in turns with the verses'.

Qualitative research generally involves collecting data in at least one of the following ways: conducting interviews, running discussion or focus groups, observing a situation or individuals, writing field notes and collecting documents (anything from health promotion literature to minutes of meetings). All of these can provide data for analysis. What you actually do in terms of data collection and analysis depends upon a number of factors, ranging from the philosophical to the severely practical (as we discuss later in this chapter). However, the first decision to make is whether or not to conduct a qualitative study in the first place.

Box 12.3

## How To . . .

# Choose between a qualitative and a quantitative study

In considering whether or not to carry out a qualitative study, the following might serve as a guide.

| Qualitative | Quantitative |
| --- | --- |
| I believe that one cannot represent the experiences of this group of people through quantitative research. | *The phenomenon I am interested in can be measured quantitatively.* |
| All previous research in this area has been qualitative in nature | *All previous research in this area has been quantitative in nature.* |
| There are very few individuals, possibly even only one or two, available for study in this area. | *There is a large pool of potential participants.* |
| I am prepared to devote time to the analysis of interview transcripts and so on. | *I have only half a term left to do my study and my time is very limited.* |
| My supervisor is happy for me to do a qualitative study. | *My supervisor is uncomfortable with qualitative methodology, or is not supportive.* |
| I would like my research to be qualitative, but I want to incorporate a quantitative element. | *I would like my research to be quantitative, but I want to incorporate a qualitative element.* |

## 12.3 Qualitative or quantitative?

The decision about the methodology to use in your study may depend on some or all of the points we present in Box 12.3, and there may be other points relevant to you that we do not mention. If, having read this, you are still undecided, it may help to read the rest of this chapter.

## 12.4 Representing the experiences of the individual

Many of us have felt, at one time or another, that a quantitative study has failed to get to the heart of an issue. By reducing an experience to numbers, the researchers seem to have missed or lost something important. This type of reaction to quantitative research is more common at the social end of the research continuum than it is at the experimental end. For example, in reading a report of a survey of smoking behaviour in young people, in which it was found that most participants had negative attitudes towards smoking but a proportion continued to smoke, you might feel that the researchers failed to address what smoking actually meant or symbolised to those young participants. Or you may have had the experience yourself of completing a questionnaire on attitudes towards some issue, and felt that the researchers were not asking the 'right' questions, or were not allowing you to express the complexities of your attitudes, beliefs and values, and how these relate to the ways you behave on different occasions. Qualitative research allows you to address areas such as these; you can allow your participants to express the inconsistencies in their feelings, cognitions and behaviours, and the meanings they ascribe to these phenomena, and, through analysis, you can help the reader make sense of the experiences of your participants.

## 12.5 Previous research

A lot of undergraduate research (and post-graduate, for that matter) follows on from the work of other researchers. Consequently, on many issues there already exists a body of knowledge explaining and describing what happens in different situations. When your own study aims to extend existing theory, or to test or modify hypotheses, then you are beginning your work from a particular standpoint, and this may be clearly associated with either a qualitative or quantitative methodology. In many instances, therefore, you will choose to adopt a similar approach to that used by other authors in your area. In this way you can draw direct comparisons and talk sensibly about trends and developments in ways closed to you if you were to use a completely different methodology. Indeed, a common piece of advice given by supervisors is that their students look at how previous research has been carried out in the area, to give them an idea of how to plan their own work. However, there will be instances in which adopting the same approach as that taken by previous authors will be counterproductive. Sometimes, a different methodology will throw up findings and perspectives on a situation which would have been missed had the traditional approach been adhered to. See Box 12.4 for an example.

Box 12.4

## A Closer Look At . . .

# Different perspectives

In a study of young people's attitudes towards smoking, a questionnaire was constructed in which participants were asked to rate a number of items reflecting beliefs, attitudes, norms and smoking behaviour. Among other findings, the results indicated that the majority had negative attitudes towards smoking, but that attitudes explained only 15% of the variance of smoking behaviour, with sociodemographic variables explaining a further 5%.

A follow-up study used a different approach. Semi-structured interviews and small group discussions replaced the earlier structured questionnaire, and a number of themes emerged: for example, for some participants, smoking represented personal freedom in otherwise constrained circumstances, while for others, smoking represented a way of coping with pressure. These representations or meanings appeared to be quite distinct from the beliefs and attitudes measured in the original study, and appeared to explain why some continued to smoke while believing that smoking was damaging to health.

## 12.6 Availability of participants

Generally speaking, quantitative research involves large numbers of participants, because the value or power of many statistics increases with the numbers of individuals contributing to the data. In practical terms, this means that if your study centres on the experiences of a group of people who are small in number – for example, women who are mothers to triplets – then it makes sense to adopt a qualitative approach from the start.

## 12.7 Time factors

It often takes more time to conduct a qualitative study than it does to conduct a quantitative study. Although you might be involving only a few participants rather than, for example, 150, you will be collecting far more data, and it often takes more time to interview a small number of people than it does to distribute large numbers of questionnaires. Although it can seem time consuming to have to code and enter numerical data, and to conduct statistical tests, it takes more time to transcribe and analyse interviews. The activities involved in qualitative analysis – for example, transcription, reading and re-reading text, searching for themes – cannot be completed in an afternoon. If there are time constraints on your study, it may not be possible to conduct a qualitative study, or at least not one of an ambitious nature. This is an important consideration for many undergraduates, especially if the study has to be conducted within a term or semester.

## 12.8   Your supervisor

In our experience, supervisors vary a great deal in the extent to which they are prepared to supervise students who wish to conduct research very different from their own. Some supervisors will happily supervise both quantitative and qualitative studies, while others have a clear preference in one or other direction. All we can say at this point is that if you want to conduct a qualitative study, it will be easier for you if your supervisor is supportive, and is conversant with qualitative methods.

## 12.9   Mixing methods

It is not always the case that a particular study need be wholly qualitative or quantitative. Clearly, there are cases in which only one of these approaches will be appropriate, but some topics can be researched using a mixture or combination of methods. Consider the example outlined in Box 12.4. Here, the qualitative approach suggested that smoking could have a number of symbolic meanings for participants, and these meanings, and their impact on behaviour, were not captured by the structured questionnaire. One possibility would be to begin this study with a qualitative phase, and from there to develop theory and hypotheses that could be explored in a subsequent quantitative phase. While this may be too ambitious for an undergraduate study, it is worth bearing in mind that the two approaches are not mutually exclusive. Similarly, if your study is essentially quantitative in nature, you could add in a qualitative element to explore some issue or finding in further detail. An example is given in Box 12.5.

Box 12.5

## A Closer Look At . . .

## Mixed methods

Contrary to popular belief, laboratory-based research need not be entirely quantitative. In a study designed to measure the effects of group pressure on the expression of attitudes, participants first completed, in isolation, a questionnaire on attitudes towards the environment. Following this, they participated in group discussions on environmental issues, in which they were asked to express their own attitudes to other group members. Later, participants completed the initial questionnaire for a second time.

Following the statistical analysis (using a test of repeated measures), a small number of participants were interviewed by the researcher to find out more about their experiences of the group discussion, and of the way in which this discussion had influenced (or failed to influence) their initial attitudes towards environmental issues.

Box 12.6

# Checklist . . .

## Choosing to conduct a qualitative study

Reasons for choosing to conduct a qualitative study:

- You want to explore the experiences of a particular group of people without making prior assumptions about the nature of those experiences.
- You believe that the existing body of research on a particular topic fails to address or to represent the complexities of the participants' experiences.
- You believe that the existing body of research on a particular topic is weak because the researchers have failed to ask the right questions, but you are not sure what the right questions might be.
- You have read published papers of studies using qualitative methods and you can see how these methods could be applied to a topic that interests you.
- You are interested in qualitative methodology and in the philosophy behind it.

Other points to consider:

- You are prepared to put in the extra time it might take to conduct a qualitative study.
- You are prepared to get training, if necessary, in interviewing or in other aspects of the qualitative research process.
- You have a supervisor who is comfortable with qualitative methodology, or you have access to an experienced qualitative researcher who is prepared to advise you.
- You are aware of the ethical issues involved, and you are prepared to take the necessary steps to ensure that your participants suffer no ill effects from taking part in your study.

## 12.10    Some approaches to qualitative research

Before taking a more detailed look at the issues involved in qualitative research, we present brief descriptions of some of the main approaches, constructs and forms of analysis. Qualitative researchers still have to provide a more thorough rationale for their methodology than do those taking a quantitative approach, and this means that they have to understand, and present, something of the underlying philosophy of the approach they have chosen. This may seem unfair, but the knowledge gained by this process can be helpful, particularly when analysing and reporting the results. So, if you decide to conduct a qualitative study, you will certainly need more detailed texts, and we provide suggestions for further reading as appropriate.

### 12.10.1    Ethnography

**Ethnography** is, broadly speaking, a **phenomenological** approach concerned with describing social groups or situations; delineating, for example, behaviours and shared beliefs of a particular group of people, and through this gaining an understanding of how and why the participants function and behave as they do within their culture. The approach is often associated with the discipline of anthropology, and the emphasis is very much on the social group, at a cultural level. Typically, the researcher (ethnographer) joins a group of people for a period of time to find out as much as possible about the group. The aim is to understand something of participants' lives from the inside (as opposed to observing from afar), to find out what goes on and why, and to understand meanings of behaviours and beliefs within the social context.

An ethnographic approach might be taken to study what happens in particular well-defined environments, such as a classroom, a hospital ward, or a factory; or in a particular group with a common purpose, such as a football team, or a local action group. Typically, theories and hypotheses are generated and explored during the research process and there is an assumption that researchers will put aside their own beliefs and values before exploring those of the target group. The research starts as soon as the researcher goes into the new situation. The methods used to collect data will be varied and suited to the context: the researcher may read documentation (such as documents published by, or used by, the group), observe what appears to be happening, talk to the people involved both formally and informally; later, the researcher may use more structured methods to explore the

Plate 12.2    Researchers can use one of a number of qualitative approaches to a study of ward hygiene.
*Source*: Getty/Keith Brofsky

issues, theories or hypotheses which have arisen. Information is gathered about the context, about the target group, and about what happens, in the form of documentation, interview transcripts, field notes and diaries or logbooks.

Take, as an example, a study based in a hospital ward. The research question centres on hand washing on the ward, particularly by the nurses. A researcher taking an ethnographic approach would spend a great deal of time on the ward, getting to know the environment and the people who inhabit that environment. She might read the hospital's documentation on hand washing, attend meetings as an observer, make observations of hand washing on the ward and interview staff in group or one-to-one settings. She would make no assumptions about what she might find before starting her study, and would perhaps resist formulating a more precise research question until she has spent some time on the ward: in this way, she would not be making assumptions about the extent to which nurses did or did not follow hospital guidelines on hand washing. She might alter her research strategy during the course of the study to find out more about specific phenomena: for example, if she noticed that one or two members of staff washed their hands less often than other members of staff, she might interview them to find out more about this, without making assumptions before speaking to them about the cause of their behaviour. Useful descriptions of ethnography are provided by Atkinson (1990); Fielding (1993); Hammersley and Atkinson (1995); LeCompte and Goetz (1982); Potter (1998); and Rachel (1996).

### 12.10.2   Grounded theory

**Grounded theory** is an approach to research whereby a theory is grounded in actual data rather than imposed *a priori* (i.e., in advance of the data collection). Grounded theory, as described by Glaser and Strauss (1967), represented a reaction within sociology against the unwarranted imposition of existing theories upon situations or contexts. It has its roots in a construct termed **symbolic interactionism**, so that the emphasis within this approach is on the symbolic meanings that people attribute to 'events', and the ways in which these meanings interact with the social roles that people fill. The relationships among people's perceptions, the roles or categories with which they associate themselves, and the wider social context, are of central concern within this approach. Data are gathered mainly from interviews, although other sources may also be used. The analysis, however, is typically focused on the search for the kind of patterns and relationships which can generate theories and hypotheses, with processing continuing until adequate theories emerge to explain the phenomenon under investigation. This tends to be exhaustive, in that it continues until all aspects of the data are accounted for, using a process called constant comparison: the researcher keeps comparing the codes or categories she has already noticed in the data with those she notices in new data. As with ethnography, researchers are assumed to come to the study without preconceived ideas. The grounded theory approach is probably most appropriate in situations that are bounded in some way, and when the central issues are salient or important to the participants. However, the approach is essentially social, and the analysis tends to focus on the group rather than on the individual.

To return to our hand washing example, the researcher taking a grounded theory approach would use some of the techniques used by the ethnographer. Thus, she would probably spend time on the ward, make observations and so on, and she would certainly be entering the environment without prior assumptions about what she might find. She would also avoid developing any theories about hand washing before she started her study. Compared with the ethnographer, our grounded theory researcher would devote more attention to the nurses as a group and to how they relate to one another, and she would focus attention on what hand washing actually meant to the nurses in the context of the team, the ward and their other social roles. Detailed accounts of grounded theory are given by Charmaz (1995); Pidgeon (1996); Pidgeon and Henwood (1996); and Strauss and Corbin (1994).

### 12.10.3   Hermeneutics

**Hermeneutics** concerns the theory and practice of interpretation, and it has a long history. For our purposes, hermeneutics is concerned with language, or rather the process of using language to make experience understandable or comprehensible. Within this approach, it is assumed that the researcher's own background will have a bearing on the investigation and interpretation. Thus there is an assumption of consciousness and knowledge of the phenomenon or situation at the heart of the investigation, and in this respect hermeneutics differs from more **realist** research. Thus, **reflexivity** is a key construct, in terms of conscious and 'thoughtful' reflection on the interaction between researcher and participant, and on the researcher's role within that interaction. Interpretation depends upon the insight, openness and patience of the researcher, such that the researcher's personal qualities are brought to the fore. Although these qualities are important in other approaches to qualitative research, they are perhaps given more emphasis in the hermeneutic approach.

The hermeneutic approach to the hand washing study might be taken by a nurse on the ward, or by someone with experience of nursing. Unlike the ethnographer or the grounded theory researcher, the hermeneutic researcher would not be putting her own experience and prior assumptions to one side before starting the study. The study would probably centre on interviews with individual nurses, and our researcher would be using her own experiences and knowledge to guide the interviews and the analysis to some extent. During the interviews, she would be consciously exploring the values, assumptions and experiences of both her interviewee and herself. For further details of hermeneutics, see Kvale (1983) and Leonard (1989).

### 12.10.4   Action research

**Action research** involves identifying problems in particular settings, generating hypotheses about the causes and 'cures', acting on these and evaluating the impact. The process can take different forms, depending upon the extent to which the researchers rely on participants to generate the hypotheses and implement the changes. It differs from ethnographic research in that changes are implemented and their effects evaluated during the period of research. In many cases, action research will be beyond the scope of the undergraduate project; however, the approach is interesting in its own right and it may be possible to incorporate aspects of action research into a small scale study.

The researcher's involvement in the process of change can vary considerably, depending on the extent to which the participants are involved in generating ideas and implementing strategies for change themselves. Other relevant factors include the level of cohesion within the group, the power structure, and degree of organisational and environmental constraint. The whole process of action research is interactive, participative and dynamic. Ideally, it is based upon co-operation and collaboration, between the researcher and the group, and amongst members of the group. Problems can arise if the researcher does not share central values with the participants, if the researcher is perceived to be in some way critical of the group or its members, or if the factions within the group have different agendas.

To return to our hand washing study, the action researcher would use some of the methods of data collection used by our other researchers, and she would probably interview and observe in the first instance. However, she would also be involving the nurses in the research process to some degree, so that she would be involving them in the search for effective interventions to improve rates of hand washing, and also in the conduct of these interventions. Finally, she would be evaluating the effectiveness of the interventions from various viewpoints, including those of the nurses themselves. For reviews of action research, see Argyris, Putnam and Smith (1985); Rheinharz (1983); Tappen (1989); Taylor (1994); and Whyte (1984).

### 12.10.5    Participatory research

Within a **participatory** study, the participants themselves take a central role; they are involved to a greater or lesser extent in setting the research agenda, designing the study, and collecting the data. The named researcher, therefore, acts more as a facilitator, helping the participants in effect to conduct their own study. This approach has a number of benefits: because participants dictate the agenda, the chance of exploitation is reduced, and it is more likely that the questions or issues most important to the participants are those which are addressed. It also gives the research the kind of credibility or face validity which is vital to ensure full co-operation and involvement, and the quality of the data may be greatly enhanced as a result. On the other hand, participatory research can be difficult to set up if the research population consists of different factions with different agendas; there may not be a single or central way of viewing the issue or topic. Finally, it may not always be easy to steer participants away from 'unresearchable' topics; the researcher's role here can demand more tact and diplomacy than is usually required.

The participatory researcher interested in hand washing would start by exploring the research question with the nurses on the ward. The nurses themselves might not feel rates of hand washing to be a problem; only with their co-operation and involvement could our researcher pursue this topic. However, if the nurses agree themselves that this is a worthy topic to research, then the participatory researcher can help them to plan the conduct of the research, such that the nurses themselves would conduct the observations, and perhaps interview other members of staff. The participatory researcher would be guiding the research, supporting the nurses in their efforts, and acting as a troubleshooter. She may help them formulate and conduct intervention strategies, but only if the nurses themselves agree to this. For more information, see Reason and Heron (1995); and Whyte (1991). Box 12.7 illustrates various ways to study hand washing.

### 12.11    Qualitative approaches that involve the analysis of text

The qualitative approaches considered in the following sections are slightly different, in that they are more directly concerned with the analysis of text or transcripts.

Box 12.7

A Closer Look At . . .

# A study of hand washing

A qualitative study of hand washing by nurses on a hospital ward could be conducted in a number of different ways:

> Ethnographic study: Without making prior assumptions, the researcher spends time in the ward environment. Sources of data include interviews, focus groups, observations, field notes and relevant documentation.

> Grounded theory study: Similar to an ethnographic study, but with less emphasis on the environment and more on the perceptions of staff as a group. Sources of data could include any of those used by the ethnographer, but will probably centre on interviews and focus groups. Central to this approach is the goal of developing theories about hand washing from the nurses' perspectives.

> Hermeneutic study: Unlike the ethnographer and the grounded theory researcher, this researcher explicitly acknowledges her own knowledge, assumptions and experience. The main source of data will probably be interviews, with the researcher consciously exploring the situation from the points of view of both her interviewee and herself. Another source of data could be available documentation.

> Action research study: This researcher involves the nurses in the study to a greater or lesser degree, and she develops, implements and evaluates intervention strategies from several viewpoints. Sources of data are similar to those used by the ethnographer.

> Participatory study: The nature of the study is determined by the nurses themselves, and the researcher guides, advises and assists the nurses in their efforts.

## 12.11.1   Content analysis

**Content analysis** is way of analysing communication, such as text or speech. It is objective and systematic in focus, and it centres on the observable qualities of the text. For example, to determine the most salient aspects of a phenomenon for participants, content analysis could be used to examine the frequency with which particular words or phrases occur, or the observable context within which these words and phrases are used. Content analysis can therefore be used to generate quantitative data. In qualitative research, content analysis offers a way of categorising and classifying text. Given the emphasis on the objective and the observable, content analysis is reliable, in that the analysis is not dependent upon the interpretation of the analyst. In this way, it differs from other qualitative methods that draw upon phenomenology. For further reading, see Krippendorff (2004) and Roberts (1997).

## 12.11.2   Discourse analysis

Broadly speaking, **discourse analysis** entails a close analysis of a text, transcript or interaction, with the aim of highlighting the social structures and assumptions embodied in the language. The language is taken to be a reflection of a wider social phenomenon. However, it is difficult to find a single definition which does justice to all variations of discourse analysis: 'it is a field in which it is perfectly possible to have two books on discourse analysis with no overlap in content at all' (Potter & Wetherell, 1987, p. 6). This comment reflects the extent of the current debate about the nature and scope of the technique.

Discourse analysis centres mainly on the function of language (e.g., Potter & Wetherell, 1987), or on how people construct meaning through particular forms of discourse (e.g., Parker, 1994). However, discourse analysis is not concerned with the cognitions that might underpin the words: from the perspective of discourse analysis, language is not a way of understanding cognition, but the means by which we negotiate relationships, meaning, or the construction of the social context. For further reading, see Burman and Parker (1993); Edwards and Potter (1992); Munslow (1997); Nikander (1995); Parker (1994); Potter (1998); Potter and Wetherell (1987); Tosh (2002); and Wetherell, Taylor and Yates (2001a, 2001b).

### 12.11.3 Interpretative phenomenological analysis

**Interpretative phenomenological analysis (IPA)** has a similar pedigree to that of grounded theory, since it emerged from the traditions of phenomenology and symbolic interactionism. However, it centres on the analysis of speech, language or dialogue, typically obtained through one-to-one interviews and discussions. In contrast with the discourse approach, IPA attempts to uncover the cognitions, thought processes and associated meanings that underpin language. There is an acknowledgement of what the researcher brings to the situation; the researcher interprets the participant's speech and behaviour through his or her own understanding. IPA has proved useful in the field of health psychology, but may be appropriate for any research issue that centres on the individual's perception of something that is personally relevant. For more on IPA, see Reid, Flowers and Larkin (2005); Smith (1996); Smith, Flowers and Osborn (1997); and Smith, Jarman and Osborn (1999). Box 12.8 offers an overview of text analysis.

## 12.12 Planning a qualitative study

Perhaps you have decided to conduct a qualitative study, but you are not sure what approach to take. Or perhaps you are still trying to decide whether your study should be qualitative or quantitative. Qualitative methods can, in theory, be applied to many areas of psychology, but the method should match the research question: clarify what it is you want to find out and then find the most appropriate method to apply. However, it is important to remember that the process of planning and conducting a qualitative study does not run in a straight line: you will probably find yourself going back and forth within and between stages, and each time you revisit a stage, your thinking may change. This is part of the process, but it can be unsettling at first.

### 12.12.1 Research questions and the conceptual framework

First of all, consider what it is that you want to find out. In other words, try to clarify your primary research questions. For example, you may want to know whether people taking an exercise class to reduce their blood pressure experience physical and psychological

A Closer Look At . . .

# Analysis of text

Here is a quote from a nurse interviewed as part of a study on hand washing on the ward:

> I try to wash my hands after seeing each patient or whatever, I really do. But sometimes it's just that . . . you do wash them when you can but sometimes it kind of depends on the patient and how busy you are and where you are and things like that. I mean they're always telling us to wash your hands, wash your hands. But sometimes your hands just get sore, or there's no basin right there and I think any nurse would tell you the same. The patients I see aren't ill, usually, it's not like working in A and E.

A content analyst might look at the frequencies of words such as 'patient', 'nurse' and 'they' (i.e., hospital authorities). She might also look at the conjunction of certain terms, or repetitions of certain phrases. She may have made a decision before commencing analysis to concentrate on certain aspects of the text, and she will not go beyond the observable features.

A discourse analyst might look at the way certain words are used to convey social roles, and the kind of language (or discourse) with which these words are associated: for example, the context in which the interviewee refers to people as 'patients' and the hospital authorities as 'they'. The analyst might also consider the way that language is used by the interviewee to justify his or her own hand washing behaviour, or to distance the interviewee from other nurses (e.g., those working in Accident and Emergency departments). While the analyst may go beyond the observable features of the text (in that she may categorise discourses in a way that is not immediately obvious from the text), she will not try to interpret or label the cognitions that underpin the words.

An interpretative phenomenological analyst might also take the discourse into account, but she will focus more on the cognitions that appear to underpin the words: for example, while she might interpret 'any nurse would tell you the same' as a justification of hand washing behaviour, she would also try to understand the cognitive process through which this justification was achieved.

benefits, and what their perceptions of those benefits are; or you may want to know about the different ways students prepare for exams, and about their perceptions of their own exam strategies. Miles and Huberman (1994) suggest a useful series of strategies to help at this stage. First, you could try to map out a conceptual framework of the topic of interest: drawing boxes to encompass the relevant constructs, and making the connections between those boxes. The boxes in the first instance might be simple and descriptive: for example, you could differentiate between the potential physical and psychological effects of exercise, such as increased physical fitness or increased self-esteem. This may be problematic for researchers wishing to limit the imposition of their own preconceptions, but it can help mark the scope of a project. Second, try to formulate some research questions which are consistent with the conceptual framework: for example, the extent to which people feel better as a result of exercise, and whether *they* in fact differentiate between physical and psychological benefits. This may be a rather circular process involving a redrawing of the framework as the questions emerge. For example, having raised the question of whether people differentiate between physical and psychological benefits of exercise, you may wish to reconsider putting these effects in different boxes or categories to begin with.

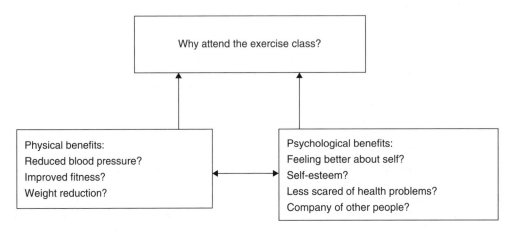

A first attempt at a conceptual framework.

At this stage, the research questions may of necessity be rather vague, but formulating the questions can help you to understand your own preconceptions and biases (such as your expectation that exercise will lead to beneficial outcomes, or that these beneficial outcomes will be seen as desirable by your participants). These can then be made explicit, a crucial underpinning to much qualitative research. More pragmatically, the process of formulation can highlight problems: some questions may not in fact be 'researchable' and although it is not always possible to spot this at an early stage, the more thought and deliberation that goes into planning the less likely it is that the study will fail. Finally, at this stage, we would urge you to limit the number of research questions you are working with: somewhere between one and four should be sufficient.

### 12.12.2  Deciding on the method

When you have formulated research questions, think about the best way to answer them. If you have any hypotheses (or even hunches), formulate these too. What do you need to find out? What would it take to answer your question? It is likely that this process will take a while, and you may have to revisit the issues more than once. For our purposes, the first issue to address concerns the method. Both questions mentioned above, concerning the benefits of the exercise class and perceptions of exam strategies, could be addressed in a number of ways. To take the latter study as an example, you could conduct focus groups or hermeneutic interviews (assuming that you also have to prepare for exams); or you could subject interview transcripts to discourse or content analysis; or you could even conduct an action research study by promoting different exam strategies and evaluating their impact. It may be that you have to weigh up the pros and cons of different approaches, although sometimes the decision will be clear cut. This process will also help you refine your research questions, and it will help you determine whether the scope of the proposed project is appropriate. As an undergraduate, your time and resources are limited and you have to be practical about what you can actually achieve. If possible, get advice on these points from an experienced qualitative researcher.

The next step might be to consider the methods that are typically used to research the topic you have chosen. Reading around the area is always a good start to planning any study, and it gives you a feel for the traditions and for the underlying philosophies. To revisit a point made earlier, don't automatically assume that qualitative methods are inappropriate for a topic that is typically researched quantitatively; for example, it may be interesting to find out the extent to which the perceptions of people taking the exercise class are consistent with the theories derived from quantitative studies on the physiological benefits of exercise. Find out as much as you can about the approach taken by other authors, so that you understand why, for example, a researcher used discourse analysis rather than content analysis. A further bonus to this early reading is that these books and journal articles can provide you with models of the best way to conduct your study, analyse your data and present your results. However, there is much argument about the extent to which the researcher should go into the field with preconceived ideas or even questions, and you need to be aware of those arguments. We agree with Miles and Huberman's (1994) thoughts on this: that the inexperienced qualitative researcher should probably have an idea about the boundaries of his or her project. As a student working on your own to a tight time schedule, you may be able to collect data from only some of the relevant people on only some of the relevant topics, and you need to be aware of the implications of these restrictions from the outset, if possible.

To go back a stage, consider whether you have clear hypotheses or hunches, or if you have no idea about what you might find. There is a tension here between immersing yourself in the literature and the theories on the one hand, and, on the other, allowing yourself to approach your study without preconceptions. For the undergraduate student, the middle ground is probably the best option: you need to know something about the topic (not least because you might have to write a rationale or proposal at an early stage) and you don't want to find that your research question has already been answered more than adequately by countless other researchers. At the other extreme, if you are overly aware of the theories and findings of previous researchers, you may not ask the questions that could lead to new territory.

### 12.12.3  Piloting

**Piloting**, in whatever form, is important. You need to know if the proposed methods of collecting data (and perhaps analysing those data) 'work' in terms of achieving the goals. However, piloting may not take place until the research is actually under way. It thus becomes part of the process in a way not usually found within quantitative research. It may not even be described as piloting, but at some stage most researchers have to find out whether or not their chosen methods actually produce data or information which can be used. This applies to the more open-ended or unstructured methods as well as to the more structured. In all forms of piloting, however, it is crucial to keep detailed notes, to record all of the factors, both situational and personal, which inform the decisions about methodology. These notes can then be submitted as part of the final write-up of the project.

Box 12.9

## How To . . .

# Plan your qualitative study

### First of all, formulate some research questions:

OK, I'll start with this: What do people with high blood pressure get out of exercise classes?

### Draw up a rough conceptual framework:

| Physical benefits | Psychological benefits |
| --- | --- |
| Reduction in blood pressure? | Feeling better about self? |
| Increased physical fitness? | Self-esteem? |
| Weight reduction? | Less scared of health problems? |
| | Company of other people? |

**Other factors**

Motivation?

Other health problems?

Sociodemographic factors?

Practical issues (e.g., distance from gym)?

Ambivalence about costs/benefits of exercise?

Aspects of identity (labelling, etc.)?

Stigma?

### Consider whether you have any hypotheses or hunches:

Yes, that people who continue with the exercise class do so because they feel better, physically and psychologically, for doing so. But my research question does not reflect this, so I had better rephrase it. How about: In a group of people with high blood pressure, what differentiates those who continue with exercise classes from those who drop out? And I had better redraw my conceptual framework . . .

### Consider what it will take to address the research question:

Semi-structured interviews with people with high blood pressure who have attended an exercise class? I should include some who are regular attenders and some who have dropped out. But should they all come from the same exercise class? Should they be similar or varied in sociodemographic terms? What do I mean by regular attendance and dropping out?

### Consider the types of qualitative research available to you:

I could attend a couple of classes if I am allowed to do so, so I could add an ethnographic element to my study. However, I am going to rely on the interviews for data. So what kind of interview should I conduct? What kind of analysis? What have other qualitative researchers done with these kinds of topics . . . ?

Have another look at your research questions and conceptual framework, clarify your thoughts and determine the boundaries of your study:

OK, I have to recognise my limits. I will try to interview six men from the same exercise class, all of whom started around the same time. I will try to interview three who still attend the class three months after starting and three who stopped attending after the first month. I will focus on the perceived costs and benefits of attending the class, but will try not to impose further limits on the interview topics. I will use IPA to analyse the interviews, because this seems to be applicable to health issues. But perhaps I need to do some more work on this . . .

## 12.13 Other points to consider

### 12.13.1 Your reason for choosing the topic

A question to ask yourself at this stage concerns your reason for choosing this topic. In other words, what is your interest or stake in this topic? This is a question that we don't normally ask of the quantitative researcher, but the extent to which the qualitative researcher has prior experience of the topic can make a difference to all aspects of the research process. It is not always necessary or appropriate for you to declare your interest in a topic (for example, that you have a particular health problem, or have experienced a difficult situation in your own life), but you should at least be honest with yourself at the outset. Your own experiences will probably influence how you first start thinking about the topic, and it may be that your experiences inform data collection and analysis. The more experienced you are, the easier it becomes to deal with such issues. At this stage, we would urge you to think very carefully about this issue (and we return to this below), and to work with the situation rather than fight against it. If you have prior knowledge and experience, this will direct you at the outset and may help you establish rapport with your participants. If you don't, then you have the potential advantage of neutrality. Experienced researchers can work under either set of circumstances, but they know how to acknowledge and work with those circumstances. The other point to remember is that we all have our own strengths and weaknesses. If you know from the outset that you will find certain views or findings difficult to deal with, perhaps because of your own values or experiences, then choose another topic.

### 12.13.2 Self-disclosure

You should consider very carefully the issue of disclosing personal information to your participants. There are, of course, important issues to be considered surrounding the extent to which self-disclosure influences the research process, and about the ethics of self-disclosing or otherwise. However, the issue also has personal ramifications. You may not be comfortable disclosing something that is very important to you, that you do not generally talk about with other people, and if this is the case then think carefully ahead of time about what you are doing and the implications of any decisions you make. If possible, talk to someone with experience in this area.

At a practical level, self-disclosure can help establish a comfortable and open relationship between researcher and interviewee and it can facilitate certain topics: for example, if the interviewee with high blood pressure learns that you also have this problem, the interview may open up considerably. However, self-disclosure can also have a negative impact on the interview. Personal information can be intrusive and off-putting to the interviewee. A researcher who expresses their own point of view or their own experiences at every turn can inhibit the flow of the interview, particularly if the researcher and interviewee do not share common values or experiences. Some interviewees will not want to know anything about the person who is interviewing them. Such issues should be considered carefully before interviewing or data collection commences.

### 12.13.3 Philosophical issues

During this planning stage, a number of what might be called philosophical issues should be carefully considered. Thus, you need to consider the extent to which you are able to bracket or ignore your own experiences and preconceptions, and, indeed, your position on the extent to which this is possible. You need to consider the use of recording equipment, not only in terms of data collection, but also the extent to which it might influence what is said or what happens. You need to consider your own role in the research process, and the potential effects of your research on the lives of participants. And you should also consider the nature and role of reflexivity, as it applies to your proposed study. Arguments surround each of these issues, and you, as a researcher, need to be aware of these arguments. Further, you need to make decisions about where you stand and what you will do in your study. For further reading on the use of recording equipment (and on the researcher's influence on the research process), see Hammersley (2003) and Speer and Hutchby (2003); and on reflexivity, see Finlay (2002).

### 12.13.4 Ethical issues

Ethical issues must be addressed at the planning stage of a qualitative study. You may have to operate within two or more sets of ethical guidelines, and you will probably find that your university or college sets limits on the kinds of research that undergraduate students can do. Your supervisor will be able to advise you on this, but at the very least you should consider the guidelines published by the British Psychological Society (BPS). Some of these issues have already been raised in Chapter 6; in this section we focus more specifically on the ethics of qualitative research.

At the time of writing, the most recent BPS guidelines (2004) centre on the protection of participants, with emphasis on informed consent, non-coercion, the right to withdraw, anonymity and confidentiality, and duty of care. Thus the guidelines clearly state that all participants must give informed consent, and that they must be given the opportunity to withdraw at any time from the research (even if they have signed a consent form). Potential participants should be provided with information about the study ahead of time, in writing and in person, and they should be asked to read and sign consent forms. Every effort should be made to keep participation anonymous (so that the recording of names and addresses is kept to a minimum) and confidentiality must be maintained at all times.

There is an art to writing information sheets and consent forms, and it is worth getting representatives of the target population to read early versions. These representatives can point out ambiguities, jargon and omissions. Indicate the nature and purpose of the research; information should be as clear, straightforward and honest as possible, detailing the demands that will be placed on participants (e.g., the topics to be covered in an interview and the time it will take). Give a contact name, address and telephone number. Indicate the process of recruitment. If information sheets and consent forms are to be mailed to potential interviewees, enclose a stamped addressed envelope. Sensitivity should be used because not everyone can read and write: in this case, the researcher should explain the study to potential participants in a relatively neutral way, allowing them to ask questions, and indeed to refuse to participate.

While people cannot be interviewed without their permission, they can be coerced into doing so, and such coercion is unethical. In a sense, an interview is based on a contract between the researcher and the interviewee, and this should be negotiated explicitly. Even if someone agrees to be interviewed, he or she should be given the opportunity to terminate the interview at any point. The interviewee should also be told who will have access to the record of the interview, and about the methods that will be used to ensure anonymity and confidentiality. These issues are important: they are related not just to potential exploitation of interviewees but also to the development of trust, and thus to the quality of the research.

Interviewing can be demanding of the skills and qualities of the interviewer, and it is important to get training and experience in this before setting out on your own. Training and experience support the ethical principles within which we operate, because an experienced interviewer will be less likely to upset the interviewee and will be more able to help and support him or her should problems arise. Before you start your interviewing, consider what to do if things don't go according to plan. Talk these issues over with your supervisor or an experienced interviewer. What will you do if your interviewee becomes upset, or discloses something that you feel you should tell someone about? What will you do if you are asked for help and you are unable or unwilling to provide that help? What will you do if *you* become upset, scared or angry? This brings us to duty of care. The BPS guidelines state clearly that we should not pretend to have expertise or knowledge or experience that we do not in fact possess, and most undergraduates will not be in a position to offer the necessary support for troubled interviewees. However, there are a number of strategies that undergraduate students can adopt to make sure that ethical standards are adhered to. In addition to obtaining experience, students can ensure that their supervisors are either present during the interview, or close at hand. Further, they can prepare for the interview by collecting leaflets, addresses, web sites and telephone numbers that might prove useful to their interviewees. Interviews should always be taken seriously, even if the topic is lighthearted or apparently straightforward: for example, an interview on a seemingly neutral topic such as exam preparation may unexpectedly trigger a painful emotion in your interviewee, and you need to be on the lookout for the changes in expression and body language that signal discomfort.

A number of ethical issues should be considered before observing participants, or before delving into archive material. These include the extent to which people should be observed without their knowledge, the extent to which stored information should be accessed without consent, confidentiality, and feedback on results to participants. While it may seem harmless to make video recordings of people in public places, it may not seem so to the people involved. Advice should be sought not only from ethical committees but also from representatives of your potential pool of participants. Sometimes researchers wish to observe people's behaviour in settings where knowledge of being observed might change the behaviour. In such cases, the researcher should consider the extent to which this might cause embarrassment or distress to such people; it is often unnecessary to take video recordings, for example. For further reading, see BPS *Ethical Guidelines* (2004); Cartwright (1983); Kvale (1996); Moustakas (1994); and Rogers (1996). Box 12.10 presents some key points on ethics.

### Checklist . . .

# What an ethics committee might want to know about a qualitative study

- Your participants. Give details of selection and exclusion criteria. Give details on your method of recruitment.
- Your methods. Indicate the ways you plan to collect data. If you plan to interview, include an interview schedule or list of topics with your application. If you plan to observe, indicate how and where this will be done, and what you plan to observe.
- Information and informed consent. It makes sense to include copies of information sheets and consent forms with your application.
- Procedures for ensuring that your participants are not upset or harmed in any way by taking part in your study. These could include training; access to an experienced researcher or psychologist if a participant requires help or advice; and the provision of written information and so on.
- Procedures for ensuring that information about participants (in written or recorded format) is kept confidential and anonymous.
- Procedures for ensuring your own safety and wellbeing, if appropriate.

## 12.14 Collecting data

### 12.14.1 Interviewing

The term *interview* here is used here to describe anything from an informal chat with someone to a highly structured question and answer session. In qualitative research, interviews are generally semi-structured at most, meaning that the interviewer has a set of questions or topics but goes into the interview prepared to deviate, to a greater or lesser extent, from that set. As noted above, experience is crucial, and it is worth taking the time to plan and prepare for your interviews because this preparation will allow you to focus more of your attention on the interviewee and what he or she is actually saying. Ideally, you should not have to look at your interview schedule during the interview.

Decide on your potential interviewees. For example, are you going to take participants from a number of different exercise classes, or all from the same class? Students

Plate 12.3    The interview is one method of collecting data in qualitative research.
*Source*: Getty/Mike Powell

from just one class or module? Consider how many interviews you would like to do (e.g., 10 or more) and how many you are actually able to do (e.g., 4 or 5). Decide on the criteria to be used in selecting your interviewees, and also define your exclusion criteria – from an ethical standpoint, you should exclude people who are particularly vulnerable or who may require the kind of support that you are unable to provide. Consider the ways in which you can gain access to the names of potential interviewees, and negotiate these as soon as possible: ethics committees and decision-making boards can take a while to grant permission.

Make sure that you have done your preparatory work. Draw up a provisional interview schedule with any topics or questions that you wish to explore. Pilot this and continue to adapt or change your interview schedule until it easily elicits the information you are looking for. Develop ways of prompting your interviewees to say more about topics of interest, without putting words into their mouths. The actual process of interviewing will vary according to the approach you are taking, or the type of analysis you intend to do, but in most cases, the aim is to minimise your input and to maximise the input of your interviewee. Further, you should do everything you can to ensure that you do not limit your interviewee's contribution, or his or her understanding, with your own preconceptions of what might be said. This takes practice. Make sure that at least some of your pilot interviews are with people representative of your target group, and use these pilot interviews to establish a style of interviewing which suits the purpose of your research, and with which you and your interviewees are comfortable. On a practical note, you will also gain a sense of the time required of the interviewee: this is important when fixing up a time for the interview. Try out your audio or video recorder if you intend to use one, and make sure that it works. Record all the decisions you make during this phase of your research.

Consider the ethics of your study, and the steps you should take to ensure that you do not cause unnecessary upset or distress to your interviewees. Consider confidentiality and anonymity: for example, you should ensure that tapes or transcripts are identified by number only, that they are stored in a safe place with a lock, and that the documentation linking name to participant number is stored elsewhere (also in a locked place). Consult representatives of your target group as well as your supervisor and any relevant ethics committees.

Make your decisions about the use of recording devices and about self-disclosure. If you have decided to use audio-recording equipment, you should negotiate this with each interviewee and respect the interviewee's wishes. If the interviewee initially agrees to the use of a tape-recorder but then seems uncomfortable with that decision, offer to switch it off. If you have decided to disclose your own interest in the research topic, you need to be aware of the potential impact of this on the interview process: so you need to decide the point at which to self-disclose. Whatever your decision about self-disclosure, you need to say enough to make your interviewee comfortable with the situation, and you also need to be aware that interviewees vary a great deal in the extent to which they express interest in their interviewers.

Plan a timetable for interviewing and begin to contact your potential interviewees. At this stage you can tell them how long the interview is likely to last and you can negotiate a place in which to interview them. If you are interviewing in a particular setting, you could try to find a private room in which to interview people. However, you should respect the wishes of the interviewee: they may prefer to be interviewed at home, or in the company of a friend.

Finally, you can start interviewing. An interview is a social event, an interaction between two or more people. Do what you can to make a person comfortable. You can do much to establish the tone of the interview in the first few minutes, in terms of seating, posture, appearance and language. While informality and equality might seem ideal (and may indeed be so for many people) some interviewees may be more comfortable with a more formal approach, and their wishes should be respected. At the start, explain the research again and ensure that the interviewee knows that the interview can be stopped at any time. If the interview becomes difficult, or if the interviewee becomes upset, switch off the tape-recorder and take some 'time out'. You may both decide to terminate the interview at this stage. Take time at the end of the interview to address any issues that have arisen and to allow the interviewee to ask questions of you.

When you are doing your interviews, keep records of where and when the interview was conducted and how long it took. As soon as possible after the interview, check that your tapes are audible or that your notes are legible, and write out full notes, including your own thoughts and reflections about the interview. If your recording equipment failed in some way, you may still be able to salvage something from the interview if you do this quickly enough. Review Box 12.11 for tips on interviewing.

### 12.14.2   Focus groups

**Focus group** methodology emerged from studies of the effects of mass communications or mass media, using 'focused interviews' (Merton & Kendall, 1946). Focus groups represent another way to collect data: a group of people are brought together to discuss a specific topic, under the direction or guidance of a moderator and the resulting conversation is recorded and/or observed. The decisions to be made about focus groups, and the practical issues, are similar to those surrounding the use of interviews, but there are some additional issues to be taken into account.

# Interviewing

- If you have not already done so, decide on your potential interviewees and start the process of obtaining names and addresses. You also need to draw up information sheets and consent forms for your potential interviewees.
- Draw up an interview schedule, and start preparing and piloting. Get training if possible. Practice your interview technique.
- Consider the ethical issues and make decisions about ways to deal with potential problems.
- Decide how you are going to record interviews, taking the ethical and philosophical issues into account.
- Consider the issues for and against self-disclosure and come to a decision.
- Consider the best way to conduct your interviews, but be flexible.

Focus groups can be useful at various stages of a project: they can provide the researcher with background knowledge of an area, they can help generate interview topics or questionnaire items, and they can help the researcher judge the adequacy of an analysis or interpretation of a situation. However, the focus group is not an easy way to interview a group of people at once. There is a vast amount of evidence from the field of social psychology to show that people are changed in the company of others: what people say and do, and even perhaps what they think, will be affected by the presence of other people. Sometimes this social influence will work in favour of the researcher, such that other people may spark a line of thought or an interaction which yields more than would emerge from an individual interview. However, it may also hinder the research process. It takes experience to be able to tell the difference.

The quality of the data gathered from a focus group will depend on the make-up of the group and the skills of the moderator. Obviously, the members of the group should have an interest in, or experience of, the topic under discussion: if you want to know about the strategies that students adopt for exam preparation, and the effects of those strategies, ask students who have taken exams recently rather than those who graduated some time ago. But a good group will not compensate for a poor moderator. Even when all group members are willing to talk, a good moderator is required, if only to ensure that people speak in turn (and can therefore be heard or recorded). The most important point to remember is that the focus group is not an easy option. Having said this, we can recommend a number of useful and practical guides: Asbury (1995); Greenbaum (1998); Morgan (1988); and Morgan and Krueger (1998).

## 12.14.3    Observation

Observation is used in both qualitative and quantitative research in a number of different ways. It can be used to establish what actually happens in various settings, to generate hypotheses and theories, to illuminate findings or examine situations more closely, and to evaluate the impact of interventions. It is in some ways a straightforward and easily

Plate 12.4    Observation can be used in both qualitative and quantitative research.
*Source*: Alamy

understood way of collecting data, but it requires as much preparatory thought as any other method. Decisions must be made before beginning the observations (or during the piloting phase) and the nature and causes of these decisions should be made explicit.

The first thing to do is to consider the ethical issues surrounding your proposed observation. Make contact with the relevant committees and official organisations, and also discuss your plans with representatives of those you wish to observe.

Do a number of 'informal' observations to begin with. Use these to make decisions about whom, where and what you are going to observe. Think about where you should position yourself or where to position equipment. If you are going to use a video recorder, try it out: can you clearly see the behaviours or events that you are interested in? These activities will also make your presence (and that of your equipment) more familiar to the people to be observed.

Prepare detailed descriptions or definitions of the events or behaviours that are to be observed. These may be refined later but it is important to be as clear as possible from the outset. Conduct a pilot study. Is the equipment reliable? Are you observing what you planned to observe? Can you record all of the necessary details in the time allowed? If you are conducting the study alone, you can enlist the help of colleagues to investigate the reliability of your interpretations: if another person interprets the events or behaviours in different ways then your descriptions of behaviour or events should be reconsidered. If you are working with another person, spend time at this stage in establishing agreement and make full records of the decisions made.

Keep records of observations. Make these as detailed as possible, including details of times, the situation and context, the potential range of participants, and anything else that was going on at the time of the observation. Also keep records of your own reflections about what happened. For example, the behaviour of students in a seminar might be affected by a party held at the students' union the night before. If you think that something was influencing the situation under observation, talk to the people concerned: there may be an explanation. Start your analysis or interpretation of observations as soon as possible. You may become aware of flaws in your approach which could be remedied before it is too late.

## 12.15  Dealing with qualitative data

The analysis of qualitative data is an ongoing process that is best begun early, as soon as the data collection begins in fact. Writing up should also be started early on: analysis and writing up are closely intertwined in qualitative studies. Typically the process of analysis is arduous and the researcher often goes through a phase of feeling disheartened in one way or another. Although this might not seem like a particularly helpful comment, it is worth knowing that it is a common experience and that it does not signify failure. Perseverance usually pays off.

### 12.15.1  Transcription

Burman (1994) pointed out that researchers dealing with interviews have to decide on the precise source of their 'raw data': is the analysis to be conducted on the transcript (such that the transcript becomes the source) or on the interview, including the social context in which the interview was conducted? This is not always an easy distinction (or decision) to make but it may be helpful to consider the extent to which the major focus is on the language used by the interviewee or on the interaction between interviewee and interviewer. Important decisions have to be made, therefore, about the way in which interviews are transcribed, including the extent to which pauses and other speech acts are represented. Various ways of systematising transcripts have been developed (e.g., Jefferson, 1985) which take account of pauses, inflections, intonations and stresses. You also need to consider ways of reflecting a local accent or way of speaking. Some researchers reproduce accents in the spelling of words while others use standard spelling whenever possible: compare 'I know masel' I shouldnae be daeing it but it's jist you're addicted tae it' (from an interviewee with a Glaswegian accent talking about smoking) with 'I know myself I shouldn't be doing it, but it's just you're addicted to it'. There are arguments for and against both approaches, and your approach should be consistent with the analysis you intend to conduct. At the very least, you need to consider your responsibility to your interviewees, the extent to which you are representing what they actually said, and the extent to which quotes will be intelligible to readers.

A full transcript will be a necessary condition for certain forms of analysis, and it makes other forms of analysis much easier to undertake. It is, however, time consuming: Potter (1998) estimated that it could take around 20 hours to transcribe 1 hour of tape, but in our experience that time can be reduced to around 8 hours, if the transcription method is simple, and if you have good keyboard skills and good equipment (e.g., mini-disk player, digital voice recorder, transcription equipment). Sometimes information can be extracted by listening to audio-tapes without transcription, but this leaves the researcher in a rather vulnerable position since the source is not available to others, and detailed analysis is very difficult to achieve.

### 12.15.2    Analysis of interviews

The way that you analyse your interview transcripts depends crucially on the approach you have decided upon: for example, IPA and discourse analysis are very different in aim and therefore different in process. However, it could be said that analysis is likely to involve a search for consistencies on the one hand and variations on the other. The level at which these qualities are sought will vary and it is common for the researcher to consider different levels within the same analysis. Thus the analysis might focus on the use of particular words or phrases, or a response to a particular question, or a theme which has emerged without prompting, or a narrative on a particular issue. In addition, the researcher might be looking for both individual and group consistencies and variations, moving between the different levels in an effort to find meaning.

Some undergraduate students will have access to software packages designed specifically to assist in qualitative analysis. These packages can help you organise your material, and are particularly useful in making links between different sources, such as field notes, documentation, and interview transcripts: different units of text can be tagged and ascribed to any number of different files which can represent themes or categories. While this may be a more tidy way of doing things and can certainly help with the management of the analytical process, the software does not ascribe any meaning to the categories and it can take the new researcher some time to become familiar with the software. Often, at undergraduate level, that time would have been better spent on the analysis itself. See Langdridge (2004) and Miles and Huberman (1994) for discussions on the ways in which computer software can be used effectively to manage and analyse qualitative data.

Any analysis of text will involve a number of stages. If you are about to start this process, we recommend reading a more detailed account on your chosen approach than we can provide here: for example, Hammersley and Atkinson (1995); Potter (1998); Smith, Jarman and Osborn (1999); and Wetherell, Taylor and Yates (2001b). However, we can provide an overview. Assuming that you have the interview transcripts as document files on your computer, the first step is a practical one: format the documents in double-spacing, with large margins or indents on either side of the text, so that the text is in the middle of the page. This format will allow you to write in your comments on either side of the text.

The first level of coding is one common to a number of approaches. At this level, you are trying to see what your participants are saying, keeping as open a mind as possible. As you read the transcript, make notes or comments down one side of the margin as you go along, and keep adding to these as you re-read the transcript. Try not to censor your thoughts too much at this stage, or to try to fit what you are reading into pre-existing categories (unless you are doing a structured content analysis). If appropriate, you can use the spaces to make notes or memos, too. When you feel that you have completed this phase, you can start looking for themes or categories, and these can be recorded in the other margin. For example, you may find that a student you have interviewed sometimes compares his exam strategy with those used by his friends or other students. Sometimes this comparison is favourable (in that he feels he uses a better strategy), sometimes it is unfavourable. At this stage, these would be left as separate themes, until you get some sense of if, or how, these themes are linked. The next stage involves a further organisation of these themes or categories, although the way that this is done is highly dependent on the analytical approach and the aims of the study. However, you should probably go through at least the first two stages with each transcript or document that you are working with before going on to the next.

It is common to feel overwhelmed at this stage. The interviews may have elicited any number of themes or 'repertoires', and you may have to decide on what to write up and what to discard. One way to begin the process is to go back to your research questions. From there, you could focus on responses to a particular question or topic. For example, how did people describe their experiences at the exercise class, or what kind of discourse did they use to talk about the benefits of exercise? What different exam strategies were identified by students and how were these categorised by the students themselves? Or look to the themes and categories that you have managed to identify and start thinking about the ones to focus on, the ones to summarise, and the ones to discard. Sometimes the themes or categories that you did not expect to find are the more interesting or important. Somewhere along the line, you need to go back to the literature on your topic, and this in itself may help focus your attention on how to present your findings.

### 12.15.3  Field notes

**Field notes** are the notes made (or scribbled) during and immediately after visits to the location and they cover events, information and the thoughts and reflections of the researcher. The best way to approach the analysis of field notes is to write them up in some structured way; the most useful structures will depend on the focus and orientation of the research (see Miles & Huberman, 1994). One way to go about this would be to start with a description of the contact with participants on that day, giving details of the people involved and the events or situations that were witnessed. Following this, details would be given of the main themes or issues that emerged. You might then indicate your own part in the activities, your reflections, and any other potentially relevant observations. Field notes relating to interviews could include reflections on the process, and these can be added in some way to the interview transcript. These remarks might cover your perceptions of the relationship formed with the interviewee, thoughts on what was said and how it was said, thoughts on the quality of the interview, and reactions and 'mental notes'.

### 12.15.4  Observational data

Observational data can be analysed in different ways. If the observations include discrete behaviours or events, then it might be possible to create categories. For example, if the observation was focused on interactions between people, then it would be possible to discriminate between different forms of interaction. It would then be possible to examine the frequencies of these different forms of interaction, as well as considering the situations in which these occurred, and the outcomes and implications for those concerned. Categorisation is generally a process during which the researcher has to consider the extent to which new events or behaviours can be slotted into existing categories or whether it is necessary to create a new category. Categories should be meaningful in terms of the aims of the research: it becomes difficult to deal with a large number of categories, but collapsing events into a small number of categories can mean that important or relevant variation is missed. A large 'miscellaneous' category usually means that the category system is flawed in some way. It is important to keep clear and detailed records of the process of categorising: the criteria used to select categories, and to assign an event to one category rather than another, should be made explicit in the final report.

Categorisation is the point at which the overlap between a quantitative and a qualitative approach can become apparent: frequencies can be reported, numbers can be applied. Many researchers prefer not to submit their observations to strict categorisation. This can be because they are interested in a sequence of behaviours or events which unfolds during the observation. However, others may resist attempts to apply an implicit interpretation of events, preferring an explicit interpretation during which they and others have access to the process. The categorisation of people and social situations is essentially a flawed and subjective process: for example, mistakes can be made when categorising people according to social class or ethnic origin, and it is better to describe people rather than to ascribe labels which may not be accurate.

## 12.16 The quality of the research

There is much debate around the question of judging the quality of qualitative work. Some authors have argued that the criteria used to judge quantitative research are not always appropriate here (e.g., Tindall, 1994). This does not mean, however, that the quality of the work is unimportant. In fact, many qualitative researchers are committed to improving and maintaining quality, not only for their own peace of mind, but also because of the responsibility they feel towards their participants. For a recent debate on this topic within psychology (although it would also apply to the other social sciences), see Elliott, Fischer and Rennie (1999); and Reicher (2000).

Since qualitative research typically centres on a particular context, event or situation, and since each researcher brings to the study his or her own orientations, qualities and skills, there are no grounds for expecting consistencies across studies. However, there are grounds for expecting the researcher to provide sufficient information about the process to permit others to assess the extent to which the interpretation might be idiosyncratic. One of the problems faced by qualitative researchers is that they are subject to the same biases as everyone else. For example, a particularly vivid event or description tends to be remembered and recalled more easily than the more mundane; this is a problem when the vivid description is not particularly representative. Researchers should take the time to pull back and consider the extent to which they are reporting the whole picture and not just the aspect to which they are attracted. Miles and Huberman (1994) stressed the importance of considering outliers, or cases which appear to disconfirm interpretations; they should be discussed rather than ignored. Similarly, alternative explanations and interpretations should be fully explored in the report.

**Triangulation** is the term usually used to describe the ways in which the reliability of a study can be assessed. The term describes the way in which a second point of view on a phenomenon creates a triangle. Triangulation can be used in different ways: to assess the extent to which different participants or sources provide the same information; the extent to which different researchers perceive the phenomena in the same ways; the extent to which different methods, such as observations and interviews, provide consistent information; and the extent to which different theories or explanations provide adequate accounts of the same data. Useful accounts of the ways in which triangulation can be used are provided by Miles and Huberman (1994) and Tindall (1994).

Validity is an important component of qualitative research to the extent that the researchers should be aiming to provide an adequate account of the phenomenon under investigation. At the very least, they owe this to their participants. In fact, it is sometimes held to be good practice to show the participants the findings before finalising the report; if they disagree with the interpretation then this can be taken into account. The field notes and observations made by the researcher during the process of research are vital to assessing the validity or 'trustworthiness' of a report. Readers should have access not only to the ways in which all important decisions were made but also to the reflections of the researcher on his or her role in the study. Such detail is not generally included in reports of quantitative studies, but with qualitative work it is important to provide clear indications of the ways in which the work might have been weakened (or strengthened) by the researcher's involvement. It is also important to honestly indicate the limitations of the work.

## 12.17   Points to consider when writing up

We cover this topic in detail in Part 7, so we will just make a few general points here. First of all, it should be noted that there is no one 'correct' way of writing up a qualitative study and many different formats can be used to impart the relevant details to the reader. As with any study, the final report should be adequately referenced and should take the work of other authors in the field into account. However, each qualitative study is unique in some way, and the structure of the final report should be adapted to fit the demands of the study rather than the other way round. For example, it may make more sense to discuss the findings as they emerge, rather than have a separate discussion section, so that the reader can follow the process of interpretation more closely. Some researchers write up their work almost as a narrative, telling the story of the study from its inception, including details of key decisions in chronological order. This often makes good sense, particularly if things did not go according to plan. Whatever the format, it is important to describe key decisions relating to methodology in detail. These include decisions about the research agenda, the framing of the research questions, and methods of analysis and interpretation. All of these details will help the reader to understand and evaluate the study.

## Review

This chapter has briefly described some of the main approaches to qualitative research, ways of collecting data and the points which should be taken into account before commencing such a study. We acknowledge that those of you who wish to conduct qualitative research will have to go elsewhere for detail, but we hope that we have given you a starting point, and we recommend that you follow up at least some of the references we have provided. We hope that we have not deterred anyone from trying out these methods: qualitative research is time consuming, but it can be very involving and deeply satisfying.

## Suggested further reading

Banister, P., Burman, E., Parker, I., Taylor, M., & Tindall, C. (Eds.). (1994). *Qualitative methods in psychology: A research guide*. Buckingham: Open University Press.

Elliott, R., Fischer, C. T., & Rennie, D. L. (1999). Evolving guidelines for publication of qualitative research studies in psychology and related fields. *British Journal of Clinical Psychology, 38*, 215–229.

Henwood, K., & Pidgeon, N. (1992). Qualitative research and psychological theorizing. *British Journal of Psychology, 83*, 97–111.

Langdridge, D. (2004). *Introduction to research methods and data analysis in psychology*. Harlow, Essex: Pearson/Prentice Hall.

Miles, M. B., & Huberman, A. M. (1994). *Qualitative data analysis* (2nd ed.). Thousand Oaks, CA: Sage.

Silverman, D. (1993). *Interpreting qualitative data: Methods for analysing talk, text and interaction*. London: Sage.

Willig, C. (2001). *Introducing qualitative research in psychology: Adventures in theory and method*. Buckingham: Open University Press.

# Writing up research

## Part 7

**Introducing research**

**Planning a research project—the design**

**Carrying out research—methods & procedure**

**Describing research findings—descriptives**

**Analysing research findings—inferential statistics**

**Carrying out qualitative research**

**Writing up and presenting the findings of research**

Alamy

This part considers all the important elements which comprise a research report and offers guidance on clear and concise methods for writing up the various activities involved in any piece of psychological research, be it quantitative or qualitative. Since the material presented here is of a much more practical nature than the material covered in previous parts, a great deal of what follows is of the *what to do–what not to do* variety. The following topics are covered:

- what should go into a report and why it should be there
- where it should go
- style
- reporting results
- referencing
- writing up qualitative work

# 13 Writing up research

You have now completed a state-of-the-art, cutting-edge, incisive and comprehensive study (or at least, this is your belief). However, other people can only know of the brilliance of this research by being told about it in some way, usually through a written report, which will offer details on what you have done, why it was done and what the outcomes were. For an undergraduate, a large proportion of marks in a research module will probably be assigned to the final report, and success will depend almost entirely on the quality of the writing and presentation. It is therefore important to consider the way in which this work will be presented from the earliest stages through to the concluding comments; this is true whether the research was quantitative or qualitative and what follows will in large part be applicable to both approaches.

Ideally, a study should be written up as it progresses (it really is easier this way, rather than trying to remember what you did after the fact, which is the usual way for the majority of students). Mapping out the main points of the literature review as you do it will often serve as a guide in the formulation of hypotheses and will clarify design and methodological issues – points made right at the beginning of this book in Parts 1 and 2. Writing up the methodology section while it is still fresh in your mind will save you hours of work at a later stage, as will keeping a careful record of your references from the beginning (this goes for a bibliography as well, though note that a bibliography is quite different from a reference section: see section 13.6). The point here is that, if you are going to (or might) cite material in the body of your report, it must be properly referenced (see Box 13.15), with authors, year, journal title, etc. Noting this information at an early stage will avoid frantic scrabbling through scores of papers when it comes to writing up. One of the most common mutterings overheard in university libraries (from students and authors of textbooks alike) is, 'what did I do with that reference?'

Another area where it is important to keep track of what you are doing is in the results section – writing up your results as you conduct the analysis will identify any significant gaps while there is still sufficient time to fill them. Alternatively, this might also help you to recognise when further analysis is unnecessary: a common problem with many undergraduate reports is over-analysis of data, which creates needless work for both the student and the supervisor. However, even the most conscientious of researchers may have to make amendments to their report at the last minute, and it is only when discussions and conclusions have been written that the overall structure may be assessed (this is the reason why you should always write the abstract *last*). It is important to allow yourself the time to read your work critically before it has to be submitted, to reflect on its contents and to make any necessary changes. This is why you should make notes as you go along, and Box 13.1 should serve as a guide.

Box 13.1

Practicalities . . .

# Keeping track

- File complete references of articles or books that you have read, with details of the main points of studies or theories.

- Write down the arguments behind your hypotheses – it is all too easy, during the course of a lengthy project, to lose sight of what the original aims were. Being able to return to some statement of intent will serve as a reminder as to why you are doing this. This may seem an odd point to make but students often experience periods of alarm when, bogged down by scores of questionnaires, rating scales and transcripts, they feel they have lost direction. This seems to become a particular problem at the data analysis stage and many supervisors are used to their students looking uncomfortable when asked why they carried out *this* analysis instead of *that*.

- Carefully record the means whereby you recruited participants, with details of the numbers agreeing or refusing to participate. This can become an important issue if you are hoping to generalise from your sample to a wider population – participant numbers and sampling procedures will be key limiting factors in how much you will be able to say here.

- Note any changes that you may have made to questionnaires or other instruments, and the arguments behind the changes. It is important to demonstrate how your research developed and one of the elements a supervisor will be interested in concerns your choice of, for example, questionnaire items: Why ask these questions? Why in this format? Why a Likert scale as opposed to a rating scale?

- Record details of pilot studies, and any modifications made as a result of those studies: as with the previous point, it is important to show how your research developed and how you ended up adopting a particular approach. Pilot studies often play a key role in determining the final structure and format of research; they should therefore be described in detail.

- Maintain a log of the exact procedures you employed, with appropriate justification. Much of the criticism levelled at undergraduate projects revolves around procedural problems – for example, not enough detail, or no explanation of why an approach was adopted.

- Keep track of coding procedures. Not only will you be expected to give an account of this in your report but, from a practical point of view, it is easy to forget which particular numerical values you used to denote responses on a multi-item questionnaire or to distinguish participants in a control group from those in an experimental group. To change a coding frame in the middle of a study can be fatal.

▪ Keep a detailed record of all analyses carried out and why you did them. Apart from the obvious necessity of reporting this as part of your write-up, there is a risk of losing sight of what you are trying to do at this stage; wading through pages of SPSS output showing descriptive statistics, numerous $t$-tests and the odd analysis of variance can be confusing (what an understatement), not to mention a major contributor to the sense of panic which often strikes at the analysis stage of a research project. Faced with a tearful student wielding the results of umpteen correlations a supervisor will typically ask, "What was it you were trying to do?"

There are different ways to keep notes, although perhaps a diary or labbook format is the simplest; keeping up with reading, meetings with supervisors and notes needs a certain amount of self-discipline, and it is surprising how often one simply cannot remember such details at a later stage. You really will be saving yourself time and trouble if you keep an accurate running record of your research activities in some organised format. Relying on memory alone, or random scraps of paper, will not be effective; your supervisor will (or should) keep a diary of your progress and it is very much in your own interests to do the same.

## 13.3  The structure of a psychology report

The basic structure of your write-up should normally follow the familiar layout of a standard laboratory report, in that it should consist of the four major sections: Introduction, Method, Results, and Discussion, in that order, headed by a title and abstract and followed by a reference list and any appendices. Part of the reason for keeping to this conventional format is that the reader will know just where to find each piece of essential information about your research. You should therefore make sure that your report conforms to this layout as much as possible, and that relevant information is where it should be.

The report of a substantial research project is likely to be weightier than the average laboratory report. A common question from undergraduates is 'how long should the report be?' The answer, no matter how unsatisfactory, must be: *as long as it takes to report the research concisely, but clearly, accurately and completely*. Having said this, most student researchers will probably have some sort of length indication specified by their department or tutor (e.g., about 10,000 words). This is always a rough indication, since an assessor is not actually going to count the words (big surprise, especially to those of you who like to include a word count as part of submitted work), but any such limit is worth bearing in mind and a report should always endeavour to end up somewhere within the recommended range. One of the most annoying aspects of undergraduate reports for supervisors is unnecessary length – a product of over-writing and a sense that every concept, theory or piece of previous research must be explained in great detail, especially in the introduction. In most cases this is not necessary and a general overview of established theory is sufficient, except when a particular study or issue forms the basis for the current piece of research, in which case detail is essential. Box 13.2 offers a summary of how a report should be structured, while the sections which follow consider the elements of a typical report in detail.

Box 13.2

## A Closer Look At . . .

# The structure of a typical project report

### Title

Should be brief, clear, accurate; don't try to be funny or whimsical (10–12 words at most).

### Abstract

Approximately 100–150 word summary. Say briefly what it's about, what was done and what was found. Write this last!

### Introduction

What was this research all about? What relevant previous work was there? What did they find? Is there a central theory, or a debate about different theories? Was the present study the same (a replication) – if not, how was it different? In either case, what were you trying to do (aims)? And what did you expect to find (the hypotheses)?

### Method

Four sub-headings, setting out the structure of the study, as follows:

| | |
|---|---|
| ***Design*** | What sort of study was it (e.g., an experiment, a survey, a case-study)? |
| | Repeated measures design, independent groups, or a mixed design? |
| | What were the dependent variables (what was measured)? |
| | What were the independent variables (what varied across different participants)? |
| ***Participants*** | How many? Any *relevant* description. |
| ***Apparatus*** | What materials or equipment were used? |
| ***Procedure*** | Briefly describe what happened. Quote instructions given to the participants. |

### Results

A written presentation of summary or descriptive statistics, not individual participant data. For example, give the mean and standard deviation for the dependent variable for each different condition. If any graphs or tables help clarify the results, put them in here, but don't merely duplicate tabular data – figures are useful only if they clarify or highlight data in a manner not possible with tables. Report the statistics used, and say briefly whether or not the results supported the hypotheses.

### Discussion

An examination of your results in light of your hypotheses or research questions, and in comparison with previous findings. What conclusions do your results point to? How do you interpret your findings? You could also suggest improvements or variations in the design, or further hypotheses which might be tested.

### References

List only references actually cited earlier in the report. If it is important to mention other sources used, though not explicitly cited, these should be given in a separate bibliography.

### Appendices

This is the location for the raw materials used in the study – stimuli, examples of question-naires and so on. Raw data and computer printouts are not recommended, unless there is a case for inclusion. Supervisors will normally inform you of their expectations here.

### 13.3.1  Title

This should be concise but informative, and should give a clear indication of what the project is about: for example, 'Individual differences in the perception of embedded figures', or 'Gender and age stereotypes of emotionality'. Readers should be able to tell from the title alone whether a report is of interest to them, or of relevance to their own research. A title that is too general may be at best uninformative and at worst misleading: for example, the title 'Gender and memory' gives no indication of which aspects of either gender or memory were investigated. If a report is likely to be placed on library access, or in other ways made available to a broader readership, it is important that the title contains the relevant keywords that any interested readers would be likely to use in their literature search (e.g., 'individual differences', 'perception' or 'embedded figures'). This is of particular importance today when, increasingly, researchers are using the Internet and other electronic databases to carry out keyword searches. Box 13.3 looks at common errors in titles.

**Box 13.3**

**A Closer Look At . . .**

## Common errors in the title

Some authors try to apply snappy titles to their work, incorporating puns, innuendo or otherwise playing on words, presumably in the hopes of appealing to journal editors (or amusing supervisors enough to gain an extra few marks).
For example:

*New treatment in substance abuse: Not to be sniffed at*

Or

*Altered states – dream on*

Amusing as these may be, they don't actually offer much information about the studies and would be likely to be overlooked in the early stages of a literature review for this reason. And in case anyone is wondering, editors and supervisors would not be impressed.

### 13.3.2  Abstract

The abstract is a short summary of the main information contained in the project report as a whole. It should ideally be about 100 or 150 words in length, although some journals (and supervisors) now prefer structured abstracts. While the abstract is positioned at the beginning of the report, it is often the last part to be actually written – it will certainly be easier to write the abstract when the report is finished than the other way around. Normally the abstract should, very briefly, identify the problem studied; the hypotheses tested; the method employed, including the number and kind of participants; the results obtained; and the main conclusions drawn. Statistical details should usually be excluded, unless you have used a novel type of analysis, or have departed from the norm in any other important way (e.g., used a non-standard probability level). In short, an abstract should be like an extremely condensed version of the full report, providing key information from the introduction, method, results and discussion sections. Box 13.4 discusses common errors in abstracts.

---

Box 13.4

## A Closer Look At . . .

## Common errors in the abstract

In the search for brevity, some writers reduce the information content of an abstract to the point where it becomes impossible to judge the nature of a study without reading the entire report. This is a particularly common problem among undergraduate students, but it is not exclusive to them.

> A study on consumerism among a stratified sample failed to demonstrate significant differences between any of the comparison groups on any of the 15 differentiating behaviours. In all cases the null hypotheses were accepted.

An abstract of this nature is virtually useless – there is no real indication of what the study was about, which aspects of consumerism were being studied, or the type of participant used. Nor is there any indication as to what kind of statistical analysis was carried out in order to test the hypotheses, whatever they happened to be.

Equally unhelpful is the two-page abstract in which the writer is incapable of summarising the important elements of the study:

> In a study carried out over five days between April 1 and April 5, one hundred participants took part in a between-groups experiment on choice behaviour, with choice being determined as a preference for vegetarian versus non-vegetarian food in a canteen environment. The participants were initially drawn from a local population comprising primarily university undergraduates, all of whom lived within the campus area, except for a small group who commuted from a neighbouring district. Of these, the population was known to comprise 80% males and 20% females, with an age distribution roughly . . .
> Arghh!

This amount of detail, if extended to the rest of the study, would provide an abstract almost as long as the report itself, which is as counterproductive as the previous minimalist example.

*Checklist . . .*

# The abstract

A good abstract should contain the following information:

- The research issue being explored – this would comprise the research question, or the theory being investigated in the study.
- The hypotheses being tested – the specific predictions which form the basis of the study.
- The design of the study – the way in which it has been set up to explore the hypotheses, expressed in the language of design (e.g., repeated measures, counterbalanced).
- The key (relevant) characteristics of the participants – for example, there is little point in offering detail on age in the abstract unless age influenced, or explained, the findings in some way.
- The key (relevant) characteristics of any apparatus used – for example, if findings can be explained only by reference to the specifics of apparatus, or if replication could not take place without this particular information.
- The outcome of the study – for example, whether the hypotheses are accepted or rejected, or the key findings.
- Conclusions, and a comment on any unusual features of the study, if appropriate.

Writing a good abstract (one that conveys key information clearly and accurately, without exceeding the length limit) is difficult, but it is important. Like the title, the abstract may be accessed by online search systems, so it should contain enough specific information to enable a researcher to find the work in the first place, and then to decide whether to read the whole thing. This is becoming increasingly important with the advent of modern databases since the abstract (and the title) will often be the first point of contact others will have with a researcher's work. It is therefore important to get it right (see Box 13.5).

### 13.3.3 Contents

If the purpose of a write-up is a final report rather than an article intended for publication (which, alas, is something few undergraduates actually consider), a list of contents could be provided, based on section or chapter headings. Also included here should be details of any appendices, and this is probably an appropriate point at which to remind you to number the pages – again, something often forgotten by keen (or late) students.

### 13.3.4 Introduction

This is the first major section of the report. A good introduction should provide the reader with the essential background to the project, starting out with a broad description of the particular research topic that is being dealt with, and moving on through a clear and accurate account of the previous research which has led up to the project. You should be able to show that your particular study is a natural development of this previous work, and that it adds something – even if that something is only that an effect is (or is not) replicated with a different sample. It is also important to show that you are aware of current or recent work which is relevant to the study, and that the important theoretical issues are understood.

There is no one correct way to begin an introduction, but it is probably a good idea to start off with a brief overview of the area of study to set the scene for what is to follow. For example, if a study concerns the relationship between exercise and psychological wellbeing, one could begin by describing the general assumptions made about this relationship, followed by a delineation of the aspects of exercise and wellbeing to be considered in further detail in the report. If a study concerns ways of coping with a particular illness, you could begin by describing the aspects of the illness which may be found stressful, followed by an outline of the model of stress and coping which you use as a framework for analysis. The introductory paragraphs should therefore outline, in a general way, what the study is about and which aspects of a given issue you are exploring.

The central part of an introduction should cover the relevant research which forms a background to the project. If the research is based on one major published study, describe this in some detail, including the number and type of participants used, the design of the original study, the measures taken, and the method of analysis. This amount of detail is necessary since, in your own study, you will probably be using a similar design, with similar types of people. If the aim is to refute or criticise a previous piece of research, you will still need this level of detail, if only to demonstrate how, for example, by using a different mode of analysis you generate completely different findings. Following on from this you should comment on the study which is serving as a platform for your own work, taking into account such issues as the adequacy of the sample, measures, design and analysis used, the extent to which the results may be generalised to other populations, and any theoretical implications of the results. You can then describe other studies in the area using this general framework, although unless they relate directly to the research issue, or provide a further foundation for what you are going to do, these should not be presented in anything like this amount of detail. In this way, the major areas of interest, related issues and matters pertaining to the particular approach you are taking, can be clarified as you proceed. Consequently, hypotheses or research questions when they are finally offered – usually in the concluding phase of the introduction – should not come as a surprise to the reader: every aspect of the hypotheses should have been mentioned at an earlier point in the introduction and should follow on naturally and logically from what has gone before. It is a common experience of supervisors to come to the aims, objectives and hypotheses section of a report and then to have to go back through the introductory discussion to try and find out where these hypotheses came from and what their rationale might happen to be. It is worth mentioning that this can be extremely irritating for a supervisor, so consider yourself warned. Box 13.6 lists common errors occurring in introductory text.

The introduction should normally lead towards an overview of what the study will actually do (but saving the details for the next section) and should conclude with a statement of the hypotheses. It is often useful to state these twice: first as a general prediction of outcomes (e.g., that exercise would be related to wellbeing); and then more precisely. For example:

It was therefore hypothesised that significant differences in psychological wellbeing would be observed between the two conditions (exercise vs. non-exercise), such that participants in the exercise condition would gain higher scores on the measure of

# Common errors in the introduction section

- Writing an anecdotal, subjective background which is based more on personal opinion than a sound knowledge of the field.

- Trying to cover the entire history of research in the field: be selective, and review only that which is directly relevant to your own study. This is especially important in areas which have proved popular among researchers (imagine trying to review the last 50 years of research into personality and you will get the point).

- Explaining too much: you may assume some theoretical knowledge on the part of your reader. You should not have to define common terms – unless, of course, you are using them in a specialised way. (It is worth considering the nature of your readership here: a report for publication in a scientific journal will not have to spell out the characteristics of various measurement scales in questionnaire design. A presentation to undergraduates, on the other hand, might require that the structure of, for example, a Likert scale be explained.)

- Explaining too little: we are not all experts in your field, so write as if for the intelligent, interested, non-specialist. In practical terms a balance will have to be struck between this and the previous point.

- Failing to show how your review of the relevant literature leads up to, and provides a rationale for, your particular study.

- Failing to state just what it is that your study is seeking to accomplish. A frequent form of this error is failing to state your hypotheses at the end of the introduction.

wellbeing than would participants in the non-exercise condition. It was further hypothesised that this effect would be moderated by gender, such that differences between the two conditions would be greater for females than for males.

It is also useful at this stage to identify (as much for your own benefit as the reader's) the independent and dependent variables so that it is always clear what is being tested: the more precise your hypotheses, the more straightforward the analysis. (And the more likely you will be able to recover from the sense of panic common to the middle stages of a project, when there is a danger of losing sight of what it was you were trying to do.)

Pilot studies may also be mentioned in the introduction if they have contributed to the development of hypotheses or research questions. Otherwise, the convention is that details of pilot studies are given in the method section, especially where they relate to developing questionnaire items or strategies for data gathering.

## 13.3.5 Method

The method section is the next major part of a research write-up, in that it gives all the information about how the research was actually carried out. Its purpose is to present a detailed description of the conduct of the study in such a way that the reader can follow the natural timeline, or sequence of events, which characterised the study, from general introduction through specific hypotheses to actual testing and data gathering. This is an important section since it provides the opportunity to explain what you actually did. Most of the material covered in the introduction is concerned with theory and hypotheses. The method section is concerned with the concrete: Who participated? How were participants assigned to groups? What was measured? What checks were made on extraneous factors? These are typical questions posed by anyone reviewing or assessing a report and the answers should be readily available in this section, simply because of the detail offered by the researcher. From a practical point of view, the method section also provides a supervisor with insight into the extent to which a student has been careful and systematic in the conduct of a study. This is the section in which design flaws become highlighted and the limitations of the study underlined. Often, when criticising the findings of a study, a supervisor will return to the method section with comments such as, 'you cannot make this generalisation with such a small sample', or, 'by doing it this way you overlooked an important issue . . .' Frightening as this revelation must be to many undergraduate readers, it nonetheless makes the point that this part of a report is central to the way in which a piece of research will be evaluated. If a study is flawed it will show up here but, if the researcher understands enough about the issues and how they were tackled, the limitations outlined here will form the basis of much of the later discussion section in which the writer will attempt to justify the conclusions drawn, demonstrate that she understands why hypotheses were not supported, and be able to outline ways in which the issues might be more effectively explored.

A second reason for providing a detailed method is to allow replication of the study; perhaps the study has broken new ground in its field, or perhaps its findings are unexpected, or even suspect in some way. Or perhaps a researcher wants to know if particular effects can be reproduced under different circumstances, or by using different types of participant. Whatever the case, replication is possible only if sufficient detail is provided on the conduct of the original study. Now realistically, this will rarely be true of most undergraduate research – as we have previously stated, studies at this level are more often carried out for demonstration and experiential purposes than to genuinely extend our understanding of the human condition. Yet, as part of this process, an ability to produce replicable methodology is an important skill for anyone intending to pursue their interest in psychology beyond the graduate level.

Below, we discuss the major divisions or sub-sections which comprise a typical method section, and describe the ways in which this part of a report would be structured.

### 13.3.6   Design

This, the initial part of the method section, describes the formal structure of the study. It is usually brief and concise, but lacking in specific details about participants and procedure, and it is generally couched in the technical language of a research design (between-groups, repeated measures, counterbalanced, etc.). First, you must specify what kind of investigation you carried out (for example, an experiment, an observational study, a survey, a case study, and so on). You should then define the variables either measured or manipulated in the study, making the distinction between independent variables (or predictors) and dependent variables (or outcome measures). This ought to be a straightforward task, since these matters will have been sorted out in the early stages of a study. However, supervisors are often surprised at the confusions which appear over the description of variables present in a study, even in cases where the rest of the work is of a high standard. (If this is remains a problem, a review of Part 2 will be helpful.)

Box 13.7

A Closer Look At . . .

# A typical design

In a 2 × 3 quasi-experimental design, male and female patients were randomly assigned to one of three exercise conditions. The dependent variable was post-operative recovery time, measured in days to a pre-determined level, and the between-groups independent variables were gender (male or female) and exercise regime (none, moderate and regular). Age was controlled for in the analysis.

This difficulty of correctly identifying variables can sometimes be aggravated in correlational studies where identification is sometimes less clear – variables are related or associated with one another but not always in an obvious cause-and-effect manner. However, you should usually be able to distinguish between the variables that you want to find out about (outcome), and the variables that you are just using to get there (predictors). You should also specify any important extraneous variables: that is, factors which under other circumstances might be considered independent variables in their own right, but which in this case might have to be controlled for. (Our discussion on the distinction between multiple regression and partial correlation in Part 5 is a useful guide to the issue of when a variable is extraneous or not.)

Another important design element is whether you have used repeated measures (within-subjects design), independent groups (between-groups design), or a combination of the two (mixed design). (See Part 2 for more detail.) This should be accurately reported, especially in experimental studies (note that correlational designs by definition use repeated measures). The factor levels which form the experimental conditions should be described if appropriate, as should the method by which the participants were assigned to groups. Box 13.7 provides an example of the information expected in a typical design.

A common mistake made by undergraduates is to confuse design and procedural matters. It must be remembered that the design of a study is the plan of campaign, formulated before the study proper is implemented. Consequently when decisions are made it is not always possible to know how many participants would actually respond to your questionnaire, or that your particular experimental manipulation would produce a revolt among one of your groups. This is why the design is a formal statement of intent, expressed in general terms and using the language of experimentation (if appropriate). If you are still in doubt about this, have another look at Part 2. Box 13.8 also illustrates this point.

If your project is at the more qualitative end of the spectrum, you should still try to give a formal and objective description of your project under this heading. Thus you should clarify the method (e.g., observation, or semi-structured interview), the main issues under consideration, corresponding to dependent variables (e.g., types of non-verbal behaviours, expressed sources of stress at work), other variables or factors corresponding to independent variables and covariates (e.g., gender, age, employment status), and time factors, such as the frequency of repeated observations.

The final element in this section is shown in Box 13.9, comprising a checklist of key points which you should review before you consider any other developments in your study. It is worth remembering that if you have come up with an inappropriate design, or if you are unclear about key design elements, everything which follows will be affected.

Box 13.8

## A Closer Look At . . .

# Common errors in the design section

Many people, and especially those new to the research report, readily confuse procedural elements with the design. By way of example, what follows is an outline of procedural matters rather than design:

> Eighty subjects were used in the study, 40 males and 40 females, of varying ages and backgrounds. Both groups were treated identically, being shown a video (see Appendix 1), prior to the experimental manipulation, in which the procedural details were explained (see Appendix 2). The manipulation itself comprised a small parts assembly exercise in which a number of rivets, washers and bolts were assembled in a predetermined order and then inserted into a pegboard. On completion of the experiment each subject completed a questionnaire which rated various attitudinal factors on a 1–5 scale . . .

The author has not clarified the type of study (is it between-groups or within-subjects, or mixed?); the dependent variables (is the main dependent variable time taken to complete the task, or attitudinal scores, or both?); or the independent variables (presumably gender is an independent variable, but this is not clearly stated). The key point about a design is that it should serve almost as a schematic map or diagram of a study in which the major elements – and only those – are illustrated. Most of the details in our example are procedural.

### 13.3.7 Participants

Give *relevant* details of those who participated in your research, including the number of individuals who comprised your sample, their age and gender, and on what basis they were allocated to subgroups. Any participant profile characteristics which might have affected their responses or behaviour should be mentioned, and you should explain how these were dealt with (e.g., 'to control for possible gender effects, equal numbers of male and female participants were allocated to each of the groups'). You should also state how

Box 13.9

  Checklist . . .

# The design section

Your design should contain the following information:

- ▢ The nature of the study (e.g., experiment, survey, case study).
- ▢ The structure of the design (e.g., repeated measures, between-groups).
- ▢ The independent and dependent variables.
- ▢ Extraneous variables and any controls used to reduce their effect.

A Closer Look At . . .

# A section on participants

Sixty undergraduate students (30 males, 30 females) participated in the study. All were members of the university participant panel, and all responded to a formal written request for participants placed on the appropriate notice board: the first 60 volunteers were recruited for the study. The median age of participants was 19 years (range 17–23 years). Participants were assigned to either the hedgehog group or the newt group on a quasi-random basis, such that equal numbers of males and females were included in each group. Given the nature of the task, the participants were screened to ensure that their eyesight was normal or corrected to normal.

the participants were obtained, and give refusal rates if appropriate. You should aim to give sufficient detail to enable you and the reader to decide the extent to which your participants were representative of the population. For example, if you recruited participants through a self-help group or through a newsletter, you may have distributed 100 questionnaires but had only 40 returns. This should be stated, since it may imply that your results are applicable only to a subsection of the target population. While this may be a limitation of your project it is not something to be hidden, or indeed to be ashamed of. In this case, the possible limitations of your results should be considered in the discussion element of your report. See Box 13.10.

## 13.3.8 Apparatus (or materials)

Give full details of all equipment, apparatus and materials used. Trade names and model numbers of pieces of equipment should be given. The full names of published tests should be given, with references. Details of pilot studies may be given here, if they confirmed the utility of apparatus or materials, or, alternatively, if they indicated the need for changes or alterations. If questionnaires or other test materials have been changed in any way, give full details and a rationale for the changes made. For example, you may have changed the wording of certain items from a questionnaire originating in the United States to make it more suitable for a UK population, or you may have omitted an item because it was unethical or irrelevant within the context of your project.

If you have used a fairly lengthy questionnaire or interview schedule, you may wish to give some representative examples of items in this section, and refer the reader to an appendix where the entire list can be found. If your questionnaire incorporates a number of different sections or subscales, make it clear what these are and how they are to be calculated. If you have written a computer programme for your study, give a careful explanation of what it actually does. The programme itself can be listed in full in an appendix.

You may have devised an interview schedule for your project. In this case, describe the main areas covered in the interview and indicate the sources of any particular questions or wording. Give the interview schedule in full in an appendix.

### 13.3.9 Procedure

Describe exactly what was done, and include verbal instructions given to participants. If instructions were provided in handouts or with test materials, include these in an appendix. Bear in mind that the function of this section is to give the reader sufficient detail to repeat the study (although we accept that rarely will anyone wish to replicate an undergraduate study, except under exceptional circumstances). And of course, we mustn't forget the key role of the procedure in assessment – for your supervisor, the procedure is an important element of your report.

Indicate the circumstances under which the participants responded or were tested (e.g., in a designated room on their own, in groups, in their own homes, in the library), the order in which test items were completed (e.g., whether the order was randomised or fixed, and if fixed, what the order was) and the approximate length of time required of participants. You should also clarify the extent to which participants were offered anonymity, the instructions participants were given with regard to terminating their involvement in the project, any payment offered, and debriefing or feedback procedures. If a consent form was used (and it ought to be) this should be referred to and an example of a blank form shown in an appendix. You may have given some of this information in earlier sections; however, it is important to provide a full and clear description of procedure in this section, even at the risk of repeating yourself.

The method is the second major section of the report, but is often the first to be written. The reason for this is that most of the technical details, the structure, and the practical details of the study have to be decided in advance. The method section is also the easiest to write, since you do not have to invent anything or be creative in any way: you are simply reporting factual information about your study.

### 13.3.10 Results

If you have conducted a quantitative study, this section should contain all the objective outcomes of your study: the factual results, as generated from analyses and without any attempt at discussion, inference or speculation. This should be presented in conventional text format, as in the rest of the report (that is, give the main results in writing, with appropriate $t$-values, $F$-ratios or whatever). The temptation to expand and speculate here is admittedly huge – after all, this represents the point at which you have finally learned whether or not your predictions have been justified, hypotheses upheld or theories supported. However, the discussion section is the place to argue about the implications, not the results section. (The names given to these different parts of a report, by the way, ought to be something of a give-away!)

First of all, present the descriptive statistics, which should summarise your data in a standard form. Then present the inferential statistics, which test whether your results can be distinguished from chance and hence whether your hypotheses have been rejected or upheld. It is not usually appropriate to report individual participants' raw data unless your study requires it (for example, a case study). Probably the easiest way to think of this is that the reader, having read through the introduction and focused on the aims and hypotheses, will now want to find out what you actually found – moving to the results ought to show, clearly and concisely, whether or not hypotheses were accepted, theories supported or indeed whether or not the experiment (if that's what it was) worked.

Descriptive statistics would normally consist of the means and standard deviations of your main outcome variables (which may be compared with any available published

Table 13.1 Mean error rate and standard deviations (SD) for three groups differentiated by cycling experience (novice, probationer, experienced).

|  | Mean errors | SD | N |
|---|---|---|---|
| Novice | 35 | 2.76 | 15 |
| Probationer | 32 | 2.15 | 15 |
| Experienced | 17 | 0.27 | 15 |

norms), including not only global summary measures, but also those for any appropriate sub-groups or conditions. For example, you may wish to give separate means and standard deviations for males and females, or those in different age groups. However, if your main outcome variable is categorical rather than continuous, you should give percentages and numbers, as appropriate. The descriptive statistics can often be conveniently presented in a table (see Table 13.1), or alternatively in a figure (see Figure 13.1) if the nature of tabulated data is potentially misleading, or if there is so much of it that the information to be expressed is obscured. (It is worth noting, though, that tables and figures should be used as either-or alternatives – it is not appropriate to present the same data twice, once in each format. What would be the point?) The use of tables and figures in a report is discussed in detail in a later section, while Box 13.13 provides a summary of guidelines for the production of tables and figures.

If you are using a questionnaire or materials that other authors have used, compare your results with theirs at this stage. Thus you should be able to demonstrate that your sample has provided data which fall within an expected range (or not), and that these data are suitable for further statistical analysis. Both of these points may be raised in the discussion.

If your sample appears to be different from other samples in some important way (e.g., they have different profile characteristics, or they obtain markedly higher or lower measures on particular questionnaire items), you may still be able to carry out further analysis, but you should indicate the nature of the difference and show that steps (such as data transformation or recoding) have been taken to remedy the problem. The presentation of descriptive statistics is important, and forms the logical starting point of further analysis.

Figure 13.1 Mean error rates for three groups differentiated by cycling experience.

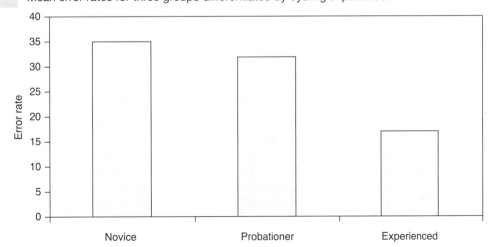

Moreover, as experienced researchers and reviewers are aware, inspection of descriptive statistics is often sufficient, on its own, to determine the outcome of a quantitative study – for instance, when two mean scores are close to one another it is often clear that no real difference exists between the groups, obviating the need for any further analysis. Indeed, many a supervisor will criticise a student for proceeding with a comprehensive and complex inferential analysis of data, when inspection of (and understanding of) the descriptive statistics would have clearly indicated that no effects were present. A useful thing for students to know! For this reason it is worth having a good look at these relatively straightforward statistics before moving on to the main analysis.

The results of the statistical analysis should then be presented in a clear and logical way. The most obvious approach is to deal with each hypothesis in turn, in the order given at the end of your introduction. The aim is to show clearly what your data say about each one, and then to state simply whether the evidence supports it or not. Generally speaking this requires you to report the appropriate significance test, giving the value of the statistic, the degrees of freedom and the associated probability. You should then help the reader by translating (briefly) what the test is telling you into a straightforward verbal statement, while avoiding the temptation to expand or speculate. For example, in a variant of our exercise and wellbeing study, psychological wellbeing scores were compared for two groups, one taking no exercise over a given period and one taking regular exercise. A one-way ANOVA was used to determine whether the two groups differed on wellbeing. (Note that we could have used an independent samples $t$-test.) The convention for statistical reporting of significance tests requires the following elements:

- state the test used
- state the variables being tested
- state the significance level applied to the test, or report the exact probability
- state the findings (in words)
- express the findings in terms of the statistic ($t$-value, $F$-ratio); the degrees of freedom; and the probability value, either as an exact probability, or greater than or less than a given alpha level
- state whether the statistic is significant
- translate the finding for the reader, and relate the finding to the hypothesis

In the present example, this could be expressed as follows:

A one-way ANOVA was used to determine whether the scores of the two groups (exercise vs. non-exercise) differed significantly on wellbeing scores. A significant difference was found between the two groups: $F(1, 31) = 12.14, p < .05$, or $p = .002$. As can be seen from Table X, which displays the means and SDs of wellbeing scores for each group, those in the exercise group gained significantly higher wellbeing scores than did those in the non-exercise group. The hypothesis was therefore supported.

If you are examining differences between or among groups, remember that the reader will need to know the mean scores (and SDs) for each group; refer the reader to a table, or present the information at this point in the text. Without this information, the reader will not be able to understand your results. Note also that we have shown two versions of the statistical findings, one relating statistics to a pre-determined significance level, and one reporting the exact probability. Both are acceptable provided consistency is maintained over a number of tests in a report. See Box 13.11 for a comprehensive guide to the reporting of significance tests.

# Report the results of analyses

At the .01 level of significance, a significant negative correlation was observed between cyclists' age and number of hedgehogs run over: $r$ (29) $= -.43, p < .01$.

A zero-order correlation analysis indicated that a significant positive relationship existed (at the 5% level) between sunspot activity and incidence of road rage: $r$ (20) $= .89, p < .05$. However, a first-order partial correlation analysis indicated that this relationship was not significant when temperature was partialled out: $r_{xy.z}$ (17) $= .32, p > .05$. [$x =$ the predictor (sunspot activity); $y =$ the criterion (road rage); $z =$ the variable partialled out (temperature).]

Exam performance was regressed on study time. A significant positive relationship was noted: $r$ (11) $= .93, p = .002$. Exam performance and study time shared 84% of their variance ($r^2 = .84$). The regression equation was as follows: Estimated exam performance $= 19.46 + 5.66$ study time.

The criterion variable, error rate, was regressed on the three predictors of age, extraversion, and experience (measured in months). The results were as follows: $R = .75; F$ (3, 94) $= 41.78, p < .05; R^2 = .55$. Thus, 55% of the variance of error rate was explained by the three predictors. The regression equation was as follows: Estimated error rate $= 5.69 - 0.05$ age $+ 0.21$ extraversion $- 0.52$ experience.

(Note: a table of beta coefficients, $t$-values and probabilities is necessary to demonstrate the relationships between the predictors and the criterion variable, and some reference to these relationships should be made in the text at this point.)

No significant difference in blood pressure level was observed between the two groups at the .05 level: $t$ (22) $= 1.51, p > .05$.

(Note that the same format is appropriate for paired $t$-tests.)

At the .05 level, a significant main effect of fishing experience was observed on the numbers of trout landed in competition: $F$ (2, 99) $= 14.52, p < .05$. No main effect of lure was observed on the numbers of trout landed during competition: $F$ (1, 99) $= 1.77, p > .05$. However, a significant Experience X Lure interaction was observed: $F$ (2, 93) $= 9.72, p < .05$.

(Note: a table of means would be required to indicate the relationships among the variables. A figure would be required, or appropriate post hoc testing, to indicate the nature of the significant interaction.)

The association between gender and response to the dichotomous questionnaire item (Are you enjoying the book so far?) was not significant: $\chi^2$(1, $N = 54$) $= 2.75, p > .05$.

Always bear in mind that you must clarify your results for the reader. It is tempting to use short-hand when describing certain variables, particularly in tables. Tables derived from computer printout usually bear the abbreviated labels used to code variables rather than the full variable name. If you do have to use shortened names in tables, provide a key underneath the table.

Table x.   Means and standard deviations (SD) for two
           variables: cholesterol levels in overweight
           cyclist group, and error rate.

| Variable | Mean | *SD* |
|----------|------|------|
| Ichygrp | 7.53 | 0.09 |
| Squish | 16.39 | 0.22 |

Ichygrp – Incidence of cholesterol in the overweight cyclist group
Squish – Number of hedgehogs run over

Although the results section often contains a large amount of numerical and statistical information, it is nevertheless part of the text of your report and should be written in English. It is not acceptable simply to present a series of tables or diagrams without a clear accompanying text which explains in plain language what your illustrations show. Even less appropriate would be to base this section on computer printouts which are notoriously minimalist. Moreover, unless you have gone to the trouble of labelling your data during the initial data-entry stage, groups and sub-divisions in SPSS will be presented by their numerical code. One of the most common criticisms of the results section of a write-up is that tables and graphs are unclear. If you have lengthy or complex results, however, clarity is often greatly helped by including appropriate illustrative tables or figures. These can be a real help to the reader in understanding the overall pattern of your results, and therefore in following the argument. Sometimes, however, they can simply be confusing and counter-productive, or irrelevant and annoying. See Box 13.12 for a checklist relating to the results section.

Box 13.12

✔ *Checklist . . .*

# The results section

▪ Have you presented descriptive statistics, and do these represent the data fairly and adequately?

▪ Do the results deal with each of your hypotheses?

▪ Are your results presented appropriately?

▪ Are all tables and figures correctly labelled?

▪ Is it possible to assess the outcome of the study by consulting the results alone, without the need to refer to other sections of the report?

▪ Have you included results that are not relevant to the research issue in general or the hypotheses in particular, or to which you do not refer again?

Tables are easily produced by a word-processor, a spreadsheet package or even by the statistics package used for analysis. They usually consist of summary data (e.g., means and standard deviations, percentages, etc.), presented within a system of rows and columns representing various categories (e.g., different samples, categories within samples or experimental conditions). See Table 13.1 for an example.

Figures usually present the data in pictorial form (e.g., bar charts, histograms, scatter-plots, etc.), and are either produced directly by your statistics package or indirectly by means of specialist software for diagrams and graphics. Increasingly, many integrated word-processing/spreadsheet/drawing packages offer this facility, bringing the opportunity to create effective illustrations within everyone's grasp. Generally speaking, the data contained in tabular form are precise (actual numerical values are used) whereas figures offer a less exact though often more immediate impression. Compare the earlier Figure 13.1 with Table 13.1.

All tables and figures must be numbered (e.g., Table 1, Figure 1) and should be given titles which are self-explanatory. Titles may appear above or below, but the location of titles should be consistent within a report. The reader should be able to understand what a table or figure is all about without digging through the text to find out. At the same time, the information displayed in tables or figures should not be mysteriously independent of the text: it *must* be discussed, explained or otherwise used in some relevant way. Common comments from supervisors with regard to tables and figures include the following: "What is this?" "What does this show?" "Why have you included this chart?"

The whole point of using figures and tables is to report, accurately and clearly, the outcome of a study. However, this section of any written report is often the main source of misleading, inaccurate and inappropriate information. Figure 13.2 shows a typical example. Here the researcher is guilty of two errors. On the one hand, there is simply too much information offered on the line graph and it becomes almost impossible to identify any trend or pattern in the data. On the other hand, there is no information on what each of the plotted lines is measuring: the legend for the graph is missing. Furthermore, this

**Figure 13.2**    Exam performance scores in five subjects across three degree programmes.

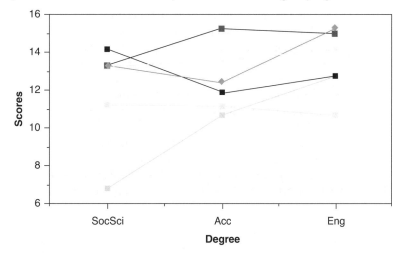

Figure 13.3 Mean scores for male and female participants on the measure of perception of discrimination against women in work.

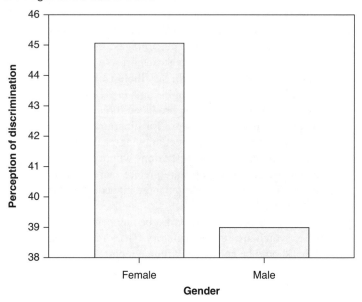

particular researcher seems to have lost the ability to count, as can be observed by closer inspection of the figure in question.

In the next example, Figure 13.3 demonstrates how a sneaky researcher can manipulate the vertical and horizontal axes of a figure to maximise an effect. Presenting data in this form suggests that there are indeed huge differences between males and females on a measure of attitudes – in this instance, perceptions of active discrimination against women in work.

Compare this with the final illustration in this section, Figure 13.4, in which the axes have been manipulated in a different but equally misleading way. The data are the same as for the previous figure, but the impression created is totally different, achieved by manipulating the vertical (*y*) axis.

This kind of manipulation is not recommended and the sophisticated reader is likely to pick up on such attempts to deceive quite quickly. If in any doubt how best to present data fairly and objectively, most current statistical software uses a recognised format for graphs which provides an acceptable standard. If still in doubt, there is an old adage beloved of statisticians long gone now, that the vertical axis should always be three-quarters the length of the horizontal! Combine this with axes showing true zero points and extending just beyond the highest data value and you have solved the problem, or at least attained consistency.

The question of when to use either of these features is a recurring one and students are always asking supervisors if they should use a graph or a table to describe some finding. At least they appreciate that it is an either-or event. Generally speaking most tutors would prefer a table because of its precision, and this tends to be the view of most journal editors also. A figure is appropriate when tabulated data become too complex to indicate trends, and a picture offers a quick, at a glance way of making a point. Similarly, when describing interactions – as in the two-way ANOVA case – a figure is often the only way such relationships can be expressed with any clarity. Figures are also useful when

Mean scores for male and female participants on the measure of perception of discrimination against women in work.

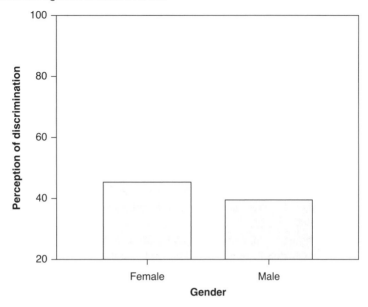

presenting data to a statistically inexperienced readership; hence they are much favoured by newspapers. This is unlikely to be an issue for the student of psychology preparing work for a class assignment (hopefully). And finally, at the initial screening stage of data analysis, the use of figures offers an ideal overview of the shape of the data and can offer an early indication of departures from normality and other unusual occurrences.

This section concludes with a checklist in Box 13.13 to serve as a reminder of what tables and figures are supposed to be doing. Readers may also find a review of Part 4 useful.

*Checklist . . .*

# Tables and figures

Tables

■ A table complements the content of the text. It should not duplicate it but should add something to the clarity of expression which is not possible within the text alone. Otherwise there is no need for a table.

■ A table should be referred to in the text by its identifying number with key points noted.

■ A table should be self-explanatory. If the reader has to refer to the text to understand what the table is showing or why it is there, the table has failed in its purpose.

■ Tables should be numbered sequentially as they appear. Letter suffixes are not recommended. (Note, though, our discussion on suffixes in Part 4 concerning the use of tables within a textbook.)

- Tables should be identified by a title which is intelligible and supported by footnotes if abbreviations or special features are to be explained.
- The format of tables should be standardized. The APA (2001) guidelines encourage the use of horizontal lines to subdivide a table and discourage the use of vertical lines. See Table 1 for an illustration.

### Figures

- Everything which offers a pictorial presentation is termed a figure. This includes photographs, drawings and charts, although in most undergraduate reports the chart is the most frequent form of figure.
- A figure complements the content of the text. It should add something to the clarity of expression which is not possible within the text alone or which would be unclear from a table. Otherwise there is no need for a figure.
- A figure should be referred to in the text by its identifying number with key points noted.
- A figure should be self-explanatory with the axes clearly labelled and scaled. If the reader has to refer to the text to understand what the figure is showing or why it is there, the figure has failed in its purpose.
- Figures should be numbered sequentially as they appear. As with tables, letter suffixes are not recommended.
- Figures should be identified by a title which is intelligible and supported by footnotes if abbreviations or special features are to be explained.
- The format of figures should be standardized within a report, especially if comparisons are to be drawn.
- Over-embellishment is to be discouraged. Figures should be simple and offer an immediate impression of the data. If figures need to be closely inspected to determine trends they have lost any advantage they might have over a table.

If these guidelines are followed, your figures and tables will be relevant and intelligible. For more information on this topic, refer to the APA (2001) guidelines.

## 13.5 Discussion

This is the section that probably demands the most of your creativity and intellect, where you try to make sense of it all, to relate your findings to previous research and explain what happened in your study – in particular, this is where the hypotheses are reviewed in the light of the results. The best guidance would be to start off by providing a summary of the main results of your study, indicating the implications of these results for your hypotheses. Then you can draw on the main points of your introduction: for example, you can indicate whether your results are consistent or inconsistent with the findings of other researchers, or whether they support one theory rather than another.

You have to present some explanations for your results – this may be easy if your results were entirely in the expected directions and all of your hypotheses were supported. It may be less straightforward (although more interesting) if your results were not consistent with the results of other researchers. Under these circumstances, you have to review all of the potentially relevant points made earlier in the report: you may have used a different participant pool, used a slightly different procedure, changed the test materials in some way, and all of these may have affected your results. You should not attempt to hide any such discrepancies; rather, the effects of discrepancies and variations should be highlighted, since they tell you something very important about the strength or robustness of any predicted effects. Moreover, being honest and 'up-front' like this indicates that you appreciate the limitations of your study, which in itself is commendable. More importantly, from an assessment point of view, if you don't do this your supervisor certainly will. One of the most irritating characteristics of tutors everywhere is their unerring knack of finding the flaws in the research of their students.

Overall, you should ensure that you cover all of the main points raised in your introduction. Thus if you mentioned the possibility of gender differences in the introduction, you should raise this issue again in your discussion, even if you were not able to examine gender differences (for example, because of limitations within the participant pool). One of the aims of the discussion is to highlight the limitations of your project and areas worthy of further investigation. You are not expected to conduct a study which covers every option; on the other hand, you are expected to discuss the strengths, weaknesses and limitations of your work in a clear and objective tone. (Remember the point made above about supervisors.) You should also consider ways in which your project might have been improved, and the direction of any future work which may be profitably undertaken in this area.

A very important point to note is that the failure to uphold your hypotheses does not mean that the study has 'failed', which is often the view of students new to research. To show that something is *not* the case can be as important as showing that it *is* the case: a null result does not mean that you have nothing to say. You should not, therefore, write your discussion of a null outcome in an apologetic way; yes, we all like to get a 'significant result', but the rejection of an hypothesis can be equally informative, and may lead to new ideas.

The converse of this is also true: rejecting a null hypothesis does not necessarily mean that a study has 'worked'. A truly huge sample, for instance, will allow you to demonstrate significance in almost anything, but to little point, and while admittedly this will not be an issue in most undergraduate research, small samples can be influenced by extreme scores, and deviations from normality can make interpretation of significance problematic.

The discussion should end with a paragraph or two of conclusions. It may be tempting at this stage to make rather sweeping statements. Remember the limitations of your study and try not to go beyond your own results. A useful checklist for the discussion section appears in Box 13.14.

## 13.6 References

The reference section of a report offers an alphabetical listing (by first author's surname) of all the sources mentioned or referred to in the main text of the report: journal articles, book chapters, commentaries and quotations – any material in fact to which you have made reference in the body of a report must be cited. An important point here, and one

Box 13.14

## The discussion section

- Have you discussed all of the important issues raised in your introduction?
- Have ideas crept in to the discussion which are not really related to the study?
- Does the discussion concentrate purely on the findings, or does it consider broader issues?
- Conversely: does your discussion take sufficient note of the actual findings?
- Are there any findings which you have not discussed?
- Have you considered whether your data might support an explanation other than the one you prefer?
- Does the discussion point to original thinking?
- Are your conclusions clear?

which is a traditional source of confusion to many undergraduates, concerns the difference between a reference section and a bibliography. References, as already mentioned, relate to work actually cited. A bibliography, on the other hand, is a listing (again alphabetically, by first author) of any work which was consulted, browsed or which in some way contributed to the background, formulation and conduct of your study. For instance, in reviewing the type of research carried out in a particular area you might have read several journal articles and book reviews, none of which provided specific material to which you referred in your report. However, insofar as they did contribute to the overall foundations of your work, they would be listed in the bibliography – an opportunity for you to provide an overview of your own research into a topic. Note, however, that the inclusion of a bibliography is not always acceptable, and it is worth checking the guidelines offered by your own department or institution on this point.

The format for presenting references tends to vary slightly from publication to publication, but many psychology journals conform to formats favoured by the major journals and approved by both the APA and the BPS, the essence of which we have used in offering our own guidelines, as follows.

Citations in the text itself should be by author's surname and date only – which is the minimum information needed to correctly identify the full reference where it appears at the end of the report (see Box 13.15 for examples). Any other information, such as the title of the publication or the author's initial, is usually redundant here and serves only to distract. In multiple citations in the text (where you give a list of authors, in brackets, to support a point), reference your sources in alphabetical order (date order may also be acceptable). If you cite more than one article published by a single author in the same year, use the letters *a*, *b*, *c*, etc. after the date: for example, Boelen (1992a) and Boelen (1992b). The identifiers (*a, b, c*) are used in the order in which you cite them in your final reference list (and so in alphabetical order), and not in the order in which they were published in the particular year in question – they are *your* suffixes, not those of the author or publisher. And of course, the identifiers accompany the full reference in the reference section.

# Reference, in accord with APA (2001) guidelines

## 1. Journal articles

### Single authorship

Likert, R. A. (1932). A technique for the measurement of attitudes. *Archives of Psychology, 140*, 55.

### Joint authorship

Johnson, M. H., Karmiloff-Smith, A., & Patry, J. L. (1992). Can neural selectionism be applied to cognitive development and its disorders? *New Ideas in Psychology, 10*, 35–46.

Note that (*a*) capital letters are not used in the titles of the articles except at the beginning of sections (or when proper names are used); (*b*) inverted commas are not used; (*c*) journal names are given in full; (*d*) journal names and volume numbers are italicised (or underlined, if you are not using a word-processor).

## 2. Books and chapters in books

### Single authorship

Cohen, J. (1988). *Statistical power analysis for the behavioral sciences* (2nd ed.). Hillsdale, NJ: Erlbaum.

### Joint authorship

Potter, J., & Wetherell, M. (1987). *Discourse and social psychology: Beyond attitudes and behaviour*. London: Sage.

### Chapter

Burman, A. (1994). Interviewing. In P. Banister, E. Burman, I. Parker, M. Taylor, & C. Tindall (Eds.), *Qualitative methods in psychology: A research guide* (pp. 49–71). Buckingham: Open University Press.

Note that (*a*) capitals are not used in the titles except at the beginning of sections (although it is acceptable to use capitals for main words in book titles); (*b*) inverted commas are not used; (*c*) book titles are italicised (but not chapter titles); (*d*) page numbers are given if specifically referred to or quoted from in the text; (*e*) place of publication, then publishers, are cited last.

## 3. Citations in the text

In the text itself, sources are cited by surnames and date only. Citation can be direct or indirect:

### Direct

Archer (1991) found higher testosterone levels in the more aggressive group.

### Indirect

Higher testosterone levels were found in the more aggressive group (Archer, 1991).

Quotations are best avoided unless the full quotation given is of direct relevance to your own work. If you do quote verbatim from an author, give the page number as well as the author's name and date: e.g., 'Comparisons . . . revealed higher testosterone levels in the more aggressive group' (Archer, 1991, p. 21). If there are two authors, give both surnames using *and* for direct citation and & for indirect, e.g.,

**Direct:**   Barry and Bateman (1992)

**Indirect:**   (Barry & Bateman, 1992)

If there are more than two authors, give all the names the first time the source is cited (e.g., Johnson, Karmiloff-Smith, & Patry, 1992). For subsequent mentions, use *et al.* (e.g., Johnson et al., 1992).

### 4. Internet sources

The APA and BPS provide detailed guidelines on referencing material found on the Internet. Briefly, the aim of any reference is to provide the reader with sufficient information to track down the source. Since Internet sources can be updated, you should indicate the date on which you found or downloaded the material, and the source or URL.

#### Online periodical

Author, A., Author, B., & Author, C. (date). Title of article. *Title of periodical, volume*, start page–end page. Retrieved month, day, year, from source/URL.

#### Online document

Author, A. (date). Title of work. Retrieved month, day, year, from source/URL.

## 13.7 Appendices

These should include all test materials and examples of any stimuli used in the study. Any questionnaires developed by the researcher must be shown in full, although standardised instruments are not required. It can be assumed that the reader is familiar with the 16PF, or that detailed information on a particular test is readily available (through published test and administration manuals). Tables of norms should be given if they are relevant to the interpretation of the research findings. Note that most tutors and examiners will not welcome reams of computer output, even in an appendix, or raw data (although there is an understanding that they are available for inspection should it be required). If your study is qualitative in nature, however, you may wish to include interview transcripts and so on. Again, if in doubt, consult the typical format used in a standard journal (or ask your supervisor).

## 13.8 Presentation and style

Remember that presentation is important. Try to ensure that your work is free from spelling and grammatical errors. Check your work for errors before you hand it in. The style of writing should be plain and relatively formal, and you should use the past tense throughout and write in the third person; many novice researchers frequently use "I" and "we" in their writing ("we felt repeated measures were more appropriate"), but this tends to create an impression of informality and lack of scientific rigour. And, whether accurate or not, impressions do count. It is much better to place some distance between yourself and the report, as in: "It was found that/observed/noted" (except for a qualitative report in which the views of the author may be central).

## 13.9 Writing up qualitative research

Those of you who have conducted a qualitative study may feel uncertain as to how to present and write up your work. There is no one 'correct' way of writing up a qualitative study and many different formats can be used to impart the relevant details to the reader. However, the following discussion may help you when it comes to writing up your work.

### 13.9.1 The background to a qualitative report

The first point to make is that the aims of a qualitative study are likely to be different from those of a quantitative study, such that the aim is less likely to centre on an existing theory. For example, in grounded theory research, the researcher is unlikely to have posed any hypotheses at all, and the theory emerges after the study has been completed – which is, in fact, the point of this approach. An ethnographic study aims to describe cultures or groups with which the researcher was initially unfamiliar. It follows that research of this type cannot be theory-driven. In studies of this sort, the important points about theory are made in the discussion rather than in the introduction.

The second point we need to make here is that that there are a number of different techniques and traditions associated with qualitative research. Far from converging on an agreed set of procedures, these have tended to develop into distinct approaches to the conduct, analysis and presentation of research. This means that there is no one set of guiding principles, although a number of authors have published thoughtful and useful guidelines on this topic (see, for example, Elliott, Fischer, & Rennie, 1999; Finlay, 2002; Miles & Huberman, 1994; Smith, Jarman, & Osborn, 1999; Wetherell, Taylor, & Yates, 2001b). We can offer some general guidelines here, but bear in mind that what you are trying to do is to ensure that your reader understands and appreciates your study.

## 13.10 Guidelines on writing up qualitative research

The report on a qualitative study will normally take the form of a narrative or 'story', typically comprised of four sections. We deal with each of these in turn.

### 13.10.1 The introduction

This should cover the background to the study, the context and the nature of the research. You might first want to offer a rationale for the study: the reader will want to know what prompted the research, what it aimed to show or illustrate and why (the potential implications). Then you would present the context of the research, which would include any existing work in the area, or the factors that were likely to be relevant to the participants. Taking the study on the relationship between blood pressure and exercise as an example, your introduction should cover the basic issues, such as what is meant by high blood pressure, and the literature relating exercise to blood pressure. You would also want to consider the issue from the participants' point of view, such as the symptoms people commonly experience with high blood pressure, and the impact that the symptoms may have upon their lives, activities and subjective wellbeing. Then you need to present the nature of the research, with some justification for the approach taken. While some of this detail might be better suited for the method section, it will help the reader to learn something of the approach at this stage: for example, you might indicate that you have taken a phenomenological approach (and why you have done so), or that you have interviewed participants.

Given the central role of the researcher in a qualitative study, the researcher's thoughts, feelings, reflections and reactions are usually highly relevant. As we have said in Part 6, you need to think carefully about the extent to which you are willing or able to disclose personal information about yourself: you should not feel obliged to say anything in the report that you might later regret. On the other hand, if it is not too personal, it might be relevant to indicate any experience that relates to the topic at hand. So, you might indicate whether you have had experience of people with high blood pressure, and the nature of that experience. If your topic is one that is quite alien to you, or which affects people who are quite different from you, then you might make this point here. For example, if the topic affects middle-class white males, and you share none of those characteristics, it could be worth saying this. On a more pragmatic note, it sometimes makes more sense for the researcher to describe himself or herself as 'I' in the written report than as 'the researcher', but opinions vary on this point and we would advise you to check this up with your supervisor before submitting the final report.

### 13.10.2   The method

This is a major part of the report. Some researchers write up their work almost as a narrative, telling the story of the study from its inception, including details of key decisions in chronological order. This often makes good sense, particularly if things did not go according to plan. Generally speaking, the method section should cover the following points: the approach taken, with justification for this (and perhaps also justification for excluding other approaches); the recruitment of participants; the data collection methods used (in sufficient detail that the study could be repeated by the reader); how the study evolved or changed over the course of study; and what the researcher did to ensure that he or she represented the experiences of the participants. The issues concerning the approach taken must be considered in detail, demonstrating a clear understanding of any assumptions taken on board. Give examples if that helps the reader to understand exactly what happened and why. Remember that the reader (your supervisor and other markers) needs to follow the progress of the study, to understand what you did and why, and the reader also needs to be able to judge how well you carried out your study.

### 13.10.3   The results and discussion

In a qualitative report, it often makes sense to discuss the findings as you go along, rather than to have two separate sections. Again, the aim is to make it easy for your reader to follow what you have found. The first issue is generally that of analysis, unless you have covered this in the method section: explain carefully the procedures used to analyse the data, and the ways in which you drew up any themes, categories or topics. These themes and categories can then be used to structure your results, and you may find a table or diagram useful at this point. In your writing, sufficient original data should be provided to enable the reader to evaluate the interpretation. This brings us to the issue of quotation. Having decided on the themes or topics you are going to present, you may want to illustrate these with quotes from interview transcripts or the texts you were using. It is often tempting to include several quotes for each theme, but too many quotes can actually detract from the quality of your work. As a rule of thumb, two or three quotes for each theme should be sufficient. The best quotes do something in addition to illustrating a theme; for example, a good quote can also demonstrate an ambivalence or shift in the participant's perspective, it can illustrate a metaphor you have used and it can be used to demonstrate your analytical technique. Quotes are an important part of your 'evidence', and also part of your narrative, but they should illustrate rather than constitute your results/discussion sections. On a practical note, quotations are easier to read if they are indented (around 1.5 cm), and you should identify the participant with a number or pseudonym, depending on the conventions you are using.

### 13.10.4    Conclusions

In this final section of your report, you should review your study both in terms of its conduct and its findings. This may be the section where you present your theory, and if so, then you need to make some links with the existing literature. You should also review the quality of your study, and consider strengths, shortcomings and limitations (see Part 6, particularly section 12.16).

### 13.11    Giving a presentation of your study

There is an increasingly common expectation – if not a requirement – that undergraduates offer an oral presentation of their work to staff and fellow students at some stage during the conduct of a project. Timings vary, with some colleges and universities scheduling presentations before data collection begins, while others wait until the entire project is completed. Either way, presentations are now a familiar part of undergraduate life and they serve a variety of functions. At the most obvious level they provide the student with an opportunity to show off as it were – after all, a great deal of reading has probably gone into the development of a research project, only a fraction of which is ultimately used in the study proper. How satisfying to be able to demonstrate to your tutors that you have actually put considerable effort into your work (especially useful in those cases where presentations comprise an assessable component of a research methods module). Presentations also demonstrate the depth of your familiarity with a topic and tutors will often ask probing questions about issues which, even if they did not form a part of your study, you might be expected to know something about if your reading really was comprehensive.

If presentations occur at an intermediate stage then they serve the extremely useful function of generating constructive feedback, with an audience being given the chance to offer advice ('you need a larger sample for this type of analysis', or 'have you read . . . ?'). And of course, finally, having to prepare and give a presentation is now regarded as an important element of general research methods training – anyone hoping to pursue a career in the field will find that the presentation is an important way to disseminate information. A few guidelines on presentation techniques might come in useful.

A good starting point is to consider the purpose of the presentation. The aim is usually to describe, in the course of a 10-minute talk (sometimes longer), your study. During the presentation you must identify the research issue you have explored, outline the research background to the issue and provide a rationale for what you have done (or are about to do). The actual study must be described in sufficient detail that an audience can follow your design and procedure, and results (if appropriate) should be offered in a format which describes the outcome without confusion. Finally, you should be able to present your view of the implications of the study, and all in a manner which is interesting, informative and accurate. All in all, a pretty terrifying prospect!

In structure, a presentation should be like a trimmed-down version of a standard research report, comprising more or less the same major sections and sub-divisions. It will have a title, much like the report title, followed by a brief statement of what the study was about. This is not quite like an abstract since data and findings would not be offered at this stage, but more like an expanded explanation of the title, highlighting the general research area and stating the research questions ('an observational study in the area of . . . and exploring the specific issue of . . .').

A review of the background to the research is important, and this will take the form of a summarised version of the literature review found in the written report. Naturally, key studies would have to be mentioned, with their findings, along with any research which provided a rationale for the study, ending with a statement of the hypotheses explored.

An outline of the procedure would be offered next, with illustrations provided of questionnaires or stimuli. Data should be described in descriptive terms, followed by details of results. While most of the other sections would tend to be presented in general terms, this results section should be full and precise. It remains only to make concluding comments about the conduct of the study, how the findings relate to the research issue in general and the hypotheses in particular.

## 13.12 Practicalities: Giving a presentation

The previous section outlined the content of a typical presentation, but said little about how this material might be presented. This section attempts to offer some practical advice.

A key point to remember, when preparing for a presentation, is that an oral exposition of a piece of work differs from a text version. In the write-up you have ample opportunity to explain in detail the conduct of previous research in your field, to include the results of complex statistical analyses and to discuss at length your findings. In a presentation it is not possible to present such detailed material. For one thing, there are time constraints and, contrary to popular undergraduate belief, 10 minutes is not really that long; what you say has to be a much condensed version of your study, but one which nevertheless contains the essence of what you did. For another, while a reviewer or assessor can re-read the contents of a report, or follow up material in appendices, a presentation is a 'one-shot' affair – you have a single opportunity to say what you want, to make your points and show that you have done a good job. So how do you do this?

The starting point is your written report: if this is completed before presentations are given (as is the norm) then you already have all the information necessary for an oral version. You actually have too much information, so the report should be read carefully and important information extracted. Box 13.16 offers a summary of what is required.

The next stage is to decide how best to present the information gleaned from the full report: some undergraduates will simply write a summary, based on their notes, and the presentation comprises a rather tedious reading aloud of this summary. This is not a particularly effective method of giving a presentation – it tends to be dull, it doesn't allow the audience to focus on key elements and it can also be intimidating for the speaker; with no other source of stimulation the audience's entire attention is focused on the oral presentation itself.

Box 13.16

Practicalities . . .

# Presenting research

The following is a suggested listing – with comments – of the major elements which should comprise an oral presentation. They appear in the typical order in which they would be introduced to an audience. They also represent the likely content of a series of slides or overheads which would be used as a basis for a presentation.

1. **A title for the presentation**, which will be based on the title of the study itself. Accompanying notes would expand on this title, identifying the research area in which your study was based, and outlining the research questions posed.

2. **An outline of key research in the area.** An overhead would display the authors of research, the date of the published work and the research findings – these might be in terms of mean scores for different groups, or a description of factors identified in the research: for example, 'Cattell (1969): 16 personality factors identified . . .' Accompanying notes would expand on the studies cited, explaining the findings in more detail and demonstrating how they formed a basis for your work.

3. **A statement of the aim of the study**, in general terms, and statements of the hypotheses being tested. Notes would expand on the aim, reminding the audience of how the stated aim has developed from previous research (or whatever), and each hypothesis would be explained in turn: what the basis for each hypothesised prediction was, and what the expected outcomes were.

4. **A description of procedural elements**, such as the sample characteristics (where relevant to the conduct and findings of the study), details of any apparatus used, including questionnaires and standardised test instruments. In the case of tests or questionnaires, examples of items, coding and scoring systems can be displayed. Full copies might also be distributed among the audience. Notes here would provide descriptive details of how samples were drawn, why certain characteristics were controlled for (e.g., extraneous variables) and how participants were assigned to groups, if appropriate; and whether or not the design was within-subjects or between-groups. Details would also be given on questionnaires, including pilot study data if appropriate. An explanation of the development of items would be given and the role and composition of sub-scales discussed. (Note: a lot of information is covered in this section and this might be represented in a number of slides. For instance, one might deal with participant characteristics, there might be two or more giving examples of test items and there might be an additional slide reviewing the findings of a pilot study.)

5. **A summary statement identifying independent and dependent variables and noting any extraneous factors.** Notes would briefly review the procedure, reminding how independent variables were manipulated and explaining how outcome measures were taken.

$\longrightarrow$

6. **Presentation of results.** Key findings would be illustrated, firstly in the form of summary statistics, and then in terms of analysis. These would include means, $t$-values, $F$-ratios and correlation coefficients, for example. Probability values would also be shown. Notes would indicate how the statistics were derived and what tests were carried out and any significant effects highlighted. Figures are often appropriate here for their visual impact.

7. **More results.** If additional analysis was carried out to further explore a finding, or you wish to highlight some unusual or worthy finding, this should be presented next. Notes would explain why additional analysis was necessary (e.g., 'it was noted that mean scores for males in the sample were higher than previous reported norms'), and any figures would be discussed.

8. **Hypotheses would be re-stated** and upheld or rejected in light of the results. Notes would expand upon the relationship between the findings and the predicted outcomes. Explanation would then extend to re-considering the entire research issue in view of the study just outlined. The presentation at this point is likely to return to the kind of general discussion of issues introduced at the very beginning.

A far better solution is to make use of some form of visual aid – overheads, slides and computer-generated screen graphics are all ideal and most departments will happily make facilities available for students. The advantages of this approach are considerable:

1. Key points of a study can be put on an overhead or slide allowing you to emphasise to your audience the important elements of the study. For instance, you might display the hypotheses as you explain procedural matters, making it easier for your audience to appreciate why you carried out your study *this* way, as opposed to *that* way.

2. Complex information can be presented more effectively in this format than by verbal explanation. Just imagine trying to explain the results of a multiple group comparison analysis verbally. A table or a graph projected onto a screen will describe at a glance what might take you several minutes to explain.

3. A series of slides tends to impose its own structure on a presentation, covering the logical sequence of activities which comprised the study (e.g., you will probably have, in order, slides displaying the title of the study, examples of previous work, statement of hypotheses, procedural matters, results, etc.). They also serve as *aides memoire*, reminders of what you need to talk about next, or which part of your notes to consult. Relying totally on notes, without this kind of external structure, can lead to confusion and loss of place, especially if the notes are extensive.

4. Using visual displays takes pressure off the presenter, especially useful for the nervous undergraduate who can panic quite freely in a corner while everyone's attention is focused on a projected image somewhere else.

Clearly there are advantages in using presentation aids, but be cautious. Firstly, the temptation to cover your slides with everything you want to say should be avoided at all costs. The purpose of these aids is to present key points and illustrations – any more than this and it would be as easy to provide each audience member with a text version of your talk. Legibility is another issue: if you've never used overheads before it's important to find out how big writing or font sizes need to be so that an audience can read them. And thirdly, organisation is important. There is nothing guaranteed better to destroy a nervous presenter's confidence than to discover their slides are in the wrong order, or that one is missing. Take it from two lecturers who know.

Material in support of overheads has to be considered. Previously it has been suggested that a slide can act as an *aide memoire*, triggering recall in the mind of the presenter and reminding him or her what to say next. In fact, only skilled presenters and lecturers are likely to be able to do this well and, unless a talk is well rehearsed, students are advised to use notes to accompany each overhead. Even experienced lecturers are often caught out by an overhead whose existence, never mind content, comes as a complete surprise to them, recognisable when a lecturer is caught staring blankly at a screen for some time.

Examples of test materials can also be made available to an audience, especially if a questionnaire has been custom-designed for a study. Even copies of standardised tests might be distributed if an audience includes fellow students who might not be familiar with specialised instruments.

To conclude this section on presentations, it is worth noting that giving a presentation is a skilled activity, and therefore requires practice to develop. Few undergraduates are going to be superb at this task but, with a bit of organisation and a lot of preparation, presentations can be made competent and interesting.

## 13.13 Assessment

Any study, no matter how elaborate and irrespective of its contribution to the fount of human knowledge, will ultimately be judged on the written exposition of the background, design, conduct and findings of the research. This is true whether the report is based on an undergraduate project, represents a submission to a periodical editor or is a published article in an international journal. In every case, a reader, tutor or reviewer is looking for the same kind of thing – evidence that the study has been well carried out, the data competently analysed and the research issue fully explored. A judgement here can only be based on the written report or article and, while your own research might not necessarily set the world of academia alight, if you have followed all the guidelines in this chapter, you will at least guarantee yourself a fair and objective hearing. Box 13.17 is the concluding illustration in this chapter and it offers a summary of the main points a reviewer or tutor will be looking for in a written report.

Box 13.17

 *Checklist . . .*

# Typical assessment criteria

### Originality

To what extent are the choice of topic and methdodology your own? Does the work show some originality in design or approach?

### Initiative

Have you shown initiative in collecting data or in preparing test materials?

## Introduction

How well have the research issues been identified and explained? Is the review of the literature relevant and thorough? Has the scope of the project been clearly presented? Are the hypotheses unambiguously stated, and is it clear how they relate to previous work? Is the rationale for the aims of the study and the specific hypotheses clear?

## Design

Is the design of the project appropriate for the research question? Have issues concerning sampling and control been addressed? Have independent and dependent variables been correctly identified? Has this section been expressed in the appropriate language of design?

## Participants

Were the participants representative of the population? Have their relevant characteristics been described? Are recruitment strategies presented? Are response and refusal rates recorded?

## Apparatus/materials

Have the details of apparatus been recorded? Have the details of questionnaires, etc. been presented? Are justifications provided for the choice of materials, and for any changes made to published materials? In what ways do the materials provide data for analysis?

## Procedure

Is it possible to understand exactly what procedures were followed in collecting data? Are these procedures appropriate? Could the study be replicated on the information provided?

## Results

Are the results clearly presented? Is the analysis appropriate for the level of data? Does the analysis actually address the hypotheses or research questions under consideration?

## Discussion

Are the results discussed with reference to the issues raised in the Introduction? Are the results discussed with reference to previous findings and relevant theory? Are any problems or limitations of the study fully understood and discussed?

## References

Are all references given in full? Are they presented in a standard format?

## Presentation

Is the project well presented? Is it free from spelling errors? Is it well written? Are arguments clearly and carefully presented?

(Note: the comments on initiative and originality, while relevant for any piece of research, are likely to be particular issues for undergraduate studies.)

## Review

In this chapter, we have discussed the issues you need to think about when you are writing up your research. You should now be familiar with the following topics:

- the functions of each of the main sections of the report
- how to write an abstract
- what to put in the introduction section
- what to put in the methods section
- how best to present your results
- what to cover in the discussion section
- how to reference the work of other authors
- how to give an effective oral presentation of your work

## Suggested further reading

American Psychological Association. (2001). *Publication manual of the American Psychological Association* (5th ed.). Washington, DC: American Psychological Association.

Cresswell, J. W. (1998). *Qualitative inquiry and research design: Choosing among five traditions.* Thousand Oaks, CA: Sage.

Day, R. A. (1989). *How to write and publish a scientific paper* (3rd ed.). Cambridge: Cambridge University Press.

Denzin, N. K., & Lincoln, Y. S. (Eds.). (1994). *Handbook of qualitative research.* Thousand Oaks, CA: Sage.

Howard, K., & Sharp. J. A. (1983). *The management of a student research project.* Aldershot, Hants: Gower.

Kantowitz, B. H., Roediger III, H. L., & Elmes, D. G. (1994). *Experimental psychology: Understanding psychological research* (5th ed.). St. Paul, MN: West Publishing.

Leedy, P. D., & Ormrod, J. E. (1989). *Practical research: Planning and design* (7th ed.). Upper Saddle River, NJ: Prentice Hall.

Miles, M. B., & Huberman, A. M. (1994). *Qualitative data analysis* (2nd ed.). Thousand Oaks, CA: Sage.

# Appendix A

## Area under the normal curve

How to interpret the tables showing the area under the normal curve:

1. Columns headed A contain $z$-scores, which are transformed scores from original raw values
2. Columns headed B show the proportion of the area which lies between the mean and the $z$-score
3. Columns headed C show the proportion of the area which falls beyond $z$
4. Values in columns B and C can be expressed as percentages, such that between the mean of a distribution and the value corresponding to a $z$-score of 0.54, 20.54% of observations fell
5. Since normal distributions are uniform −ve $z$-scores can be interpreted by symmetry
6. To determine the total area falling below a given (+ve) $z$-score, add the area shown in column B to 0.5 (since 0.5 of the total area lies below the mean)

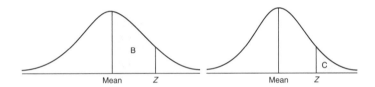

| (A) z | (B) area between mean and z | (C) area beyond z | (A) z | (B) area between mean and z | (C) area beyond z | (A) z | (B) area between mean and z | (C) area beyond z |
|---|---|---|---|---|---|---|---|---|
| 0.00 | .0000 | .5000 | 0.15 | .0596 | .4404 | 0.30 | .1179 | .3821 |
| 0.01 | .0040 | .4960 | 0.16 | .0636 | .4364 | 0.31 | .1217 | .3783 |
| 0.02 | .0080 | .4920 | 0.17 | .0675 | .4325 | 0.32 | .1255 | .3745 |
| 0.03 | .0120 | .4880 | 0.18 | .0714 | .4286 | 0.33 | .1293 | .3707 |
| 0.04 | .0160 | .4840 | 0.19 | .0753 | .4247 | 0.34 | .1331 | .3669 |
| 0.05 | .0199 | .4801 | 0.20 | .0793 | .4207 | 0.35 | .1368 | .3632 |
| 0.06 | .0239 | .4761 | 0.21 | .0832 | .4168 | 0.36 | .1406 | .3594 |
| 0.07 | .0279 | .4721 | 0.22 | .0871 | .4129 | 0.37 | .1443 | .3557 |
| 0.08 | .0319 | .4681 | 0.23 | .0910 | .4090 | 0.38 | .1480 | .3520 |
| 0.09 | .0359 | .4641 | 0.24 | .0948 | .4052 | 0.39 | .1517 | .3483 |
| 0.10 | .0398 | .4602 | 0.25 | .0987 | .4013 | 0.40 | .1554 | .3446 |
| 0.11 | .0438 | .4562 | 0.26 | .1026 | .3974 | 0.41 | .1591 | .3409 |
| 0.12 | .0478 | .4522 | 0.27 | .1064 | .3936 | 0.42 | .1628 | .3372 |
| 0.13 | .0517 | .4483 | 0.28 | .1103 | .3897 | 0.43 | .1664 | .3336 |
| 0.14 | .0557 | .4443 | 0.29 | .1141 | .3859 | 0.44 | .1700 | .3300 |

(continued)

| (A) z | (B) area between mean and z | (C) area beyond z | (A) z | (B) area between mean and z | (C) area beyond z | (A) z | (B) area between mean and z | (C) area beyond z |
|---|---|---|---|---|---|---|---|---|
| 0.45 | .1736 | .3264 | 0.96 | .3315 | .1685 | 1.47 | .4292 | .0708 |
| 0.46 | .1772 | .3228 | 0.97 | .3340 | .1660 | 1.48 | .4306 | .0694 |
| 0.47 | .1808 | .3192 | 0.98 | .3365 | .1635 | 1.49 | .4319 | .0681 |
| 0.48 | .1844 | .3156 | 0.99 | .3389 | .1611 | 1.50 | .4332 | .0668 |
| 0.49 | .1879 | .3121 | 1.00 | .3413 | .1587 | 1.51 | .4345 | .0655 |
| 0.50 | .1915 | .3085 | 1.01 | .3438 | .1562 | 1.52 | .4357 | .0643 |
| 0.51 | .1950 | .3050 | 1.02 | .3461 | .1539 | 1.53 | .4370 | .0630 |
| 0.52 | .1985 | .3015 | 1.03 | .3485 | .1515 | 1.54 | .4382 | .0618 |
| 0.53 | .2019 | .2981 | 1.04 | .3508 | .1492 | 1.55 | .4394 | .0606 |
| 0.54 | .2054 | .2946 | 1.05 | .3531 | .1469 | 1.56 | .4406 | .0594 |
| 0.55 | .2088 | .2912 | 1.06 | .3554 | .1446 | 1.57 | .4418 | .0582 |
| 0.56 | .2123 | .2877 | 1.07 | .3577 | .1423 | 1.58 | .4429 | .0571 |
| 0.57 | .2157 | .2843 | 1.08 | .3599 | .1401 | 1.59 | .4441 | .0559 |
| 0.58 | .2190 | .2810 | 1.09 | .3621 | .1379 | 1.60 | .4452 | .0548 |
| 0.59 | .2224 | .2776 | 1.10 | .3643 | .1357 | 1.61 | .4463 | .0537 |
| 0.60 | .2257 | .2743 | 1.11 | .3665 | .1335 | 1.62 | .4474 | .0526 |
| 0.61 | .2291 | .2709 | 1.12 | .3686 | .1314 | 1.63 | .4484 | .0516 |
| 0.62 | .2324 | .2676 | 1.13 | .3708 | .1292 | 1.64 | .4495 | .0505 |
| 0.63 | .2357 | .2643 | 1.14 | .3729 | .1271 | 1.65 | .4505 | .0495 |
| 0.64 | .2389 | .2611 | 1.15 | .3749 | .1251 | 1.66 | .4515 | .0485 |
| 0.65 | .2422 | .2578 | 1.16 | .3770 | .1230 | 1.67 | .4525 | .0475 |
| 0.66 | .2454 | .2546 | 1.17 | .3790 | .1210 | 1.68 | .4535 | .0465 |
| 0.67 | .2486 | .2514 | 1.18 | .3810 | .1190 | 1.69 | .4545 | .0455 |
| 0.68 | .2517 | .2483 | 1.19 | .3830 | .1170 | 1.70 | .4554 | .0446 |
| 0.69 | .2549 | .2451 | 1.20 | .3849 | .1151 | 1.71 | .4564 | .0436 |
| 0.70 | .2580 | .2420 | 1.21 | .3869 | .1131 | 1.72 | .4573 | .0427 |
| 0.71 | .2611 | .2389 | 1.22 | .3888 | .1112 | 1.73 | .4582 | .0418 |
| 0.72 | .2642 | .2358 | 1.23 | .3907 | .1093 | 1.74 | .4591 | .0409 |
| 0.73 | .2673 | .2327 | 1.24 | .3925 | .1075 | 1.75 | .4599 | .0401 |
| 0.74 | .2704 | .2296 | 1.25 | .3944 | .1056 | 1.76 | .4608 | .0392 |
| 0.75 | .2734 | .2266 | 1.26 | .3962 | .1038 | 1.77 | .4616 | .0384 |
| 0.76 | .2764 | .2236 | 1.27 | .3980 | .1020 | 1.78 | .4625 | .0375 |
| 0.77 | .2794 | .2206 | 1.28 | .3997 | .1003 | 1.79 | .4633 | .0367 |
| 0.78 | .2823 | .2177 | 1.29 | .4015 | .0985 | 1.80 | .4641 | .0359 |
| 0.79 | .2852 | .2148 | 1.30 | .4032 | .0968 | 1.81 | .4649 | .0351 |
| 0.80 | .2881 | .2119 | 1.31 | .4049 | .0951 | 1.82 | .4656 | .0344 |
| 0.81 | .2910 | .2090 | 1.32 | .4066 | .0934 | 1.83 | .4664 | .0336 |
| 0.82 | .2939 | .2061 | 1.33 | .4082 | .0918 | 1.84 | .4671 | .0329 |
| 0.83 | .2967 | .2033 | 1.34 | .4099 | .0901 | 1.85 | .4678 | .0322 |
| 0.84 | .2995 | .2005 | 1.35 | .4115 | .0885 | 1.86 | .4686 | .0314 |
| 0.85 | .3023 | .1977 | 1.36 | .4131 | .0869 | 1.87 | .4693 | .0307 |
| 0.86 | .3051 | .1949 | 1.37 | .4147 | .0853 | 1.88 | .4699 | .0301 |
| 0.87 | .3078 | .1922 | 1.38 | .4162 | .0838 | 1.89 | .4706 | .0294 |
| 0.88 | .3106 | .1894 | 1.39 | .4177 | .0823 | 1.90 | .4713 | .0287 |
| 0.89 | .3133 | .1867 | 1.40 | .4192 | .0808 | 1.91 | .4719 | .0281 |
| 0.90 | .3159 | .1841 | 1.41 | .4207 | .0793 | 1.92 | .4726 | .0274 |
| 0.91 | .3186 | .1814 | 1.42 | .4222 | .0778 | 1.93 | .4732 | .0268 |
| 0.92 | .3212 | .1788 | 1.43 | .4236 | .0764 | 1.94 | .4738 | .0262 |
| 0.93 | .3238 | .1762 | 1.44 | .4251 | .0749 | 1.95 | .4744 | .0256 |
| 0.94 | .3264 | .1736 | 1.45 | .4265 | .0735 | 1.96 | .4750 | .0250 |
| 0.95 | .3289 | .1711 | 1.46 | .4279 | .0721 | 1.97 | .4756 | .0244 |

(continued)

| (A) z | (B) area between mean and z | (C) area beyond z | (A) z | (B) area between mean and z | (C) area beyond z | (A) z | (B) area between mean and z | (C) area beyond z |
|---|---|---|---|---|---|---|---|---|
| 1.98 | .4761 | .0239 | 2.44 | .4927 | .0073 | 2.90 | .4981 | .0019 |
| 1.99 | .4767 | .0233 | 2.45 | .4929 | .0071 | 2.91 | .4982 | .0018 |
| 2.00 | .4772 | .0228 | 2.46 | .4931 | .0069 | 2.92 | .4982 | .0018 |
| 2.01 | .4778 | .0222 | 2.47 | .4932 | .0068 | 2.93 | .4983 | .0017 |
| 2.02 | .4783 | .0217 | 2.48 | .4934 | .0066 | 2.94 | .4984 | .0016 |
| 2.03 | .4788 | .0212 | 2.49 | .4936 | .0064 | 2.95 | .4984 | .0016 |
| 2.04 | .4793 | .0207 | 2.50 | .4938 | .0062 | 2.96 | .4985 | .0015 |
| 2.05 | .4798 | .0202 | 2.51 | .4940 | .0060 | 2.97 | .4985 | .0015 |
| 2.06 | .4803 | .0197 | 2.52 | .4941 | .0059 | 2.98 | .4986 | .0014 |
| 2.07 | .4808 | .0192 | 2.53 | .4943 | .0057 | 2.99 | .4986 | .0014 |
| 2.08 | .4812 | .0188 | 2.54 | .4945 | .0055 | 3.00 | .4987 | .0013 |
| 2.09 | .4817 | .0183 | 2.55 | .4946 | .0054 | 3.01 | .4987 | .0013 |
| 2.10 | .4821 | .0179 | 2.56 | .4948 | .0052 | 3.02 | .4987 | .0013 |
| 2.11 | .4826 | .0174 | 2.57 | .4949 | .0051 | 3.03 | .4988 | .0012 |
| 2.12 | .4830 | .0170 | 2.58 | .4951 | .0049 | 3.04 | .4988 | .0012 |
| 2.13 | .4834 | .0166 | 2.59 | .4952 | .0048 | 3.05 | .4989 | .0011 |
| 2.14 | .4838 | .0162 | 2.60 | .4953 | .0047 | 3.06 | .4989 | .0011 |
| 2.15 | .4842 | .0158 | 2.61 | .4955 | .0045 | 3.07 | .4989 | .0011 |
| 2.16 | .4846 | .0154 | 2.62 | .4956 | .0044 | 3.08 | .4990 | .0010 |
| 2.17 | .4850 | .0150 | 2.63 | .4957 | .0043 | 3.09 | .4990 | .0010 |
| 2.18 | .4854 | .0146 | 2.64 | .4959 | .0041 | 3.10 | .4990 | .0010 |
| 2.19 | .4857 | .0143 | 2.65 | .4960 | .0040 | 3.11 | .4991 | .0009 |
| 2.20 | .4861 | .0139 | 2.66 | .4961 | .0039 | 3.12 | .4991 | .0009 |
| 2.21 | .4864 | .0136 | 2.67 | .4962 | .0038 | 3.13 | .4991 | .0009 |
| 2.22 | .4868 | .0132 | 2.68 | .4963 | .0037 | 3.14 | .4992 | .0008 |
| 2.23 | .4871 | .0129 | 2.69 | .4964 | .0036 | 3.15 | .4992 | .0008 |
| 2.24 | .4875 | .0125 | 2.70 | .4965 | .0035 | 3.16 | .4992 | .0008 |
| 2.25 | .4878 | .0122 | 2.71 | .4966 | .0034 | 3.17 | .4992 | .0008 |
| 2.26 | .4881 | .0119 | 2.72 | .4967 | .0033 | 3.18 | .4993 | .0007 |
| 2.27 | .4884 | .0116 | 2.73 | .4968 | .0032 | 3.19 | .4993 | .0007 |
| 2.28 | .4887 | .0113 | 2.74 | .4969 | .0031 | 3.20 | .4993 | .0007 |
| 2.29 | .4890 | .0110 | 2.75 | .4970 | .0030 | 3.21 | .4993 | .0007 |
| 2.30 | .4893 | .0107 | 2.76 | .4971 | .0029 | 3.22 | .4994 | .0006 |
| 2.31 | .4896 | .0104 | 2.77 | .4972 | .0028 | 3.23 | .4994 | .0006 |
| 2.32 | .4898 | .0102 | 2.78 | .4973 | .0027 | 3.24 | .4994 | .0006 |
| 2.33 | .4901 | .0099 | 2.79 | .4974 | .0026 | 3.25 | .4994 | .0006 |
| 2.34 | .4904 | .0096 | 2.80 | .4974 | .0026 | 3.30 | .4995 | .0005 |
| 2.35 | .4906 | .0094 | 2.81 | .4975 | .0025 | 3.35 | .4996 | .0004 |
| 2.36 | .4909 | .0091 | 2.82 | .4976 | .0024 | 3.40 | .4997 | .0003 |
| 2.37 | .4911 | .0089 | 2.83 | .4977 | .0023 | 3.45 | .4997 | .0003 |
| 2.38 | .4913 | .0087 | 2.84 | .4977 | .0023 | 3.50 | .4998 | .0002 |
| 2.39 | .4916 | .0084 | 2.85 | .4978 | .0022 | 3.60 | .4998 | .0002 |
| 2.40 | .4918 | .0082 | 2.86 | .4979 | .0021 | 3.70 | .4999 | .0001 |
| 2.41 | .4920 | .0080 | 2.87 | .4979 | .0021 | 3.80 | .4999 | .0001 |
| 2.42 | .4922 | .0078 | 2.88 | .4980 | .0020 | 3.90 | .49995 | .00005 |
| 2.43 | .4925 | .0075 | 2.89 | .4981 | .0019 | 4.00 | .49997 | .00003 |

*Source*: Haber, A. and Runyon, R. P. (1973) *General Statistics*, 2nd edition, Addison Wesley.

# Appendix B

## Critical values of $U$ and $U'$ for a one-tailed test at $\alpha = 0.025$ or a two-tailed test at $\alpha = 0.05$

To be significant for any given $n_1$ and $n_2$: Obtained $U$ must be equal to or *less than* the value shown in the table. Obtained $U'$ must be equal to or *greater than* the value shown in the table. Note that $U'$ values are shown underlined.

In each cell the upper number is $U$ and the lower (underlined) number is $U'$, shown here as $U$ / $U'$.

| $n_2$ \ $n_1$ | 1 | 2 | 3 | 4 | 5 | 6 | 7 | 8 | 9 | 10 | 11 | 12 | 13 | 14 | 15 | 16 | 17 | 18 | 19 | 20 |
|---|---|---|---|---|---|---|---|---|---|---|---|---|---|---|---|---|---|---|---|---|
| 1 | — | — | — | — | — | — | — | — | — | — | — | — | — | — | — | — | — | — | — | — |
| 2 | — | — | — | — | — | — | — | 0/16 | 0/18 | 0/20 | 0/22 | 1/23 | 1/25 | 1/27 | 1/29 | 1/31 | 2/32 | 2/34 | 2/36 | 2/38 |
| 3 | — | — | — | — | 0/15 | 1/17 | 1/20 | 2/22 | 2/25 | 3/27 | 3/30 | 4/32 | 4/35 | 5/37 | 5/40 | 6/42 | 6/45 | 7/47 | 7/50 | 8/52 |
| 4 | — | — | — | 0/16 | 1/19 | 2/22 | 3/25 | 4/28 | 4/32 | 5/35 | 6/38 | 7/41 | 8/44 | 9/47 | 10/50 | 11/53 | 11/57 | 12/60 | 13/63 | 13/67 |
| 5 | — | — | 0/15 | 1/19 | 2/23 | 3/27 | 5/30 | 6/34 | 7/38 | 8/42 | 9/46 | 11/49 | 12/53 | 13/57 | 14/61 | 15/65 | 17/68 | 18/72 | 19/76 | 20/80 |
| 6 | — | — | 1/17 | 2/22 | 3/27 | 5/31 | 6/36 | 8/40 | 10/44 | 11/49 | 13/53 | 14/58 | 16/62 | 17/67 | 19/71 | 21/75 | 22/80 | 24/84 | 25/89 | 27/93 |
| 7 | — | — | 1/20 | 3/25 | 5/30 | 6/36 | 8/41 | 10/46 | 12/51 | 14/56 | 16/61 | 18/66 | 20/71 | 22/76 | 24/81 | 26/86 | 28/91 | 30/96 | 32/101 | 34/106 |
| 8 | — | 0/16 | 2/22 | 4/28 | 6/34 | 8/40 | 10/46 | 13/51 | 15/57 | 17/63 | 19/69 | 22/74 | 24/80 | 26/86 | 29/91 | 31/97 | 34/102 | 36/108 | 38/114 | 41/119 |
| 9 | — | 0/18 | 2/25 | 4/32 | 7/38 | 10/44 | 12/51 | 15/57 | 17/64 | 20/70 | 23/76 | 26/82 | 28/89 | 31/95 | 34/101 | 37/107 | 39/114 | 42/120 | 45/126 | 48/132 |
| 10 | — | 0/20 | 3/27 | 5/35 | 8/42 | 11/49 | 14/56 | 17/63 | 20/70 | 23/77 | 26/84 | 29/91 | 33/97 | 36/104 | 39/111 | 42/118 | 45/125 | 48/132 | 52/138 | 55/145 |
| 11 | — | 0/22 | 3/30 | 6/38 | 9/46 | 13/53 | 16/61 | 19/69 | 23/76 | 26/84 | 30/91 | 33/99 | 37/106 | 40/114 | 44/121 | 47/129 | 51/136 | 55/143 | 58/151 | 62/158 |
| 12 | — | 1/23 | 4/32 | 7/41 | 11/49 | 14/58 | 18/66 | 22/74 | 26/82 | 29/91 | 33/99 | 37/107 | 41/115 | 45/123 | 49/131 | 53/139 | 57/147 | 61/155 | 65/163 | 69/171 |
| 13 | — | 1/25 | 4/35 | 8/44 | 12/53 | 16/62 | 20/71 | 24/80 | 28/89 | 33/97 | 37/106 | 41/115 | 45/124 | 50/132 | 54/141 | 59/149 | 63/158 | 67/167 | 72/175 | 76/184 |
| 14 | — | 1/27 | 5/37 | 9/47 | 13/57 | 17/67 | 22/76 | 26/86 | 31/95 | 36/104 | 40/114 | 45/123 | 50/132 | 55/141 | 59/151 | 64/160 | 67/171 | 74/178 | 78/188 | 83/197 |
| 15 | — | 1/29 | 5/40 | 10/50 | 14/61 | 19/71 | 24/81 | 29/91 | 34/101 | 39/111 | 44/121 | 49/131 | 54/141 | 59/151 | 64/161 | 70/170 | 75/180 | 80/190 | 85/200 | 90/210 |
| 16 | — | 1/31 | 6/42 | 11/53 | 15/65 | 21/75 | 26/86 | 31/97 | 37/107 | 42/118 | 47/129 | 53/139 | 59/149 | 64/160 | 70/170 | 75/181 | 81/191 | 86/202 | 92/212 | 98/222 |
| 17 | — | 2/32 | 6/45 | 11/57 | 17/68 | 22/80 | 28/91 | 34/102 | 39/114 | 45/125 | 51/136 | 57/147 | 63/158 | 67/171 | 75/180 | 81/191 | 87/202 | 93/213 | 99/224 | 105/235 |
| 18 | — | 2/34 | 7/47 | 12/60 | 18/72 | 24/84 | 30/96 | 36/108 | 42/120 | 48/132 | 55/143 | 61/155 | 67/167 | 74/178 | 80/190 | 86/202 | 93/213 | 99/225 | 106/236 | 112/248 |
| 19 | — | 2/36 | 7/50 | 13/63 | 19/76 | 25/89 | 32/101 | 38/114 | 45/126 | 52/138 | 58/151 | 65/163 | 72/175 | 78/188 | 85/200 | 92/212 | 99/224 | 106/236 | 113/248 | 119/261 |
| 20 | — | 2/38 | 8/52 | 13/67 | 20/80 | 27/93 | 34/106 | 41/119 | 48/132 | 55/145 | 62/158 | 69/171 | 76/184 | 83/197 | 90/210 | 98/222 | 105/235 | 112/248 | 119/261 | 127/273 |

# Appendix C

## Critical values of *t*

For any given *df*, the table shows the values of *t* corresponding to various levels of probability. Obtained *t* is significant at a given level if its absolute value is equal to or *greater than* the value shown in the table.

| | Level of significance for one-tailed test | | | | | |
| | .10 | .05 | .025 | .01 | .005 | .0005 |
| | Level of significance for two-tailed test | | | | | |
| df | .20 | .10 | .05 | .02 | .01 | .001 |
|---|---|---|---|---|---|---|
| 1 | 3.078 | 6.314 | 12.706 | 31.821 | 63.657 | 636.619 |
| 2 | 1.886 | 2.920 | 4.303 | 6.965 | 9.925 | 31.598 |
| 3 | 1.638 | 2.353 | 3.182 | 4.541 | 5.841 | 12.941 |
| 4 | 1.533 | 2.132 | 2.776 | 3.747 | 4.604 | 8.610 |
| 5 | 1.476 | 2.015 | 2.571 | 3.365 | 4.032 | 6.859 |
| 6 | 1.440 | 1.943 | 2.447 | 3.143 | 3.707 | 5.959 |
| 7 | 1.415 | 1.895 | 2.365 | 2.998 | 3.499 | 5.405 |
| 8 | 1.397 | 1.860 | 2.306 | 2.896 | 3.355 | 5.041 |
| 9 | 1.383 | 1.833 | 2.262 | 2.821 | 3.250 | 4.781 |
| 10 | 1.372 | 1.812 | 2.228 | 2.764 | 3.169 | 4.587 |
| 11 | 1.363 | 1.796 | 2.201 | 2.718 | 3.106 | 4.437 |
| 12 | 1.356 | 1.782 | 2.179 | 2.681 | 3.055 | 4.318 |
| 13 | 1.350 | 1.771 | 2.160 | 2.650 | 3.012 | 4.221 |
| 14 | 1.345 | 1.761 | 2.145 | 2.624 | 2.977 | 4.140 |
| 15 | 1.341 | 1.753 | 2.131 | 2.602 | 2.947 | 4.073 |
| 16 | 1.337 | 1.746 | 2.120 | 2.583 | 2.921 | 4.015 |
| 17 | 1.333 | 1.740 | 2.110 | 2.567 | 2.898 | 3.965 |
| 18 | 1.330 | 1.734 | 2.101 | 2.552 | 2.878 | 3.922 |
| 19 | 1.328 | 1.729 | 2.093 | 2.539 | 2.861 | 3.883 |
| 20 | 1.325 | 1.725 | 2.086 | 2.528 | 2.845 | 3.850 |
| 21 | 1.323 | 1.721 | 2.080 | 2.518 | 2.831 | 3.819 |
| 22 | 1.321 | 1.717 | 2.074 | 2.508 | 2.819 | 3.792 |
| 23 | 1.319 | 1.714 | 2.069 | 2.500 | 2.807 | 3.767 |
| 24 | 1.318 | 1.711 | 2.064 | 2.492 | 2.797 | 3.745 |
| 25 | 1.316 | 1.708 | 2.060 | 2.485 | 2.787 | 3.725 |
| 26 | 1.315 | 1.706 | 2.056 | 2.479 | 2.779 | 3.707 |
| 27 | 1.314 | 1.703 | 2.052 | 2.473 | 2.771 | 3.690 |
| 28 | 1.313 | 1.701 | 2.048 | 2.467 | 2.763 | 3.674 |
| 29 | 1.311 | 1.699 | 2.045 | 2.462 | 2.756 | 3.659 |
| 30 | 1.310 | 1.697 | 2.042 | 2.457 | 2.750 | 3.646 |
| 40 | 1.303 | 1.684 | 2.021 | 2.423 | 2.704 | 3.551 |
| 60 | 1.296 | 1.671 | 2.000 | 2.390 | 2.660 | 3.460 |
| 120 | 1.289 | 1.658 | 1.980 | 2.358 | 2.617 | 3.373 |
| ∞ | 1.282 | 1.645 | 1.960 | 2.326 | 2.576 | 3.291 |

*Source*: Haber, A. and Runyon, R. P. (1973) *General Statistics*, 2nd edition, Addison Wesley.

# Appendix D
# Critical values of *T* at various levels of probability

The symbol *T* denotes the smaller sum of ranks associated with differences that are all of the same sign. For any given *N* (number of ranked differences), the obtained *T* is significant at a given level if it is equal to or *less than* the value shown in the table.

| | Level of significance for one-tailed test | | | | | Level of significance for one-tailed test | | | |
|---|---|---|---|---|---|---|---|---|---|
| | .05 | .025 | .01 | .005 | | .05 | .025 | .01 | .005 |
| | Level of significance for two-tailed test | | | | | Level of significance for two-tailed test | | | |
| *N* | .10 | .05 | .02 | .01 | *N* | .10 | .05 | .02 | .01 |
| 5 | 0 | — | — | — | 28 | 130 | 116 | 101 | 91 |
| 6 | 2 | 0 | — | — | 29 | 140 | 126 | 110 | 100 |
| 7 | 3 | 2 | 0 | — | 30 | 151 | 137 | 120 | 109 |
| 8 | 5 | 3 | 1 | 0 | 31 | 163 | 147 | 130 | 118 |
| 9 | 8 | 5 | 3 | 1 | 32 | 175 | 159 | 140 | 128 |
| 10 | 10 | 8 | 5 | 3 | 33 | 187 | 170 | 151 | 138 |
| 11 | 13 | 10 | 7 | 5 | 34 | 200 | 182 | 162 | 148 |
| 12 | 17 | 13 | 9 | 7 | 35 | 213 | 195 | 173 | 159 |
| 13 | 21 | 17 | 12 | 9 | 36 | 227 | 208 | 185 | 171 |
| 14 | 25 | 21 | 15 | 12 | 37 | 241 | 221 | 198 | 182 |
| 15 | 30 | 25 | 19 | 15 | 38 | 256 | 235 | 211 | 194 |
| 16 | 35 | 29 | 23 | 19 | 39 | 271 | 249 | 224 | 207 |
| 17 | 41 | 34 | 27 | 23 | 40 | 286 | 264 | 238 | 220 |
| 18 | 47 | 40 | 32 | 27 | 41 | 302 | 279 | 252 | 233 |
| 19 | 53 | 46 | 37 | 32 | 42 | 319 | 294 | 266 | 247 |
| 20 | 60 | 52 | 43 | 37 | 43 | 336 | 310 | 281 | 261 |
| 21 | 67 | 58 | 49 | 42 | 44 | 353 | 327 | 296 | 276 |
| 22 | 75 | 65 | 55 | 48 | 45 | 371 | 343 | 312 | 291 |
| 23 | 83 | 73 | 62 | 54 | 46 | 389 | 361 | 328 | 307 |
| 24 | 91 | 81 | 69 | 61 | 47 | 407 | 378 | 345 | 322 |
| 25 | 100 | 89 | 76 | 68 | 48 | 426 | 396 | 362 | 339 |
| 26 | 110 | 98 | 84 | 75 | 49 | 446 | 415 | 379 | 355 |
| 27 | 119 | 107 | 92 | 83 | 50 | 466 | 434 | 397 | 373 |

Note: Slight discrepancies will be found between the critical values appearing in the table above and in Table 2 of the 1964 revision of F. Wilcoxon, and R. A. Wilcox, *Some Rapid Approximate Statistical Procedures*, New York, Lederle Laboratories, 1964. The disparity reflects the latter's policy of selecting the critical value nearest a given significance level, occasionally overstepping that level. For example, for *N* = 8

the probability of a *T* of 3 = 0.0390 (two-tail)

and

the probability of a *T* of 4 = 0.0546 (two-tail).

Wilcoxon and Wilcox select a *T* of 4 as the critical value at the 0.05 level of significance (two-tail), whereas Table J reflects a more conservative policy by setting a *T* of 3 as the critical value at this level.

*Source*: Haber, A. and Runyon, R. P. (1973) *General Statistics*, 2nd edition, Addison Wesley.

# Appendix E

## Table of $\chi^2$

| Degrees of freedom df | P = .99 | .98 | .95 | .90 | .80 | .70 | .50 | .30 | .20 | .10 | .05 | .02 | .01 |
|---|---|---|---|---|---|---|---|---|---|---|---|---|---|
| 1 | .000157 | .000628 | .00393 | .0158 | .0642 | .148 | .455 | 1.074 | 1.642 | 2.706 | 3.841 | 5.412 | 6.635 |
| 2 | .0201 | .0404 | .103 | .211 | .446 | .713 | 1.386 | 2.408 | 3.219 | 4.605 | 5.991 | 7.824 | 9.210 |
| 3 | .115 | .185 | .352 | .584 | 1.005 | 1.424 | 2.366 | 3.665 | 4.642 | 6.251 | 7.815 | 9.837 | 11.341 |
| 4 | .297 | .429 | .711 | 1.064 | 1.649 | 2.195 | 3.357 | 4.878 | 5.989 | 7.779 | 9.488 | 11.668 | 13.277 |
| 5 | .554 | .752 | 1.145 | 1.610 | 2.343 | 3.000 | 4.351 | 6.064 | 7.289 | 9.236 | 11.070 | 13.388 | 15.086 |
| 6 | .872 | 1.134 | 1.635 | 2.204 | 3.070 | 3.828 | 5.348 | 7.231 | 8.558 | 10.645 | 12.592 | 15.033 | 16.812 |
| 7 | 1.239 | 1.564 | 2.167 | 2.833 | 3.822 | 4.671 | 6.346 | 8.383 | 9.803 | 12.017 | 14.067 | 16.622 | 18.475 |
| 8 | 1.646 | 2.032 | 2.733 | 3.490 | 4.594 | 5.527 | 7.344 | 9.524 | 11.030 | 13.362 | 15.507 | 18.168 | 20.090 |
| 9 | 2.088 | 2.532 | 3.325 | 4.168 | 5.380 | 6.393 | 8.343 | 10.656 | 12.242 | 14.684 | 16.919 | 19.679 | 21.666 |
| 10 | 2.558 | 3.059 | 3.940 | 4.865 | 6.179 | 7.267 | 9.342 | 11.781 | 13.442 | 15.987 | 18.307 | 21.161 | 23.209 |
| 11 | 3.053 | 3.609 | 4.575 | 5.578 | 6.989 | 8.148 | 10.341 | 12.899 | 14.631 | 17.275 | 19.675 | 22.618 | 24.725 |
| 12 | 3.571 | 4.178 | 5.226 | 6.304 | 7.807 | 9.034 | 11.340 | 14.011 | 15.812 | 18.549 | 21.026 | 24.054 | 26.217 |
| 13 | 4.107 | 4.765 | 5.892 | 7.042 | 8.634 | 9.926 | 12.340 | 15.119 | 16.985 | 19.812 | 22.362 | 25.472 | 27.688 |
| 14 | 4.660 | 5.368 | 6.571 | 7.790 | 9.467 | 10.821 | 13.339 | 16.222 | 18.151 | 21.064 | 23.685 | 26.873 | 29.141 |
| 15 | 5.229 | 5.985 | 7.261 | 8.547 | 10.307 | 11.721 | 14.339 | 17.322 | 19.311 | 22.307 | 24.996 | 28.259 | 30.578 |
| 16 | 5.812 | 6.614 | 7.962 | 9.312 | 11.152 | 12.624 | 15.338 | 18.418 | 20.465 | 23.542 | 26.296 | 29.633 | 32.000 |
| 17 | 6.408 | 7.255 | 8.672 | 10.085 | 12.002 | 13.531 | 16.338 | 19.511 | 21.615 | 24.769 | 27.587 | 30.995 | 33.409 |
| 18 | 7.015 | 7.906 | 9.390 | 10.865 | 12.857 | 14.440 | 17.338 | 20.601 | 22.760 | 25.989 | 28.869 | 32.346 | 34.805 |
| 19 | 7.633 | 8.567 | 10.117 | 11.651 | 13.716 | 15.352 | 18.338 | 21.689 | 23.900 | 27.204 | 30.144 | 33.687 | 36.191 |
| 20 | 8.260 | 9.237 | 10.851 | 12.443 | 14.578 | 16.266 | 19.337 | 22.775 | 25.038 | 28.412 | 31.410 | 35.020 | 37.566 |
| 21 | 8.897 | 9.915 | 11.591 | 13.240 | 15.445 | 17.182 | 20.337 | 23.858 | 26.171 | 29.615 | 32.671 | 36.343 | 38.932 |
| 22 | 9.542 | 10.600 | 12.338 | 14.041 | 16.314 | 18.101 | 21.337 | 24.939 | 27.301 | 30.813 | 33.924 | 37.659 | 40.289 |
| 23 | 10.196 | 11.293 | 13.091 | 14.848 | 17.187 | 19.021 | 22.337 | 26.018 | 28.429 | 32.007 | 35.172 | 38.968 | 41.638 |
| 24 | 10.856 | 11.992 | 13.848 | 15.659 | 18.062 | 19.943 | 23.337 | 27.096 | 29.553 | 33.196 | 36.415 | 40.270 | 42.980 |
| 25 | 11.524 | 12.697 | 14.611 | 16.473 | 18.940 | 20.867 | 24.337 | 28.172 | 30.675 | 34.382 | 37.652 | 41.566 | 44.314 |
| 26 | 12.198 | 13.409 | 15.379 | 17.292 | 19.820 | 21.792 | 25.336 | 29.246 | 31.795 | 35.563 | 38.885 | 42.856 | 45.642 |
| 27 | 12.879 | 14.125 | 16.151 | 18.114 | 20.703 | 22.719 | 26.336 | 30.319 | 32.912 | 36.741 | 40.113 | 44.140 | 46.963 |
| 28 | 13.565 | 14.847 | 16.928 | 18.939 | 21.588 | 23.647 | 27.336 | 31.391 | 34.027 | 37.916 | 41.337 | 45.419 | 48.278 |
| 29 | 14.256 | 15.574 | 17.708 | 19.768 | 22.475 | 24.577 | 28.336 | 32.461 | 35.139 | 39.087 | 42.557 | 46.693 | 49.588 |
| 30 | 14.953 | 16.306 | 18.493 | 20.599 | 23.364 | 25.508 | 29.336 | 33.530 | 36.250 | 40.256 | 43.773 | 47.962 | 50.892 |

Source: Haber, A. and Runyon, R. P. (1973) General Statistics, 2nd edition, Addison Wesley.

# Glossary

**accidental sampling** a procedure in which everyone in a particular place at a particular time becomes a member of a sample, purely as a matter of convenience. Much undergraduate research is of this nature and the approach makes no attempt at representativeness.

**action research** a form of qualitative research that involves the following: the identification of problems in particular settings; the generation of hypotheses about the causes of the problems and ways of solving them; an intervention; and an evaluation of the intervention.

**alternate form reliability** a measure of reliability obtained by administering equivalent or parallel forms of a test to the same participants on separate occasions. Using different forms of a test in this way is seen as a control for memory effects.

**analyse** in the context of SPSS this is a menu item which makes available the various commands for describing data.

**ANOVA** the common expression of the technique of analysis of variance. See also *one-way analysis of variance (ANOVA)*.

**area sampling** sampling a population in one specific geographical area or location.

**between-groups design** a design in which comparisons on some outcome variable are made between different groups of participants.

**between-groups variance** a measure of the variation among individual scores when participants are compared across two or more groups.

**bivariate** research involving a relationship between two variables. It is applied most commonly to correlational designs.

**Bonferroni procedure** a technique for reducing the possibility of a Type I error when multiple comparisons are made among a number of group means. This is part of the process of identifying exactly where an effect has occurred in an analysis of variance.

**boxplot** a type of graph used to represent interval-scaled data, emphasising the median, the interquartile range (IQR) and the minimum and maximum values.

**case study** intensive and detailed study of a very small number of participants – and sometimes only one. The case study is a common qualitative approach.

**central tendency** the frequently observed phenomenon whereby measurements of any trait or behaviour tend to cluster around some typical or central value, such as an average.

**chi-square** a procedure for comparing the observed frequency of response with expected frequencies in a nominal-nominal study; that is, when both the independent and dependent variables comprise categories. The difference between what is observed and what is expected is evaluated in terms of the likelihood of obtaining particular discrepancies by chance. This test is used in between-groups designs.

**closed-ended question** a type of questionnaire or interview item in which the range of responses open to a respondent is determined by the researcher.

**codebook** a detailed breakdown (usually accompanying secondary data) of the contents of a research data set, likely to include a description of the variables examined in a study, information on how categories were generated and explanations of the numerical codes used to identify various groups.

**coding** the process of transforming information or responses into numerical values. For example, $1 =$ male; $2 =$ female.

**coefficient of determination** a statistic obtained by squaring a correlation value. This provides a measure of the amount of variation in a criterion variable which is explained by, or predicted by, a predictor variable in a correlation design.

**concurrent validity** a version of criterion-related validity in which the comparison measures are taken at the same time as the test findings.

**condition** a participant profile characteristic or element of an experimental manipulation which distinguishes one group of participants from another (in between-subjects designs), or one observation period from another (in within-groups designs).

**confidence interval** the range of values within which we are confident that a population mean is likely to lie. Confidence is given as a probability, usually 95%.

**construct validity** the type of validation necessary for any test attempting to measure some psychological concept or construct. This is not really a measure in itself nor does it describe one single procedure – rather, construct validity is demonstrated using a variety of techniques.

**content analysis** in this context, a way of analysing text. A systematic and objective analysis of the content of a text, typically centring on thematic and symbolic elements. Can be used in qualitative or quantitative analysis.

**content validity** demonstrated when the content of a test – in terms of the type and scope of items – comprises a fair and representative reflection of the opinion, attitude or event which is the focus of interest.

**contingency table** tabulated output of a crosstabulation.

**control** any mechanism, device or manipulation that functions to minimise the effects of some extraneous or confounding influence in a study.

**control group** a group which receives no treatment in an experiment, usually to provide a basis for comparison with an experimental group on some outcome measure, or to demonstrate that, in the absence of a treatment or intervention, there is no effect.

**convenience sampling** a procedure whereby a sample comprises everyone in a particular place at a particular time. An undergraduate might administer questionnaires to everyone in the psychology section of the library for instance, or to everyone standing in a bus queue, as a matter of convenience. Also known as accidental sampling.

**corrected model** in two-way ANOVA combines all possible factor levels to determine whether or not a significant difference is present.

**correlation** a measure of the association between two continuous variables. Expressed as a statistic $r$, which indicates both the strength and direction of a relationship.

**correlation coefficient ($r$)** a numerical value which indicates the magnitude and nature of a correlation. Expressed as a value between 0 and $+/-1$, and thus either positive or negative.

**counterbalancing** a method of manipulating the order in which participants experience experimental treatments in a within-subjects design. The technique eliminates, or reduces, the effects of repetition, in particular the possibility of order effects. It does not eliminate practice effects.

**criterion-related validity** a method of demonstrating test validity by comparing test findings to some other measure, or criterion.

**criterion variable** in correlation research, measures which are associated with predictor variables. In an experiment, they would be referred to as dependent variables.

**cross-sectional designs** refers to research in which all measures are taken at the same point in time.

**crosstabulation** a procedure in which the proportion of cases or observations falling across two nominal or ordinal variables is noted. The type of table in which the outcome of this procedure is presented is a contingency table. This is also an option under the Descriptive Statistics menu of SPSS.

**cut-off assignment** a procedure whereby participants are assigned to conditions or categories of an independent variable as a result of scoring above or below a specified cut-off value on a continuous measurement scale. An example might be classifying undergraduate volunteers as either young or mature, depending on whether their ages are more or less than 25 years.

**cut off (score)** a value in a distribution of scores which acts as a boundary between different categories of score. In a distribution of extraversion scores, for example, a particular cut off score can be selected to distinguish between extraverts and introverts. See *cut off assignment*.

**data view** The particular view of a data file in SPSS in which we can enter data and in which we have access to the various commands for describing and performing analyses.

**dependent variable** the outcome measure in a study.

**descriptive** An option in the Descriptive Statistics menu of SPSS which provides a limited range of measures on a single, interval-scaled variable. Typically the mean and standard deviation are offered.

**descriptive statistics** In the context of SPSS, one of the sub-commands available in the Analyse menu, which offers various ways of describing data.

**descriptive techniques** a series of procedures that summarise, simplify and illustrate data.

**dichotomous scales** scales on which there are only two kinds of response (as in Yes/No).

**discourse analysis** a term used to describe a number of qualitative approaches, all of which centre on the analysis of text or language. In the field of psychology, discourse analysis usually concerns the function of language and the construction of meaning.

**dispersion** the tendency for scores in a distribution to vary around some middle value.

**double-blind control** a method of eliminating the effects of knowledge of the experiment on the outcome of an experiment, in which neither the participants nor the experimenter know the nature of a manipulation. The term 'double' is appropriate since both elements of the experimental situation (participants and experimenter) are blind to the manipulation. See also *single-blind design*.

**equivalent-groups design** an experimental design in which groups being compared are deemed to be equivalent, usually as a result of the random allocation of participants to groups. It should be noted that such equivalence is probabilistic and not actual, since different participants will be present in the different groups.

**ethnography** a form of qualitative research. The study of social groups through involvement with those groups, typically taking a phenomenological standpoint.

**experiment** a procedure for gathering data which involves the researcher manipulating key aspects of a study, such as the way in which participants are assigned to groups, the experiences they encounter and the way in which measures are taken.

**experimental design** a research approach characterised by manipulation of participants into groups, of independent variables, and of experimental treatments.

**experimental group** a group which is subjected to some form of treatment in an experiment.

**explore** an option in the Descriptive Statistics menu of SPSS which provides the full range of measures of central tendency and dispersion for a continuous, interval-scaled variable. These measures are also available for different categories of a corresponding nominal variable (e.g., average and range of income can be explored separately for males and females).

**extraneous variable** a variable present in an experiment which might interfere with or obscure the relationship between an independent and a dependent variable.

**face validity** a characteristic of measurement instruments whereby a test seems to be measuring what it claims to be measuring. This is an aspect of a test's appearance and its apparent relevance to participants. The term is potentially misleading since it provides no indication of true, objective validity, but it does influence the attitudes of participants to the research and their level of co-operation.

**factorial design**  a design with two or more factors, or categorical independent variables (for example, gender and social class).

**factorial research**  research in which the influence of several factors on some dependent variable are explored.

**field notes**  the records made during qualitative research. In tone, can be objective (e.g., people present at meetings, topics of discussion) or subjective (e.g., the researcher's reactions, feelings and thoughts).

**field study**  a procedure for gathering data in which the researcher manipulates key factors within a natural setting.

**focus group**  a type of discussion group established to explore particular issues. A method used to generate qualitative data. A group of people brought together to discuss a specific topic, under the direction or guidance of a moderator.

**frequencies**  an option in the Descriptive Statistics menu of SPSS which offers a simple count of the number of cases falling into different categories (e.g., the number of males and females in a sample).

**frequency tables**  a table in which the frequencies of cases, participants or observations are presented, either as numbers, percentages, or both. Such tables are useful for describing the distribution of cases across the categories of a single, nominal or ordinal variable.

**generalisation**  the ability to apply findings gleaned from a sample to the population at large. This is only possible when samples truly reflect population characteristics, otherwise findings are situation specific.

**generalisation problem**  a common difficulty in research in which the findings of a study might not be typical of, or generalisable to, the population at large.

**Greenhouse-Geisser**  an alternative approach to the calculation of an $F$-ratio, which makes a correction for the absence of sphericity in the calculation of a repeated measures ANOVA.

**grounded theory**  a form of qualitative research first described by Glaser and Strauss, and related to symbolic interactionism and phenomenology. No theory is imposed *a priori* (prior to data collection). The aim is to generate theory from the data gathered during the research process.

**hermeneutics**  a term with a long and interesting history. In this context, a form of qualitative research and analysis, such that the interpretation and understanding of communication and social events centres on the meanings ascribed to the communication or events by people in the context of their culture.

**histogram**  a type of graph, similar to a bar graph, used to represent interval-scaled data.

**homogeneity**  in the independent samples $t$-test, refers to the extent to which the variances of the two groups are similar.

**homogeneous**  a description applied to a population in which the members share consistent and similar characteristics.

**hypothesis**  a specific prediction about some aspect of the universe, based on the more general beliefs which comprise a theory. For example, 'there will be a significant difference between male and female participants on the mean performance scores on a choice-dilemma problem-solving task'.

**independent-groups design**  a between-groups design.

**independent-samples *t*-test**  a test which compares the means of two different groups measured on some outcome variable. The magnitude of the observed difference is evaluated in terms of probability. This test is used in between-groups designs and is also known as unrelated $t$-test, unpaired $t$-test, between-groups $t$-test, and independent-samples $t$-test.

**independent variable**  the variable manipulated by a researcher in an experiment.

**inferential statistics**  forms of analysis which allow predictions to be examined and hypotheses to be accepted or rejected.

**informed consent** the agreement of a participant to participate in research, based on a full understanding of the aims of a study, and of their own rights in respect of confidentiality and ethical treatment.

**interaction effect** when the effect of one independent variable on some outcome measure depends on the presence of another independent variable.

**internal validity** a quality associated with a true experiment, or the extent to which a causal relationship can be assumed between the independent and dependent variables.

**interpretative phenomenological analysis (IPA)** a form of qualitative analysis of text (usually derived from transcriptions of interviews), with a phenomenological focus. The analysis centres on the individual, with the aim of understanding the cognitions that underpin the language.

**interquartile range (IQR)** the difference between the values of the lower and upper quarter of an ordered array of values.

**interval scale** a system of measurement in which observations are made on a scale comprising equal intervals. (The distance between two adjacent units on this scale is the same as the distance between any other two adjacent units.) Temperature, for example, is usually measured on an interval scale. See also *nominal, ordinal* and *ratio scale*.

**kurtosis** a measure of the steepness or shallowness of the curve which forms part of the shape of a distribution.

**leptokurtic** describing a distribution characterised by peakedness and a narrow spread of data about the mean.

**level** the commonly used term for a condition in factorial designs.

**level of measurement** the term identifying variables as being measured on nominal, ordinal, interval or ratio scales.

**Likert scale** a type of rating scale in which the numbers are replaced by response categories, usually in terms of how much a participant agrees with a particular statement. For example: strongly agree; agree; neither agree or disagree; disagree; strongly disagree.

**literature review** the section of a written report of a study that considers the work of other authors, as part of the justification for that study.

**local sampling effect** a possible consequence of a practical constraint on some research, describing an effect of restricting sampling to a local community. Inadvertently such samples can become overloaded with unusual or extreme localised characteristics. See also *sample bias* and *situation specificity*.

**longitudinal** research in which repeated observations are made on a sample of the same participants over a period of time.

**main effect** the influence exerted by an independent variable on some outcome measure, free from the effects of any other factor.

**Mann-Whitney *U*-test** a non-parametric equivalent to the independent samples *t*-test. Calculations of *U* and *U'* are based on the ranks of different scores or observations.

**matching** a process whereby participants in each group in a between-groups design are matched on a number of key characteristics (between-subjects, matched groups design).

**Mauchly test of sphericity** A test of sphericity in repeated measures designs. Given in SPSS as part of the ANOVA output.

**mean** the arithmetic average of an array of scores or measurements, calculated by summing all the scores and dividing by their number. A measure of central tendency.

**median** the middle value of an ordered array of scores. This statistic is sometimes used in preference to the mean when extreme scores are present.

**meta-analysis** a procedure for combining the results of a number of independent studies into what is effectively a single, large-scale study of a particular topic.

**mixed design** an experimental design which incorporates both between-groups and within-subjects elements. Some mixed designs combine equivalent and non-equivalent groups.

**mode** the most frequently occurring value in an array of scores.

**multiple category scale** a response scale that includes a number of different categories for the respondent to choose from.

**multiple correlation** a procedure whereby a number of predictors are correlated, in combination, with a single criterion variable.

**multiple regression** procedure in which the contribution of several variables to variation on some outcome measure is assessed.

**Murphy's Law** a clichéd American colloquialism which claims that if something can go wrong it will. It should serve as a warning to all researchers to plan their work in advance and anticipate problems before they emerge.

**negative correlation** a relationship in which, as measures on one variable increase, measures on the other decrease.

**nominal scale** A scale in which the participants of a study are distinguished by the group or category to which they belong. Differences between or among categories are qualitative and imply no sense of magnitude. The variable gender is nominally scaled. See also *ordinal*, *interval* and *ratio scale*.

**non-equivalent-groups design** an experimental design in which groups being compared are deemed not to be probabilistically equivalent. Includes designs incorporating naturally occurring groups (e.g., males and females).

**non-parametric data** nominally scaled or ordinally scaled data are non-parametric: they cannot be meaningfully described in terms of means and standard deviations.

**non-probability sampling** sampling procedures in which not every member of a population stands an equal probability of being sampled.

**normal distribution** a term describing the characteristic arrangement of observations on any variable, with most scores clustering around some central value and fewer and fewer observations occurring with the distance from this average measure.

**norms** measures of typical or normal performance on questionnaires or psychometric instruments, usually given in terms of mean scores and measures of spread for specific subsections of the population. Sometimes presented as a proportion or percentage of a sample producing particular scores.

**null hypothesis** the prediction that participants in different groups are drawn from the same population (and will not, therefore, differ on the criterion variable).

**observational research** research based on observations of participants in particular contexts or situations.

**one sample *t*-test** a test that compares a sample statistic against a known population parameter.

**one-tailed test** A one-tailed test (as opposed to a two-tailed test) can be used when the hypothesis states the direction of the predicted effect: for example, that the mean of one group on the dependent variable will be greater than that of another group.

**one-way analysis of variance (ANOVA)** a between-groups, independent-samples parametric test comparing three or more groups or conditions. See also *ANOVA*.

**open-ended question** a type of questionnaire or interview item in which there are no restrictions on the range of responses possible to a respondent.

**order effect** a possible occurrence in repeated measures designs in which the order in which conditions are encountered by participants influences outcomes, often in unpredictable ways.

**ordinal scale**  A scale in which the participants of a study are distinguished by the group or category to which they belong. Differences between or among categories are quantitative but only at the level of 'greater than' or 'less than'. Assigning research participants to an age category (young, middle-aged, elderly) places them on an ordinal scale. See also *ordinal*, *interval* and *ratio scale*.

**outcome variable**  an alternative term for dependent, or criterion variable.

**paired *t*-test**  this test compares the means of two variables derived from a single group, usually on two different occasions: for example, it can be used to determine whether test performance varies over time. The test is commonly applied to within-subjects designs in which comparisons are made on a 'before and after' basis, or according to treatment. Related terminology: correlated *t*-test; within-groups *t*-test; related *t*-test; repeated measures *t*-test; dependent samples *t*-test.

**parametric data**  data which meet a number of statistical criteria: they are continuous scaled; they are normally distributed; and they can be meaningfully expressed in terms of their key summary characteristics or parameters – the mean and standard deviation.

**partial correlation**  a correlation between two variables from which the effects of a third have been statistically removed.

**participant observation**  observation of a group of people, whereby the researcher joins the group and makes the observations while part of the group. For example, an observation of a seminar group by someone who is a member of that seminar group.

**participatory research**  forms of qualitative research wherein the participants take a central role in setting the research agenda, designing the study and collecting the data.

**percentiles**  a cumulative measure of the proportion of individuals who score at, or below, particular points on a measuring scale.

**phenomenology**  in this context, a central construct in many forms of qualitative research. An approach centred on the perceptions (in the broadest sense) of participants, such that the researcher (*a*) accepts the participants' representations of events and situations as the real account, and (*b*) does not impose his or her own representations on the research process.

**piloting**  the term used to describe preparatory work in developing ways of collecting data, typically the stage during which methods of collecting data are tried out on small numbers of participants. Changes are made in response to the participants' reactions and to any problems experienced.

**platykurtic**  describing a distribution which is squashed in appearance, characterised by a relative flatness in the centre and a wide spread of data about the mean.

**population**  the entire set of entities which comprise the group, or sub-group, of participants which is the object of study, and in which the entire range of an outcome measure is represented.

**positive correlation**  a relationship in which, as measures on one variable increase, measures on the other variable increase also.

**post hoc tests**  a term applied to tests made after an analysis of variance, the purpose of which is to identify the exact source of a significant effect. See also *Bonferroni procedure*.

**post-test**  a term found in repeated measures or within-subjects designs to refer to measures taken after an intervention, task or passage of time.

**post-test randomised between-groups experimental design**  a design that can be called a true experiment, in that participants are randomly assigned to groups.

**power**  the power of a statistical test is $1 - \beta$, where $\beta$ (beta) is the probability of a Type II error. The ability of the test to detect a real effect.

**practice effects**  a tendency for performance on certain types of test to improve over time simply as a result of practice. The effect can often lead to artificially reduced measures of reliability.

**PRE (proportional reduction in error)**  in a crosstabulation analysis, this indicates the extent to which the independent variable actually predicts the dependent variable.

**predictive validity** a version of criterion related validity in which the comparison measures are taken sometime in the future, after test findings have become available.

**predictor variable** the preferred term in correlation research for what otherwise might be called the independent variable in an experimental design.

**pre-test** a term found in repeated measures or within-subjects designs to refer to baseline measures.

**primary data** data collected by the researcher, and used to address the aims of the study for which it was intended.

**probability** a measure of likelihood, based on the ratio of particular events to the total number of events possible. Statistical decisions about hypotheses are based on probability.

**probability sampling** the principle behind random sampling procedures in which every member of a population from which a sample will be drawn has an equal probability of being selected as every other member.

**procedural variations** an occasional tendency for apparent differences among participants on particular tests to reflect variations in testing procedures as opposed to actual variations on some quality.

**profile data (participant data)** descriptive information on the participants who take part in a study. Typically the participant's age, gender, social category and so on.

**project** an undertaking (for the purposes of this textbook) whereby a study is devised and carried out as part of a formal undergraduate course. Such an undertaking is usually assessed.

**projective techniques** methods whereby we 'project' or express some element of our individual nature, attitudes or personality, as when we respond to open-ended questions in a survey, or make up stories about what we see in a Rorschach Ink Blot.

**psychometric test** a test designed to measure some psychological construct. The quality and utility of such a test would usually be assessed in terms of reliability and validity.

**purposive sampling** a procedure whereby a particular population group is identified as possessing particular predictive qualities for the wider population and sampling is restricted (on purpose) to that group.

**quasi-experiment** a design that is not strictly experimental in that it makes use of naturally occurring groups, such as gender. However, the design shares features associated with a true experiment.

**quota sampling** a procedure of drawing fixed quotas of participants from different strata within a population; quotas usually reflect the relative representativeness of particular groups within the wider population.

**random sampling** a procedure of drawing participants from a population in a totally random fashion; every single individual has an equal probability of being selected.

**randomisation** a procedure in which participants are assigned to different groups in an experimental design, such that each individual has an equal probability of being assigned to either a control or an experimental group. The procedure contributes to an equivalent-groups design.

**randomised control trial (RCT)** a term found in the medical literature to refer to an experiment, or quasi-experiment, in which participants are randomly assigned to a group prior to an intervention.

**range** a simple measure of dispersion – the difference between the lowest and highest values.

**rating scales** response scales offering the participant a range of possible responses.

**ratio scale** a system of measurement in which observations are made on a scale comprising equal intervals and on which there is a true zero point. Measurement of response time on an experimental task would be on a ratio scale. See also *nominal*, *ordinal*, and *interval scale*.

**realist** A realist view, or realism, describes a philosophical position whereby we can know or access the world directly. An idealist view, on the other hand, describes the position or belief that what we know about the world is always mediated by our own cognitions, beliefs, emotions, etc.

**reflexivity** An aspect of a number of qualitative approaches. The conscious, explicit and questioning examination of the researcher's own role in the research process, including analysis.

**regression line** expresses the relationship between a pair of correlated variables as a straight line.

**reliability** a term to describe the consistency of a test.

**reliability coefficient** a statistic that offers a numerical indication of test reliability. The statistic is based on a modified version of correlation, in which such factors as the number of items in a test are controlled for. A common measure here is Cronbach's alpha ($\alpha$).

**repeated measures design** a type of experimental design in which a series of observations are repeated on the same participants within a single experiment or study. See also *within-groups designs*.

**repetition effects** the possible influence of repeated trials or treatments in a within-subjects design. Can be of due to such factors as practice and order of presentation.

**representative** in psychometrics, the term refers to a highly desirable characteristic of tests, in which the item coverage is a fair reflection, or representation, of the area under investigation. In sampling procedures, it refers to the importance of ensuring that the sample is a fair reflection, or representation, of the population from which it is drawn.

**research** a process of investigating, scrutinising or studying an issue, usually conducted according to a set of pre-determined guidelines and procedures.

**research area** the general area of interest in which the research is carried out (e.g., cognitive, developmental, occupational).

**research design** the formal plan of a research study in which all the elements necessary to test a hypothesis are identified and detailed – such elements include independent and dependent variables, extraneous elements and controls, relevant experimental manipulations and significance levels to be applied. Sometimes abbreviated to *design*.

**research question** an issue within an area of interest which provides the basis for a study; for example, 'are there sex differences in certain elements of cognitive functioning?' Sometimes referred to as the research issue.

**sample** the group of participants taking part in a study. It is assumed that the sample will be representative of the population from which it has been drawn such that observations on the sample will allow inferences to be made about the population.

**sample bias/sampling bias** the result of a particular sample being over- or under-represented on some characteristic which makes the sample atypical of the population from which it was drawn. This has the effect of limiting the extent to which inferences about the population can be made.

**sampling error** the difference between a sample and the population from which it has been drawn. Partly a function of sample size, it influences the extent to which population characteristics can be predicted from sample statistics.

**sampling frame** a listing of every individual in a population. Since random sampling procedures require that every member of a population has an equal chance of being sampled, sampling frames must be comprehensive.

**scatterplot** a type of graph in which the relationship between two variables is plotted.

**scientific method** a set of established procedures for the conduct of research, common to all disciplines.

**secondary data** data that have been collected for another purpose or study, or that have been taken from a secondary source.

**secondary research** research based on data collected by other researchers, or on an existing database.

**semantic differential** the responses available lie at two extremes of a single continuum: for example, good and bad.

**sentence completion** a procedure sometimes used for measuring attitudes in which the respondent is presented with an incomplete sentence and asked to continue in his or her own words.

**single-blind design** an experimental design in which participants are unaware of the particular experimental condition they are participating in – control or experimental. The term 'single' is appropriate since only one element of the experimental relationship (the participants) is blind to the precise nature of the manipulation. See also *double-blind control*.

**situation specificity (situational bias)** describes the tendency for many research findings to be relevant only to the sample or situation in which the study was carried out. A function of rigorous sampling and controls which remove a particular study too far from real life.

**skew** a measure of the extent to which a real distribution deviates from the normal distribution shape, as influenced by an unusual number of cases falling at one particular end of a distribution.

**snowball sampling** a procedure whereby the members of a (usually small) sample obtain additional participants through personal contacts or privileged access. The procedure can be used when the primary researchers would not themselves have access to a particular group.

**sphericity** In repeated measures analysis, refers to the correlations among scores at different levels of the within-subjects factor. Similar to the requirement of homogeneity of variance in between-groups research.

**Split-half reliability** a measure of reliability which measures the relationship among the items of a particular test. By splitting a test into two halves, and comparing the scores of participants on each half, it is possible to measure the internal consistency of a test.

**SPSS** a modern statistical computer package developed to organise, describe and analyse research data.

**squared multiple correlation** a measure which expresses the amount of variation in a criterion variable as a result of the combined effects of several predictors.

**standard deviation** a common measure of dispersion, based on the extent to which each individual score in a distribution varies from the mean.

**standard error** the standard deviation of a distribution of means; the denominator in the formula for the independent *t*-test.

**standard error (of the mean)** a statistic based on the standard deviation of a (theoretical) group of sample means, which provides a measure of how close the sample mean might be to the population from which it has been drawn.

**standard normal distribution** the term given to the theoretical distribution which serves as a model for all real, normal distributions.

**standardisation** in the context of psychological testing, standardisation refers to the process of ensuring identical procedures for administration, data collection and scoring.

**standardisation sample** the particular subset of a population who first experience a particular test, the aim being to identify typical or normal scores (norms).

**statistic** a symbol, along with its numerical counterpart, which represents, summarises or defines important characteristics of a variable. The symbols themselves are usually taken from the Greek alphabet.

**statistically significant** a term applied to an event when its likelihood of occurrence is so rare as to exceed a pre-determined probability level, usually taken as the 5% or .05 level.

**stemplot** alternative term for stem-and-leaf plot, which provides an unusual visual image of tabulated data.

**stratified sampling** a way of drawing participants from a population according to some pre-determined strategy. Normally, if a population is seen to comprise certain strata (socio-economic divisions, ethnic groupings, etc.) a sample should reflect the same structure and in the same proportions.

**study** a planned investigation of a specified topic or issue involving a systematic process of reading, exploration, experimentation and research.

**survey**  a method of collecting data from large numbers of participants on a particular topic (e.g., opinions, intentions). Can involve self-report questionnaires or highly structured interviews.

**symbolic interactionism**  a central construct in some forms of qualitative research, particularly grounded theory. In this context, it centres on the meanings ascribed to phenomena by the participants, such that these meanings are explored by the researcher through engagement and active interpretation.

**test reliability**  a measure or indication of the extent to which a test produces consistent results across time and situations.

**test validity**  an indication of the extent to which a test is actually measuring what it is supposed to be measuring. Unlike reliability, validity is not necessarily demonstrated statistically, although there are instances in which it can be.

**test-retest reliability**  a measure of reliability obtained by administering the same test to the same participants on two separate occasions.

**theory**  a general set of beliefs about some aspect of the universe which may or may not be supported by evidence.

**treatment**  the experimental manipulation to which participants are exposed in an experiment.

**triangulation**  a term used in qualitative research to describe ways in which the reliability of the research or analysis can be assessed. The term describes the way in which a second point of view on a phenomenon creates a triangle.

**true experiment**  a design that conforms in all respects to the definition of an experiment. Participants are randomly assigned to groups.

**two-tailed test**  a test used when the direction of predicted difference is unknown. See also *one-tailed test*.

**two-way ANOVA**  a parametric test in which different levels of two or more factors are compared on some dependent measure.

**Type I error**  said to occur when an observation or event is deemed to be statistically significant when in reality it falls within the bounds of acceptability. An example might be when we accept that an observed difference between the means of two groups is significant, when in fact what we are observing is a naturally occurring, if extremely unusual event.

**Type II error**  said to occur when an observation or event is deemed to be only rare but within the bounds of acceptability when it is in fact significant. An example might be when we accept that an observed difference between the means of two groups is a naturally occurring, if unusual event, when in reality we are observing a significant difference.

**unstructured items**  questionnaire items which allow the respondent to answer in an unlimited fashion.

**value label**  additional information used to describe and explain the coded values which represent the different categories in a variable in SPSS.

**variable label**  additional information used to describe a named variable in SPSS. In variable view of the current SPSS release, abbreviated variable names can be expressed in more detail here.

**variable name**  the name used to identify a variable in SPSS – usually limited to eight characters and requiring expansion under the variable label element.

**variable view**  the particular view of a data file in SPSS in which we can define and describe important characteristics of our variables. We can provide a fuller explanation of variables, assign numerical values to categories and so on.

**variance**  a measure of dispersion based on the actual values in a distribution and describing the average squared deviation of scores around a mean.

**visual analogue scale**  a measurement scale which is expressed as a single horizontal line, of standard length (100 millimetre) and anchored by two extreme and opposing attitudinal values.

**Wilcoxon signed rank test**  a non-parametric equivalent to the paired *t*-test when the same participants are measured under two conditions.

**within-group parametric comparison test**  a test in which two repeated measures are taken on a single group.

**within-group variance**  a measure of the total variation among individual scores within a group or sample.

**within-subjects design**  an experimental design in which the same participants are tested on some outcome measure at different times, or under different conditions. Sometimes known as a repeated measures design.

**word association**  a procedure in which the respondent is asked to respond with the first thing which comes to mind following the presentation with a stimulus word.

**z-scores**  the numerical values produced when actual scores in a distribution are transformed into the same scale and system of measurement as the standard deviation.

# References and reading list

Altman, D. G., & Dore, C. J. (1990). Randomisation and baseline comparisons in clinical trials. *Lancet, 335*, 149–153.

American Psychological Association (2001). *Publication manual of the American Psychological Association* (5th ed.). Washington, DC: American Psychological Association.

American Psychological Association (2002). Ethical principles of psychologists and code of conduct. *American Psychologist, 57*, 1060–1073.

Argyris, C., Putnam, R., & Smith, M. C. (1985). *Action science: Concepts, methods and skills for research and intervention*. San Francisco, CA: Jossey-Bass.

Asbury, J. E. (1995). Overview of focus group research. *Qualitative Health Research, 5*, 414–420.

Atkinson, P. (1990). *The ethnographic imagination: Textual constructions of reality*. London: Routledge.

Baddeley, A. (1993). Working memory or working attention. In A. Baddeley & L. Weiskrantz (Eds.), *Attention, selection, awareness and control: A tribute to Donald Broadbent*. Oxford: Oxford University Press.

Banister, P., Burman, E., Parker, I., Taylor, M., & Tindall, C. (Eds.). (1994). *Qualitative methods in psychology: A research guide*. Buckingham: Open University Press.

Beech, J. R., & Harding, L. (Eds.). (1990). *Testing people: A practical guide to psychometrics*. Windsor: NFER-Nelson.

British Psychological Society. (2004). *Ethical guidelines: Guidelines for minimum standards of ethical approval in psychological research*. Leicester: British Psychological Society.

British Psychological Society (2005). *Code of conduct, ethical principles and guidelines*. Leicester: British Psychological Society.

British Psychological Society Scientific Affairs Board (1985). Guidelines for the use of animals in research. *Bulletin of the British Psychological Society, 38*, 289–291.

Bryman, A. (1988). *Quantity and quality in social research*. London: Unwin Hyman.

Bryman, A. (2001). *Social research methods*. Oxford: Oxford University Press.

Bulmer, M. (Ed.). (1982). *Social research ethics*. London: Macmillan.

Burman, E. (1994). Interviewing. In P. Banister, E. Burman, I. Parker, M. Taylor, & C. Tindall (Eds.), *Qualitative methods in psychology: A research guide* (pp. 49–71). Buckingham: Open University Press.

Burman, E., & Parker, I. (Eds.). (1993). *Discourse analytic research: Repertoires and readings of texts in action*. London: Routledge.

Cartwright, A. (1983). *Health surveys in practice and in potential: A critical review of their scope and their methods*. London: King Edward's Hospital Fund for London.

Charmaz, K. (1995). Grounded theory. In J. A. Smith, R. Harré, & L. Van Langenhove (Eds.), *Rethinking methods in psychology* (pp. 27–49). London: Sage.

Christensen, L. B. (2004). *Experimental methodology* (9th ed.). Boston: Allyn & Bacon.

Cohen, J. (1988). *Statistical power analysis for the behavioral sciences* (2nd ed.). Hillsdale, NJ: Erlbaum.

Cooper, P., & Tower, R. (1992). Inside the consumer mind: Consumer attitudes to the arts. *Journal of the Market Research Society, 34*, 299–311.

Cresswell, J. W. (1998). *Qualitative inquiry and research design: Choosing among five traditions*. Thousand Oaks, CA: Sage.

Day, R. A. (1989). *How to write and publish a scientific paper* (3rd ed.). Cambridge: Cambridge University Press.

Denzin, N. K., & Lincoln, Y. S. (Eds.) (1994). *Handbook of qualitative research*. Thousand Oaks, CA: Sage.

de Vaus, D. A. (1996). *Surveys in social research* (4th ed.). London: University College London Press.

Dex, S. (Ed.). (1991). *Life and work history analysis: Qualitative and quantitative developments*. London: Routledge.

Diekhoff, G. (1992). *Statistics for the social and behavioral sciences: Univariate, bivariate, multivariate*. Dubuque, IA: Wm. C. Brown Publishers.

Dometrius, N. C. (1992). *Social statistics using SPSS*. New York: Harper Collins.

Dracup, C. (1995). Hypothesis testing—what it really is. *The Psychologist, 8* (8), 359–362.

Dyer, C. (1995). *Beginning research in psychology: A practical guide to research methods and statistics.* Oxford: Blackwell.

Edwards, D., & Potter, J. (1992). *Discursive psychology.* London: Sage.

Elliott, R., Fischer, C. T., & Rennie, D. L. (1999). Evolving guidelines for publication of qualitative research studies in psychology and related fields. *British Journal of Clinical Psychology, 38*, 215–229.

Eysenck, H. J., & Eysenck, S. B. G. (1964). *Manual of the Eysenck Personality Inventory.* London: University of London Press.

Eysenck, H. J., & Eysenck, S. B. G. (1991). *Manual of the Eysenck Personality Scales (EPS Adult).* London: Hodder & Stoughton.

Eysenck, H. J., & Eysenck, S. B. G. (1975). *Manual for the Eysenck Personality Questionnaire.* London: Hodder & Stoughton.

Field, A. (2000). *Discovering statistics using SPSS for Windows: Advanced techniques for beginners.* London: Sage.

Fielding, N. (1993). Ethnography. In N. Gilbert (Ed.), *Researching social life* (pp. 154–171). London: Sage.

Finlay, L. (2002). 'Outing' the researcher: The provenance, process, and practice of reflexivity. *Qualitative Health Research, 12*, 531–545.

Galton, F. (1888). Co-relations and their measurement. *Proceedings of the Royal Society of London, 45*, 135–145.

Galton, F. (1889). Correlations and their measurement, chiefly from anthropometric data. *Nature, 39*, 238.

Glaser, B. G., & Strauss, A. L. (1967). *The discovery of grounded theory: Strategies for qualitative research.* Chicago: Aldine.

Goldberg, D. P. (1972). *The detection of psychiatric illness by questionnaire.* Maudsley Monograph, No 21. Oxford: Oxford University Press.

Goldberg, D. P., & Blackwell, B. (1970). Psychiatric illness in general practice. A detailed study using a new method of case identification. *British Medical Journal, 2* (5705), 439–443.

Goldberg, D., & Williams, P. (1988). *A user's guide to the General Health Questionnaire.* Windsor: NFER-Nelson.

Greenbaum, T. L. (1998). *The handbook for focus group research* (2nd ed.). Thousand Oaks, CA: Sage.

Hammersley, M. (Ed.). (1993). *Social research: Philosophy, politics and practice.* London: Sage.

Hammersley, M. (2003). 'Analytics' are no substitute for methodology: A response to Speer and Hutchby. *Sociology, 37*, 339–351.

Hammersley, M., & Atkinson, P. (1995). *Ethnography: Principles in practice* (2nd ed.). London: Routledge.

Henwood, K., & Pidgeon, N. (1992). Qualitative research and psychological theorizing. *British Journal of Psychology, 83*, 97–111.

Horn, R. (1996). Negotiating research access to organisations. *The Psychologist, 9* (12), 551–554.

Howard, K., & Sharp. J. A. (1983). *The management of a student research project.* Aldershot, Hants: Gower.

Howell, D. C. (1997). *Statistical methods for psychology* (4th ed.). Belmont, CA: Duxbury.

Howitt, D., & Cramer, D. (2000). *An introduction to statistics in psychology* (2nd ed.). Harlow, Essex: Pearson/Prentice Hall.

Howitt, D., & Cramer, D. (2003). *A guide to computing statistics with SPSS 11 for Windows.* Harlow, Essex: Pearson/Prentice Hall.

Jadad, A. R. (1998). *Randomised controlled trials: A user's guide.* London: BMJ Books.

Jefferson, G. (1985). An exercise in the transcription and analysis of laughter. In T. A. van Dijk (Ed.), *Handbook of discourse analysis: Vol. 3. Discourse and dialogue* (pp. 25–34). London: Academic Press.

Kantowitz, B. H., Roediger III, H. L., & Elmes, D. G. (1994). *Experimental psychology: Understanding psychological research* (5th ed.). St. Paul, MN: West Publishing.

Kinnear, P. R., & Gray, C. D. (2000). *SPSS for Windows made simple: Release 10.* Hove, East Sussex: Psychology Press Ltd.

Krippendorff, K. (2004). *Content analysis: An introduction to its methodology* (2nd ed.). Thousand Oaks, CA: Sage.

Kvale, S. (1983). The qualitative research interview: A phenomenological and hermeneutical mode of understanding. *Journal of Phenomenological Psychology, 14*, 171–196.

Kvale, S. (1996). *Interviews: An introduction to qualitative research interviewing.* London: Sage.

Langridge, D. (2004). *Introduction to research methods and data analysis in psychology.* Harlow, Essex: Pearson/Prentice Hall.

LeCompte, M. D., & Goetz, J. P. (1982). Ethnographic data collection in evaluation research. *Educational Evaluation and Policy Analysis, 4*, 387–400.

Leedy, P. D., & Ormrod, J. E. (2001). *Practical research: Planning and design* (7th ed.). Upper Saddle River, NJ: Prentice Hall.

Leonard, V. (1989). A Heideggerian phenomenological perspective on the concept of the person. *Advances in Nursing Science, 11,* 40–55.

Likert, R. A. (1932). A technique for the measurement of attitudes. *Archives of Psychology, 140,* 5–55.

Lofland, J., & Lofland, L. H. (1995). *Analyzing social settings: A guide to qualitative observation and analysis* (3rd ed.). Belmont, CA: Wadsworth.

McGhee, J. W. (1985). *Introductory statistics.* St. Paul, MN: West Publishing.

Merton, R. K., & Kendall, P. L. (1946). The focused interview. *American Journal of Sociology, 51,* 541–557.

Micceri, T. (1989). The unicorn, the normal curve, and other impossible creatures. *Psychological Bulletin, 105,* 156–166.

Miles, M. B., & Huberman, A. M. (1994). *Qualitative data analysis* (2nd ed.). Thousand Oaks, CA: Sage.

Morgan, D. L. (1988). *Focus groups as qualitative research.* London: Sage.

Morgan, D. L., & Krueger, R. A. (1998). *The focus group kit, Vols. 1–6.* London: Sage.

Morgan, M. (1996). Qualitative research: a package deal? *The Psychologist, 9* (1), 31–32.

Morgan, M. (1998). Qualitative research…science or pseudo-science? *The Psychologist, 11* (10), 481–483.

Moustakas, C. (1994). *Phenomenological research methods.* Thousand Oaks, CA: Sage.

Munoz, P. E., Vazquez-Barquero, J. L., Pastrana, E., Rodriguez, F., & Oneca, C. (1978). Study of the validity of Goldberg's 60-item GHQ in its Spanish version. *Social Psychiatry, 13,* 99–104.

Munslow, A. (1977). *Deconstructing history.* London: Routledge.

Myers, I. B., & McCaulley, M. H. (1985). *Manual: A guide to the development and use of the Myers-Briggs type indicator.* Palo Alto, CA: Consulting Psychologists Press.

Nikander, P. (1995). The turn to the text: The critical potential of discursive social psychology. *Nordiske Udkast, 2,* 3–15.

Paivio, A. (1971). *Imagery and verbal processes.* New York: Holt, Reinhart and Winston.

Parker, I. (1994). Qualitative research. In P. Banister, E. Burman, I. Parker, M. Taylor, & C. Tindall (Eds.), *Qualitative methods in psychology: A research guide* (pp. 1–16). Buckingham: Open University Press.

Pearson, K. (1894). Contribution to the mathematical theory of evolution. *Philosophical transactions of the Royal Society, Series A, 185,* 71–110.

Pearson, K. (1895). Skew variation in homogeneous material. *Philosophical Transactions of the Royal Society of London, Series A, 186,* 343–414.

Pearson, K. (1896). Regression, heredity, and panmixia. *Philosophical Transactions of the Royal Society of London, Series A, 187,* 253–318.

Pidgeon, N. (1996). Grounded theory: Theoretical background. In J. T. E. Richardson (Ed.), *Handbook of qualitative research methods for psychology and the social sciences* (pp. 75–85). Leicester: British Psychological Society.

Pidgeon, N., & Henwood, K. (1996). Grounded theory: Practical implementation. In J. T. E. Richardson (Ed.), *Handbook of qualitative research methods for psychology and the social sciences* (pp. 86–101). Leicester: British Psychological Society.

Potter, J. (1998). Qualitative and discourse analysis. In N. R. Schooler (Ed.), *Comprehensive clinical psychology,* Vol. 3: *Research and methods* (pp. 117–144). Amsterdam: Elsevier.

Potter, J., & Wetherell, M. (1987). *Discourse and social psychology: Beyond attitudes and behaviour.* London: Sage.

Rachel, J. (1996). Ethnography: Practical implementation. In J. T. E. Richardson (Ed.), *Handbook of qualitative research methods for psychology and the social sciences* (pp. 113–124). Leicester: British Psychological Society.

Reason, P., & Heron, J. (1995). Co-operative inquiry. In J. A. Smith, R. Harré, & L. Van Langenhove (Eds.), *Rethinking methods in psychology* (pp. 122–142). London: Sage.

Reicher, S. (2000). Against methodolatry: Some comments on Elliott, Fischer and Rennie. *British Journal of Clinical Psychology, 39,* 1–6.

Reid, K., Flowers, P., & Larkin, M. (2005). Exploring lived experience. *The Psychologist, 18*(1), 20–23.

Rheinharz, S. (1983). Phenomenology as a dynamic process. *Phenomenology and Pedagogy, 1,* 77–79.

Richardson, J. T. E. (Ed.). (1996). *Handbook of qualitative research methods for psychology and the social sciences.* Leicester: British Psychological Society.

Roberts, C. W. (Ed.). (1997). *Text analysis for the social sciences: Methods for drawing inferences from texts and transcripts.* Mahwah, NJ: Lawrence Erlbaum.

Robson, C. (1993). *Real world research: A resource for social scientists and practitioner-researchers.* Oxford: Blackwell.

Rogers, J. (1996). Ethical issues in survey research. In L. DeRaeve (Ed.), *Nursing research: An ethical and legal appraisal*. London: Bailliere Tindall.

Salmon, P. (2003). How do we recognise good research? *The Psychologist, 16* (1), 24–27.

Salmon, W. C. (1981). John Venn's logic of chance. *Proceedings of the 1978 Pisa conference on the history and philosophy of science*. II (pp. 125–138). Dordrecht/ Boston, MA: Reidel.

Sarantakos, S. (1998). *Social research* (2nd ed.). London: Macmillan Press.

Shaughnessy, J. J., & Zechmeister, E. B. (1994). *Research methods in psychology* (3rd ed.). New York: McGraw-Hill.

Silverman, D. (1993). *Interpreting qualitative data: Methods for analysing talk, text and interaction*. London: Sage.

Smith, J. A. (1996). Beyond the divide between cognition and discourse: Using interpretative phenomenological analysis in health psychology. *Psychology and Health, 11*, 261–271.

Smith, J. A., Flowers, P., & Osborn, M. (1997). Interpretative phenomenological analysis and the psychology of health and illness. In L. Yardley (Ed.), *Material discourses of health and illness* (pp. 68–91). London: Routledge.

Smith, J. A., Jarman, M., & Osborn, M. (1999). Doing interpretative phenomenological analysis. In M. Murray & K. Chamberlain (Eds.), *Qualitative health psychology: Theories and methods* (pp. 218–240). London: Sage.

Speer, S. A., & Hutchby, I. (2003). From ethics to analytics: Aspects of participants' orientations to the presence and relevance of recording devices. *Sociology, 37*, 315–337.

Stevens, S. S. (1946). On the theory of scales of measurement. *Science, 103*(2684), 677–680.

Stevenson, C., & Cooper, N. (1997). Qualitative and quantitative research. *The Psychologist, 10* (4), 159–160.

Stewart, D. W., & Kamins, M. A. (1993). *Secondary research: Information sources and methods* (2nd ed.). London: Sage.

Strauss, A. L., & Corbin, J. (1994). Grounded theory methodology: An overview. In N. K. Denzin & Y. S. Lincoln (Eds.), *Handbook of qualitative research* (pp. 273–285). London: Sage.

Tabachnik, B. G., & Fidell, L. S. (2001). *Using multivariate statistics* (4th ed.). Needham Heights, MA: Allyn & Bacon.

Tappen, R. M. (1989). *Nursing leadership and management: Concepts and practice*. Philadelphia: F. A. Davis.

Taylor, M. (1994). Action research. In P. Banister, E. Burman, I. Parker, M. Taylor, & C. Tindall (Eds.), *Qualitative methods in psychology: A research guide* (pp. 108–120). Buckingham: Open University Press.

Terman, L. M., & Merrill, M. A. (1960). *Stanford-Binet Intelligence Scale: Manual for the third revision, Form L-M*. Boston: Houghton-Mifflin.

Tesch, R. (1990). *Qualitative research: Analysis types and software tools*. New York: Falmer Press.

Tindall, C. (1994). Issues of evaluation. In P. Banister, E. Burman, I. Parker, M. Taylor, & C. Tindall (Eds.), *Qualitative methods in psychology: A research guide* (pp. 142–159). Buckingham: Open University Press.

Tosh, J. (2000). *The pursuit of history: Aims, methods and new directions in the study of modern history* (3rd ed.). Harlow, Essex: Longman/Pearson Education.

Tukey, J. W. (1972). Some graphic and semigraphic displays. In T. A. Bancroft (Ed.), *Statistical Papers in Honor of George W. Snedecor* (pp. 293–316). Ames, IA: Iowa State University Press.

Tversky, A., & Kahneman, D. (1974). Judgement under uncertainty: Heuristics and biases. *Science, 185* (4157), 1124–1131.

Valentine, E. (1998). Out of the margins. *The Psychologist, 11* (4), 167–168.

Wetherell, M., Taylor, S., & Yates, S. J. (Eds.). (2001a). *Discourse theory and practice: A reader*. London: Sage.

Wetherell, M., Taylor, S., & Yates, S. J. (Eds.). (2001b). *Discourse as data: A guide for analysis*. London: Sage.

Whyte, W. F. (1984). *Learning from the field*. London: Sage.

Whyte, W. F. (1991). *Participatory action research*. London: Sage.

Willig, C. (2001). *Introducing qualitative research in psychology: Adventures in theory and method*. Buckingham: Open University Press.

Worsley, A., Walters, W. A. W., & Wood, E. C. (1977). Screening for psychological disturbance amongst gynaecology patients. *Australian and New Zealand Journal of Obstetrics and Gynaecology, 17*, 214–219.

# Index

Note: Material in tables, figures, photos and boxes is denoted by special characters when it is not included in the page-locator span for the subject. Tables are indicated by a *t* after the page number, figures by *f*, photos by *photo,* and boxed material by *box.*

absolute zero, 34, 50
abstract section of written report, 368, 370–1
accidental sampling, 96, 97*box*
accreditation for tests, 135
action research, 341–2, 343
advanced analysis. *See* tests for advanced analysis
agree/disagree questions, 129–30
alternate form reliability, 142–3
American Psychological Association (APA)
    ethical guidelines, 121
    *Psychological Abstracts*, 22
    reference guidelines, 389–90
animal research, 3, 124
anonymity of subjects, 14, 120, 122, 350, 354
ANOVA (one-way analysis of variance),
    261–75
    advantage over *t*-tests, 263
    aim of, 264–5
    Bonferroni correction and, 286, 287
    factorial (two-way) ANOVA, 310–13
    how to perform, 274, 287
    independent variable/factor in, 262
    language of, 266–7
    locating an effect in, 313–19
    multi-factorial (two-way) ANOVA, 310–13
    non-parametric equivalents to, 275
    one-way ANOVA, 282–7
        successive, 311
    post hoc testing in, 272–5, 316–19
    two-way ANOVA, 310–13
        corrected model, 312
    in written report, 381
anthropologists, 11*photo*, 12–13
APA. *See* American Psychological
    Association
apparatus
    in data-collection, 118
    in written report, 268, 377
appendices in written report, 390
area sampling, 93
assessment/assessment criteria, 397–8
association. *See* tests of association
assumption of equivalence, 65
assumption of linearity, 77–9
astrological signs, 47
attitudinal research, 132
average. *See* central tendency; mean

bar charts, 157, 166
    in SPSS program, 208–9
bar graphs. *See* bar charts
before-and-after designs, 62, 64
beginning a research project, 4–6, 18–21
    choosing a research area, 18–19
    deciding on type of study, 21
    evaluating research, 25–7
    formulating the research question, 19–20
    literature review, 21–5
    proposing a testable hypothesis, 20–1
    structuring a research project, 27
behavioural research, 104, 132, 134
best fit, line of. *See* regression line
between-group comparisons. *See under* tests of difference
between-groups designs, 57–60, 202
    achieving equivalence, 60*box*
    defined, 57
    equivalence in, 57
    many-groups designs, 58
    mixed designs, 68–9
    participant variables, 62
    versus within-subjects designs, 60, 61
between-subjects effects, 312*t*
bias, 7–8
    criterion contamination, 147
    double blind controls, 43
    in judgement, 10, 12, 15
    observer effect, 9–10
    in qualitative research, 349, 350
    sampling bias, 92, 99, 182
        margin of error, 104
        non-probability sampling, 94
        quota sampling, 95
        snowball sampling, 96
    single-blind designs, 43
    *See also* reliability; validity
bivariate correlation, 320, 321–2
bivariate methods, 73, 83
Bonferroni correction, 286, 287
boxplot, 167–70
    how to generate, 168–9
    in SPSS program, 214, 225
BPS. *See* British Psychological Society
British Psychological Society (BPS)
    accreditation for tests, 135
    ethical guidelines, 121, 122–4, 350

case number in SPSS, 201, 223
case studies, 14–15, 91, 113
categorical variables
    in figures/graphs, 156–9
    in tables, 154–6
categories, 62, 65
    selection of, 34, 52–3
    *See also* nominal (category) scales; nominal
        (category) variables
categorisition, 359–60
category scales. *See* nominal (category) scales
category variables. *See* nominal (category) variables
cause-and-effect relationships
    between-groups designs, 56, 57–8, 60
    correlational designs, 72–3
    cut-off assignment, 65
    factorial designs, 67, 68, 70
    independent versus dependent variables, 34
    misleading correlations, 79–81
    mixed designs, 69
    non-equivalent-groups designs, 65–6
    observational research, 9
    questionnaires, 16
    with small effects, 61–2
    between variables, 37, 44
Celsius scale, 50
Census, National (UK), 113
Central Office for Research Ethics (COREC), 123
central tendency, 128, 140, 173–4
    norms, 137
    in SPSS program, 210–11
chi-square ($\chi^2$) test, 288–94
    calculations of chi-square statistic, 292, 292*t*
    how to perform in SPSS, 294
    Lambda statistic, 283, 294
    Pearson chi-square, 292–3, 292*t*, 294
    Proportional Reduction in Error (PRE), 293
    table of chi-square, 407
    in written report, 381
citation format, 388–90
    *See also* literature
Citation Indexes, 24–5
classification systems, 45
    *See also* measurement scales
Clever Hans, 42–3, 43*photo*
clinical research. *See* medical model/medical research
closed-ended questions, 125–7, 129–31, 132
co-operation, participant, 100–1
codebook, 114–16, 195
coding
    data in SPSS, 192–203
    defined, 195
    interview data, 358–9
    recoding of variables, 52–3
    in written report, 36*box*
    *See also* case number
coefficient of correlation, 77, 298–9
coefficient of determination, 77, 302
cognitive psychology, 91, 98
Cohen, Jacob, 239

collecting data. *See* data collection
comparing samples and populations, 241–5
comparison groups generation, 65
computer analysis. *See* SPSS (Statistical Package for
    the Social Sciences)
computer software. *See* statistical software
conclusions section of written report, 387
concurrent validity, 145
conditions, defined, 65
confidence interval, 245
confidence level, 103*box*, 104–6
confidentiality, 14, 119, 120, 340, 350
    in qualitative studies, 351–4
consent. *See* informed consent
consistency, internal, 142
construct validity, 147
content validity, 144
contents section of written report, 371
contingency tables, 155
continuous data, 197–201
continuous variables
    boxplot, 167–70
    coding and recoding in SPSS, 197–201
    figures/graphs and, 165–7
    tables and, 160–3
controls, 7, 41–4
    Clever Hans example, 42–3, 43*photo*
    control groups, 57, 58–9
        between-groups designs, 58, 68
        randomised controlled designs, 68
        within-subjects designs, 60–1
    counterbalancing, 62–4
    defined, 41
    double-blind, 43–4
    matching, 41
    randomised controlled trials, 42, 68
    single-blind, 43
convenience sampling (accidental sampling), 96, 97*box*
COREC (Central Office for Research Ethics), 123
correlated *t*-test. *See* paired *t*-test
correlation, 72–85, 295–9
    bivariate, 320, 321–2
    coefficient of, 77, 298–9
    defined, 295
    mathematical solution, 323–4
    misleading, 79–81
    multiple, 83–5
    negative, 75
    partial, 81–2, 319–24
    Pearson, 321*t*, 322
    positive, 75
    in SPSS program, 303–8
    strength of, 73–4
    in written report, 381
    *See also* correlational designs; partial correlation
correlation coefficient (*r*), 77, 298–9
correlational designs, 72–85
    coefficient of determination, 77, 302
    correlation coefficient, 77, 298–9
    criterion variables, 74, 158

linearity, 77–9
misleading correlations, 79–81
multiple correlation and regression, 83–5
nature of correlation, 73–6
partial correlation, 81–2
predictors (predictor variables), 74, 158
*See also* correlation; experimental
  research designs; research design
counterbalancing, 62–4
CRB (Criminal Records Bureau), 123
Criminal Records Bureau (CRB), 123
criterion contamination, 147
criterion measures, 73, 74
  *See also* outcome measures
criterion-related validity, 145
criterion variables, 74
  effect of multiple predictors on, 324
  multiple correlation and, 83–4
  partial correlation and, 81
  shown on *y*-axis, 158
critical values of *t* and *T*, 405, 406
critical values of *U* and *U*′, 404
cross-sectional approach, 61
crosstabulation, 156
  combined with chi-square ($\chi^2$)
    test, 288–94
  Crosstabs command, 215–17
  graphs and, 221–3
  practicalities of use, 220–1
  in SPSS program, 217–23
curvilinear relationships, 78–9
cut-off assignment, 65
cut-off scores, 65


data
  interval, 160–1, 246
  nominal, 246
  ordinal, 246
  parametric and non-parametric, 245–7
  primary, 17
  in qualitative versus quantitative research, 333
  ratio, 246
  secondary, 17–18
  *See also* data collection; data description
data collection, 117–49
  codebooks, 114–16, 195
  ethical guidelines, 117–24
  in ethnography, 339–40
  focus groups, 354–6
  participant co-operation, 100–1
  pilot research, 134–5
  procedures, 117–24
    apparatus, 118
    ethics, 120–4
    procedural issues, 119–21
    sampling, 118
  psychological tests, 136–49
    alternate form reliability, 142–3
    norms, 137–9, 140–1*box*

reliability, 139–42
standardisation, 136–7
test-retest reliability, 142
validity, 143–9
  in qualitative research, 334, 336
questionnaires, 16–17, 124–32
  questionnaire design, 124–5
  types of questions, 125–6, 131–2
  types of scale, 125–32
special techniques, 132–6
standardised instruments, 135
by surveys, 15–16
time factors and, 336
data description, 153–89
  boxplot, 167–70
  categorical variables, 154–9
  common sense in, 154
  comparison of methods, 170–2
  continuous variables, 165–70
  descriptive techniques, 154, 170–1
  figures/graphs, 156–9, 165–7
  frequency distribution, 161–3
  interval data, 160–1
  missing data values, 224
  numerical representation, 153–4
  outliers and extreme scores, 224–5
  statistics, 172–89
  stemplot, 163–5
  tables, 154–6, 160–3
  *See also* SPSS (Statistical Package for the
    Social Sciences)
deception, 119, 123–4, 125
  and face validity, 144, 146
dependent *t*-test. *See* paired *t*-test
dependent variables, 34–5, 53–4*box*
  individual variability and, 61
  more than one, 36–7
  sample representativeness, 92
  two-way ANOVA and, 311
  versus independent/extraneous
    variables, 40*box*
  *See also* cause-and-effect relationships;
    measurement scales; variables
describing data. *See* data description
descriptive analysis. *See* SPSS (Statistical Package
  for the Social Sciences)
descriptive techniques, 154, 170–1
design. *See* research design
design section of written report, 268, 374–6
determination, coefficient of, 77, 302
diagnostic tests, 145
dichotomous scales, 126
difference, tests of. *See* tests of difference
discussion, section of written report, 368,
    386–7
discussion groups, 133
dispersion, 175–8
  interquartile range, 175–6
  measures in SPSS program, 211–12
  range, 175

standard deviation, 176–8
double-blind controls, 43–4

electronic searching, 22–5
EPI. *See* Eysenck Personality Inventory
EPQ. *See* Eysenck Personality Questionnaire
equivalence
    achieving, 60*box*
    assumption of, 65
    between groups designs, 56–60
    in true experimentation, 65
    within-subjects designs, 60–1
    *See also* non-equivalent-groups designs
equivalent-groups designs. *See* between-groups designs
errors
    margin of error (sampling error), 103*box*, 104
    ratio scale of measurement, 51
    standard error, 183, 211
    standard error statistic, 103*box*
    statistical, 234
        type I, 234, 239, 272
        type II, 234, 239
    unknown factors and, 69
ethics, 350–2
    animal research, 124
    BPS guidelines, 350
    checklist, 352*box*
    committees, 14, 99, 118, 123
        qualitative studies and, 352
        sampling and, 96
    guidelines
        for data collection, 117–24
        on participation, 101*box*
        summarized, 122–4
        for undergraduate research, 98
    information sheets, 350–1
    informed consent, 13, 14, 98, 119–24, 350–2
    interviews, 351, 353–4
    in qualitative research, 350–2
    recordings, 351–2
    *See also* deception; participants' rights
ethnography, 13, 338–40, 343
evaluating research, 25–7
experimental research, defined, 55–6
experimental research designs, 55–71
    between-groups designs, 57–60, 60
    factorial designs, 66–8, 70–1
    introduction, 56–7
    mixed designs, 68–70
    non-equivalent-groups designs, 65–6
    randomised controlled designs, 68
    versus correlational designs, 72–3
    within-subjects designs, 60–5
    *See also* correlational designs; research design; *specific design types*
experimenter effect, 9–10
extraneous variables
    controls and, 41
    defined, 39

non-equivalent groups as, 66
    researchers as, 42–4
    test performance, 136
    versus independent variables, 39–41
    within-subjects designs, 61–2
    *See also* cause-and-effect relationships; variables
extraversion scales, 65
extreme ranges, 179–80, 212
Eysenck Personality Inventory (EPI), 139
Eysenck Personality Questionnaire (EPQ), 65, 110, 136–7, 138, 140–1*box*, 197

F-statistic/value, 264–5, 268, 269, 285
face validity, 144–5, 146
factorial ANOVA. *See* two-way ANOVA
factorial designs, 66–8
    mixed designs, 68–70
    reservations on, 70–1
factorial research, 66
field studies, 13–14
figures, 156–9
    checklist for, 385–6*box*
    comparison of, 171–2
    continuous variables and, 165–7
    how to ruin, 159
    in written report, 383–6
    *See also* graphs; tables
Fisher, Ronald, 262
Fisher's F-statistic, 264–5, 268, 269
focus groups, 132–4, 354–5
frequency distribution, 161–3
frequency polygon, 167
frequency tables, 155–6

Galton, Francis, 73, 73*photo*
gender effects, 376
General Health Questionnaire (GHQ), 148
General Household Survey, 113
generalisation problem, 8
GHQ (General Health Questionnaire), 148
Gosset, William, 239, 247, 250
graphs, 156–9
    bar chart/bar graph, 157, 166
    categorical variables and, 156–9
    combination variety, 157
    comparison of, 170–2
    components of, 157–8
    continuous variables and, 165–7
    crosstabulated data, 221–3
    frequency polygon, 167
    histograms, 166–7
    how to ruin, 159
    scatterplot, 74
    *x*-axis, 158
Greenhouse-Geisser, 285, 285*t*, 287
grounded theory, 340–1, 343
groups

comparison, 65
control, 57, 58–9, 60–1, 68
discussion, 133
equivalent and non-equivalent, 68–9
experimental, equivalence between, 56–60
focus, 132–4, 354–5
pre-existing/natural, 65–6, 69, 83
subgroups, 95
*See also* participants; sampling
guidelines
data collection, 117–24
ethical, summarised, 122–4
participation, 101*box*
undergraduate research, 98, 99–100,
100–1, 106

Hawthorne effect, 9–10
hermeneutics, 341, 343
histograms, 166–7
in SPSS program, 213, 226–7
holistic research, 9, 13
horizontal (*x*) axis, 74, 158
human behavior, complexity of, 7
hypotheses, 6
case studies and, 15
cause-and-effect judgements, 38
examples of, 53–4
generation of, 132, 133
null hypothesis, 239–40
in qualitative research, 346, 347, 366
revisited in written report, 386, 387
testable, 20–1
testing of, 6–9, 33, 107–10, 113
variables and, 35

ideas for research projects, 18–19
independent groups designs. *See*
between-groups designs
independent-samples *t* test, 250–5
in SPSS program, 255
in written report, 381
independent variables, 35–9, 53–4*box*
conditions, 65
criterion contamination, 147
defined, 35–7
factorial designs and, 66–8
levels, 65
limiting the number of, 112
more than one, 37–9
multiple correlation, 83–5
non-equivalent-groups designs, 65
and two-way ANOVA, 311
versus extraneous variables, 40*box*
within-subjects designs, 62
*See also* cause-and-effect relationships; measurement
scales; variables
individual variability, 61
inferential statistics. *See* statistics, inferential

information sheets, 350–1, 352
informed consent, 13, 14, 98, 122–4
forms, 119, 120–1
in qualitative studies, 350–2
requirements, 119
instruments, data collection, 135
intelligence studies, 179–80
intelligence tests, 144
interaction effect, 311
interactions, 67–8, 70
interfering factors, 90
internal validity, 57
Internet resources, 22–5
interpretative phenomenological analysis (IPA), 344
interquartile range (IQR), 128, 175–6
in SPSS program, 212
interval data, 160–1, 246
interval predictors, 319–24
interval scales, 45, 46*box*, 50–1
*See also* interval variables
interval variables, 54*box*
correlational designs, 84
defined, 46*box*
non-equivalent-groups designs, 65
statistical studies, 51
*See also* interval scales
interventions, 342
interviews, 352–7
in action research, 342
analysis of, 358–9
checklist, 355*box*
defined, 352
ethical issues, 351, 353–4
in hermeneutics, 341
pilot programs, 353
in qualitative research, 352–4
time required for, 336
transcripts in appendices, 390
introduction section of written report, 368, 371–3
IPA (interpretative phenomenological
analysis), 344
IQR. *See* interquartile range
issues identification, focus groups, 132–4

Kelvin scale, 50
Kruskal-Wallis test, 275
kurtosis, 180–3
in SPSS program, 212–13

Lambda statistic, 283, 294, 294*t*
language
function (discourse analysis), 343–4
use (hermeneutics), 341
leading questions, 125
least squares line. *See* regression line
leptokurtic distribution, 181
level of confidence. *See* confidence level
levels, defined, 65

levels of measurement, 44–6
    changing, 52–3
    defined, 65
    measurement scales, 44–6
    qualitative versus quantitative, 45–6
    variables and, 44
    *See also* measurement scales
Levene's test, 254–5, 274
Likert scale, 129–30, 245
limitations statement, 99, 106, 112
line of best fit. *See* regression line
linearity, 77–9
literature, 366
    APA (2001) guidelines, 389–90*box*
    Citation Indexes, 24–5
    citation rules, 388–90
    electronic searching, 22–5
    evaluating research in, 25–7
    Internet resources for, 23
    *Psychological Abstracts* (PAs), 22
    reference checklist, 388*box*
    references in written report, 387–90
    research journals, 22
    review, 21–5, 31
longitudinal research, 61
lower-bound, 285*t*

main effects, 67, 68, 313
manipulations, experimental, 14
Mann-Whitney *U*-test, 107–8, 255–61
*Manual of the Eysenck Personality Scales*, 140*box*, 143*box*
many-independent variable studies. *See* factorial designs
margin of error (sampling error), 103*box*, 104
market research, 47–8, 95, 132–3
matching, 41, 57
Mauchly test of sphericity, 285, 287
Mead, Margaret, 11*photo*
mean
    arithmetic, 173–5
        norms, 137, 140
        in SPSS program, 210–11
    and assignment of subjects, 65
    mean of the sample means (MSM), 244–5
    standard error of the, 183, 242–5
        how to calculate, 244–5
*Mean squares between*, 265, 267
*Mean squares within*, 265, 267
measurement objectives. *See* dependent variables
measurement scales, 44–54
    changing levels of, 52–3
    comparison of interval and ratio scales, 51
    interval, 45, 46*box*, 50–1
    multiple category, 49–50, 126–7
    nominal (category), 34, 44–8, 84
    ordinal, 46*box*, 48–50
    rating scales, 127–9
    ratio, 34, 45, 46*box*, 50–1, 65
    types of, 45, 46*box*, 125
measurement, small effects, 61–2

median, 173–5
    interquartile range and, 175–6
    in SPSS program, 211
medical model/medical research, 42, 68, 91, 105
mere presence effect, 9–10
meta-analysis, 18
method section of written report, 268, 373–8
Minitab, 60, 191
missing data values, 224
modal interval, 163
modal value, 175
mode, 163, 175
*MSbetween*, 265, 267
MSM (mean of the sample means), 244–5
*MSwithin*, 265, 267
multi-causality, 37
multi-correlational design, 83
multi-factor ANOVA. *See* two-way ANOVA
multi-factor approach. *See* factorial designs
multiple-category scales, 49–50, 126–7
multiple-choice questions, 47
multiple correlation, 83–5
multiple regression, 83–5, 324–8, 381
Murphy's Law, 33
Myers-Briggs personality typology, 47

National Census (UK), 113
National Health Service (NHS) regulations, 99
Necker cubes, 11*f*
negative correlation, 75
NHS. *See* National Health Service (NHS) regulations
nominal (category) scales, 45, 46–8, 127
    *See also* nominal (category) variables; ordinal scales
nominal (category) variables, 46–8, 53–4*box*
    correlational designs, 84
    quantitative relationships among, 48–50
    *See also* nominal (category) scales; ordinal variables
nominal data, 246
nominal predictor, 319
nominal scales, 34
non-equivalent-groups designs
    cause-and-effect relationships, 65–6
    combined with equivalent groups, 68–9
    participant selection, 90, 99
non-linear associations, 78–9*box*
non-normal distributions, 182, 225–6
non-parametric data, 245–7
non-parametric tests, 275
non-probability sampling, 94–7, 97*box*
normal distribution, 178–82
    area under the normal curve, 401–3
    characteristics of, 184
    defined, 184
    kurtosis, 180–2, 212–13
    leptokurtic distribution, 181
    peakedness of, 180–2
    platykurtic distribution, 181–2
    skewness, 179–80, 182, 212
    in SPSS program, 212–13

standard normal distribution, 183–9
   symmetry of, 184*f*
   z-scores and, 187–8
   *See also* standard deviation
norms, 137–9, 140–1*box*
null hypothesis, 239–40
number of participants. *See* sample size
number, participant or case, 201, 223
numerical representation, 153–4


observation, 9–13
   judgement/bias in, 10, 15
   observational data, 359–60
   observational research, 9–10, 97, 360–1
observer effect, 9–10
one-sample *t*-test, 238–9
one-tailed tests, 234–9
   critical region for, 237–8*f*
   critical values of *U* and *U'* for, 404
   one-sample *t*-test, 238–9
one-way analysis of variance. *See* ANOVA
one-way ANOVA, related, 282–7
open-ended questions, 131–2
order effects, 59, 62–4
ordinal data, 246
ordinal scales, 46*box*, 48–50, 128
ordinal variables, 48–50, 54*box*
organisational psychology, 109
outcome data, 194–5
outcome measures, 56
   correlational designs and, 84
   criterion measures, 73
   individual variability and, 61
   order effects and, 62, 63
   standardised instruments and, 135
   *See also* criterion measures; research design
outcome variables. *See* dependent variables


PAs. *See Psychological Abstracts*
paired *t*-test, 275–8
   how to perform in SPSS, 278
parametric and non-parametric data, 245–7
parametric data, 128
partial correlation, 81–2, 319–24
   defined, 320
   how to compute in SPSS, 324
   mathematical solution, 323–4
   in written report, 381
participant number in SPSS, 201, 223
participant sampling and recruitment, 89–116
   ensuring co-operation, 100–1
   how to choose participants, 90*box*
   non-probability sampling, 94–7
   number of participants, 101–13
   obtaining participants, 97–100, 97–9
   representativeness, 91–2
   sampling techniques, 92–4
   secondary research, 113–16

summary of procedures, 97*box*
   undergraduate research guidelines, 98, 99–100, 100–1, 106
   *See also* participants; sample size; sampling
participant variables (profile variables), 62
participants, 7–8, 10–13
   availability of, 336
   characteristics, as extraneous variables, 61
   co-operation, 100–1
   equivalence between groups, 56–60
   individual variability, 61
   matching, 41, 57
   obtaining, 61, 97–100
   participant data, 192–3
   randomisation, 41–2
   refusal rate, 377
   representing experiences of, 335
   role in action research, 341–2
   role in participatory research, 342
   stress, 119, 121, 122
   variables (profile variables), 90
   vulnerable groups, 119, 121, 123, 134
   in written report, 268, 376–7
   *See also* ethics; participant's rights;
      sampling
participants' rights, 350–4
   anonymity, 14, 120, 122, 350, 354
   confidentiality, 14, 119, 120, 340, 350, 351–4
   informed consent, 13, 14, 98, 119–24, 350–2
   voluntary participation, 119, 122
   withdrawal from study, 14, 119, 351
   *See also* ethics
participatory research, 342, 343
peakedness of a distribution, 180–2
Pearson chi-square, 292–3, 292*t*, 294
Pearson correlation, 321*t*, 322
Pearson, Karl, 73
Pearson's *r*, 298–9
percentiles, 139, 140
performance measures, 34, 37, 38
performance studies, repetition effect and, 62
permission, 351
personality research, 65
personality scales, 140*box*, 143*box*
personality tests, 140*box*, 141, 143*box*
Pfungst, Oskar, 43
phenomenological approach, 338–40
pilot studies, 132, 134–5, 347, 353, 366*box*
placebo, 43
platykurtic distribution, 181–2
political research, 95, 133
POM (Profile of Mood States), 148
populations, 91, 91–2, 102–6
   *See also* groups; sampling
positive correlation, 75
post hoc testing, 272–5, 316–19
post-test, 57, 58–9
power
   effect size and, 239–40
   of research procedures, 109–10
   of tests, compared, 107–8*box*

practice effects, 62, 142
PRE (Proportional Reduction in Error), 293
pre-tests, 57, 59
predictions. *See* coefficient of determination
predictive validity, 145–7
predictors (predictor variables)
    correlational designs, 74
    interval (continuous), 319–24
    multiple correlation and regression, 83–4
    nominal, 319
    partial correlation, 81
    shown on *x*-axis, 158
presentation of research, 393–7
previous research, 31, 335–6
primary data, 17
prior research, 31, 335–6
probabilistic equivalence, 57
probability, 232–40
    closer look at, 240
    critical values of *T*, 406, 405
    explained, 232–4
    statistical significance, 234
    values, 107
probability sampling. *See* random sampling
procedural variations, 136
profile data, 192–3
Profile of Mood States (POM), 148
profile variables (participant variables), 62, 90
projective techniques, 131
Proportional Reduction in Error (PRE), 293
*Psychological Abstracts* (PAs), 22
psychology
    aims of, 3–4
    a definition of, 3
    scope of, 4
psychometric tests, 16, 118, 135
purposive sampling, 95–6, 97*box*

qualitative research, 331–62
    approaches to, 338–42
        action research, 341–2
        comparison of, 343
        ethnography, 338–40
        grounded theory, 340–1
        hermeneutics, 341
        participatory research, 342
    choosing, versus quantitative research, 334–5, 338*box*, 349
    data analysis, 357–60
        field notes, 359
        interview analysis, 358–9
        observational data, 359–60
        transcription, 357–8
    data collection, 352–7
        focus groups, 132–4, 354–5
        interviewing, 352–4
        observation, 355–7
    differences from quantitative research, 331–2, 333–4
    ethical issues, 350–2

    example of, 332–4
    interviewing checklist, 355*box*
    mixing methods, 337
    observation, 355–7
    open-ended questions, 132
    participant availability, 336
    participant experiences represented, 335
    philosophical issues, 350
    planning, 344–99, 348–9*box*
        method decisions, 346–7
        piloting, 347
        research questions/conceptual framework, 344–6
    previous research, 335–6
    quality of, 360–1
    recordings, 350
    self-disclosure, 349–50, 354
    supervisors, 337, 338*box*
    text analysis, 342–4, 345*box*
        content analysis, 343
        discourse analysis, 343–4
        interpretative phenomenological analysis (IPA), 344
    time factors, 336, 338*box*
    triangulation, 360–1
    written report, 361, 391–3
    *See also* interviews; questionnaires
quantitative research
    mixing methods with qualitative research, 337
    versus qualitative research, 331–2, 333–4
quantitative variables, 45, 128
quasi-experimental research/design, 65–6, 90, 99
questionnaires, 16–17, 124–32
    changes in, 366
    design, 124–32
        focus groups, 134
        participant cooperation, 100–1
        pilot studies, 134–5
    ethical guidelines, 118, 120–1
    Eysenck Personality Questionnaire, 65, 110, 136–7, 138, 140–1*box*, 197
    full questionnaires in appendices, 390
    General Health Questionnaire (GHQ), 148
    question types, 125–7, 129–31, 132
    standardised instruments, 135
    tabular sample description, 156
    types of scale, 125–32
        dichotomous scales, 126
        Likert scale, 129–30
        multiple-category scales, 126–7
        nominal scales, 47, 126, 127
        ordinal scales, 49–50
        rating scales, 127–9
        semantic differential, 130
        visual analogue scales, 130–1
    *See also* ethics; questions; survey research
questions
    agree/disagree, 129–30
    closed-ended, 125–7, 129–31, 132
    leading, 125

multiple-choice, 47
open-ended, 131–2
sentence completion, 131
unstructured items, 131
word association, 131
Yes/No, 47, 48, 126–7
*See also* research question
quota sampling, 94–5, 97*box*


*r* (correlation coefficient), 77, 298–9
random sampling, 92–4, 97*box*
randomisation
    as extraneous variable control, 41
    post-test randomised between-groups
        experimental designs, 57, 58–9
    random number generation, 60
    random number tables, 93
randomised controlled trials (RCTs), 42, 68
range, 175
    extreme ranges, 179–80, 212
    interquartile range (IQR), 175–6, 212
    in SPSS program, 200, 212
rating scales, 127–9
ratio data, 246
ratio scales, 34, 45, 50–1
    defined, 46
    non-equivalent-groups designs, 65
    statistical studies, 51
ratio variables, 34, 50–1, 65
RCT. *See* randomised controlled trials
realist research, 341
recoding of variables, 52–3
recordings, 350, 351–2
reductive analytic model, 8
references. *See* literature
references section of written report, 369, 387–90
reflexivity, 341
refusal rate for participants, 377
regression, 78, 83–5, 299–305
    multiple, 83–5, 324–8
        in SPSS program, 328
    simple, 299–305
        regression line, 299–302
        in SPSS program, 303–8
    in written report, 381
regression line, 299–308
related-samples *t*-test. *See* paired *t*-test
reliability
    alternate form, 142–3
    reliability coefficients, 143
    retests, 142
    split-half, 142–3
    test, 144
    of tests, 139–43, 143*box*
repetition effects, 62–4, 142
replicability, 118
report. *See* writing up research
representativeness
    of psychological tests, 136

of sampling, 91–2, 94, 95, 96
standardisation samples, 137, 139
versus participant willingness, 98
*See also* sample size; sampling
research, 4–5
    evaluation, 25–7, 99
    limitations of, 106*box*
    meta-analysis, 18
    objectiveness of, 331
    psychological, defined, 3–4
    purpose of, 90
    secondary, 17–18
    types of studies/techniques, 6–18
    *See also* beginning a research project; research design
research area, 18–19
research design, 31–54
    complex designs, analyses for, 310–28
    controls, 41–4
    defined, 31
    dependent variables, 34–7
    extraneous variables, 39–41
    independent variables, 35–9
    levels of measurement, 44–6, 52–3
    measurement scales, 45–54
    principles and language of, 33–4
    problems with, 32–3
    purpose of, 31–2
    variables in, 34
    *See also* correlational designs; experimental
        research designs
research question, 19–20, 31, 34–5, 90
research report. *See* writing up research
research types
    attitudinal, 132
    behavioural, 104, 132–4
    cognitive, 91, 98
    market, 47–8, 95, 132–3
    medical, 91, 105
    opinion, 144
    political, 95, 133
    questionnaire, 16–17, 124–32
    secondary, 113–16
    survey, 15–16, 92, 94
    *See also* research design
response data, 194–5
results section of written report, 368, 378–82
review of literature, 21–5, 31

sample size, 101–13
    confidence level, 104–6
    in estimating population characteristics, 102–6
Sample size (*contd.*)
    factorial designs and, 70–1
    in hypothesis testing, 107–10
    margin of error, 104
    power and, 109–10
    small, 14–15, 108, 182–3
    variability and, 102–4, 110–13
    within-subjects designs and, 61
    *See also* sampling

sampling, 89–116
  accidental sampling, 96, 97*box*
  area sampling, 93
  bias, 92, 99, 182
    margin of error, 104
    non-probability sampling, 94
    quota sampling, 95
    snowball sampling, 96
  comparing samples, 241–5
    mean of the sample means (MSM), 244–5
    standard error of the mean, 242–5
  ethics and, 118
  how to get participants, 97–100
  local sampling effects, 98
  margin of error (sampling error), 103*box*, 104
  non-probability sampling, 94–7, 97*box*
  probability sampling, 97*box*
  problems, 16, 17, 182–3
  purposive sampling, 95–6, 97*box*
  quota sampling, 94–5, 97*box*
  random sampling, 92–4, 97*box*
  representativeness of, 91–2, 96, 98, 99
    over-represented groups, 94
    subgroups, 95
  samples, defined, 91
  sampling frame, 93
  snowball sampling, 96, 97*box*
  special groups, 99–100
  statistical significance, 105
  stratified sampling, 93–4, 97*box*
  summary of procedures, 97*box*
  undergraduate research guidelines, 98, 99–100,
    100–1, 106
  *See also* sample size
scales
  dichotomous, 126
  measurement, 44–54
    interval scales, 45, 46*box*, 50–1
    multiple category scales, 49–50, 126–7
    nominal (category) scales, 34, 44–8, 84, 127
    ordinal scales, 46*box*, 48–50
    ratio scales, 34, 45, 46*box*, 50–1, 65
  psychological, 45, 46*box*, 125–32
    extraversion scales, 65
    Likert scale, 129–30, 245
    personality scales, 140*box*, 143*box*
    rating scales, 127–9
    semantic differential, 130
    visual analogue scales, 130–1
scatterplots, 74
Science Citation Index, 24–5
scientific method, 5–6
Scottish Criminal Records Office (SCRO), 123
screening data, 224–7
SCRO (Scottish Criminal Records Office), 123
*SD. See* standard deviation
secondary data, 17–18
secondary research, 113–16
self-disclosure, 349–50, 354
semantic differential, 130

sentence completion, 132
significance, statistical, 105, 109, 234
simple regression. *See* regression, simple
single-blind designs, 43
situation specificity, 92
situational bias, 92
skewness, 108*box*, 179–80, 182–3
SMC. *See* squared multiple correlation
snowball sampling, 96, 97*box*
social facilitation/inhibition effect, 9–10
Social Sciences Citation Index, 24–5
social surveys, 113–14
software. *See* statistical software
Sphericity Assumed, 285, 285*t*, 287
sphericity, Mauchly test of, 285, 287
split-half reliability, 142–3
SPSS (Statistical Package for the Social Sciences),
    190–227
  coding data, 192–203
    codebook, 195
    continuous data, coding and recoding, 197–201
    how to code data, 196–7
  creating files, 191–2
  Data Editor, 198–201
  data entry, 191–2, 201–6
    between-groups designs, 202
    naming variables, 201–6
    setting up data files, 203–6
    within-groups designs, 202–3
  data view, 192
  descriptive statistics, 206–23
    Crosstabs command, 215–17
    crosstabulation, 217–23
    Descriptives command, 209
    Explore command, 209–17
    Frequencies command, 208
    full descriptive output, 209–17
    how to generate, 206–8
    interquartile range, 212
    kurtosis, 212, 212–13
    measures of central tendency, 210–11
    measures of dispersion, 211–12
    measures of normality, 212–13
    missing values, 224
    outliers and extreme scores, 224–5
    screening data, 224–7
    selecting cases, 223
    skewness, 212
    standard deviation, 212
    standard error/confidence interval, 211
    variance, 211
  group statistics, 253–4
  menus, 193, 207
  missing column, 204–5, 224
  multifactor output, 312
  participant or case number, 201, 223
  random number generation, 60
  values box/column, 200, 204–6
  variables
    naming/defining, 201–6

setting up/data entry, 191–2
    variable view, 192
  viewing data, 194–5
  *See also specific statistical tests*
squared multiple correlation (SMC), 83
SS (sum of squares), 265, 267
standard deviation, 103*box*, 137, 176–8
  defined, 128
  how to calculate, 176–7
  standard normal distribution and, 185
  in written report, 378–80
  z-scores and, 187–8
standard error, 183, 242–5
  defined, 243
  how to calculate, 244–5
  in SPSS program, 211
  statistic, 103*box*
  in written report, 379
standard normal distribution. *See* normal distribution
standardisation
  psychological tests, 136–7
  standardisation samples, 136, 139
  standardised instruments, 135, 148–9
starting a research project. *See* beginning a research project
Statistica, 191
statistical analysis. *See* statistics
Statistical Package for the Social Sciences. *See* SPSS
  (Statistical Package for the Social Sciences)
statistical significance, 105, 109, 234
statistical software, 190–1
  Minitab, 60, 191
  PC versus MAC, 190
  SPSS, 190–227
  Statistica, 191
  *See also detailed entries under SPSS*
statistical tests. *See* tests
statistics, 172–89
  central tendency, 173–4
  dispersion, 175–8
  errors
    standard error, 183
    type I and II errors, 234, 239, 272
  kurtosis, 180–3
  mean, arithmetic, 173–5
  median, 173–5
  mode (modal value), 175
  non-normal distributions, 182, 225–6
  normal distribution, 178–82
  partial, 81–2
  ratio and interval scales, 51
  skew, 108*box*, 179–80, 182–3
  standard deviation, 176–8
  standard error, 183, 242–5
    how to calculate, 244–5
  standard normal distribution, 183–9
  statistic, defined, 172
  statistical significance, 105, 109, 234
  symbols and their meaning, 178
  *See also specific tests*; statistical software;
    statistics, inferential

statistics, inferential, 231–47
  comparing samples and populations, 241–5
  confidence interval, 245
  effect size and power, 239–40
  errors, 234
    type I error, 234, 239, 272
    type II error, 234, 239
  null hypothesis, 239–40
  one- and two-tailed tests, 234–9
  parametric and non-parametric data, 245–7
  probability, 232–40
  standard error of the mean, 242–5
    how to calculate, 244–5
  statistical significance, 234
  *See also* tests for advanced analysis; tests
    of association; tests of difference
stem-and-leaf diagram (stemplot), 163–5
  how to generate, 164–5
  in SPSS program, 214–15
stemplot. *See* stem-and-leaf diagram
Stevens, S. S., 45, 51, 72
stratified sampling, 97*box*
stress, participant, 121, 122
Student's *t*-test. *See under t*-tests
subjects. *See* participants
sum of squares (SS), 265, 267
survey research, 15–16, 49
  General Household Survey, 113
  importance of sample choice, 92
  nominal variables and, 47–8
  non-equivalent-groups designs and, 66
  secondary research/surveys, 113–14
  stratified sampling, 94
  tabular sample description, 156
  *See also* questionnaires
symbolic interactionism, 340
symbols, statistical, 178

*t*, 109
  critical values of, 405
*t*-tests, 108*box*
  correlated, 275–8
  dependent, 275–8
  independent-samples, 250–5
  one-sample, 238–9, 247–75
  paired, 275–8
  related-samples, 275–8
  Student's independent, 239, 250–5
  Type I errors and, 272
  versus ANOVA, 263
*T*, critical values of, 406
tables, 154–6
  categorical variables and, 154–6
  checklist for, 385–6*box*
  components of, 155
  contingency, 156
  continuous variables and, 160–3, 165–7
  crosstabulation, 156
  frequency, 155–6

of norms, 390
in written report, 383–6
*See also* figures; graphs
tachistoscope, 118
temperature, as interval-scaled variable, 50–1, 51, 54
tests
accreditation for, 135
between-subjects effects, 312*t*
one- and two-tailed tests, 234–9
personality, 140*box*, 141, 143*box*
power of, compared, 107–8*box*
psychological, 136–49
alternate form reliability, 142–3
norms, 136–9, 137, 139, 140–1*box*
reliability, 139–43, 142–3, 143*box*, 144
standardisation, 136–7
psychometric, 16, 118, 135
reliability of, 139–44
alternate form reliability, 142–3
split-half reliability, 142–3
test reliability, 139–42
test-retest reliability, 142
Tukey HSD test, 318, 319*t*
validity of, 143–9
concurrent validity, 145
construct validity, 147
content validity, 144
criterion related validity, 145
face validity, 144–5, 146
predictive validity, 145–7
standardised testing instruments, 148–9
test validity, 143–4, 148*box*
*See also t*-tests; tests for advanced analysis; tests of association; tests of difference
tests for advanced analysis, 310–28
locating an effect in ANOVA, 313–19
multiple regression, 324–8
partial correlation, 319–24
two-way ANOVA, 310–13
tests of association, 288–309
chi-square ($\chi^2$), 288–94
chi-square statistic, 292, 292*t*
coefficient of determination, 302
correlation, 295–9, 303–8
crosstabulation, 288–94
simple regression, 299–302, 303–8
tests of difference, 247–87
between-group comparisons, 247–75
independent-samples *t* test, 250–5
Mann-Whitney *U*-test, 107–8, 255–61
one-sample *t* test, 238–9, 247–50
one-way analysis of variance (ANOVA), 261–75
post hoc testing in ANOVA, 272–5
within-group comparisons, 275–87
one-way ANOVA, related, 282–7
paired *t*-test, 275–8
tests of within-subjects effects, 285
Wilcoxon signed rank test, 278–82

text analysis, 342–4, 345*box*, 358
theory, 5–6
*See also* hypotheses
time factors, 336
title of written report, 368, 369
transcription, 357–8
treatment present/treatment absent designs, 56, 64
triangulation, 360–1
true experiment, 57
Tukey HSD test, 318, 319*t*
Tukey output, 273
two-tailed tests, 234–9
critical regions for, 237*f*
critical values of *U* and *U'* for, 404
two-way ANOVA, 310–13
type I errors, 234, 239, 272
type II errors, 234, 239

*U* and *U'*
critical values of, 404
Mann-Whitney *U*-test, 107–8, 255–61
undergraduate research guidelines, 98, 99–100, 100–1, 106

validity, 26, 143–9, 361
concurrent, 145
construct, 147
content, 144
criterion related, 145
face, 144–5, 146
internal, 57
predictive, 145–7
test, 143–4, 148*box*
values. *See* ethics
values fields, in SPSS program, 200, 204
variability
rating scales, 128
sample size and, 102–4, 110–13
variables, 34–41
causal versus coincidental associations, 72–3
changing over time, 61
defined, 44
dependent, 34–5
different types of, 53–4
extraneous, 39–41
independent, 35–9
interval, 46, 51
limiting the number of, 112
nominal (category), 46–50
ordinal, 46, 48–50
partialling out (removing), 81–2
ratio, 45, 46, 50
restructuring/recoding of, 52–3
*See also* correlation; factorial designs; *specific variable types*
variance, 103*box*
analysis explained, 262–71

ANOVA (one-way analysis of variance), 261–75
two-way ANOVA, 310–13
comparing within one sample, 254
interaction effect, 311
Levene's test for Equality of Variances, 254–5
measures in SPSS, 211
variation measures in SPSS, 211–12
Venn diagrams, 82, 84
Venn, John, 82
vertical (y) axis, 74, 158
visual analogue scales, 130
visual imagery, 11
voluntary participation, 119, 122
Von Osten, Wilhelm, 42–3
vulnerable groups, 119, 121, 123, 134

Wilcoxon signed rank test, 278–82
how to perform in SPSS, 282
within-group comparisons. *See under* tests of difference
within-group parametric comparison test.
*See* paired *t*-test
within-groups designs, 202–3
within-subjects designs, 60–5
counterbalancing, 62–4
mixed designs, 69
multi-condition designs, 63–5
within-subjects effects, 285
word association, 131
writing up research, 365–99
APA (2001) guidelines, 386, 389–90
appendices, 390
assessment/assessment criteria, 397–8
composite look at, 368–9
ethics for, 118

giving a presentation, 393–7
keeping track, 366–7*box*
presentation and style, 390–1
problems, 32
purpose of, 365
qualitative research, 391–3
results, how to report, 391–2
structure of report, 367–82
abstract, 368, 370–1
appendices, 369
conclusions, 387
contents, 371
discussion, 368, 386–7
introduction, 368, 371–3
method, 268, 373–8
references, 369, 387–90
results, 368, 378–82
tables and figures, 383–6
title, 368, 369
study limitations statement, 99, 106, 112
tables and figures, 383–6
writing guidelines, 265–7
Wundt, Wilhelm, 3

*x*-axis, 74, 158

*y*-axis, 74, 158
Yes/No questions, 47, 48, 126–7

z-scores, 187–8
Zener cards/task, 110–11
zero points, 50